ANTHROPOLOGY
CONTEMPORARY PERSPECTIVES

SIXTH EDITION

ANTHROPOLOGY
CONTEMPORARY PERSPECTIVES

SIXTH EDITION

Edited by

PHILLIP WHITTEN
Harvard University

DAVID E.K. HUNTER
Yale University

HarperCollins*Publishers*

*This book is dedicated
to my mother, Sylvia,
with love,
appreciation, and
admiration for her
strength and courage;*

*and to my father,
Clifton, whose
kindness and love of
learning were an
inspiration to all who
were fortunate enough
to know him.*

—P.W.

*To Elaine and Lisa—
flowers in the desert.*

—D.E.K.H.

Library of Congress Cataloging-in-Publication Data

Anthropology : contemporary perspectives / edited by Phillip Whitten
and David E.K. Hunter—6th ed.
    p.   cm.
  ISBN 0-673-52074-9
  Includes bibliographical references.
  1. Anthropology.   I. Whitten, Phillip.   II. Hunter, David E.K.
GN29.A59   1990
306—dc20   89-39941
                                                    CIP

    4 5 6—MAL—94 93 92

PREFACE

Anthropology is an exciting discipline—and why not? It encompasses all of the human experience: from the evolutionary processes that have molded the human race; to civilizations, both ancient and modern; to the way people communicate with each other; to the kaleidoscopic variety of human culture.

Anthropology is also a fast-changing discipline—enlivened by new discoveries, theories, problems, and debates on issues of fundamental importance to the understanding of human nature, society, and behavior. In this, the sixth edition of *Anthropology: Contemporary Perspectives*, we have attempted to convey the excitement and relevance of contemporary anthropology to beginning students. The needs and interests of these students were foremost in our minds when we selected the articles for this anthology. The selections had to strike a balance between academic quality and level of difficulty. They had to be intrinsically interesting to students, both in subject matter and in writing style. They also had to relate to the introductory course in anthropology as it is taught in most North American colleges and universities. The resulting collection thus reflects both the important ongoing work of modern anthropology and the ways introductory anthropology is taught, as well as providing interesting, enjoyable reading for the college undergraduate.

This sixth edition of *Anthropology: Contemporary Perspectives* is a substantial revision of the book, primarily in terms of subject matter. Some 35 percent of the articles are new to this edition. New articles explore such topics as human evolution; sociobiology; human diversity ("race"); sickle-cell anemia; current and future advances in archaeology and biological anthropology; the nature of human language; Koko the gorilla; the sacred cows of India; voodoo; the impact of modernization and industrialization on small, marginal societies throughout the world; the Stone-Age diet; birth as an American ritual; and, in the final, disquieting article, the extinction of the human race. Articles retained from the first five editions are those judged most successful in a poll of instructors who have adopted the book and students in introductory anthropology classes during the 1987–88 school year. As in previous editions, the authors include prominent anthropologists such as Barry Bogin, Laura Bohannan, Napoleon A. Chagnon, Yehudi Cohen, Jared Diamond, Robert C. Dunnell, Agnes Estioko-Griffin, Robbie Elizabeth Davis-Floyd, Robert A. Foley, Ernestine Friedl, Stephen Jay Gould, Marvin Harris, William W. Howells, Albert Jacquard, Laurel Kendall, Melvin Konner, Jeffrey T. Laitman, Jane B. Lancaster, Richard Borshay Lee, David Maybury-Lewis, Horace Miner, Monique Borgerhoff Mul-

der, Martin K. Nickels, Colin Renfrew, Lauriston Sharp, Barbara Smuts, Eric Wolf, Peter M. Worsley, and Henry T. Wright, as well as professional science writers and leading individuals in other social and behavioral sciences.

The articles come from a broad range of sources, including major books and such journals and popular magazines as *American Anthropologist*, *Anthropology Today*, *Archaeology*, *Discover*, *Harvard Magazine*, *Horizon*, *Human Nature*, *Human Organization*, *McCall's*, *Michigan Quarterly Review*, *Mosaic*, *Mount Sinai Review*, *Natural History*, *Psychology Today*, *Science*, *Science Digest*, *Scientific American*, *Smithsonian*, *Society*, *The Sciences*, and the *Unesco Courier*. Some articles were written specifically for this volume. Most of the articles are very recent: over 59 percent date from the 1980s, 43 percent were first published in the last five years, and two articles bear 1990 copyrights. Many of these articles reflect new discoveries and changes in the discipline of anthropology, but we also have included a number of the "classic" articles. In particular, the articles address some of the most important and exciting issues with which anthropologists are grappling today:

• In the area of human evolution, for example, important fossil finds have been unearthed in the badlands of East Africa and elsewhere with startling regularity since the mid-1970s. At the same time, the role of Neanderthal in the sequence of human evolution has been reevaluated. Each discovery has broadened the understanding of evolutionary history while simultaneously raising new and intriguing problems. In fact, these finds have so altered anthropologists' ideas about the evolution of the human species that in the last three editions of this anthology we have been compelled to rework the entire section on human evolution.

• The publication of Edward O. Wilson's influential book *Sociobiology* (1975) raised anew (and at a more sophisticated level than before) the question of the extent to which human behavior is governed by genetic inheritance. Are humans, indeed, captives of their own genes—or, to put it more scientifically, is there a human biogram? Are certain behaviors influenced more by our biological rather than by our cultural heritage? These are some of the questions anthropologists have tackled with gusto. From the research and writing—not to mention the storm of controversy—they have engendered, no doubt will come a deeper understanding of just what kind of creature *Homo sapiens* is.

• The relationship between human beings and their closest living primate relatives—the chimpanzees and gorillas—also has been brought to the fore in recent years. Molecular biology has demonstrated that humans share almost 99 percent of our genetic endowment with chimpanzees. In fact, humans are more closely related to chimps than horses are to zebras. Longitudinal fieldwork studying apes living in the wild—pioneered in the 1960s by Jane Goodall, Dian Fossey, and others—has shown that these creatures are far more sophisticated than previously imagined. Current studies of West African chimpanzees, due to be published early in the 1990s, have discovered distinct chimpanzee cultures passed on from generation to generation, and a sophisticated division of labor by sex. As one primatologist recently told us: "We're finding out these chimps are more like australopithecines than we thought the australopithecines were!" Finally, efforts to teach apes, such as Koko the gorilla, to communicate using American Sign Language have been remarkably fruitful. Koko can use over 500 symbols; she can combine them in new ways, she can joke, she can lie—in short, she can use language in most of the ways considered uniquely human. Presently, she is being taught to read. Ironically, just as humans are learning to understand and appreciate their primate cousins, they are on the verge of extinction in their natural habitats, primarily as a result of human encroachment.

- Sex roles is another topic of intense and heated debate these days. And it is a debate to which anthropology can contribute a great deal. Are the sex roles that humans grow up with "natural," that is, biologically ordained? Or are they cultural conventions, created in the past to solve challenges posed by the environment and hence subject to modification as the physical and social environment changes? If the latter, what are the benefits and costs—both to the individual and to society as a whole—of radically altering a society's traditional sex roles? In the mid-1980s, this controversy was rekindled and brought to a boiling point by the publication of Derek Freeman's *Margaret Mead and Samoa: The Making and Unmaking of an Anthropological Myth* (1983). In his book Freeman attacks both Margaret Mead's scientific integrity and her research on Samoan society as reported in her classic book *Coming of Age in Samoa* (1928). Because anthropology, far more than any other behavioral science, takes a cross-cultural perspective, it can bring a great deal of research and knowledge to bear on the question of the diversity in human sex roles and other related questions.

ORGANIZATION

We have retained the basic organization of the fifth edition of *Anthropology: Contemporary Perspectives* because of its compatibility with the leading textbooks in both introductory anthropology and cultural anthropology, and because this organization allows it to be used as the only book in either of these courses.

- There are six main parts of the book, with parts 2 through 5 corresponding to the major subdisciplines within anthropology: biological anthropology, archaeology, language and communication, and cultural anthropology.
- Within the six parts there are fifteen topics, corresponding to the subject matter common to virtually all texts and courses in introductory anthropology: human evolution; primatology and human behavior; human diversity; archaeol-

ogy; language, thought, and communication; fieldwork; kinship and marriage; political and economic organization; sex roles; belief and ritual; and so on.

- In addition, we have significantly expanded both the part and topic introductions, explaining important basic concepts and providing students with a carefully detailed framework that will enhance their understanding and appreciation of the selections that follow.
- We have added an entirely new topic—Contemporary Applications—to illustrate the utility and relevance of anthropology.
- An extensive Glossary contains definitions for more than five hundred important terms used in the book.
- Finally, we have retained the popular fascimile format of the book, keeping original photographs and artwork wherever possible.

ACKNOWLEDGMENTS

We are deeply indebted to the following instructors who not only provided in-depth critiques of the fifth edition and our plans for its revision, but who also provided specific suggestions for new articles, many of which we used: Jonathan G. Andelson, Grinnell College; Barry Bogin, University of Michigan, Dearborn; Vaughn M. Bryant, Jr., Texas A & M University; Janeen Arnold Costa, University of Utah; Raymond D. Dunstan, SUNY College of Technology at Farmingdale; Charles Edwards, SUNY College, Brockport; David Hakken, SUNY College of Technology at Utica; Rose Mary Hall, Diablo Valley College; Philip A. Hasley, Niagara Community College; James H. Mielke, University of Kansas; Lloyd Miller, Des Moines Area Community College; John H. Moore, University of Wisconsin; Brian Siegel, Furman University; and Malcom C. Webb, University of New Orleans.

Several other instructors also offered valuable, in-depth critiques of the fifth edition, for which we are grateful: William Fisher, Columbia University; Charlotte J. Frisbie, Southern Illinois University at Edwardsville; Thomas C. Greaves, Bucknell University; and Lawrence S. Leshink, Pace University.

We would also like to thank the following individuals for the outstanding research they did in assisting us with this revision: Linda Muterspaugh; Elizabeth Whiteside; and Russell Whitten.

We are also indebted to the higher education division at Scott, Foresman/Little, Brown, with whom we worked so effectively; and, in particular, to our editor, Harriett Prentiss, who provided many valuable suggestions in revising the book.

Finally, we owe a debt of gratitude to the authors whose articles appear in *Anthropology: Contemporary Perspectives*. Without their work, along with their permission (and that of their publishers) to reprint it, this book would not have been possible.

Phillip Whitten
David E.K. Hunter

BRIEF CONTENTS

CONTENTS

processes leading to urbanization began. Considering our evolutionary heritage, "the wonder is not that man has trouble getting along in cities, but that he can do it at all," writes Pfeiffer. (*Horizon*, Autumn 1972)

culturally prescribed rules of convention. This makes generalizing across cultures tricky, and the research studies Thayer reports on in this article are mostly from the U.S. Nevertheless, intuitively it seems true that northern European cultures prohibit touching more than do cultures from southerly regions. This may have important consequences for how people grow up thinking and feeling about themselves and others. (*Psychology Today*, March 1988)

ANTHROPOLOGY
CONTEMPORARY PERSPECTIVES

SIXTH EDITION

Driftwood Creek (16)

Girl's Hill (16)

Putu (16)

Old Crow (16)

Bering Land Bridge (16)

The Eskimo (Inuit) (32)

Purgatory Hill (3)

The Naskapi (32)

Kansas City (22)

The Shoshoni (32)

Calico Hills (16)

Anzick (16)

The Iroquois (36)

The "Nacirema" (26)

W. Virginia (41)

Santa Rosa Island (16)

Del Mar (16)

U.S.A. (22, 47, 48, 49)

The Paiute (32)

Folsom (16)

Cahokia (18)

The Garbage Project (14)

Gainesville (22)

Puerto Rico (22)

Haiti (42)

Teotihuacan (19)

Mayans (15, 19)

Valley of Mexico (17, 19)

Panama (22)

Colombia (22)

Mesoamerica (19)

The Yanomamö (9, 23, 28, 46)

Costa Rica (22)

Tlapcoya (16)

The Machiguenga (32, 33)

The Mehinacu (32)

Peru (19)

Bolivian Tin Miners (40)

Huaca Prieta (17)

Pikimachay Cave (16)

Fell's Cave (16)

Sweden

Neander Valley (4, 5)

Paris (22)

Cro-Magnon (4)

La Chapelle-aux-saints (18)

La Ferrassie (4)

Mladec (4)

Predmost (4)

Jebel Irhoud (4)

W. Africa (12)

The Tiv (24)

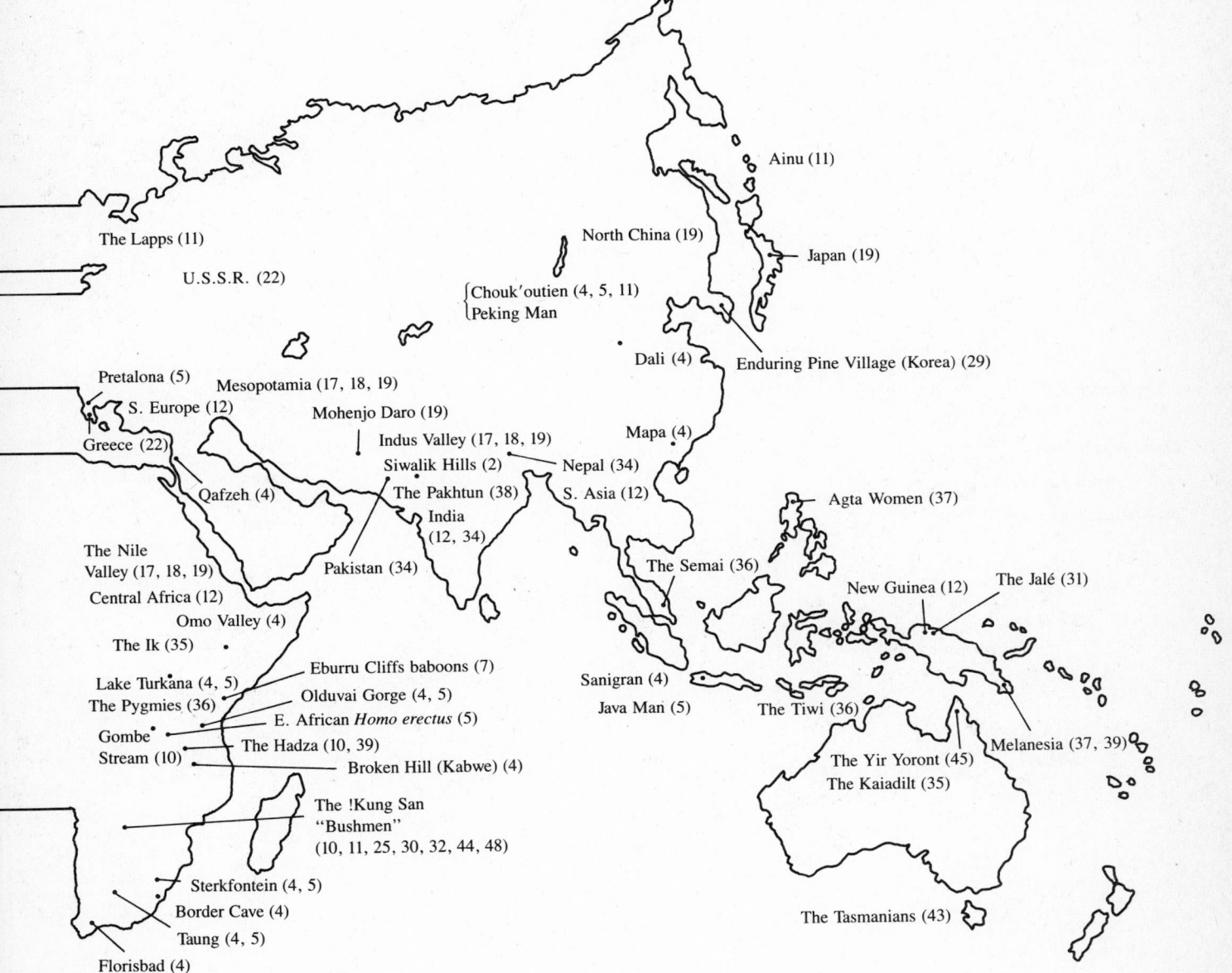

The Lapps (11)

U.S.S.R. (22)

Pretalona (5)

Mesopotamia (17, 18, 19)

S. Europe (12)

Mohenjo Daro (19)

Greece (22)

Indus Valley (17, 18, 19)

Qafzeh (4)

Siwalik Hills (2)

The Pakhtun (38)

India (12, 34)

The Nile Valley (17, 18, 19)

Pakistan (34)

Central Africa (12)

Omo Valley (4)

The Ik (35)

Lake Turkana (4, 5)

Eburru Cliffs baboons (7)

The Pygmies (36)

Olduvai Gorge (4, 5)

Gombe Stream (10)

E. African *Homo erectus* (5)

The Hadza (10, 39)

Broken Hill (Kabwe) (4)

The !Kung San "Bushmen" (10, 11, 25, 30, 32, 44, 48)

Sterkfontein (4, 5)

Border Cave (4)

Taung (4, 5)

Florisbad (4)

North China (19)

Chouk'outien (4, 5, 11)

Peking Man

Dali (4)

Mapa (4)

Nepal (34)

S. Asia (12)

Ainu (11)

Japan (19)

Enduring Pine Village (Korea) (29)

Agta Women (37)

The Semai (36)

Sanigran (4)

Java Man (5)

New Guinea (12)

The Jalé (31)

The Tiwi (36)

Melanesia (37, 39)

The Yir Yoront (45)

The Kaiadilt (35)

The Tasmanians (43)

1

Introduction to Anthropology

This collection of articles will introduce you to some of the many facets of anthropology. In each part we provide a general framework and some historical comments to help you understand the significance of the readings within the general discipline of anthropology. The introductory notes are especially extensive in Part 2 (Biological Anthropology) and Part 3 (Archaeology), because these topics are more likely than others to lie outside of the realm of the daily world of discourse of most students.

We introduce you to anthropology in Topic 1, The Study of Anthropology. Here, we sketch both the historical roots and the modern subdisciplines of anthropology in order to provide you with an overall framework that you can use to organize your reading of the articles collected in this reader.

The Study of Anthropology

What is anthropology? For one thing, it is an academic discipline whose history, subdisciplines, and major theories we trace in the article that opens this anthology. But we believe deeply that anthropology is more than just an academic discipline, for its scope embraces all of humankind—past and present. Whether or not you go on to concentrate your studies in an anthropology major, taking an introductory course in anthropology will enrich your life and broaden your perspectives. It will expose you to foreign peoples, strange places, unexpected customs, new viewpoints, and—again and again—the universals at the heart of the human condition everywhere.

We leave it to you to discover these universals, to find yourself in the enormous diversities of peoples and cultures, life-styles and world views represented in the articles reprinted here.

In the article "What Is Anthropology?" the editors of this volume provide a guide to sampling the fruit of a tree whose roots are deep and whose boughs spread wide.

In "The Prospects for Anthropology," written especially for this volume, Eric Wolf examines some of the changes the discipline of anthropology has undergone in the past four decades. He argues that anthropology must articulate basic questions and concerns as it heads into the next century.

What Is Anthropology?

By Phillip Whitten and David E. K. Hunter

....

Anthropology is a way—or rather a collection of many different ways—of studying human beings and their closest primate relatives. The term *anthropology* comes from two Greek words: *anthropos,* meaning "man" (in the sense of human being), and *logos,* meaning "to reason" (or study).

THE BRANCHES OF ANTHROPOLOGY

If one thinks of the overall discipline of anthropology as a tree, then it is a tree consisting of four major branches and many smaller branches and twigs. The four major branches are biological anthropology, archaeology, linguistics, and cultural anthropology.

1. *Biological anthropology* is the study of human biology—but not just biology alone. Whether studying the fossil remains of our ancestors, the distribution of diverse genes among the world's contemporary populations, the mechanisms of genetic inheritance, the differing shapes and colors characterizing people in various regions, or even the behavior patterns of humans and their primate relatives, biological anthropologists are concerned with the manner in which all these things are related to the natural and social environments in which the subjects are living. So biological anthropology really is the study of the biological processes of humans and their primate relatives in their natural and social contexts or environments.

2. *Archaeology* is the retrieval and study of human remains. This includes not only their bodily remains (which certainly can tell us a great deal about how they lived and died), but also the remains of the things they built, produced, and made use of. In other words archaeologists attempt to find and study all the traces that human groups have left behind—of themselves and of all their activities—and they seek to understand the ways these remains are related to each other and the environments in which they occur.

3. *Linguistics* is the study and analysis of human communication systems, but most especially of language. Some linguists attempt to reconstruct the earlier language forms from which our present languages have evolved. Others study modern languages in order to learn how they encode the range of human experiences, what grammatical forms they feature, or what separates language from the communication systems of other species. Some linguists are concerned with what language usage can reveal about the different social groups within a society. Others are interested in what can be learned about the nature of the human mind from the study of language. So linguistics is *not* what many people take it to be—the mere learning of a lot of different languages—rather it embodies the use of research into languages in order to better understand the nature of human beings as a species.

4. *Cultural anthropology* is the study of culture and cultures. Culture consists of the shared patterns of behavior and associated meanings that people learn and participate in within the groups to which they belong. Every group, down to each individual family, has its own culture, and each culture is unique. Of course some cultures are quite similar to each other (say, the family cultures of a specific community); others are very different (nomadic Arab culture and Eskimo culture, for example). Some anthropologists study the nature of culture in general as an element of human existence; others are more interested in studying a specific culture (perhaps the culture of a Norwegian fishing village or a *barrio* in Mexico City). Culture, by providing "designs for living," enables humans to be extremely flexible and resourceful in solving problems posed by the natural environment, and our species is unique in that it inhabits virtually every niche that nature has wrought on our planet. The better we understand culture, the closer we shall come to understanding what it means to be a human being.

At this point it might be helpful to return to the image of the "tree of anthropology" with which we opened this essay. Until now we have concentrated on a description of its branches—its four main branches and even a number of its smaller branches and twigs. Some readers might even be tempted to ask whether, in all this diversity of interests encompassed by anthropology, there is in fact any trunk to the tree. Is there a central core that holds the whole thing together?

That is a reasonable question, and at times even anthropologists have had cause to ask it. In fact there is a trunk to be found. It is worth looking for because it is in the trunk of the tree that we find what makes anthropology different from all the other social sciences and also what makes it a worthwhile discipline to study and practice. We shall lead you to an appreciation of the trunk somewhat indirectly, however, by first describing some of the major roots of anthropology. We do this because we think that an understanding of the origins and development of the discipline will make its current practice more comprehensible and enticing.

THE ROOTS OF THE TREE

The origins of anthropology—as indeed of so much of our civilization—can be traced back to ancient Greece and the civilization of the Middle East. Historians claim as their father a Greek named Herodotus (484?–425? B.C.), and so might anthropologists as well. He traveled widely and recorded the life-styles of some fifty different peoples. He also formulated the idea that all peoples are *ethnocentric*—that is, they consider their own way of life superior to all others, and they judge other life-styles (for the most part negatively) in terms of the norms and values of their own.

With the fall of Rome in the fifth century A.D., much of the knowledge and thought of the classical civilizations were lost to Europeans for almost a thousand years. Medieval scholars were not so much interested in human beings or even in the nature of the world around them as they were in discovering as much as could be learned about God. Of course, they attempted to learn about God by studying the universe that God had created, and they did make many important discoveries about the world. But their concern to find "divine order" and "divine principles" underlying the manifest world blinded them to many of its most interesting features. It really was not until the Renaissance emerged in the fifteenth century, bringing with it a rediscovery of the treasures of classical learning, that European scholars began to investigate the natural environment as well as human societies with a view to understanding them on their own terms.

Already in medieval times, however, Europeans had been exposed to the existence—on distant shores accessible only to the hardiest of travelers—of many "strange and exotic" peoples. Throughout the Renaissance and Enlightenment periods, as Europe extended its economic interests ever farther abroad, exploration and colonization enabled scholars to visit these faraway places and make records (often fantastically misinformed and distorted) of the peoples they discovered and observed. By the eighteenth century, the vast riches to be made through control of the populations and resources of Africa, Asia, and the Americas induced governments and private enterprises to take more seriously the value of careful study of these so-called primitive peoples. After all, the better one understood them, the more efficiently one could set about exploiting them.

The Church too was quick to grasp the opportunity to extend its influence through missionary activities. Naturally, in order for their activities to be successful, these missionaries required information about the languages and customs of the people they would seek to convert to Christianity.

For many reasons, then, Europeans came to be interested in acquiring information about foreign peoples. Travelers, missionaries, sea captains, colonial administrators, adventurers, traders, and soldiers of fortune ranged across the world recording their impressions of the peoples they encountered. They brought these accounts back with them to European "armchair scholars," who attempted to study them by comparing them to each other—and to European society—in a more or less systematic manner. Inevitably, these efforts tended to "prove" the superiority of European society over all the "primitive" societies thus studied. These eighteenth- and nineteenth-century researches developed into what has come to be called the *comparative method* of social science research. Through the application of this method, a great many schemes of social and cultural evolution were put forward, all of which placed the institutions of European society securely at the top of the evolutionary pyramid.

Until the middle of the eighteenth century, there was no separate discipline that one might call social science. To the extent that society was studied, it was done within the all-purpose framework of history. But by around 1750, the study of society had become sufficiently specialized to deserve the label "social science"—a separate discipline having split off from historical studies and embarked on its own development. For about one hundred years, the study of human nature and society evolved along the lines we have already described, embodying loosely all the different approaches to the building of a science of humankind.

A century later Darwinian evolutionism arrived. The impact of Darwinism on human thought was profound, and its effects on social science were no less dramatic. The two outstanding changes in the study of human nature and society that resulted were (1) the application of evolutionary theory to virtually all aspects of the study of humankind, and (2) the split of such studies into increasingly specialized, separate disciplines.

The Emergence of Evolutionary Thought

The Christian doctrine that Creation had been a single event (pinpointed at 9:00 P.M. on October 23 in 4004 B.C. by Archbishop James Ussher in the early 1600s, who deduced that time from a careful study of Genesis) became more and more troublesome. Already in the sixteenth century Vasco Núñez de Balboa discovered that America was not an extension of Asia but, rather, a separate continent—and the origin of the "Indians" became a source of heated argument. This debate rapidly expanded into controversy about the degree of relatedness—and inherent levels of ability—of all the diverse peoples around the world.

To the *polygenists* the differences between human groups were so vast that they could not accept even a common origin for all people. Rebelling against a narrow acceptance of Genesis, they insisted that scientific inquiry must prevail over the Bible (a courageous position at the time). They argued that God must have created human beings a number of times in different places and that all people were not then descendants of Adam and Eve. Their numbers included many of the period's leading skeptics and intellectuals, such as Voltaire and David Hume. It is hardly surprising that these thinkers, attaching as they did such great significance to human physical variation, should have been racial determinists and indeed racists, ascribing to their own "stock" superior mental abilities. Voltaire, for instance, discussing the state of civilization among Africans, argued:

> If their understanding is not of a different nature from ours, it is at least greatly inferior. They are not capable of any great application or association of ideas, and seemed [sic] formed neither for the advantages nor the abuses of philosophy (quoted in Harris 1968:87).

Monogenicism defended the Scriptures' assertion of a single origin for all humans. Isolated groups, such as the "Indians," were accounted for by the claim that they had come from Atlantis (a mythical continent that was believed to have stretched from Spain to Africa before sinking beneath the waters of the Atlantic Ocean) or that they were the descendants of one of the lost tribes of Israel. Monogenists accounted for "racial" differences in terms of populations adapting to the problems posed by different environments—an idea that would become central to Darwin's principle of natural selection. But they also tended to believe, along with the French biologist Jean Baptiste de Lamarck (1744–1829), that physical characteristics acquired by an individual in the course of his or her lifelong development could be passed on biologically from one generation to the next (an idea rejected by Darwin and the mainstream of subsequent evolutionary thought).

Because monogenists tended to defend the validity of the Biblical version of human origins, they also accepted the very recent dates that Biblical scholars had established for human creation. Thus although they, like the polygenists, divided the human species into "races," they deduced that these "races" must be of very recent origin and that, although people exhibited differences in response to environmental pressures, these differences were of minimal importance with regard to basic human abilities. For instance, Johann Friedrich Blumenbach (1752–1840), a German physician who developed an interest in comparative human anatomy, published a study in 1775 in which he identified five "races": Caucasian, Mongolian, Ethiopian (including all sub-Saharan blacks), Malayan, and American. For this effort he is frequently called the "father" of physical anthropology. However, Blumenbach was far from convinced that these categories were anything more than artificial constructions of convenience in the service of science: "When the matter is thoroughly considered, you see that all [human groups] do so run into one another, and that one variety of mankind does so sensibly pass into the other, that you cannot mark out the limits between them." And he adds, with a tone of wryly modern wisdom, "Very arbitrary indeed both in number and definition have been the varieties of mankind accepted by eminent men" (cited in Montagu 1964:41).

(The debate between monogenists and polygenists raged on through the nineteenth century and continues to this day. Although most human biologists since Darwin have aligned themselves in the monogenist camp, the writings of Carleton S. Coon (1904–1981), a contemporary anthropologist, were firmly polygenist. He argued in *The Origin of Races* (1963)—a controversial work—that the human species evolved five different times into the five "races" that he believed constitute the population of the world today.)

Let us return, however, to our account of the emergence of the theory of evolution. By the late eighteenth and early nineteenth centuries, discoveries (especially in biology and geology) were gradually forcing scholars to reassess their acceptance of a date for the creation of the earth derived from scriptural study. More and more geological strata in the earth's crust were coming to light, and it became clear that the thickness of some strata, and the nature of the mineral contents of many, demanded a very long developmental process. In order to account for this process, these scientists faced the need to push back the date of Creation, as we will see shortly. In addition, the fossilized record of extinct life forms accumulated, obliging scientists to produce plausible explanations for the existence and subsequent disappearance of such creatures as the woolly mammoth and the saber-toothed tiger.

In 1833, Sir Charles Lyell (1797–1875) published the third and last volume of his *Principles of Geology*, a work that had a tremendous influence on Darwin. Lyell attacked such schools of thought as *diluvialism*, whose followers claimed that Noah's flood accounted for what was known of the earth's geological structure and history, and *catastrophism*, whose adherents proposed that localized catastrophes (of which the Biblical flood was merely the most recent) accounted for all the layers and cracks in the earth's crust. He argued that the processes shaping the earth are the same today as they always were—uniform and continuous in character—a position that has come to be called *uniformitarianism*. However, Lyell was unable to free himself entirely from a doctrinaire Christian framework. Although he could envision gradual transformations in the inanimate world of geology, when he discussed living creatures, he continued to believe in the divine creation of each (unchanging) species, and he accounted for the extinction of species in terms of small, localized natural catastrophes.

Some biologists did comprehend the implications of comparative anatomy and the fossil record. For instance, Lamarck advanced his "developmental hypothesis," in which he arranged all known animals into a sequence based on their increasing organic complexity. He clearly implied that human beings were the highest product of a process of organic transformation and had been created through the same processes that had created all other species. However, Lamarck's imagination was also bound by theological constraints, and he did not carry his research through to its logical conclusion. Rather than limiting himself to natural forces as the shapers of organic transformation, Lamarck assumed an underlying, divinely ordered patterning.

Before scholars could fully appreciate the antiquity of the earth and the processes that gave rise to all species—including the human species—they had to free themselves from the constraints of nineteenth-century Christian theology. A revolution of perspective was necessary, a change of viewpoint so convincing that it would overcome people's emotional and intellectual commitment to Christian dogma. The logic of the new position would have to be simple and straightforward and would have to rest on a unified, universally applicable principle.

As we shall see shortly, students of human *society* had been grappling with these issues for almost a century. Herbert Spencer (1820–1903) developed the theory of evolution as applied to societies and based it (in the now immortal phrase) on the "survival of the fittest." His writings and those of Thomas Malthus (1766–1834), the political economist who pessimistically forecast a "struggle for survival" among humankind for dwindling resources, profoundly influenced two naturalists working independently on the problem of the origins of species: Both Alfred Russel Wallace (1823–1913) and Charles Robert Darwin (1809–1882) arrived at the solution at the same time. They hit on the single, unifying (and natural) principle that would account for both the origin and the extinction of species—*natural selection*. In 1858, they presented joint papers on this topic, and the next year Darwin published *On the Origin of Species*, a book that captured scholars' imaginations and became the first influential work that popularized the concept of evolution as applied to the world of living organisms.

What is natural selection? It can be put simply and straightforwardly: *Natural selection is the process through which certain environmentally adaptive features are perpetuated at the expense of less adaptive features.*

Two very important points must be stressed with regard to natural selection: (1) *It is features—not individuals—that are favored,* and (2) *no features are inherently "superior."* Natural selection is entirely dependent on the environment. Change the environment, and the favored adaptive features change as well.

Evolutionism in Social Thought

As we have mentioned, since medieval times, Europeans had been exposed, through the reports of adventurous travelers, to the existence of many "strange" peoples living in "exotic" places on distant shores. Thus, European scholars accumulated a body of information (much of it quite unreliable) about foreign societies, and quite a few set about trying to compare societies in more or less systematic ways. By the late eighteenth century and throughout the nineteenth century, the *comparative method* of social science resulted in the elaboration of theories of social and intellectual progress that developed into full-blown evolutionary theories, frequently referred to as *classical* or *unilineal evolutionism*. The Marquis de Condorcet (1743–1794), for instance, identified ten stages of social evolution marked by the successive acquisition of technological and scientific knowledge: From the limited knowledge needed for hunting and gathering, humanity passes through the development of pastoralism, agriculture, writing, and the differentiation of the sciences, then through a temporary period of darkness and the decline of knowledge in the Middle Ages, leading to the invention of the printing press in 1453, the skeptical rationalism of René Descartes' philosophy, then to the founding of the French Republic of Condorcet's day, and eventually, through the application of scientific knowledge, to a world of peace and equality among the nations and the sexes. His *Outline of the Intellectual Progress of Mankind* (1795) is viewed by many as the outstanding work of social science produced in eighteenth-century Europe, even though its ethnocentric bias is blatant (Harris, 1968:35).

Auguste Comte (1798–1857), who is sometimes called one of the "fathers" of social science, followed Condorcet's approach to social evolution. For him, too, the progress of the human intellect moved social evolution forward. However, he identified only three stages of evolution, characterized respectively by "theological thought," in which people perceive the universe as animated by a will much like their own (evolving from animism through polytheism to monotheism); "metaphysical thought," in which abstract laws of nature are discovered; and finally "positive thought," represented by the scientific method (of which his own writings were the embodiment in the social sciences). By the way, it is interesting to note that Comte also believed that each person passes through these three stages in the course of his or her individual development.

The writings of Herbert Spencer on social evolution were preeminent during much of the middle and late nineteenth century. As mentioned earlier, it was he who first introduced the term *evolution* into the scientific literature. And in his classic *First Principles*, published in 1862,[1] he provides a definition of the term that has not significantly been improved upon to this day. *Evolution*, Spencer points out, *is not merely change*. It is "change from an indefinite, incoherent homogeneity to a definite, coherent heterogeneity; through continuous differentiations and integrations." In other words, to Spencer *evolution is the progress of life forms and social forms from the simple to the complex*.

Spencer's work is often neglected by contemporary anthropologists, who tend to trace their historical roots to two other major nineteenth-century evolutionists, Sir Edward Burnett Tylor (1832–1917) and Lewis Henry Morgan (1818–1881). Morgan's work in many ways is derived from that of Spencer. Like Spencer, he viewed social evolution as the result of societies adapting to the stresses of their environments. In his classic study, *Ancient Society* (1877), Morgan identified seven stages of social evolution:

    I. Lower Status of Savagery
        Marked by simple food gathering

   II. Middle Status of Savagery
        Marked by knowledge of fishing and the invention of fire

---

1. The word *evolution* does not appear in Darwin's *On the Origin of Species* until the 1872 edition!

  III. Upper Status of Savagery
        Marked by the invention of the bow and arrow

  IV. Lower Status of Barbarism
        Marked by the invention of pottery

   V. Middle Status of Barbarism
        Marked by the domestication of plants and animals, irrigation, and stone and brick architecture

  VI. Upper Status of Barbarism
        Marked by the invention of iron working

 VII. Civilization
        Marked by the invention of the phonetic alphabet

Sir Edward Tylor lacked the concern with social systems of Spencer and Morgan. He was more concerned with *culture* than with society, defining culture all-inclusively as "that complex whole which includes knowledge, belief, art, morals, law, custom, and any other capabilities and habits acquired by man as a member of society" (1958:1; orig. 1871). Tylor attempted to demonstrate that culture had evolved from simple to complex and that it is possible to reconstruct the simple beginnings of culture by the study of its "survivals" in contemporary "primitive" cultures.

In spite of the fact that their individual evolutionary schemes differed from one another in important ways, these classical evolutionists shared one overriding conviction: Society had evolved from simple to complex through identifiable stages. Although it could not be claimed that every single society had passed through each of the stages they described, nevertheless they believed they had found sequences of developmental stages through which a "preponderant number" of societies had passed (Carneiro 1973:91) and that these sequences represented progress. At the turn of the century, this position came under furious assault by Franz Boas and his students and vanished from the American intellectual scene. It reemerged in the 1940s to become one of the major conceptual tools that prehistorians and archaeologists use to reconstruct the human past.

The Emergence of Specialized Disciplines

As we noted earlier, until the mid-eighteenth century, the social sciences had no separate identities—the study of history embodied them all. And it wasn't until the rise of evolutionary theory in the nineteenth century that the social sciences began to differentiate themselves, began to split off from each other through a specialization of interests and research methodologies.

Perhaps the major splitting of the social sciences in the mid-nineteenth century was the emergence of the separate disciplines of sociology and anthropology, which to this day have maintained their distinct and individual identities. Sociologists tended to follow the positivist approach of Auguste Comte described earlier and shared with Comte a preoccupying interest in European society. Anthropologists, on the other hand, remained interested in a far broader range of data: archaeological finds, the study of "races" and the distribution of diverse human physical traits, human evolution, the comparative study of cultures and cultural evolution—all more or less unified by evolutionary theory. And whereas sociologists focused on European society, anthropologists, in their worldwide search for data, tended to concentrate on the "primitive" or preindustrial societies (Voget 1975:114–116.) It is in this context that the four main branches—physical anthropology, archaeology, linguistics, and cultural anthropology—emerged as separate, but still interrelated, subdisciplines.

THE TRUNK OF THE TREE

As you have seen, the roots of anthropology go very deep and they spread wide across the world. Its branches, large and small, are numerous and diverse. Where then is its trunk? What holds anthropology together?

In order to work—to plan, execute, and evaluate their research—all scientists must be trained in the sets of beliefs and practices that characterize their disciplines in a fundamental way. This set of beliefs and practices—in essence the core and underpinning of a scientific discipline—is sometimes termed the *paradigm* of that science. Although no scientist will ever fully utilize all the elements of a paradigm in his or her research, nevertheless such research is planned, undertaken, and evaluated by other scientists in terms of the ways in which it contributes to and reflects the paradigm as a whole.

Anthropology has such a paradigm—which is the trunk of the tree. It consists of five themes that have developed gradually as anthropology has emerged as a distinct discipline. These are the *comparative*, the *holistic*, the *systems and process*, the *case study*, and the *"insider-outsider"* themes. Before we explain and elaborate on each of these, we wish to emphasize one important point: Not all anthropologists conduct their day-to-day work in terms of all five themes, but all anthropologists do appreciate their importance and understand their own and others' work within the context these themes provide.

The Comparative Theme

As we mentioned above, a major aspect of the split between anthropology and sociology in the nineteenth century was that whereas sociology focused on Western society, anthropology continued the tradition of comparing and contrasting peoples and cultures throughout the world. These comparisons are made in two ways: (1) by *synchronics*, which is the comparison of anthropological data across a wide geographical area (including many peoples and cultures) at one point in time (usually the present or recent past); and (2) by *diachronics*, which involves comparison of such data through a very extended period of time but limited to one geographical region (and only a few peoples and cultures), thus revealing patterns of evolution (be it biological, social, or cultural).

The Holistic Theme

Another feature of the sociology-anthropology split was that sociologists came to concentrate their attention on society and social systems, whereas anthropologists continued to attempt to tie together all aspects of human biology and behavior—that is, biology, society, culture, and even psychology. The concern with the *whole* picture of the human condition is termed *holism*, and it is a fundamental aspect of anthropology. That is one reason anthropologists find themselves at odds with so many contemporary scholars and popularizers who wish to account for human behavior by reducing it to one simple underlying determinant, such as "race," territoriality, sexual dimorphism, or the structure of the human brain.

The Systems and Process Theme

Herbert Spencer introduced the concept of the *social system* in the early nineteenth century. In the last few decades anthropologists have rediscovered the fact that it is not very productive to describe and analyze societies and cultures in terms of static lists of their traits. Rather societies and cultures are understood as open systems, each possessing many subsystems and all such systems containing their own patterned processes. For example, archaeologists are no longer satisfied merely to catalog the material remains that they retrieve from prehistoric societies. Rather, they attempt to understand what such remains can tell us about the ways these societies adapted to and utilized the elements of their natural environment, how they organized themselves into social groups, the ways such groups interacted among themselves and with each other, and so forth. Biological anthropologists have essentially abandoned the static concept of "race" as useless and have turned instead to investigating the ways in which genes express themselves changeably in different environments. This concern with systems, processes, and dynamics has greatly enriched the discipline of anthropology.

The Case Study Theme

You will recall that anthropology developed on the fringes of European society and continued with a preoccupation with distant and remote peoples and places. Those hardy souls who ventured forth to study such out-of-the-way societies found themselves cut off, for long periods of time, from contacts with their homes. They lost track of current events in European affairs and consequently immersed themselves in the detailed study and description of the daily happenings among the people they were studying. It was a challenge to keep their objectivity while at the same time working to gain people's trust and even their affection. This form of social research is called *participant observation*. It is characteristic of much of the research undertaken by anthropologists, who seem on the whole to be much less comfortable with grand abstractions than with the concrete world of stones and bones, phonemes and morphemes, rituals, economic transactions, and pottery sherds. For every grand (and grandiose!) theory of society or human behavior that is so lightly bandied about in the popular media, one is sure to hear a quiet but insistent anthropological gadfly asking, "But what about the case of the Eskimos?" or "But how does that fit with what we know about forest-dwelling baboons?" Sadly, the wider public remains for the most part uninformed of the objections anthropologists have raised to the widely proliferated, pseudoscientific writings claiming "proof" for such things as prehistoric extraterrestrial visitors.

The "Insider-Outsider" Theme

Because anthropologists, more than other social scientists, have concentrated so much of their research on studying remote peoples with life-styles, mores, values, subsistence systems, and languages very different from our own, it has fallen on anthropologists to grapple with the problem of translating the *perspective of the people being studied* (the "insider's" view) into the *perspective of Western social science* (the "outsider's" view). Neither view is inherently correct, of course, and both complement and supplement each other. But it is easy to get them mixed up both during the process of learning about the people one is studying, and again after having completed one's research when trying to make it meaningful to colleagues, students, and even the public at large. After all, anthropologists are just as vulnerable as anybody else to succumbing to the insidious distortions of ethnocentric thought. Guarding against this is an important element of anthropological research. Because anthropologists are sensitized to the many and subtle ways people look down upon one another, the study of anthropology can be a valuable contribution to an individual's maturation and education.

THE TREE OF ANTHROPOLOGY

In this brief introductory essay, we have presented you with the branches, roots, and trunk of the "tree of anthropology." The articles that follow are many of its fruits. Naturally, we have selected this offering to make the study of anthropology enticing. We think the articles are clear and informative, and not a few of them are warmed by a sense of humor. We have been careful, however, to allow as many as possible of the voices of our discipline to be heard in these pages. The differences of opinion, the disputes and controversies that currently enliven the lives of anthropologists, are offered to you for your own consideration.

We hope that you will pause a while at the tree of anthropology, that you will taste of its fruit and rest in its shade. We hope that some of you will be moved to climb up into its branches, to see the world from the unique vantage points they offer. But most of all, we hope that those of you who choose to wander on through the other niches of the garden of academia will have found your stay here refreshing, that you will have acquired a new set of perspectives, perhaps a new understanding or awareness. If that is the case, then this awareness will enrich all of your future travels.

References

Carneiro, Robert
    1973 "The Four Faces of Evolution," in John J. Honigmann (ed.), *Handbook of Social and Cultural Anthropology*, Chicago: Rand McNally, pp. 89–110.

Coon, Carleton S.
    1963 *The Origin of Races*, New York: Alfred A. Knopf.

Harris, Marvin
    1968 *The Rise of Anthropological Theory: A History of Culture*, New York: Thomas Y. Crowell.

Montagu, Ashley
    1964 *Man's Most Dangerous Myth: The Fallacy of Race* (4th ed., rev.), New York: Meridian Books.

Tylor, Sir Edward Burnett
    1958 (orig. 1871) *The Origins of Culture*, Part I of *Primitive Culture*, New York: Harper Torchbooks.

Voget, Fred W.
    1975 *A History of Ethnology*, New York: Holt, Rinehart and Winston.

Looking Toward the 21st Century:
The Prospects for Anthropology

By Eric Wolf

....

As anthropology approaches the twenty-first century, it is a discipline undergoing profound changes. These changes will surprise those who hold a traditional image of anthropology. This image grew out of widely read books, written by Ruth Benedict and Margaret Mead in the 1930's, which depicted primitive cultures as personalities "writ large" and argued that each culture produces a characteristic pattern of individual development. Dr. Mead drew on her field work in Samoa and New Guinea to address a wide range of public issues in our own society, becoming a spokesman for what anthropology could offer the world at large.

That approach has not been central to anthropology for many years, but Dr. Mead herself continued to play an important role as a tribal elder. Her death in 1978 symbolically closed an earlier chapter in American anthropology. During her lifetime, the discipline became less a vocation and more a profession, and moved toward increasing specialization. Specialization brought fragmentation, which in turn has raised a troublesome question: What, these days, constitutes the discipline of anthropology?

Although, as the previous article indicates, American anthropology is still distinguished from other traditions by its "four-field approach," the practitioners of those fields—archaeologists, linguists, biological anthropologists, and social or cultural anthropologists—increasingly have pulled apart, meeting and publishing separately. Social-cultural anthropologists have also split into subdivisions, turning themselves into applied, cognitive, economic, ecological, legal, political, psychological, urban, or even psychopharmacological anthropologists. Area specialization has grouped anthropologists working in a particular geographical area with, say, Latin Americanists or Middle Easternists from other disciplines. Such lines of tension were deepened by opposition between older and younger members of the profession, between anthropologists at the "major" and at the "minor" institutions, and between those teaching within academe and those working outside. Moreover, conflicts during the 1960's over the role of anthropology in the American involvement in Southeast Asia and the developing issues of affirmative action exacerbated the other fissures.

Yet this restlessness of the tribe is intellectual as well as professional. An earlier anthropology had achieved unity under the aegis of the culture concept. It was culture, in the view of anthropologists, that distinguished humankind from all the rest of the universe, and it was the possession of varying cultures that differentiated one society from another. Each people was seen as having a distinctive, internally coherent repertoire of artifacts and customs, which—passed from generation to generation—created an enduring compact between the living and the dead. Looking at culture in this way, anthropologists had found seemingly secure explanations of why people behaved in certain ways and not others: it was "in their culture." Similarly, changes in the way people behaved could be accounted for by pointing to changes "in their culture." Other disciplines, especially psychology, sociology and history, acknowledged anthropology's special jurisdiction over the study of cultural phenomena.

The past four decades have undermined this intellectual sense of security. The relatively inchoate concept of "culture" was attacked from several theoretical directions. As the social sciences transformed themselves into "behavioral" sciences, explanations for behavior were no longer traced to culture; behavior was to be understood in terms of psychological encounters, strategies of economic choice, strivings for payoffs in games of power. Culture, once extended to all acts and ideas employed in social life, was now relegated to the margins as "world view" or "values." In 1958, the anthropologist Alfred Kroeber, long associated with the University of California at Berkeley, and the Harvard University sociologist Talcott Parsons, each the dean of his respective profession, drew up a joint statement on the concepts of culture and of social system, restricting culture to "values, ideas, and other symbolic-meaningful systems." In the division of spoils, sociology was permitted to claim all the social action and anthropology retained the residual "values."

Soon afterward there came word from Paris that Claude Lévi-Strauss had done away with the notion of distinctive cultures altogether. For Lévi-Strauss, culture was generated

Reprinted by permission of the author.

neither in human action oriented toward practical ends nor in the passing on of cultural forms from generation to generation, but in the convolutions of the human brain. This brain, common to all humans, continuously spawns logical and analogical oppositions, forever replacing binary opposites already installed with new ones, in an ultimately fruitless round—fruitless because the human brain cannot transcend the matrix of nature that had given rise to it.

A third movement assailed the concept of culture itself. In the 50's, the anthropological study of how cultures adapted to and used their physical environments had produced a "cultural ecology" that concerned itself with the specifically cultural acts and artifacts deployed in the transformation of the natural world. In the 60's, however, this cultural ecology increasingly gave way to a general ecological approach, which began to treat humans as organisms among other organisms—measuring, for example, the intake and expenditure of calories in different environments. Such an approach abrogated the boundary between the human and the nonhuman aspects of the world and threatened to deal with culture as just another organismic appendage, like the sonar radar of the bat or the antlers of the Irish stag.

The upshot of this revision and displacement of the traditional culture concept has been an acrimonious debate between "materialists," who claim to study the observable behaviors involved in concrete action, and students of meaning, who claim to study the mental universes constructed by the natives themselves. Each side actually represents a variety of different positions but gains a spurious unity in denigrating the opposition. Marvin Harris, who now teaches at the University of Florida, and who is the most vigorous spokesman for materialism, castigates the "obscurantists" and "eclectics" bent on impeding the "struggle" to transform anthropology into a science of human social life. His opponents counter by deriding Harris's attempts to reduce the complexities of culture to mechanical processes of protein consumption or population control. The main prescription for the further study of meaning, by Clifford Geertz, a resident at the Institute for Advanced Studies at Princeton, calls for the "reading" of cultures as "texts." Offered a choice between biological reductionism and literary criticism, most anthropologists have preferred to go about their work unencumbered by theoretical consistency.

Luckily so, perhaps, for the strength of anthropology has always lain in its eclecticism, or—what may be the same thing—its respect for reality. The anthropological enterprise grew out of the confrontation of the West with variegated and unfamiliar cultures elsewhere. For anthropologists, the arrangements of the Western world will always remain but one set of possibilities among others; a new and unexpected configuration is always waiting across the next tributary of the Amazon or the next Papuan mountain—or in the next neighborhood of their own home town. To learn about yet another set of human possibilities demands prolonged engagement with and patient apprenticeship to the people one hopes to understand.

The result of anthropology's eclecticism is that the field continues to astound by its diverse and colorful activity. New findings are reported about Bushman demography, the use of hallucinogens in tropical South America, the decipherment of Mayan hieroglyphics. Anthropologists are now as likely to study peasant and urban subcultures as those of primitives, and increasingly they are investigating how such cultures are remolded by their inclusion into larger regional, national and global systems. Feminist concerns are generating new research on the import of gender in different cultures, not only uncovering specifically female domains of culture but also altering our understanding of the male domains. Despite the challenge of increasing specialization to the "four-field approach," it continues to open up new avenues of inquiry. Thus, a "new" archaeology makes use of ecology and ethnography, as well as sophisticated quantitative methods and state-of-the-art high technology, to build models of the past. Current approaches to human evolution interpret the fossil record by drawing on archaeology, ecology, comparative studies of social behavior, sociobiology, genetics, and the ethnology of still-extant hunters and gatherers. Studies of meaning employ methods derived from structural linguistics. Ethnohistory joins the study of written documents to oral history, archaeology, linguistic reconstruction, and considerations of political economy. Beyond the academy, anthropologists working in health care, education, social services and a variety of other settings bring their special skills of observation and diagnosis to bear on an understanding of complex institutions. The annual meeting operates as a giant fair, in which these diverse activities and their results are exhibited, discussed and savored.

Yet this multifarious activity is accompanied by a sense of unease, which feeds on that very proliferation of purposes and tasks. What was once a secular church of believers in the primacy of Culture has now become a holding company of diverse interests, defined by what the members do rather than by what they do it for. There are unvoiced concerns within the profession about what anthropology has become and where it is headed. The old culture concept is moribund. But in its time, it unified the discipline around a concern with basic questions about the nature of the human species, its biological and socially learned variability, and the proper ways to assess the similarities and differences. Ultimately, a discipline draws its energy from the questions it asks. Whether anthropology's basic questions are still those that marked its beginnings or new ones, the task of articulating them becomes imperative as we approach the twenty-first century.

PART 2

Biological Anthropology

Biological anthropology has broadened a great deal over the last four decades, and it now includes many subjects that overlap with other disciplines. In a loose way, we may define biological anthropology as the study of primate biology in its natural and social environments—with a special emphasis on the study of our own species. Yet it is useful to break apart this large and rather loosely connected branch of anthropology into two major subbranches: *paleontology*, the study of our extinct ancestors (through their fossilized remains); and *neontology*, the comparative study of living primate groups.

Many scholars trace the origins of modern biological anthropology to the work of Johann Blumenbach (1752–1840), who systematically undertook to collect and study human skulls from many populations around the world. He devised ways of making very precise measurements on these skulls and used these measurements to produce an encyclopedic work on what he called the races of the world.

One of Blumenbach's central ideas was that the "races" developed as biological responses to environmental stresses. This notion was elaborated upon in the nineteenth century by numerous scholars, such as Anders Retzius (1796–1860), who in 1842 devised a formula for computing long-headedness and narrow-headedness:

$$\frac{\text{head breadth}}{\text{head length}} \times 100 = \text{cephalic index}$$

A low cephalic index indicates a narrow head; a high cephalic index a broad head. Fourteen years later, Retzius published a survey of cranial indexes based on the measurement of skulls from private collections, in which he distinguished a vast number of "races" determined by virtue of their cephalic indexes.

Others followed the lead of Blumenbach and Retzius, and a wide number of techniques were developed through which the human body could be systematically measured. Such measuring is called *anthropometry* and remains to the present day an important aspect of biological anthropology. Anthropometry contributes to our understanding of fossil remains by providing scholars with precise methods for studying them. It also provides concrete data on variations in body shape among human populations, replacing what previously had been rather impressionistic descriptions. Thus body measuring became one of the major tools for determining "racial" classifications. However, by the end of the century, it was being attacked by scholars who pointed out that anthropometric traits of all ranges could be found represented among individuals within each of the so-called races.

After the publication of Charles Robert Darwin's *On the Origin of Species* in 1859, natural selection became the core concept of biological anthropology, and evolution its primary concern. Thomas Huxley (1825–1895), a naturalist who enthusiastically took up Darwin's theories, added great impetus to the study of human evolution by showing that the human species was not qualitatively distinct from other primates, but rather only the most complex in an evolutionary continuum ranging from the primitive lower primates to monkeys, the great apes, and finally humankind.

The study of the fossil evidence for human evolution was slow in developing. By 1822, reports had come from Germany about findings of the fossilized remains of many extinct animals in limestone caves. These reports impelled William Buckland (1784–1856), reader of geology at Oxford University, to investigate the limestone Paviland Cave on the Welsh coast. There Buckland found the same kinds of extinct animals as had been reported in Germany—as well as flint tools and a human skeleton. This skeleton came to be called the Red Lady of Paviland, because it had become stained with red ochre. (Subsequently it was determined that the skeleton was that of a male.) As a Christian minister, Buckland was hard pressed to explain this human presence among extinct creatures. He resorted to the contorted conclusion that the animal remains had probably been swept into the cave by flooding and that the human skeleton had been buried there long after Noah's flood by local inhabitants.

Similar mental gymnastics kept scholars from acknowledging what, in fact, their eyes were seeing: ancient human remains among extinct animals, attesting to a vastly longer human existence than Christian doctrine permitted. Only after the Darwinian revolution could people permit themselves to make accurate interpretations of these fossil materials. In 1860, for example, Edouard Lartet (1801–1873), while investigating a cave near the village of Aurignac in southern France, found human remains associated with the charred bones of such extinct animals as the woolly mammoth, the woolly rhinoceros, the cave bear, and the bison. The evidence he reported finally convinced many people, including the prominent geologist Charles Lyell, of the antiquity of humankind. It is hardly coincidental that these events happened the year after the publication of Darwin's *On the Origin of Species.*

Eight years later, in 1868, Louis Lartet followed his father's lead and excavated an ancient rock shelter that had been exposed in the course of the construction of a railway in the Dordogne region of France. He found five human skeletons: three adult males, one adult female, and one unborn baby. These people were associated with the same kinds of extinct animals and cultural artifacts as those found by his father at Aurignac. They came to be viewed as representatives of the so-called Cro-Magnon population (fully modern humans) that produced the impressive Aurignacian Upper Paleolithic culture.

In 1857, fragments of a human skeleton were found in a limestone cave near Düsseldorf in Germany. The skull cap, however, displayed what at the time seemed to be shockingly apelike features. It was extraordinarily thick, had massive ridges over the eyes, and had little in the way of a forehead. This specimen, which came to be called Neanderthal man (sometimes spelled Neandertal, in keeping with current German spelling), raised for scholars the possibility of finding fossil populations of primitive people who were ancestral to the Cro-Magnon types and, thus, to modern human beings. In 1889, Eugène Dubois (1859–1940) traveled to Southeast Asia with the deliberate intention of finding such fossilized evidence of human evolution. There, during 1891 and 1892, in a site on the bank of the Solo River on the island of Java, he found some molars, a skull cap, and a femur (thigh bone) of such primitive nature that he thought them at first to be the remains of an ancient chimpanzee. By 1892, he revised this assessment and decided that he had indeed found an evolutionary ancestor of the human species, a creature he eventually called *Pithecanthropus erectus* (erect apeman). Naturally, as with all such finds, a great debate about its evolutionary status ensued; but today we agree with Dubois that his Solo River find is indeed a human ancestor, one of many that have since been found and are now grouped together under the term *Homo erectus* (erect man).

Although biological anthropology emerged as a fully developed discipline only after the theory of evolution had established itself in the minds of Europe's leading thinkers, in the 1700s, scholars were already engaged in the serious study of human population biology—as in the researches of Blumenbach and Retzius. However, as we indicated in "What is Anthropology?" (Hunter and Whitten), with which we opened this reader, eighteenth-century research on human biology was marred by the polarizing effects of the great debate of the day: the bitter feud between the *polygenists* and the *monogenists*. The former saw the biological and behavioral differences between the world's populations as being so substantial in nature that they could not accept a common origin for all the world's peoples. They argued (contrary to the teachings of the Scriptures) that God must have created people a number of different times in a number of different places. Monogenists, on the other hand, argued for a single origin for all peoples. Whereas polygenists perceived "racial" characteristics as permanent and immutable, monogenists insisted that they were changeable and came about as a result of the influence of the natural environment upon local groups.

Blumenbach himself was a member of the monogenist camp and recognized that the five "races" he posited were as much a matter of classificatory convenience as they were a reflection of the real world. Nevertheless, this debate proved rather fruitless until a means was found to resolve it. That means was the revolutionary theory proposed jointly by Alfred Russel Wallace (1823–1913) and Charles Robert Darwin (1809–1882) in 1858, and popularized by the publication in the following year of Darwin's masterpiece, *On the Origin of Species.*

If there is any one concept that united the discipline of biological anthropology, it is the theory of evolution. Its assumptions, axioms, hypotheses, and premises are the foundations upon which virtually all work in this area rests. It is important that you grasp how all-pervasive evolutionary thought is—how it has been assimilated into virtually all the social and biological sciences. Many of the readings in this and other sections of this book make explicit and implicit reference to evolutionary theory. We shall let them speak for themselves, but first we wish to clarify one aspect of evolutionary theory that is widely misunderstood and yet is its central principle—the principle of *natural selection.*

Simply, natural selection can be defined as *the process through which certain environmentally adaptive features are perpetuated in organisms at the expense of less adaptive features.* That really is it. But its simplicity is deceptive, and the concept frequently (perhaps generally) is misunderstood. Here we shall address two widely held misconceptions about natural selection:

1. There is no such thing as an evolutionary favored individual. *Features* are favored, not individual organisms. (Actually, since the 1980s, most evolutionary biologists have accepted the notion that it is *individual genes* that are the units of selection. In any event, it is *not* individual organisms.)

2. There is no such thing as an inherently superior fea-

ture (let alone an inherently superior organism). What is meant by the term *superior* is the degree to which a feature is adapted to its environment. Change the environment, and a "superior" feature may well become an "inferior" feature.

Natural selection, then, is relative—relative to the environment. And because the environment is always changing, natural selection is an ever-changing process. No group, in-dividual organism, or specific feature will ever reside permanently on top of the evolutionary ladder. Here, as elsewhere, the one constant is change.

In the context of this general introduction, we now present the articles of this part. They are grouped into three topics: Human Evolution, Evolution and Primate Behavior, and Human Diversity. We discuss each of these separately.

TOPIC 2

Human Evolution

When the editors of this reader were college undergraduates (in the early 1960s) taking their first anthropology courses, the academic world still was in uproar over the fossil skull and teeth found by Mary and Louis Leakey in 1959 at Olduvai Gorge in northern Tanzania (East Africa). These fossilized remains, named *Zinjanthropus boisei* by the Leakeys, were dated at 1.75 million years old—almost a million years older than similar fossils that had been found in southern Africa. The possibility that the australopithecines—the direct ancestors of human beings (at least that is what they were thought to be then)—could be over a million years old was absolutely shocking.

The past three decades have seen the unearthing of previously undreamed of riches in fossil finds. Most of these finds have not been limited to specimens of *Homo erectus* (generally regarded today as our most recent direct ancestor) or of Neanderthals (now seen as an isolated population of European hominids who were our evolutionary cousins). Rather, most of the finds have been of much older hominids and even of their remote ancestors—the earliest primates. In "Our Forebears' Forebears," Phillip Whitten and Martin K. Nickels survey what the latest discoveries have taught us about the evolution of the early primates. They discuss how plate tectonics (continental drift) and changing climatological conditions helped shape primate evolution, and they explore the major controversies surrounding our early ancestors.

As more fossils, and more ancient fossils, have been unearthed, scholars have not reacted calmly. Almost every significant new find has produced a flurry of heated debate over (1) its taxonomic status (that is, its place in the evolutionary hierarchy) and (2) its significance (that is, the degree to which it confirmed or invalidated previous views of human evolution). At first, settling the debates was merely a matter of pushing back the emergence of human ancestors earlier and earlier: The australopithecines became "older" throughout the 1960s, 1970s, and 1980s—first one, then two, then three, and now perhaps five million years old. But then, as more and more fossils were found, the questions became more profound and subtle. For instance, what was

the relationship between the emergence of erect bipedalism (walking on two legs) and the evolution of the large, complex human brain? Did large brains favor the invention of tools or, the other way around, did the invention of tools promote the enlarging of the brain?

One of the most recent and, in many ways, the most interesting debate concerns hominid finds from East Africa. There Mary Leakey and her son Richard Leakey, working respectively at Laetoli (thirty miles south of Olduvai Gorge) and at Lake Turkana (in Kenya), have found remarkable hominid specimens. They identify these specimens, some of which are as old as 3.35 to 3.75 million years, as belonging to our own genus *Homo*. Their main antagonist is Donald Johanson, whose fieldwork has been mainly in the Afar Triangle (in Ethiopia), west of the lower end of the Red Sea. Johanson's finds are the same age or slightly older than the Leakeys', and one of them, a skeleton he calls Lucy, is remarkably complete (over 40 percent of her bones were found). Johanson gives his finds the taxonomic label *Australopithecus afarensis*. He claims that the Leakey finds older than 2 million years are members of that same species, and that this species is the earliest example of a true hominid ancestor to human beings.

One of the most puzzling problems that had been confronting students of human evolution was the fact that the interpretations of early hominid fossil remains did not fit in with the studies comparing human and ape amino acid molecules. Scientists studying amino acid molecules had, for over a decade, shown that systematic comparisons of these molecules from related species could be used to compute how far back in the evolutionary past their ancestors had split apart. Using these methods, Allan Wilson and Vincent Sarich of the University of California at Berkeley arrived at a date of 5 to 6 million years ago for the split between pongids (apes and their ancestors) and hominids (humans and their ancestors). On the other hand, fossil studies, which counted *Ramapithecus* as the first true hominid, set the date of that split some 9 million years earlier. There seemed to be no way out of this dilemma other than to favor one view or the other (and most anthropologists favored the latter). Some authors even went so far as to suggest that the amino acid time clock might be accurate for the whole animal kingdom except for human beings. Two developments contributed to a solution to this puzzle: (1) the reinterpretation of ramapithecine remains and (2) the discovery of Lucy.

David Pilbeam of Harvard has been one of the world's foremost students of ramapithecines, the small ape-like creatures who inhabited Africa and Asia 8 to 15 million years ago and whose jaws seemed to show true hominid features. In the 1980s, after more complete remains of *Ramapithecus* were discovered (before then only ramapithecine jaws had been found), Pilbeam realized that *Ramapithecus* (and a related form, *Sivapithecus*) was not in the human family line at all, but most likely was ancestral to the orangutan. Another possibility is that a later fossil population would be found, one that might qualify as the earliest hominid. This would make possible a meeting of the minds between those who have studied fossils and those who have studied amino acid time clocks. The first fully hominid fossils might indeed be only 5 or 6 million years old.

But is there such a fossil population? Richard Leakey thinks he and his associates have found one—a creature he has named *Homo habilis* ("handy man"). *Homo habilis,* which dates back over 2 million years, produced stone tools and had a brain one-third to one-half as large as our own. This population clearly was ancestral to *Homo erectus,* the immediate ancestors of *Homo sapiens.* But what was the origin of *Homo habilis*?

Leakey believes that *Homo habilis* evolved directly from a much earlier pongid ancestor, possibly the cat-sized pongid *Aegyptopithecus* (Egyptian ape), whose remains, found near Cairo, date back some 28 million years. Therefore, Leakey considers the other main fossil populations that are similar to, and precede or are contemporary with, *Homo habilis* to be parallel side branches of hominids—that is, evolutionary deadends.

This is where Johanson's discovery of Lucy becomes important. When discovered, she was the earliest, most complete, fully erect and bipedal hominid remain ever found. As mentioned earlier, Johanson coined the term *Australopithecus afarensis* for the population of fossils to which Lucy belongs. In 1984, David Pilbeam announced the discovery of some *Australopithecus afarensis* fossils dating back over 5 million years, the earliest hominid remains yet uncovered. Though it walked on two legs, *Australopithecus afarensis* had a smaller brain than *Homo habilis,* and Johanson believes that *Australopithecus afarensis* is the ancestor of the "handy man," the link between *Homo habilis* and the

pongid (ape) line. In this view, *Homo habilis* joins *Australopithecus afarensis* and *Australopithecus africanus* (found in southern Africa) as one single, continuous evolutionary line. (In this view the more rugged, robust line of australopithecines remains an evolutionary cul-de-sac.)

At least one very important issue is at stake in the Leakey–Johanson debate. If Leakey's view is right, it would appear that bipedalism and large brains evolved more or less together and that they were associated with the manufacture and use of tools. If Johanson's view is right, then our ancestors first evolved an upright posture and tool use, and only afterwards did the brain become enlarged.

In "The Emergence of *Homo Sapiens,*" Boyce Rensberger takes up the tale at a later but equally important time. He accepts the Johanson interpretation of early hominid origins and focuses on the evolution of *Homo sapiens,* our direct ancestor, from *Homo erectus.* Here, too, there is debate, especially over the position of the large-headed, heavy-browed, stoop-shouldered Neanderthals. The replacement hypothesis portrays Neanderthals as evolutionary deadends, whereas the unilinear hypothesis views them as an early form of our own species who evolved into modern Europeans.

Rensberger lays out the arguments and data offered by both sides of the debate—and in the end suggests that it is too early to take sides. However, by 1990, the preponderance of evidence seemed to point clearly to the Neanderthals as our close cousins, but *not* in the evolutionary line that led to ourselves, *Homo sapiens.*

This view is reinforced in Stephen Jay Gould's "Bushes All the Way Down." Gould reviews the latest evidence—from fossil studies to analysis of mitochondrial DNA—and argues that *all* people alive today are descended from *Homo erectus* populations that lived exclusively in Africa until as recently as two hundred thousand years ago or less.

Gould also dispenses with the metaphor of the ladder in explaining human evolution—the idea that earlier forms, from bacteria to apes, represented rungs in a ladder that led inexorably to modern human beings, the crown of creation. This metaphor, which derives from the nineteenth-century notion of the inevitability of progress, should now be abandoned. In its place, Gould offers the metaphor of the bush, with humans representing only a recent twig. This theme is reinforced by British biological anthropologist, Robert A. Foley, in "The Search for Early Man." Foley examines the advances that have been made recently in understanding human evolution, looks at ongoing research, and projects what we may have learned by the year 2050.

Our Forebears' Forebears

By Phillip Whitten and Martin K. Nickels

FOUR TO FIVE MILLION YEARS AGO, the earliest humanlike creatures first strode upright across the rolling savannas of East Africa, gazed over the vast plain, and began competing with much stronger, faster, and deadlier carnivores for a place in the sun. But long before our remote forebears built the first fire and huddled around it to ward off the night (about one and a half million years ago), eons before their predecessors fashioned the first crude stone tools (almost four million years ago), or even began to walk on two legs, primates had inhabited the Earth for well over fifty million years, evolving the set of physical characteristics—grasping hands, binocular vision, short snouts, and large cortexes—that they would later pass on to *Homo sapiens*. And while Africa was undoubtedly the birthplace of our own immediate ancestors and the genus *Homo* itself, the earliest primates appear to have arisen not in Africa or Asia, but on the North American continent.

Despite the variety within the order of primates, the nearly two hundred living species are bound by a common ancestral lifestyle that has shaped their distinctive features. The distant relatives of today's prosimians (lemurs, tarsiers, lorises, and galagos or bush-babies), monkeys (both Old World and New World forms), apes (chimpanzees, gorillas, orangutans, gibbons, and siamangs), and humans all shared a life history that began in and amongst the trees. Some spent all of their lives in the branches, while others most likely concentrated their activities close enough to the trees so that they could flee into them during times of danger and sleep in them at night, safe from ground-stalking predators. But all primates developed dexterous fingers and toes with nails (rather than claws) ideal for grasping and clinging to branches as well as for capturing small insects and lizards; and all of them developed eyes that faced forward with overlapping fields of vision that enabled them to judge accurately the distance to the next perch or the next meal. As vision became more important for their survival and their eyes moved from the sides of the head to the front, the primates' olfactory apparatus diminished both in importance and size. Finally, the selective pressures of arboreal life caused the primate brain to change. The visual cortex became enlarged and elaborated as it processed more information. At the same time, complex cortical motor control areas developed to coordinate rapid movements through trees.

The first primate (or proto-primate), however, was not a very impressive fellow. From the rather meager fossil record of only a few teeth, we can tell that it was a rodent-like animal (before there were true rodents). It probably spent much of its time either hunting for insects or avoiding being unceremoniously squashed by the dinosaurs that ruled as unchallenged lords for more than 160 million years, dominating both land and sea until they disappeared about 65 million years ago.

Oddly enough, the fossilized remains of this early form have been found only in North America, a continent with no indigenous primate species today. Its remains, along with those of fearsome dinosaurs like *Triceratops,* were discovered in 1964 by scientists from the University of Minnesota, in Montana's Bug Creek area, among the chalky rubble of Purgatory Hill (hence the primate's name, *Purgatorius*). As if to confirm the American origins of the first primate, other bones appeared nearby. Last year, in Wyoming, Robert T. Bakker, of Johns Hopkins University, discovered the fossil foot bones of a fifty-two-million-year old lemurlike animal called *Cantius.* These fossils are the oldest evidence of a grasping big toe, a characteristic that some scientists consider more important than teeth for tracing primate evolution.

It is tempting to conclude from these discoveries that the origin of all primates may have been on this continent, but the fossil evidence is both skimpy and controversial. And even though the oldest bones we now have come from North America, it is always possible that still older and more conclusive evidence may be found elsewhere. Furthermore it is difficult to argue, with only a handful of North American teeth and foot bones, that primates first arose on this continent. After all, except for South American monkey fossils, most fossil evidence relating to the evolutionary rise of the higher primates (humans included) comes from Africa, Asia, and Europe.

Still the question nags: What of the bones found in North America? They date from the dawning of the Paleocene epoch (the earliest division of the Cenozoic era), when North America and Eurasia were one continuous continent called Laurasia; when South America and Africa may still have been linked by a land bridge; and when North and South America were not yet connected. Flowers, deciduous trees, and grasses were beginning to spread out, creating forest, bush, and savanna habitats that covered the northwestern United States and Europe with lush tropical rain forests.

ONE OF THE CREATURES that lived during this green era some sixty-five million years ago was *Plesiadapis,* a squirrel-sized animal very much like a rodent, whose remains have been found in both North America (Colorado) and Europe (France). *Plesiadapis* itself is not thought to be a direct ancestor of later primates—it had claws instead of nails, relied more on smell than sight, and had teeth specially adapted to eating fruits, seeds, and vegetables. But this rodentlike creature had already adapted to climbing and living in trees, the distinctive ecological niche occupied by almost every primate form. In fact, *Plesiadapis* so resembles the prosimians that came later that it is sometimes classified as one even today.

The indisputable evolutionary attributes of the primates did not appear until the next Cenozoic epoch, the Eocene. Like their Paleocene predecessors, the fossilized remains of Eocene primates come almost exclusively from the Eurasian-North American landmass. Unlike their predecessors, they had more manipulative digits, protected by flat nails instead of claws, and a body structure that allowed them to cling, hop, and leap, as some modern prosimians do. Fossil evidence of this period, which is the most complete for any of the early primate eras, also attests to the great diversity and adaptive success of these animals. Probably both nocturnal and diurnal, lemurlike and tarsierlike forms abounded. But despite their adaptive success, even these primates died out.

New mammalian groups, especially the rodents, began to invade the prosimians' econiches, and climatic changes forced many prosimians either into more restricted zones or into extinction. Prosimian supremacy among the primates eventually gave way to the superior arboreal adaptations of the anthropoids, the suborder that includes monkeys, apes, and humans. The earliest known anthropoids had larger and more complex brains than the prosimians, quite possibly color vision, more mobile and dexterous digits, and perhaps even more complex social adaptations. And by this time primate evolution had shifted toward the Asian half of the Eurasian-North American landmass. In 1980, when a team of Burmese and American scientists discovered fossilized fragments of the earliest known anthropoid primates—*Amphipithecus* and *Pondaungia*—in the hills of northern Burma, they noted that both creatures were about the size of a modern gibbon, and that their jaws were strikingly similar to those of present-day humans. Most astounding of all was their age: the fossils were dated to forty million years ago, more than ten million years before the earliest anthropoid remains found in Africa.

These earliest known anthropoid primates, though, also turned out to be virtually the last on the North American-Eurasian landmass, for the cooling climate that began at the end of the Eocene continued into the next epoch, the Oligocene. The northern and middle latitudes cooled so much that the forests that had flourished during the Paleocene and the Eocene turned into grasslands. And the primates, which had adapted to forest life, soon began to vanish. In fact, only two primates from this epoch have been found in North America, reflecting the disappearance of the climate that was once so congenial to them. The next primate to occupy this continent would be *Homo sapiens,* who migrated here from eastern Asia less than fifty thousand years ago.

In the Americas, primate evolution shifted during the Oligocene to South America, where the climate was milder. The oldest known specimen comes from Bolivia and has features of both monkeys and prosimians. However, the actual origin of primates in South America is still uncertain and highly controversial. Since there was no isthmus connecting North and South America at this time, the possibility of an African origin cannot be ruled out.

In the Old World, the stage for primate evolution moved to North Africa, to a fossil-rich area known as the Fayum depression, near present-day Cairo. These primates may have traveled from Asia to Africa beginning about thirty-five million years ago. Though the Fayum today is a desolate, wind-swept desert, then it was lush and tropical. Among the tall trees growing along its river banks lived at least six different kinds of primates: two genera of monkeys and four of apes, but apparently no prosimians. The virtually simultaneous appearance of monkeys and apes in the Fayum deposits and their similarities—small size, teeth designed for fruit eating, and four-legged posture—strongly indicate that they evolved either from some common anthropoid ancestor or from separate prosimian ancestors, but not one from the other.

About twenty-eight million years ago, some sixty million years after that unimpressive rodentlike animal appeared in North America, the first ape emerged from the basic stock of the Old World anthropoids. This cat-sized creature, known as the Egyptian ape, *Aegyptopithecus,* was discovered by Elwyn Simons, of Duke University, in 1960. Like the prosimians, it had a long snout, suggesting that its sense of smell was still relatively important. But its eyes faced directly forward and its brain, though smaller than that of comparably sized modern monkeys, was distinctly anthropoid. Presumably a social animal like most anthropoids, it lived mainly in the arboreal canopy high above the Fayum delta. But unlike some modern apes, it did not swing through the trees hand over hand, but rather ran among the branches on all four legs as monkeys do. This creature is especially important for understanding later events: Simons thinks it was ancestral to the apes that came to dominate the primate world in the next epoch and, in turn, almost certainly gave rise to modern apes and humans.

APE AND PLANET evolved together during the next epoch, the Miocene. India, which until that time had been an island in the Indian Ocean, drifted north and collided with southern Eurasia, forming the Himalayan Mountains. The Arabian Peninsula joined Africa and Eurasia together, and the Mediterranean Sea apparently evaporated, sometime between six and twelve million years ago, allowing animals (including primates) to pass between North Africa and southern Europe across the Arabian peninsula. Another land bridge connected Alaska with Siberia during the middle part of the Miocene. And around five million years ago, Central America arose from a bed of lava between North and South America. The Earth became drier as well.

While the forests of southern Europe and Asia dried into open grasslands, inadequate for apes, the African forests of the early Miocene richly supported the ape way of life. And so the Miocene in Africa was the heyday of the apes, the time when they reached their evolutionary peak. Simons estimates that there were about twenty times more kinds of apes than monkeys during this period. It was also in Africa some eighteen to twenty million years ago that a small tree-dwelling ape, known as *Proconsul,* stepped onto the evolutionary path that ultimately led to the development of the human species. First discovered half a century ago, *Proconsul'*s status as a human ancestor has been debated ever since. Based on analyses of a remarkably complete skeleton that Alan Walker, of the Johns Hopkins University School of Medicine, and Martin Pickford, of the National Museums of Kenya, reconstructed, Walker argues that *Proconsul* was almost certainly the direct ancestor of the dryopithecines, the most common apes of the Miocene.

Proconsul dates to the mid-Miocene in Africa, and soon thereafter migrated to Asia and Europe, where a new genus, *Dryopithecus,* evolved. Though *Dryopithecus* was very successful, surviving some ten million years, it began to disappear as its forest habitat gave way to expanding grasslands. By ten million years ago, the combination of receding forests and competition, especially from monkeys, proved too much for most of the Miocene apes, and they vanished from the Earth. Some species of this ape may have evolved into the still surviving orangutan, gorilla, and chimpanzee, but even these modern apes live in steadily shrinking forest habitats and are likely to become extinct in the wild by the end of this century.

The last and possibly most important ape form in the Miocene epoch was *Ramapithecus* (and its close cousin, *Sivapithecus*), which lived eight to fourteen million years ago, when the great forests were shrinking and the savannas expanding. Ever since the first ramapithecine jawbone was unearthed from the Siwalik Hills of northwest India, in the first decade of this century, anthropologists have argued over the status of this enigmatic primate with its mixture of apelike and humanlike features. Remains have since been found in Africa, Pakistan, Hungary, and Greece, as well as India, confusing rather than resolving the mystery of this ape. Was *Ramapithecus* the first ancestral hominid, a cousin of our true ancestor, or just an evolutionary dead end?

Some have argued that its thickly enameled molar teeth indicate that *Ramapithecus,* like *Homo sapiens,* ate mostly hard-covered fruits, nuts, and seeds, rather than the softer forest fruits and vegetation that most monkeys and apes feasted on. Others have held that *Ramapithecus* may have stood upright and walked on two legs, a prelude to human posture. But most of these early conclusions have been revised or abandoned in recent years. The number of alleged ancestral humanlike features have been either steadily reduced or seen in other, related forms, such as *Gigantopithecus* and *Sivapithecus*. And with the recent discovery of some fossilized limb bones, it now appears that *Ramapithecus* was more quadrupedal than previously thought, and quite likely more arboreal than terrestrial, even though it may well have been able to move on the ground on occasion, perhaps much as the modern chimpanzee and gorilla do today but without their more specialized "knuckle-walking" gait.

In the past ten years, many scholars have moved further and further from according hominid status to *Ramapithecus*. But the debate continues. Recently, there have been two significant developments. In 1981, Richard F. Kay, an anatomist at Duke University Medical Center, published an analysis of ramapithecine molars, in which he argues that this gentle creature was, indeed, probably our own great-great-grandfather, many times removed. On the other hand, last January, David Pilbeam, an anthropologist at Harvard University, reported on an eight-million-year-old skull from Pakistan, which he considers evidence that neither *Ramapithecus* nor *Sivapithecus* belong in the hominid lineage. Pilbeam even suggests that these forms more properly belong in the ancestral closet of the orangutan.

Regardless of whether *Ramapithecus* was the first hominid or a proto-orangutan, there is about a four-million-year gap in the fossil record after its disappearance and before the arrival of *Australopithecus* (southern ape) on the plains of eastern and southern Africa four million years ago. Late last year, Hidemi Ishida, of Osaka University, in Japan, and Richard E. Leakey, director of the National Museums of Kenya, announced the discovery in Kenya of a hominoid fossil that they argue may provide some of the missing pieces. Leakey describes the humanlike jawbone with five teeth as "a critical specimen—definitely a hominoid, and clearly neither a dryopithecine nor an australopithecine." He is cautious about fixing a firm date for the fossil pending the results of potassium-argon analyses, but he feels confident that it does date from about eight million years, judging from the fossilized fauna found in association with it. If Ishida and Leakey are correct, the fossil may provide the first evidence of the evolutionary divergence of humans and apes. However, the odds are small that it represents the last common ancestor of hominids and apes.

For the next form, the hominid *Australopithecus,* there is abundant fossil evidence. Larger-brained than *Ramapithecus* and fully erect, this creature walked as efficiently on two legs as we do. The adults stood less than five feet tall and weighed only 50 to 130 pounds. But they probably found safety in numbers. Walking the savannas in small bands, they likely gathered nuts, fruits, and berries, and perhaps even hunted and scavenged for meat. Despite their numbers, *Australopithecus* often fell prey to the larger and more powerful hunters of the African plain, particularly lions and leopards.

Within one million years after *Australopithecus* appeared, between two and three million years ago, hominid forms abounded on the vast African grasslands. One of them had a slightly larger brain and more modern-looking teeth than its australopithecine contemporaries.

Like them, it was a small, erect, bipedal creature that probably lived in nomadic bands. But its proficiency in shaping and using stone tools distinguished it from the others and suggested its name, *Homo habilis*—handy man. An evolutionary odyssey that seems to have begun ninety million years ago with an unpretentious ratlike creature thus eventually produced the first member of our own genus, *Homo*. And the story of human life on Earth began to unfold.

The Emergence of *Homo sapiens*

By Boyce Rensberger

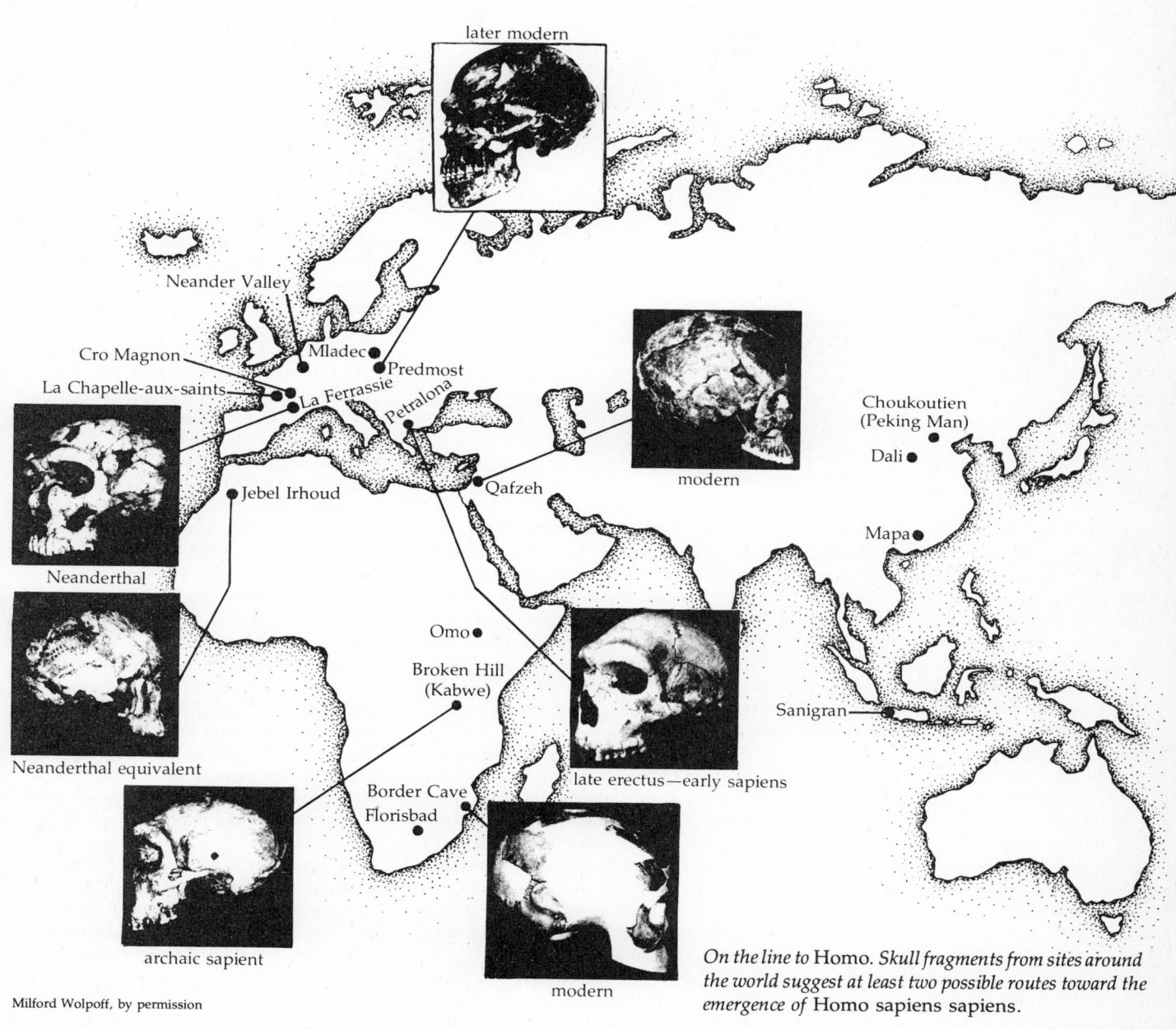

later modern

Neander Valley

Cro Magnon

La Chapelle-aux-saints

Mladec

La Ferrassie

Predmost

Petralona

Qafzeh

modern

Choukoutien
(Peking Man)

Dali

Mapa

Neanderthal

Jebel Irhoud

Omo

Neanderthal equivalent

Broken Hill
(Kabwe)

late erectus—early sapiens

Sanigran

Border Cave
Florisbad

archaic sapient

modern

Milford Wolpoff, by permission

On the line to Homo. Skull fragments from sites around the world suggest at least two possible routes toward the emergence of Homo sapiens sapiens.

Reprinted from MOSAIC, National Science Foundation, November/December 1980.

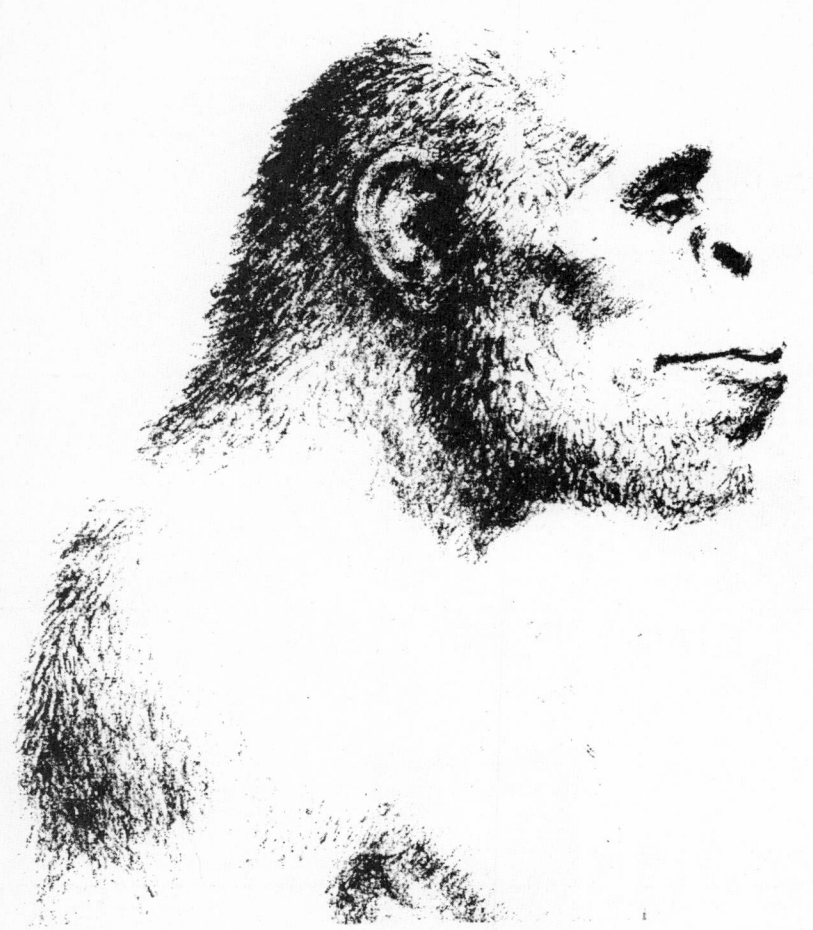

Australopithecus afarensis

According to one side of paleoanthropology's most enduring controversy, a confrontation that was to become humanity's most dramatic clash of two cultures took place in Europe's Upper Paleolithic period, some 35,000 years ago. On the one hand there were the Neanderthals, ostensibly beetle-browed hulks who trudged about Europe and the Middle East for more than 30 millennia, starting at least 70,000 years ago. Massively built people, they purportedly made up in brute strength what they lacked in wit and cunning.

At the same time, somewhere beyond Neanderthal's mostly European range—perhaps in Africa or Southwest Asia—a new breed of human being was on the rise, fully modern, anatomically and intellectually indistinguishable from ourselves. These people would soon produce magnificent cave paintings and sculpture. The most durable evidence of their culture is sophisticated weaponry indicative of a hunting prowess well beyond that of the Neanderthals.

In a geological moment, as some interpret the stratigraphy of excavations all over Europe, the Neanderthals disappeared. They were succeeded instantly by the moderns, sometimes called Cro-Magnon after the French site where several specimens were found. By 35,000 BP (before the present) the Neanderthals were gone. Fully modern people were the sole surviving form of human being on earth.

Where did the Cro-Magnons and their ilk come from? Did they exterminate the native Neanderthals? Did they simply outcompete them for food and other resources? Did they interbreed, producing genetic mixtures that survive as today's Europeans? Or was there no sharp division at all but rather a gentle evolutionary blurring as one form of creature developed naturally into another more suited to changing times?

The replacement hypothesis—the notion that a group from outside invaded the Neanderthals' range and superseded them through extermination, outcompeting or in-

terbreeding—is only the most popular guess as to what actually happened to the Neanderthal. As with so many other questions in paleoanthropology, the data that must be relied upon to answer this one have vexingly limited reliability. Many fossils are not securely dated, skeletons are often only fragmentary and it is frequently unclear whether a group of skeletons from the same site represents one or many populations. Honest but widely divergent opinions are common. The evidence supporting Neanderthal replacement, for example, can also be read to suggest a unilinear hypothesis: that fully modern human beings descended directly from the Neanderthals with relatively little contribution from outside of Europe or the Middle East.

Neanderthal's place

Since the original discovery of a Neanderthal skull in the Neander Valley of Germany in 1856—the first extinct form of human being ever found—scientific thinking about the emergence of fully modern humans has been in more or less continuous ferment. The evidence is, in some ways, more obscure than that for the earlier stages of human evolution. In recent years the effort to understand the final steps in human evolution—the steps that gave rise to our own kind, to people indistinguishable from us—has been overshadowed, at least in public perception. More attention, for example, has been drawn to the search for the earliest hominids, the first, still-apelike creatures considered to be on the direct evolutionary line to *Homo*, even though kinship to us might lie in hardly more than two-legged locomotion. (For a fuller discussion of human evolution up to the hominid divergence see the *Mosaic* special on human origins: Volume 10, Number 2.)

The earliest known creatures that are undisputedly hominids (members of the human family after it diverged from the pongid, or ape, family) date from 3.8 million years ago. They are of the species known as *Australopithecus afarensis*, a two-legged animal with a body of rather human proportions, but not much more than a meter tall and with a head only slightly different from an ape's. According to a newly emerging interpretation, *A. afarensis*, named in 1978, could have been the common ancestor of two lineages. One included the two previously known forms of *Australopithecus: A. africanus* and *A. robustus*. The other lineage was *Homo*. The oldest *Homo* known, usually called *Homo habilis*, is represented by the famous skull 1470 from Kenya, dated at about 1.8

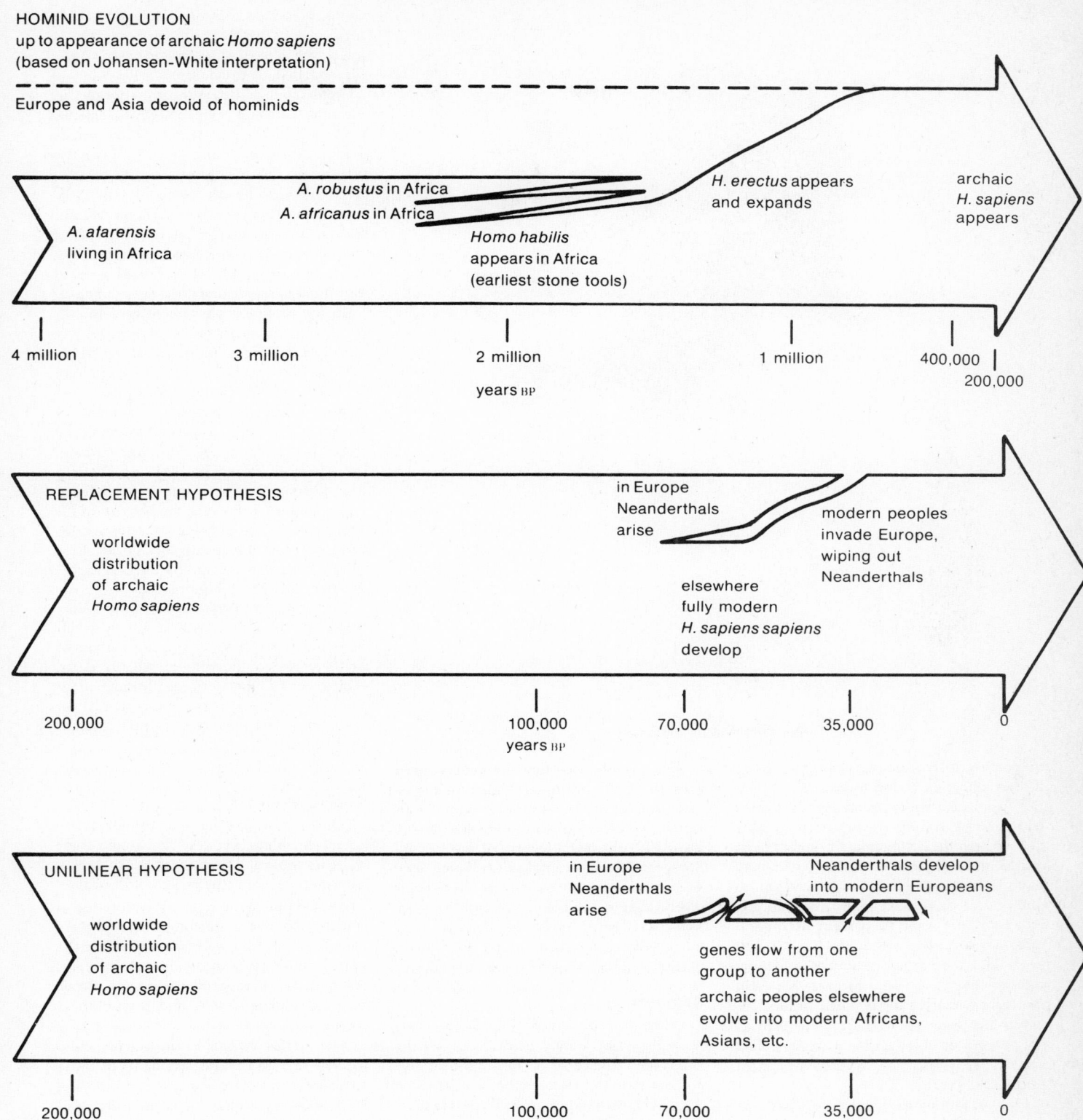

HOMINID EVOLUTION
up to appearance of archaic *Homo sapiens*
(based on Johansen-White interpretation)

– –
Europe and Asia devoid of hominids

A. robustus in Africa
A. africanus in Africa

A. afarensis
living in Africa

Homo habilis
appears in Africa
(earliest stone tools)

H. erectus appears
and expands

archaic
H. sapiens
appears

| 4 million | 3 million | 2 million | 1 million | 400,000 |

years BP

200,000

REPLACEMENT HYPOTHESIS

worldwide
distribution
of archaic
Homo sapiens

in Europe
Neanderthals
arise

modern peoples
invade Europe,
wiping out
Neanderthals

elsewhere
fully modern
H. sapiens sapiens
develop

| 200,000 | 100,000 | 70,000 | 35,000 | 0 |

years BP

UNILINEAR HYPOTHESIS

worldwide
distribution
of archaic
Homo sapiens

in Europe
Neanderthals
arise

Neanderthals develop
into modern Europeans

genes flow from one
group to another
archaic peoples elsewhere
evolve into modern Africans,
Asians, etc.

| 200,000 | 100,000 | 70,000 | 35,000 | 0 |

years BP

The place of Neanderthals. Time line represents hominid evolution and two theories of Neanderthals' place in the line to modern Homo: *In the unilinear hypothesis, they are in the main stream; in the replacement hypothesis, they were bypassed.*

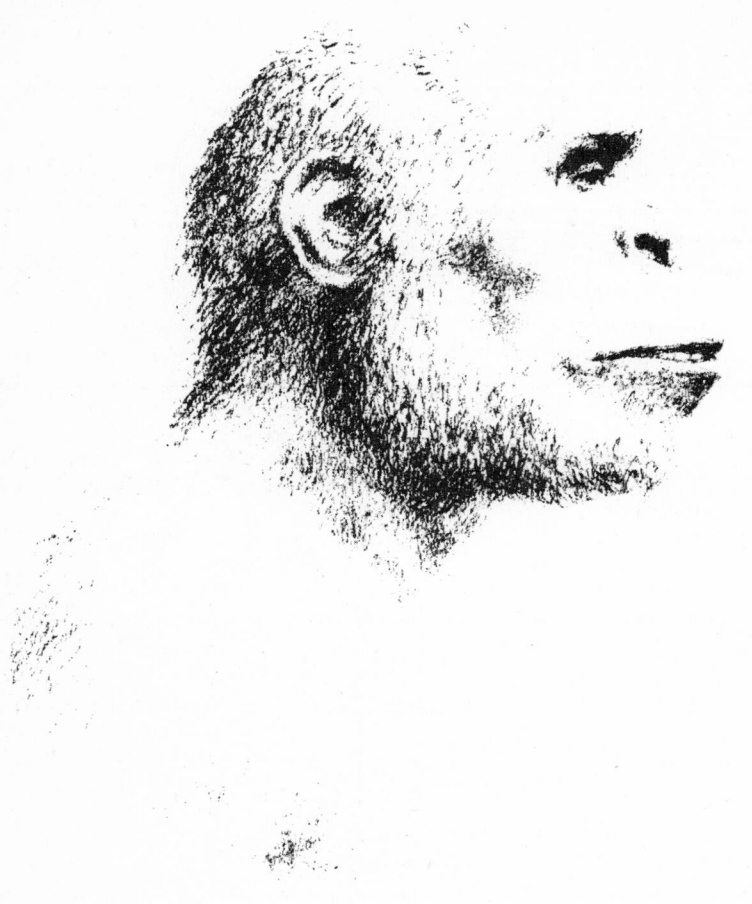

Australopithecus robustus

million years. Its brain was only half the size of that of people living today.

By about 1.5 million years ago, *H. habilis* had evolved into *H. erectus*. This appears to have been the first hominid to spread from Africa into Eurasia. Peking Man, who may have lived anywhere from 700,000 BP to 400,000 BP, is one well-known example. Not until the final 10 percent of the 3.8 million-year span—within the last 400,000 years—did the earliest examples of *Homo sapiens* emerge. These, however, were still not fully modern people. Their brains, for one thing, were only about 83 percent as big as ours on the average. Usually called "archaic sapiens," they ranged over most of the Old World.

Only in still more recent times—perhaps around 70,000 years ago—did they evolve, in Europe, into the classic Neanderthals, who are designated *Homo sapiens neanderthalensis*. The archaic sapiens also evolved into fully modern peoples, *Homo sapiens sapiens*.

There is evidence that the evolutionary growth of the brain—a trend that began early and slowly in hominid evolution—attained its present level something like 115,000 years ago—the last 3 percent of the 3.8 million years of the hominid career. Some say it was not until the last one percent. It remains one of the great challenges of anthropology to discover which of those figures is so: by what route—through, around or over Neanderthal—archaic sapiens became modern.

Another way

While the replacement hypothesis is perhaps the most widely held answer to the challenge, advocates of the unilinear hypothesis have not been overborne. They hold that the transition in Europe from Neanderthal to fully modern people may not have been as instantaneous as is often implied. Many thousands of years can disappear into a geological instant and, advocates note, the skeletons called Neanderthal show a high degree of variation that cannot be ignored.

Some Neanderthals are decidedly more modern looking than others; some specimens even appear transitional between classic Neanderthals and moderns.

After all, the differences between the Neanderthals and their modern successors are largely matters of degree. Brains are already at their maximum size. Nearly all the differences involve decreases in the robustness of bones. People become less heavily muscled and bones become correspondingly lighter and thinner. Skeletal buttressing diminishes. Once-massive brow ridges become smaller, and what is left of a snout continues to recede under the eyes and nose.

In the unilinear view there was no cultural clash, just a gradual evolution, largely confined to Europe in the case of the Neanderthals, though similar changes would have been taking place independently and perhaps, though not necessarily, coincidentally in Africa and Asia as well. Australia, like the New World, remained uninhabited until quite recently. People first reached Australia around 40,000 BP. They appear to have been fully modern. Entry into the New World is more controversial, with most estimates ranging from 12,000 to 30,000 BP. (See "Pre-Clovis Man: Sampling the Evidence," *Mosaic*, Volume 11, Number 5.)

For years the Neanderthal controversy rested at this point, with few new developments pointing either way. Adherents of neither side could point to reliably dated remains of fully modern people much older than about 35,000 years, and certainly not from anywhere outside of Europe and the Middle East.

Ancient moderns

Then a controversial new interpretation of ancient human bones—first found some 40 years ago in Border Cave in South Africa, 400 meters from the Swaziland border—suggested that modern people were living in southern Africa a startling 115,000 years ago. This was fully 45,000 years before the more primitive Neanderthals first appeared. As some view it, the replacement hypothesis received a major boost, and the unilinear hypothesis a major setback, at Border Cave.

Was Africa the real birthplace of *Homo sapiens sapiens*? Did descendants of those early Africans spread north through the Middle East to swamp the Neanderthals and become the ancestors of today's Europeans? Or did modern peoples evolve independently in Africa and Europe and, presumably, in Asia too? Those are among the questions that hang on the Border Cave dates. Unfortunately, the dates are far from secure;

again, vexingly, the evidence can be read several ways.

"There's no doubt that the Border Cave specimens are fully modern," says G. Philip Rightmire of the State University of New York at Binghamton. His detailed study of the single, adult partial skull found there (the other remains are an infant skull and an adult mandible) has established that fact. Using a statistical analysis of 11 measurements of the partial skull (including such things as the projection of the brow ridges and the distances between various bony landmarks), Rightmire has established that the Border Cave *Homo* falls within the range of variation exhibited by living peoples. Further, it comes closest to resembling today's so-called Hottentots, a South African ethnic group similar to the Bushmen (or San) but rather distinct from African Negroes. "The idea that fully modern humans appeared only 35,000 to 40,000 years ago is certainly subject to quite drastic change....

"The problem is, though, that the dating isn't that solid. There's a good deal of assumption-making going on before one can arrive at the date of 115,000 years," Rightmire observes.

The scientist principally responsible for the date, Karl W. Butzer of the University of Chicago, is rather more confident. And he sees major implications not only in such an early emergence of modern humans but in that it may have taken place in Africa. Since most anthropologists are of European ancestry, he observes, it has been almost a foregone conclusion that Europe must be the homeland of modern human beings. "Border Cave completely explodes contemporary thinking about *Homo sapiens sapiens*," says Butzer.

Assumptions and inferences

Like many other fossils and artifacts from the crucial period in human evolution between 400,000 BP, when *Homo erectus* died out, and about 35,000 BP, when modern forms become well established, the Border Cave remains are not easily datable. They are too old for such reliable standbys as radiocarbon dating and not suitable for potassium/argon dating, which requires volcanic minerals. One new method, amino acid racemization, has yielded a date at Border Cave that supports the 115,000-year estimate. The technique, however, is controversial and not widely accepted. Another, molecular evolution, requires soft tissue. More sensitive methods of radiocarbon dating are in development and within a few years may be able to reach about 100,000

Australopithecus africanus

years or more. (For more on these subjects, see "Pre-Clovis Man; Sampling the Evidence," in *Mosaic*, Volume 11, Number 5; "Molecular Evolution; A Quantifiable Contribution," *Mosaic*, Volume 10, Number 2; "The Significance of Flightless Birds," *Mosaic*, Volume 11, Number 3; and "Extending Radiocarbon Dating," *Mosaic*, Volume 9, Number 6.)

The chain of assumptions and inferences necessary to reach any date at all for Border Cave is typical of the problems anthropologists face at many of the key sites that bear on this crucial stage of human evolution. Butzer's Border Cave date is based on a detailed analysis of sedimentary deposits in the cave. There are some 20 layers of dust, grit, rubble and the detritus of human occupation. Each layer has distinctive geological and chemical attributes. Some, for example, contain extensive amounts of rock particles that flaked off the cave roof because of frost weathering. These layers indicate a period of colder climate. Other layers show certain

mineral transformations that require protracted warm and humid periods.

The younger sediments in the cave, back to one laid down about 50,000 years ago, have been radiocarbon dated. Using intervals between the radiocarbon dates, Butzer has calculated rates of sediment accumulation and extrapolated the rates to older sediments. He has also correlated the cave's cold-phase sediments with climatological data from ocean cores. By these methods, Butzer calculates that the skeletal remains at issue came from sediments deposited 115,000 years ago during a period of cool and moderately wet climate. From the bones of animal species found at the same level, it has been deduced that the habitat was then a mosaic of woodland and savanna.

The assumptions necessary to calculate a finite date in Border Cave are enough to inspire skepticism among some anthropologists, although such methods are commonly relied upon after expression of certain caveats. At Border Cave, one additional caveat is

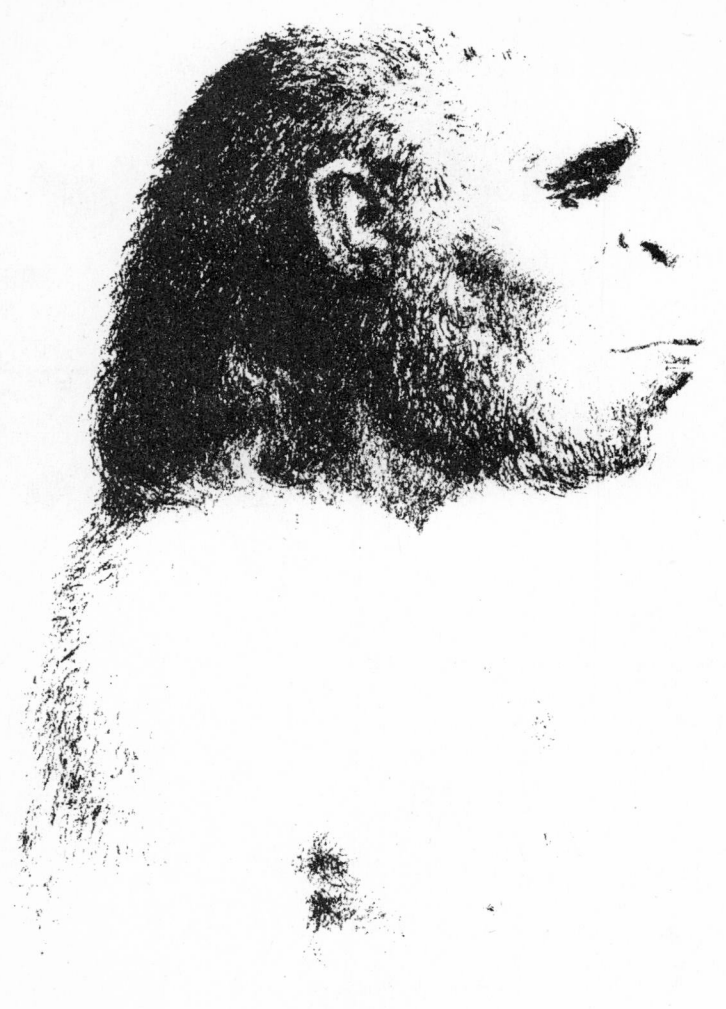

Homo habilis

that the critical adult skull did not come from a controlled excavation. It was found in a dump outside the cave, having been tossed there in 1940 by someone digging in the cave for guano.

An important link between the skull and the 115,000-year-old layer is that bits of sediment wedged into cracks in the bone match most closely the sediments of that layer. Even more important, in Butzer's view, was a 1941 excavation that *did* carefully document an infant skull in the same beds. And in 1974 a fully modern adult jaw was excavated from a layer estimated at 90,000 BP. It was well below the layer radiocarbon-dated to more than 50,000 years. "Dating of the key fossils to between 90,000 and 115,000 years is not proved beyond a reasonable doubt," Butzer concedes, "but

it's very probable. The probabilities of being mistaken are very small."

In Butzer's view, anatomically modern people probably originated in southern Africa some time before 115,000 BP. The area meets certain geographic criteria: that evolution is thought to take place chiefly on the periphery of a species' range and that in such locales environments are often different enough from those at the core of the range, so that different traits are favored by natural selection. Southern Africa, at one extreme of the hominid range, which included much of Africa and Eurasia, would seem an ideal site. It had the added advantage, Butzer suggests, of offering a wide variety of habitats within a small area. The range, from seacoast to plains to desert to mountains, should have favored the survival

of people with a high degree of intelligence and adaptability.

Archaic sapients

Locality aside, there is general agreement among paleoanthropologists that *Homo erectus* was the ancestor of all later forms of human beings. From about 1.5 million years ago until perhaps 400,000 years ago *Homo erectus* was the sole human species on the planet. Specimens are known from many parts of Africa, Europe, China and Indonesia.

The transition from *Homo erectus* to *Homo sapiens* could have taken place anywhere in this vast range. Fossil skulls with features that seem intermediate between *Homo erectus* and modern people—those usually termed archaic sapients—have been found in Europe, Asia and Africa.

The best known African specimen of archaic *Homo sapiens* was once called Rhodesian man. It is a remarkably complete skull that was found in 1921 near what was then Broken Hill in Northern Rhodesia and is today Kabwe, Zambia. It was once estimated to be 40,000 years old; newer evidence, putting it in line as a possible ancestor to the Border Cave people, suggests it is at least 125,000 years old and perhaps much older.

Butzer believes the case for a southern African origin of modern human beings is now strong. From there, the Chicago researcher suggests, this evolutionary trend toward more modern features gradually spread northward, reaching the Middle East by about 50,000 BP. This date is based on some fairly modern-looking human remains from Qafzeh, in Israel. The Qafzeh bones have proved difficult to date (various methods have yielded widely differing dates), but a reasonable compromise puts the bones at around 50,000 BP. From the Middle East, gateway from Africa to Eurasia, Butzer speculates, modern peoples spread out, to replace the Neanderthals and their ilk.

Strong dissent

While several American, British and South African anthropologists tend to agree with Rightmire and Butzer about the significance of the Border Cave, there are prominent dissenters. Among them is Richard G. Klein of the University of Chicago. He has specialized in interpreting the hunting skills of peoples living over the last 130,000 years, especially in southern Africa.

"Those Border Cave remains didn't come out of excavations. They came out of dumps," says Klein, recalling the guano diggers churning through the cave deposits. (They never did find any guano.) "To me that's not evidence. I remain to be convinced that the bones are as old as they say. We've all too often been misled by this kind of thing."

Like many paleoanthropologists dealing with what they consider to be equivocal or isolated pieces of evidence, Klein prefers to set this one aside. It is better, he feels, to try to make sense of unarguable data. In Klein's view this approach leaves the title of oldest anatomically modern *Homo sapiens* with the Qafzeh people in Israel, if one accepts an age for them of around 50,000 years. (Various methods have given dates from 33,000 to 56,000 BP.)

Klein believes there was a replacement of Neanderthals by modern people, but that the Middle East probably makes a better candidate place of origin than does Africa. His analysis of European sites suggests that, while the replacement in any one place may have been rapid, it took some 5,000 years (from 40,000 to 35,000 BP) for the wave of replacement to sweep from the Middle East westward to the Atlantic.

Among advocates of the replacement hypothesis there is debate about whether the invaders slaughtered the natives or interbred. Most suspect both and argue about the ratio. Klein, however, takes an extreme position, rejecting flatly the notion of interbreeding: "I would think that the behavioral gulf between these two very different kinds of people would have been so great that there would have been no desire at all to mate."

Klein remains unconvinced, for example, that the Neanderthals, along with other archaic *Homo sapiens*, had crossed the mental threshhold that makes modern peoples distinctive. He disputes the contentions of other scientists that Neanderthals, who produced no art, buried their dead with grave goods. (See "On the Emergence of Language," *Mosaic*, Volume 10, Number 2.) More important, Klein argues that the Neanderthals were unable to make superior weapons. They were "rotten hunters," he declares.

Additionally, from his studies of South African sites where the bones of prey animals were preserved, Klein has deduced that people of the African Middle Stone Age, who were culturally comparable to the European Neanderthal of the period called the Middle Paleolithic, were able to bring down only the weakest and least dangerous animals. Using fossil teeth to determine the maturity of the prey species, Klein has proposed that Middle Stone Age hunters generally killed animals under a year old. Very few animals in their prime are represented in the preserved garbage of those times. The

Homo sapiens (archaic)

prey-age distribution is comparable to that of lions. The two exceptions are the eland and the bastard hartebeest. Unlike other bovids, both can be driven in herds. Klein suspects that Middle Stone Age hunters learned this and drove entire herds off cliffs.

Fully modern people from the Later Stone Age, comparable to Europe's Upper Paleolithic, Klein has found, were able to kill any animal they chose. Bones from such sites reflect an age distribution closer to that of living groupings and also include remains of more dangerous animals such as wild pigs.

The difference, Klein suspects, was in the weaponry. Armed with little more than rocks and clubs, neither the Middle Stone Age *Homo* nor the Neanderthal could get close enough to an animal in its prime and they dared not approach dangerous prey. They

lacked the ability to invent such superior weapons as the spear thrower or the bow and arrow that make it possible to kill from a distance. The remains of such weapons have been found in sites of modern peoples in Africa and Eurasia, but not in sites occupied by their evolutionary predecessors. Later sites also show abundant remains of fish and flying birds, species absent from earlier sites. Since fishing and fowling require specialized tools and skills, Klein suspects these findings help differentiate the mental abilities of archaic and modern *Homo sapiens* on any continent.

New skills

Once the transition from Neanderthal to modern occurred, whether by competition, breeding or succession, there appears to have

Homo erectus

been a great population explosion. It has been estimated that the density of post-Neanderthal humans was anywhere from 10 to 100 times that of Neanderthals. Erik Trinkhaus of Harvard has suggested that one reason may have been the Neanderthals' greater need for food energy. He estimates that, on the basis of the massiveness of Neanderthal skeletons and the necessary corresponding musculature, they may have needed twice as many calories to stay active as their more slender successors. This, however, would account for only part of the population difference. Klein argues that, since the basic resources available to both groups were the same, modern people could have been so numerous only if they were more effective exploiters of their environment.

"I don't know what it was," Klein says, "but the people who appeared 35,000 years

ago knew how to do an awful lot of things their predecessors didn't. Something quite extraordinary must have happened in the organization of the brain."

It could not have been an increase in brain size, for Neanderthal brains were already just as large as ours today. Much of the older literature, in fact, asserts that they were larger, though this is now thought to be the result of early Neanderthal samples that included mostly males. Even among people today male brains are, on the average, considerably larger than female brains with, obviously, no difference in intellectual power.

"I'm quite convinced," Klein says, "that in Europe it was a physical replacement of one kind by another. And I'm prepared to bet that that's what happened in Africa too and at about the same time."

The unilinear view

Milford H. Wolpoff would take that bet. Wolpoff, at the University of Michigan, is one of the leading advocates of the unilinear hypothesis—the view that there was no sudden, single replacement of one kind by another. Rather, he suggests, the Neanderthals by and large evolved into today's Europeans. The anatomically modern population represented at Qafzeh did not invade Europe but, instead, having derived from an archaic *Homo sapiens* there, gave rise to today's Middle Easterners and North Africans. The Border Cave people, whatever their age, then would be the ancestors of today's southern Africans. Other fossil remains from Asia, such as the Neanderthal-like people represented at Mapa and Dali in China, are in the line that led to modern Asians.

"Any theory of human evolution," Wolpoff notes, "has got to account for the differences among modern populations. A modern European skull looks different from a modern African skull. And both of them look different from a modern Chinese or a modern Australian."

Indeed, while all living peoples unquestionably belong to the subspecies *Homo sapians sapiens,* most members of each population—sometimes designated a race or ethnic group—share certain distinctive skeletal features. In fact, using the kind of statistical comparison of measurements that Rightmire applied to the Border Cave skulls, it is often possible to distinguish between rather closely related groups such as the Bushmen and the Hottentots.

"You look at what the distinctive features of modern Europeans are and then you look at the fossil populations to see where those features first appear, and you find them in the Neanderthals," Wolpoff says. One feature he likes to cite is the big nose. European anthropologists tend to euphemize the feature, including it in what they call the "midfacial prominence," but it is clear that people of other races find Europeans distinctive because, among other things, of their noses. Europeans have the most prominent noses of the living races. It begins jutting out at a fairly sharp angle just below the brow. In Africans and Asians, the nasal bone descends well below the browline before curving outward. The fleshy part of the nose may be broader in some groups but it rarely protrudes farther than or begins to protrude as high as the Europeans'.

Neanderthals had big noses. Only half jokingly, Wolpoff says their noses must have resembled that typified by Charles de Gaulle. In Neanderthals the feature is often considered an adaptation to a cold climate, because a larger nose is presumed better for warming inhaled air. Anatomically-modern fossil populations from outside Europe, such as the people of Qafzeh or of Border Cave, lack this feature.

Wolpoff cites a variety of other anatomical features that, in the same way, are characteristic of a modern race and that first appear in the archaic *Homo sapiens* fossils from the same area. These include various subtle contours of the skull bones: for example the more flattened face of Asian peoples and the slight bulge that bridges the brow ridges above the nasal root in the African skull.

"To me it makes the most sense to assume that those distinctive features were inherited from the people who were already living in the area and who already had the feature," Wolpoff says. For most other parts of the world, most anthropologists accept such parsimony, he declares, but not for Europe.

Neanderthal types

One of the chief reasons, in Wolpoff's unilinear view, that the Neanderthal controversy continues is too great a reliance on typological thinking. In other words, when people think of the Neanderthals, one particular skull—often beetle-browed—or a closely related group of skulls comes to mind. And when people think of more modern successors, they think of another set of distinctive skeletal traits, including less prominent, loftier brows. Between the two stereotypes there are great differences, and they lead to the view that the earlier could not have given rise to the later in so brief a time.

"People forget just how much variation there is in every population," Wolpoff observes, pulling, as he talks, various casts from cabinets in his laboratory and arranging them on a table. (He maintains what is considered to be the most complete collection of fossil hominid casts in the United States.) "Every feature that is considered to distinguish modern Europeans from Neanderthals can be found in [one or another] Neanderthal sample."

Modern features are rare among Neanderthals and certainly not typical, he concedes, but this is exactly what would be expected of evolution. Natural selection works by acting on traits that are already expressed. A trait may be represented at a very low frequency in a given population; if it becomes advantageous, after many generations it will come to predominate.

The Neanderthals, in Wolpoff's view, were far from homogeneous either at any one time or throughout the 35,000 or so

Homo sapiens neanderthalensis

years they existed. Modern traits—less massive bones or higher foreheads, for example—are present but rare in the earliest specimens. In the later Neanderthal populations, such traits become more common. There are even some skulls that appear to be a blend of Neanderthal and modern features, so much so that some authorities have guessed them to be hybrids. Unilinear advocates, on the other hand, see them as evidence of evolutionary transition.

Even *Homo erectus*, the immediate ancestor of *neanderthalensis* and other *Homo sapiens*, and often said to have been remarkably stable in its million-year career, actually changed with time. Brain size, for example, grew some 20 to 25 percent between the earliest and latest specimens.

And the transition from *H. erectus* to *H. sapiens* was gradual. There is no gen-

erally accepted way to define the boundary. There are specimens that look like hybrids of the two types and might have been taken for such if they were not dated to about 400,000 BP, when the transition was in progress. There are similarly gradual transitions elsewhere in human evolution. There are, for example, specimens that look intermediate between the archaic sapiens and classic Neanderthals. And there are, among the fossils called "anatomically modern," many examples that are considerably more archaic in appearance than are living people.

Again, because of the lack of reliable dates for many of the specimens, it is not always possible to arrange them in chronological order. But by using estimated dates and archaeological associations, it is possible to produce what amounts to a morphological continuum from *H. erectus* to *H. sapiens*

Homo sapiens sapiens (Cro Magnon)

sapiens into which *H. sapiens neaderthalensis* fits nicely.

Wolpoff holds that the Neanderthals were simply European representatives of a phase of human evolution through which people also evolved in Asia and Africa. This has sometimes been misunderstood as an assertion that archaic sapients from Asia and Africa were Neanderthals. Rather simplified, Wolpoff's idea is this: Since·the parent stock of all modern peoples was *Homo erectus*, and since modern people today despite minor differences all differ from *Homo erectus* in the same way, people everywhere had to evolve through intermediate stages that exhibit similar intermediate features.

These intermediate features, along with the results of natural selection in the unique European environment, in Europe produced a classic Neanderthal. In Africa, the same gradation is represented by specimens found in Ethiopia's Omo Valley, at Florisbad in South Africa and at Jebel Irhoud in Morocco. They lack certain distinctive Neanderthal features; instead, they have uniquely African traits. Comparable Asian specimens would be the skulls from Mapa and Dali in China.

Mainstream Neanderthals

Wolpoff also asserts that the Neanderthals were not the dull-witted brutes that Klein envisions. In fact, he sees no reason to doubt that they were anything other than squarely on the intellectual continuum, almost if not already the equal of modern human beings.

One recent discovery in France lends new support to this view. Bernard Vandermeersch of the University of Paris has found a Neanderthal skeleton in clear and direct association with stone tools more sophisticated than the Mousterian tools that are typical of most Neanderthals. These advanced tools are of a type known as Chatelperronian. The kit includes such Mousterian examples as scrapers and irregularly shaped flakes for cutting. But it also includes some of the long, regularly shaped blades, struck from a flint core, that are typical of the tool kit of more modern people.

Until now the finer, Chatelperronian tools have always been considered early examples of the work of modern people. Now it appears that Neanderthals were capable of just that transition to more advanced technologies. Additionally, the modern people of Qafzeh, considered by replacement advocates as possible sources of the invasion, made and used the cruder Mousterian tools. "What is all comes down to," Wolpoff argues, "is that if you look at all the European evidence, there is no great jump. You don't need invasions."

But are there inconsistencies? Would the people of Border Cave, assuming they were fully modern 115,000 years ago, have bided their time in Africa while less advanced peoples occupied Eurasia? Wolpoff is reserving his opinion on the reliability of the Border Cave date. But, he argues, it makes little difference how old those people are. Citing Rightmire's conclusion that they most closely resemble modern Hottentots, Wolpoff suggests that they were simply the ancestors of today's southern Africans. The distinctively African features in the Border Cave skeletons do not appear in any European fossils. From this, Wolpoff concludes that the Border Cave people are unlikely to have contributed in any large part to modern European ancestry.

The unilinear hypothesis should not be understood to rule out mating between otherwise separated groups. Indeed, most authorities assume it must have been a common occurrence. It is the norm today in many traditional cultures for men and women to seek their mates from other bands or clans or villages. This practice, if extended indefinitely, means that genes are flowing more or less continuously over the entire inhabited range. One effect of this practice, well documented for living peoples, is that physical traits that are predominant in one area slowly diffuse to the surrounding areas. If a trait is advantageous in all environments, it will quickly spread. But if the environment of the surrounding area does not favor the trait, the introduced gene will remain at a low frequency. If bearers of this gene in the surrounding area chance to mate with someone from an area still more distant from the trait's center, the gene will be spread farther but still at a frequency related to its utility.

Shared traits

Many physical traits among modern peoples (skin color, height, head shape, etc.) are distributed in this way and will continue to exist in continua so long as there is outbreeding at the range margins. So long as the environment at the core of the area exhibiting the trait continues to favor that trait, it should remain common there. Like ripples on a pond, the trait should continue spreading so long as the force making the ripples remains active.

In this way, Wolpoff suggests, traits that are only locally advantageous will spread some distance away but will remain rare at that distance. On the other hand, traits that are advantageous in all environments, such as a larger brain, will spread throughout the inhabited region and reach high frequencies throughout.

The flow of universally advantageous genes, Wolpoff suggests, would be likely to spread them to neighboring peoples before the originating population progressed so far that it could use the advantage to invade or exterminate its neighbors.

Replacement advocates, of course, disagree. They envision early peoples as so widely dispersed that, from time to time, groups became cut off—perhaps isolated by a desert or a mountain range. These insular groups would not spread any of their newly evolved advantages until they had developed well beyond their contemporaries elsewhere and then breached the isolating constraints. Thus big-brained peoples, if isolated long enough, might eventually break out and replace their small-brained contemporaries.

There is no clear sign that the controversy over the emergence of anatomically modern peoples will be resolved soon. Undoubtedly more fossils will be found. But perhaps more important, existing discoveries must be reanalyzed with the aid of new techniques, new or extended dating methods and fresh eyes. One very serious handicap to any single investigator is the difficulty of access to most of the original fossils (which are housed in isolated collections around the world) or even to casts of the bones (which are either expensive or unavailable). Hominid fossils are often treated as the personal property of their discoverer and sometimes access is granted only to a favored few. A full description of the bones may be years or decades in coming, and until then convention dictates that no one else may analyze or interpret the material in detail.

Compared to the rich and active lives led by thousands or millions of members of now extinct hominid species in the many past environments of the planet, the bits of bone that have been found in the past century—in all only a few score—are a pitifully meager basis from which to develop a believable story of human evolution. Still the broad outline of a fairly coherent story has emerged. Indeed, the origin of human beings in apelike ancestors is among the best documented speciation events in paleontology. Only the details remain troublesome.

And as the details come closer to illuminating the differences and similarities among living peoples, we may rightly become more rigorous and, inevitably, more contentious in evaluating the evidence. Clues to many of the most important events or processes in human evolution may never amount to proof, at least in the eyes of other disciplines.

And yet it is nothing less than the heritage of our species that is at stake. We have, after all, come a long way from the view of the shocked lady who is alleged to have said, when Darwin's ideas of descent from the animals first burst forth, "Let us hope that it is not true, but if it is, let us pray it does not become generally known."

Like orphans searching for our parents, we want to know where we came from, how we got here, how we are really related to the rest of the living world. It can be argued, in fact, that providing this knowledge is paleoanthropology's highest use. In this light, even the smallest quibbles about how human evolution took place are matters of vital substance for us all.

Bushes All the Way Down

By Stephen Jay Gould

An old English rhyme captures, quaintly but succinctly, a central truth of nature's dilemma:

> Pale Ebeneezer thought it wrong to fight
> Puffing Bill who killed him thought it right.

Or, in American translation, "There ain't room enough here for the both of us."

The tale of Ebeneezer and Bill epitomizes a rule of thumb in ecological and evolutionary theory called the principle of "competitive exclusion." This doctrine holds that if two coexisting species are "too close" in their ecologies and mode of life, they cannot both persist in the same area. We cannot imagine that both will pursue their common modes of life with an absolutely equal efficiency; one must perform at least ever so slightly better, and this species will, in course of time, eventually supplant the other (so long as space and resources are limited, as they always are in our finite world).

Yet, manifestly, species of similar form and relationship do often coexist in stability. In these cases, biologists argue that the domain of ecological difference is large enough to permit joint survival. (The principle can become meaningless if we use the fact of coexistence as a priori evience for sufficient difference, and evolutionists have often so erred. But if we search for such cases of coexistence in order to test the principle by a subsequent study of ecological disparity, then competitive exclusion may have scientific value.)

In any case, the principle of competitive exclusion became the centerpiece of an explicit hypothesis about human evolution that enjoyed a great vogue in the 1960s and 1970s but has now been disproved—the "single species hypothesis," the last bastion for the metaphor of the ladder in studies of human evolution.

In the classic statement of the single species hypothesis ("Competitive Exclusion Among Lower Pleistocene Hominids: The Single Species Hypothesis," *Man*, vol. 6, 1971, pp. 601–14), M.H. Wolpoff quoted Ernst Mayr, our greatest living evolutionary theorist, on the interpretation of competitive exclusion:

The logical consequence of competition is that the potential coexistence of two ecologically similar species allows three alternatives: (1) the two species are sufficiently similar in their needs and abilities to fulfill these needs so that one of the two species becomes extinct, either (a) because it is "competitively inferior" or has a smaller capacity to increase or (b) because it has an initial numerical disadvantage; (2) there is a sufficiently large zone of ecological nonoverlap (area of reduced or absent competition) to permit the two species to coexist indefinitely.

The single species hypothesis held that no two human species ever coexisted and that our evolution has progressed as a series of successive stages on a single pathway leading to modern *Homo sapiens*. Wolpoff and his colleague C.L. Brace applied their single species hypothesis particularly to the record of early human evolution in Africa—arguing that the two classic lineages of australopithecines, the so-called graciles and robusts, must belong to a single species, with pronounced geographic and sexual variation previously misinterpreted as evidence for multiple lineages.

But why did Wolpoff and Brace hold so strongly to this view of competitive exclusion, especially since the principle permits coexistence of two species if their domain of ecological overlap is small enough? The single species hypothesis rested upon the specific argument that the uniqueness of human life styles precluded such small overlap between coexisting species. Wolpoff identified culture as the reason for necessary competition to the point of exclusion. Other animals can become narrow specialists on a particular type of food or within a limited space in a rich environment. Such specializations can minimize competition with relatives committed to different foods and spaces—and permit close evolutionary cousins to dwell together in stability.

But culture defines human uniqueness, and culture is, by definition, expansive. We become learning animals and develop ways to exploit more kinds of foods and places. Our evolution must proceed toward greater generality—that is, toward the domain of overlap, where competitive exclusion must operate if two human species inhabit the same area. Even though australopithecine culture scarcely rivaled our own, Wolpoff deemed it rich enough to build an ecological niche so broad that only one hominid species could inhabit Africa at any time. Wolpoff wrote:

> *Culture acts to multiply, rather than to restrict, the number of usable environmental resources. Because of this hominid adaptive characteristic implemented by culture it is unlikely that different hominid species could have been maintained. . . . Competition would most likely cause each hominid species to develop the ability to utilize a wider range of resources and thus increase the amount of competition. One surely must succeed at the expense of the other.*

As an extension of the single species hypothesis, Wolpoff and Brace sought to interpret other supposed cases of apparent interaction between two differing peoples as evolutionary sequences of direct transformation—in particular, Neanderthal evolving into modern humans, rather than Neanderthal interacting with, and replaced by, a discrete group of invaders (Cro-Magnons of modern type), as dramatized in the popular novels of Jean Auel. (If Brace is right, then Ayla's struggle is fiction in more ways than one.)

In fact, Brace often derided hypotheses of interaction and replacement, labeling all such ideas as "hominid catastrophism"—a reversion to the bad, old pre-evolutionary habits of special pleading: to avoid an interpretation of direct evolutionary transformation, we suppose that a new species migrants in from elsewhere and wipes the "primitives" out.

If the single species hypothesis be valid, then Brace's ridicule is justified—for no other species can exist to form the phalanx of an invasion, and all temporal sequences should be interpreted as cases of evolutionary transformation. But if the single species hypothesis is wrong, and if human evolution follows nature's conventional topology of the bush (rather than our culturally bound hope for a ladder of progress), then "hominid catastrophism" should be an anticipated consequence of evolution, not a term of reproach. If splitting and twigginess are primary themes of human evolution, then different species may exist to meet and interact.

As the single species hypothesis had set its roots in a claim about our long African prehistory (from our split with the chimpanzee lineage some five to eight million years ago to the exodus of *Homo erectus* from Africa about a million years ago), so too did it fall in Africa. By 1976, the hypothesis had already faded, since most paleontologists had concluded that gracile and robust australopithecines represented separate lineages, not males and females of a single species. In that year Richard Leakey and Alan Walker described two hominids from the same geological formation (about 1.5 million years old) so different in appearance that no one could dispute their separate status ("*Australopithecus, Homo erectus*, and the Single Species Hypothesis," *Nature*, vol. 261, pp. 572–74). Fortunately (for clarity in conclusion, but not for the single species hypothesis), these two skulls displayed extremes of gracile and robust tendencies—thus accentuating differences to the point of resolution.

One skull represents the so-called hyper-robust form *Australopithecus boisei*, a small-brained creature with a protruding face and massive brow ridges. The other, quite modern in appearance, has been placed in *Homo erectus*, the species supposedly ancestral to modern humans. Thus, much of human prehistory in Africa included at least two coexisting lineages—our own and the surviving robust australopithecines. (Richard Leakey sees even more bushiness in our African story, for he argues that three hominid species coexisted just before this time—*H. habilis*, presumed ancestor of *H. erectus*; the robust lineage; and surviving populations of the gracile lineage, *A. africanus*. As is the case with the apes, our knowledge may not be near the asymptote of hominid bushiness.) So Africa has fallen to bushiness, but how far can we extend this favored metaphor? Surely, at some point we must reach a twig that grows straight out without further branching to modern *Homo sapiens*. Where is the teeny ladder of this ultimate twig?

About a million years ago, after our long and exclusively African prehistory, some populations of *H. erectus* migrated out of Africa (while others stayed) to colonize parts of Europe and Asia. (As Java man and Peking man, we knew about these Asian *H. erectus* even before we had discovered their australopithecine forebears in Africa.) Some paleontologists have identified *H. erectus* as a bottom rung of the ultimate ladder, arguing that this ancestral species transformed itself, in toto and in various places, into modern humans (*H. erectus* and *H. sapiens* become, in this interpretation, grades of structural improvement within a single evolving lineage, not proper species by the usual criterion of branching). Carleton Coon advanced the extreme form of this argument when he claimed, in his popular book *The Origin of Races* (1962), that five separate groups of *H. erectus* had independently evolved in parallel, in Africa, Europe, and Asia, to *H. sapiens*.

The alternative viewpoint, following the metaphor of the bush, still interprets *H. erectus* as our ancestral species but seeks a later and local point of origin for modern humans. After all, *H. erectus* thrived on three continents. Why insist that all its populations moved upward and onward to our current glory? Why not argue that *H. sapiens*, like most species, branched from one of these populations and then spread out, eventually to displace *H. erectus* populations (or their descendants) in other parts of the world—a classic case of "hominid catastrophism" as a legitimate pattern of evolution?

The hints have been with us for a decade, but strong evidence has just emerged for a radical version of bushiness to this bitter end. To summarize the conclusions baldly (the evidence follows in a moment): all modern humans are products of a very recent twig that lived exclusively in Africa until 90,000 to 180,000 years ago. We therefore branched from *H. erectus* in Africa, the center of origin for all hominid species discovered so far. Modern *H. sapiens* migrated from Africa to the rest of the world (reaching Europe and Asia quickly, Australia some 40,000 years ago, and the Americas some 10,000 to 20,000 years ago). All modern humans are a product of this split and migration; the previous emigration of *H. erectus* to Asia left no descendants. (Lest this seem improbable or complex, consider the story of horses. Remember that T.H. Huxley mistakenly concocted a European ladder of horses from four separate lineages that migrated sequentially to Europe, where each became extinct without issue.) Fossil hominids older than this date of splitting for *H. sapiens* in Africa—including the Asian *H. erectus* and probably the famous Neanderthals of Europe—are separate lineages on the hominid bush and played no role in our ancestry. For African *H. sapiens*—the forebears of us all—as for Judah the Maccabee:

See the conquering hero comes!
Sound the trumpet, beat the drums!

(although we have no evidence for martial replacement by African invaders; the indigenous people of Europe and Asia may have disappeared earlier or for other reasons).

The hints are in stone and bone. Sophisticated blade tools appeared in Africa nearly 100,000 years ago, long before they replaced simpler flake tools in Europe or Asia. Concomitantly, the oldest modern humans have been found in African sediments some 100,000 to 140,000 years old. Moreover, some paleontologists are now arguing that the Asian populations of *H. erectus* developed a suite of anatomical specializations absent both from modern humans and from African fossils usually called *H. erectus*. If this tentative claim is affirmed, then Asian *H. erectus* would be debarred from the ancestry of modern humans, while African forms remain admissible. (I leave for another time the interesting implication for taxonomic realignment—that African populations now placed in *H. erectus* may require redesignation as a separate species. The name *Homo erectus* must, by rules of nomenclature, remain with the Asian forms that first received this label.)

The firmer evidence lies in molecules, for we all carry genetic tracers of our ancestry. During the past decade, molecular evolutionists have recognized the power of mitochondrial DNA for unraveling the histories of recently evolved groups. Mitochondria are the energy factories of all complex (eukaryotic) cells. They presumably originated, more than a billion years ago, as entire cells of primitive (prokaryotic) type that began living as symbionts within the ancestors of eukaryotic cells. As a heritage of their independent origin, mitochondria have their own DNA—arranged as a short, circular molecule.

Mitochondrial DNA has two favorable features for the reconstruction of evolutionary histories. First, it evolves about ten times faster, on average, than nuclear DNA—thus permitting sufficient resolution for such recent and rapid events as the origin and spread of modern humans. Second, compared with nuclear DNA, its pattern of inheritance is simple and direct. Since the business end of a sperm is all nucleus, mitochondrial DNA is strictly maternally inherited. We can therefore trace lineal paths of descent, rather than the complex crisscrossing of family lines for nuclear genes that may come from either parent. Moreover, the entire mitochondrial genome is inherited as a unit. Prokaryotic cells (like modern bacteria and the precursors of mitochondria) do not have paired chromosomes; DNA is arranged instead as a single continuous molecule. When chromosomes pair, as in all nuclear DNA of eukaryotic cells, exchanges occur between the two members in each generation. Nuclear chromosomes are, therefore, continually fractured and reconstituted. But the mitochondrial genome is a stable entity, passed intact from mother to offspring and altered only by mutation. It is therefore an ideal tracer for genealogical histories.

Rebecca L. Cann, Mark Stoneking, and Allan C. Wilson have just published our most extensive data on variation in human mitochondrial DNA ("Mitochondrial DNA and Human Evolution," *Nature*, January 1987, pp. 31–36). They studied 147 people drawn from five geographic populations (Africans, Asians, Caucasians, aboriginal Australians, and New Guineans) and succeeded in surveying about 9 percent of the entire mitochondrial genome of 16,569 base pairs.

Cann and her colleagues found 133 variants among the 147 subjects (most people are unique, but very little different from many others). As the next (and crucial) step, they arranged these 133 mitochondrial types into an evolutionary tree. We now encounter an important property of such molecular information: the data themselves are abundant and "hard"; but interpretations rest upon assumptions that, although reasonable and proper, must be stated and evaluated. In principle, a vast number of evolutionary trees may be constructed from 133 variants. How shall we decide which to prefer?

In such cases, we generally invoke the assumption of parsimony—that is, we build the evolutionary tree that requires the minimal number of mutational changes to link the 133 variants. (This procedure matches our intuitions: confronted with mouse, rat, and human, we would assume a closer tie between mouse and rat rather than the unparsimonious solution that mouse evolved to human and human back to rat—for this second, unparsimonious tree would require a much longer pathway of linkages, namely, a double run both up and down the long rodent-to-human road, rather than a single excursion, as in the first solution. But parsimony is a procedural asumption that might be wrong in any particular case, not an a priori truth of nature.) In the mitochrondrial example, we may worry less about the parsimony assumption because conclusions are, in the profession's jargon, so "robust"—that is, a large family of most parsimonious and nearly parsimonious alternative trees all yield the same basic solution.

The minimal length tree for 147 humans has a simple and striking topology. It includes two major branches joining at the base. One contains only Africans, the second includes other Africans plus everybody else. Cann and colleagues compared this most parsimonious tree with several alternatives. The conceptually opposite tree for example—one that links each of the five geographic groups to an independent root and corresponds to Coon's old theory about separate origins from different stocks of *H. erectus*—would require fifty-one more mutations to make all the linkages.

These data provide two strong reasons for viewing Africa as the unique source of modern humans: first, of course, the form of the tree itself, with its African root; second, the greater mitochondrial diversity maintained by peoples of African descent. The older a group, the longer the time available for generating diversity. Cann found as much variation *within* the African populations as between Africans and any other geographic group.

The tree's form tells us "where," but not "when." Since mitochondrial trees say nothing about the anatomy of our common African ancestor, we need subsidiary information from paleontology—and this requires knowledge of timing. If the two great branches of the mitochondrial tree joined in Africa more than a million years ago, then our most recent common ancestor would presumably have looked like *H. erectus*. If the joining occurred much later, then our common roots are much more shallow—and we all probably branched from a subset of a population that had already become *H. sapiens*.

To derive such an estimate of timing, we must make an additional assumption, more tenuous than the previous statement about parsimony. We assume that mitochondrial DNA changes by mutation at a constant average rate over considerable stretches of time. Such an assumption is not required by evolutionary theory, and alternative ideas of greatly variable rates (due to differing intensities of natural selection) can easily be defended. The justifications for this assumption are primarily twofold: first, the presupposition of constancy, though initially derided by many evolutionary theorists, has worked in many cases where we can check a molecular tree against known dates of branching from the fossil record. Second, the tree derived under this assumption is also robust; large departures from constancy would be required to change its form or its timings substantially. In any case, the figures reached under the principle of constancy must be viewed as ballpark numbers tied to their assumptions, not as established facts.

Many studies of diverse animal groups yield the same estimate of 2 to 4 percent change in mitochondrial DNA per million years. Combining this figure with measured distances among the 147 people, we derive a time scale for diversification and spread of modern humans. This exercise suggests a conclusion surprising to many (though not to me and other devotees of the bush) and stunning in its implications about human unity: despite our external differences of skin color, hair form, and size, all modern humans have a remarkably recent, or "shallow," common ancestry, occurring well after our anatomical transformation to *H. sapiens* in Africa.

The assumption of constancy at 2 to 4 percent suggests that the common ancestor for all existing human mitochondrial DNAs lived in Africa between 140,000 and 290,000 years ago. This branch then split into the two main limbs of Cann's tree, and members of the second limb left Africa later—only 90,000 to 180,000 years ago. All non-African racial diversity arose within this geological millisecond, and the underlying unity of all humans is, as I have argued before, a "contingent fact of history," not a hope of liberal ideology.

If these dates are right, we must also accept the conclusion that older inhabitants of Europe and Asia died out without contributing anything to our genetic heritage. European Neanderthals, for example, predate this time of migration from Africa. If the invading Cro-Magnons had hybridized with Neanderthals or if Neanderthals had simply evolved to humans of modern form (both hypotheses have been popular), then the mitochondrial tree would not have its unique and shallow African root—for older mitochondria from Neanderthals would be found in European populations. Of course, a larger sample of humans might yield different mitochondrial variants of greater distinction, but the data as now known suggest no such heterogeneity in human ancestry.

Before leaving this subject, I must correct one striking misinterpretation that has begun to flood popular accounts of this discovery. Noting that all human mitochondrial DNA can be traced to a single African type, some have dubbed this conclusion the "Eve hypothesis" and have actually claimed an implication that we all owe our ancestry to a single female who lived about a quarter of a million years ago. The data do mean that all modern humans may contain, in their genealogical ancestry, one African female (or a few with the same mitochondrial type), but such a perfectly orthodox, almost necessary conclusion says little about the *size* of our ancestral population at this time of origin. To say that we all include one woman in our ancestry is not to claim that only a single woman existed at that time—although this is the ludicrous misinterpretation that has spawned some lurid press accounts. After all, the ancestral human population may always have included, say, 50,000 people during the time of its African origin, but all modern humans may still trace a mitochondrial genealogy to just one female among these 50,000.

In fact, such a pattern of boom for one and bust for everyone else is not at all surprising but an expected and predicted result in our tough and random world, exposing each and every one of us to the continuous slings and arrows of outrageous fortune. Most genealogical processes work this way. Consider human family lines, for example. If we started with a population of twenty family names, with twenty people per name, and maintained the population at constant size for many generations under uncertain conditions of human life (disease, conquest, infertility), most names would eventually die out and we would all be Smiths or Goldsteins (if we didn't confound the process by adopting new names as the old lines expired). Yet this later uniformity would permit no conclusion that a certain Ms. Goldstein had lived alone in Eden way back when—for the population had always numbered 400.

This principle rests upon a well-established mathematics beyond the scope of this column and its author. Its conclusions are firm, though surprising to those (most of us, alas) who do not understand the nature and power of random processes. For example, in a purely random system even for a large population begun with 15,000 unrelated females, we can calculate a 50 percent probability that, 18,000 generations later, all members of the population would be descendants of but one female among these 15,000.

This stunning demonstration of the temporal shallowness of our roots has a precious property shared by very few of the new discoveries that inundate us daily. It provides one of those rare items of information that might make us think in a fundamentally different way about a subject of great importance—our own origins and the nature of evolution. First, the generality: no matter how high we tune the power of our microscope, we cannot escape an evolutionary topology of branching and bushiness. We are all products of a recent African twig, not termini of a general evolutionary advance. The metaphor of the bush (and the falsity of the ladder) permeates evolution at all genealogical scales, from the history of a species to the unfolding of life's entire tree. Bushiness is a pattern of self-similarity that emerges whenever we magnify successively smaller segments of life's tree.

We might have anticipated a different conclusion—a change from bushes to ladders once we looked at sufficiently small segments of life's history. We might have supposed that while life, in toto, must be a bush, each little twig might grow straight. Since the human lineage is a tiny twig, why not hold that *H. sapiens* might be the top rung of a tiny ladder, even while the history of all primates forms a bush. But life's tree is a fractal, and tiny parts, when magnified, look much like the whole.

This shallowness of ancestry also teaches a more particular lesson for us as a species. Modern *H. sapiens* is an entity, not an evolutionary tendency. We have a definite point of recent origin and a history of later spread. We are not a grade of structural advance in mentality, the expected termination of the hope of ages; we are a discrete historical thing, a fragile little twig of recent origin and unparalleled subsequent success. Our unities of mythology, of what we call human "essence" or "nature," perhaps even of language (if the Indo-European branch can be connected, as some scholars maintain, with other families of language to a single rooted tree), need not reflect mysterious immanences of the soul or deep archetypes of the psyche, but need only record a recent history of common origin. We are close enough to our African origins to hope for the preservation of unity in both action and artifact. We are used to thinking of ourselves as an essence, or a type—one, moreover, that holds hegemony over nature by virtue of evolved superiority. We are no such thing; we are an item of history—an entity, not a tendency.

The Search for Early Man

By Robert A. Foley

EAST AFRICA, JAN. 1, 2050— *It was announced today that Dr. Leakey has discovered a new fossil hominid in a remote part of what used to be northern Kenya. Dr. Leakey's find is the oldest and most complete yet unearthed and is likely to lead to a major revision of our current understanding of human evolution. . . .*

Not Louis, Mary, or Richard Leakey, of course, but a great (or great great) grandchild. Given the family's tenacity, it is entirely possible that the big news of 2050 will be the latest in a long series of discoveries by the Leakeys, stretching over 100 years, each one more dramatic than the last.

Not every student of human evolution, however, will be setting up camp in East Africa, as the Leakeys have done. Some researchers will be making remarkable discoveries by using computers and related technologies. And still others will be unraveling the story of our species in the genetics laboratory— following the intricate threads of our DNA. In the end, the year 2050 may well see a revolution in evolutionary science that will crown the achievements made by Charles Darwin 200 years before.

In the face of such dazzling prospects, one takes a certain pleasure in the assurance that some things will stay the same. Finding fossils is the heart of palaeoanthropology— the study of human evolution— and progress over the past century can be measured by the discoveries of

new fossils: the neanderthals in the late nineteenth century; the pithecanthropines (or *Homo erectus* as they are now known) at the turn of the century; the australopithecines of South Africa in the 1920s; and the wealth of early material discovered in East Africa, starting with *Zinjanthropus* in 1959. Without these discoveries, there would be no development in our understanding, no new synthesis of the pattern of human evolution.

It would not be surprising, therefore, to find developments over the next 60 years firmly based on exciting new finds. Although the fossil record of human evolution is still by no means complete, it is incomparably better than it was just 60 years ago. In 1924 there was only one fossil hominid from the African Plio-Pleistocene; today there are 1,700. If that rate of discovery were to continue, then in another 60 years the gaps in the record should be far fewer, the human tree much more complete.

There remain, however, some important areas of human evolution for which there is virtually no fossil record. We currently think that hominids separated from the great apes of Africa around eight million years ago. But there are no fossils that provide satisfactory evidence about the three million or four million years preceding the separation. The first fossil evidence we have for a hominid lineage is dated at five million years ago. Between that time and three million years ago,

there are only a few fragmentary remains, and even the period between three and two million years ago is poorly known. In other words, if hominids have been around for eight million years, only the final quarter of that existence is known in any detail. Consequently there is a desperate need for fossils that flesh out the details— indeed, provide the basic skeleton— of not only the early stages of human evolution but also the entire evolutionary history of African apes.

Even the past two million years are characterized by many significant gaps in the fossil record. Two small areas of Africa— in South and East— have yielded more than 90 percent of the evidence we have. All sorts of vital fossil evidence, about which we know nothing, may lie in other parts of Africa. India, which was probably occupied by hominids about one million years ago, is virtually terra incognita with regard to fossil evidence. Thus, although we have a larger number of fossils from these later periods, they come from only a few areas.

It is simple to predict, therefore, that major developments of the next half century will include the discovery of new fossils. The strategy for the future is quite clear: new techniques must be developed to enhance the efficiency of fossil recovery, and more and more expeditions must be mounted to seek out fossils in places that have not been investigated.

But not all the discoveries will be

Reprinted with permission from *Archaeology*, January/February 1989

made by expeditions. By the year 2050, there will likely be sophisticated new techniques available for plugging the gaps in the fossil record. Of these, remote sensing may be the most significant. For example, by 2050, the resolution of satellite imagery will probably be sharp enough to determine whether certain ground deposits contain fossils. Perhaps more significantly, subsurface topography will be detectable. Such techniques are already capable of mapping subterranean drainage systems beneath the Sahara Desert. Since fossils are likely to occur in sediments associated with water systems, this will help future palaeoanthropologists locate promising deposits.

Furthermore, the use of coring systems to sample deeply buried sediments — so important in the development of marine geology — is likely to have a major impact on the methods of archaeological and palaeontological excavation. The potential of these techniques may be seen by considering Olduvai Gorge. Although the gorge is just a small gash in the overall landscape of the Serengeti, the deposits that are exposed there must extend underground to either side. Today it is only in this narrow gorge that palaeoanthropologists have access to the deposits, but with remote-sensing and coring techniques the total landscape of the Olduvai hominids may become accessible.

All this suggests a rosy, fossiliferous future. But there is a built-in paradox. With each new fossil find, we are usually less certain about the nature and pattern of human evolution than we were before. As a result, the clear-cut evolutionary trees of the earlier part of this century will have given way to multiple-choice schemes and a myriad of alternative dotted lines linking putative ancestor with putative descendant.

Why do new fossils seem only to complicate matters? The effects of new fossil discoveries are a function of sample size. Only 2,500 pre-Holocene hominid fossils are known to us, but estimates suggest that more than five billion hominids lived between the origin of the group eight million years ago and the end of the Pleistocene 10,000 years ago. Consequently, the chance that the 2,500 hominids known to us represent all the variability of the hominid family is extremely small — after all, we are only finding one in every 200 million of them! Even if we can quadruple the size of the fossil record over the next 60 years, we are not going to alter the situation very much. We are still a long way from a stable understanding of human evolution, and no doubt the fossil record will continue to surprise us (although hopefully to a lesser and lesser extent).

Crucial as they are, however, fossil discoveries alone are not the key to the future. More and more, we can learn about human evolution not from the fossils in isolation but from their comparative context. One kind of context is the geological, palaeontological, and sedimentological context in which a fossil lies. Context can provide information about the environment in which a hominid lived and ultimately died. Distinct from the geological is the anatomical context of each fossil. Through a comparison of the bones and soft tissue of living and extinct animals, we are able to infer evolutionary relationships and functions. For example, Thomas Huxley established in the nineteenth century, through basic comparative primate anatomy, that the apes are our closest relatives. His conclusion was based on observation of gross anatomical features — the broad similarities of the bones, musculature and other soft tissue of apes and humans.

However, a new comparative framework is emerging, based not on gross anatomy but on molecular anatomy. Comparisons between species are now being carried out at the level of the molecule, and the results have been stunning, further eroding the biological pedestal on which humans have placed themselves. The genetic differences between humans and apes, it turns out, are relatively small — certainly far fewer than anatomy and behavior would lead us to expect. Superficial anatomical comparisons can actually be misleading. Anatomically the African apes (chimpanzees and gorillas) appear to be more similar to the great Asian apes (the orangutans) than either group is to modern humans. However, on the molecular and genetic level — which provides us with direct evidence of evolutionary relatedness — we and the African apes share a very close relationship. It is the orang which is the most divergent.

Molecular biology, the direct study of the building blocks of life, is the centerpiece of modern biology. An exciting example of its potential is the recent work on mitochondrial DNA (the genetic material found outside the nucleus) by Allan Wilson and his colleagues at the University of California at Berkeley. Assuming a constant rate of mutation over the millennia, they analyzed the mitochondrial DNA of modern people. Given a constant rate, the number of genetic changes can be used to determine when our own species began; and the amount of mitochondrial DNA variation in modern groups can indicate how closely related their genetic material is to that of the first *Homo sapiens sapiens*. The best explanation of the results obtained by Wilson place the origins of our own species in Africa between 150,000 and 200,000 years ago.

The implication of work on DNA *outside* the nucleus is that the origins of modern humans are relatively recent within hominid history. Complete mapping of the mitochondrial

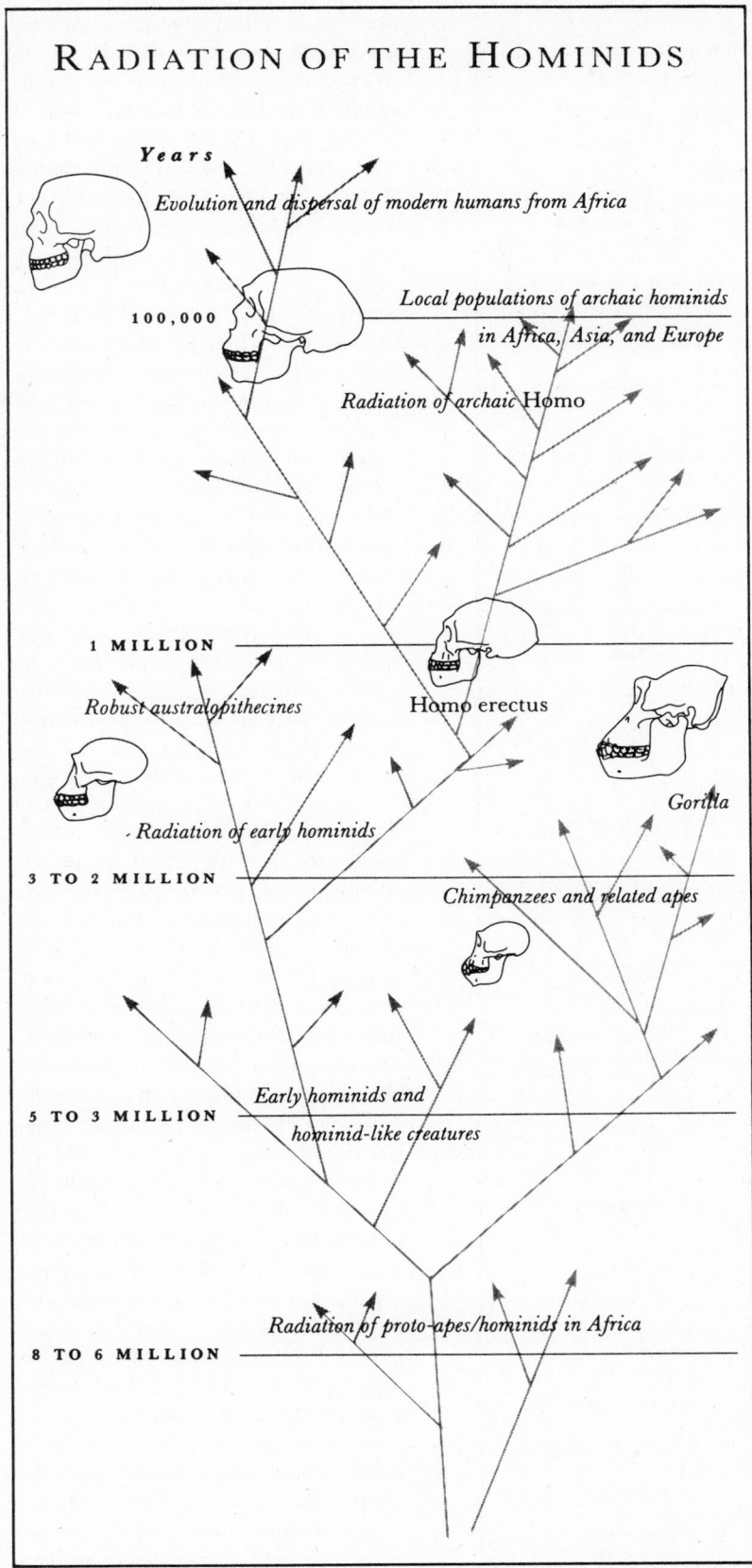

RADIATION OF THE HOMINIDS

Years

Evolution and dispersal of modern humans from Africa

100,000

Local populations of archaic hominids in Africa, Asia, and Europe

Radiation of archaic Homo

1 MILLION

Robust australopithecines

Homo erectus

Gorilla

Radiation of early hominids

3 TO 2 MILLION

Chimpanzees and related apes

5 TO 3 MILLION

Early hominids and hominid-like creatures

Radiation of proto-apes/hominids in Africa

8 TO 6 MILLION

DNA is possible because of its relatively limited size. In comparison, nuclear DNA is a complex, extensive, and complete sequencing of the entire human genome. Mapping of the complete human genome is at an early stage, but major molecular biology laboratories are currently racing to complete this project. The work will probably be completed within the next decade or so, certainly by 2050, and it will release a mass of new information about human evolution. One exciting prospect is that it will corroborate or refute the current model of a recent African origin for modern humans suggested by mitochondrial DNA studies. Moreover, complete genetic mapping will yield greater understanding of the function of the genes themselves, and molecular biology will gradually move into the field of behavioral genetics.

Biologists will have the tools to determine how much behavioral patterns in modern humans do—or do not—reflect the genetic basis of individuals and populations. In particular, the genetic basis for the differences between humans and the African apes will be measurable directly, bringing to an end 200 years (as it will be then) of speculation, philosophical debate, and tortuous theology about the chasm separating humans from their animal relatives. The evidence for evolution lies not just in the fossils we unearth, but in the molecules of which we are made.

What, though, will be the consequences of these developments for the way we think human evolution has occurred? The "how and why" questions will be as central in the year 2050 as they are today. At the risk of constraining the future in the straitjacket of the present, I shall concentrate on the issues that are currently at the center of debates and controversies—reassured to some extent by the fact that these debates have been central as long as human evolution has been a subject of study.

Darwin himself first put forward the idea of an African origin, so it is a hypothesis that has survived more than 100 years of scrutiny—and I suspect it will survive the next hundred. With each new discovery, whether in the field or in the genetics laboratory, the links between humans, the ancient hominids, and the African apes become more solid. We need progress not in finding a new cradle for humanity, but in understanding better *Why* Africa is so central; what is it about this continent that generates such evolutionary novelty? The answer to this will come not from studies of humans and hominids in isolation, but only from a better understanding of the mechanisms of evolution and the interactions between coexisting and competing species. The answer to "Why Africa?" in human evolution lies in the animals and plants that evolved with the hominids. I also suspect that 60 years from now, the issue may no longer be "Why Africa?" but why a particular *part* of the continent. For surely the key question is whether the East African Rift Valley is just a repository for excellent fossils or is itself the true cause—for a variety of ecological and geological reasons—of why humans exist at all. This does not relegate the rest of the world to a marginal place in palaeoanthropology—it just means that we should be asking different questions in continents that hominids colonized than in those in which they evolved.

Then, too, what of the scale of human evolution? Human evolution is both African and, under current models, a relatively recent event. Gone is the long line of hominids stretching back into the middle and early Miocene (20 to 25 million years ago), now replaced by a short sequence of Pliocene (about one and a half to five million years

CHRONOLOGY OF HUMAN EVOLUTION

Years Before Present

PRESENT

· *Extinction of archaic hominids/ dispersal of anatomically modern humans/colonization of Australia and the New World*

· *Evolution of neanderthals in Europe*

· *Evolution of anatomically modern humans in Africa*

½ MILLION
· *Archaic hominids widely dispersed*

First hominids out of Africa/
· *colonization of Asia and Africa*

1 MILLION

· *Origins of* Homo erectus

2 MILLION

· *Origins of the genus* Homo
· *Radiation of the australopithecines*

5 MILLION

· *First hominids*

10 MILLION

· *Evolution of the African hominoid stem that gave rise to hominids*

MAIN EVENTS IN PALAEOANTHROPOLOGY

1970 ·	*Period of major discoveries in East Africa*
1960	*The Leakeys discover the first early hominid in East Africa*
1950 ·	*Piltdown forgery exposed*
1940	
1930 ·	*Discoveries of* Homo erectus *in China*
1920	· *The first australopithecine discovered in South Africa*
	· *Piltdown man discovered*
1910	
1900	
1890	· *Dubois' discovery of* Homo erectus *in Java*
1880	
1870	· *Publication of* Descent of Man
1860 ·	*Publication of* Origin of Species
1850	· *Discovery of Neander specimen*
	· *First "neanderthal" discovered at Gibraltar*

ago) apes. Until recently, the emphasis was always on the oldest specimens. The goal of many researchers was to put the human family further and further back in time. The effect of this was also to broaden the gap between humans and other animals, for the more ancient the lineage, the greater the evolutionary distance from other creatures. As a result, humans retained their special status—on a pedestal—in the living world. The shorter time scale with which we now work offers new and exciting possibilities. We no longer envision long sequences of change along a single evolutionary ladder; rather, we think of an array of coexisting, competing hominid species. It is now often more interesting to discover the youngest specimen—the last surviving robust australopithecine or neanderthal, the ones that did not become our ancestors. Evolution is an experimental process, the trial and error of survival. The success of our own species over a very short period should not mislead us into assuming that the evolutionary success of hominids was inevitable. The story of human evolution is as much one of failure as it is of success, with many species surviving for many hundreds of thousands of years but ultimately disappearing, leaving no descendants. A key to understanding our own evolution lies in unraveling the extinctions of all other hominids.

This should be good news for the poor old neanderthals. As the first non-modern fossil hominids to be discovered, they have always been central to discussions about the pattern of human evolution. Their rugged and robust features have generally placed them in a position peripheral to the mainstream of human evolution; it was only for a brief period between 1960 and the 1980s that there has been strong support for neanderthals having a more central, ancestral role relative to modern humans. But the picture I have outlined for the next half century does not augur well for the neanderthals if their only claim to fame lies in their proximity to ourselves. I think that in the future they may be recognized even more firmly as an isolated European population of the last glaciation. (Indeed by 2050, with developments in molecular biology and the ability to retrieve DNA from fossilized material, it may actually be possible to prove this one way or the other.) Interest in them, however, should not stop there, for what makes the neanderthals so interesting from a truly evolutionary perspective is that they are a species of hominid so close to us in time, and yet so different. They underline a major lesson of the Darwinian revolution; there are more ways to be a hominid than by being a modern human. And these extinct hominids may well offer us our best chance within evolutionary biology to study a complex animal—its ecology, behavior, and society—that no longer exists.

Ultimately, though, it is the way we *think* about human evolution that is critical to how we interpret the fossils and their contextual evidence. To the Victorians, the meaning of evolution lay in the ladder it provided, upon each rung of which could be placed the grades of evolutionary complexity—with, of course, modern humans at the top. Early evolutionary biology looked at the history of the animal world in terms of progress or development. Only in the past 20 years has evolutionary theory been rejuvenated and the notion of progress within evolution abandoned. The emphasis now centers on adaptation—on evolutionary changes as the product of selection operating at the level of the individual. Evolutionary changes reflect changes in reproductive success—and therefore patterns in the fossil record need to be explained in terms of changing adaptations and reproductive strategies. In this perspective, humans are not an inevitable outcome of evolution but the product of a series of short-term responses to very specific selective conditions. Understanding human evolution, both in the technical sense of sorting out the pattern of fossils and in the more general sense of appreciating our place in nature, depends on relating our unique adaptive features to the conditions in which they evolved.

The approach that can achieve this end is not anthropology or anatomy or geology, but evolutionary, and especially behavioral, ecology. The first half of the twenty-first century will almost certainly see the expansion of this approach—incorporating more and more of human behavior within the overall study of comparative animal behavior. This must be the inevitable conclusion of the Darwinian revolution started in 1859: the full incorporation of hominid evolution within comparative evolutionary biology. In 2050, nearly 200 years after Darwin's *Origin of Species*, the evolution of our species should be understandable in terms of ordinary processes of natural selection—with the human being seen as just another animal, not the pinnacle of evolution. Paradoxically, the achievement of that goal may also mean the end of a discipline, for it will result in the full absorption of palaeoanthropology within evolutionary and biological science. The human species will no longer occupy a pedestal—but will have earned honor enough by coming down from it.

Evolution and Primate Behavior

Human beings are mammals, members of the order *Primates*. And we are very closely related to some other living primates, most notably chimpanzees (with whom we share almost 99% of our genetic material), gorillas, and orangutans. As primates, human beings have certain evolutionary traits in common with other primates (and other mammals as well); but our species is also distinctly different from all other animal species. At this moment, scholars are actively debating the degree to which it is possible to understand or explain human behavior in terms of the behavior patterns that seem to be innate in other species, particularly other primates.

In the first article in Topic 3, "What Are Friends For?" Barbara Smuts explores some of the complexities of baboon societies. Baboons are monkeys, and among the most successful of all primates. Like human beings, their ancestors long ago climbed down from the trees to pursue a lifestyle that is largely terrestrial. Smuts has been observing baboons in the wild for almost twenty years. Her observations have enriched our knowledge of these primate relatives of ours and have often shown how humanlike baboons can be. In this article, Smuts describes the world of baboon friendship (often including sexual intimacy) between males and females, and the protective role males often take toward the infants of their female friends. She argues that perhaps for our ancestors, as for baboons today, sex and friendship went hand-in-hand.

Edward O. Wilson has been a very controversial figure ever since 1975, when he published a book called *Sociobiology: The New Synthesis*. In this book he gathered together all the information biologists had accumulated about genetically transmitted behavior among the world's animals. But he went one step further: he argued that, contrary to the cherished beliefs strongly held by many anthropologists, human behavior also has fundamentally innate patterns. Three years later, in 1978, Wilson developed these views at length in his next book, *On Human Nature*.

Initially, Wilson's arguments stimulated heated debate which, at times, became ugly and personal. Several of his colleagues at Harvard organized the Sociobiology Study Group of Science, which became a forum for attacking Wilson and his followers. The study group argued that any attempt to account for human behavior genetically will inevitably cater to reactionary politicians seeking to protect the interests of groups with social, economic, and political power in society. In a letter to *The New York Review of Books*, they proclaimed that "Wilson joins the long parade of biological determinists whose work has served to buttress the institutions of their society by exonerating them from responsibility for social problems" (Dec. 11, 1975:60–61).

A careful reading of Wilson's books reveals, however, that he has made no direct, declarative statements tying human behavior to genes. Rather, he uses what to his critics is a maddening suppositional style: he *supposes* there *might* be genes that would favor certain forms of social behavior, then proceeds to ponder how such genes might be expressed. His critics point out, with some justification, that many lay readers are apt to miss this reserve and read Wilson's speculations as definitive. (Indeed, subsequent works by others have done so, most egregiously in the area of the study of sex roles, where Wilson himself is apt to use language decidely deterministic in flavor. See Topic 12 for a fuller discussion of these materials.)

Both Wilson and his adversaries have recently toned down their public rhetoric. But the debate and its bitterness do show that science is not pursued in a vacuum. Its findings can be and often are appropriated for social, economic, and political purposes—regardless of scientists' intentions. Thus, in a society still organized to some degree along "racial" (and sexual) lines in its distribution of wealth and access to institutions of power, scientific theories and findings that even suggest the possibility that social institutions may, to whatever degree, be rooted in innate biological traits will be used to justify the status quo and undermine pressures for change. For example, if certain research suggests that intelligence is unevenly distributed among the "races" of our society, some pressure groups will use these findings to justify terminating programs, such as Head Start, which are designed to compensate for social inequalities. It was fear of such misuse of Wilson's work that fueled the bitterness of his critics' attacks.

The last three articles in Topic 3 address these issues. In "On Becoming Human," Boyce Rensberger reviews Wilson's work and concludes that human behavior is a result of a complex interplay between our biological heritage and our culture. Monique Borgerhoff Mulder examines what sociobiology has taught us about human behavior in "Progress in Human Sociobiology." She looks at such classic issues as kin selection, altruism, reproductive success, wealth, and marriage through the sociobiological lens. In the final article, "Sharing in Human Evolution," Jane B. Lancaster and Phillip Whitten attack the notion first popularized by Konrad Lorenz that innate aggression is so powerful in human beings that it will overwhelm all social structures designed to curb it. They argue that to the extent that there is a human "biogram" (as Wilson would put it), the evidence from both fossil remains and cross-cultural comparisons with still-surviving hunting-and-gathering groups demonstrates that human beings are characterized primarily by a predisposition toward cooperation and sharing, rather than toward violence and aggression. This article shows how looking for biological foundations for human behavior rooted in our evolutionary past need not reduce human beings to naked apes.

What Are Friends For?

By Barbara Smuts

....

Virgil, a burly adult male olive baboon, closely followed Zizi, a middle-aged female easily distinguished by her grizzled coat and square muzzle. On her rump Zizi sported a bright pink swelling, indicating that she was sexually receptive and probably fertile. Virgil's extreme attentiveness to Zizi suggested to me—and all rival males in the troop—that he was her current and exclusive mate.

Zizi, however, apparently had something else in mind. She broke away from Virgil, moved rapidly through the troop, and presented her alluring sexual swelling to one male after another. Before Virgil caught up with her, she had managed to announce her receptive condition to several of his rivals. When Virgil tried to grab her, Zizi screamed and dashed into the bushes with Virgil in hot pursuit. I heard sounds of chasing and fighting coming from the thicket. Moments later Zizi emerged from the bushes with an older male named Cyclops. They remained together for several days, copulating often. In Cyclops's presence, Zizi no longer approached or even glanced at other males.

Primatologists describe Zizi and other olive baboons (*Papio cynocephalus anubis*) as promiscuous, meaning that both males and females usually mate with several members of the opposite sex within a short period of time. Promiscuous mating behavior characterizes many of the larger, more familiar primates, including chimpanzees, rhesus macaques, and gray langurs, as well as olive, yellow, and chacma baboons, the three subspecies of savanna baboon. In colloquial usage, promiscuity often connotes wanton and random sex, and several early studies of primates supported this stereotype. However, after years of laboriously recording thousands of copulations under natural conditions, the Peeping Toms of primate fieldwork have shown that, even in promiscuous species, sexual pairings are far from random.

Some adult males, for example, typically copulate much more often than others. Primatologists have explained these differences in terms of competition: the most dominant males monopolize females and prevent lower-ranking rivals from mating. But exceptions are frequent. Among baboons, the exceptions often involve scruffy, older males who mate in full view of younger, more dominant rivals.

A clue to the reason for these puzzling exceptions emerged when primatologists began to question an implicit assumption of the dominance hypothesis—that females were merely passive objects of male competition. But what if females were active arbiters in this system? If females preferred some males over others and were able to express these preferences, then models of mating activity based on male dominance alone would be far too simple.

Once researchers recognized the possibility of female choice, evidence for it turned up in species after species. The story of Zizi, Virgil, and Cyclops is one of hundreds of examples of female primates rejecting the sexual advances of particular males and enthusiastically cooperating with others. But what is the basis for female choice? Why might they prefer some males over others?

This question guided my research on the Eburru Cliffs troop of olive baboons, named after one of their favorite sleeping sites, a sheer rocky outcrop rising several hundred feet above the floor of the Great Rift Valley, about 100 miles northwest of Nairobi, Kenya. The 120 members of Eburru Cliffs spent their days wandering through open grassland studded with occasional acacia thorn trees. Each night they retired to one of a dozen sets of cliffs that provided protection from nocturnal predators such as leopards.

Most previous studies of baboon sexuality had focused on females who, like Zizi, were at the peak of sexual receptivity. A female baboon does not mate when she is pregnant or lactating, a period of abstinence lasting about eighteen months. The female then goes into estrus, and for about two weeks out of every thirty-five-day cycle, she mates. Toward the end of this two week period she may ovulate, but usually the female undergoes four or five estrous cycles before she conceives. During pregnancy, she once again resumes a chaste existence. As a result, the typical female baboon is sexually active for less than 10 percent of her adult life. I thought that by focusing on the other 90 percent, I might learn something new. In particular, I suspected that routine, day-to-day relationships between males and pregnant or lactating (nonestrous) females might provide clues to female mating preferences.

Nearly every day for sixteen months, I joined the Eburru Cliffs baboons at their sleeping cliffs at dawn and traveled several miles with them while they foraged for roots, seeds, grass, and occasionally, small prey items, such as baby gazelles or hares (see "Predatory Baboons of Kekopey," *Natural History*, March 1976). Like all savanna baboon troops, Eburru Cliffs functioned as a cohesive unit organized around a core of related females, all of whom were born in the troop. Unlike the females, male savanna baboons leave their natal troop to join another where they may remain for many years, so most of the Eburru Cliffs adult males were immigrants. Since membership in the troop remained relatively constant during the period of my study, I learned to identify each individual. I relied on differences in size, posture, gait, and especially, facial features. To the practiced observer, baboons look as different from one another as human beings do.

As soon as I could recognize individuals, I noticed that particular females tended to turn up near particular males again and again. I came to think of these pairs as friends. Friendship among animals is not a well-documented phenomenon, so to convince skeptical colleagues that baboon friendship was real, I needed to develop objective criteria for distinguishing friendly pairs.

I began by investigating grooming, the amiable simian habit of picking through a companion's fur to remove dead skin and ectoparasites (see "Little Things That Tick Off Baboons," *Natural History*, February 1984). Baboons spend much more time grooming than is necessary for hygiene, and previous research had indicated that it is a good measure of social bonds. Although eighteen adult males lived in the troop, each nonestrous female performed most of her grooming with just one, two, or occasionally, three males. For example, of Zizi's twenty-four grooming bouts with males, Cyclops accounted for thirteen, and a second male, Sherlock, accounted for all the rest. Different females tended to favor different males as grooming partners.

Another measure of social bonds was simply who was observed near whom.

When foraging, traveling, or resting, each pregnant or lactating female spent a lot of time near a few males and associated with the others no more often than expected by chance. When I compared the identities of favorite grooming partners and frequent companions, they overlapped almost completely. This enabled me to develop a formal definition of friendship: any male that scored high on both grooming and proximity measures was considered a friend.

Virtually all baboons made friends; only one female and the three males who had most recently joined the troop lacked such companions. Out of more than 600 possible adult female–adult male pairs in the troop, however, only about one in ten qualified as friends; these really were special relationships.

Several factors seemed to influence which baboons paired up. In most cases, friends were unrelated to each other, since the male had immigrated from another troop. (Four friendships, however, involved a female and an adolescent son who had not yet emigrated. Unlike other friends, these related pairs never mated.)

Older females tended to be friends with older males; younger females with younger males. I witnessed occasional May–December romances, usually involving older females and young adult males. Adolescent males and females were strongly rule-bound, and with the exception of mother–son pairs, they formed friendships only with one another.

Regardless of age or dominance rank, most females had just one or two male friends. But among males, the number of female friends varied greatly from none to eight. Although high-ranking males enjoyed priority of access to food and sometimes mates, dominant males did not have more female friends than low-ranking males. Instead it was the older males who had lived in the troop for many years who had the most friends. When a male had several female friends, the females were often closely related to one another. Since female baboons spend a lot of time near their kin, it is probably easier for a male to maintain bonds with several related females at once.

When collecting data, I focused on one nonestrous female at a time and kept track

At nine months or so, young baboons often begin seeking out their male friends whenever their mothers are not around. Here a young baboon hitches a ride on the back of his adult male friend.

Photo: Courtesy of Irven DeVore/Anthro-Photo

of her every movement toward or away from any male; similarly, I noted every male who moved toward or away from her. Whenever the female and a male moved close enough to exchange intimacies, I wrote down exactly what happened. When foraging together, friends tended to remain a few yards apart. Males more often wandered away from females than the reverse, and females, more often than males, closed the gap. The female behaved as if she wanted to keep the male within calling distance, in case she needed his protection. The male, however, was more likely to make approaches that brought them within actual touching distance. Often, he would plunk himself down right next to his friend and ask her to groom him by holding a pose with exaggerated stillness. The female sometimes responded by grooming, but more often, she exhibited the most reliable sign of true intimacy: she ignored her friend and simply continued whatever she was doing.

In sharp contrast, when a male who was not a friend moved close to a female, she dared not ignore him. She stopped whatever she was doing and held still, often glancing surreptitiously at the intruder. If he did not move away, she sometimes lifted her tail and presented her rump. When a female is not in estrus, this is a gesture of appeasement, not sexual enticement. Immediately after this respectful acknowledgement of his presence, the female would slip away. But such tense interactions with nonfriend males were rare, because females usually moved away before the males came too close.

These observations suggest that females were afraid of most of the males in their troop, which is not surprising: male baboons are twice the size of females, and their canines are longer and sharper than those of a lion. All Eburru Cliffs males directed both mild and severe aggression toward females. Mild aggression, which usually involved threats and chases but no body contact, occurred most often during feeding competition or when the male redirected aggression toward a female after losing a fight with another male. Females and juveniles showed aggression toward other females and juveniles in similar circumstances and occasionally inflicted superficial wounds. Severe aggression by males, which involved body contact and sometimes biting, was less common and also more puzzling, since there was no apparent cause.

An explanation for at least some of these attacks emerged one day when I was watching Pegasus, a young adult male, and his friend Cicily, sitting together in the middle of a small clearing. Cicily moved to the edge of the clearing to feed, and a higher-ranking female, Zora, suddenly attacked her. Pegasus stood up and looked as if he were about to intervene when both females disappeared into the bushes. He sat back down, and I remained with him. A full ten minutes later, Zora appeared at the edge of the clearing; this was the first time she had come into view since her attack on Cicily. Pegasus instantly pounced on Zora, repeatedly grabbed her neck in his mouth and lifted her off the ground, shook her whole body, and then dropped her. Zora screamed continuously and tried to escape. Each time, Pegasus caught her and continued his brutal attack. When he finally released her five minutes later she had a deep canine gash on the palm of her hand that made her limp for several days.

This attack was similar in form and intensity to those I had seen before and labeled "unprovoked." Certainly, had I come upon the scene after Zora's aggression toward Cicily, I would not have understood why Pegasus attacked Zora. This suggested that some, perhaps many, severe attacks by males actually represented punishment for actions that had occurred some time before.

Whatever the reasons for male attacks on females, they represent a serious threat. Records of fresh injuries indicated that Eburru Cliffs adult females received canine slash wounds from males at the rate of one for every female each year, and during my study, one female died of her injuries. Males probably pose an even greater threat to infants. Although only one infant was killed during my study, observers in Botswana and Tanzania have seen recent male immigrants kill several young infants.

Protection from male aggression, and from the less injurious but more frequent aggression of other females and juveniles, seems to be one of the main advantages of friendship for a female baboon. Seventy times I observed an adult male defend a female or her offspring against aggression by another troop member, not infrequently a high-ranking male. In all but six of these cases, the defender was a friend. Very few of these confrontations involved actual fighting; no male baboon, subordinate or dominant, is anxious to risk injury by the sharp canines of another.

Males are particularly solicitous guardians of their friends' youngest infants. If another male gets too close to an infant or if a juvenile female plays with it too roughly, the friend may intervene. Other troop members soon learn to be cautious when the mother's friend is nearby, and his presence provides the mother with a welcome respite from the annoying pokes and prods of curious females and juveniles obsessed with the new baby. Male baboons at Gombe Park in Tanzania and Amboseli Park in Kenya have also been seen rescuing infants from chimpanzees and lions. These several forms of male protection help to explain why females in Eburru Cliffs stuck closer to their friends in the first few months after giving birth than at any other time.

The male–infant relationship develops out of the male's friendship with the mother, but as the infant matures, this new bond takes on a life of its own. My coworker Nancy Nicolson found that by about nine months of age, infants actively sought out their male friends when the mother was a few yards away, suggesting that the male may function as an alternative caregiver. This seemed to be especially true for infants undergoing unusually early or severe weaning. (Weaning is generally a gradual, prolonged process, but there is tremendous variation among mothers in the timing and intensity of weaning. See "Mother Baboons," *Natural History*, September 1980.) After being rejected by the mother, the crying infant often approached the male friend and sat huddled against him until its whimpers subsided. Two of the infants in Eburru Cliffs lost their mothers when they were still quite young. In each case, their bond with the mother's friend subsequently intensified, and—perhaps as a result—both infants survived.

A close bond with a male may also improve the infant's nutrition. Larger than all other troop members, adult males monopolize the best feeding sites. In general, the personal space surrounding a feeding male is inviolate, but he usually tolerates intrusions by the infants of his female friends, giving them access to choice feeding spots.

Although infants follow their male friends around rather than the reverse, the males seem genuinely attached to their tiny companions. During feeding, the male and infant express their pleasure in each other's company by sharing spirited, antiphonal grunting duets. If the infant whimpers in distress, the male friend is likely to cease feeding, look at the infant, and grunt softly, as if in sympathy, until the whimpers cease. When the male rests, the infants of his female friends may huddle behind him, one after the other, forming a "train," or, if feeling energetic, they may use his body as a trampoline.

When I returned to Eburru Cliffs four years after my initial study ended, several of the bonds formed between males and the infants of their female friends were still intact (in other cases, either the male or the infant or both had disappeared). When these bonds involved recently matured females, their long-time male associates showed no sexual interest in them, even though the females mated with other adult males. Mothers and sons, and usually maternal siblings, show similar sexual inhibitions in baboons and many other primate species.

The development of an intimate relationship between a male and the infant of his female friend raises an obvious question: Is the male the infant's father? To answer this question definitely we would need to conduct genetic analysis, which was not possible for these baboons. Instead, I estimated paternity probabilities from observations of the temporary (a few hours or days) exclusive mating relationships, or consortships, that estrous females form with a series of different males. These estimates were apt to be fairly accurate, since changes in the female's sexual swelling allow one to pinpoint the timing of conception to within a few days. Most females consorted with only two or three males during this period, and these males were termed likely fathers.

In about half the friendships, the male was indeed likely to be the father of his friend's most recent infant, but in the other half he was not—in fact, he had never been seen mating with the female. Interestingly, males who were friends with the mother but not likely fathers nearly always developed a relationship with her infant, while males who had mated with the female but were not her friend usually did not. Thus friendship with the mother, rather than paternity, seems to mediate the development of male–infant bonds. Recently, a similar pattern was documented for South American capuchin monkeys in a laboratory study in which paternity was determined genetically.

These results fly in the face of a prominent theory that claims males will invest in infants only when they are closely related.

If males are not fostering the survival of their own genes by caring for the infant, then why do they do so? I suspected that the key was female choice. If females preferred to mate with males who had already demonstrated friendly behavior, then friendships with mothers and their infants might pay off in the future when the mothers were ready to mate again.

To find out if this was the case, I examined each male's sexual behavior with females he had befriended before they resumed estrus. In most cases, males consorted considerably more often with their friends than with other females. Baboon females typically mate with several different males, including both friends and nonfriends, but prior friendship increased a male's probability of mating with a female above what it would have been otherwise.

This increased probability seemed to reflect female preferences. Females occasionally overtly advertised their disdain for certain males and their desire for others. Zizi's behavior, described above, is a good example. Virgil was not one of her friends, but Cyclops was. Usually, however, females expressed preferences and aversions more subtly. For example, Delphi, a petite adolescent female, found herself pursued by Hector, a middle-aged adult male. She did not run away or refuse to mate with him, but whenever he wasn't watching, she looked around for her friend Homer, an adolescent male. When she succeeded in catching Homer's eye, she narrowed her eyes and flattened her ears against her skull, the friendliest face one baboon can send another. This told Homer she would rather be with him. Females expressed satisfaction with a current consort partner by staying close to him, initiating copulations, and not making advances toward other males. Baboons are very sensitive to such cues, as indicated by an experimental study in which rival hamadryas baboons rarely challenged a male–female pair if the female strongly preferred her current partner. Similarly, in Eburru Cliffs, males were less apt to challenge consorts involving a pair that shared a long-term friendship.

Even though females usually consorted with their friends, they also mated with other males, so it is not surprising that friendships were most vulnerable during periods of sexual activity. In a few cases, the female consorted with another male more often than with her friend, but the friendship survived nevertheless. One female, however, formed a strong sexual bond with a new male. This bond persisted after conception, replacing her previous friendship. My observations suggest that adolescent and young adult females tend to have shorter, less stable friendships than do older females. Some friendships, however, last a very long time. When I returned to Eburru Cliffs six years after my study began, five couples were still together. It is possible that friendships occasionally last for life (baboons probably live twenty to thirty years in the wild), but it will require longer studies, and some very patient scientists, to find out.

By increasing both the male's chances of mating in the future and the likelihood that a female's infant will survive, friendship contributes to the reproductive success of both partners. This clarifies the evolutionary basis of friendship-forming tendencies in baboons, but what does friendship mean to a baboon? To answer this question we need to view baboons as sentient beings with feelings and goals not unlike our own in similar circumstances. Consider, for example, the friendship between Thalia and Alexander.

The affair began one evening as Alex and Thalia sat about fifteen feet apart on the sleeping cliffs. It was like watching two novices in a singles bar. Alex stared at Thalia until she turned and almost caught him looking at her. He glanced away immediately, and then she stared at him until his head began to turn toward her. She suddenly became engrossed in grooming her toes. But as soon as Alex looked away, her gaze returned to him. They went on like this for more than fifteen minutes, always with split-second timing. Finally, Alex managed to catch Thalia looking at him. He made the friendly eyes-narrowed, ears-back face and smacked his lips together rhythmically. Thalia froze, and for a second she looked into his eyes. Alex approached, and Thalia, still nervous, groomed him. Soon she calmed down, and I found them still together on the cliffs the next morning. Looking back on this event months later, I realized that it marked the beginning of their friendship. Six years later, when I returned to Eburru Cliffs, they were still friends.

If flirtation forms an integral part of baboon friendship, so does jealousy. Overt displays of jealousy, such as chasing a friend away from a potential rival, occur occasionally, but like humans, baboons often express their emotions in more subtle ways. One evening a colleague and I climbed the cliffs and settled down near Sherlock, who was friends with Cybelle, a middle-aged female still foraging on the ground below the cliffs. I observed Cybelle while my colleague watched Sherlock, and we kept up a running commentary. As long as Cybelle was feeding or interacting with females, Sherlock was relaxed, but each time she approached another male, his body would stiffen, and he would stare intently at the scene below. When Cybelle presented politely to a male who had recently tried to befriend her, Sherlock even made threatening sounds under his breath. Cybelle was not in estrus at the time, indicating that male baboon jealousy extends beyond the sexual arena to include affiliative interactions between a female friend and other males.

Because baboon friendships are embedded in a network of friendly and antagonistic relationships, they inevitably lead to repercussions extending beyond the pair. For example, Virgil once provoked his weaker rival Cyclops into a fight by first attacking Cyclops's friend Phoebe. On another occasion, Sherlock chased Circe, Hector's best friend, just after Hector had chased Antigone, Sherlock's friend.

In another incident, the prime adult male Triton challenged Cyclops's possession of meat. Cyclops grew increasingly tense and seemed about to abandon the prey to the younger male. Then Cyclops's friend Phoebe appeared with her infant Phyllis. Phyllis wandered over to Cyclops. He immediately grabbed her, held her close, and threatened Triton away from the prey. Because any challenge to Cyclops now involved a threat to Phyllis as well, Triton risked being mobbed by Phoebe and her relatives and friends. For this reason, he backed down. Males frequently use the infants of their female friends as buffers in this way. Thus, friendship involves costs as well as benefits because it makes the participants vulnerable to social manipulation or redirected aggression by others.

Finally, as with humans, friendship seems to mean something different to each baboon. Several females in Eburru Cliffs had only one friend. They were devoted companions. Louise and Pandora, for example, groomed their friend Virgil and no other male. Then there was Leda, who, with five friends, spread herself more thinly than any other female. These contrasting patterns of friendship were associated with striking personality differences. Louise and Pandora were unobtrusive females who hung around quietly with Virgil and their close relatives. Leda seemed to be everywhere at once, playing with infants, fighting with juveniles, and making friends with males. Similar differences were apparent among the males. Some devoted a great deal of time and energy to cultivating friendships with females, while others focused more on challenging other males. Although we probably will never fully understand the basis of these individual differences, they contribute immeasurably to the richness and complexity of baboon society.

Male–female friendships may be widespread among primates. They have been reported for many other groups of savanna baboons, and they also occur in rhesus and Japanese macaques, capuchin monkeys, and perhaps in bonobos (pygmy chimpanzees). These relationships should give us pause when considering popular scenarios for the evolution of male–female relationships in humans. Most of these scenarios assume that, except for mating, males and females had little to do with one another until the development of a sexual division of labor, when, the story goes, females began to rely on males to provide meat in exchange for gathered food. This, it has been argued, set up new selection pressures favoring the development of longterm bonds between individual males and females, female sexual fidelity, and as paternity certainty increased, greater male investment in the offspring of these unions. In other words, once women began to gather and men to hunt, presto—we had the nuclear family.

This scenario may have more to do with cultural biases about women's economic dependence on men and idealized views of the nuclear family than with the actual behavior of our hominid ancestors. The nonhuman primate evidence challenges this story in at least three ways.

First, long-term bonds between the sexes can evolve in the absence of a sexual division of labor or food sharing. In our primate relatives, such relationships rest on exchanges of social, not economic, benefits.

Second, primate research shows that highly differentiated, emotionally intense male–female relationships can occur without sexual exclusivity. Ancestral men and women may have experienced intimate friendships long before they invented marriage and norms of sexual fidelity.

Third, among our closest primate relatives, males clearly provide mothers and infants with social benefits even when they are unlikely to be the fathers of those infants. In return, females provide a variety of benefits to the friendly males, including acceptance into the group and, at least in baboons, increased mating opportunities in the future. This suggests that efforts to reconstruct the evolution of hominid societies may have overemphasized what the female must supposedly do (restrict her mating to just one male) in order to obtain male parental investment.

Maybe it is time to pay more attention to what the male must do (provide benefits to females and young) in order to obtain female cooperation. Perhaps among our ancestors, as in baboons today, sex and friendship went hand in hand. As for marriage—well, that's another story.

On Becoming Human

By Boyce Rensberger

Edward O. Wilson has a theory about what makes people act the way they do. He thinks that broad categories of human behavior—things such as male dominance, incest taboos, and other patterns perpetuated by tradition and cultural practice—are not merely cultural inventions. Instead Wilson believes that social behaviors like these are under a degree of genetic control built into the brain. He thinks these behaviors have been shaped by a special kind of evolution in which genes and culture—the forces of nature *and* nurture—worked together.

But in the two years that Wilson has been promoting his provocative theory, he has learned that many humans find it hard to accept the idea of any genetic control of their behavior. So he likes to explain his theory by taking people on an imaginary trip to another galaxy. There he shows them two species of intelligent beings—the Eidylons and the Xenidrins, who represent extreme examples of the two possible ways of explaining the forces that might govern human behavior.

Eidylons and Xenidrins both look rather human, but they differ in one respect. The Eidylons (Greek for "skilled ones") behave strictly according to genetic control. The Xenidrins (from the Greek for "strangers") act only according to cultural influence.

Eidylons are as intelligent as Earthlings, but they can respond only one way to a given set of circumstances. During embryonic development Eidylon genes build brains that are "hard wired" and thus capable of learning only one set of social behaviors. All Eidylon societies have the same political and economic systems. Details of language, art, and other elements of their cultures may vary, but the basic structures are unchangeable. At Eidylon festivals ritual hymns stir feelings of deep pleasure in the audience, but the music is always the same, note for note. Eidylons teach and learn all that they know, but they are capable of learning only one thing in each category—one language, one creation myth, one courtship ritual. Like the white-crowned sparrows of California, they must hear the song of their species in order to learn it, but it is the only song they can learn.

At the opposite end of the spectrum are the Xenidrins, who are born with minds that are truly blank slates. Their every behavior is shaped by their culture. Like Eidylons, they must be taught in order to learn, but they can learn any form of behavior. In some Xenidrin societies the culture leads men to dominate women, but in as many others the culture leads women to dominate men. Some prohibit incest; others encourage it. Smiles are not the universal language among the Xenidrins; in some Xenidrin cultures the tradition is instead to wrinkle the nose or shake the head.

If Earthlings were guided entirely, or predominantly, by culture, as social scientists often hold, a survey of Earthling societies ought to reveal a species something like the Xenidrins. Or, if human behavior were entirely genetic in control, it ought to resemble that of the Eidylons.

Not even Wilson suggests that humans are genetic automatons like the Eidylons. But he does propose that it is time to move away from the opposite bias, one that had its origin decades ago as a reaction to another, more objectionable brand of genetic determinism. Early in this century many biologists went to extremes in proclaiming that genes governed not only anatomy but behavior. Their views quickly developed into the eugenics movement, which sought to improve humanity by eliminating genetically "inferior" peoples.

Recoiling from this, top anthropologists such as Franz Boas and Alfred Kroeber denied any effect of genes on behavior. For evidence Boas sent his student Margaret Mead to Samoa to find a culture lacking the stressful adolescence that eugenicists said was innate. She found it, and her controversial book, *Coming of Age in Samoa*, was seen as proof of cultural determinism. Between anthropology and biology Kroeber proclaimed an "eternal chasm."

When the eugenics movement faded, partly because of the rise of cultural determinism and partly because extremist eugenics turned into virulent racism, biologists largely withdrew from questions of human behavior. But the issue never quite died within the social sciences. As the influence of Boas and Kroeber began to decline in the 1930s and '40s, some social scientists adopted more moderate stands, sometimes embracing a degree of genetic influence.

Not until Wilson, a shy and mild mannered Harvard professor who specialized in insect societies, took up the question in his epochal 1975 book, *Sociobiology*, did biologists reenter the debate in large numbers. Some did so with vehement opposition, asserting that sociobiology was only the racist ghost of the eugenics movement. In 1978, for example, when Wilson started to address a packed scientific meeting, demonstrators rushed the dais shouting "Nazi!" "Racist!" "Fascist!" and dumped a pitcher of water on the startled man's head. Wilson, hobbled by a broken foot at the time, could do little more than wipe his face, dry his glasses, and, after accepting a standing ovation from the audience, continue his paper.

Beyond invoking a degree of genetic influence over behavior, Wilson's theories have little in common with the eugenics movement. Specifically, Wilson contends that the genes construct a brain organized in such a manner that it processes certain kinds of information and certain kinds of thoughts more readily in one way than another. When an individual is faced with a choice (and is preparing to exercise willful control of behavior), the biological properties of the brain will make it more likely—though not inevitable—for one alternative to be favored.

Wilson can talk for hours about these ideas, citing evidence from this anthropologist's study or that psychologist's findings, conducting

the kind of interdisciplinary tour de force that made *Sociobiology* command such respect. That book's last chapter—the only part that dealt with human beings rather than animals—triggered a major furor, monopolizing academic conferences for years in anthropology, psychology, sociology, and other social and behavioral sciences. Although some specialists in each field championed sociobiology as applied to humans, the reaction was largely critical.

Wilson pressed on anyway and, two years ago, published an obtuse, math-laden book, *Genes, Mind, and Culture,* arguing that human social behaviors arose as the result of a special evolutionary process in which genetic evolution—specifically that affecting the brain—is yoked in a feedback loop with cultural evolution. Human genes and human culture, Wilson claimed along with coauthor Charles J. Lumsden, have been irrevocably tied for many thousands of years. They called their hypothesis gene-culture coevolution. It is high time, the pair said, to alloy the social sciences and biology into a new, Darwinized human science.

That was two years ago, and although many social scientists still scoff, more than a few anthropologists and psychologists have rallied to the new view. A small but growing number consider Wilson a seminal thinker, the catalyst of a paradigm shift that could someday unify the social sciences and the natural sciences. Major centers of sociobiologically oriented social science have grown up not only at Harvard but at the University of Michigan, Northwestern University, and University of Washington.

Now Wilson and Lumsden have a new book, mercifully free of mathematics, and it takes their case even further. They suggest that genetic evolution and cultural evolution became locked onto one another perhaps a couple of million years ago, each fueling the other and igniting a "Promethean fire"

(the new book's title) that drove the evolutionary growth of the mind at a pace unprecedented for any other organ. Gene-culture coevolution, they say, is what made the modern human mind and the culture to which it is bound.

If *Promethean Fire* creates as much of a stir as have Wilson's earlier books, it will not be because of the theory; that was already set forth in more scientific trappings two years ago. It will be because Wilson now asserts that a biologically based human science promises to yield new methods by which society can consciously redesign human nature. Wilson does not shrink from advocating what he calls social engineering. In other words, he thinks society may someday decide, for example, that people are too aggressive and that subsequent generations ought to be made less aggressive. It might be done, Wilson feels, by altering the environmental factors with which the child's genes interact to produce an adult with a fully developed human nature.

"One result of a strong human science," Wilson points out in *Promethean Fire,* "might be the creation of a sophisticated form of social engineering, one that touches the deepest levels of human motivation and moral reasoning."

David Barash winced and then rolled his eyes to the ceiling when he heard that quote. "I admire Ed a lot," he allowed. "I think he's going to be remembered as one of the most important thinkers in biology, but I wish he wouldn't say things like that." Barash is a University of Washington sociobiologist and one of the top researchers in the field. He is one of Wilson's strongest scientific allies and, in fact, is asked so often to lecture in place of the almost Darwinishly reclusive Wilson that Barash says he's getting tired of being "Ed's West Coast Huxley."

Talk of social engineering, Barash says, is much too premature and, in any case, leads to such negative connotations for most people that they are inclined to reject sociobiology altogether. That, to Wilson, would be unthinkable, given what we now know. "Nobody," he says, "can deny biology any more." He holds that anthropological and psychological studies provide evidence of a deeply seated human nature shared by all peoples.

One of the more obvious, if trivial, examples of a genetic constraint on behavior has to do with the words people use to name colors. Physicists know that the colors of visible light form a continuous spectrum. Yet a study of 20 societies around the world found that practically all perceive a spectrum as composed mainly of discrete color categories. Most recognize four basic ones: red, yellow, green, and blue. "This beautiful illusion," Wilson says, "is genetically programmed into the visual apparatus and brain." It turns out that the eye's retina has nerve endings that are especially sensitive to the wavelengths of light approximating three of these basic colors. Superficially, cultures may have different names for, say, blue, but people everywhere have evolved a nervous system that is particularly sensitive to light with a wavelength of 440 nanometers. The genes, then, *do* influence human color vocabularies, which are a simple kind of behavior.

Facial expressions appear to reflect another form of genetic control. Photographs of Americans acting out anger, surprise, loathing, happiness, and fear were correctly described by New Guinea tribesmen. Pictures of the tribesmen registering the same emotions in their own way were, likewise, immediately recognized by Americans. Support for the idea that the brain is genetically programmed to recognize facial expressions has come from study of a rare brain disorder called prosopagnosia. It is caused by lesions in particular regions of the brain and leaves the victim unable to recognize other people by their faces. Sufferers can still recognize nonfacial images but must learn to differentiate people by their voices.

Still another kind of evidence that Wilson cites involves phobias, the unreasoning fears of specific things that, in extreme cases, can incapacitate sufferers with reactions of the autonomic nervous system such as nausea and cold sweat. Wilson observes that phobic reactions are most easily evoked by many of the great dangers that early humans would have faced—heights, thunderstorms, snakes, spiders. If phobias were the result of cultural conditioning, as is often said, why, he asks, are they rarely brought on by modern dangers such as explosives, electric sockets, and automobiles? Wilson suggests that evolution has programmed the brain to regard certain natural phenomena as dangerous and that phobias are extreme examples of this. Evolution has not had time to do the same for dangerous modern inventions.

Perhaps the most important evidence that Wilson cites involves a much more socially complex behavior—the nearly universal practice of incest avoidance. As it happens, incest avoidance has figured prominently in much social science thinking. Anthropologists such as Leslie White and Claude Levi-Strauss have even held that the origin of an incest prohibition, usually expressed through some cultural device such as a taboo, marked the evolutionary transition of animals to humans. These authorities, like Freud and Bronislaw Malinowski half a century earlier, considered incest avoidance mechanisms to be strictly cultural inventions.

Wilson insists that its origin is genetic. For one thing, many lower animals lacking culture have behavior patterns that avoid incest. For another, inbreeding is known to increase the chances of producing defective offspring. Simple Darwinian natural selection would tend to weed out such individuals and to favor others possessing any inborn mechanism that discouraged inbreeding.

Wilson believes anthropologists have discovered the mechanism in human beings and that it illustrates the process by which genes and culture interact to produce human nature. The best evidence comes

from now-classic studies of Israeli kibbutzim, communal living arrangements shared by many families. Typically, the children spend their days in one big day care center. Although the pioneers of the kibbutz movement encouraged children to marry within their own kibbutz, just the opposite has happened. According to one study of 2,769 marriages of children raised in kibbutzim, none were between men and women raised together since birth.

To Wilson this study suggests that some mechanism deeper than culture is at work. After all, the culture encouraged marriage within the kibbutz. Wilson calls the mechanism an epigenetic rule, his name for the genetically determined influence, or bias, that will be triggered by certain cultural conditions. In this case, the epigenetic rule says that children raised closely together during their earliest years will feel little or no sexual attraction toward one another when they grow up. This is the rule, Wilson says, that discourages brothers and sisters from marrying. In kibbutz conditions, where children are raised as closely as if they were siblings, the genes are, in a sense, fooled.

Confirmation of a sort has come from a study of certain Chinese families that adopted brides for their sons when both were young children. Of 19 adoptions in one village, 17 couples refused to consummate the marriage when they reached adulthood. In both consummated marriages the girls were considerably older when adopted, presumably too old to trigger the epigenetic rule.

"Sociobiology has given us the first really cogent explanation for this phenomenon of incest avoidance," says Pierre L. van den Berghe, a University of Washington sociologist. "This is a question that has obsessed lots of sociologists, anthropologists, and psychologists for over a hundred years. For me there is no question any more that we are genetically programmed to avoid inbreeding. And, through sociobiology, we can make a case that holds water scientifically. It's been a long time since any social scientist could do that."

Van den Berghe, in fact, considers sociobiology the salvation of his field. "Sociology today is very much a dead-end discipline. It isn't really a science, and it's not even a good humanity. Wilson is showing us how to get scientific, and I predict that 10 years from now it will be old hat. But right now most sociologists remain blissfully unaware of what has hit them."

When their awareness dawns, there will be work for them to do. The human mind, Wilson believes, contains epigenetic rules guiding many realms of human social behavior. He concedes that most of the rules are unknown but contends that social scientists have not been collecting the kind of data from various cultures to identify them.

Each of the epigenetic rules is presumed to be the product of neural structures. Although the nature of these structures is as yet unknown, they are assumed to have been built in each human mind, like any other brain structure, through the guidance of genes selected over eons of evolution. Wilson does not say—and this is a distinction often overlooked by critics—that the neural structures invariably produce a given behavior in all individuals or even in one individual all the time. Nor does he say that the structures prohibit the development of a culture that contradicts the genetic influence; he does say these should be rare.

Sometimes the behavioral response may be virtually inescapable, as in color naming. More often the genes only bias the choice an individual makes, rendering it more likely that one behavior will be favored over an alternative. In other words, a behavior that is genetically influenced need not be universally displayed. Couples who *wanted* to practice incest, for example, could exercise free will to override any anti-incest genes.

The first book by Lumsden and Wilson, *Genes, Mind, and Culture,* presented lots of elaborate mathematical models to demonstrate what they called the coevolutionary

circuit, the central tenet of gene culture coevolutionary theory. It is a sequence of ideas that runs as follows: The genes dictate the patterns of neural structures (and related hormonal systems). These structures impose the regularities in thinking and behavior that Wilson calls epigenetic rules. Since the rules are shared by many minds in a society, they readily find expression in the form of cultural institutions or traditions. The coevolutionary circuit is completed when these cultural traditions act the role of the physical environment in ordinary natural selection. Just as a hard freeze favors plants with genes for cold tolerance, human cultural traditions favor individuals with genes for the right epigenetic rules.

Incest avoidance again provides an example. If an epigenetic rule is shared by many minds in a society, it may give rise to a corresponding cultural practice or tradition such as a law, taboo, or ritual. These cultural factors can be as effective in weeding out the wrong genes as would be the biological consequences of inbreeding.

The mathematical models, contributed chiefly by Lumsden, whose background is in math and the physical sciences, indicate that this cyclic feedback mechanism can start with a very small genetic bias—a weak epigenetic rule—and build it into a major cultural institution in only a few thousand years.

Because of typographical errors in the formulas as given in *Genes, Mind, and Culture,* scientists who could follow the math originally said it failed to do what the authors claimed. "Once you correct the misprints, though, there are no conceptual errors in the model," says Montgomery Slatkin, a mathematician turned evolutionary biologist at the University of Washington. "But as far as I'm concerned, you don't need the math at all. It seems to me that the issues Lumsden and Wilson are raising are self-evident."

Gene-culture coevolution, however, is decidedly *not* self-evident to most social scientists.

"Sociobiology is a cultish thing," says Marshall Sahlins, a University of Chicago anthropologist who was a leading critic when Wilson published his 1975 book. "There are so many intellectual concessions one has to make to do sociobiology, but frankly, I don't want to have any more to say about it. Journalistic hype is what keeps it alive."

More vocal in denouncing Wilson's theories is Marvin Harris of the University of Florida, a widely respected anthropologist who has written several books on his own theory of cultural origins. His theory rejects genetic causes. "No respectable anthropologist who knows anything at all about sociocultural evolution could be concerned with gene-culture coevolution," Harris says. "Don't get me wrong. I'm a great enthusiast of sociobiology applied to primates, protohumans, early hominids, and maybe even early human beings up to Neandertal times. But that's all."

Harris holds that the major steps of human cultural evolution—such as the rise of agriculture, the origins of the state and of modern industrial systems—have all occurred too recently and too quickly for genetic evolution to have played a role. Harris accepts genes as shaping human nature up to the time of humanity's first great economic revolution, the switch from hunting and gathering to agriculture. ("Every anthropologist says there is a human nature. Nobody really has any trouble with that.") What sociobiology fails to explain, Harris says, is the revolutionary cultural changes that have taken place in the last 10,000 or so years.

"There are cultural forces around us that have accounted for these major changes," Harris says, "and gene-culture coevolution can't explain them." Harris holds that his own theory of cultural materialism can. He thinks the major transformations of human culture, as well as regional cultural practices, can be explained as adaptations to ecological and economic conditions. Societies, he says, repeat cycles of exploiting a new technology, overpopulating their land,

and intensifying the use of resources to the point of ecological catastrophe, whereupon a new technology or resource is devised to start a new cycle.

Wilson has heard criticisms like this aplenty. His response is to compare the traditional intellectual approaches of natural scientists with those of social scientists.

Natural scientists tend to be reductionist, assuming that complex phenomena can be broken down into simpler components and that one must start by studying these. Only after the simple and the specific are understood does the natural scientist move on to examine the complex. The biologist who hopes to understand the human body starts by trying to figure out how cells work. If even cells are too complex, the reductionist looks to the molecules. Thus was born molecular biology. And thus, Wilson likes to think, will be born a new biologized human science.

Social scientists, on the other hand, usually abhor reductionism. The whole, they say, is often greater than the sum of its parts. Unforeseeable properties emerge when simpler components act in concert. The mind, social scientists have long held, is something more than a collection of brain cells; culture is one of the emergent properties of a collection of human minds.

"If you want to be an influential social scientist," Wilson suggests, "you must present a fully mature theoretical system. In the natural sciences that's easily dismissed, and people tend to look for the most promising seed project. Lumsden and I tried to work within the natural sciences.

"Science is the art of the soluble," he goes on, "and you have to start with simple systems. When the social scientists find somebody taking the natural science approach, many of them tend to react negatively. They say it's not really going to tell us what we want to know about the origin of political systems or the other major questions of the social sciences. So they often tend to reject the rudimentary approach of the natural sciences. The natural scientists know the value of an

embryo."

Still, Wilson does concede ground. "There may be some substance to the objection that some social science questions are too complex, too technically intractable to be solved," he says. He notes that most of the behavioral examples he has studied, such as incest avoidance, involve simple two-choice alternatives. Wilson compares his situation to that of physicists who can easily calculate the forces acting between two bodies of matter but who find "many-body problems" insoluble. No physicist assumes that the forces governing many-body interactions are different from those in two-body interactions. "It could turn out that the gene-culture interactions underlying complex behavioral situations are insoluble. But I'm not ashamed to admit that. It doesn't invalidate the entire approach."

Maybe not. But some of Wilson's closest allies think it *does* mean that it is much too soon to talk about social engineering. Sociologist van den Berghe, for one, says he must part company with Wilson on this point. "Wilson is an amiable optimist. He looks only at the use of knowledge for good ends," says van den Berghe. "I'm a cynical pessimist. I'm not sure we'll ever have the knowledge to do it, but if we do, it'll be used for bad, selfish ends."

Wilson makes no specific engineering proposals beyond suggesting that modern humans carry a burden of outmoded epigenetic rules adapted to the Stone Age. He cites aggression and xenophobia. And he suggests that ways might be found to enhance traits that remain useful, such as the propensity for altruism and cooperation.

Since nobody knows the epigenetic rules for these traits, Wilson uses incest avoidance as a purely hypothetical example of how sociobiological knowledge might permit social engineering. Assume the engineer's goal is to encourage incest. Since the relevant genes cannot be identified, much less engineered, the cultural partner in the gene-culture interaction must be modified. For example, if the epigenetic rule is that people do not become

sexually attracted to children with whom they grew up, the social engineer must separate siblings in infancy. Raised apart during the crucial years, a brother and sister would presumably lack an innate revulsion at the idea of incest.

"Close self-examination and planned manipulation of values can be a distasteful exercise," Wilson and Lumsden write in the final chapter of their new book. "But in a world growing steadily more complicated and dangerous, the alternatives are not promising. A society that chooses to ignore the existence of the innate epigenetic rules will nevertheless continue to navigate by them and at each moment of decision yield to their dictates by default." If society continues to live by what it considers "conscience" and "God's will," without challenging "the ancient hereditary oracle dwelling within the epigenetic rules," Wilson and Lumsden suggest, there is little chance of creating a stable and benevolent world.

"On the other hand, the deep scientific study of the epigenetic rules will call the oracle to account and translate its commands into a precise language that can be understood and debated. People who know human nature in this way are more likely to agree on universal goals within the constraints of that nature and recognize absolute ethical truths, if such can be shown to exist. And although societies cannot escape the inborn rules of epigenesis and would lose the very essence of humanness if they even came close to succeeding, they can employ knowledge of the rules to guide individual behavior and cultural evolution to the ends on which their members may someday agree."

Many scientists have pursued their work with epic visions, but few have made so bold as to put them in print in quite such terms. Fewer still have been taken as seriously as the Harvard zoologist whose first love, before he became the standard-bearer of sociobiology, was the flawlessly tuned social structure of ants.

Progress in Human Sociobiology

By Monique Borgerhoff Mulder

EVOLUTIONARY BIOLOGICAL THEORY

At a recent conference on evolutionary theory in Cambridge, Sir Peter Medawar threw to a packed auditorium the question 'What has sociobiology taught us about human behaviour?'. The answering silence suggested that the audience was either sceptical or largely unaware of the recent progress of evolutionary biological studies within anthropology. So what are the achievements of human sociobiology and what of the criticisms it has incurred?

Let us be clear from the start that the term 'human sociobiology' is merely a fashionable label for the use of evolutionary biological theory in the study of human social behaviour. It is often mistakenly equated with the more explicitly genetically based model of kin selection (see below), whereas the proper role of human sociobiology is to examine a much wider issue: how the diversity of human societies reflects the adaptation of individuals to their social and ecological environments. For this reason it is increasingly becoming known as behavioural ecology.

What distinguishes this evolutionary perspective from those employed by anthropologists in the past is that it is explicitly Darwinian: behaviour is viewed as adaptive, and potentially shaped by natural selection, if an individual, as a consequence of this behaviour, accrues relative *reproductive* benefits compared with others who do not behave in this way. I stress at the outset that this Darwinian position does not require that behavioural differences stem from genetic differences. The point is simply this: if a particular pattern of behaviour causes a person to leave more descendants than those who do not exhibit such behaviour, it will come to predominate, or be naturally selected, *irrespective* of the mechanism of transmission from parents to offspring.[1]

The Darwinian concepts central to evolutionary biological theory—adaptation and natural selection—have without doubt enormously increased our understanding of animal social behaviour.[2] The question I want to address here is this: are these concepts of use to anthropology? Many anthropologists, and also some biologists, think not; but this is largely because of the series of chauvinistic myths and phoney statements that have come to characterize human socio-

biology, especially since E.O. Wilson's purported 'founding' of the field in 1975. The biological arguments have become muddled, and most anthropologists now rightly find them obscure and unnecessarily deterministic. Human sociobiology has become a derogatory term, and is generally rejected out of hand. This, I aim to show, is wrong.

The popularization of the human sociobiology debate has distracted attention from a growing body of empirical studies, particularly in North America, that test evolutionary hypotheses. It is from these studies, and not the popular literature, that an answer to Medawar's question is emerging. It is that humans are particularly prone to favour their kin, to use wealth and status to their reproductive advantage, and to marry and raise offspring in ways that can be predicted from evolutionary principles. While the supporting evidence for this answer is quite strong (as I shall show), any conclusive statements about the power of evolutionary explanations for human behaviour would be entirely premature. What sociobiologists in the field are trying to do is generate new and testable hypotheses for the cultural diversity of mankind. This is no radical departure from Radcliffe-Brown's goal, a science of society.

NEPOTISM AND RECIPROCAL ALTRUISM

Human sociobiologists first focused attention on the importance of kin selection (nepotism) in explaining patterns of social behaviour. The theory of kin selection states that it is in an individual's genetic interests to behave altruistically when the recipient of the altruistic act is related through descent from a common ancestor. More specifically, an altruistic gene enjoys a net benefit when the benefit to the recipient (B), times the degree of relatedness to the recipient (r), is greater than the cost suffered by the altruist (C) or $Br > C$.[3] The theory, in its weakest form, states that, other things being equal, cooperative behaviour most commonly occurs between closely related individuals.[4] As I point out later, this weak formulation of kin selection theory can lead to simplistic hypotheses. First, however, I shall examine some examples of kin selection applied to humans.

While almost all primitive societies studied by anthropologists are organized around groups of kin, Napoleon Chagnon's work with the Yǎnomamö Indians of Venezuela specifically demonstrates the importance of genealogical relationships in structuring events he observed during his fieldwork.[5] For instance, in large villages tensions develop between the villagers and they often fission into two or more new groups. Chagnon's data show that such villages usually split apart along kinship lines; indeed the degree of relatedness between villagers is consistently higher after than before fissioning. This is adaptive, Chagnon argues, because of the customary way in which Yǎnomamö, who practise bilateral cross-cousin marriage, acquire wives: groups of closely related males enter into alliances with other such groups, swapping their daughters and sisters in marriage. As such, brothers and close cousins play an important role in helping each other to acquire large numbers of wives, both through negotiations and raids, and can therefore benefit from co-residence. Indeed Chagnon shows some association between the numbers of a man's co-resident primary allies and his probability of finding a wife.

As further evidence of the importance of genealogical relationship, Chagnon and Bugos have shown how fights tends to polarize along kinship lines. An axe fight that occurred in a Yǎnomamö forest village in 1971 has subsequently been analysed (from film). A group of visitors, who had previously belonged to the village, overstayed their welcome at a feast, eating ravenously, making insulting remarks and finally beating up a woman. Bad feelings boiled over into a fight in which about thirty people, men and women, armed themselves with weapons (mainly clubs). The action culminated around two individuals, Mohesiwä and Keböwä. Analysis showed that those who participated actively on behalf of Mohesiwä bore more relationship to each other than they did to the supporters of Keböwä, and vice versa for the supporters of Keböwä. This was so even though members of the two groups were extremely familiar with one another, having shared the village until a few months previously. The authors conclude that while relatedness alone cannot account for all the tactics of recruitment, it is an important factor in structuring fights.

It can be concluded from studies like these only that kin selection is *consistent* with the facts, not that it is a better explanation than any previously offered for the observed behaviour, nor even that kin selection has been demonstrated. Indeed, non-evolutionary-biological anthropologists have quite different ideas about the importance of kinship in simple societies. Sahlins, for example, notes that the critical factor structuring human activity is not genealogical relationship *per se*, but the way in which relatives, and even non-relatives, are *classified* as kinsmen.[6] While some societies do seem to put a good deal of emphasis on genealogi-

cal ties, others elaborate many fictitious bonds such as godfathers, blood brothers, extended classificatory kin networks and adoption.

The response of evolutionary biological anthropologists to this challenge was to show that biological brothers or offspring are favoured over individuals who are simply *classified* as 'brother' or 'child'.[7] Several ethnographies mention the difficulties encountered by adopted children. For example, Martin Daly and Margo Wilson have shown that in American and Canadian cities, child abuse and neglect occur more commonly in families with adopted children, controlling for other socio-economic differences between these families. As the tales of wicked stepmothers in European folklore would have us believe, people generally treat their real relatives rather better than adopted members of the family. Blood does seem to run thicker than water. And in fact, where adoption occurs in traditional societies, those adopted are usually already closely related to the adopting family.[8]

A further example of the importance of genealogical relationship *per se* comes from the study of inheritance patterns. Matrilineal descent occurs predominantly in societies where men are frequently away from their wives, on absences of a military or economic nature, and consequently uncertain of whether or not they fathered their wives' children. Under such conditions it is better (reproductively speaking) for a man to leave his worldly goods to the children of his sister, with whom he knows he bears at least some relationship through their shared mother.[9]

How do we reconcile these two positions? Sociobiologists are right in noting that genealogical relations are an important factor in structuring human activity. They are also right in noting that real kin are often favoured over fictitious kin. However, anthropologists are right in pointing out that classificatory principles are important components of the variability in kinship systems. We seem to have reached an impasse, pitting biological versus cultural factors in the structuring of human activity.[10] However, to characterize the debate as such entails a profound misunderstanding of evolutionary biology, and two points must be made to clarify the sociobiologists' position.

First, as mentioned before, it is simplistic to expect individuals to direct altruism to others simply in proportion to the degree of relatedness, without our considering the costs and benefits of dispensing altruism to particular individuals. Calculating these costs and benefits is crucial to Hamilton's equation, although sociobiologists until recently have omitted to do so. Individuals should favour closest kin only when it is in their reproductive interests to do so. In certain cases a rich and distantly related neighbour will be a far more effective ally than a close kinsman who might be impotent, senile or simply uncooperative.

Second, social behaviour is equally likely to be shaped by reciprocal altruism, namely the trading of altruistic acts between individuals to the advantage of both. Social allies will be chosen for their ability to procure or provide whatever in that particular environment is necessary for an individual and his family to survive and reproduce; such unrelated allies may subsequently be classified as fictitious kin, or even become marriage partners. Thus among East African pastoralists for example, residentially distant men will be selected as cattle loaning partners, to insure a family's herd against localized problems such as drought, sickness or theft, and may subsequently become kin through marriage.

In sum, the objections raised by Sahlins and others, that kinship is not just blind biology, are not a serious challenge to the sociobiological enterprise. Nevertheless, in view of these objections, evolutionary biological anthropologists should stop focusing narrowly on the fit between the coefficients of relatedness and the occurrence of altruism; rather they should attempt to determine the ecological and social circumstances in which it is advantageous for an individual to cooperate with different categories of people, not just relatives.

REPRODUCTIVE SUCCESS OR WEALTH?

An important goal of humans in many parts of the world, not just western societies, is the acquisition of wealth (power or rank). The orthodox anthropological position has been to interpret human behavioural variability in terms of the maximization of utilities such as these. So are people maximizing wealth or offspring?

One approach to this problem might be to ask people what they are maximizing when they make decisions. But this does not get to the root of the problem. The evolutionary argument is essentially that decisions, choices and customary patterns of behaviour have the ultimate effect of increasing reproductive success, whether this is a conscious goal or not. Models derived from evolutionary theory use a form of cost-benefit analysis. The unit to be maximized in this cost-benefit assessment is the number of descendants an individual leaves. When evolutionary biologists talk about behaviour X being 'more successful' than behaviour Y, they mean that the reproductive consequences of X are greater than those of Y. Like all maximizing theories, evolutionary models require the individual to be able to weigh the relative costs and benefits of any particular behavioural strategy; however, it should be stressed that he or she need not necessarily be *aware* of weighing these options. Asking people what they do, while of utmost importance in understanding *how* individuals behave, and a central interest of all anthropologists (both evolutionary and other), neither clinches nor refutes an evolutionary explanation.

So if we cannot ask people *what* they are maximizing, we must examine whether their behaviour makes more sense as reproductive or economic maximization strategies. Reproductive strategies are more clearly in evidence than are economic strategies in some societies, such as the Yạnomamö

and most hunter-gatherer groups, perhaps because there is little scope for unequal acquisition of material goods. Yạnomamö headmen, for example, have more than twice as many children (8.6, on average) as do other men of comparable age (4.2), even though headmen are in no material sense richer than anyone else. However, where opportunities exist for a rigid differentiation in wealth we have to ask whether individuals strive for wealth, power and status as a means of increasing their reproductive success, or for material and social returns as goals in themselves. In some cases these goals can be separated. William Irons, for example, has shown that Yomut Turkmen men of Iran take second wives, despite suffering economically as a result of second marriages.[11]

Other studies address the question of whether large families represent economic or reproductive strategies from another angle. Anthropologists, relaying the views of people of many non-western cultures, have often argued that people want to have as many children as possible so as to benefit from the economic assistance they can expect from these children when they grow up. After reaching the age of about six years children in many cultures begin helping with household chores. Paul Turke's cross-sectional study of Ifalukian society in the Caroline Islands shows that parents invest more effort and time in their offspring than they receive as recompense from them later on in life, suggesting that children, at least on the Ifalukian Atoll, are more of a cost to parents than a source of labour and economic security.[12] While difficult problems arise in quantifying such equations, these studies are trying to separate Darwinian from other types of maximization models for human behaviour, and test one against the other.

There is, however, a point beyond all this. What the economic models lack, and the Darwinian models do not, is a reason why particular behaviour patterns are predicted to occur. Anthropologists characteristically see the maximization of wealth, pleasure (or whatever other utility) as a *sufficient* explanation for human behaviour. Biologists, by contrast, are less complacent, claiming that natural selection cannot operate on differential wealth accumulation, or differential achievement of any other utility, unless this leads to reproductive advantages.

MARRIAGE AND INHERITANCE

Recently sociobiologists have been looking into the adaptive significance of other aspects of human behaviour, such as variability in patterns of marriage, choice of wife, inheritance patterns, foraging strategies and child development. In each case the new approach is beginning to provide insights into cultural diversity.

Take for example the occurrence of monogamy and polygyny in humans. Research among many different species of birds and mammals has revealed principles that determine where polygyny will occur. Polygynous mating is more likely if the quality of male territories is highly variable; this is because, from the female point of view, it is better to be the second female sharing a good territory than a single female on a territory of lesser quality. This same principle may account for the distribution of polygyny in traditional human societies as well. Studies have shown that the most rigidly stratified societies almost consistently practise polygyny whereas the most egalitarian groups, notably hunter-gatherers, are predominantly monogamous. Furthermore, within social groups, it is the wealthiest men who have the most wives.[13]

Polyandry too can be examined from the point of view of what is the optimal strategy for reproduction under highly constrained ecological circumstances. Tibetan studies show that polyandrously married women achieve larger family sizes than monogamously married women. But why do the young men agree to share their elder brother's wife? Recent studies by John Crook and his colleagues show that with cultivable land limited to small alluvial fans in an otherwise barren area, there is no feasible reproductive option open to a young man other than to stay on the family farm.[14]

Such insights into the ecological bases of monogamy and polygyny are not of course the prerogative of evolutionary biologists. Anthropologists have long recognized associations between polygyny and stratification, polyandry and resource limitation, and again the issue of the sufficiency of explanations arises. Evolutionary biologists, having identified associations between resources and mating systems, start to wonder why humans should adopt reproductive solutions to particular ecological conditions that are so similar to those of males and females in other species. This then leads them into an explanation of whether marital behaviour reflects the optimal reproductive strategies of individuals within the particular social and ecological constraints of the society. Evolutionary biologists expand, rather than supplant, traditional anthropological explanations.

Sociobiologists can provide *novel* insights into aspects of behavioural variability. Let us look at inheritance patterns. I have already discussed matrilineal systems, but what of the thorny old question of why resources are in most human societies bequeathed to males? For the Darwinian, this is not an awkward reflection of (perhaps) the greater strength of males, but a question open to empirical test. Evolutionary theory predicts that parents should distribute their resources (including inheritance) among offspring according to the ability of each to use these resources to become successful parents; in short, a parent's strategy is to redistribute the inheritance in such a way as to maximize the number of his or her descendants (grand, or even great grand offspring). In polygynous societies, where sons can use parental resources to acquire many wives, parents should give resources preferentially to sons, whereas in monogamous societies inheritance should be more equally divided between sons and daughters.[15] Conversely, in stratified hypergynous social contexts, parents may do better (in terms of numbers of descendants) to endow their daughters and accrue reproductive benefits from high-ranking grandchildren.[16]

WHY ANTHROPOLOGISTS OBJECT

The evolutionary biological approach is beginning to shed light on cultural diversity, or at least to stimulate some interesting questions? So why do anthropologists object to sociobiology and behavioural ecology?

One reason is the genetic implications sometimes associated with evolutionary models of behaviour. In fact, the assumed role of genes in determining behavioural differences has become grossly inflated because of the confusing stylistic shorthand sociobiologists commonly use—a gene for this and a gene for that. As stated at the outset, the mechanisms whereby behavioural patterns are transmitted between parents and offspring need not necessarily be genetic for the theory of natural selection to be relevant. It is in fact very difficult to show that there are any genetic differences either within or between populations that are of major importance to the study of social behaviour. There is currently extremely little evidence, in any species, of behavioural differences that are determined genetically; behavioural differences are assumed to result from an interaction between genotype and variable environmental and social conditions.[17] Moreover, there is as yet no clear evidence that differences in aptitudes or behavioural tendencies, either within or between groups, stem *even in part* from genetic differences.

Another objection anthropologists make is 'What about culture?'. While human sociobiologists see culture as a consequence of individual behaviour, many traditional anthropologists, particularly in the USA, hold the Durkheimian perspective of culture as a superorganic entity. Cultural differences, in this latter sense, are thought to be either beyond explanation or subject to some kind of cultural logic which bears little relationship to what individuals actually do. The tension between explanations for group and individual level phenomenon has long divided social scientists and biologists. While group level explanations have proved to be much less powerful than individual level explanations in most nonhuman species, the human sociobiologists have perhaps given insufficient attention to this issue, and the possibility of emergent properties of systems should not be ruled out.

PROSPECTS FOR THE FUTURE

So if human sociobiologists are to show that evolutionary biology has something to offer the social sciences, what should they do?

Current studies suggesting that behaviour is shaped by natural selection, or has been in the past, immediately raise questions regarding both the mechanisms involved in the occurrence of adaptive behaviour and the specifics of individual cases.[18] While evolutionary theory generates stochastic models that can be tested against empirical data, the ins and outs of why an individual pursues a particular course of action at a given time cannot be understood out of context. As yet, sociobiologists have paid insufficient attention to these motivational factors, although interesting suggestions are being offered.[19] Perhaps more reprehensible has been the tendency of sociobiologists to underemphasize the historical and institutional factors that influence behaviour.

Indeed one could imagine circumstances in which cultural factors might impede the adoption of the most adaptive behavioural strategy, at least in the short term. For instance, take a society where, because of chronic warfare, men are likely to be uncertain as to their paternity; sociobiological logic would predict that males should behave more nepotistically to their sisters' children than to their own 'supposed' offspring. What if we find that this society practises patrilineal and not matrilineal inheritance, in contradiction to this prediction? Historical factors may well have played an important role. For example, an earlier imposition of a religion such as Islam, stressing descent through the father, might have inhibited people from reckoning descent through women. Clearly cultural heritage, in this case religious beliefs, will limit the power of any simplistic use of the concept of adaptation.

The future of human sociobiology lies in an approach which integrates the perspectives of more traditional anthropologists with the insights of evolutionary theory. Ethologists also stress an integrative approach. They ask questions not only about adaptation, but investigate how behaviour is controlled in a given set of circumstances; how behaviour is acquired, perhaps through learning or imitation, during development; and how the evolutionary history of an organism and its environment imposes constraints on the extent to which individuals can differentially survive and reproduce. In the study of humans these questions respectively relate to issues such as motivation, intention and decision-making; to socialization and individual differences, and to the importance of historical and cultural constraints on behaviour. The holistic discipline of anthropology may prove to be a particularly favourable arena for combining these levels of analysis, with its diverse interests in cognitive, physical, developmental, cultural and archaeological studies. As human sociobiology adopts a more integrative approach to the study of man, it will perhaps come to be viewed less as a subversive conspiracy, more as a unifying theme.

The answer to Medawar's question is this: good evidence exists that individuals favour genetic over classificatory kin, that patterns of residence, descent and marriage are in part affected by reproductive considerations, and that wealth and status are converted into reproductive advantage. The contribution of sociobiology so far has been to reveal correla-

tions between social, economic and reproductive behaviour that might not otherwise have been detected. New studies must examine how individuals enhance their reproductive success, and how these strategies contribute to cultural diversity. And then we must ask what is happening in modern industrial society: are our ultimate goals different from those of propagation and, if so, why and when have we gone 'off track'?

Notes

[1] See for discussion of this use of the term adaptation: Clutton-Brock T.H. & P.H. Harvey. 1979. Comparison and adaptation. *Pro. Royal Soc. of London. B.* 205, 547–565. Dunbar, R.I.M. 1984. *Reproductive Decisions.* Princeton: Princeton U.P. Caro, T.M. & M. Borgerhoff Mulder. In press. The problem of adaptation in the study of human behaviour. *Ethology and Sociobiology.* Ref. 15.

[2] For a good recent review see Trivers, R. 1985. *Social Evolution.* Menlo Park, Calif: Benjamin-Cummings.

[3] Hamilton, W.D. 1963. The evolution of altruistic behavior. *American Naturalist* 97, 354–6.

[4] For a clear treatment of sociobiological predictions see Gray, P.J. 1985. *Primate Sociobiology.* New Haven, Conn: HRAF Press.

[5] Chagnon, N.A. & P.E. Bugos Jr. 1979. Kin selection and conflict: an analysis of a Yanomamö ax fight. In *Evolutionary Biology and Human Social Behavior.* (eds) N.A. Chagnon & W. Irons. North Scituate, Mass: Duxbury P. See also Chagnon, N.A. 1982. Sociodemographic attributes of nepotism in tribal populations: Man the rule breaker. In *Current Problems in Sociobiology.* (eds) King's College Sociobiology Group. Cambridge: Cambridge U.P.

[6] Sahlins, M.D. 1976. *The Use and Abuse of Biology.* Ann Arbor: Univ. of Michigan P.

[7] For example: Daly, M. & M. Wilson. 1985. Child abuse and other risks of not living with both parents. *Ethology and Sociobiology* 6, 197–210.

[8] Silk, J.B. 1980. Adaptation and Kinship in Oceania. *Am. Anthrop.* 82, 799–820.

[9] For supporting evidence see Hartung, J. 1985. Matrilineal inheritance: new theory and analysis. *Behavioral and Brain Sciences* 8, 661–88.

[10] Borgerhoff Mulder, M. 1983. Social organization and biology. *Man* (N.S.) 18, 786–7.

[11] Irons, W. 1979. Cultural and biological success. In *Evolutionary Biology and Human Social Behavior* (eds) N.A. Chagnon & W. Irons. North Scituate, Mass: Duxbury P. See also Irons, W. 1980. Is Yomut social behavior adaptive? In *Sociobiology: Beyond Nature/Nurture?* (eds) G. Barlow & J. Silverberg. Boulder: West View.

[12] Turke, P.W. In press. Helpers at the nest: childcare networks on Ifaluk. In *Human Reproductive Behaviour* (eds) L.L. Betzig, M. Borgerhoff Mulder & P.W. Turke. Cambridge: Cambridge U.P.

[13] Betzig, L.L. 1986. *Despotism and Differential Reproduction.* Chicago: Aldine. Borgerhoff Mulder, M. In press.

On cultural and reproductive success: Kipsigis evidence. *Am. Anthrop*.

[14]Crook, J.H. & S.J. Crook. In press. Tibetan polyandry: problems of adaptation and fitness. In *Human Reproductive Behavior* (eds) L.L. Betzig, M. Borgerhoff Mulder & P.W. Turke. Cambridge: Cambridge U.P.

[15]Hartung, J. 1982. Polygyny and the inheritance of wealth. *Curr. Anthrop*. 23, 1–12.

[16]See, for example, Dickemann, M. 1979. Female infanticide and the reproductive strategies of stratified human societies: a preliminary model. In *Evolutionary Biology and Human Social Behavior* (eds) N.A. Chagnon & W. Irons. North Scituate, Mass: Duxbury P. Also, Boone, J.L. In press. Parental investment and elite family structure and preindustrial states. *Am. Anthrop*. 88.

[17]This position has been clearly argued in many sources. See, in particular: Alexander, R.D. 1979. *Darwinism and Human Affairs*. Washington, Seattle: Washington U.P. Irons, W. 1979. Natural selection, adaptation and human social behavior. In *Evolutionary Biology and Human Social Behavior* (eds) N.A. Chagnon & W. Irons. North Scituate, Maxx: Duxbury P. See also footnotes 4 and 15.

[18]Betzig, L.L., M. Borgerhoff Mulder & P.W. Turke. In press. Mating and parenting in Darwinian perspective. In *Human Reproductive Behaviour* (eds) L.L. Betzig, M. Borgerhoff Mulder & P.W. Turke. Cambridge: Cambridge U.P.

[19]Draper, P. & H. Harpending. 1982. Father absence and reproductive strategies: an evolutionary perspective. *J. anth. Res*. 38, 255–273.

Sharing in Human Evolution

By Jane B. Lancaster and Phillip Whitten

. . . .

"There is evidence," wrote famed ethologist Konrad Lorenz in 1963, "that the first inventors of pebble tools—the African australopithecines—promptly used their weapons to kill not only game, but fellow members of their species as well. Peking Man, the Prometheus who learned to preserve fire, used it to roast his brothers: beside the first traces of the regular use of fire lie the . . . roasted bones of *Sinanthropus pekinensis* himself."

Thus was promulgated the view of humans as clothes-wearing "killer apes." Despite the fact that this concept ignores a vast array of cultural anthropological data and relies on misinterpretations and erroneous extrapolations of ethological observations, it undoubtedly has caught on. Books by Lorenz (*On Aggression, Behind the Mirror*), Robert Ardrey (*African Genesis, The Territorial Imperative, The Social Contract*), Desmond Morris (*The Naked Ape, The Human Zoo*), Lionel Tiger and Robin Fox (*Men in Groups*), and others all have sold remarkably well—some even making the best-seller charts. According to this view, humans, unlike their primate relatives, are innately territorial and warlike. Indeed, it is argued, this unique propensity for killing and violence is the one most responsible for our evolutionary success.

Proponents of the killer-ape theory make what appears at first glance to be a strong case. One does not need to look far to find evidence of human violence and destruction. In fact, however, the theory is wrong on both counts: aggression is *not* the characteristic that distinguished our early ancestors from the apes; and humans are *not* the only primates who kill their fellows.

Jane Goodall and her colleagues in Tanzania's Gombe Stream Reserve have observed a community of chimpanzees that split in two in 1970. By 1972 the observers noted a cooling of relations between the two groups. In 1974 several males from the original group attacked a single male from the splinter group, beating him savagely for about twenty minutes until he died. Since that time, a series of brutal gang attacks—including one in which a rock was thrown at a prostrate victim—has completely wiped out the second chimp community (*Science News*, 1978).

If aggression is not the trait that distinguished our forebears from other primates, what is? The answer lies in a distinctively human characteristic—sharing—and the evolutionary mechanism that made it possible.

BIPEDALISM

Sometime between five and ten million years ago our ancestors began to spend much of their time on the ground, walking on two legs. Long before we had developed large brains, before we had language with which to communicate, and before we could manipulate the environment to our own ends, we were bipedal.

Bipedalism was one of the earliest evolutionary changes that distinguished the human way of life from that of the ape. Some experts claim that hominids (the family of primates that includes human beings and our earlier fossil ancestors) first stood in order to run, or to fight, or to free their hands for using tools. But these scenarios are unlikely. The first adventurers on two legs, like toddlers learning to walk, were probably very clumsy and inefficient. Such awkwardness would be of little value in combat or in flight. Similarly, tool using by itself cannot explain the significance of bipedalism, since tools can be used as easily while sitting down as standing up. More likely the adaptive value of bipedalism lay in the social behavior that it helped bring about—cooperation and sharing.

Walking on the hindlimbs while clutching food to be shared with others in the forelimbs would have been an advantage to a primate group utilizing a large home range. In this context, bipedalism could evolve slowly over hundreds of thousands of years—as it undoubtedly did. Thus, rather than being violent killer apes, our ancestors—and we—can more accurately be described as *sharing* apes.

Unfortunately, we know very little about the original differentiation and emergence of the human family. The period between five and ten million years ago is virtually an archaeological blank. The fossil record picks up about four and a half million years ago with scraps of hominid bone and teeth, and later with simple stone tools. By about three to one-and-a-half million years ago, a new way of life had been firmly established—a way of life fundamentally different from that of the apes and distinctly human in its broadest features. This original adaptive system of the hominids was very successful, lasting several million years—most of the history of the human line.

There are only a limited number of ways we can use to reconstruct this stage in human evolution. The archaeological record, though reasonably full, is limited to accidents

Reprinted by permission from the authors.

of preservation. However, we can expand our interpretation of the record by making judicious comparisons between the behavior of humans and of our closest living relatives, monkeys and apes. Other evidence can be gleaned from studies of the world's few remaining hunting-and-gathering societies.

THE BASIC PRIMATE PATTERN

There are few generalizations that can be made about all the higher primates. But some patterns seem to be so widespread among the Old World monkeys and apes that we can cautiously assume they must be very ancient and fundamental to the higher primate adaptation of life in social groups. The most significant of these patterns is the relationship between young animals and adults.

In all higher primate species, young animals spend years in physical and social dependence upon adults. This long dependence begins at birth, when the newborn first establishes a close one-to-one relationship with its mother. Unlike many other mammals, higher primates are not born into litters and hidden away in dens or nests. Instead, a single offspring is born, which for the first months of its life stays continuously in contact with its mother, clinging to her while she is moving, and resting in her arms to sleep. As Blurton-Jones (1972)

has pointed out, adaptations for continuous contact with mother involve many different anatomical, physiological and behavioral systems. These range from the anatomy of the hands and feet, distribution of body fat, composition of breast milk, sleep and sucking patterns, ease of satiation, tendency to vocalize, to the need for body contact for feeling secure.

Although this basic pattern holds true for all the higher primates (Old World monkeys, apes, and humans), there is a striking contrast in how this continuous contact relationship between mother and infant is maintained. Among all the Old World monkeys the responsibility of maintaining the relationship rests heavily with the infant. From the moment of birth, an infant monkey must be able to cling to its mother for long periods of time while she feeds, travels, grooms, or even leaps to safety. Infants unable to maintain body contact are likely to be eliminated through accident or predation from the gene pool. Monkeys need all four limbs for locomotion; clutching a weak or sick infant to the chest while trying to hobble on three legs is difficult and leaves the pair vulnerable to predators.

The same basic pattern is true for the great apes—though newborn apes are less developed than monkeys and are poor at clinging for the first few weeks of life. Mother apes help their poorly coordinated infants by walking on three legs and by restricting their movements and social interactions for several weeks after giving birth.

The close, continuous relationship between mother and infant gradually loosens as the infant is weaned and gains independence in locomotion. Once a young monkey or ape is weaned, it has sole responsibility for feeding and drinking. If it is too weak from illness or injury to do so, it will die before the concerned eyes of its mother. The mother will defend her youngster, groom it, sleep with it cradled in her arms, but feeding it solid foods is beyond her comprehension. Although isolated instances of food sharing among chimpanzees have been observed, basically the nonhuman primates are individual foragers.

In contrast with their early independence in feeding behavior, young monkeys and apes are dependent upon adults for protection for many years. Young primates remain at least until puberty in the safety of the group in which they were born; many never leave it. The prolonged period of juvenile development occurs in all the higher primates. During the years of development, the young primate has plenty of time to play, as well as to learn and practice the social and physical skills needed in adulthood.

CHIMPANZEE AND HUMAN BEHAVIOR

The general cleverness of chimpanzees has long been known. But it was not until the long-term field studies in Central Africa that particularly humanlike aspects of chimpanzee behavior were observed (Goodall, 1976; van Lawick-Goodall, 1971; Teleki, 1974, 1975). One of the most striking of these was the wide variety of tool use by chimpanzees in everyday life. These tools include the now-famous grass blades, vines or sticks used to "fish" for ants and termites in their nests; leaf sponges used to collect water, honey or wipe dirt off the body; twigs and sticks used to investigate and probe unfamiliar objects; rough hammer stones used to break open nuts; leafy twigs used as fly whisks; and finally sticks, stones and vegetation used as missiles in aggressive display. Chimpanzee tool use is similar to human in the sense that tools are an adaptive means to meet a wide variety of problems posed by the environment.

One of the marked differences between the use of tools by humans and chimpanzees is in the casualness and impermanence of the ape's tools. Although chimpanzees make their own tools in the sense that they strip a stick of leaves and side branches or chew up a mass of leaves for a sponge, they do not try to keep a particularly well-made tool for future use. Chimpanzees discard their tools because it is difficult for them to carry anything for long distances. When Goodall and her colleagues established a central feeding station at the Gombe Stream Reserve that provided bananas for the wild chimpanzees in the area, many came to load up a supply of bananas. They tried to carry bananas in every possible way: held in their mouths, hands and feet, tucked under armpits and chins, even slipped between flexed thighs and groins. Loaded up in this way, they retreated to climb nearby trees, dropping bananas every step of the way.

Another aspect of chimpanzee behavior that has excited students of human evolution is their sporadic attempts at the collective killing of small game. Sometimes these hunts involve several adult and subadult males who coordinate their movements to encircle the prey, some acting as diversions while others slip close enough to dash in for the capture. Prey (usually small gazelles) are killed and eaten immediately, the participants in the hunt dividing the prey simply by tearing it to pieces. Latecomers may get a mouthful by persistent attempts to pull off a piece or by begging.

The killing and eating of meat is clearly a special event in chimpanzee life. Witnesses of a kill show great interest and excitement and a clear desire for even a taste. The highly social, as opposed to nutritional, nature of chimpanzee cooperative killing and eating of prey has been noted by Geza Teleki (1975), who observed that a dozen or more chimpanzees may take a whole day to consume an animal weighing less than 10 kg (22 lbs). The small size of game killed by primates (baboons have also been reported to hunt small mammals on occasion) is very striking. The largest prey is under 10 kg—well under the body weight of an individual hunter. Shared foods are most often minuscule scraps, more social tokens than major sources of protein.

In spite of their tool use and hunting, the behavior of modern chimpanzees still fits squarely into the pattern described earlier for other primates. They are in no way quasi human. Like other monkeys and apes, they are basically individual foragers who live in long-term social groups. The infant is dependent on the mother for many years, but this relationship is based on a physical and psychological need for the mother's protection. Once weaned, young chimpanzees feed themselves. The basic diet is typical of many primates living in the tropics: vegetables, fruits and nuts, with some animal protein in the form of insects, small vertebrates and occasional small mammals. The important contrast between the feeding habits of human and nonhuman primates is not so much in what is eaten; rather it lies in whether each individual must forage for itself or whether there is a collective responsibility for gathering and sharing food between adults and young.

MODERN HUNTER-GATHERERS

In recent years the ways of life of hunter-gatherers have attracted renewed interest (Lee and Devore, 1968, 1976). Although only a few hunting-gathering groups remain in the modern world, they take on special significance when it is recalled that fully ninety-nine percent of human history was spent in the hunting-gathering stage. The peculiar demands of this life-style may well have left imprints on modern human biology and behavior.

There are certain ecological relationships and social behaviors found in all known tropical hunter-gatherers, which stand out in sharp relief when contrasted with the behavior of monkeys and apes. The first of these is a diet based on a balance of plant and animal foods. This balance is highly flexible and varies according to season, geographic location and long-term cycles in food availability. Our understanding of sex roles and the ecological basis of early human societies has shifted away from an emphasis on females as camp and infant tenders and males as food providers (Isaac, 1976; Tanner and Zihlman, 1976). In the process, our concept of "man, the hunter" has been modified to "humans, the hunter-gatherers."

Data from modern hunter-gatherers in the tropics indicate that meat is an important part of the diet, but always comprises well under fifty percent of the total. The basic day-to-day diet is provided by the collecting efforts of adult women, and consists mainly of vegetable foods and animal protein in the form of insects and nestling birds or eggs. Animal protein in large "packages"—that is, animals weighing over 20 kg—is provided by the efforts of adult males. Hunting, even in the tropics, is a risky occupation. It not only is potentially dangerous, but it is often unpredictable. Richard Lee (quoted in Hassan, 1975:35) found that among the San of the Kalahari, most hunters kill only one or two large animals a year. Among the Hazda of East Africa, as many as half the adult males fail to kill even one large animal a year, and some men kill only one or two in a lifetime. The question of whether or not a growing child eats or starves does not depend on the uncertain hunting success of a few adult males. As Isaac (1971:279) noted some time ago, the evolution of human behavior from a primate pattern involved not simply an increasing intensity of predation, but the unusual development of "a flexible system of joint dependence on plant and animal foods."

It is informative to look at the basic material possessions of a hunting-gathering woman who lives in the tropics. She must be able to carry all her possessions herself when she moves, because men are responsible for their own hunting equipment and for protecting the group. The most important items a woman possesses include a digging stick, a sling or net bag for carrying her infant, and a variety of bark and skin trays and containers for carrying and preparing food. This is all she needs to provide for her family. Significantly, none of these materials leaves a trace in the archaeological record.

The importance of carrying infants in a sling should be underscored because it is a major factor in human evolutionary history. Unlike Old World monkeys and apes, human infants are unable to cling to their mothers. In fact, they are dependent on their mothers to hold them for many months. Hunting-gathering women keep their infants with them continuously during their daily foraging. They use a sling, which suspends the infant from the mother's shoulder while leaving her hands and arms free. It appears that one of the costs our species paid for evolving larger brains was a prolonged period of infant helplessness. The invention of such a simple tool as a skin sling to carry an infant may have been a crucial turning point in human history because it permitted the survival of infants born with small, immature brains and the potential for major growth after birth.

The lives of hunter-gatherers differ sharply from those of other primates in the tropics by virtue of one very important behavior pattern: carrying and sharing. The carrying of infants, tools, or food to be shared allowed our ancestors to shift away from individual foraging to a pattern emphasizing the sharing of gathered and hunted foods within the social group. Among the Kalahari hunter-gatherers plant foods collected by women are shared among close family members. Meat—food which comes in much larger packages—is shared in a larger network.

The success of a system of sharing foods depends on one other behavioral innovation which sets humans off from other primates. This is the evolution of the home base, or camp. A home base need not be permanent. It can be nothing more than an agreed-upon location where members of the group can meet in order to share foods. Many monkeys and apes have favorite clumps of sleeping trees, where they often return for the night. A home base, however, is not just a location for sleeping. Rather it serves a much more important function as the site for the sharing of food among members of the social group. Like the shift from individual foraging to sharing, this represents a way novel among primates of utilizing a niche.

THE ARCHAEOLOGICAL RECORD

Glynn Isaac (1976), an archaeologist at the University of California at Berkeley, suggests that these behavioral elements—a flexible diet of plant and animal foods, food sharing, the carrying of food and equipment, and a home base—form a behavioral platform upon which the distinctly human way of life was established. The evidence for the early building of this behavioral platform comes from the fossil record, although not all elements of the pattern are equally clear. Accidents of preservation, and the bias against perishable plant foods and materials in favor of stone and bone, give a skewed view of the past.

Some of the earliest evidence of the shift in diet from foraging to hunting-gathering can be found at Olduvai Gorge and Koobi Fora in East Africa—sites dating from around three million to one-and-a-half million years ago. Here early stone tools are found in association with broken up mammal bones. These animals range in size from small

rodents to elephants, but it is clear that many are far larger than the 10 kg mentioned by Teleki as the largest prey taken today by nonhuman primates. The dismembering of a large mammal like an elephant or a hippopotamus suggests strongly that meat was not only killed cooperatively, but shared as well.

Evidence about the equipment of early hominids is very limited. Both at Olduvai and Koobi Fora, the two basic classes of stone tools—core tools and flakes—can be found. The rest of the probable technology and equipment of the early hominids—sharpened sticks for digging and stabbing, and slings and nets for carrying and gathering—will probably never be found in the archaeological record. At Olduvai a semi-circular stone windbreak has been discovered, perhaps the oldest structure built by our hominid ancestors. Concentrations of stone tools and broken bones here and at other sites attest to an essential element of the adaptive platform: a home base. The artifacts and bones tend to be located in particular ecological settings: patches about five to twenty meters in diameter, a size similar to the campsites of modern hunter-gatherers. They are usually located next to sandy streams, the kind which today provide strips of shade and are bounded by fruit trees. These bases were home for our remote ancestors. They were places where the hominids gathered together at night for warmth and protection against the great carnivores, and to share food.

The creatures living in these camps were fully bipedal, with brains somewhat larger than might be expected if they were apes. Although their molar teeth were massive by modern standards, there were no protruding canines like those used by other primates in aggression. The relatively small size of their crania clearly shows that the human adaptation of bipedalism, tool use, and home base long preceded the expansion of the brain and elaboration of culture so obvious later in the archaeological record. It is doubtful that these early hominids had language in any modern sense of the word. The small size of the brain argues against it, and their hunting and gathering activities and manufacture of simple tools did not demand language. Their life in small, face-to-face social groups suggests a communication system like that of modern chimpanzees.

SHARING AND SOCIAL ORGANIZATION

The elementary human adaptation, the one upon which all else is built, depends on a simple but unique change in ecological and social relations. This change was the shift from the individual foraging and feeding pattern of other primates to a system of sharing and cooperation, in which adults feed infants and juveniles. Associated with this assumption of responsibility to feed the young was a new economic interdependence between the sexes, one in which females gathered and males hunted. This ancient division of labor, permitting the flexible, joint dependence on plant and animal food, probably accounts for the early success of the first hominids. After all, they were small-sized, small-brained primates moving into a niche already crowded with highly successful group hunters such as lions, hyenas and wild dogs.

It is interesting to speculate on the effect of the economic division of labor on the social organization of early hominids. Comparative studies of Old World monkeys and apes indicate that attachment based on descent is one of the prime organizers of monkey and ape societies (Lancaster, 1975). This ancient principle is based on the attachment of an infant to its mother. In multigenerational primate societies, the early attachment is expanded to include other close relatives and descendents of the mother. It is reasonable to assume that the first social network through which hominids shared food was joined by female links. Much of the food was probably gathered by females. Male hunting must have added a new element to the equation. For the first time in primate evolution, males and females shared responsibility for feeding their offspring. Eventually this mutual economic interest probably led to the formation of a second set of emotional attachments, ones that linked specific males to specific females. It is unlikely that the early hominids had anything like the institution of marriage. But it is not unreasonable to speculate that couples formed special, more-or-less-enduring attachments that facilitated the feeding of offspring.

HUMANS: THE SHARING APES

What distinguishes our own species from our primate relatives is not any innate proclivity toward violence and aggression. Rather we can accurately be described as cultural animals whose outstanding characteristics are cooperation and sharing. What separated our family from the apes was a reorganization of the relationships between the sexes and between adults and young. This shift, which favored cooperative activities, permitted early hominids to exploit a niche new to primates. The ability to exploit this new niche rested on a few, rather simple behavioral patterns. These included bipedalism, the use of tools, the division of labor between male hunters and female gatherers, a home base, and most important—cooperation and sharing.

The archaeological record, the study of modern primates, and the behavior of present-day hunter-gatherers all attest to the significance of sharing in human evolution. It is the rock upon which all human culture is built; it is what makes us human.

REFERENCES

Blurton-Jones, N. 1972. Comparative aspects of mother-child contacts. In N. Blurton-Jones (ed.), *Ethological Studies of Child Behaviour.* London: Cambridge University Press.

Goodall, Jane. 1976. Continuities between chimpanzee and human behaviour. In Isaac and McGown (eds.), *Human Origins.* Menlo Park, CA: Staples Press, pp. 81–96.

Hassan, F.A. 1975. Determination of the size, density, and growth rate of hunting-gathering populations. In S. Polgar (ed.), *Population, Ecology, and Evolution.* The Hague: Mouton, pp. 27–52.

Isaac, Glynn. 1971. The diet of early man: aspects of archaeological evidence from lower and middle Pleistocene sites in Africa. *World Archaeology* 2:278–298.

Isaac, Glynn. 1975. The activities of early African hominids: A review of archaeological evidence from the time span two and a half to one million years ago. In Isaac and McGown (eds.), *op. cit.,* pp. 483–514.

Lancaster, Jane B. 1975. *Primate Behavior and the Emergence of Human Culture.* New York: Holt, Rinehart and Winston.

Van Lawick-Goodall, Jane. 1971. *In the Shadow of Man.* Boston: Houghton Mifflin.

Lee, Richard B. and I. DeVore (eds). 1968. *Man the Hunter.* Chicago: Aldine.

Lee, Richard B. and I. DeVore (eds). 1975. *Kalahari Hunter-Gatherers.* Cambridge, MA: Harvard University Press.

Science News. 1978. Chimp killings: Is it the 'man' in them? *Science News* 113:276.

Tanner, N. and A. Zihlman. 1976. Women in evolution. Part 1: Innovation and selection in human origins. *Signs* 1:385–602.

Teleki, Geza. 1975. Primate subsistence patterns: collector-predators and gatherer-hunters. *Journal of Human Evolution* 4:125–184.

TOPIC *4*

Human Diversity

....

Since the beginnings of recorded history, the physical differences characterizing human populations have been of interest to both scholars and lay persons. *Neontology*, which includes the study of the distribution of modern human biological traits, is a major area of interest to biological anthropologists.

You will recall from the essay introducing Part II that in the eighteenth century Johann Blumenbach developed rigorous standards for measuring physical traits and used clusters of these measurements to identify "races." The concept of race quickly was incorporated into scientific thought, and much of the subsequent research on human diversity has been undertaken using this concept. *The term* race *generally is used to refer to a population that is distinguished from all other groups by virtue of displaying a cluster of innate biological traits.* Indeed, the concept of race has won general, widespread acceptance—so much so that if you were to tell your neighbor today that races do not exist, you would likely be dismissed as a fool.

Yet *do* races exist as biological facts of nature? In his now classic work *The Mismeasure of Man*, the biologist Stephen Jay Gould argues that all attempts to measure biological differences among human populations have reflected the biases of those groups that had the political power to do the measuring. In painstaking detail he reanalyzes quantitative studies of everything from human head size to IQ and shows that the research conducted by even the most eminent scholars of their time is marred again and again—by such severe distortions as leaving out data (or explaining facts away) that did not fit the popular social preconceptions of the times, by serious statistical malpractice, and even by outright fabrication of "facts." His conclusion is that "claims for a direct biological mapping of human affairs have recorded cultural prejudice and not nature. . . ."

Of course it is possible, as Boyce Rensberger observes in the article "Racial Odyssey," which opens Topic 4, to define human groups using any biological trait one wishes—hair color, facial shape, height, skin color, and on and on—but there are no known features or clusters of features that neatly divide the human species into clearly defined groups

(which is what one would expect if the concept of race had any biological meaning). Therefore, the kind or number of "races" depends on the purpose of the classification system one uses. Rensberger illustrates this by selecting a large number of biological traits and illustrating that no matter what way one wants to organize them, they still wind up cutting across "racial" lines. The conclusion is clear: human diversity is real, but rather than trying to force the mosaic of human biological traits into a predetermined design, we should try to discover what adaptive utility such diversity provides our species.

The second article in Topic 4 does just that. In "Blood, Genes, and Malaria," Jared Diamond illustrates the way modern biological anthropologists study the adaptive significance of different biological traits. Sickle-cell anemia often has been referred to as the black man's disease, though it does not affect only blacks or only men, and it is not, strictly speaking, a disease. Diamond shows how the genetic mutation of the sickle cell actually is an evolutionary adaptation that protects most individuals against malaria. It is true that when two people who are heterozygous for sickle-cell mate, one-fourth of their children will die from sickle-cell anemia. But *a much larger number* will be protected by their genetic inheritance against malaria and will survive.

In the final article of Topic 4, "'Race': Myths Under the Microscope," Albert Jacquard looks at some of the connections between "race" and racism. *Racism is something very real indeed; it consists of those beliefs that have been used to justify the subjugation, exploitation, and even extermination of one group by another, when the basis of the distinction between the groups is defined as biological.* He points out that there is much greater genetic variation among individuals within any group than there is between the "average" genetic frequencies of groups as wholes. Further, he notes that genetic diversity is a fundamental source of evolutionary robustness, not the threat to "racial purity" over which racist elites raise such alarm.

Anthropology has made two fundamental contributions to the understanding of human diversity: first, by systematically studying the adaptive significance of specific traits in relation to the environments in which they are found most frequently, and second, by demonstrating that the feelings of superiority that are to be found in virtually all human groups (known as *ethnocentrism*) are cultural products, not biological products.

Racial Odyssey

By Boyce Rensberger

The human species comes in an artist's palette of colors: sandy yellows, reddish-tans, deep browns, light tans, creamy whites, pale pinks. It is a rare person who is not curious about the skin colors, hair textures, bodily structures and facial features associated with racial background. Why do some Africans have dark brown skin, while that of most Europeans is pale pink? Why do the eyes of most "white" people and "black" people look pretty much alike but differ so from the eyes of Orientals? Did one race evolve before the others? If so, is it more primitive or more advanced as a result? Can it be possible, as modern research suggests, that there is no such thing as a pure race? These are all honest, scientifically worthy questions. And they are central to current research on the evolution of our species on the planet Earth.

Broadly speaking, research on racial differences has led most scientists to three major conclusions. The first is that there are many more differences among people than skin color, hair texture and facial features. Dozens of other variations have been found, ranging from the shapes of bones to the consistency of ear wax to subtle variations in body chemistry.

The second conclusion is that the overwhelming evolutionary success of the human species is largely due to its great genetic variability. When migrating bands of our early ancestors reached a new environment, at least a few already had physical traits that gave them an edge in surviving there. If the coming centuries bring significant environmental changes, as many believe they will, our chances of surviving them will be immeasurably enhanced by our diversity as a species.

There is a third conclusion about race that is often misunderstood. Despite our wealth of variation and despite our con-stant, everyday references to race, no one has ever discovered a reliable way of distinguishing one race from another. While it is possible to classify a great many people on the basis of certain physical features, there are no known feature or groups of features that will do the job in all cases.

Skin color won't work. Yes, most Africans from south of the Sahara and their descendants around the world have skin that is darker than that of most Europeans. But there are millions of people in India, classified by some anthropologists as members of the Caucasoid, or "white," race who have darker skins than most Americans who call themselves black. And there are many Africans living in sub-Sahara Africa today whose skins are no darker than the skins of many Spaniards, Italians, Greeks or Lebanese.

What about stature as a racial trait? Because they are quite short, on the average, African Pygmies have been considered racially distinct from other dark-skinned Africans. If stature, then, is a racial criterion, would one include in the same race the tall African Watusi and the Scandinavians of similar stature?

The little web of skin that distinguishes Oriental eyes is said to be a particular feature of the Mongoloid race. How, then, can it be argued that the American Indian, who lacks this epicanthic fold, is Mongoloid?

Even more hopeless as racial markers are hair color, eye color, hair form, the shapes of noses and lips or any of the other traits put forth as typical of one race or another.

NO NORMS

Among the tall people of the world there are many black, many white and many in between. Among black people of the world there are many with kinky hair, many with straight or wavy hair, and many in between. Among the broad-nosed, full-lipped people of the world there are many with dark skins, many with light skins and many in between.

How did our modern perceptions of race arise? One of the first to attempt a scientific classification of peoples was Carl von Linne, better known as Linnaeus. In 1735, he published a classification that remains the standard today. As Linnaeus saw it there were four races, classifiable geographically and by skin color. The names Linnaeus gave them were *Homo sapiens Africanus nigrus* (black African human being), *H. sapiens Americanus rubescens* (red American human being), *H. sapiens Asiaticus fuscusens* (brownish Asian human being), and *H. sapiens Europeaeus albescens* (white European human being). All, Linnaeus recognized, were members of a single human species.

A species includes all individuals that are biologically capable of interbreeding and producing fertile offspring. Most matings between species are fruitless, and even when they succeed, as when a horse and a donkey interbreed and produce a mule, the progeny are sterile. When a poodle mates with a collie, however, the offspring are fertile, showing that both dogs are members of the same species.

Even though Linnaeus's system of nomenclature survives, his classifications were discarded, especially after voyages of discovery revealed that there were many more kinds of people than could be pigeonholed into four categories. All over the world there are small populations that don't fit. Among the better known are:

● The so-called Bushmen of southern Africa, who look as much Mongoloid as Negroid.

● The Negritos of the South Pacific,

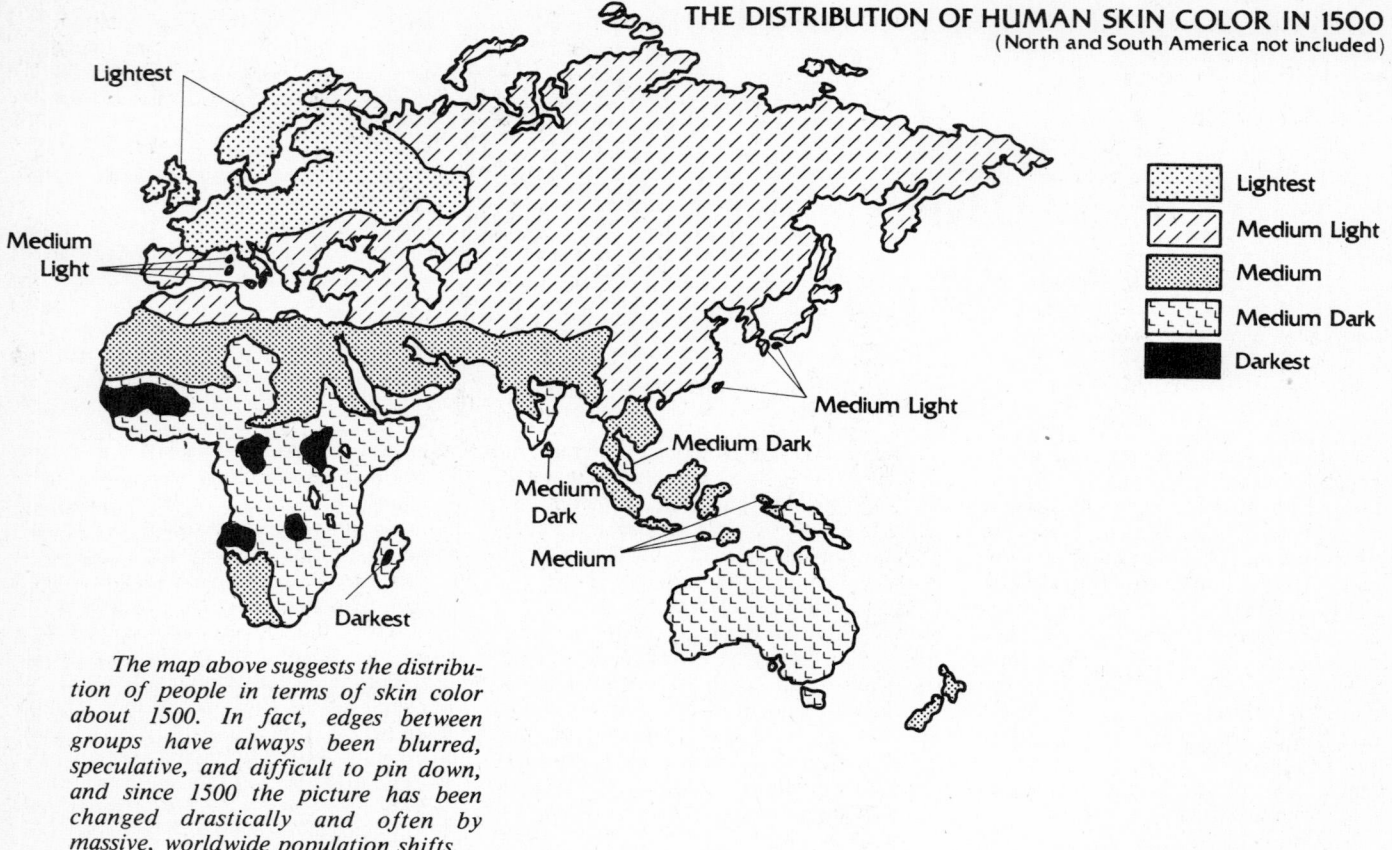

THE DISTRIBUTION OF HUMAN SKIN COLOR IN 1500
(North and South America not included)

Lightest

Medium Light

Medium Light

Medium Dark

Medium Dark

Medium

Darkest

Lightest
Medium Light
Medium
Medium Dark
Darkest

The map above suggests the distribution of people in terms of skin color about 1500. In fact, edges between groups have always been blurred, speculative, and difficult to pin down, and since 1500 the picture has been changed drastically and often by massive, worldwide population shifts.

who do look Negroid but are very far from Africa and have no known links to that continent.

● The Ainu of Japan, a hairy aboriginal people who look more Caucasoid than anything else.

● The Lapps of Scandinavia, who look as much like Eskimos as like Europeans.

● The aborigines of Australia, who often look Negroid but many of whom have straight or wavy hair and are often blond as children.

● The Polynesians, who seem to be a blend of many races, the proportions differing from island to island.

To accommodate such diversity, many different systems of classification have been proposed. Some set up two or three dozen races. None has ever satisfied all experts.

CLASSIFICATION SYSTEM

Perhaps the most sweeping effort to impose a classification upon all the peoples of the world was made by the American anthropologist Carleton Coon. He concluded there are five basic races, two of which have major subdivisions: Cau-

casoids; Mongoloids; full-size Australoids (Australian aborigines); dwarf Australoids (Negritos—Andaman Islanders and similar peoples); full-size Congoids (African Negroids); dwarf Congoids (African Pygmies); and Capoids (the so-called Bushmen and Hottentots).

In his 1965 classic, *The Living Races of Man,* Coon hypothesized that before A.D. 1500 there were five *pure* races—five centers of human population that were so isolated that there was almost no mixing.

Each of these races evolved independently, Coon believed, diverging from a pre-*Homo sapiens* stock that was essentially the same everywhere. He speculated that the common ancestor evolved into *Homo sapiens* in five separate regions at five different times, beginning about 35,000 years ago. The populations that have been *Homo sapiens* for the shortest periods of time, Coon said, are the world's "less civilized" races.

The five pure races remained distinct until A.D. 1500; then Europeans started sailing the world, leaving their genes—as sailors always have—in every port and planting distant colonies. At about the same time, thousands of Africans were

captured and forcibly settled in many parts of the New World.

That meant the end of the five pure races. But Coon and other experts held that this did not necessarily rule out the idea of distinct races. In this view, there *are* such things as races; people just don't fit into them very well anymore.

The truth is that there is really no hard evidence to suggest that five or any particular number of races evolved independently. The preponderance of evidence today suggests that as traits typical of fully modern people arose in any one place, they spread quickly to all human populations. Advances in intelligence were almost certainly the fastest to spread. Most anthropologists and geneticists now believe that human beings have always been subject to migrating and mixing. In other words, there probably never were any such things as pure races.

Race mixing has not only been a fact of human history but is, in this day of unprecedented global mobility, taking place at a more rapid rate than ever. It is not farfetched to envision the day when, generations hence, the entire "complexion" of major population centers will be different. Meanwhile, we can see such changes taking place before our eyes, for they are a part of everyday reality.

HYBRID VIGOR

Oddly, those who assert scientific validity for their notions of pure and distinct races seem oblivious of a basic genetic principle that plant and animal breeders know well: too much inbreeding can lead to proliferation of inferior traits. Crossbreeding with different strains often produces superior combinations and "hybrid vigor."

The striking differences among people may very well be a result of constant genetic mixing. And as geneticists and ecologists know, in diversity lies strength and resilience.

To understand the origin and proliferation of human differences, one must first know how Darwinian evolution works.

Evolution is a two-step process. Step one is mutation: somehow a gene in the ovary or testes of an individual is altered, changing the molecular configuration that stores instructions for forming a new individual. The children who inherit that gene will be different in some way from their ancestors.

Step two is selection: for a racial difference, or any other evolutionary change to arise, it must survive and be passed through several generations. If the mutation confers some disadvantage, the individual dies, often during embryonic development. But if the change is beneficial in some way, the individual should have a better chance of thriving than relatives lacking the advantage.

NATURAL SELECTION

If a new trait is beneficial, it will bring reproductive success to its bearer. After several generations of multiplication, bearers of the new trait may begin to outnumber nonbearers. Darwin called this natural selection to distinguish it from the artificial selection exercised by animal breeders.

Skin color is the human racial trait most generally thought to confer an evolutionary advantage of this sort. It has long been obvious in the Old World that the farther south one goes, the darker the skin color. Southern Europeans are usually somewhat darker than northern Europeans. In North Africa, skin colors are darker still, and, as one travels south, coloration reaches its maximum at the Equator. The same progression holds in Asia, with the lightest skins to the north. Again, as one moves south, skin color darkens, reaching in southern India a "blackness" equal to that of equatorial Africans.

This north-south spectrum of skin color derives from varying intensities of the same dark brown pigment called melanin. Skin cells simply have more or less melanin granules to be seen against a background that is pinkish because of the underlying blood vessels. All races can increase their melanin concentration by exposure to the Sun.

What is it about northerly latitudes in the Northern Hemisphere that favors less pigmentation and about southerly latitudes that favors more? Exposure to intense sunlight is not the only reason why people living in southerly latitudes are dark. A person's susceptibility to rickets and skin cancer, his ability to withstand cold and to see in the dark may also be related to skin color.

The best-known explanation says the body can tolerate only a narrow range of intensities of sunlight. Too much causes sunburn and cancer, while too little deprives the body of vitamin D, which is synthesized in the skin under the influence of sunlight. A dark complexion protects the skin from the harmful effects of intense sunlight. Thus, albinos born in equatorial regions have a high rate of skin cancer. On the other hand, dark skin in northerly latitudes screens out sunlight needed for the synthesis of vitamin D. Thus, dark-skinned children living in northern latitudes had high rates of rickets—a bone-deforming disease caused by a lack of vitamin D—before their milk was routinely fortified. In the sunny tropics, dark skin admits enough light to produce the vitamin.

Recently, there has been some evidence that skin colors are linked to differences in the ability to avoid injury from the cold. Army researchers found that during the Korean War blacks were more susceptible to frostbite than were whites. Even among Norwegian soldiers in World War II, brunettes had a slightly higher incidence of frostbite than did blonds.

EYE PIGMENTATION

A third link between color and latitude involves the sensitivity of the eye to various wavelengths of light. It is known that dark-skinned people have more pigmentation in the iris of the eye and at the back of the eye where the image falls. It has been found that the less pigmented the eye, the more sensitive it is to colors at the red end of the spectrum. In situations illuminated with reddish light, the northern European can see more than a dark African sees.

DISEASE ORIGINS

The gene for sickle cell anemia, a disease found primarily among black people, appears to have evolved because its presence can render its bearer resistant to malaria. Such a trait would have obvious survival value in tropical Africa.

A person who has sickle cell anemia must have inherited genes for the disease from both parents. If a child inherits only one sickle cell gene, he or she will be resistant to malaria but will not have the anemia. Paradoxically, inheriting genes from both parents does not seem to affect resistance to malaria.

In the United States, where malaria is practically nonexistent, the sickle cell gene confers no survival advantage and is disappearing. Today only about 1 out of every 10 American blacks carries the gene.

Many other inherited diseases are found only in people from a particular area. Tay-Sachs disease, which often kills before the age of two, is almost entirely confined to Jews from parts of Eastern Europe and their descendants elsewhere. Paget's disease, a bone disorder, is found most often among those of English descent. Impacted wisdom teeth are a common problem among Asians and Europeans but not among Africans. Children of all races are able to digest milk because their bodies make lactase, the enzyme that breaks down lactose, or milk sugar. But the ability to digest lactose in adulthood is a racially distributed trait.

About 90 percent of Orientals and blacks lose this ability by the time they reach adulthood and become quite sick when they drink milk.

Even African and Asian herders who keep cattle or goats rarely drink fresh milk. Instead, they first treat the milk with fermentation bacteria that break down lactose, in a sense predigesting it. They can then ingest the milk in the form of yogurt or cheese without any problem.

About 90 percent of Europeans and their American descendants, on the other hand, continue to produce the enzyme throughout their lives and can drink milk with no ill effects.

It has been suggested that Europeans developed lighter eyes to adapt to the longer twilights of the North and their greater reliance on firelight to illuminate caves.

Although the skin cancer-vitamin D hypothesis enjoys wide acceptance, it may well be that resistance to cold, possession of good night vision and other yet unknown factors all played roles in the evolution of skin colors.

Most anthropologists agree that the original human skin color was dark brown, since it is fairly well established that human beings evolved in the tropics of Africa. This does not, however, mean that the first people were Negroids, whose descendants, as they moved north, evolved into light-skinned Caucasoids. It is more likely that the skin color of various populations changed several times from dark to light and back as people moved from one region to another.

Consider, for example, that long before modern people evolved, *Homo erectus* had spread throughout Africa, Europe and Asia. The immediate ancestor of *Homo sapiens, Homo erectus,* was living in Africa 1.5 million years ago and in Eurasia 750,000 years ago. The earliest known forms of *Homo sapiens* do not make their appearance until somewhere between 250,000 and 500,000 years ago. Although there is no evidence of the skin color of any hominid fossil, it is probable that the *Homo erectus* population in Africa had dark skin. As subgroups spread into northern latitudes, mutations that reduced pigmentation conferred survival advantages on them and lighter skins came to predominate. In other words, there were probably black *Homo erectus* peoples in Africa and white ones in Europe and Asia.

Did the black *Homo erectus* populations evolve into today's Negroids and the white ones in Europe into today's Caucasoids? By all the best evidence, nothing like this happened. More likely, wherever *Homo sapiens* arose it proved so superior to the *Homo erectus* populations that it eventually replaced them everywhere.

If the first *Homo sapiens* evolved in Africa, they were probably dark skinned; those who migrated northward into Eurasia lost their pigmentation. But it is just as possible that the first *Homo sapiens* appeared in northern climes, descendants of white-skinned *Homo erectus*. These could have migrated southward toward Africa, evolving darker skins. All modern races, incidentally, arose long after the brain had reached its present size in all parts of the world.

North-south variations in pigmentation are quite common among mammals and birds. The tropical races tend to be darker in fur and feather, the desert races tend to be brown, and those near the Arctic Circle are lighter colored.

There are exceptions among humans. The Indians of the Americas, from the Arctic to the southern regions of South America, do not conform to the north-south scheme of coloration. Though most think of Indians as being reddish-brown, most Indians tend to be relatively light skinned, much like their presumed Mongoloid ancestors in Asia. The ruddy complexion that lives in so many stereotypes of Indians is merely what years of heavy tanning can produce in almost any light-skinned person. Anthropologists explain the color consistency as a consequence of the relatively recent entry of people into the Americas—probably between 12,000 and 35,000 years ago. Perhaps they have not yet had time to change.

Only a few external physical differences other than color appear to have adaptive significance. The strongest cases can be made for nose shape and stature.

WHAT'S IN A NOSE

People native to colder or drier climates tend to have longer, more beak-shaped noses than those living in hot and humid regions. The nose's job is to warm and humidify air before it reaches sensitive lung tissues. The colder or drier the air is, the more surface area is needed inside the nose to get it to the right temperature or humidity. Whites tend to have longer and beakier noses than blacks or Orientals. Nevertheless, there is great variation within races. Africans in the highlands of East Africa have longer noses than Africans from the hot, humid lowlands, for example.

Stature differences are reflected in the tendency for most northern peoples to have shorter arms, legs and torsos and to be stockier than people from the tropics. Again, this is an adaptation to heat or cold. One way of reducing heat loss is to have less body surface, in relation to weight or volume, from which heat can escape. To avoid overheating, the most desirable body is long limbed and lean. As a result, most Africans tend to be lankier than northern Europeans. Arctic peoples are the shortest limbed of all.

Hair forms may also have a practical role to play, but the evidence is weak. It has been suggested that the more tightly curled hair of Africans insulates the top of the head better than does straight or wavy hair. Contrary to expectation, black hair serves better in this role than white hair. Sunlight is absorbed and converted to heat at the outer surface of the hair blanket; it radiates directly into the air.

White fur, common on Arctic animals that need to absorb solar heat, is actually transparent and transmits light into the hair blanket, allowing the heat to form within the insulating layer, where it is retained for warmth.

Aside from these examples, there is little evidence that any of the other visible differences among the world's peoples provide any advantage. Nobody knows, for example, why Orientals have epicanthic eye folds or flatter facial profiles. The thin lips of Caucasoids and most Mongoloids have no known advantages over the Negroid's full lips. Why should middle-aged and older Caucasoid men go bald so much more frequently than the men of other races? Why does the skin of Bushmen wrinkle so heavily in the middle and later years? Or why does the skin of Negroids resist wrinkling so well? Why do the Indian men in one part of South America have blue penises? Why do Hottentot women have such unusually large buttocks?

There are possible evolutionary explanations for why such apparently useless differences arise.

One is a phenomenon known as sexual selection. Environmentally adaptive traits arise, Darwin thought, through natural selection—the environment itself chooses who will thrive or decline. In sexual selection, which Darwin also suggested, the choice belongs to the prospective mate.

In simple terms, ugly individuals will be less likely to find mates and reproduce their genes than beautiful specimens will. Take the blue penis as an example. Women might find it unusually attractive or perhaps believe it to be endowed with special powers. If so, a man born with a blue penis will find many more opportunities to reproduce his genes than his ordinary brothers.

Sexual selection can also operate when males compete for females. The moose with the larger antlers or the lion with the more imposing mane will stand a better chance of discouraging less well-endowed males and gaining access to females. It is possible that such a process operated among Caucasoid males, causing them to become markedly hairy, especially around the face.

ATTRACTIVE TRAITS

Anthropologists consider it probable that traits such as the epicanthic fold or the many regional differences in facial features were selected this way.

Yet another method by which a trait can establish itself involves accidental selection. It results from what biologists call genetic drift.

Suppose that in a small nomadic band

a person is born with perfectly parallel fingerprints instead of the usual loops, whorls or arches. That person's children would inherit parallel fingerprints, but they would confer no survival advantages. But if our family decides to strike out on its own, it will become the founder of a new band consisting of its own descendants, all with parallel fingerprints.

Events such as this, geneticists and anthropologists believe, must have occurred many times in the past to produce the great variety within the human species. Among the apparently neutral traits that differ among populations are:

Ear Wax—There are two types of ear wax. One is dry and crumbly and the other is wet and sticky. Both types can be found in every major population, but the frequencies differ. Among northern Chinese, for example, 98 percent have dry ear wax. Among American whites, only 16 percent have dry ear wax. Among American blacks the figure is 7 percent.

Scent Glands—As any bloodhound knows, every person has his or her own distinctive scent. People vary in the mixture of odoriferous compounds exuded through the skin—most of it coming from specialized glands called apocrine glands. Among whites, these are concentrated in the armpits and near the genitals and anus. Among blacks, they may also be found on the chest and abdomen. Orientals have hardly any apocrine glands at all. In the words of the Oxford biologist John R. Baker, "The Europids and Negrids are smelly, the Mongolids scarcely or not at all." Smelliest of all are northern European, or so-called Nordic, whites. Body odor is rare in Japan. It was once thought to indicate a European in the ancestry and to be a disease requiring hospitalization.

Blood Groups—Some populations have a high percentage of members with a particular blood group. American Indians are overwhelmingly group O—100 percent in some regions. Group A is most common among Australian aborigines and the Indians in western Canada. Group B is frequent in northern India, other parts of Asia and western Africa.

Advocates of the pure-race theory once seized upon blood groups as possibly unique to the original pure races. The proportions of groups found today, they thought, would indicate the degree of mixing. It was subsequently found that chimpanzees, our closest living relatives, have the same blood groups as humans.

Taste—PTC (phenylthiocarbamide) is a synthetic compound that some people can taste and others cannot. The ability to taste it has no known survival value, but it is clearly an inherited trait. The proportion of persons who can taste PTC varies in different populations: 50 to 70 percent of Australian aborigines can taste it, as can 60 to 80 percent of all Europeans. Among East Asians, the percentage is 83 to 100 percent, and among Africans, 90 to 97 percent.

Urine—Another indicator of differences in body chemistry is the excretion of a compound known as BAIB (beta-amino-isobutyric acid) in urine. Europeans seldom excrete large quantities, but high levels of excretion are common among Asians and American Indians. It has been shown that the differences are not due to diet.

No major population has remained isolated long enough to prevent any unique genes from eventually mixing with those of neighboring groups. Indeed, a map showing the distribution of so-called racial traits would have no sharp boundaries, except for coastlines. The intensity of a trait such as skin color, which is controlled by six pairs of genes and can therefore exist in many shades, varies gradually from one population to another. With only a few exceptions, every known genetic possibility possessed by the species can be found to some degree in every sizable population.

EVER-CHANGING SPECIES

One can establish a system of racial classification simply by listing the features of populations at any given moment. Such a concept of race is, however, inappropriate to a highly mobile and ever-changing species such as *Homo sapiens*. In the short view, races may seem distinguishable, but in biology's long haul, races come and go. New ones arise and blend into neighboring groups to create new and racially stable populations. In time, genes from these groups flow into other neighbors, continuing the production of new permutations.

Some anthropologists contend that at the moment American blacks should be considered a race distinct from African blacks. They argue that American blacks are a hybrid of African blacks and European whites. Indeed, the degree of mixture can be calculated on the basis of a blood component known as the Duffy factor.

In West Africa, where most of the New World's slaves came from, the Duffy factor is virtually absent. It is present in 43 percent of American whites. From the number of American blacks who are now "Duffy positive" it can be calculated that whites contributed 21 percent of the genes in the American black population. The figure is higher for blacks in northern and western states and lower in the South. By the same token, there are whites who have black ancestors. The number is smaller because of the tendency to identify a person as black even if only a minor fraction of his ancestors were originally from Africa.

The unwieldiness of race designations is also evident in places such as Mexico where most of the people are, in effect, hybrids of Indians (Mongoloid by some classifications) and Spaniards (Caucasoid). Many South American populations are tri-hybrids—mixtures of Mongoloid, Caucasoid and Negroid. Brazil is a country where the mixture has been around long enough to constitute a racially stable population. Thus, in one sense, new races have been created in the United States, Mexico and Brazil. But in the long run, those races will again change.

Sherwood Washburn, a noted anthropologist, questions the usefulness of racial classification: "Since races are open systems which are intergrading, the number of races will depend on the purpose of the classification. I think we should require people who propose a classification of races to state in the first place why they wish to divide the human species."

The very notion of a pure race, then, makes no sense. But, as evolutionists know full well, a rich genetic diversity within the human species most assuredly *does*.

Blood, Genes, and Malaria

By Jared Diamond

....

The headaches that I had been having for several days grew rapidly worse during my physiology lecture to UCLA medical students. By the end of the hour it was painful to look at a light, and I felt as if knives were being pressed against my eyes from inside my skull. I barely got through the lecture, went out into the hall, vomited, and checked into a UCLA hospital bed. There I broke out in a sweat, pushed all the bedcovers off, then felt so cold that I pulled up the covers and two blankets, only to become hot and drenched in sweat again. My physician, who had drawn a sample of my blood, soon confirmed what I already suspected: I had malaria.

I cursed my bad luck. If only I had been quicker at swatting those damned mosquitoes in New Guinea a few months ago, perhaps I wouldn't be lying in a hospital in such absolute misery.

A year later, I instead was feeling lucky. After seven more attacks of diminishing severity at intervals of forty-eight days, my malaria disappeared. I wasn't stuck with it for life, as some people are, nor did I have to resort to dangerous and sometimes lethal drugs to eradicate it, as other people do.

In another sense, though, I could still be called unlucky. Hundreds of millions of people born where malaria is endemic belong to populations that have evolved a resistance to malaria. Because my ancestors came from malaria-free regions of Europe, I was genetically unprotected.

Malaria is the world's most important infectious disease, affecting more than a hundred million people each year. In some areas it kills nearly 10 percent of the population in childhood. Today, those malaria victims who are lucky enough to share my access to modern medicine get treated, with varying success, with antimalarial drugs. Most victims, however, have to rely on their body's own genetic antimalarials. Just as plant species native to regions with

browsing mammals evolved many natural antibrowser defenses (such as sharp spines and toxic chemicals), so humans in malarial regions have evolved dozens of chemical defenses against malaria.

Sickle-cell hemoglobin is probably the best-known genetic antimalarial. Like other such defenses, it provides some protection against one disease, while causing another—in this case sickle-cell anemia. Taken collectively, genetic antimalarials constitute the commonest single-gene disorders in the world and are carried by more than 300 million people. In their paradoxical combination of protecting against one disease while causing another, they give us our best-understood paradigm for the origin of other, widespread genetic diseases.

Genetic antimalarials also provide a paradigm of human evolution. We often consider the evolution of the human body to have ended by Cro-Magnon times 35,000 years ago, but genetic antimalarials have been continuing to evolve in the last few centuries, practically under our noses. Finally, they have proved unexpectedly interesting to historians, through leaving genetic mileposts by which to reconstruct the trans-Saharan caravan trade, as well as the countries of origin of American blacks. Thus, the infectious disease that most concerns me personally also draws the interest of physicians, evolutionary biologists, and historians. I acknowledge with pleasure my debt to three physicians—Louis Diamond (my father) of UCLA Medical School, Y. W. Kan of the University of California Medical School, San Francisco, and Ronald Nagel of Albert Einstein College of Medicine in New York—for helpful discussions of recent discoveries in this field.

The first evidence of a genetic antimalarial came from study of the disease that it causes, rather than of the disease against which it protects. In 1910 a Chi-

cago physician treating an anemic black student noticed that some of the patient's red blood cells, instead of having their usual shape of a filled doughnut, were sickle shaped. It turned out that many black Africans suffer from such an anemia, characterized by sickle-shaped red cells and leading to bacterial infections, painful episodes of blocked circulation, and degeneration of some organs. Until the advent of modern medicine, many victims died in childhood.

The cell sickling is in turn caused by hemoglobin (the oxygen-binding protein that gives our blood its red color) forming crystals within red cells in capillaries, where oxygen concentrations are low. Genetic studies proved that sickle-cell disease is due to a single gene for which patients are homozygous, that is, the patients inherit one copy of the gene from their father and a second copy from their mother. So-called heterozygotes, or people who inherit only one copy of the gene, experience either a much milder anemia or no symptoms at all.

In 1949 the great chemist Linus Pauling and three colleagues showed that the hemoglobin of sickle-cell patients is itself abnormal. Heterozygotes have a mixture of the abnormal hemoglobin (termed hemoglobin S, for sickle-cell hemoglobin) and the normal hemoglobin A. Recall now that hemoglobin and other proteins consist of twenty different building blocks called amino acids, arranged in chains of usually one hundred or more. (By comparison, words consist of twenty-six building blocks called letters, arranged in chains of usually a dozen or less.) Hemoglobin itself consists of two pairs of different chains, two so-called alpha chains of 141 amino acids and two beta chains of 146 amino acids. In 1956 Vernon Ingram proved that the sole difference between sickle-cell and normal hemoglobin is that the former has the amino acid valine at the

Joe LeMonnier

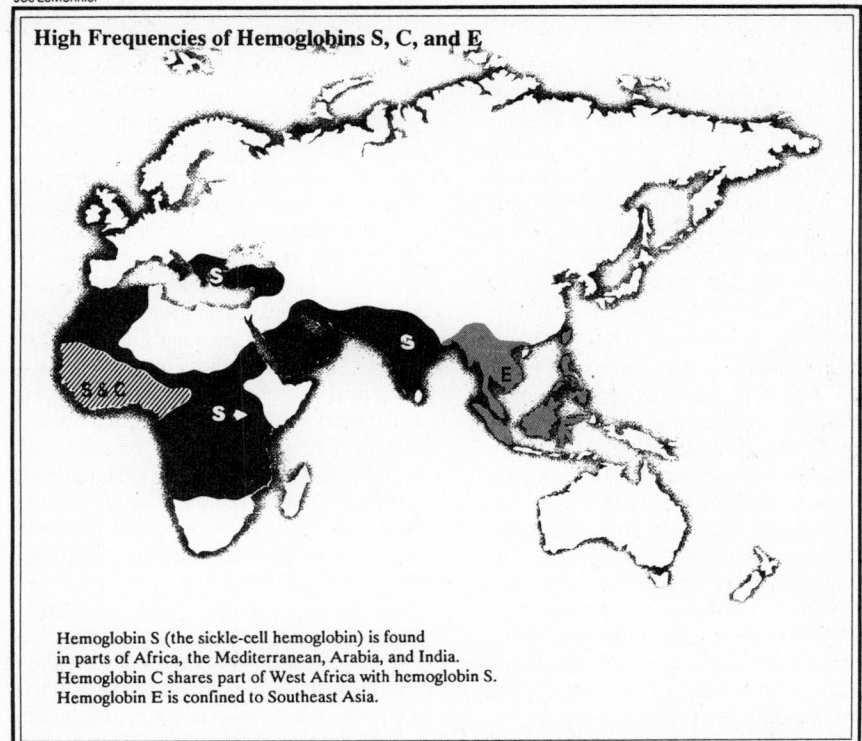

High Frequencies of Hemoglobins S, C, and E

Hemoglobin S (the sickle-cell hemoglobin) is found
in parts of Africa, the Mediterranean, Arabia, and India.
Hemoglobin C shares part of West Africa with hemoglobin S.
Hemoglobin E is confined to Southeast Asia.

sixth position of the beta chain, where the latter instead has the amino acid glutamate.

Thus, a mutation in one out of the 287 amino acids in one of the body's thousands of different proteins is ultimately responsible for all the symptoms of a serious disease. Even more than for its elucidation of sickle-cell anemia, this remarkably simple discovery is remembered for having launched the molecular study of disease that has revolutionized modern medicine.

Since patients in rural Africa who were homozygous for the sickle-cell gene usually died in childhood, it was initially a mystery why natural selection hadn't quickly eliminated the sickle-cell gene by killing off its bearers. The first clue to this mystery emerged about 1946, when a physician in Rhodesia noticed that children heterozygous for the sickle-cell gene had an advantage over normal children: their blood contained fewer malaria parasites. This suggested that the sickle-cell gene might have persisted by doing both good and harm: harm, because homozygotes tended to die of anemia; but good, because heterozygotes might be less likely than normal people to die of malaria.

In animals it would have been easy to put this malaria-protection hypothesis to a decisive experimental test. One need only

have injected both normal and sickle-cell heterozygous animals with malaria parasites to see if more of the normal animals became infected. Of course, ethical considerations today should bar this experiment in humans. Incredibly, however, the human experiment was nevertheless performed in the 1950s on thirty African volunteers. Fourteen of the fifteen who lacked the sickle-cell gene became infected, but only two of the fifteen sickle-cell heterozygotes fell ill.

While these results supported the malaria-protection hypothesis, the number of experimental subjects was too few (thank God!) to be decisive. Instead, five indirect types of evidence have been gathered in support of the hypothesis:

The natural distribution of sickle-cell genes is confined to certain areas of the world where malaria has long been endemic. These are tropical sub-Saharan Africa, plus parts of North Africa, Mediterranean Europe, Arabia, and India. In some areas of Africa 40 percent of all people carry the gene as heterozygotes. The slave trade brought the gene to the New World, where it now occurs in about one out of every ten American blacks.

In malarial regions of Africa, children under five are twice as likely to have heavy natural infections of malaria parasites,

and far more likely to die if they lack the sickle-cell gene than if they carry it.

In those same regions the fraction of the population carrying the gene increases from birth until age five (for example, from 24 percent to 29 percent in Nigeria) because that fraction suffers fewer deaths from malaria by age five than does the fraction not carrying the gene. African couples in which one partner is a sickle-cell heterozygote and the other is normal have more children who survive, and fewer who die, than do couples in which both partners lack the sickle-cell gene. The reason is that by the laws of genetics, half the children of the former marriage are heterozygous for the sickle-cell trait and thus less likely to die of malaria.

In red cells of sickle-cell heterozygotes, infection by the malaria parasite triggers sickling, and the sickled cells are subsequently destroyed by the patient's body. Those infected cells that survive provide a poor environment for the parasite's further growth. Since malaria parasites have to go through a stage of growing inside red cells, these responses of sickled cells to infection may explain why sickle-cell heterozygotes are resistant to malaria.

Taken together, these five types of indirect evidence provide strong support for the malaria-protection hypothesis. In malarial areas, people heterozygous for the sickle-cell gene are more likely to survive malaria, produce children, and pass on their genes. It's true that when two heterozygotes marry, one-quarter of their children are apt to be homozygotes and die of sickle-cell anemia. But the advantage enjoyed by the more numerous heterozygotes balances the deaths of the rarer homozygotes, hence the gene persists.

In some malarial areas, no one carries the gene. There, other red cell genetic abnormalities may be functioning as antimalarials, although the evidence is less complete than in the case of the sickle-cell gene. Often, the same human population, and even the same individual, carries more than one of these genetic antimalarials. Most of these other antimalarials offer weaker protection against malaria and produce milder diseases of their own than does the sickle-cell gene.

Two of these other antimalarials, hemoglobins C and E, common in West Africa and Southeast Asia, respectively, also have abnormal amino acid chains. Many other antimalarial genes do not affect hemoglobin structure, but cause the protein to be synthesized at abnormally low rates.

Such rate disorders are termed thalassemias, from the Greek word *thalassa,* for "sea," because physicians first recognized them in people living near the Mediterranean Sea. (I still recall from my high-school Greek the climax of Xenophon's *Anabasis,* when Xenophon's Greek army, after fighting its way through the interior of the Persian empire, finally glimpsed the sea again. The joyous cry of "thalassa!" swept through the army's ranks, and many of those overjoyed soldiers were probably thalassemics, as are most of my native friends in coastal New Guinea.) Widespread deficiencies of the red cell enzyme glucose 6-phosphate dehydrogenase (G6PD) also appear to function as genetic antimalarials. So does a red cell shape disorder termed elliptocytosis.

We don't know exactly how any of these genes protect against malaria; perhaps they all make the red cell membrane more rigid and difficult for malaria parasites to penetrate. Or perhaps each protects in a different way.

Let's now move from these medical questions to evolutionary ones. How long have genetic antimalarials been present in human populations at high frequencies? Here we have to speculate, since thalassemias and abnormal hemoglobins

haven't yet been diagnosed in ancient bones or mummies.

Many physicians favor the interpretation that malaria became a common human disease only after the rise of agriculture had created the ponds in which malaria's mosquito vectors breed abundantly in sub-Saharan Africa. Theoretical calculations show that, starting out with a sickle-cell mutation, natural selection by malaria could boost the sickle-cell gene to Africa's present high frequency within only 1,000 to 2,500 years. That would allow plenty of time, since the rise of agriculture began about 4,000 years ago in sub-Saharan Africa and earlier in the Mediterranean, Asia, and New Guinea.

It is also possible that malaria and genetic antimalarials have been with us for much longer. In Southeast Asia and India, the mosquito vectors of malaria breed in hill forests or fast-flowing streams and don't depend on agricultural ponds. In Asia, but not in Africa, human malaria occurs in wild monkeys, providing a natural reservoir of infection even before agriculture brought on a human population explosion. Africa's Eastern Pygmies, though not the Western Pygmies, have been reported to have a high frequency of the sickle-cell gene despite being nonagri-

cultural hunter–gatherers. Thus, I regard it as still uncertain whether genetic antimalarials were already widespread among human hunter–gatherers or whether they rose to high frequency only since the rise of agriculture.

In contrast, natural selection has certainly been causing genetic antimalarials to disappear rapidly in some populations. Recall that the sickle-cell gene tends to kill off its homozygous bearers. Heterozygous bearers may also face an increased risk of death during heavy exertion, as suggested by an analysis of otherwise unexplained deaths of U. S. Army black recruits during basic training. In malarial regions these drawbacks of the sickle-cell gene are offset by the protection it affords against malaria. In the absence of malaria, however, this benefit would disappear, and natural selection should gradually tend to eliminate the gene by preferentially killing its bearers—especially in the era before modern medicine.

This is exactly what seems to have happened in two New World black populations whose ancestors brought the sickle-cell gene from Africa. The gene is less common in blacks who live on the malaria-free Caribbean island of Curaçao than in blacks from nearby, malaria-ridden Surinam, although the ancestors of both populations had similar African origins. In Georgia blacks the sickle-cell gene is much less common than are other African genes. Since Curaçao and Georgia blacks both began migrating from Africa to their new homes only a few centuries ago, the gradual elimination of their sickle-cell genes by natural selection in malaria's absence has been proceeding virtually before our eyes. These examples will be unwelcome to creationists, who deny that humans evolved through natural selection and dismiss evolution as an inferred postulate rather than an observation.

Why have different genetic antimalarials evolved in different malarial regions? For instance, is it pure chance that Africa has much hemoglobin S, Southeast Asia has much hemoglobin E but no S, and New Guinea has much alpha-thalassemia and elliptocytosis but neither hemoglobin E nor S? This situation could have come about if each mutation were so rare that each malarial region of the globe ended up only with the one mutation that happened to arise there.

In fact, these and related mutations are not so rare. More than 300 different mutant abnormal human hemoglobins have

Joe LeMonnier

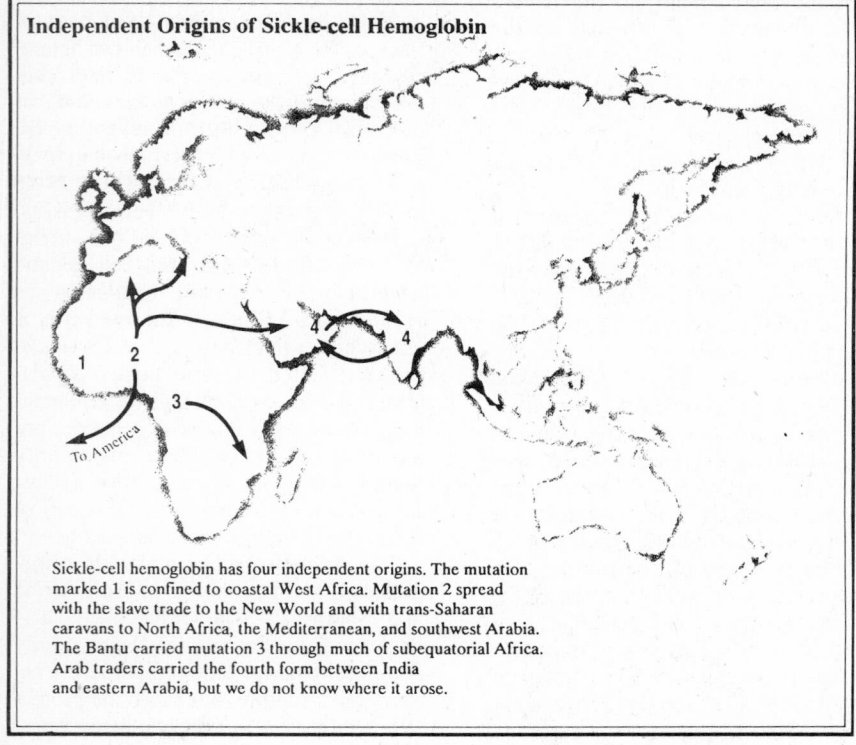

Independent Origins of Sickle-cell Hemoglobin

1

2

3

4

4

To America

Sickle-cell hemoglobin has four independent origins. The mutation marked 1 is confined to coastal West Africa. Mutation 2 spread with the slave trade to the New World and with trans-Saharan caravans to North Africa, the Mediterranean, and southwest Arabia. The Bantu carried mutation 3 through much of subequatorial Africa. Arab traders carried the fourth form between India and eastern Arabia, but we do not know where it arose.

been identified, and more than 16 of these have been observed to have arisen spontaneously in a contemporary generation (that is, to occur in a child but not in the child's parents). Many different types of G6PD deficiency are known, as are many types of thalassemias involving decreased synthesis of each of hemoglobin's two types of chains. Thus, mutations produced abundant variety on which natural selection could operate.

Studies of the fine structure of some common genetic antimalarials indicate that the same gene product probably arose independently by different mutations in different places. (The fine structures are termed haplotypes, or polymorphic restriction endonuclease sites, by molecular geneticists.) Sickle-cell hemoglobin appears to have arisen at least four times: on West Africa's Atlantic coast; somewhere in central West Africa between Togo and Nigeria; among Bantu Africans; and in India or eastern Arabia. Hemoglobin E, the Southeast Asian specialty, arose independently in one Czech family and one other northern European family but did not spread, since northern Europe lacks malaria. Alpha-thalassemia has arisen at least six times in New Guinea.

These seem to me beautiful examples of how evolution works in our own species. Malaria, one of the world's leading killers of humans, has been a prime target for natural selection. Mutations produced thousands of red cell abnormalities, most of which are useless for protecting against malaria. Dozens did prove useful and have repeatedly arisen identically or with slight variations. All these useful antimalarials rose independently to high frequencies through natural selection. Most differ in detail, but they resemble each other in the result: antimalarial efficacy. Their similarities are an example of convergent evolution at the molecular level, just as the similarly streamlined bodies of whales,

sharks, and extinct marine reptiles constitute convergent evolution at the level of gross anatomy.

But why was hemoglobin S repeatedly selected for in Africa, while hemoglobin E instead was selected for in Southeast Asia? I'd guess that more than pure chance was involved. Specifically, I would guess that mutations for hemoglobin S did occur in Southeast Asia, and that hemoglobin E mutations also occurred in Africa, but that neither became established. One factor might have been other genetic differences between Asians and Africans, since other genes (such as those for fetal hemoglobin production) modify the severity of sickle-cell anemia. A second factor could be competition and cooperation between different genetic antimalarials, since hemoglobin E plus beta-thalassemia proves to be a particularly nasty combination, while hemoglobin S plus alpha-thalassemia is more benign. Still another factor could be regional differences in malaria's transmission, such as forest mosquito vectors and monkeys being significant for human malaria in Asia but not Africa. Different conditions might also select for antimalarials of different efficacy: hemoglobin S offers more protection to heterozygotes than does C, which is in turn more efficacious than E. (The harm to homozygotes decreases in the same sequence.) At present, these four suggestions are all speculative, but I expect that it will soon be possible to start assessing them.

Finally, what about the interest of genetic antimalarials for historians? I'll give two examples. First, the transatlantic slave trade that brought millions of Africans to the New World tore them brutally from roots all over black Africa. Many white Americans, but few black Americans, can precisely trace their Old World origins through written records such as birth certificates. But sickle-cell hemoglo-

bin arose independently in at least three parts of Africa, each time with a different fine genetic structure. By analyzing frequencies of hemoglobin genes of black Americans living in Baltimore, Ronald Nagel obtained molecular estimates of their family trees: about 18 percent of their ancestors came from Bantu Africa, 15 percent from West Africa's Atlantic coast, and most (62 percent) from central West Africa.

The second example of interest to historians involves the sickle-cell gene in North Africa and Mediterranean Europe. It turns out not to represent a distinct origin but instead to be in most cases identical with the gene of central West Africa. Those African genes are a legacy of the trans-Saharan caravan trade that flourished before written records. To central West Africa, the caravans brought horses, cattle, salt, copper, and manufactured goods. To Europe, they brought ivory, gold, slaves, and among the slaves' genes, a genetic antimalarial new to Europe.

Now that much is understood about genetic antimalarials, they provide a model for trying to understand the persistence of other genetic diseases. In the Old World tropics, malaria has been the most important infectious disease, and we now know that it elicited red cell disorders as a genetic response. In northern Europe the leading infectious diseases instead included smallpox, measles, bubonic plague, tuberculosis, and bacterial diarrheas. At the same time, northern Europe evolved a different set of genetic diseases, including cystic fibrosis, Tay-Sachs, diabetes, and genetically based ulcers. We're just starting to ask which of these northern genetic diseases provided protection against which of those northern infectious diseases. But the story of that search will have to wait for a future column.

"Race": Myths Under the Microscope

By Albert Jacquard

....

Racism has historical roots. It has not been a universal phenomenon. Many contemporary societies and cultures show little trace of it. It was not evident for long periods in world history. Many forms of racism have arisen out of the conditions of conquest, out of the justification of Negro slavery and its aftermath of racial inequality in the West, and out of the colonial relationship. Among other examples is that of anti-Semitism, which has played a particular role in history, with Jews being the chosen scapegoat to take the blame for problems and crises met by many societies.

Man is a creature endowed with the fabulous power of self-construction, the ability to participate in his own creation; but the price of this capacity is investment with its opposite: that of self-destruction. The latter may take violent forms—even the collective suicide of the species has now become possible, because of the existence of nuclear weapons. But it also manifests itself in mean, shifty, surreptitious types of behaviour, among which racism is surely the most widespread.

Scorn for others because they belong to a different group is by no means a recent phenomenon, but it is one which during the present century has developed along new lines, with the assertion that "recent discoveries of modern science" and "biologically proven models" justify the classification of human populations in hierarchical order.

If scientific progress had indeed led to such conclusions, we would be obliged to take them into account, irrespective of our moral, philosophical or religious opinions. But what science tells us today, notably where the most relevant discipline—genetics—is concerned, is the exact opposite: to claim, on biological grounds, that certain individuals within a given group, or certain groups, naturally constitute an élite is totally to misunderstand the message of biology.

Awareness that scientists should be given the opportunity of stating their views on the subject, unequivocally and before the widest possible audience, led Unesco to organize in Athens, in the spring of 1981, a symposium where representatives of various disciplines could set out their most recent findings, and where racist arguments could be countered in a reasoned, dispassionate manner.

Twenty-two scientists were thus able to spend a week discussing the issues involved in a totally frank and open atmosphere, bringing from a wide spectrum of countries that included Lebanon, Tunisia, Morocco, Israel, Mexico, France, Ivory Coast, Norway, the USA and the USSR, contributions in the fields of anthropology, ethnology, psychology, genetics, sociology, history, mathematics, law and philosophy.

The diversity of cultures and disciplines represented strengthened, rather than weakened, the intensity of the debates; the genuine interdisciplinarity which characterized the exchange of views enabled each participant to understand the ideas communicated by the others and to share with them his own questionings and commentaries.

Racism was successively examined in relation to the following branches of learning: genetics; psychology and neurobiology; sociology; anthropology and ethnology; history and prehistory.

At the conclusion of the Symposium, the participating scientists, together with the representatives of Unesco, drew up a joint Appeal, the terms of which were discussed at length and unanimously approved.

GENETICS AND RACISM

Advances in the field of genetics have made it possible to determine with accuracy the content of the biological heritage of human populations; whereas, during the past centuries, attempts at racial definition were based on observable, external features such as skin colour, hair texture, and cranial structure, examination of these characteristics has now been replaced by the investigation of the genetic structures which determine them.

The overall frequency with which various genes are encountered in the members of a given group constitutes the genetic structure of that group. The differences between the structures of two populations can be synthesized by establishing a "distance" calculated from frequencies observed in each group. The definition of races thus involves grouping together populations between which genetic distances are small, and attributing to different races populations between which genetic distances are wide.

Where the human species is concerned, however, this procedure proves fruitless. Migratory movements have taken place on such a scale, and the isolation of individual groups has been so short-lived that differentiations between groups have not reached a level which makes it possible to trace boundaries between separate, relatively homogeneous populations. The variability of the human species, which is considerable, is not to be explained in terms of the differences between the average genetic distances between various groups, but in terms of the differences to be found in individual members of the same group. According to findings published by Richard Lewontin in 1974, the average genetic distance between two individuals increases by only 7 or 8 per cent when they belong to two different nations, and by only 15 per cent when they belong to two different "races."

Consequently, the type of grouping described above can only be arbitrary. For the geneticist the concept of race corresponds to no stable or objective reality where humankind is concerned.

Genetics also provides us with an argument to set against the second proposition of racist theory: that races can not only be defined, but can also be classified by order of superiority.

In fact, investigation of mechanisms of selection reveals that their effect is not to retain the "best" and to eliminate what is less satisfactory, but rather to preserve the coexistence of a great variety of characteristics. Wealth, in biological terms, is not synonymous with "good" genes, but with genetic diversity: the "best" group is that which has conserved the widest variety of genes, irrespective of the composition of that variety.

From this point of view, therefore, it is obviously impossible to invoke biological arguments to justify some sort of "natural" hierarchy of individuals or populations.

PSYCHOLOGY, NEUROLOGY, AND RACISM

When psychology became "scientific" in the mid-nineteenth century, it set itself the task of comparing the intellectual performances of individuals and groups. This analysis of differences was quickly replaced by attempts to establish relationships of superiority and inferiority. Techniques of testing were devised whereby human beings were classified in relation to an implicitly accepted norm, the average behaviour of modern Western society. As a general rule, the results of such tests are presented in numerical form, as the Intelligence Quotient, or IQ. This measurement is widely used, but it is rarely interpreted in a way which takes into account the limits of its significance.

The mere fact of expressing the IQ in numerical form creates the illusion that it measures a magnitude with an independent existence. In reality, however, comparisons between individuals of different cultures or between groups which are made using IQ are, by virtue of the definition of IQ itself, devoid of any real meaning.

Misunderstandings about the IQ are particularly dangerous when they are related to the problem of "innate and acquired" characteristics. Abuse of the concept of heritability, devised by geneticists, has led certain psychologists to attribute variations in IQ between individuals or groups to a combination of genetic and environmental factors (the ratio being generally of the order of 80 per cent for the former and 20 per cent for the latter). In fact, none of the conditions necessary to validate the measurements of heritability are here present; the figures advanced are thus not even inaccurate, they are meaningless.

SOCIOLOGY AND RACISM

Racism should not be considered as the inevitable product of a necessary sequence of cause and effect. More particularly, it is false to see racism as a mere consequence of economic phenomena, when it is in fact an interaction in which racial animosity and the quest for a scapegoat combine and focus on a minority the aggressivity engendered by failures and setbacks of all kinds, notably economic.

It is not objective economic situations that encourage racism, but the subjective interpretations of those situations. The manner in which a situation is perceived is of greater consequence than the situation itself. The process is thus one in which political action plays a decisive role, and where the media, by virtue of the notions to which they give currency and the manner in which they present the facts, also play a decisive part. The invocation of a "threshold of tolerance" is a good example of the use of a mechanism presented as natural, in order to justify the rejection of minorities. In fact, such thresholds cannot be measured, and correspond to nothing that can be objectively defined.

The situation of those who are oppressed because of their "race" is not the outcome of an inevitable malediction; it is simply an observable state of affairs which cannot be justified in any way.

The often distorted propagation of certain arguments advanced by sociobiologists can prove extremely dangerous. Sociobiology deals with the causes and circumstances, including those of a genetic nature, which determine the organization of animal societies, ranging from termites to primates. The extrapolation of its findings to humankind is obviously risky and should only be undertaken with the greatest care. For example, the assertion that most human behaviour is genetically conditioned rests on no serious evidence. Little caution is shown by certain journalists who claim that theories which are still the subject of debate are "scientifically proved"; other writers conceal dogmatic attitudes behind what they claim is scientific evidence.

ANTHROPOLOGY, ETHNOLOGY, AND RACISM

Anthropology sets out to make a global study of man, integrating the physical, genetic, cultural and historical points of view. In all these domains, individuals differ from each other, and anthropology endeavoured, over a long period, to take these differences into account in preparing classifications and where possible in tracing the outlines of more or less homogeneous groups, or "races." The latter were thus defined as the product of a division of humanity according to transmissable physical characteristics. But this analysis is of doubtful value because of the importance of the genetic exchanges occurring between groups, the intensity of which has varied in different ages and regions. Such exchanges have increased during the past few centuries, and consequently groups which might have been defined as "races" in the past have disappeared, giving place to other, provisional regroupings.

But the essential contribution of anthropology is to show that the feelings of superiority found in most human groups is related to their culture, and not to their biological heritage; their sentiments are ethnocentric, and not racist. Racism, as a belief in the natural superiority of a given group, is of comparatively recent origin. It developed parallel to the colonial expansion of the European powers, finding scientific justification in a mistaken extrapolation of the theories of Darwin, social Darwinism. Reaching its height during the period of Nazism, it has subsequently declined appreciably, despite the rearguard actions of certain groups (which appear notably in *The Mankind Quarterly*), or individuals, such as the psychologist Arthur Jensen.

Anthropologists have reacted forcefully; for example, an important study by R. Sinha, of India, has shown that "there is no innate difference in intellectual capacities between the different racial groups."

In the last analysis, the problem with which we are confronted is not one of justifying or invalidating racist attitudes, but rather that of understanding why such attitudes persist, despite a total absence of justification.

HISTORY, PREHISTORY, AND RACISM

Over the centuries, racist theories have developed in response to the requirements of dominant groups. Not infrequently, they have embodied contradictory premises. The eighteenth century, for example, saw the simultaneous adoption of the myth of the "noble savage" as opposed to the "wicked sophisticate," and the uninhibited practice of slavery, while, at the present time, when the findings of science are demolishing the very foundations of racism, there are those who consistently invoke science in their attempts to promote its resurgence.

Historical studies enable us to compare the mechanisms which determine the evolution of a racist society (which inevitably drifts into a state of tension between dominant and dominated groups and in which the range of alternatives grows steadily smaller), and those which govern the development of a progressive, pluralist society (open to interchange and to all the different forms of creativity which become possible thanks to a permanent ferment of ideas and action).

The resurgence of racism presents a challenge to which we must respond by a steadfast call for the social diversification which it is in our power to achieve: diversification through science and technology, through culture, through recourse to our origins and through freedom available to all.

PART 3

Archaeology

....

Archaeology is the systematic retrieval and study of the remains (both of people and their activities) that human beings and their ancestors have left behind on and below the surface of the earth. Like biological anthropology, archaeology gradually emerged as a separate discipline in the course of the nineteenth century. It split off from the generalized study of ancient history as scholars—mostly geologists, initially—began to focus on finding material remains of ancient precivilized populations in Europe.

Actually, it was a geological debate that helped lay the groundwork for the emergence of archaeology. The prevailing view among geologists until well into the nineteenth century was that the various strata that compose the earth's crust were the result of either Noah's flood (diluvialism) or a series of catastrophes of which the flood was the most recent (catastrophism). One of the first geologists to dispute these notions was William Smith (1769–1839). Dubbed "Strata" Smith by his detractors, he assembled a detailed table of all the known strata and their fossil contents and argued a uniformitarian position: that the eternally ongoing processes of erosion, weathering, accumulation, and the movement of the continents accounted for the large number of strata. He was supported by James Hutton (1726–1797) in his influential work *Theory of the Earth*, published in 1795.

The combat was joined by the greatly respected William Buckland (the discoverer of the "Red Lady of Paviland," which we discussed in the introduction to Part 2), who in 1823 published his work *Reliquiae Diluvianae, or Observations on the Organic Remains contained in Caves, Fissures and Diluvial Gravel, and on Other Geological Phenomena attesting to the Action of an Universal Deluge*, in which he vigorously attacked the uniformitarian views that so directly contradicted Church dogma. Only the appearance of Sir Charles Lyell's *Principles of Geology* (1830–1833) managed finally to turn the tide of scholarly sentiment in favor of the uniformitarian view of the earth's history.

Because of the nature of their work, it was for the most part amateur and professional geologists who most frequently encountered fossilized human remains, generally embedded in strata in the floors of limestone caverns. In the roughly six decades following the 1790s, an impressive array of evidence with regard to human antiquity was found in a number of such caves in Europe and England, but the finds were dismissed or their importance unrecognized. As early as 1797, for example, John Frere (1740–1807) found chipped flint tools twelve feet deep in his excavation at Hoxne (northeast of London). These stone tools were closely associated with the remains of extinct animal species. To Frere, these finds suggested a very ancient human existence, even older than the commonly accepted 6,000-year antiquity of Creation. Nobody listened. Forty years later, in 1838, Boucher de Perthes (1788–1868), a customs collector at Abbeville in the northwest of France, disclosed news of some flint "axes" he had found in gravel pit caves on the banks of the Somme River. The world laughed at his assertion that these tools were manufactured by "antediluvial man," even though they had been found in the immediate vicinity of the bones of extinct cold-adapted animals. In 1846, he published *Antiquités Celtiques et Antediluviennes*, in which he formally argued his thesis—and was attacked as a heretic by the Church.

We have already discussed William Buckland's inability in 1822 to comprehend the significance of his own find, the so-called Red Lady of Paviland. The powerful grip of Christian theology on scholars' minds blinded the intellectual establishment of the period, keeping them from seeing and appreciating the overwhelming pattern that these and numerous other finds presented. As we have emphasized repeatedly, it was the emergence of Darwinism in 1859 that freed people's vision and enabled them to face and reinterpret these materials correctly. The evolutionary perspective, then, was of critical importance for the emergence of archaeology. Without it, there was no way to interpret accurately the significance of the ancient remains that were being turned up with increasing frequency.

The excavation of rock shelters revealing human cultural remains of great antiquity was only one of several kinds of archaeological research being undertaken in the nineteenth-century. The excavation and description of large prehistoric monuments and burial mounds, begun in the wake of emergent nationalism in the seventeenth century and eighteenth centuries, continued. So did the retrieval and preservation of materials accidentally brought to light by road, dam, and building excavations as the industrial revolution changed the face of the earth. By the 1800s, vast quantities of stone and metal implements had been recovered and had found their way into both private and public collections. As the volume of such artifacts mounted, museum curators were faced with the problem of how to organize and display them meaningfully.

In 1836, Christian Jurgensen Thomsen (1788–1865), curator of the Danish National Museum, published a guide to its collections in which he classified all artifacts in terms of the material from which they were made. He argued that the three classes he thus identified represented stages in cultural evolution: a *Stone Age* followed by a *Bronze Age* and then an *Iron Age*. The idea was not new—it had been proposed by Lucretius in ancient Rome—but it was new for its time. However, the *Three-Age System* fit well with the contemporary writings of early nineteenth-century social evolutionists and was of such usefulness that it quickly spread to other countries.

The Three-Age System was clearly evolutionary (and hence radical). It contained a geological perspective in that it proposed clearly defined sequences of cultural stages modeled after geological strata. It was of tremendous value in providing a conceptual framework through which archaeologists could begin systematically to study the artifacts they retrieved from the earth, and in tending to support those scholars arguing for a greatly expanded vision of human antiquity.

Combined with Darwinian evolutionism, the Three-Age System became an even more powerful conceptual tool. In 1865, Sir John Lubbock (1834–1913) published his tremendously influential book *Prehistoric Times*, in which he vastly extended the Stone Age and divided it in two. He thus proposed that human prehistory be viewed in terms of the following stages: the *Paleolithic* (Old Stone Age, marked by flint tools); the *Neolithic* (New Stone Age, marked by the appearance of pottery); the *Bronze Age*; and the *Iron Age*. Although this system has continued to be refined, it still forms the basis of our understanding of world prehistory, and we continue to make use of its terminology.

At about the time Lubbock was formulating his broad outline of the stages of cultural evolution, Edouard Lartet (whom we discussed earlier) and his English colleague Henry Christy were exploring the now famous rock shelters in the Dordogne region of France. In one cave, called La Madeleine, Christy and Lartet found not only an abundance of spectacular cave art and small engravings of extinct species, such as the woolly mammoth, but also a magnificent collection of tools, including intricately carved implements of antler bone and ivory. These became the *type complex* for the identification of the Magdalenian culture, easily the most advanced and spectacular culture of Upper Paleolithic times.

Using the art work they found in the ten or so caves they explored in this region, Lartet and Christy developed a system to classify the materials they uncovered. Their approach was based on the fact that renderings of different species of animals predominated during different periods. The succession of stages they worked out for the Dordogne region was the following: (1) the Age of the Bison, (2) the Age of the Woolly Mammoth and Rhinoceros, (3) the Age of the Reindeer, and (4) the Age of the Cave Bear.

Gabriel de Mortillet (1821–1898) took the work of Lartet and Christy a step further by developing a chronology of the same region based on the tool industries found at *type sites* (sites used to represent the characteristic features of a culture). The series he ultimately settled on in the 1870s had six stages: Thenaisian, Chellean, Mousterian, Solutrean, Magdalenian, and Robenhausian. Although these materials have been reinterpreted a great deal since that time, prehistoric archaeologists still use Mortillet's approach to naming archaeological cultures and even most of the names he proposed.

The archaeologist of the late nineteenth century who most attracted public attention was probably Heinrich Schliemann (1822–1890). After intensive study of the Homerian epics, Schliemann set out to find the ancient city of Troy. He accomplished this in 1871 at a place called Hissarlik, near the western tip of Anatolia (modern Turkey). He was a romantic figure, and his quest to find the sites of Homeric legend excited public fancy and brought forth private funds to support both his own and other archaeological research. Unfortunately, he was not a very skilled excavator: While digging up the highly stratified site at Hissarlik he focused his attentions on what turned out to be the wrong layer—and virtually destroyed the real Troy in the process.

As the frontiers of knowledge about human origins expanded in Europe with the emergence of increasingly specialized subdisciplines, a parallel development was taking place in the Americas. Wild speculation about the origins of Native Americans gave way to increasingly systematic research by scholars and learned amateurs. In 1784, for example, Thomas Jefferson (1743–1826) excavated an Indian burial mound in Virginia. Although his digging techniques were crude, he approached his task in a very modern manner. Rather than setting out simply to collect *artifacts*, Jefferson cut into the mound to collect *information*. His cross-section of the mound revealed ancient burial practices similar to those of known historic groups and refuted the popularly held notion that the mound builders had buried their dead in an upright position.

By the 1840s, John Lloyd Stephens and Frederick Catherwood had established new standards for care in the recording of details in their magnificent reports about, and drawings of, the ruins of the Mayan civilization in the Yucatan peninsula, published in works such as Stephens's *Incidents of Travel in Central America: Chiapas and Yucatan* (1842).

The mounds of the southeastern United States attracted a number of excavators, most notably E. G. Squier and E. H. Davis, who described their research in an important monograph published in 1848. By the middle of the century, sufficient work had been done to justify a long synthesis of American archaeology by Samuel Haven, published in 1856.

Archaeology in the New World was always very tightly connected to cultural anthropology—much more so than in Europe. This stemmed from the fact that whereas Europeans engaged in archaeological research as an extension of their researches backward from known historical times to their distant prehistoric past, Americans were investigating foreign societies—whether they were digging in their own backyards or engaging in ethnographic research with their displaced (and decimated) Native American neighbors. To this day this difference persists: In Europe archaeology is usually thought of as a humanity (an adjunct to history), whereas in the United States archaeology is practiced as a subdiscipline of anthropology and is viewed as a social science.

TOPIC 5

Doing Archaeology

. . . .

How do we learn about the past? What kinds of evidence remain behind after ancient societies have vanished? How do we go about retrieving these remains, studying them, interpreting them? These are the concerns of archaeology.

Archaeological remains are the material things left behind both by people and by their environment—and are located or retrieved by trained specialists. Such remains may be collected from the surface of a site, retrieved from caves or under water, or dug up out of the ground. Basically, archaeologists study three kinds of materials: remains of the environment, remains created (on purpose or inadvertently) by human activities, and human remains themselves.

Archaeologists have developed sophisticated and highly specialized techniques to retrieve and interpret this evidence from the past. After an area has been surveyed for the presence of archaeological remains, after sites (areas containing concentrations of archaeological remains) have been found, then a crucial decision must be made: should a given site be excavated (and thereby irretrievably destroyed), or should it be preserved for possible future excavation when technological advances may vastly enhance what may be learned from it?

In "What's New In Archaeology," the first of the two articles of Topic 5, the distinguished British archaeologist Colin Renfrew describes some of the latest techniques—

from the highly technological to the merely ingenious—that archaeologists and the specialists from other disciplines they work with have developed to allow us glimpses into the previously hidden lives of people long dead.

In the past several decades, archaeology has increasingly adapted the resources, tools, and techniques of other sciences—from satellite mapping to computer-assisted analysis—in order to learn more about the past. However, in "Hope for an Endangered Science," Robert C. Dunnell argues that "intellectually, archaeology is in deep trouble" if it does not become a full-fledged science. One of the shortcomings of the discipline, Dunnell observes, is that we have no generally accepted standards for judging the relative worth of competing explanations of the archaeological record. He also argues that, for the purposes of archaeology, culture should be redefined as a "trait transmission process analogous to genetics." Finally, he lists those archaeological techniques and methods that he thinks will be developed in the coming century. While we think his acceptance of the frequently made distinction between humanism and science is simplistic (see, by way of contrast, the article by Wright, "The Rise of Civilization: Mesopotamia to Mesoamerica" in Topic 6), we agree that he is correct to call for a rethinking of the field of archaeology.

What's New in Archaeology?

By Colin Renfrew

....

OVER the past two or three decades, archaeology—the study of the human past through the material remains of human activity—has changed profoundly in nature. Archaeology was once widely regarded as some sort of backward extension of recorded history. For times when written records were available it was seen as a useful addition, as simply some sort of illustration of the written narrative. For the prehistoric period, prior to the availability of written testimony, it offered some kind of shadowy reconstruction of the past, an illiterate substitute for a proper historical record.

Today, rather suddenly, archaeology, seems *relevant* and relevant in a very international way. Every continent has its own rich archaeological record, whether or not it has its own written records into the remote past. Moreover we can see more clearly that what happened in the Americas, for instance, or in Africa two or three thousand years ago is just as relevant to our general understanding of human history as events occurring at that time in Asia or in Europe, areas with a longer written record.

Several developments have come together to create a new awareness that the archaeology of all these areas—and let us not leave out Australia and the Pacific—is part of *our* archaeology, the record of the history and achievements of our own species, and a part of the cultural heritage of *our* world.

In the first place, the development of new dating techniques, especially radiocarbon dating, has allowed the archaeological finds from every part of the globe to be dated reliably, without recourse to written history. The application of other techniques from the sciences, along with more rigorous excavation methods, has given the archaeologist a whole array of approaches which he or she can use to investigate past economies, the development of technology and early social systems (see article page 12).

Secondly, with the development of what has come to be called the "New Archaeology", research workers have redefined their aims. We are no longer simply seeking to reconstruct the past, and form some simple narrative of what happened in early times. We are trying in addition to understand *why* things changed and why they became what they are. This aim requires the development of a clearer theoretical framework for archaeology and involves the questioning of old beliefs. And if our goal is to understand how and why things change, the study of the processes at work in one part of the world may give us very valuable insights into those operating in another. The New Archaeology is therefore not ethnocentric, or at least it tries not to be.

Thirdly, with the increased pace of development in many parts of the world, both in towns and in the countryside through the mechanization and intensification of agriculture, many components of the archaeological record are under threat. The awareness that this is so has given rise to "rescue archaeology" as a national policy in many countries, sometimes referred to as Culture Resource Management. This implies both the effort to protect important sites against damage, and an acknowledgement of the need to conduct systematic excavations at those whose destruction cannot be prevented, so as to learn what we can from them before the site has been destroyed. Along with the national, public investment in rescue archaeology has come a deeper awareness of the significance of the early past for each nation's own identity. Our past matters: it is a fundamental part of what we have become. And archaeology is the only way we can find out about our early origins.

Up until a century ago, no-one had any very clear idea of how old the world was, and very little notion of the antiquity of humankind. In most countries there were creation stories, often suggesting that the

first appearance of humankind was the act of god, or of the gods. But no one could say with any precision how long ago this occurred.

It was not until 1859, the same year in which Charles Darwin published *The Origin of Species,* that the antiquity of man was established. Flint tools were then shown to have been found together with the bones of extinct animals, and it was demonstrated that the animals and the humans who made the tools must have lived many thousands of years ago.

Work over the century following these revelations made many things clear. It was shown that our species had first emerged in Africa and that most of the globe had first been peopled during what is termed the Old Stone Age, well before 10000 BC. Evidence for the local origins of farming was found in several parts of the world. In some of these areas, early cities developed for the first time and writing was invented.

But when? To give a precise date to these developments was extremely difficult. It was not until the 1950s that progress in atomic physics allowed new analytical techniques to come to the aid of archaeology. From the application of potassium-argon dating applied to these two elements found in rocks of volcanic origin, we know that the first tool-making hominids emerged in Africa around two million years ago. They were not, of course, very much like modern humans. But even the earliest hominids, of the genus *Australopithecus,* had the human ability of walking upright, of using the hand to hold things in a prehensile grasp, of binocular vision, and other abilities distinguishing them from many other species.

By 35,000 years ago, the first members of our own species, *Homo sapiens sapiens* are seen. Modern humankind dates from then and this date for the appearance of modern humankind is given to us by radiocarbon analysis. This technique of radiocarbon dating is another spin-off from atomic physics, and it allows any piece of organic matter (that is to say, material derived from once living things, whether animal or plant, and which contains carbon) to be dated in the laboratory, so long as it is not more than about 40,000 years old.

For prehistoric Europe, these results have produced a revolution in our thinking. They showed that many of the very early European developments were not derived from the east Mediterranean area, as had once been thought. For instance it is no longer true that the pyramids of Egypt are the earliest stone-built monuments in the world. Some of the stone-built tombs of Europe are earlier, and Stonehenge in England or the temples of Malta are now the contemporaries of the pyramids not their younger relatives.

The broader significance of radiocarbon dating is much wider even than this. It means that for the first time, those areas which did not have an early written history can have their own secure chronology. We know now, for instance, that Australia had a human population, the ancestors of the modern aborigines, as early as 25,000 years ago. We can now date properly the early developments in the Americas, to take another example. It has been shown that the origins of the Maya civilization of Mexico and neighbouring countries date back as early as 2000 BC. We can now begin to understand the African iron age, and recognize properly the true originality of the terracotta and the bronze sculptures of Nigeria, some of them dating back to around 600 BC.

These are just a few examples of the many which could be brought forward from each area of the globe. All of this means then, that it is now possible to speak in terms of a world prehistory. For each area the long sequence of human development can be built up. As a result of this dating revolution, each country can have its own, well-dated prehistory.

Dating techniques represent, however, only one group of the techniques of archaeological science, even though they are probably the most important. Another line of investigation is the laboratory analysis of artefacts—stone tools, for instance, or pottery—which can often give clear indications of the original source of the material used. This allows us to learn something of the trade and exchange of goods among the early populations and of the system of distribution of the goods to the areas where they were used, buried and later discovered by the archaeologist.

The life sciences too have made their contribution. From the study of the rubbish of early societies it is now possible to build up a very clear picture of their diet, and hence of their subsistence economy. For instance,

Above, excavating a tumulus in fair weather and foul, as depicted in the Gentleman's Magazine, *1852.*

carbonized seeds from rubbish dumps, when studied by a specialist, can reveal precisely what food crops were being cultivated by early farmers. Investigations of animal bones can indicate which wild animals were being hunted, and whether or not domestic animals were being kept and in what numbers and proportions.

Modern archaeology, it has been said, is sometimes just the study of poor man's rubbish. This is often quite true! For by studying these rather modest remains we can build up a whole picture of the developing economy of early societies which may tell us more about life in them than the most precious objects of gold or jade.

In many ways, however, the most exciting recent developments in archaeology have not been those achieved in the laboratory, in the perfection of dating methods or the study of the early environment. They have come rather, from a change in outlook, and of philosophy. The "New Archaeology" began in the 1960s, in the United States and in Britain, arising from a dissatisfaction with the assumption and outlook of the traditional archaeology, which often seemed to reach conclusions framed in very simplified historical terms. Its leading exponent has been Professor Lewis R. Binford of the University of New Mexico at Albuquerque, and his great achievement has been to show that in order

Photo Alexis Vorontzoff. Unesco

Prehistoric megalithic temple complex at Ggantija, on the island of Gozo, Republic of Malta. Modern scientific dating techniques have shown that some of Malta's prehistoric stone temples, characterized by a very skillful use of local materials, were built before 3000 BC, much earlier than was once thought. Unesco is cooperating with the Maltese Government on the preservation and presentation of Malta's important monuments and sites.

to understand the past it is not sufficient just to dig up the artefacts of past ages and to write some intuitive story based on one's impressions of them.

Instead, our concern should be the study of culture process—that is to say how and why human cultures change. We have to ask much more carefully what is the explanation for all the differences, the variability which we see in the archaeological record. This means that we have to develop a better theory, a better methodology for archaeological interpretation.

Processual archaeologists, then, seek to understand why things changed, and this means developing explanations through a willingness to generalize. It implies the construction of theories in the same sort of way that the scientist works when understanding the world of nature. These theories can then be assessed, and sometimes they can be tested against new archaeological findings.

To take an example, we may want to understand how a particular city came to be built, and how civilization emerged in an area—whether we are talking of ancient Rome, or of Moenjodaro in Pakistan, or whatever. To do this properly we need to seek some more general understanding of the processes which lead to increasing growth and complexity in different human cultures. We can then study how far the case of Rome or Moenjodaro fits into the general picture, and try to examine the special features of each.

The "New Archaeology" is more optimistic than the traditional approach. It does not accept the assertion that we cannot learn through archaeology about the social organization or the religious life of past societies as many traditional archaeologists have asserted. Rather we have to try and develop sound arguments which will allow us to interpret the data about these aspects of society, as well as about diet and about technology and so forth.

Processual archaeology is very concerned also to think more carefully about how the archaeological record itself is formed—about exactly how the sites which we dig up, and the objects which we find in them, come to be found where they are. The new field of ethnoarchaeology has developed in order to investigate these issues. It involves going out to live in a suitable contemporary community, which has a way of life that is in some respects similar to the prehistoric or historic one that one seeks to understand. The ethnoarchaeologist studies how the modern archaeological record in that contemporary society comes about.

Lewis Binford was one of the first archaeologists to go and do this. His interest was in the hunter-gatherers of the Mousterian period, 40,000 years ago. He saw clearly that the best way to understand the archaeological record of those long-dead hunter-gatherers was to go out and study in detail the archaeological record of a living community of hunter-gatherers. He chose the Nunamiut eskimos of Alaska. He lived in a suitable community, taking part in hunting expeditions. And because he was not a very good hunter, he did the butchery for the group. This gave him the opportunity of studying how rubbish is discarded in such a community, and his work has contributed greatly to the study of early hunter-gatherers.

The same techniques of study can be applied to urban communities also. In Tucson, Arizona, the "Garbage Project" under the direction of Professor William J. Rathje has studied the rubbish discarded by families in different districts of the city. Since they do not simply throw rubbish away, but deposit it in trash cans, the Garbage Project has had to turn itself into a rubbish-disposal squad, collecting the garbage from the trash cans and studying it in the laboratory. It may sound odd, but the results are very interesting.

This project illustrates the point that the techniques of archaeology are relevant to the material culture of human societies at all times and places, ancient and modern. The contemporary archaeologist no longer thinks in terms of "primitive" and "advanced" cultures. The hunter-gatherer of today or yesterday is as interesting as the city-dweller: both are part of the rich variety of human culture—although it must be admitted that hunter-gatherers have contributed to it for a hundred times as long as city-dwellers!

There is another reason why modern archaeology really does deserve its place in the modern world. The traditional archaeology often explained things in terms of the "diffusion" of culture. The assumption was made that the major advances came about only in one or two areas, and were transmitted to the barbarian fringe by the "diffusion" of culture. In recent years, researchers have come to realize that this was sometimes a rather colonialist viewpoint, implying that the interesting developments came about only in a few crucial, privileged centres.

Today we see that, to understand the changes taking place, you have to understand the processes that are operating locally in the area under study. It is necessary to study the changes in social structure, the developing population, the economy and technology. Exchanges with other areas, and the importation of new ideas can admittedly play and do play a part in that process, but they are not necessarily of dominant importance.

To take one example, it was assumed for many years that the ruins of Great Zimbabwe, in the country which today takes its name from that monument, must have been the work of skilled immigrants from the north, or perhaps the result of contacts with Arab traders. It simply was not accepted that they could be the work of the local inhabitants, that is to say, of the African population. Yet today all the evidence (including the radiocarbon evidence) goes to show that this was in fact the case. We don't

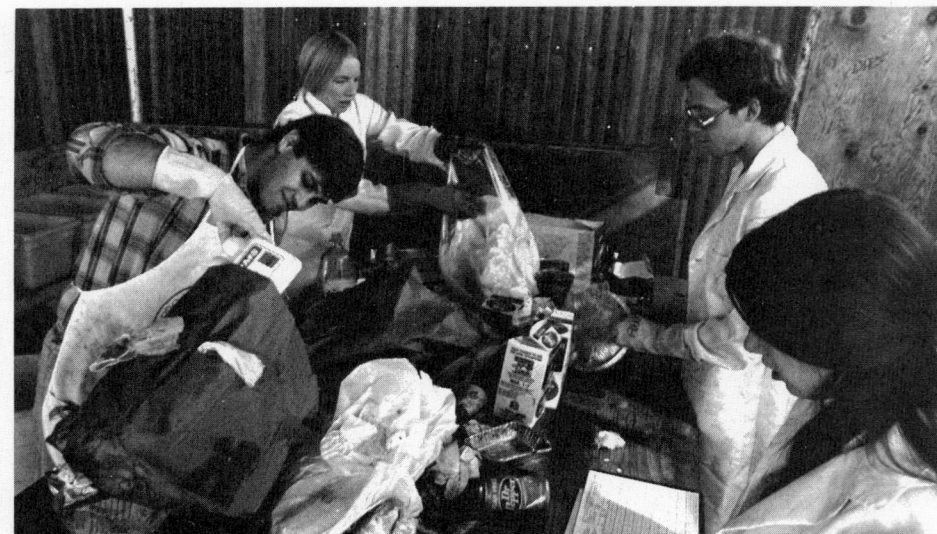

Photo © W.L. Rathje, Tucson, Arizona

The Tucson Garbage Project. *The brainchild of a group of anthropologists at the University of Arizona, the Tucson Garbage Project was launched in 1973 in order to study the material culture of a modern city by "excavating" its garbage, considered as evidence of its residents' way of life. In the words of the Project's director, Professor William L. Rathje, "We believed that assumptions about the way material culture is related to behaviour in past civilizations can be tested in a familiar, on-going society. Second, we felt that applying archaeological methods to such a society can produce valuable insights into that society itself." Above, Rathje's student workers carefully sort, record and weigh household garbage for evidence of what contemporary society buys and how it lives. This attempt to take a systematic look at modern society in the United States from the archaeological viewpoint is the prototype of similar studies conducted elsewhere in the United States as well as in Mexico City and Sydney, Australia.*

need immigrants, or a trading mission, to account for the monument, which we can explain better in terms of the local working of the society of the time. Just the same is true of Stonehenge in England which used to be thought of as the product of contacts and skills of the Mediterranean world. Today we think of it in local terms. We don't need Mediterranean colonists to explain it.

This does not mean that we should always think of each land in isolation. But it does encourage us to believe that every nation should encourage the investigation by archaeological means of its own past. Today most countries are proud of their own cultural heritage and some of them have remarkable museums, like those in Mexico City and in Cairo, to display it.

There is also a growing concern for the conservation of the cultural heritage. Unesco is sponsoring a number of projects, such as its major campaign to save the remains of the great early city of Moenjodaro in Pakistan (see article page 32); and most nations have their own programme for safeguarding monuments. These are now seen as international problems. Some of them will be discussed at the World Archaeological Congress, to be held in September 1986 in Southampton and Lon-

don (see note page 38). The U.K. national secretary, Professor Peter Ucko of Southampton University, is expecting that representatives from most countries in the world will attend. They will discuss problems of conservation and of interpretation, in the light of the newly-emerging international consciousness about our early past.

Archaeology used to be the pursuit of a few leisured amateurs, often based in the more prosperous centres of the industrial west. Today it is a field of great interest to many people in every country in the world. This is partly because it gives each of us an opportunity to understand more fully our own national history. But to focus on one's own nation alone is mere chauvinism. Archaeology also offers us the opportunity to see the early history of each land as one part of the broader history of the human species as a whole. And processual archaeology invites us to try to understand better the greater diversity of human culture, now and in the past. This has been made easier both by the battery of techniques made available by the sciences, and the rigour and the self-awareness which have been part of the "New Archaeology".

Hope for an Endangered Science

By Robert C. Dunnell

....

Outwardly, archaeology is a robust and healthy discipline. There are more archaeologists employed today than ever before; there is more money devoted to archaeological fieldwork and analysis than there was only a decade ago. Archaeologists have borrowed advances in the natural sciences and technology to great advantage.

These gains are real and substantial. But intellectually, archaeology is in deep trouble, trouble that has been brewing for more than a century and has now reached crisis proportions. Behind this grave threat are defects in archaeological theory and method.

Archaeologists have always aspired to be scientific — eminent nineteenth-century scholars such as Cyrus Thomas and William Henry Holmes lamented that archaeology was not yet an "exact science." The so-called "new archaeology," which has dominated the profession for the past two decades, is a modern affirmation of the desire to make archaeology a science. That desire is nowhere more plainly stated than in the titles of widely used archaeological texts: *Explanation in Archaeology, An Explicitly Scientific Approach* and *Archaeological Explanation, The Scientific Method in Archaeology*. Simply put, archaeology must become a science if it is to survive. Yet the attempt to place archaeology on a firm scientific footing has failed.

Our lack of success is nowhere more evident than in our failure, after decades of discussion, to improve the quality of archaeological explanation. The "Classic Maya collapse" is a perfect case in point. Ever since archaeologists noticed the abrupt end of the Classic Maya in the Peten, they have attempted to identify the cause. They have advocated many explanations, ranging from climatic change to ecological imbalances, to social or political disruption, to warfare and migration. But we still have no clear-cut reason to prefer one explanation over another. The same can be said for other "big questions," such as the origins of agriculture or the rise of civilization. Consequently, as we watch archaeological interpretations change with startling rapidity, we must ask if archaeological "explanations" are anything more than just-so stories.

There have been various reactions to this problem. Many archaeologists committed to a scientific approach have retreated into subdisciplines like geoarchaeology, zooarchaeology, and archaeometry, where nonarchaeological scholarship supplies the essential theory. Others have retreated into interpretive "schools" of archaeological theory. We now have ecological, economic, and population pressure approaches, to name a few, but no compelling reason to prefer one over another. For the most part, these different schools continue the traditional aspiration (pretense?) to science, but in the past decade some (the structuralist and symbolic approaches) have abandoned scientific methodology altogether. However we want to characterize its parts, archaeology in the 1980s is in greater intellectual disarray than ever before, and its century-old commitment to science is weakening. How we now deal with this problem — the lack of a scientific basis for interpreting the archaeological record — will decide the course of archaeology in the next century.

The future of archaeology may lie with evolutionary theory. Archaeologists and anthropologists have now taken the first steps in reworking evolutionary theory by redefining our concept of culture as a trait transmission process analogous to genetics. The major features of biological evolution derive from the integration of Darwinism and genetics in the 1930s, genetics supplying the mechanism of trait transmission lacking in Darwin's formulation. In the case of human beings, however, most significant trait transmission is effected not genetically but culturally. While culture traditionally was taken to be a *configuration* of traits (beliefs, language, technology), in evolutionary theory it becomes a *mechanism* by which traits are passed on from generation to generation.

We cannot, however, use this new approach simply to reinterpret the results of earlier studies. This is because archaeologists have traditionally pursued a typological view of the archaeological record, classifying artifacts and assemblages into types or kinds. Since these typolo-

Reprinted with permission from *Archaeology*, January/February 1989

gies are based on the similarities among artifacts, they tend to suppress the recording of variations in favor of recording similarities. Because mechanisms of evolution, such as natural selection, operate on variation, our archaeological "facts" — the descriptions of artifacts and assemblages that we have developed — are flawed. Redescribing the archaeological record is not only an unsettling prospect, it is a daunting physical task. It must be done, however, if we are to have a scientific archaeology grounded in evolutionary theory.

A major change is required in the way in which we go about doing archaeology, ranging from how we do fieldwork to how we analyze the finds. The methods employed both in the field and in the laboratory can be expected to change dramatically over the next 50 years. One important advance we have already made is the recognition that the archaeological record is produced not just by human activity but by a variety of causes we call *formation processes*. Prominent among them are soil formation, weathering, erosion, and disturbances by plants and animals, all of which can have a profound impact on what we excavate. The implications of this realization are just beginning to be understood. For example, we can no longer assume that the items found within a pit or a house necessarily tell us when or for what those structures were used. This realization forces us to call into question earlier interpretations that we now recognize to be naive. In the long term, archaeologists will have to be more careful and collect additional information, both field observations and artifact analysis, in order to determine whether the association of objects and structures is meaningful or merely a chance result of formation processes.

There has been a general trend in archaeology to recover a broader range of objects and to pay attention to objects of smaller sizes. This trend will accelerate, and in 50 years, artifacts from two millimeters down to ionic sizes will be the backbone of archaeological research. Larger objects, now the focus of most research, will play a complementary role in interpretation.

In the next century, excavation, once the hallmark of archaeology, will be employed only when all other means of data acquisition have been exhausted. This shift, which has already begun, is the result of advances in our understanding of the archaeological record as well as conservation considerations. Site formation studies have confirmed that artifacts found on the surface of a site accurately reflect the buried deposits. Surface surveys, then, can provide information about sites over large areas at a low cost while doing little damage to the archaeological record. In contrast, excavation is expensive, destructive to the record, and at best yields great detail about a few widely separated sites.

The increased attention we give to surface deposits will change how we observe the archaeological record. Remote sensing is a burgeoning field; we already use aerial photographs and other means, such as ground-penetrating radar, to locate sites and to study them. Future research will be directed to discovering why sites produce distinct aerial "signatures" and how we can extract more information from remote-sensing data. For example, the differences in vegetation that mark sites are produced not just by moisture conditions and the amount of organic matter in the soil, but also by soil chemistry. Perhaps we will be able to use information about soil chemistry, as reflected in the plant cover, to tell us more about sites. Satellite and shuttle imagery has been attractive to archaeologists, but its utility has been limited to large-scale archaeological phenomena (e.g., roads) and general environmental studies. Increased sensor resolution and new kinds of sensors (especially in the microwave ranges) promise to make satellite imagery more generally useful, though it will not replace intermediate- and close-range sensing.

A variety of techniques included within remote sensing are used to study subsurface deposits, either minimizing or eliminating the need for excavation. Even now resistivity and magnetometry are proven field techniques that can provide data about subsurface deposits. Ground-penetrating radar is an emerging technology of considerable promise. In the future, improvements in image resolution and new kinds of sensors will increase the usefulness of remote-sensing techniques. Major near-term improvements are likely to be in the computer-assisted analysis of the information these techniques generate.

Photogrammetry (the use of metric properties of photographs and images) is well developed in other disciplines but is little used in archaeology. Anything that appears distinctly in an image can also be mapped three-dimensionally; in this way photogrammetry can be used to improve mapping accuracy in archaeology while greatly reducing the cost. The impact will be greatest with large sites, since with photogrammetry and remote sensing, they can be mapped and analyzed at only slightly greater cost than small sites. Close-range photogrammetry will replace the plans and profile drawings that now constitute the bulk of excavation records; photographs are a permanent record that can be analyzed and reanalyzed as archaeological knowledge grows.

Archaeology will also benefit from general advances in technology. Already we see electronic distance meters (EDMs) and laser transits replacing traditional surveying equipment, extending the range of ground-based surveying and mapping while improving accuracy. Labor cost is today a limiting factor in excavation, so if the economics are favorable, machines may do much of the routine archaeological "work" in the next century. Certainly much of the technology already exists; agricultural equipment even provides some prototypes (e.g., rock pickers for surface collecting).

Dating is the heart of much archaeological research, yet current methods of dating are based in other sciences, usually chemistry or physics. We will continue efforts to refine dating methods like accelerator radiocarbon dating and dendrochronology and to develop methods that span the whole period of human existence. Current dating methods have limitations. Radiocarbon dating of a wood or bone sample, for example, dates the death of a plant or animal — that is, when the sample became isolated from the atmospheric carbon reservoir. It does not date the deposit in which the wood or bone is found or the artifacts found with the sample. Thermoluminescent dating (TL) and obsidian hydration are two methods that may come into prominence by 2050. They date events that can be directly linked to archaeological events. TL dates the last time an object was heated; for instance, when a pot was fired. Obsidian hydration dates the creation of a new surface, such as the newly flaked edge of an obsidian tool, by the rate of water absorption. TL and hydration dating are already in use, but both require further development if they are to become more generally useful. The use of protein transformations — the decay of amino acids and collagen — for dating seems less promising than these other methods, at least for the near term.

By using a greater variety of methods, archaeologists will be able to include more kinds of artifacts in the development of absolute chronologies. New techniques will also reduce reliance on the use of typological dating. This is also crucial both to the further development of site-formation studies, where it is critical to date the artifacts and the enclosing sediments independently, and to the use of evolutionary theory in archaeology, since reliance on the presence of marker types of artifacts for dating overemphasizes historical connection (migration of peoples or diffusion of technologies) as the mechanism of change.

Developments in archaeological laboratory analysis will take the form of technology transfers from materials science, engineering, and the hard sciences. Advances in the analysis of materials already used by archaeologists are typically relegated to "specialist studies," where they can be regarded as optional. As a result, these advances are not integrated with the mainstream of archaeological interpretation. There must be dramatic changes in this conservative area. With better understanding of how materials behave in manufacture and use, we will be better able to distinguish between functional and stylistic variation. Many traits currently considered to be stylistic, such as the choice of ceramic tempers, may prove instead to be governed by technological and functional constraints.

All archaeologists are aware of the impact of inexpensive computing on

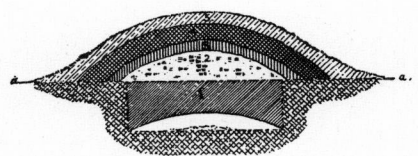

A simplistic sketch of a mound from the **Twelfth Annual Report of the Bureau of Ethnography** *reflects a naive approach to the archaeological record.*

archaeological analysis. No doubt computers will continue to shoulder an increasingly larger share of the repetitive and tedious elements of analysis. The new generation of scientific equipment is user friendly — one no longer needs to be a physicist to do perfectly competent elemental analysis. On the other hand, much of the current fascination with computing in archaeology (e.g., much of computer graphics) seems to be generated by the ready availability of a new toy rather than by any genuine archaeological utility. In large measure, the role of computing in archaeological analysis will not be defined until the character of archaeological analysis itself is better focused.

The broad scenario for archaeology in the twenty-first century I have outlined is but one path that archaeology may take. How likely is it that this, or some similar program, will be realized? Our humanistic tradition in archaeology and simple inertia, a "business as usual" attitude, are powerful barriers to scientific archaeology. Nonetheless, it is my guess that archaeology will adopt a scientific methodology, for two reasons.

Government and industry pour millions of dollars into cultural resource management, or "rescue archaeology," and federal funding supports many research excavations. This has already raised the level of accountability for archaeologists — not just among their academic peers but also to the public. We should, however, remember that all cultural values, including those currently placed on heritage and the past, are transitory. Can we assume that the public commitment to cultural heritage will prove lasting, especially if the twenty-first century brings more stringent economic conditions? Knowledge, even without immediate practical application or mass appeal, is easier to defend as the reason for preserving archaeological sites than the dated interpretations that are our current product. My suspicion is that most archaeologists are realistic enough to redirect archaeology, in spite of the major effort it will require, to a scientific methodology. Will this task be accomplished before public sympathy and funding for archaeology are withdrawn?

The second force acting in favor of scientific archaeology is the recognition by archaeologists and the general public that the archaeological record is a nonrenewable resource. Most kinds of archaeological investigation damage the record irrevocably, and decisions made today concerning what will or will not be recorded, preserved, or investigated will determine the content of the archaeological record of the twenty-first century. While a conservation ethic is not as prevalent in the profession as one might hope, recognition of the deleterious effects of tying archaeological management decisions to transitory academic fads and cultural values will lead many archaeologists to embrace the less value-bound justifications provided by scientific archaeology.

If archaeology continues along its humanistic course, I expect that it will be reduced to an arcane academic endeavor, following a trajectory not unlike philology in the past century. On the other hand, if it is successful in its century-old quest to become scientific, it promises to be a robust, exciting discipline. Archaeology can play a key role in the expansion of the historical sciences and in providing a new understanding of the world in which we live.

Whatever course archaeology takes, one thing is clear—the archaeology of the twenty-first century will bear little relation to contemporary practice.

Issues in Archaeology

In Topic 6 we approach the study of archaeology by focusing on some of the major questions that scholars are attempting to answer today. The first article looks at one of the liveliest debates in American archaeology: the question of when the New World was populated. No serious scholars doubt any longer that the Americas were populated by fully evolved human beings in hunting and food-gathering bands—probably migrating in pursuit of big game on the Siberian plains. They crossed over the Bering Strait land bridge connecting Siberia and Alaska some time during the last glacial period that marked the end of the Ice Age, and found themselves in a paradise rich in wild game and bountiful in plant life. They thrived, and their numbers grew rapidly as they migrated southward and eastward, seeking out the new and incredibly diverse environmental niches that met their needs and fit their fancies. Eventually they developed a spectacular variety of lifestyles that included advanced civilizations in the highlands and jungles of Mesoamerica, vital communities of salmon fishers on the Northwest Coast of North America, adobe cliff dwellers and complex canal builders in the American Southwest, dazzling mound builders in America's midwestern plains, advanced canal-building civilizations high in the Andes Mountains of Peru, and countless bands of semi-nomadic hunters and food gatherers from the Inuit of Alaska to the bison hunters of the Great Plains to the Yahgan of Tierra del Fuego in Argentina. The question vexing archaeologists is: *When* did the first bands cross the Bering Strait from Siberia to Alaska?

In "The First Americans: Who Were They and When did They Arrive?" Ben Patrusky is evenhanded in presenting the two main competing views. The older of the two, and still the more widely held in the United States, is that this epic migration was relatively recent—about twelve thousand years ago. Many sites have been found scattered across North America (and a few in South America, too) that date from around eleven thousand years ago and that feature, among the stone tools they exhibit, versions of the so-called Clovis point (named after a site at Clovis, New Mexico), a medium-sized, leaf-shaped projectile point with a hollow

groove in the base. In the view of many scholars, these projectile points were brought to the New World by Siberian migrants. Moreover, the rapid spread of this tool across the continent marks the rapid movement of the migrating groups, which encountered a fresh, virtually limitless, incredibly rich environment. (And, in the few centuries they perpetuated their culture, these *Clovis peoples* seem to have hunted into extinction many of the great mammals that lived there—from giant sloths to horses and elephants.)

But there are dissenters—increasing in number—who believe that human groups first crossed to America from Siberia much earlier, perhaps twenty-five to fifty thousand years ago. In the mountains of Peru, for instance, Richard MacNeish believes he has found pre-Clovis tools possibly twenty-five thousand years old. In 1988, a site in Brazil was dated at thirty-four thousand years old. MacNeish and others point to tantalizing bits and pieces of evidence indicating the presence of humans in the New World thousands of years before the Clovis culture emerged. For example, an analysis of American Indian languages seems to point to at least two, and possibly three, distinct migrations; and in 1984, an urban settlement was found in Chile, on the southernmost tip of South America, dating back about eleven thousand years. Looking at the evidence from the perspective of such findings, the Clovis horizon represents the diffusion of a new tool (not the migration of peoples) from one already established group to another. The Clovis point may have been invented in America, or it may have been brought here by a late-arriving, second-wave Siberian migration. Although the existence of pre-Clovis finds in the Americas remains controversial, we believe that eventually the latter view of the population of the New World will prove true. The data are here in Ben Patrusky's article for you to evaluate and use to decide for yourself.

The invention of agriculture was the first in a triple revolution that forever changed the lives of human beings around the world. Where and when was agriculture first invented? Until the 1980s, archaeologists believed the answer was clear. But recent discoveries have challenged many of our notions about the origin of agriculture. People living in widely scattered parts of the world—from southern Europe to western Egypt to the Nile Valley to Kenya, and also in Southeast Asia—may well have domesticated plants and animals as early as nineteen thousand years ago. That is eight thousand years before the beginnings of the great agricultural civilizations of Mesopotamia (modern Iraq). However, unlike developments in Mesopotamia, early domestication in these places did not lead quickly to the second and third great revolutions in human cultural evolution—the emergence of cities and the rise of civilizations.

In "The Origin of Agriculture," Charles B. Heiser discusses the events leading to the beginnings of plant and animal domestication in the Far East, the Middle East, and the Americas, and the profound consequences that grew out of this radical change in human lifestyle. A popular misconception is that agriculture was invented to relieve people of the unending drudgery and insecurities embodied in the hunting-and-food-gathering lifestyle. This is far from true. Research by Richard B. Lee, Marvin Harris, and others shows that agriculture requires more intensive and enduring labor than does hunting and food gathering (see the article by David E. K. Hunter, "Subsistence Strategies and the Organization of Social Life," in Topic 10). Interestingly enough, the enormous increase in available food surpluses that resulted from the mastery of agriculture never has been used to reduce the amount of energy or time expended on work; rather, it has been used again and again to enable even larger numbers of people to live crowded together into increasingly complex social groupings in increasingly unhealthy environments, that is, cities.

The emergence of agriculture, then, created the bedrock upon which was built the second great reorganization of human existence, the invention of the city. "How Were Cities Invented?" asks John Pfeiffer, and in doing so he also totals up the pros and cons of urban life. Most of us take cities for granted, but archaeology reveals how profoundly city dwelling has changed human existence in the last seven to eight thousand years. Thus, it cannot be denied that some of the most spectacular achievements in philosophy, mathematics, the natural sciences, the arts, and literature were rooted in the urban way of life. In fact, most refinements of crafts and arts were made by city dwellers. But on the other hand we must recognize that cities also created the conditions of terrible human filth and poverty by crowding together landless, unskilled, and often unemployed workers and their families. Garbage and waste disposal were (and continue to be) major public health problems for cities, and diseases were bred and spread by urban living conditions. Thus, the city, a hallmark of our own civilization, is a problematic development at best, and archaeology has much to tell us of its origins, development, possibilities, and failures.

The third great revolution in the cumulative sociocultural history of human civilization, beginning with the invention of agriculture and marked by the rise of cities, is the emergence of civilization.

Henry T. Wright, in "Rise of Civilizations: Mesopotamia to Mesoamerica," provides the final article for Topic 6. He reviews the kinds of evidence that have been amassed for the rise of civilization in each of five separate regions. For each geographical region Wright asks: "What kinds of evidence have we got to develop our understanding of events?" and then, "What further kinds of evidence would be helpful?" We think this is a most useful perspective from which to approach not only archaeology, but all anthropological research (indeed, all research whatsoever).

The First Americans: Who Were They and When Did They Arrive?

By Ben Patrusky

No serious archaeologist argues about the origins of the first human inhabitants of the Western Hemisphere or about how they arrived. These paleo-Indians strode—or drifted—in, from what is now Siberia across the Bering Strait, over a land bridge that joined the Old World to the New during the last great ice age. They came as big-game hunters on the trail of moving herds of giant elephants and other megafauna of the Pleistocene epoch. They were first occupants of Beringia—a continent-sized landmass linking Asia and North America—which lured them as it lured their game. Then shifting needs and opportunities propelled them farther east and south.

Not much of this is in question. But one big question remains: When did they come; how early were early humans in the New World? Since the early days of the 20th century, New World archaeologists have been debating the issue—often heatedly. Timetables abound. Robert L. Humphrey of George Washington University has dubbed the ongoing controversy "The Hollywood Complex, or my early man site is earlier than your early man site."

The heat of the debate doesn't surprise Dennis Stanford, director of paleo-Indian archaeology at the Smithsonian Institution. "People digging at the roots of America's ancestry tend to be highly messianic," he explains. "They've invested time, money, thought and often reputation. Sure they want their labors and finds to prove significant. Sometimes they're not very careful about interpreting their results."

The debate about humankind's dawning in the New World is far from settled. But in recent years highly trained archaeologists have begun to accumulate impressive bits of evidence that suggest migrations at a time much farther back than might have been accepted only a few years ago. Some human occupancy as much as 20,000 or 25,000 years ago is beginning to look, if not feasible, at

least arguable. Dates much older than that, however, while postulated, still strike more heat than light from among the disputants. At the present stage of knowledge and of dating technology, there is slim chance for the dispute over Western humankind's antiquity soon to be settled. But a critical look at the evidence and the inferences to be drawn from it can be highly suggestive.

Clovis and before

The pivotal point of the debate is on the order of 12,000 years ago—or 12,000 BP, for "before the present," in the parlance of the professionals. That represents the earliest totally accepted date for human appearance in the New World.

Evidence of human presence then is incontrovertible. It takes the form of a special kind of artifact: a man-made tool, a projectile point with a highly distinctive shape, a manufactured weapon for killing mammoths and other big game. The points are bifacially fluted; longitudinal flakes have been chipped from the base on both sides to form grooves. With fluting, the point could be attached to a wooden shaft for use as a spear or dart. These fluted points have been found at sites ranging from the Pacific coast to the Atlantic coast of North America and from Alaska to central Mexico. In the sites where carbon 14 dating is unequivocal, all the projectile points have been found to date within a very narrow window of time—11,500 to 11,000 BP.

Because the points were first found in abundance in a locale called Clovis in Blackwater Draw, New Mexico, the points have been designated Clovis points—and their manufacturers the Clovis Culture. The Clovis Culture is also often referred to by another name: the Llano Complex, for the Llano High Plains region of the Southwest. The designation embraces not just the fluted projectile points but the entire bone and

stone "tool kit" associated with them.

But were the bearers of the Clovis Culture the first inhabitants of the New World? Or were there earlier bands of migrant-hunters whose groping cultural evolution ultimately gave rise to the technologically advanced Clovis? That question is at the heart of the peopling of America debate.

That the Clovis people were the very first Americans is a position promulgated by Paul S. Martin of the University of Arizona. He has introduced the "overkill theory" to support his arguments. Martin contends that the Clovis people, already skilled big-game hunters, swept into the Americas from Alaska in a single, rapid migration about 12,000 years ago. There they encountered a hunter's paradise: a land teeming with mastodons and mammoths, sloths, giant cats, horses, camels and bison. The archaeological record shows that many of these species became extinct coincidentally with the advent of Clovis. Clovis, according to Martin, cut a rapacious swath through the hemisphere, exterminating these Ice Age mammals.

Other New World archaeologists contest the overkill hypothesis. In their view dramatic changes in climate and vegetation, in the wake of a significant glacial retreat, were the agents of extinction. More to the point, a number of these investigators are convinced that humans trod the soil of the New World far in advance of Clovis's distinctive appearance. Says Richard S. MacNeish, director of the Robert S. Peabody Foundation for Archeology: "There can be little doubt that man was here well before 12,000 years ago, as we have about 30 sites with more than 2,000 recognizable artifacts and with more than 60 radiocarbon determinations before 10,000 B.C.E. (Before the Common Era)." How much earlier than 12,000 years ago? MacNeish suggests that humans "may have first crossed the Bering Strait land bridge into the Western Hemisphere between 40,000 and 100,000 years ago."

Reprinted from MOSAIC, National Science Foundation, September/October 1980. The original title was "Pre-Clovis Man: Sampling the Evidence."

The pre-Llano vista

One of the most prominent figures in the controversy over New World habitation is anthropologist and geoscientist Vance Haynes, also of the University of Arizona. To Haynes, a self-styled "archaeological conservative" who has been stalking Clovis for more than two decades, has been delegated the *ad hoc* role of both arbiter and devil's advocate in the assessing and validating of evidence presumptive of prehistoric migrations into the New World. Haynes's judgment: "There is no one place where the evidence (for pre-Llano cultures) is so compelling that if you looked at it in a court of law you would want to be tried on the basis of that evidence."

The evidence to date for a pre-Llano presence in the New World is not yet "airtight," admits the Smithsonian's Dennis Stanford. "But some of what we do have looks really good and very compelling and can't be lightly dismissed."

Some of the key pieces of evidence of the existence of a pre-Llano people include:

• **Pikimachay Cave in Highland Peru,** where MacNeish has uncovered artifacts he insists date back as much as 21,000 to 25,000 years. "My excavations of Pikimachay Cave have proved to me that pre-10,000 B.C.E. and pre-20,000 B.C.E. remains of man do exist," he says unequivocally.

MacNeish discovered the cave in 1967. It is a huge rock shelter, 85 meters long and 25 meters deep, situated halfway up a hill stepped by ancient terraces. Meticulous excavation has revealed sequential strata of habitation, "a series of floors on which man had clearly lived," declares MacNeish. A roof-fall that occurred about 9,000 years ago securely sealed off the lower, earlier deposits from any

possible intrusion or artifact contamination from strata lying above and representing a later chronology.

Beneath this rocky lid lie seven strata, showing evidence of a number of occupations by man back as far as 25,000 years. Using carbon-14 dating, University of California at Los Angeles scientists assigned BP time slots of 19,660 ± 3,000; 16,050 ± 1,200; 14,700 ± 1,400, and 14,150 ± 180 to the upper four strata, respectively, though the lowest has not been so dated. The antiquity of the earliest dated level, MacNeish reports, is confirmed by an independent analysis by Isotopes, Inc., which reported an age for that stratum of 20,200 ± 1,000.

All told, says MacNeish, almost 300 "indisputable" artifacts were unearthed in association with more than 800 bones of sloths and other extinct Ice Age mammals. Perhaps the best evidence was turned up at the upper level, dated at 14,150 BP, which was found to contain 133 artifacts, including stone projectile points and scrapers. Many of the recovered artifacts are very crude, says MacNeish, and a far cry from the sophistication of Clovis, suggesting that they were the tools of unspecialized hunters and gatherers.

• **Valsequillo Basin, Puebla, Mexico,** where in the early 1960s investigators stumbled upon a trove of extinct-animal bones as well as some crude stone artifacts along a dry river bed. Subsequent stratum-by-stratum excavation turned up an ever receding chronology of hunters slaughtering Ice Age animals. At about 30 meters down, at a level dated by carbon-14 at 22,000 years, archaeologist Cynthia Irwin Williams found evidence of a mastodon dismemberment by ancient butchers.

• **Tlapacoya, Valley of Mexico, near Valsequillo,** where Mexican investigators Jose Lorenzo and Lorena Mirambell found bones in association with a shallow depression containing charcoal that yielded a carbon-14 date of 24,000 BP (give or take 4,000 years) and presumed to be the remains of an ancient hearth. Moreover, the investigators uncovered some obsidian artifacts, including a curved blade found buried under a large tree trunk, that gave the same 24,000 BP date.

• **Del Mar in Southern California.** A group of 11 human skeletons has been found along the California coast and dated by Jeffrey Bada of the University of California at San Diego, using a technique called amino acid racemization. It is based on the assumption that amino acids in protein undergo a configurational change—from the so-called *L* or left-handed sort to the *D* or right-handed kind—as bone fossilizes, and that this switching goes on at a measurable, clocklike rate until the sample reaches half-and-half equilibrium. The oldest date determined on a skull found at Del Mar gave a racemization number of 48,000 BP. Two other samples—dated at 23,000 and 17,150 BP—have been confirmed by radiocarbon dating on bone collagen performed by the University of California at Los Angeles' Rainer Berger.

• **Santa Rosa, California,** an island 25 miles off the coast of Santa Barbara, where Berger and Phillip Orr, curator of the Santa Barbara Museum, discovered a red burn area about three meters in diameter in association with stone tools and the bones of dwarf mammoths. The supposition: that the burn area actually had served as a hearth where paleo-Indians cooked the horse-sized mammoths as far back as 40,000 years ago. Carbon-14 dates derived from bits of charcoal found in the firepit suggest the age. According to Berger, during the late Pleistocene (100,000—10,000 years ago) Santa Rosa and three other nearby islands may have formed a single landmass that was joined to the mainland via a narrow neck of land across which foraging dwarf mammoths and their human predators could readily wander.

• **Meadowcroft Rockshelter, Pennsylvania.** On a sandstone outcrop 65 kilometers southwest of Pittsburgh, James M. Adovasio of the University of Pittsburgh has unearthed an assemblage of unifacial tools associated with radiocarbon ages of 13,250, 14,850 and 15,120 years. One especially significant find was a bifacial projectile point—"like a fluted point except that it has no fluting"—that dates earlier than the Clovis point and may be ancestral to it. (A detailed discussion of

Peruvian cave. Excavations of Pikimachay Cave in Peru offer evidence that humans were in the Western Hemisphere before 20,000 B.C.E.

Richard S. MacNeish, by permission

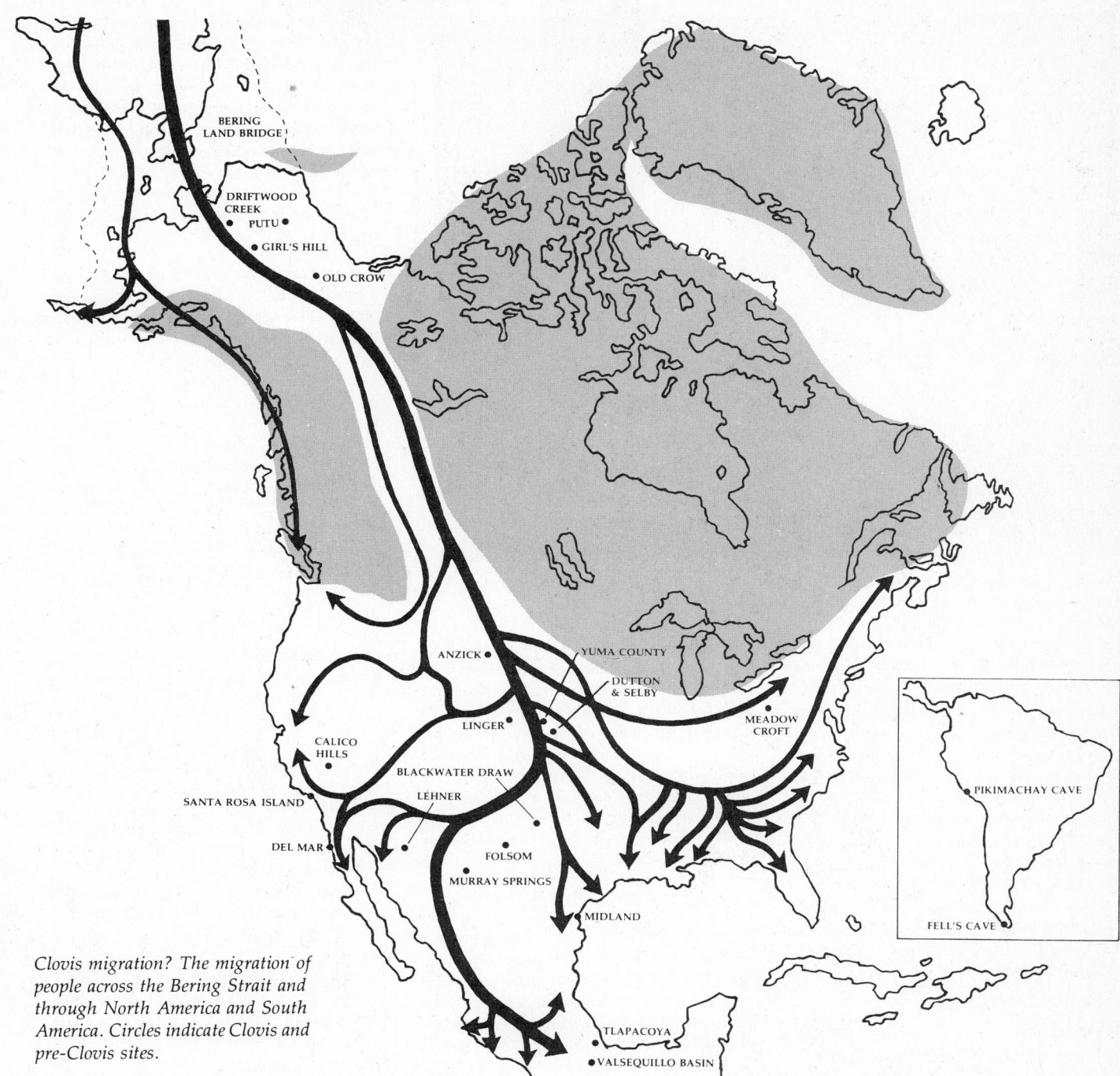

Clovis migration? The migration of people across the Bering Strait and through North America and South America. Circles indicate Clovis and pre-Clovis sites.

paleo-Indian sites in Pennsylvania and Virginia appeared in *Mosaic,* Volume 8, Number 2.)

• **The Selby and Dutton sites in eastern Colorado.** In 1975 pond-dredging crews on farms near Wray, Colorado, unearthed two Pleistocene fossil sites. Alerted to the discovery, a Smithsonian Institution archaeological team that happened to be working nearby raced to the scene. In subsequent (and as yet far from complete) excavations, under the direction of Dennis Stanford, the team initially discovered fluted projectile points and other manifestations of Clovis. Digging deeper, they found evidence of the presence of earlier cultures that included what are called bone expediency tools. These are manufactured by producing a spiral fracture in bone and using the sharp edges for butchering or hide-working. Bone flakes presumably the waste or debitage from tool production, and bone, apparently processed for the removal of marrow, were also found. The tools, made from the bones of Ice Age horse, bison, mammoth and camel, were found in "chronologically secure" layers extending back a possible 20,000 years. What makes the site especially exciting, according to Robert L. Humphrey, is that it "reveals the only evidence to date of an archaeological

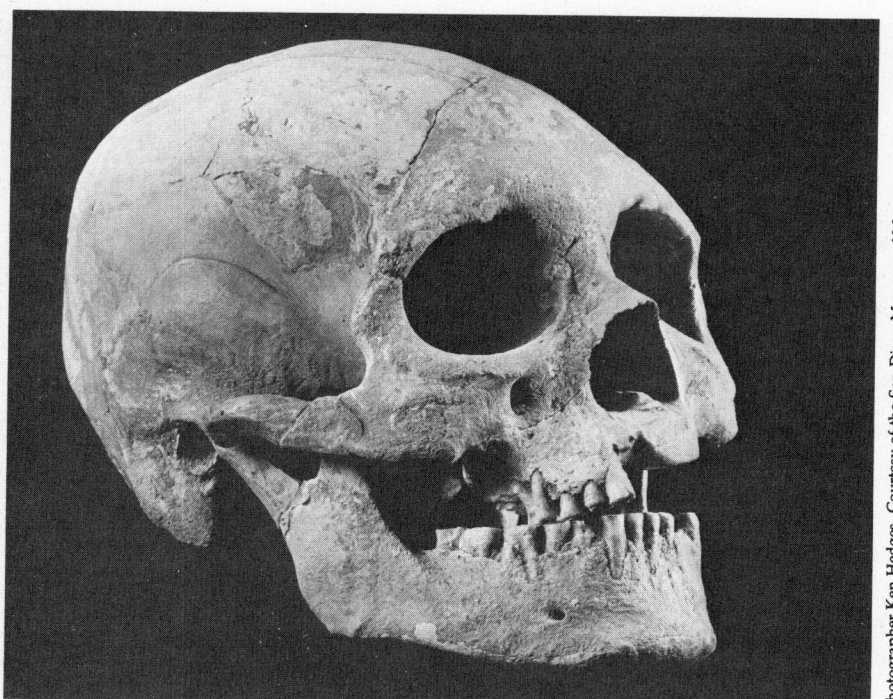

Photographer Ken Hedges, Courtesy of the San Diego Museum of Man.

Ancestral skull? This paleo-Indian skull was dated at nearly 50,000 years old through a still-controversial amino-acid dating process developed by Jeffrey L. Bada.

culture stratigraphically *in situ* below a level containing Clovis fluted points and other manifestations of the Llano Complex."

• **Old Crow Basin, Yukon Territory,** where in 1966 was discovered a caribou leg bone that had clearly been worked by human hands to produce a tool called a flesher—a backscratcher-like implement used to scrape animal hides. William Irving of the University of Toronto and Richard Morlan of the National Museum of Man, in Ottawa, who now direct major archaeological research projects in the basin, established a carbon-14 date for the flesher of 27,000 BP. Since then, other worked-bone specimens have been found and dated as far back as 41,000 years.

Not foolproof

What says Clovis specialist Haynes to all this? "Tantalizing but not foolproof. . . .I am a skeptic. I remain a skeptic. I have yet to see *unequivocal* evidence of pre-Clovis. Each (site) has some kind of uncertainty connected with it." On his list of "uncertainties," Haynes includes:

• **Skepticism about radiocarbon dates.** Samples may become contaminated by groundwater, he says, and throw the true carbon-14 date off accordingly. Case in point: the Meadowcroft site. It is possible, he says, that rainwater could have brought in dissolved

carbon from nearby coal deposits, thus disturbing the precision of the radiocarbon date. Haynes isn't saying that is what happened. "It's just that we can't be sure it didn't happen." Haynes also expresses doubts about "one of the best pieces of evidence around for a pre-Clovis presence in the New World," the Old Crow flesher. "There's no way to say for sure that the bone was not pulled out of the ground and worked over at a much later date," he says.

• **Suspicion about amino acid racemization.** In a thorough review of this dating technique, David von Endt, a research chemist at the Smithsonian Institution, writing in a monograph on pre-Llano cultures published in 1979 by the Anthropological Society of Washington, D.C., concludes: "I view no projected amino acid date as reliable." Reason: The rate of turnover from *L*- to *D*-form amino acids depends on a mix of complicated factors that have yet to be fully reckoned into the racemization clock.

• **Uncertain primary or cultural context.** "The primary requirement," says Haynes, "is. . .an assemblage of artifacts that are clearly the work of man. Next, this evidence must lie *in situ* within undisturbed geological deposits. . . .Lastly, the minimum age of the site must be demonstrable by primary association with fossils of known age or

with material suitable for reliable isotopic dating. These requirements have now been met repeatedly for the late paleo-Indian period (Clovis) but they have not yet been met repeatedly for earlier periods." Example: the "questionable" primary context of the Santa Rosa firepit. Haynes wonders whether this so-called hearth may not actually be the product of a natural brush fire—not an uncommon phenomenon on this chaparral-dense island.

• **Artifact versus geofact, or when is a tool a tool?** Haynes talks about a "bandwagon effect, where some archaeologists see artifacts everywhere they look." In many cases, he says, the artifacts are nothing more than geofacts or ecofacts, pseudotools produced by agents other than human. "I think if we were to dig anywhere there are Pleistocene, coarse-grained sediments or bones," says Haynes, "(we) would find something that could be interpreted as artifact. In other words, there is a sort of 'background noise' in the buried record of things that can be taken as artifacts." Case in point: Calico Hills in the Mojave Desert, near Yermo, California, where in 1968 archaeologists spotted what they proposed to be crude, very ancient flint artifacts in a massive deposit of alluvial gravels of Pleistocene age. The investigators contend that some of the stone specimens show flaking marks that could have resulted only from human intervention. But Haynes, who has examined the site and specimens on six different occasions, reads the "evidence" another way. As he puts it: "Evidence for artifacts remains uncompelling. . .(and) a natural origin cannot be precluded. In fact, normal natural processes are adequate to explain the origin of all the phenomena observed. Even the best specimens could have been chipped and flaked naturally, especially in view of the fact that each 'artifact' has been selected from literally hundreds of thousands of individual pieces of chert." Similarly, two criteria seem to distinguish bone artifacts: evidence of a spiral fracture (a fundamental step in tool production or marrow processing) and of polishing (indicative of tool use). But other forces, agents other than man, can break or polish bone—e.g., trampling and gnawing by other animals.

• **Absence of stone artifacts.** Thus far Old Crow and the Selby/Dutton sites (at strata below Clovis) have yielded only bone artifacts. No stone tools are in evidence and, according to Haynes, "you can't produce flake scars by hitting bone against bone. Further, there's little to support the validity of an all-bone culture. If there were stone tools at Dutton or Old Crow, where are they?'' Haynes remains skeptical about the seven tiny stone ''impact flakes'' suggestive of human origin turned up by Stanford's team at Dutton and described as tailings produced as a result of impact from a chopping tool.

Counterarguments

Needless to say, Haynes's arguments breed counterarguments among those convinced of a significant pre-Llano presence. Old Crow archaeologist William Irving, for example, suggests that stone tools may not be all that essential to the support of human life. In fact, he contends, bones that could have performed all the necessary tasks of hunting, piercing, butchering, skinning and perforating have been recovered from deposits at Old Crow and elsewhere. Two years ago, Dennis Stanford gave a dramatic demonstration of bone's versatility. Using only bone tools, Stanford showed how it was possible to butcher and process the remains of an elephant, operating on one that had died of natural causes at a Boston zoo.

As for the artifact versus geofact issue, Stanford readily concedes that archaeologists may be led astray by wishful thinking— ''seeing what they want to see.'' But, he points out, with bone, for instance, there are criteria to help the investigator with a trained eye to distinguish between tool and pseudo-tool. For example: With tools, only the ends—the working parts—tend to become polished and worn. This discriminatory polishing doesn't often happen in nature, unless only the ends have been gnawed. But then there would generally be tooth marks to help make the distinction.

Also, bones that exhibit spiral fracture by other-than-human cause are often those broken after the bone had dried or as a result of the animal's falling or twisting its leg. In both cases these bones are not likely to exhibit impact depressions suggestive of human workmanship. Moreover, says Stanford, at the Selby and Dutton sites most of the bone-artifact specimens were broken the same way; they show single and multiple points of impact located in the same area of the bone. ''These suggest a pattern that cannot be attributed to the random breakage patterns expected if the bones were either broken or polished due to natural conditions,'' he says.

In an effort to eliminate all doubt about bone-artifact authenticity, Stanford has been overseeing a number of experimental studies aimed at producing hard, quantifiable data on bone fracturing, modification and use. From his elephant-butchering trials, for instance, he has developed information regarding tool-wear patterns. Another study

Clovis tools. These Clovis fluted points are from the Naco Mammoth site in Arizona, contemporary with the Clovis site.

Courtesy of the Robert S. Peabody Foundation

has Gary Haynes, a doctoral student, feeding buffalo and horse bones to bears in the National Zoological Park in Washington, D.C., to see just how the animals break and gnaw bones. Haynes is also observing how the bones of wood bison, newly killed by wild wolves in Canada, are altered by the natural environment. In an applied offshoot, Stanford is consulting with veterinarians who are analyzing bone breaks in race horses. Are the breaks natural, or did someone break a horse's leg intentionally? The ability to discriminate has relevance for insurance companies as well as archaeologists. Stanford is hopeful that he will soon get permission to put elephant bones around a pond at the National Zoo's Conservation and Research Center near Front Royal, Virginia, to see if and how other free-to-roam animals treat the specimens.

Meanwhile, at Santa Rosa Island, museum curator Phillip Orr has built model pit barbecues to help determine whether the red-char area he and Rainer Berger discovered actually served the earliest immigrants as a hearth or whether, in fact, it was the result of a natural brush fire. His experiments produced the same kind of deep-soil burning (to a depth of about 80 centimeters) as seen in the purported pre-Llano firepit, but different from the burn pattern of a natural chaparral fire.

Whither Clovis

When Haynes, eminently known for his ''insistence on methodological exactitude,'' drops his devil's-advocate mask, he readily professes a belief in a human presence that

may far antedate Clovis, a presence he believes will become demonstrable and unquestionable in time. In fact, he now seems near-convinced about the validity of MacNeish's Pikimachay Cave finds—specifically those from the 14,150 BP level. The Valsequillo deposits, dating from 9,000 to 21,000 years ago, also enthrall him (although the picture there remains clouded by another kind of uncertainty: unsubstantiated charges that workmen may have deliberately planted some of the would-be artifacts).

But far from quashing the debate, the strong indications of a pre-Llano presence have introduced a major new wrinkle to the controversy, having to do with the origins of the Clovis Culture. Is it, as Martin, Vance Haynes and others contend, an import by a technologically advanced people who brought their Upper Paleolithic wisdom with them from Siberia? Or is it, as MacNeish, Stanford and other pre-Llano advocates maintain, a homegrown product—an evolutionary outgrowth of already-in-place, pre-Clovis cultures? Asked another way: Is the Clovis point, that superior paleo-Indian invention that allowed Llano hunters to take full advantage of the megafauna-rich Pleistocene environment of the New World, a candidate for the first truly American patent?

In Haynes's view, even if pre-Llano hunting cultures entered the Americas more than 30,000 years ago, they did not develop into technologically skilled artisans anywhere near the caliber of Clovis. As he sees it, Clovis represents an entirely independent migratory swarm, a late-glacial sweep distinct from earlier, ''inconclusive'' movements into the

New World. "It now appears," says Haynes, "that the *main* peopling of the New World took place during deglaciation, when something akin to a population explosion occurred between 11,000 and 11,500 years ago by mammoth hunters entering from Alaska and finding abundant and untapped resources."

Haynes offers up this scenario: During the peak of the most recent glacial epoch—anywhere from 14,000 to 20,000 years ago, he says—a large portion of the earth's ocean water was stored in Northern Hemisphere ice sheets, causing the sea level to drop by scores of meters. What emerged was the 1,600-kilometer-wide Bering land platform, which made Alaska as much a part of the Asian continent as the North American and which allowed for easy migration from Old World to New.

The bridge, however, was not a thoroughfare from the Old world to the *whole* of the New; two great icecaps—the Cordilleran on the west, and the Laurentide on the east—covered much of Canada and much of the United States. Joining as they did at the foot of the Canadian Rockies, the giant glaciers created an ice barrier, a wall to southerly migration.

The hunters remained mired in an Alaskan cul-de-sac until about 12,000 years ago, when a period of marked glacial retreat opened a north-south corridor between the two icecaps. The progenitors of Clovis, confined until then in central Alaska, swept south in pursuit of the mammoth and other quarry. Once through, they dispersed rapidly across all of North America and into Mexico. All Clovis dates bear this out; from east to west, north to south, the Clovis artifacts fall within that 11,000-11,500 BP slot. Nor did expansion—or technological innovation—cease. For the Clovis point gave rise to an even sleeker, more advanced projectile point, dubbed the Folsom point, after Folsom, New Mexico, where a specimen was first uncovered in association with the skeletons of extinct bison. Similar fishtail stone points have been found as far as the southernmost tip of South America—Fell's Cave in Tierra del Fuego—and dated at about 10,000 BP.

Pleistocene extinctions

The transition from the use of Clovis to Folsom points approximately 11,000 years ago coincides with the extinction of Pleistocene mammoths, horses, camels and several other varieties of megafauna—which prompted Haynes's colleague, Paul Martin, to formulate the "overkill theory," ascribing extinction to the Llano influx and insisting

that they were the first inhabitants of the Americas.

Proponents of the idea of a substantial pre-Llano presence take issue with these speculations. For one, they assail the proposition that megafauna extermination stemmed directly from an invasion of Clovis. More to blame, they say, were drastic changes in climate. With deglaciation, the desert moved north, wiping out huge areas of grassland once used for foraging. They cite the work of Russell Graham of the Illinois State Museum who, having recently completed a comprehensive examination of Pleistocene fauna, concludes: "Man's pernicious effect on the modern environment is not necessarily indicative of his impact on ancient environments. . . . Undoubtedly man's predation had an effect on the megafauna, but climatic changes are the best explanation for Pleistocene extinction." Opponents of "overkill" also wonder how it is that one of the most heavily hunted of the species, a variety of bison, is still with us, while hundreds of other animal species that Clovis and Folsom did not hunt perished. Says Dennis Stanford: "Throughout life's entire history animals have gone extinct—in most cases without any help from man."

Pre-Llano proponents also have trouble accepting the presumption of Clovis's lightning-like sweep through the hemisphere. Says Stanford: "I find it impossible to accept this idea of rapid migration. Primitive cultures tend to be conservative, hunters who explore, retreat, explore, retreat. As they move from environment to environment, they must learn to adapt, and that doesn't happen overnight." MacNeish has similar reservations: "A group of primitive people traveling into completely unknown territory would have frequently taken the wrong direction, and the group would have always been saddled with household equipment and baggage, babies, pregnant women and hobbling elders."

MacNeish proposes yet another sort of paleo-Indian-advance theory—small-group filtering or, more colloquially, the "hurry-up-and-wait" process: A band of migrants might be especially adapted for subsistence in broad ecological zones, he says, "and within these zones they would be able to move rapidly, but movement from one zone to the other would require that they build up a whole new subsistence complex; that would take considerable time. The hypothesis that Clovis and Folsom moved through dozens of radically different environmental zones from the Bering Strait to Tierra del Fuego in a thousand years thus seems unreasonable."

As such, the pre-Llano advocates suggest that Clovis, with his advanced tool kit,

developed from an indigenous population in the Americas before 11,500 years ago. "It wasn't the people that swept through America," says Stanford, "but the (technology) that diffused rapidly through already existent populations—much as the idea of tobacco use traveled from the United States through Europe to the Eskimos all in a matter of a few years."

The Siberian connection

But if paleo-Indians did indeed poke their way into the Americas long before the emergence of the Clovis Culture, who were these migrants and how did they get here, considering that a severe ice age was upon the land? Stanford: "Soviet archaeologists have found evidence that man inhabited Siberia certainly 35,000 years ago and perhaps as early as 70,000 years ago. The discovery of early occupations of Siberia greatly increases the time available for man to come across the Bering land bridge."

Moreover, he says, there is now reason to belive that the ice-free corridor from Alaska to North America was open for movement south for much longer periods than previously supposed. "In fact," says Stanford, "it may have been closed for only a short time during the whole (Ice Age) period. So it would have been possible for early hunters. . .to have entered North America long before 12,000 years ago and to have moved southward, continuing to exploit grassland environments." Further, he says, there is now even a slim possibility that an "alternative route" to the interior corridor may have been available—an ocean-side roadway that trailed down along the emerged Pacific coast.

Haynes has strong objections to this idea of a coastal route. "Even if there were such a route between the glacial ice and the ocean," he says, "it would have been an incredibly treacherous environment to negotiate. Under the prevailing circumstances it's hard to imagine people moving down the coast even in boats."

By the same token, Haynes has no problem in living with the notion of Clovis's rapid migration. As he explains: "The phenomenal dispersal of Clovis sites is more compatible with a distinct migration, related to a relatively rapid, natural event—the separation of the ice sheets to form a trans-Canadian passage—than with a sudden outgrowth from meager, indigenous cultures after 12,000 years of sluggish development for which a continuity has yet to be demonstrated."

Native technology

And how does Haynes respond to the contention that Clovis's technological know-how was born in the Americas, a product of progress in home-grown artisanship and not an import? "I do not see anything that is on a developmental sequence leading to Clovis," he says. "What you see is technology akin to Eurasia, to mammoth hunters of the Old World." He sees likenesses in the tool kits of Clovis and Old World hunters, including bifacial stone scrapers, burins (chisel-like implements), flakeknives, a bone technology of bevel-based, cylindrical points and foreshafts, shaft wrenches and the use of red ocher with burials. "The similarities are unmistakable," he says, "and to invoke independent development of all these traits in the New World from a population base for which there is only tenuous evidence does not seem reasonable as does an origin from the Siberian Paleolithic."

Conpicuously absent from the Old World tool kit, however, is the centerpiece of the Clovis Culture: the fluted projectile point. This absence is probably the key piece of evidence against those who propose an Old World origin and rapid dispersal for Clovis. Haynes, in response, explains that the development of fluted, bifacial projectile points could have taken place in Alaska or along the ice-free corridor between 14,000 and 12,000 years ago. But if so, goes the counterargument, why is there no good

evidence of Clovis points in this initial New World dwelling place as is the case elsewhere in the hemisphere?

The fact is, a few fluted points *have* been found in the Far North in recent years. However, one Alaskan find, said to date from the post-Clovis period, about 9,000 years ago, is held up as evidence that Clovis developed out of an already-extant American paleo-Indian culture, and that this new technology traveled not from north to south but from south to north, representing a cultural backwash. But two other fluted points, from the Putu site in the Brooks Range, have been related to a charcoal date of 11,500 years ago. "If this date is valid," says Haynes, "it makes at least two Alaskan fluted points as old as the oldest fluted points from interior North America."

Ultimately, settlement of the controversy over the early peopling of America will likely come only with the discovery of new archaeological sites. If, for the sake of argument, a site with a Clovis point were to be found in Central America, bearing a date beyond 14,000 years ago, that would all but demolish the Clovis fast-migration theory. One the other hand, one in Alaska more than 14,000 years old would help support it. But when and where new sites will turn up

remains unpredictable. "Most early man sites, probably 99 percent of them, tend to be destroyed by climate almost immediately or by subsequent geologic processes," says Stanford. "When we find one, we're usually dealing with a geological freak."

On balance then: The evidence, if not altogether conclusive, certainly strongly suggests that the New World was visited and settled by migrant hunting bands from the Old World in the shadowy recesses of time back far beyond 12,000 years ago. But it remains to be determined whether the Llano Complex developed from a local, as-yet-undiscovered, indigenous progenitor or whether it originated in the Old World and spread by way of rapid dispersal. At the moment, both positions seem equally defensible. Perhaps the wisest counsel for now is for New World archaeologists to wait and see—to postpone final judgment until new, clarifying evidence comes to light. In Haynes's words: "I think that if pre-Clovis man was really here, good evidence will be found. The important thing is not to rush into it. . . . What we are actually looking for is what really happened, not what we think happened."

The Origin of Agriculture

By Charles B. Heiser, Jr.

In the sweat of thy face thou shalt eat bread.

Genesis 3:19

People have been on earth for some two million years. Except for a minute fraction of that time, they have been hunters of animals and gatherers of plants, strictly dependent upon nature for their food. They must, at many times during their long history as hunter-gatherers, have enjoyed full stomachs, when vegetable foods were abundant or ample game was available. Early humans certainly must have experimented with nearly all of the plant resources, thus becoming experts on which ones were good to eat. They became excellent hunters and fishermen. Contrary to earlier opinion, recent studies suggest that they didn't always have to search continually just to find enough to eat and, at times, must have had considerable leisure.

There undoubtedly were times and places, however, in which people did have to spend most of their waking hours searching for food, and hunger probably was common throughout much of the preagricultural period. Certainly there could never have been much of an opportunity for large populations to have built up, even among the successful hunter-gatherers. People probably lived in small groups, for with few exceptions a given area would provide enough food for only a few. Disease and malnutrition probably contributed to keeping populations small, and it is likely that there were also some sorts of intentional population control, such as infanticide.

Then, about 10,000 years ago, food-producing habits began to change, and in the course of time our ancestors became food producers rather than hunter-gatherers. At first they had to supplement the food they produced with food they obtained by hunting and gathering, but gradually they became less dependent on wild food sources as their domesticated plants and animals were increased in number and improved. The cultivation of plants and the keeping of animals probably required no less effort than did hunting and gathering, but in time they gave a more dependable source of food. Having a dependable food source made it possible for larger numbers of people to live together. More mouths to feed were no longer disastrous, but rather were advantageous, for with more bodies to till and reap, food could be produced more efficiently. Although some urban centers may have developed before agriculture, food production was probably the chief stimulus for the growth of villages and eventually of cities, and with the latter came civilization.

When food production became more efficient, there was time to develop the arts and sciences. Some hunter-gathers, as was already pointed out, must have had considerable leisure, but they never made any notable advances toward civilization. An important difference between hunter-gatherers and farmers is that the former are usually nomadic whereas the latter are sedentary. But even those preagricultural people, such as certain fisherman, who had fairly stationary living sites did not develop in civilizing ways comparable to those of farmers. Agriculture probably required a far greater discipline than did any form of food collecting. Seeds had to be planted at certain seasons, some protection had to be given to the growing plants and animals, harvests had to be reaped, stored, and divided. Thus, we might argue that it was neither leisure time nor a sendentary existence but the more rigorous demands associated with an agricultural way of life that led to great cultural changes. It has been suggested, for example, that writing may have come into existence because records were needed by agricultural administrators. Plants and animals were being changed to suit needs; living in a new relation with plants and animals was, in turn, changing the way of life.

In recent years archaeological work has greatly increased our knowledge of the beginnings of agriculture, and without doubt future archaeological work will add a great deal more information. In contrast to previous generations of archaeologists who were mostly concerned with spectacular finds—tombs, and temples, the contents of which would make showy museum exhibits—recent archaeologists have taken a greater interest in how people lived, what they ate, and how they managed their environment. A few charred seeds or broken bones may appear rather insignificant in a museum, but they can reveal a great deal about early human activities. As a result of recent work in archaeology, done in cooperation with scientists from many other fields, we are beginning to understand the ecology of prehistoric people in many different parts of the world.

Our knowledge of what humans ate and did thousands of years ago comes from the remains of plants and animals recovered from archaeological excavations. Unlike many tools, which were made of stone and are indestructible, foods are perishable and are preserved only where conditions are ideal. The best sites are in dry regions, often in caves, and from such sites we obtain remains to use in the reconstruction of our ancestors' diet. Other human artifacts, such as flint sickles and stone querns, or grinding wheels, may also provide clues about diet, but they leave us to speculate about what plants were being harvested and prepared, and whether these were wild or cultivated. Obviously, the record of what prehistoric people ate is very incomplete, and for many areas of the earth, significant remains have yet to be found.

Drawings of animals, particularly from the later prehistoric periods, have come down to us and sometimes (but not always, by any means) can be fairly readily identified, but it is animal bones, or even fragments of them, that provide the best clues about the animals that were closely connected with people. An expert zoologist can identify species from bones, but it is not always possible to say whether remains are from domestic or wild animals.

Plant remains comprise a variety of forms. Most are seeds or fruits, but other parts, such as flower bracts, stalks, and leaves are sometimes found. A few remarkably well-preserved seeds are recovered, looking as if they had been harvested only a year before, but most seeds are charred and broken. A skilled botanist can identify such plant remains, and it can often be determined if they are from domesticated or wild plants.

Another source of information about the ancient diet is coprolites—fossil feces. By suitable preparation they can be restored to an almost fresh condition (sometimes, it is said, including the odor). Whole seeds have been found in coprolites, but most of the food material is highly fragmented and requires lengthy, painstaking analysis for identification. Such analysis is highly significant because it tells us what was actually eaten, in what combinations, and whether it was cooked or raw.

Unfortunately, material collected at an archaeological dig is sometimes not accurately identified, as has been shown for some of the early archaeological reports from Peru. Fortunately, however, the material recovered from archaeological sites is usually preserved in museums, and future investigators can examine the material to verify or correct identifications.

With the development of radiocarbon methods of dating it became possible to date, fairly accurately, the beginnings of plant cultivation. Sometimes radiocarbon dates, for one reason or another, may be open to suspicion, but when different materials from the same site are analyzed and several dates agree, we have fair assurance that they are correct within a few hundred years.

The evidence that has accumulated over the past several years indicates that agriculture probably had its origins in the Near East*—although not necessarily, as earlier supposed, in the fertile river valleys of Mesopotamia (which were to be important centers of early civilization), but more likely in the semiarid mountainous areas nearby. Dates determined for flint sickles and grinding stones discovered in these areas indicate that before 8000 BC humans had likely become collectors of wild grain, and there is evidence that a thousand or so years later they were actually cultivating grains and keeping domesticated animals. Several sites are now known in the Near East (see Figure 1) that give evidence of early agriculture. One of the first sites to give such evidence was at Jarmo, in Iraq, where investigations were conducted under the direction of R. J. Braidwood. In deposits dated at 6750 BC, seeds of wheat and barley and bones of goats were found. Other evidence of cultivation, dating from approximately the same time, has been found at several other sites in the Near East. Since the plants in these sites apparently represent cultivated species, we must suppose that there was an earlier period of their incipient domestication, which may have lasted for a few hundred years or more. How long it takes a plant to become fully domesticated cannot be answered precisely and it probably varies considerably from species to species. In deposits accumulated after 6500 BC we find evidence of other plants being cultivated in the Near East and Greece, and bones of various domesticated animals become more abundant.

Other centers of agriculture developed in the Old World. Whether these developments were stimulated by knowledge of agriculture in the Near East or

---

*The *Near East* (see map, Figure 1) is the term used by archaeologists to refer to the countries of southwest Asia. The term *Middle East*, widely used in the news today, includes the Near East.

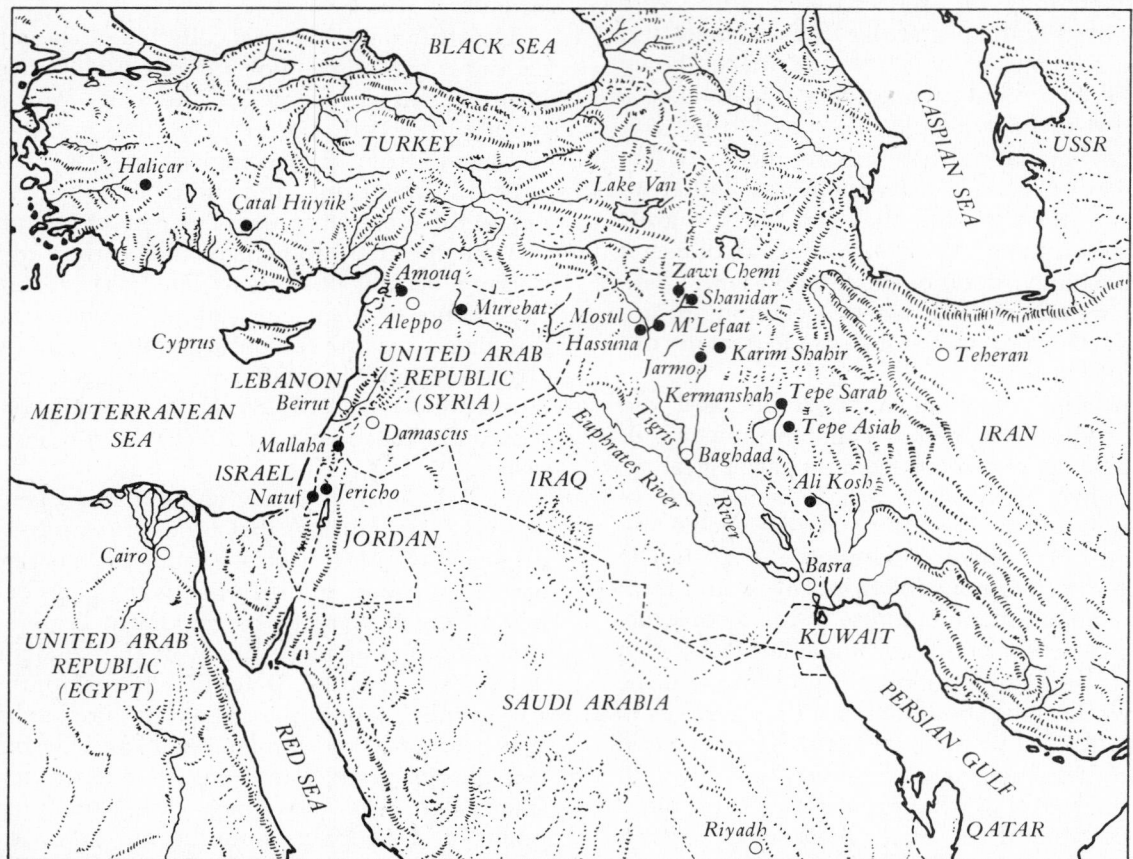

Figure 1   Selected archaeological sites that show evidence of early agriculture in the Near East (solid dots).

whether they were independent developments is not certain, but the fact that some of them were based on completely different plants from those of the Near East might support the latter view. For a long time southeastern Asia had been considered an ancient center for domesticated plants, but until recently there was no archaeological support for this view; this is not wholly unexpected, since the climate for the most part in that area of the world is hardly conducive to preservation of food remains. In 1969, however, a report was published of an assemblage of plants from Thailand, including possibly a pea and a bean, dated at 7000 BC. As it is not definitely clear whether the plants recovered represented wild or cultivated species, we cannot yet say that agriculture was practiced as early here as it was in the Near East. We do not yet know when rice, which was to become the basic food plant of southeastern Asia, was first brought under cultivation, but it was probably considerably later than the cereals of the Near East.

In the New World, agriculture began a few thousand years later than in the Near East and had its origins in Mexico and Peru. Through a series of ex-

cavations directed by R. S. MacNeish, we now have a remarkable sequence of plants giving evidence of the period of incipient domestication in Mexico. Some indication of the earliest cultivated plants is found in the mesquite-desert regions of southwestern Tamaulipas, with gourds, squashes, beans, and chili peppers being found at levels dated at between 7000 and 5500 BC.

Following investigations at Tamaulipas, MacNeish made deliberate efforts to search for evidence of the domestication of maize, which eventually became the most important plant in the Americas. A group of caves in the arid highlands near Tehuacan in south central Mexico showed promise, and a series of excavations was begun in 1961. The results give us the best picture yet of the transitional stages leading to full-scale agriculture. Humans were probably in the Tehuacan area by 10,000 BC and for several millennia they depended on wild food sources, both plant and animal. Gradually more and more plants were cultivated, some perhaps having been domesticated at this site, others introduced from other regions. The first suggestion of cultivated plants occurs in material dated at about 5000 BC, with maize, squash, chili pepper, avocado, and amaranth being found. These plants were definitely cultivated during the next period (4900–3500 BC), together with various fruits and beans toward the end of the period. During the next thousand years other plants were added, including cotton and two new kinds of beans. The dog, which is known from historic records to have been an important food item in Mexico, is first associated with humans in the archaeological record at this time. At about the beginning of the Christian era, the inhabitants of Tehuacan had also acquired the turkey. From remains of the same period there are reports of some other plants: guava, pineapple, and peanut. The presence of these plants would be of particular interest, for the peanut is definitely South American in origin and the pineapple and guava perhaps are also, which would suggest that the peoples of this area had contact with South America at this time. None of these plants has been found in any other archaeological sites in Mexico to date. A study of historical records of both peanuts and pineapple would suggest that they arrived in Mexico recently, perhaps after the coming of the Spanish.

Another early development of agriculture in the Americas occurred in Peru, perhaps even earlier than in Mexico. Two kinds of cultivated beans and a chili pepper, dated at around 6000 BC or earlier, have been recovered in a highland valley at Callejon de Huaylas in north central Peru. Previous to this discovery, archaeological plant material had been found in dry coastal sites, such as Huaca Prieta in northern Peru. Gourds, squashes, cotton, lima beans, and chili peppers are among the first plants cultivated on the coast; present evidence indicates that agriculture developed here about 2000 years later than in the highlands.

At present it is difficult to say whether agriculture in the Americas appeared first in Peru or Mexico. The fact that many of the same plants were cultivated in the two areas might suggest that agriculture spread from one of the areas to the other, but the chile peppers and the squashes of the two regions belong to different species, and it seems possible that the common bean was domesticated independently in Mexico and Peru. Thus, although the possibility remains that agriculture, or at least the idea of growing plants, diffused from one area to the other, it is just as likely that agriculture arose independently in Mexico and Peru. That there was diffusion between the two areas at a later time is clear because maize, which almost certainly had its origin in Mexico, appears in Peru by 2500–3000 BC and, as already mentioned, certain South American plants may have appeared in Mexico in pre-Columbian times.

From the foregoing account it can be seen that agriculture arose in widely separated parts of the earth, probably quite independently from place to place. But agriculture begin in the Old World more than a thousand years earlier than it did in the New—could the idea of agriculture have come to the New World from the Old? The New World was peopled by immigration across the Bering Strait long before agriculture was known, and if there were subsequent crossings at this place, it was by hunters rather than agriculturists. Thus, we would have to postulate a long ocean voyage at a very early date to account for agricultural knowledge being brought to the New World. Some anthropologists have postulated that there were such voyages in prehistoric times, but much later than the time at which agriculture was established in Mexico. Therefore, it seems highly unlikely that agriculture had but a single origin. It is, in fact, likely that it had several origins in both the Old and the New World, although some people still believe that it was invented only once.

An examination of the list of food plants from all the early sites in both the New and the Old World reveals that all of the plants were propagated by seed. A large number of present-day food plants, including such important ones as the white and the sweet potato, manioc, yams, bananas, and sugar cane are pro-

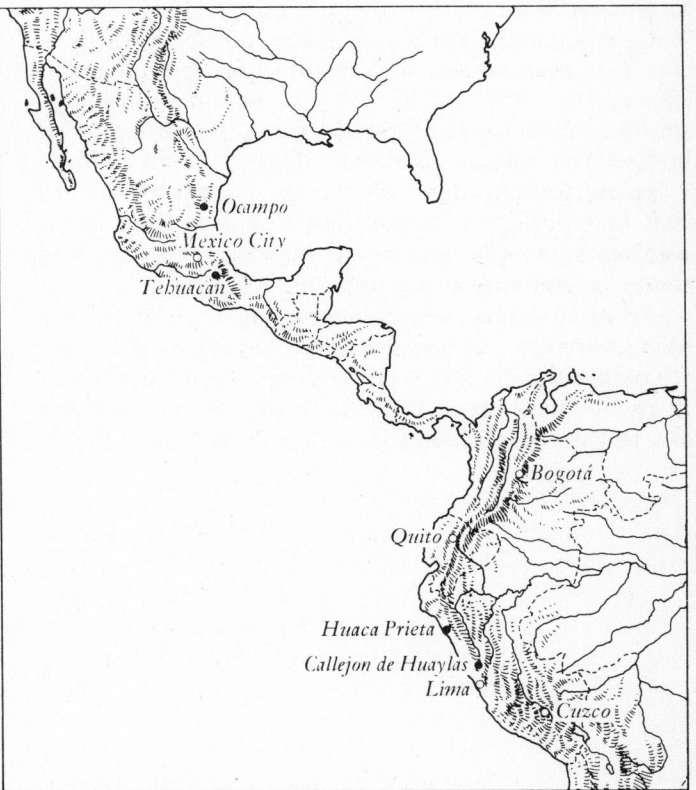

Figure 2 Selected New World archaeological sites that show evidence of early agriculture (solid dots).

pagated vegetatively—by stem cuttings, tubers, or roots—rather than from seed. Some people, notably the geographer Carl Sauer, have reasoned that cultivation of plants probably began with vegetative propagation, arguing that such cultivation is much simpler than seed planting. There is also some evidence from Old World mythology suggesting that vegetative cultivation is older than seed planting. The archaeological record, unfortunately, has not been able to provide us with clearcut answers, for many of the vegetatively cultivated plants are crops of the wet tropics, areas where the preservation of prehistoric food materials is rather unlikely. Moreover, even in dry areas, tubers and other fleshy plant parts are far less likely to be preserved than are relatively dry materials, such as seeds. While we cannot, perhaps, entirely rule out the possibility that agriculture based on vegetative propagation was earlier than seed-propagation agriculture, it seems fairly clear that it was seed planting that led to the most profound changes in our way of life. All the early high civilizations whose diets are known to us were based on seed-reproducing plants—wheat, maize, or rice—with or without accompanying animal husbandry.

Following the domestication of plants and animals, the next great advance in agriculture came with the control of water. Irrigation arose in the Near East around 5000 BC and in Mexico shortly after 1000 BC. With irrigation, considerably more food could be produced in many areas; as a result, a few people could produce enough food to feed a large population, permitting others to spend time in pursuit of the arts and crafts and of religion. Elaborate temples, many of them standing today, were constructed by early societies that had perfected methods of irrigating their crops and testify to the amount of human labor that was made available for other pursuits.

Another important development in Old World agriculture was the use of animals to prepare the fields for planting, which was never done in the New World in prehistoric times. Along with this difference there was a basic difference in planting techniques. In the Old World the cereals (wheat, for example) were planted by broadcasting handfuls of grain, whereas in the New World the grains of maize were planted individually.

With the domestication of plants and animals there should have been a dependable food supply and, so it might be thought, hunger should have disappeared from the earth. As any intelligent person is acutely aware, however, hunger is still very much with us today. Harmony with nature has yet to be established. With the advent of agriculture, humans began changing their environment drastically. Irrigation, which initially led to greater food production, eventually destroyed some of the most fertile areas. Without adequate drainage, irrigation leads to an accumulation of salts in the soil that few plants can tolerate. That this happened in prehistoric times in the Near East is evident from archaeological findings; for barley, which is more salt tolerant than wheat, replaced the latter plant in some regions after irrigation was developed. The use of animals to till the soil led to increased areas being planted, which in time must have been accompanied by increased soil erosion. Then, along with the plants and animals that people brought under their control came others that they did not want and could not control. Rusts, smuts, and weeds soon found cultivated plants and fields a fertile territory for their development, and insects, rodents, and birds moved in to appropriate the new foods for themselves. Competition for the more fertile agricultural land led to warfare on an escalating scale, for which the powers of some of the domesticated animals were used. Hunger has always accompanied war.

Deserts now occupy many of the areas where high civilizations once flourished. Natural climatic change may in part be reponsible for some of these deserts, but humankind most likely contributed through misuse of soil and water. Alteration of the environment, which began in a modest way 10,000 years ago, continues in the present on a scale never known before.

How Were Cities Invented?

By John Pfeiffer

. . . .

The most striking mark of man's genius as a species, as the most adaptable of animals, has been his ability to live in cities. From the perspective of all we know about human evolution, nothing could be more unnatural. For over fifteen million years, from the period when members of the family of man first appeared on earth until relatively recent times, our ancestors were nomadic, small-group, wide-open-spaces creatures. They lived on the move among other moving animals in isolated little bands of a few families, roaming across wildernesses that extended like oceans to the horizon and beyond.

Considering that heritage, the wonder is not that man has trouble getting along in cities but that he can do it at all—that he can learn to live in the same place year round, enclosed in sharp-cornered and brightly-lit rectangular spaces, among noises, most of which are made by machines, within shouting distance of hundreds of other people, most of them strangers. Furthermore, such conditions arose so swiftly, practically overnight on the evolutionary time scale, that he has hardly had a chance to get used to them. The transition from a world without cities to our present situation took a mere five or six millenniums.

It is precisely because we are so close to our origins that what happened in prehistory bears directly on current problems. In fact, the expectation is that new studies of pre-cities and early cities will contribute as significantly to an understanding of today's urban complexes as studies of infancy and early childhood have to an understanding of adolescence. Cities are signs, symptoms if you will, of an accelerating and intensive phase of human evolution, a process that we are only beginning to investigate scientifically.

The first stages of the process may be traced back some fifteen thousand years to a rather less hectic era. Homo sapiens, that new breed of restless and intelligent primate, had reached a high point in his career as a hunter-gatherer subsisting predominantly on wild plants and animals. He had developed special tools, special tactics and strategies, for dealing with a wide variety of environments, from savannas and semideserts to tundras and tropical rain forests and mountain regions. Having learned to exploit practically every type of environment, he seemed at last to have found his natural place in the scheme of things—as a hunter living in balance with other species, and with all the world as his hunting ground.

But forces were already at work that would bring an end to this state of equilibrium and ultimately give rise to cities and the state of continuing instability that we are trying to cope with today. New theories, a harder look at the old theories, and an even harder look at our own tendencies to think small have radically changed our ideas about what happened and why.

We used to believe, in effect, that people abandoned hunting and gathering as soon as a reasonable alternative became available to them. It was hardly a safe or reliable way of life. Our ancestors faced sudden death and injury from predators and from prey that fought back, disease from exposure to the elements and from always being on the move, and hunger because the chances were excellent of coming back empty-handed from the hunt. Survival was a full-time struggle. Leisure came only after the invention of agriculture, which brought food surpluses, rising populations, and cities. Such was the accepted picture.

The fact of the matter, supported by studies of living hunter-gatherers as well as by the archaeological record, is that the traditional view is largely melodrama and science fiction. Our preagricultural ancestors were quite healthy, quite safe, and regularly obtained all the food they needed. And they did it with time to burn. As a rule, the job of collecting food, animal and vegetable, required no more than a three-hour day, or a twenty-one-hour week. During that time, collectors brought in enough food for the entire group, which included an appreciable proportion (perhaps 30 per cent or more) of dependents, old persons and children who did little or no work. Leisure is basically a phenomenon of hunting-gathering times, and people have been trying to recover it ever since.

Another assumption ripe for discarding is that civilization first arose in the valleys of the Tigris, Euphrates, and Nile rivers and spread from there to the rest of the world. Accumulating evidence fails to support this notion that civilization is an exclusive product of these regions. To be sure, agriculture and cities may have appeared first in the Near East, but there are powerful arguments for completely independent origins in at least two other widely separated regions, Mesoamerica and Southeast Asia.

In all cases, circumstances forced hunter-gatherers to evolve new ways of surviving. With the decline of the ancient life style, nomadism, problems began piling up. If only people had kept on moving about like sane and respectable primates, life would be a great deal simpler. Instead, they settled down in increasing numbers over wider areas, and society started changing with a vengeance. Although the causes of this settling down remain a mystery, the fact of independent origins calls for an explanation based on worldwide developments.

An important factor, emphasized recently by Lewis Binford of the University of New Mexico, may have been the melting of mile-high glaciers, which was well under way fifteen thousand years ago, and which released enough water to raise the world's oceans 250 to 500 feet, to flood previously exposed coastal plains, and to create shallow bays and estuaries and marshlands. Vast numbers of fish and wild fowl made use of the new environments, and the extra resources permitted people to obtain food without migrating seasonally. In other words, people expended less energy, and life became that much easier, in the beginning anyway.

Yet this sensible and seemingly innocent change was to get mankind into all sorts of difficulties. According to a recent theory, it triggered a chain of events that made cities possible if not inevitable. Apparently, keeping on the move had always served as a natural birth-control mechanism, in part, perhaps, by causing a relatively high incidence of miscarriages. But the population brakes were off as soon as people began settling down.

One clue to what may have happened is provided by contemporary studies of a number of primitive tribes, such as the Bushmen of Africa's Kalahari Desert. Women living in nomadic bands, bands that pick up and move half a dozen or more times a year, have an average of one baby every four years or so, as compared with one baby every two and a half years for Bushman women living in settled communities—an increase of five to eight babies per mother during a twenty-year reproductive period.

The archaeological record suggests that in some places at least, a comparable phenomenon accompanied the melting of glaciers during the last ice age. People settled down and multiplied in the Les Eyzies region of southern France, one of the richest and most-studied centers of prehistory. Great limestone cliffs dominate the countryside, and at the foot of the cliffs are natural shelters, caves and rocky overhangs where people built fires, made tools out of flint and bone and ivory, and planned the next day's hunt. On special occasions artists equipped with torches went deep into certain caves like Lascaux and covered the walls with magnificent images of the animals they hunted.

In some places the cliffs and the shelters extend for hundreds of yards; in other places there are good living sites close to one another on the opposite slopes of river valleys. People in the Les Eyzies region were living not in isolated bands but in full-fledged communities, and populations seem to have been on the rise. During the period from seven thousand to twelve thousand years ago, the total number of sites doubled, and an appreciable proportion of them probably represent year-round settlements located in small river valleys. An analysis of excavated animal remains reveals an increasing dietary reliance on migratory birds and fish (chiefly salmon).

People were also settling down at about the same time in the Near East —for example, not far from the Mediterranean shoreline of Israel and on the border between the coastal plain and the hills to the east. Ofer Bar-Yosef, of the Institute of Archaeology of Hebrew University in Jerusalem, points out that since they were able to exploit both these areas, they did not have to wander widely in search of food. There were herds of deer and gazelle, wild boar, fish and wild fowl, wild cereals and other plants, and limestone caves and shelters like those in the Les Eyzies region. Somewhat later, however, a new land-use pattern emerged. Coastal villages continued to flourish, but in addition to them, new sites began appearing further inland— and in areas that were drier and less abundant.

Only under special pressure will men abandon a good thing, and in this case it was very likely the pressure of rising populations. The evidence suggests that the best coastal lands were supporting about all the hunter-gatherers they could support; and as living space decreased there was a "budding off," an overflow of surplus population into the second-best back country where game was scarcer. These people depended more and more on plants, particularly on wild cereals, as indicated by the larger numbers of flint sickle blades, mortars and pestles, and storage pits found at their sites (and also by an increased wear and pitting of teeth, presumably caused by chewing more coarse and gritty plant foods).

Another sign of the times was the appearance of stone buildings, often with impressively high and massive walls. The structures served a number of purposes. For one thing, they included storage bins where surplus grain could be kept in reserve for bad times, when there was a shortage of game and wild plants. They also imply danger abroad in the countryside, new kinds of violence, and a mounting need for defenses to protect stored goods from the raids of people who had not settled down.

Above all, the walls convey a feeling of increasing permanence, an increasing commitment to places. Although man was still mainly a hunter-gatherer living on wild species, some of the old options no longer existed for him. In the beginning, settling down may have involved a measure of choice, but now man was no longer quite so free to change locales when the land became less fruitful. Even in those days frontiers were vanishing. Man's problem was to develop new options, new ways of working the land more intensively so that it would provide the food that migration had always provided in more mobile times.

The all-important transition to agriculture came in small steps, establishing itself almost before anyone realized what was going on. Settlers in marginal lands took early measures to get more food out of less abundant environments—roughing up the soil a bit with scraping or digging sticks, sowing wheat and barley seeds, weeding, and generally doing their best to promote growth. To start with at least, it was simply a matter of supplementing regular diets of wild foods with some domesticated species, animals as well as plants, and people probably regarded themselves as hunter-gatherers working hard to maintain their way of life rather than as the revolutionaries they were. They were trying to preserve the old self-sufficiency, but it was a losing effort.

The wilderness way of life became more and more remote, more and more nearly irretrievable. Practically every advance in the technology of agriculture committed people to an increasing dependence on domesticated species and on the activities of other people living nearby. Kent Flannery of the University of Michigan emphasizes this point in a study of one part of Greater Mesopotamia, prehistoric Iran, during the period between twelve thousand and six thousand years ago. For the hunter-gatherer, an estimated one-third of the country's total land area was good territory, consisting of grassy plains and high mountain valleys where wild species were abundant; the rest of the land was desert and semidesert.

The coming of agriculture meant

that people used a smaller proportion of the countryside. Early farming took advantage of naturally distributed water; the best terrain for that, namely terrain with a high water table and marshy areas, amounted to about a tenth of the land area. But only a tenth of that tenth was suitable for the next major development, irrigation. Meanwhile, food yields were soaring spectacularly, and so was the population of Iran, which increased more than fiftyfold; in other words, fifty times the original population was being supported by food produced on one-hundredth of the land.

A detailed picture of the steps involved in this massing of people is coming from studies of one part of southwest Iran, an 880-square-mile region between the Zagros Mountains and the Iraqi border. The Susiana Plain is mostly flat, sandy semidesert, the only notable features being man-made mounds that loom on the horizon like islands, places where people built in successively high levels on the ruins of their ancestors. During the past decade or so, hundreds of mounds have been mapped and dated (mainly through pottery styles) by Robert Adams of the University of Chicago, Jean Perrot of the French Archaeological Mission in Iran, and Henry Wright and Gregory Johnson of the University of Michigan. Their work provides a general idea of when the mounds were occupied, how they varied in size at different periods—and how a city may be born.

Imagine a time-lapse motion picture of the early settling of the Susiana Plain, starting about 6500 B.C., each minute of film representing a century. At first the plain is empty, as it has been since the beginning of time. Then the pioneers arrive; half a dozen families move in and build a cluster of mud-brick homes near a river. Soon another cluster appears and another, until, after about five minutes (it is now 6000 B.C.), there are ten settlements, each covering an area of 1 to 3 hectares (1 hectare = 2.47 acres). Five

minutes more (5500 B.C.) and we see the start of irrigation, on a small scale, as people dig little ditches to carry water from rivers and tributaries to lands along the banks. Crop yields increase and so do populations, and there are now thirty settlements, all about the same size as the original ten.

This is but a prelude to the main event. Things become really complicated during the next fifteen minutes or so (5500 to 4000 B.C.). Irrigation systems, constructed and maintained by family groups of varying sizes, become more complex. The number of settlements shows a modest increase, from thirty to forty, but a more significant change takes place—the appearance of a hierarchy. Instead of settlements all about the same size, there are now levels of settlements and a kind of ranking: one town (7 hectares), ten large villages (3 to 4 hectares), and twenty-nine smaller villages of less than 3 hectares. During this period large residential and ceremonial structures appear at Susa, a town on the western edge of the Susiana Plain.

Strange happenings can be observed not long after the middle of this period (about 4600 B.C.). For reasons unknown, the number of settlements decreases rapidly. It is not known whether the population of the area decreased simultaneously. Time passes, and the number of settlements increases to about the same level as before, but great changes have occurred. Three cities have appeared with monumental public buildings, elaborate residential architecture, large workshops, major storage and market facilities, and certainly with administrators and bureaucrats. The settlement hierarchy is more complex, and settlements are no longer located to take advantage solely of good agricultural opportunities. Their location is also influenced by the cities and the services and opportunities available there. By the end of our hypothetical time-lapse film, by the early part of the third millennium B.C., the largest settlement of all is the city of Susa, which covers some thirty hectares and will cover up to a square kil-

Hillel Burger, Peabody Museum, Harvard University

Female figurine from Tepe Yahya, Iran. A variety of sites throughout the world have yielded astonishingly ancient objects created by men who farmed and built permanent dwellings such as this stone figurine found in Tepe Yahya, Iran—a settlement that was in contact with Susa before 4000 B.C.

ometer (100 hectares) of territory before it collapses in historical times.

All Mesopotamia underwent major transformations during this period. Another city was taking shape 150 miles northwest of Susa in the heartland of Sumer. Within a millennium the site of Uruk near the Euphrates River grew from village dimensions to a city enclosing within its defense walls more than thirty thousand people, four hundred hectares, and at the center a temple built on top of a huge brick platform. Archaeological surveys reveal that this period also saw a massive immigration into the region from places and for reasons as yet undetermined, resulting in a tenfold increase in settlements and in the formation of several new cities.

Similar surveys, requiring months

and thousands of miles of walking, are completed or under way in many parts of the world. Little more than a millennium after the establishment of Uruk and Susa, cities began making an independent appearance in northern China not far from the conflux of the Wei and Yellow rivers, in an area that also saw the beginnings of agriculture. Still later, and also independently as far as we can tell, intensive settlement and land use developed in the New World.

The valley of Oaxaca in Mexico, where Flannery and his associates are working currently, provides another example of a city in the process of being formed. Around 500 B.C., or perhaps a bit earlier, buildings were erected for the first time on the tops of hills. Some of the hills were small, no more than twenty-five or thirty feet high, and the buildings were correspondingly small; they overlooked a few terraces and a river and probably a hamlet or two. Larger structures appeared on higher hills overlooking many villages. About 400 B.C. the most elaborate settlement began to appear on the highest land, 1,500-foot Monte Albán, with a panoramic view of the valley's three arms; and within two centuries it had developed into an urban center including hundreds of terraces, an irrigation system, a great plaza, ceremonial buildings and residences, and an astronomical observatory.

At about the same time, the New World's largest city, Teotihuacán, was evolving some 225 miles to the northwest in the central highlands of Mexico. Starting as a scattering of villages and hamlets, it covered nearly eight square miles at its height (around A.D. 100 to 200) and probably contained some 125,000 people. Archaeologists are now reconstructing the life and times of this great urban center. William Sanders of Pennsylvania State University is concentrating on an analysis of settlement patterns in the area, while Rene Millon of the University of Rochester and his associates have prepared detailed section-by-section maps of the city as a step toward further extensive excavations. Set in a narrow valley among mountains and with its

own man-made mountains, the Pyramid of the Sun and the Pyramid of the Moon, the city flourished on a grand scale. It housed local dignitaries and priests, delegations from other parts of Mesoamerica, and workshop neighborhoods where specialists in the manufacture of textiles, pottery, obsidian blades, and other products lived together in early-style apartments.

The biggest center in what is now the United States probably reached its peak about a millennium after Teotihuacán. But it has not been reconstructed, and archaeologists are just beginning to appreciate the scale of what happened there. Known as Cahokia and located east of the Mississippi near St. Louis, it consists of a cluster of some 125 mounds (including a central mound 100 feet high and covering 15 acres) as well as a line of mounds extending six miles to the west.

So surveys and excavations continue, furnishing the sort of data needed to disprove or prove our theories. Emerging patterns—patterns involving the specific locations of different kinds of communities and of buildings and other artifacts within communities—can yield information about the forces that shaped and are still shaping cities and the behavior of people in cities. But one trend stands out above all others: the world was becoming more and more stratified. Every development seemed to favor social distinctions, social classes and elites, and to work against the old hunter-gatherer ways.

Among hunter-gatherers all people are equal. Individuals are recognized as exceptional hunters, healers, or storytellers, and they all have the chance to shine upon appropriate occasions. But it would be unthinkable for one of them, for any one man, to take over as full-time leader. That ethic passed when the nomadic life passed. In fact, a literal explosion of differences accompanied the coming of communities where people lived close together in permanent dwellings and under conditions where moving away was not easy.

The change is reflected clearly in observed changes of settlement patterns.

Hierarchies of settlements imply hierarchies of people. Emerging social levels are indicated by the appearance of villages and towns and cities where only villages had existed before, by different levels of complexity culminating in such centers as Susa and Monte Albán and Cahokia. Circumstances practically drove people to establish class societies. In Mesopotamia, for instance, increasingly sophisticated agricultural systems and intensive concentrations of populations brought about enormous and irreversible changes within a short period. People were clamped in a demographic vise, more and more of them living and depending on less and less land—an ideal setting for the rapid rise of status differences.

Large-scale irrigation was a highly effective centralizing force, calling for new duties and new regularities and new levels of discipline. People still depended on the seasons; but in addition, canals had to be dug and maintained, and periodic cleaning was required to prevent the artificial waterways from filling up with silt and assorted litter. Workers had to be brought together, assigned tasks, and fed, which meant schedules and storehouses and rationing stations and mass-produced pottery to serve as food containers. It took time to organize such activities efficiently. There were undoubtedly many false starts, many attempts by local people to work things out among themselves and their neighbors at a community or village level. Many small centers, budding institutions, were undoubtedly formed and many collapsed, and we may yet detect traces of them in future excavations and analyses of settlement patterns.

The ultimate outcome was inevitable. Survival demanded organization on a regional rather than a local basis. It also demanded high-level administrators and managers, and most of them had to be educated people, mainly because of the need to prepare detailed records of supplies and transactions. Record-keeping has a long prehistory, perhaps dating back to certain abstract designs engraved on cave walls and bone twenty-five thousand or more years ago. But in Mesopotamia after 4000 B.C. there was a spurt in the art of inventing and utilizing special marks and symbols.

The trend is shown in the stamp and cylinder seals used by officials to place their "signatures" on clay tags and tablets, man's first documents. At first the designs on the stamp seals were uncomplicated, consisting for the most part of single animals or simple geometric motifs. Later, however, there were bigger stamp seals with more elaborate scenes depicting several objects or people or animals. Finally the cylinder seals appeared, which could be rolled to repeat a complex design. These seals indicate the existence of more and more different signatures—and more and more officials and record keepers. Similar trends are evident in potters' marks and other symbols. All these developments precede pictographic writing, which appears around 3200 B.C.

Wherever record keepers and populations were on the rise, in the Near East or Mexico or China, we can be reasonably sure that the need for a police force or the prehistoric equivalent thereof was on the increase, too. Conflict, including everything from fisticuffs to homicide, increases sharply with group size, and people have known this for a long time. The Bushmen have a strong feeling about avoiding crowds: "We like to get together, but we fear fights." They are most comfortable in bands of about twenty-five persons and when they have to assemble in larger groups—which happens for a total of only a few months a year, mainly to conduct initiations, arrange marriages, and be near the few permanent water holes during dry seasons—they form separate small groups of about twenty-five, as if they were still living on their own.

Incidentally, twenty-five has been called a "magic number," because it hints at what may be a universal law of group behavior. There have been many counts of hunter-gatherer bands, not only in the Kalahari Desert, but also in such diverse places as the forests of Thailand, the Canadian Northwest, and northern India. Although individual bands may vary from fifteen to seventy-five members, the tendency is to cluster around twenty-five, and in all cases a major reason for keeping groups small is the desire to avoid violence. In other words, the association between large groups and conflict has deep roots and very likely presented law-and-order problems during the early days of cities and pre-cities, as it has ever since.

Along with managers and record keepers and keepers of the peace, there were also specialists in trade. A number of factors besides population growth and intensive land use were involved in the origin of cities, and local and long-distance trade was among the most important. Prehistoric centers in the process of becoming urban were almost always trade centers. They typically occupied favored places, strategic points in developing trade networks, along major waterways and caravan routes or close to supplies of critical raw materials.

Archaeologists are making a renewed attempt to learn more about such developments. Wright's current work in southwest Iran, for example, includes preliminary studies to detect and measure changes in the flow of trade. One site about sixty-five miles from Susa lies close to tar pits, which in prehistoric times served as a source of natural asphalt for fastening stone blades to handles and waterproofing baskets and roofs. By saving all the waste bits of this important raw material preserved in different excavated levels, Wright was able to estimate fluctuations in its production over a period of time. In one level, for example, he found that the amounts of asphalt produced increased far beyond local requirements; in fact, a quantitative analysis indicates that asphalt exports doubled at this time. The material was probably being traded for such things as high-quality flint obtained from quarries more than one hundred miles away, since counts of material recovered at the site indicate that imports of the flint doubled during the same period.

In other words, the site was taking its place in an expanding trade network, and similar evidence from other sites can be used to indicate the extent and structure of that network. Then the problem will be to find out what other things were happening at the same time, such as significant changes in cylinder-seal designs and in agricultural and religious practices. This is the sort of evidence that may be expected to spell out just how the evolution of trade was related to the evolution of cities.

Another central problem is gaining a fresh understanding of the role of religion. Something connected with enormous concentrations of people, with population pressures and tensions of many kinds that started building up five thousand or more years ago, transformed religion from a matter of simple rituals carried out at village shrines to the great systems of temples and priesthoods invariably associated with early cities. Sacred as well as profane institutions arose to keep society from splitting apart.

Strong divisive tendencies had to be counteracted, and the reason may involve yet another magic number, another intriguing regularity that has been observed in hunter-gatherer societies in different parts of the world. The average size of a tribe, defined as a group of bands all speaking the same dialect, turns out to be about five hundred persons, a figure that depends to some extent on the limits of human memory. A tribe is a community of people who can identify closely with one another and engage in repeated face-to-face encounters and recognitions; and it happens that five hundred may represent about the number of persons a hunter-gatherer can remember well enough to approach on what would amount to a first-name basis in our society. Beyond that number the level of familiarity declines, and there is an increasing tendency to regard individuals as "they" rather than "we," which is when trouble usually starts. (Architects recommend that an elementary school should not exceed five hundred pupils if the principal is to maintain personal contact with all of them, and the headmaster of one prominent prep school recently used this argument to keep his student body at or below the five-hundred mark.)

Religion of the sort that evolved with the first cities may have helped to "beat" the magic number five hundred. Certainly there was an urgent need to establish feelings of solidarity among many thousands of persons rather than a few hundred. Creating allegiances wider than those provided by direct kinship and person-to-person ties became a most important problem, a task for full-time professionals. In this connection Paul Wheatley of the University of Chicago suggests that "specialized priests were among the first persons to be released from the daily round of subsistence labor." Their role was partly to exhort other workers concerned with the building of monuments and temples, workers who probably exerted greater efforts in the belief that they were doing it not for mere men but for the glory of individuals highborn and close to the gods.

The city evolved to meet the needs of societies under pressure. People were being swept up in a process that had been set in motion by their own activities and that they could never have predicted, for the simple reason that they had no insight into what they were doing in the first place. For example, they did not know, and had no way of knowing, that settling down could lead to population explosions.

There is nothing strange about this state of affairs, to be sure. It is the essence of the human condition and involves us just as intensely today. Then as now, people responded by the sheer instinct of survival to forces that they understood vaguely at best—and worked together as well as they could to organize themselves, to preserve order in the face of accelerating change and complexity and the threat of chaos. They could never know that they were creating what we, its beneficiaries and its victims, call civilization.

Rise of Civilizations: Mesopotamia to Mesoamerica

By Henry T. Wright

IN PERHAPS AS MANY as six different regions of the world, human societies appear to have evolved — more or less independently — from simple chiefdoms to networks of small states, to empires with fully differentiated social classes and specialized systems of production. Archaeologists early in this century wrote as if these developmental patterns could be documented directly from the archaeological record. Today, we realize that this is impossible. Only the more mundane aspects of the past — a discarded potsherd, a piece of sculptured marble, an ancient text — can be documented with any degree of certainty. Nevertheless, we can use these fragmentary remains to evaluate our interpretations of past events, and even to test general theories that describe and explain the intertwined political, religious, and economic processes behind the rise of the early civilizations. Successive programs of field research and the testing of our theories has led most mid-twentieth-century archaeologists to reject most of the elegant but overly simple explanations. For example, few now seriously believe that irrigation agriculture, population growth, or long-range trade can alone explain the development of any of the early civilizations. We are now increasingly concerned with the complicated interrelationships between these developments and other variables in broader trans-regional contexts.

We are able to ask, and to begin answering, these more complex questions because the twentieth century has been one of profound changes in archaeological methods. We now have not only more precise ways to excavate and recover evidence from sites, we have remote sensing and surface survey techniques that enable us to learn a great deal about ancient regional landscapes with minimal excavation, and we have new methods for dating and artifact analysis, as well as computer facilities to handle the mountains of data that result from all these new methods.

The archaeologists of the future, however, will have a responsibility to go beyond innovation in techniques and forge new ways of thinking about the earliest civilizations. We need a synthesis of current approaches to the material aspects of life developed by anthropological archaeologists with new approaches to social life and communication now being developed by archaeologists in the humanistic traditions, linguists, and cultural anthropologists. Such a synthesis will probably be realized not by a single brilliant scholar but by many, evaluating their ideas in the context of their archaeological studies of specific civilizations. We can gain some idea of the future of such studies by looking at the accomplishments and potential of ongoing research on a selection of five of the early civilizations.

NEAR EAST

The vast nexus of urban societies that centered on the Nile and the Mesopotamian rivers — from Anatolia to Arabia, from Central Asia to the Sudan — formed the world's first great trans-regional civilization, the one that cannot have been influenced by already developed civilizations. Archaeologists working in the heartlands of these regions have the unique opportunity to retrieve some of the "waste paper" of urban economies and state polities from as early as 3400 B.C. — papyrus texts preserved by dessication in sites along the Nile and durable clay documents in Mesopotamia. These are not simply the propaganda of rulers carved in stone; they include information about day-to-day decisions about crops, labor, trade, and conflicts. These texts can be compared with the archaeological remains, the material evidence of the results of these decisions. Some archaeologists argue that decision-making is central to the functioning of culture. If this is true, then Near Eastern specialists have a powerful tool in these texts for examining the

Reprinted with permission from *Archaeology*, January/February 1989

development of decision-making hierarchies that seem to characterize all complex societies. The usefulness of these texts is, however, limited by several circumstances. First, early writing was developed in central state and temple institutions and was rarely used in family affairs or even relations among the elite. Second, early administrative texts are often laconic "grocery lists" of goods and items. These texts are difficult to read and their social context is often unclear. Finally, writing developed in the Near East, as elsewhere, long after the first steps toward economic stratification and social hierarchy had been taken. Thus the written records are most informative about the operation of the developed early states, rather than about their predecessors.

The Near East has seen the most comprehensive use of regional survey techniques. By using air photographs, systematic surface studies, and test excavations, archaeologists have been able to map landscapes with settlements, river channels and canals from as early as 5000 B.C. With better understanding of how recent geological processes have altered the archaeological record of the ancient landscape, and with better remote sensing technologies to record landscapes from satellites or aircraft, such studies will become more and more precise in the twenty-first century. Innovations in coring techniques, now being made in countries such as the Netherlands, may make it possible to extract and study soil samples from deeply buried landscapes such as those under the Nile delta and under the Euphrates alluvium.

What we will see in the Near East in the immediate future is a long overdue integration of the regional archaeological record and the textual record, along with new approaches to excavation. Humanistic archaeologists, with their keen interest in textual records, have devoted decades to the investigation of the great urban centers, understandably focusing on the great institutions where texts are more likely to be found: palaces, temples, and the like. In contrast, the few anthropological archaeologists concerned with the archaeological record of early Near Eastern civilization have spent much time salvaging information about landscapes before the evidence is destroyed by modern agriculture. They have had little chance to use the precise excavation techniques (such as representative excavation sampling, microstratigraphic control, special recovery methods for plant remains, etc.) developed by prehistorians working on the early villages that can shed light on daily activities. Somehow the time and funds must be found to apply the methods developed for early villages to the early urban centers and their subsidiary settlements. We need to recover texts in firm association with the evidence of storehouses, workshops, and homes—not only on major sites but on rural estates, border forts, etc., if we are to have a complete picture of political and economic changes.

Such innovations will require a breaking down of the institutional and disciplinary barriers to research in the Near East. Not only is better communication needed between humanistic and anthropological archaeologists, but there is also a need for better understanding between research archaeologists and the local administrative archaeologists concerned with safeguarding each nation's ancient heritage in the face of modern development. Each group in each country has different ways of recording information from archaeological surveys and excavations, different programs of publication, and different standards for the curation of archaeological remains. Tragically, most archaeological samples in the Near East are discarded after brief study simply because museum space is unavailable. The reanalysis of artifacts, soil samples, etc., as new techniques are devised will rarely be possible until the Egyptian policy of requiring the construction of large storage facilities at the site of each excavation program is generally adopted.

An area of future innovation necessary for any broader use of the Near Eastern archaeological record is that of experimental archaeology. This is because ethnoarchaeology, the study of the material remains of modern peoples, is primarily only useful for the study of questions about rural life in the Near East. The millennia that have elapsed since civilization's formative stages here have seen the destruction of the natural environment, the transformation of technology in classical times, the transformation of social orders by the rise of Islam, not to mention the recent impact of industrial civilization. However, by constructing experimental buildings, farms, and workshops, we may test ideas about both how ancient activities were performed and the processes that turned the debris of ancient activities into the archaeological record that we can excavate today.

If the comprehensive integration of Near Eastern archaeology across disciplinary and national boundaries, envisoned above, can be realized, then by 2050 we should have an unparalleled body of data for evaluating ideas about how urban economies and political hierarchies develop.

SOUTH ASIA

The first civilization on the South Asian subcontinent was centered in the alluvial plain of the Indus River, but societies on the nearby Gangetic plain, on the Afghan Plateau, and even across the Arabian Sea in Oman participated in the broader trans-regional South Asian economic system. Recent research has shown that developed village life flourished in tributary valleys of the Indus by 7000 B.C. and that networks of large settlements surrounded by subsidiary small settlements had emerged before 3000 B.C. So there are no grounds to presume that direct contact with Mesopotamia initiated the formation of complex societies along the Indus. There is, however, increasing evidence of overland and maritime trade between the developed Mesopotamian and Indus heartlands. More extensive application of underwater archaeology in the region will help to document this trade. Though relatively little is known about the early stages of the evolution of Indus civilization, much is known about its great floresence from 2500 to 1800 B.C., in spite of the fact that the rather limited kinds of written texts—apparently mostly brief names and titles carved on stone seals—from the area cannot yet be read. From the beginning of major research along the Indus during the 1920s, archaeologists there have tried to excavate both small and large communities, providing evidence of urban organization as good as that in any other area of the world. Also, researchers along the Indus have been almost unique in paying careful attention to the human biology of these first urban dwellers and their predecessors. For no other early civilization do we have the comparative information on nutrition, disease, and mortality that we have for the occupants of the Indus Valley cities and their predecessors.

What is lacking for most of South Asia is a groundwork of regional archaeological surveys. There have been few modern surveys and none are fully published. Surveys, combined with studies of past environments, will be needed on many samples of the an-

cient Indus landscape if we are to understand the basic dynamics of agriculture and population in this civilization.

In addition to archaeological surveys and to more precise excavations, there is another form of research important to developing general theories of the evolution of civilizations, one that perhaps can be undertaken in South Asia more fruitfully than anywhere else. In all the other heartlands of early civilization, the rise of the great world religions and the traumas of imperial expansion have sundered the direct ideological links with the earlier stages of civilization. Only in portions of the Indian subcontinent do large communities still flourish in which the social order, the organization of crafts, and many other aspects of life still operate under the guidance of a religious system directly developed from that of the earliest complex societies. Though many aspects of life have changed, South Asia provides unique opportunities for ethnoarchaeological study, both of the archaeological byproducts of religious activities and of the formation of urban archaeological records. This will surely be a major concern for South Asian specialists during the near future.

Given the strengths of the South Asian record—its clear evidence of town organization, crafts, trade, and ritual—and the unfortunately limited extent of its written record, it seems likely that the data from the area will contribute more to an understanding of the operation of urban economies than to that of political hierarchies. Since we yet know little of the earliest stages of the Indus civilization, before 3000 B.C., it seems likely that future research will document completely unexpected aspects of the first steps toward urban life.

EAST ASIA

Ongoing research in China is showing that the formation of the earliest East Asian civilization involved a number of interacting regions, not just the relatively well-known North China plain along the Yellow River. However, work in southern and western China has not yet reached the point at which the larger trans-regional system can be defined, as has been possible in Southwest Asia, South Asia, Mesoamerica, and the An-

des. Working in tributaries of the Yellow River, the first Chinese archaeologists were fortunate to uncover extensive areas of a state capital of the Shang, the first major Chinese dynasty. From here they recovered not only evidence of palaces and more modest homes but also a substantial cemetery with tombs ranging from those of kings to those of slaves. They also recovered a range of readable texts written on bone.

Though these are specialized divinatory texts, they contain much information on elite life, politics, and even the weather. Subsequent work has provided evidence of other towns, of areas of craft production, and of earlier centers from the formative stages of North Chinese complex polities, dating as early as 1800 B.C. Because excavations have focused on elite centers and tombs, we know a great deal about the organization of political elites and the material symbols with which they defined their high status. At present, only the Nile Valley has a record of elite art and organization approaching that available for the North China plain.

However, as in the Indus region, even the well-known North China plain lacks published regional archaeological surveys. Much information that could be assembled into a regional overview exists in local files and publications, but neither the task of integrating these data nor the intensive field surveys that will be needed to define networks of smaller settlements has been pursued. This work would be best done soon, since mechanized agriculture has revealed many sites but will soon disperse their surface remains. In the areas of southern China dominated by rice paddies, regional surface surveys will be difficult, but the success of surveys in areas such as the Nara basin, the heartland of state formation in Japan, shows that the recovery of settlement patterns is possible even in such environments.

In the near future, regional surveys, combined with the detailed study of plant and animal use in the area today, will provide an understanding of the systems of agricultural production in early Chinese civilization that we currently lack. Such research will be enhanced by the study of existing traditional Chinese agricultural production systems, many of which have long documentary histories as well. During the coming century, systematic archaeological surveys will doubtless lead to the excavation of sites other than the larger centers. It seems likely that the excavation of waterlogged sites, created by post-glacial sea level rise and by the accumulation of flood sediments in river valleys, will produce ancient economic records written on material such as bamboo (such as have been found in Japan) complementing the known texts which focus on the elite. If so, by the year 2050, Chinese archaeologists will control one of the most comprehensive bodies of data suited for the rigorous evaluation of theories relating to both early economic and early political development.

ANDEAN AMERICA

Early Andeans developed their civilization in what may have been the most diverse environments faced by any early complex society. In spite of these difficult circumstances, the historical information collected after the Spanish conquest destroyed the empire of Tiwantisuyu, the realm of the Inka (the latest phase of native Andean civilization), indicates an extraordinarily successful cultural achievement. There are difficulties facing those who study Andean civilizations, including the virtual erasure of this ancient culture by the Spanish, and the fact that among all the early civilizations, it was only here that writing did not develop. In spite of these problems, a relatively small number of archaeologists have made impressive progress in understanding the systems of terraces and canals, without which Precolumbian agriculture would have produced little, and the networks of interregional exchange that distributed materials throughout the Andes. The layouts of elite centers and cemeteries, and the meaning and use of political and religious symbols in prestate and state systems from as early as 1200 B.C., are increasingly known.

Given the extraordinary progress, and given the fact that Peru was the birthplace of modern regional survey archaeology (just after World War II) it is surprising that only two intensive archaeological surveys in the region have been completed and published. Indeed, it is tragic, because most of the coastal valleys have been leveled by modern agroindustry since 1960, and we have thus lost opportunities to study settlement patterns composed of sites so dessicated that the corncobs, cloth scraps, and even the bodies of the ancient inhabitants were often preserved. Fortunately, much survey work is currently under way, and we can hope for comprehensive publication of regional data in the near future. Perhaps as a result of this lack of work on settlement patterns, there has been only a limited study of community organization. The study of architectural features such as buildings, particularly on the coast, is only beginning, and the excavation of settlements in such a way that one can study the distribution of artifacts in rooms and dumps — and thus the changing organization of human activity — is rare.

There is no question that once such surveys and settlement studies are more advanced, the Andes will become the major testing ground for investigating the relationship between religious ideology and politics, because there is a wealth of retrievable evidence on state-subsidized agriculture works, elite architecture, military architecture, and political and religious art that cannot be matched elsewhere. In spite of centuries of treasure hunting, Peru still has royal cemeteries, which, if excavated with the best of available techniques, will provide a wealth of detail on dynastic politics and ritual in chiefdoms and states. The problem has been and will continue to be that of balancing the costs of conserving and studying this matchless record of an early civilization against the pressing needs of the modern Andean societies. Andean America's small cadre of professional archaeologists is one with a special need for support from colleagues, private foundations, and public agencies in the wealthier nations.

MESOAMERICA

Before the Spanish conquest of Mesoamerica, a single trans-regional sphere of communication united the immense region stretching from the American Southwest almost to the Isthmus of Panama. If the heartland of this nexus was in the central and southern highlands of Mexico, other regions such as the Yucatan Peninsula or parts of Guatemala were no less developed. The ruggedness of Mesoamerica has limited the amount of territory intensively surveyed, but there is no question that some of the completed surveys are among the most thorough ever done. In addition, Mesoamerica has also seen many studies of plant use, without which the results of archaeological surveys cannot be related to agricultural production systems. Finally, Mesoamericanists have, in spite of the erasure of ancient traditions during the Conquest, developed an enviable comprehension of sites as communities, not only of the architecture of elite centers, but also of the architecture of humble villages.

The most exciting current developments are related to our growing comprehension of Mesoamerican writing systems. Many inscriptions can now be shown to have political significance. They are relatively common, at least in certain parts of southern Mesoamerica, and were used in relatively early stages in the development of Mesoamerican civilization, long before the development of urban economies and even before the development of states (before 100 B.C.). Indeed, it seems that Mesoamerican writing may have had a ritual or political origin, rather than the economic origin inferred for the Mesopotamian and other writing systems. If so, this implies an interesting challenge for those attempting to construct general explanations of the development of writing. In any event, the written texts, particularly in the Maya area, provide detailed evidence of the rise and fall of dynasties, knowledge useful in evaluating ideas about the operation of systems of interrelated states.

By the middle of the next century, however, many of the issues of economic and political development may well be resolved, and scholars may be using the Mesoamerican record for very different purposes. In many ways Mesoamerica is the most different of the world's early civilizations. It arose in a land where communication was exceptionally difficult and natural disaster was frequent; its occupants had a wealth of domestic plants but few domestic animals. This meant that not only economics but also the metaphors of daily life, or of religion and politics, were different from those of other civilizations: there could neither be a "bull of heaven" nor a "lamb of god" in ancient Mexico. For all these reasons, Mesoamerica is a critical case for developing and evaluating general ideas about world view as a context for the developing cultural complexity and for the importance of what we term "religion" in the rise of the first hierarchical polities.

The study of the evolution of the early civilizations—of urban economies, of states, and of religions—is a problem that is being successfully approached within the holistic and long-term perspective of archaeology. Even now, however, it is clear that the long-standing focus on a few early civilizations is too narrow. We must diversify the roster of early civilizations. Western Africa contains a yet poorly known nexus of complex societies whose development begins in the first millennium B.C., long before any contact with the Mediterranean world. By the mid-twenty-first century, I have no doubt that Africanists will have a knowledge of such heartlands as the Inner Delta of the Niger rivaling that of Mesopotamia or the North China plain. Similarly, it is likely that Southeast Asian complex societies developed before direct relations were established with either India or China.

There is also much to be gained by contrasting these relatively independent developments with civilizations that developed in varying degrees of interaction with the established early civilizations. Did the Mediterranean, Western Europe, Central Africa, or Japan develop differently from earlier civilizations because of such interaction? The question must be asked.

To answer all the questions we wish to pose will require a range of new methods and the mass application of methods already available. We must be able to trace the sources of clays, stones, and ores if we wish to study the economic systems of these societies. We must routinely date sites and structures to the decade or even the year if we wish to answer questions about political processes. Current techniques for identifying plant tissues or studying the chemistry of human bone are only a beginning. These approaches require not only money but organization. It is a sad fact that the economic circumstances of the 1980s have led to a diminution of our organizational capacities. For example, some of the best of the young ethnobotanists and ethnozoologists trained in the optimistic 1960s and 1970s have left research because there is no stability of employment for them. We and our twenty-first-century successors must develop new organizational mechanisms, perhaps endowed institutes in-

dependent of traditional universities and museums, if there is to be more than patchwork progress in understanding the rise of civilization.

Developing useful explanations for long-completed cultural transformations can help us to resolve the global problems of tomorrow. Well-tested models representing long-term relationships between such phenomena as population growth, agricultural intensification, and social conflict will be useful in planning development for the future. However, all our rigorous theoretical explanations and sophisticated computer models will be nothing more than air castles if we lack either an archaeological record on which to test them or the means to undertake such tests. For this reason, a paramount concern must be the conservation of a representative sample of the planet's archaeological resources for future study, and the creation of a worldwide network of support for archaeological researchers. It is only fitting that the industrial nations, whose wealth depends on the accomplishments of the early civilizations, should help the descendants of those early peoples—many of whom live in poverty in environments damaged by civilization's birth-traumas—to safeguard and study what is properly the heritage (and responsibility) of everyone on the planet.

4
Language
and Communication

All animal species have methods of communication, by which we mean the transfer of information from one organism to another. Information is defined as a stimulus that changes or affects the behavior of an organism.

Of all animal species, humankind has developed the most rich, subtle, and versatile of communication systems: *language*. But what is language? Many anthropologists think of language in terms of the thirteen design features proposed by Charles Hockett. In Hockett's terms, language is characterized as follows:

1. *Vocal-auditory channel*. Language is produced through the nose and mouth and received through the ears.

2. *Broadcast transmission and directional fading*. A speaker can be heard in all directions; a listener can hear a speaker no matter which direction the signal is coming from.

3. *Rapid fading*. As soon as they are spoken, words dissipate and subsequently cannot be retrieved.

4. *Interchangeability*. All speakers of a language can both utter and understand the same words.

5. *Total feedback*. A speaker hears everything she or he says, can monitor it, and can correct or account for mistakes.

6. *Specialization*. Speech serves no other purpose than to communicate; as a specialized system, it can be used even when speaker and listener are engaged in other activities.

7. *Semanticity*. There are systematic connections between spoken words and standardly accepted meanings.

8. *Arbitrariness*. These connections between words and their meanings are a matter of convention; hence it is possible both to create new words with new meanings and to change the meanings of old words.

9. *Discreteness*. Human beings can produce an enormous range of sounds, but each language makes use of only a very small subset of these sounds, far from exhausting the human capacity.

10. *Displacement*. Humans can use language to communicate about things and events that are far removed from the immediate context in which they are interacting. These dis-

tant events may be separated by time, distance, or both—and may even include things that have never existed and never will (for example, mermaids).

11. *Productivity*. People regularly utter sentences that have never been said before in exactly the same manner, and they can talk about things (such as inventions or discoveries) that have never been observed.

12. *Traditional transmission*. It appears that human beings are genetically programmed to be predisposed to learn a language (or even more than one). However, the specific language that an individual eventually speaks is acquired solely through learning in a social context—it is not inherited genetically.

13. *Duality of patterning*. Language is patterned on at least two separate levels: *phonemes*, the sounds a language recognizes as significant but which by themselves have no meanings; and *morphemes*, the indivisible units of meaning of a language. The word *dog*, for instance, consists of three phonemes ([d], [o], [g]) and one morpheme ([dog]).

One of the earliest recorded instances of interest in language and its significance for human beings appears in the Old Testament in Genesis. First, Adam names all the creatures of the world—and through this they are placed at his disposal. Later, when through united effort in the land of Shinar humans attempted to build a tower reaching to the very heavens, God scattered them across the face of the earth and caused them to speak different tongues, thereby forever frustrating attempts at pan-human unity.

Two such themes still preoccupy modern linguists: (1) the ways in which words and the categories they represent affect their speakers' experience of, and approach to, the world around them; and (2) the evolutionary tree of langauge, or the taxonomic relationships among languages, and the ways and rates of linguistic change.

The first recorded rigorous study of a language was accomplished in the fourth century B.C. by the Indian scholar Panini. He analyzed the structure of ancient (Vedic) Sanskrit and condensed its grammatical rules to algebra-like formulas as elegant as those of any modern grammatical analysis. In doing so, he preserved a language that might well otherwise have become extinct, and he set a standard of excellence that still inspires linguistic analysts.

Some two thousand years later, another student of Sanskrit, Sir William Jones (1746–1794), systematized means to compare and contrast languages and thereby trace the relationships among them. He is considered by some, therefore, to be the modern father of comparative linguistics.

Contemporary linguistics is divided into several specialized branches and even more schools of thought. *Structural linguists* analyze individual languages, detailing their phonology (sound system), morphology (meaning representation), and syntax (the organization of language units into sequences). *Comparative (or historical) linguists* compare extant languages, trace their evolution from earlier (proto-) language forms, and attempt to reconstruct the proto-languages from which modern languages evolved. *Sociolinguists* study differences in language uses (or dialectical differences) reflecting socioeconomic groupings. And *psycholinguists* are interested in the mental apparatuses of speech perception, cognitive processes, and so on.

But human communication is not limited to language. Nonverbally, human beings communicate very important messages about many things—including their feelings about (1) themselves, (2) the person they are addressing, and (3) what they are discussing. *Kinesics* is the study of communication through gesturing, and *proxemics* is the study of the meanings of spatial patterns of people and things.

We introduce some of these and also other concerns in Topic 7, Language, Thought, and Communication.

Language, Thought, and Communication

There is a story, often told in introductory anthropology courses, that the Greek philosopher Plato one day posed to his students the question, "What sets human beings apart from all other creatures?"

One student came up with what seemed to be an irrefutable reply. "Humans," he said, "are featherless bipeds."

While the student was being congratulated by his peers, Plato is said to have slipped away for a while. Upon returning he announced, "Here is our scholar's human being!"— and threw into the crowd of students a freshly plucked chicken.

The question of what exactly separates human beings as a species from all others has continued to vex philosophers and scientists. Until recently, however, there was at least one thing that most people could agree on: only human beings have language. But was that really saying something meaningful? Does the ability to speak represent fundamental properties of our species, or is it just the epiphenomenon of having the curved tongue, short jaw, and minutely controllable lips that facilitate speech? In other words, is the use of language by humans rooted in unique mental properties, or is it something much more superficial?

Some startling studies conducted in the last two decades suggested that the answers to these questions were at hand. Various scholars, using plastic chips, hand-sign language, and other means to communicate with ape research subjects seemed to be concluding that, using nonlinguistic communication, apes are capable of the mental operations that underlie language use by humans. First, apes could learn an astonishingly large number of "words." Koko, a female gorilla, has learned more than 500. Second, and more important, they could apply rules of grammar to the use of these "words." Finally, there even appeared to be evidence that they could combine two "words" to mean something entirely new, as when the chimpanzee Washoe signed *water bird* when, for the first time, her trainer showed her a swan. Thus, it appeared that although only humans speak, other animals have the mental faculties for language use in media that they are equipped to manipulate. Language no longer was the defining characteristic of our species.

This view of apes, humans, and language captured the popular imagination. And, until very recently, it went relatively unchallenged. The data, after all, were compelling. However, a general reassessment of these studies is beginning to cast some doubt on the original findings and to dampen some of the enthusiasm with which they were received. This trend is spearheaded by psychologist Herbert Terrace, whose research originally was intended to support the view that apes had language capabilities. However, after reviewing his data, Terrace found that serious methodological problems made their interpretation problematical. And when he reviewed the methodologies of other studies, he found similar flaws.

True, some apes did learn large numbers of "words." But it was questionable whether they were using rules of grammar to combine them. For one thing, they may simply have learned sequences of signs just as you learn a telephone number—with no sense that the order *means* anything. Terrace noted that many researchers failed to record sign productions that were out of sequence; some even "corrected" sequences that were "wrong." Further, when camera film showed the humans with whom the apes were communicating, Terrace observed that often the teachers were cueing their ape students unconsciously or leading them through sequences one sign at a time. Thus, the "grammar" of the string of signs produced by the ape was, in fact, created by the human beings interacting with the apes.

Finally, Terrace pointed out that without a full description of the context, it is impossible to assess such episodes as Washoe signing *water bird* when being shown a swan. For instance, did Washoe first sign *water* and then, when her trainer asked her to sign again, sign *bird*? In other words, did Washoe ever make a mental connection between two "words"? The evidence does not allow us to judge.

However, in the first article of Topic 7, "Koko: 'Fine Animal Gorilla'," Michael Frisbie by implication asks us to consider whether Terrace's reservations are all that important. Let's accept the fact that human teachers of apes prompt them and even "read between the lines" in attempting to find meaning in their gestures—that's exactly what human parents do when teaching their own children to talk! Francine Patterson's research methodology with Koko may be flawed from the perspective of scientific rigor, but there are some things that scientific research methods simply cannot capture; the loving relationship within which it is possible for a human being to teach communication to an ape may be one of these things.

Thus, at this point is is not exactly clear whether human beings are the only creatures that can use language. Current ongoing research points increasingly to the likelihood that not only apes but also dolphins may have significant linguistic abilities. But most certainly we *are* the only creatures who can use *spoken language* (*speech*). Speech, with its infinite possibilities of expression, is the birthright of every (normal) human being. But when did this linguistic talent evolve? In "Tracing the Origins of Human Speech," Jeffrey T. Laitman describes the ingenious research he and his colleagues have carried out in attempting to answer this seemingly unanswerable question: When did our ancestors first begin to speak? We think you will find his approach fascinating.

Of course, as important as speech is to us, we do not communicate through words alone. In fact, if we were limited to speech to communicate, life would be pretty boring. Think for a moment about the many other ways in which human beings communicate—including gestures, facial expressions, distances at which they position themselves, and the special language of the eyes. All of these constitute *nonverbal communication*, which humans use to convey an enormous amount of information to each other. For one thing, nonverbal communication is constantly used to comment on what is being said verbally. In American culture, for example, rolling the eyes upwards typically is a way for a speaker to let a listener know that the speaker means exactly the opposite of what she or he has said. When it comes to expressing feelings, quite likely more information is conveyed quickly and simply through nonverbal means, such as a touch or a smile, than through words (except, perhaps, the words of poets).

One of the important ways we communicate nonverbally is through the use of space. We all have a "bubble" around us that expands and contracts as we mingle with people on the street, in the office, on the elevator, or on a date. The use of space varies by culture, and even within a culture. In "The Sounds of Silence" (1971), Edward T. Hall and Mary Reed Hall have noted that most white, middle-class Americans use four main distances in their business and social relations: intimate, personal, social, and public.

Intimate distance, which ranges from direct physical contact out to about eighteen inches, is used for our most private activities, such as making love. "At this distance," write the Halls, "you are overwhelmed by sensory inputs from the other person—heat from the body, tactile stimulation from the skin, the fragrance of perfume, even the sound of breathing—all of which literally envelop you." In our society, the public use of intimate distance is discouraged. When overcrowded conditions force us into the intimate distance with strangers, generally we feel very uncomfortable. *Personal distance*, which ranges from one-and-one-half to four feet, is generally used by spouses in public and by people who are talking to each other. In contrast, *social distance*, which ranges from four to twelve feet, is used in working relationships, business transactions, and casual social situations. Finally *public distance*, which ranges from twelve to twenty-five feet and beyond, is used by speakers at public gatherings and by many teachers in the classroom.

Another aspect of nonverbal communication is *touch*. In "Close Encounters," Stephen Thayer rounds out Topic 7 in an article discussing the power of touch to communicate, and he reports on research efforts that attempt to understand the role that touch plays in our lives. We think that you may be surprised at some of these findings.

Koko: "Fine Animal Gorilla"

By Michael J. Frisbie

Over breakfast, Penny Patterson's 14-year-old adopted daughter describes last night's dream, in which she bit her mother to get at a pair of much-admired shoes. The two laugh over the half-silly, half-scary image, and Penny gives her daughter an impulsive hug before they turn to the day's activities.

It's not an unusual scene, until you know that Penny's adopted "daughter," Koko, is a 230-pound talking gorilla.

Dr. Francine "Penny" Patterson, 38, is a psychologist who has devoted the past 13 years of her personal and professional life to a remarkable project in interspecies communication. Koko and her 12-year-old companion, Michael, another spirited but gentle lowland gorilla who shares Penny's home, "talk"—to Penny, other humans and each other—through American Sign Language (Ameslan), a system used by many deaf people. Koko regularly uses about 600 signs and has a total vocabulary of about a thousand. Michael has a smaller vocabulary, having joined the project as a three-year-old, after Koko had already been learning to talk for four years.

The gorillas' grasp of language is impressively sophisticated. They understand spoken English (Penny had to stop spelling c-a-n-d-y when Koko was just a toddler) and can fib, tell jokes, hurl insults ("you dirty toilet" is a favorite epithet of Koko's), create metaphors and even rhyme: Koko once surprised Penny by improvising a poem to describe a blossoming plant: "Flower pink, fruit stink. Fruit pink stink." And Koko named her pet kitten All Ball, which is what she thought the tailless Manx looked like. You may have seen Koko on television newscasts last year, tenderly cradling her beloved new pet and signing "Love that." Then came the report that the kitten had been hit by a car and killed.

Koko's reaction to All Ball's death dramatized the gorilla's ability to understand and discuss such abstract concepts as death and love. Told that she would never see All Ball again, Koko mourned for months, signing "Sleep cat" and "Cry, frown, sad."

Project Koko began in 1972 at the San Francisco Zoo, where one-year-old Koko had been separated from her mother as a sickly infant. Penny was a 25-year-old Stanford graduate student, newly arrived from her native Midwest, trying to discover whether gorillas had a capacity for language. She'd been inspired by hearing scientists Allan and Beatrice Gardner talk about their success in teaching sign language to a chimpanzee named Washoe, a pioneering project still going on under the direction of psychologist Roger Fouts. Recalls Penny, "Although the Gardners delivered their lecture soberly, I felt that I was hearing about something from the realm of myth or fable: Animals were capable of telling us about themselves if one knew the proper way to ask them." Penny hoped to discover whether gorillas, previously considered too unmanageable and unintelligent for such studies, could learn to talk as well as chimpanzees had.

Penny got permission to work with Koko in the zoo's glass-walled nursery. Curious crowds watched her first attempts to mold Koko's fingers into the sign for "drink" before she gave the tiny gorilla a bottle. At the beginning, Koko was happier grabbing at the bottle or simply spinning with her eyes closed, a favorite gorilla game in the wild. But within a month Koko had signed her first word—food. Her vocabulary soon included drink, more, out, dog, come, gimme, up, toothbrush and that. By the second month she was combining words; by the third she had discovered on her own how to turn a statement into a question by using gestures and facial expressions. She clearly loved talking with Penny and her assistants.

Koko began to acquire signs more rapidly and use them creatively. It is the creative use of symbols that, to Penny, marks the communication of both gorillas as genuine language. Koko frequently coins clever phrases such as "finger bracelet" to describe a ring, "bottle match" for cigarette lighter, "eye hat" for a mask, and "elephant baby" to describe a Pinocchio doll. Michael dubbed peas "bean balls" and poetically calls nectarine yogurt "orange flower sauce."

Some members of the scientific community insist that the apes are simply imitating their teachers without understanding the signs they make. But Dr. Jane Goodall, who has devoted her life to studying chimpanzees in the wild, has enough faith in Koko's language abilities to seek her advice on primate preferences. Eager to confirm her belief that chimps are more comfortable when humans sit, rather than stand, Goodall wrote Penny to ask what Koko preferred, seeking an answer "straight from the horse's mouth, as it were." (Koko replied that she likes people to sit down when they're with her.)

 Reprinted from *McCall's*, January 1986, by permission of the author. Photo: Courtesy of Ronald H. Cohn/The Gorilla Foundation

Penny's "child" has developed much like her human counterparts. Between the ages of one and six, Koko scored as slow but not retarded on standard IQ tests for human children, a feat even more remarkable considering the tests' cultural bias against gorillas. For example, Koko was shown pictures of a hat, a spoon, a tree and a house, and asked to point to the one that would provide shelter from the rain. Koko picked the tree and was marked wrong, although the answer made perfect sense to a gorilla.

Penny has seen Koko through the usual childhood stages, from the terrible twos to a defiant adolescence at age seven. "From the beginning of Project Koko I had a dual role," Penny says. "I was a scientist attempting to teach a gorilla human sign language, but I was also a mother to a child with all a child's needs and fears. I discovered the joys and stresses of parenthood. And, like a parent, I was endlessly fascinated by her development and charm." Like most children, Koko faithfully imitated her mother, pretending to talk on the phone, grooming her fingernails when

Penny did hers. And, like most children, Koko could throw herself enthusiastically into mischief, dismantling her toilet (she was trained when she was two), setting off the stove timer, pretending to hug Penny while chewing up a tape-recorder microphone pinned to her smock. "But," says Penny, "any irritation was dispelled when she'd kiss her dolls with loud smacks, tickle my ears or make me a part of her bedtime nest by arranging my arms around her, gently pushing my head down and lying down to cuddle."

At first, Penny's goals were relatively modest and short-term. She just wanted to see if a gorilla could learn sign language. She had underestimated both Koko's abilities and the emotional bond that would develop.

"When I started," she recalls, "I thought we'd end it after four years. I hadn't necessarily thought this would be a lifetime commitment." But, when four years had passed and zoo officials began pressuring Penny to give Koko back so she could be sent to the Los Angeles Zoo, she realized that Koko had much more to learn—and that the

emotional bond between them was too strong to break. "You can't just say to a mother, 'We're taking the child away,'" she explains. With her life savings and donations from gorilla lovers, Penny bought Koko and a wild-born orphan, Michael.

Since 1979, home for Koko and Michael has been the Gorilla Foundation, seven wooded acres hidden in the foggy foothills south of San Francisco. Its name may conjure up images of elaborate research facilities, but the Gorilla Foundation is in fact charmingly and at times chaotically domestic. Penny lives in the main house with Ronald Cohn, her professional and personal companion, who serves as Project Koko's official photographer and video documentarian. In their living room, computer equipment, stacks of videotapes and piles of files compete for space with a mechanical King Kong bank, Koko's "Christmas plates," on which she's drawn pictures of Santa Claus, and other pieces of gorilla memorabilia.

A few yards from the house, the gorillas live in a trailer with kitchens, bedrooms, playrooms, a bathroom and

Penny Patterson holds Koko's pet kitten "Smoky" as Koko signs "smoke."

a yard where they play on warm, sunny days, somewhat rare in the coastal foothills. Their close quarters may help fan the flames of sibling rivalry, which is unfortunate since Penny hopes the pair will someday mate. "It's difficult," she concedes, "for Koko to be attracted to someone she thinks of as her 'rotten stinker' little brother." Koko seems to relish insulting Michael. Penny has recorded this exchange:

Penny: I want to ask you a question.
Koko: Know Mike devil.
Penny: You know that Mike's a devil. That's fine, but that's not what I was going to ask you.

Koko and Michael also tattle on each other. After Penny and a colleague had been discussing whether Michael knew the sign for apple, which he was forming imperfectly, Koko chimed in, "Mike know apple . . . Mike good fake."

Koko also routinely insults Ron, whom she sees as a dominant male and something of a spoilsport. When asked, "What is funny?," Koko once replied, "Koko love Ron," and kissed him on the cheek. Yet when asked to pick her father from a set of photos—including Bwana, her biological father, Ron and other human males—she will pick Ron. Says Ron, "I think it's touching that, if they are upset or scared by something, they come right to me for protection."

Like many children, Koko and Michael sometimes offer observations that Penny diplomatically avoids translating for visitors. Koko has commented on a visitor's bad breath and nicknamed a potbellied reporter "Stomach"; when guests overstay their welcome, especially at bedtime, she may emphatically sign, "Time you go!"

Penny and Koko have grown close in their years of constant contact; Koko still occasionally cries when Penny leaves her for the night, tucked into her nest of three or four soft rugs laid over a tire. "But Michael is different," says Penny. "First of all, he was three and a half when we got him, and another woman worked with him for his first two and a half years with us. So I didn't get that strong bonding with him. He sees me not as a mother but classified with Koko as part of his harem. He seems upset if strange males get near me. And," Penny says, laughing and raising her eyebrows, "he sometimes looks at me in that odd way . . ."

Penny's two children have different personalities. "Koko is outgoing and silly, while Michael is sort of shy and sensitive. He's very artistic; he likes to express himself that way and in fact is very gifted." A painting he titled "Flowers Gorilla More" is a strikingly impressionistic blend of form and color. Though he's not as creative a conver-

sationalist as Koko, Michael values communication. "With a person he knows well, Michael is more willing than Koko to bare his soul," Penny observes. "Koko changes the subject and won't pursue anything for very long, whereas he will get into it. That quality is really interesting; it's almost as if he needs it, like the time he talked about his parents." In a heart-wrenching conversation with one of his teachers, Michael described the killing of his parents in the wild, recalling an episode of "trouble" that culminated in "red," which is the gorillas' word for violence and blood.

Koko tends to be vainer than Michael, although she sometimes responds to compliments by modestly signing "False." "What's the prettiest thing you've ever seen?" she was asked. "Think hair," she replied. "Whose hair?" "Koko's."

Koko has a strong self-image; when asked if she were human or an animal, Koko replied, "Fine animal gorilla." That doesn't keep her from preening for, and mooning over, human male visitors. "Koko tends to see men as potential candidates for her amorous intentions," says Ron. Though Koko generally ignores television, Penny says, "I once found her on her back watching *Love Boat* upside down. She was mainly interested in the partially undressed bodies of the men, I think."

On a typical day, Koko rises at eight and breakfasts on cereal and fruit as she chats with Penny. Before beginning her morning studies with Penny, she may play with Michael, her pet cats or human companions, favoring "tickle and chase" games, regardless of her playmate's species. After lunch, she studies with another teacher, with frequent breaks for recess, when Koko may play outside, color, play with dolls or adorn herself with makeup, scarves and earrings. After a vegetarian dinner at 4:30, Koko may leaf through her books and play with Michael. At bedtime she brushes her teeth (Penny does the back, she does the front), rubs baby oil on her hands and feet and settles herself into her nest.

Playing stepparent to apes is a full-time job. "We get out once in a while, but we seldom, if ever, get a vacation," says Ron, who has no regrets about giving up his career as a cell biologist to devote himself to Project Koko. "Certainly that creates a lot of tension, but we have to cope with it." The magnitude of Penny's commitment gives her pause only once during a series of lengthy, animated conversations. Asked if she would ever like to travel to Koko and Michael's natural habitat in west Africa, Penny becomes wistful. "If I could ever get away, it would be wonderful, but I don't anticipate having

a week or two-week chunk when I could feel comfortable leaving."

What's next for the gorillas? Koko and Michael are beginning yet another astonishing project: They're learning to read. Koko has always enjoyed illustrated books, frequently looking through them and signing to herself, commenting on the stories the pictures represent. Now she's showing a remarkable ability to recognize letters, phonetic groupings and words, an especially amazing achievement when you consider that Koko's primary languages—gorilla gestures and Ameslan—involve no phonetic elements. One difficulty in measuring her progress is distinguishing lack of understanding from lack of interest. "After a session in which Koko learned the written words 'nut,' 'Koko' and 'drink,' I wrote NUP, KOCO and DWINK on cards and asked her what was wrong with those words. She walked away, making no response. A few minutes later, she sauntered past and casually pointed to the C in KOCO. Later still, she strolled past the cards again and pointed to the P in NUP."

While Penny has no plans for human additions to their household, she would like to move to a site that could allow more gorillas into the family. "We're desperately trying to raise enough money to move the project to Hawaii, where Koko and Michael would have a warmer climate—closer to that of their natural habitat—and more room for them and, someday, other gorillas. When we showed Koko a picture of one of the Hawaiian sites, she emphatically signed 'Go!' "

If Penny and company move, they'll take a couple of tiny tagalongs. After the death of All Ball, Koko cried over pictures of cats. Finally she began to ask for another cat—"Tiger, please, tiger"—specifically a tailless Manx.

It took Penny some time to find a Manx kitten; Koko was so frustrated by the delay that she began referring to the promised kitten as "trouble surprise." When Penny proudly presented Koko with a reddish-gold Manx male, the gorilla showed polite interest, looked at the box from which the new pet had emerged and signed "Pick there," remembering that she had been allowed to choose All Ball from a litter. Koko was coolly cordial to the kitten, but stubbornly resisted requests to name it, perversely suggesting "Dog." To complicate matters, Michael began to refer to the kitten as "my cat." Penny solved the problem by letting Koko pick a new cat from a litter—she chose a gray Manx—and giving Michael "his cat." Now Michael and Lips and Koko and Smokey play happily together.

Penny spends as much time attending to Koko and Michael's happiness as she does gathering data for Project Koko. Some critics have suggested that Penny's concern and affection for the gorillas have clouded her perceptions as a scientist. But Roger Fouts of Project Washoe believes that emotional bonds are essential to such work. "When it comes to working with primates, heart—caring—is what it's all about."

Penny would no more withhold her warmth from her children than would any other mother. "They aren't things or even laboratory animals," she says. Penny put it simply when asked how she felt about the subject of her groundbreaking experiment. "I guess it's okay to say it," she responded. "I love Koko."

Koko's and Michael's education and care are made possible by grants and by contributions from members of The Gorilla Foundation, founded by Penny in 1976 to "promote the protection, preservation and propagation of gorillas and other endangered ape species." If you would like to help support this project, contributions may be sent to The Gorilla Foundation, P.O. Box 620-530, Woodside, Calif. 94062.

Tracing the Origins of Human Speech

By Jeffrey T. Laitman

The question of when the ancestors of modern man were first able to produce articulate speech has long puzzled scientists. We have heard many theories about when prehistoric man crossed some "vocal threshold," freeing himself from the confines of ape-like grunts and enabling him to develop the mellifluous tones of an Olivier. Most of these theories, however, have been based on deductions from archeological finds or on the inductive reasoning of the philosopher's mind.

During the last century, scientists studying paleoneurology, a field concerned with the reconstruction of the brains of human ancestors from fossil remains, have added their thoughts about the evolution of speech and language. These workers use the impressions left on the inner table of a fossil skull as a means of estimating where or how large specific areas of the individual's brain may have been. While offering valuable information, paleoneurology has not been able to tell us much about the inner workings of the brain, and as a result can only offer limited evidence about when "speech" may have evolved.

Within the last decade, however, a number of researchers, myself included, have explored a new approach in attempting to solve this old mystery. This technique, which, for lack of an easier term, we might call paleolaryngology, involves the combined use of comparative anatomy and the fossil record. With these tools we attempt to reconstruct the components of our ancestor's vocal

These diagrams depict the anatomy of the vocal tracts of an adult chimpanzee and an adult human during respiration. Some of the main structures are the epiglottis, E; laryngeal cavity, L; hard palate, H; nasal cavity, N; soft palate, S; tongue, T; and vocal fold, V. Note the high position of the larynx in the neck of the chimpanzee, similar to that of a human infant. In the vocal tract of an adult human during respiration, the larynx is much lower in the neck than in the chimpanzee or human infant. This allows room for the extensive modification of sounds produced at the vocal folds.

tract—the larynx, pharynx, tongue and associated structures. Unlike scientists who have sought to explain language origins, those of us who trace the evolution of the vocal tract have focused our attention on more specific questions: what were the anatomy and functions of the vocal tract of our ancestors, and how did this early vocal tract compare with that of present-day man? Findings that have arisen from both my own studies and those of my colleagues Edmund Crelin, professor and chief of anatomy at the Yale University School of Medicine, and Philip Lieberman, professor and chairman of linguistics at Brown University, have helped to develop a dynamic new approach to reconstructing certain behavior patterns of early man.

Swallowing and Breathing Simultaneously

My interest in tracing the origins of speech arose from my investigation of developmental change in the upper respiratory tract of mammals in general and human infants in particular. For the past eight years, Dr. Crelin, a leading expert in the anatomy of human newborns, and I have investigated the anatomical similarities and differences between the upper respiratory tract of humans and that of other mammals. In our studies we examined mammals ranging from dolphins to apes, using techniques ranging from classic postmortem dissections to sophisticated cineradiographic monitoring.

We found that the position of the larynx (or "voice-box") in the neck is of paramount importance in determining the way an animal can breathe, swallow or vocalize. Two general anatomical patterns appear to exist, each with its own functional consequences. The first we might call the "basic" mammalian pattern. In almost all mammals, at all stages of development, the larynx is found quite high in the neck, lying roughly opposite the first to third cervical vertebrae. This high position enables the larynx to literally "lock" into the nasopharynx—near the "back door" of the nasal cavity. The position of the larynx thus provides a direct air tube from the nose to the lungs. Liquid can flow around the interlocked larynx and nasopharynx through passageways known as the piriform sinuses and then on to the esophagus en route to the stomach at the same time the animal is breathing. In essence, then, a cow, cat or monkey can swallow liquids and breathe simultaneously, thanks to these separate pathways for food and air.

There is, however, a limitation to this system—at least from the human point of view. While the high position of the larynx in such mammals as cows, cats, monkeys and apes enables them to breathe and swallow simultaneously, it also severely limits the array of sounds they can produce. In these mammals and most others, the high position of the larynx leaves room for only a small airspace above it (the supralaryngeal

H. Thomas

A cut-away view of the figure on the cover reveals the anatomy of the lower head and upper neck of an australopithecine during vocalization. The volume of the throat above the larynx (see drawing on previous page for anatomical features) is much smaller than in modern adult humans. Dr. Laitman concludes that this volume is insufficient to modify sounds produced at the vocal folds, or "cords," to the extent achieved by modern humans. As a result, these australopithecines could not have produced true human speech.

The reconstructions on these pages are based on the analysis of fossil skulls of early human ancestors. This one, known as Sts 5, is an australopithecine recovered from the Sterkfontein deposits of South Africa. Sts 5 is dated at over 2 million years before the present and is thought to be the cranium of a female.

level of the pharynx). The ability of the pharynx to modify the initial, or fundamental, sounds generated at the vocal folds is thus minimal. As a result, most mammals depend largely on the structures of the oral cavity and lips to modify laryngeal sounds. While some animals can approximate some of the sounds of human speech, they are anatomically incapable of producing the range of sounds necessary for complete, articulate speech.

These drawings, based on Sts 5, show the head, neck and vocal tract of an australopithecine during normal respiration. Note the high position of the larynx and tongue. The epiglottis of the larynx is in direct contact with the soft palate, providing a direct airway from the nasal cavity to the lungs.

The Descent of the Larynx

Our studies also revealed a most significant change that occurs during the development of young human infants. Until the age of approximately 18 months to two years, the position of the larynx in human infants is high in the neck—much like that of any other mammal. Our numerous cineradiographic studies have further showed that newborns breathe, swallow and vocalize in much the same fashion as monkeys and apes. With respect to the upper respiratory tract, we might say that baby humans have the functional anatomy of monkeys.

Some time around the second year of life, the larynx of the human infant begins to "descend" into the neck, dramatically altering the way the child will breathe, swallow and vocalize. How, exactly when, or why this descent occurs is still a mystery. The end result, however, is that the larynx moves to a position completely different from that known in other mammals. The larynx of an adult human corresponds to the fourth to almost the seventh cervical vertebrae, considerably lower than that of any other species. Thus, humans have developed a unique anatomical pattern.

For the first time in mammalian history, the larynx cannot lock into the back of the nasal cavity, separating the breathing and swallowing pathways. This new, low position of the larynx in humans means that the respiratory and digestive tracts now "cross" above the larynx. This crossing can and does have unfortunate drawbacks. One is that a bolus of food can easily lodge in the entrance of the larynx. Another, obviously, is that we adult humans can no longer drink and breathe simultaneously without choking.

As compensation, however, the descent of the larynx into the neck has produced an anatomical feature of enormous value: a greatly expanded pharyngeal chamber above the vocal folds that can modify sound. This adaptation means that sounds emitted from the larynx can be modified to a greater degree than is possible for newborns or any nonhuman mammal. The expanded pharynx is, in essence, the key to our ability to produce fully articulate speech.

"Reconstructing" the Vocal Tract

During the course of these investigations, my colleagues and I noticed that the angulation, or degree of flexion, of the bottom of the skull (the base of the cranium, or basicranium) is related to the position of the larynx. This is not surprising, since the basicranium serves as the "roof" of the upper respiratory tract. We solicited the help of our long-time co-worker Raymond Heimbuch, formerly of Yale and presently manager of statistical programming at Ortho Pharmaceutical. Together we performed detailed statistical analyses of the cranial flexion of many species of mammals. Using these results, we came to the conclusion that two basic skull/larynx relationships exist. In the first, crania that are largely flat or non-flexed relate to larynges positioned high in the neck. This is the pattern found consistently in all mammals except for older humans. In the second, crania that are markedly bent, as found only in humans after the age of about two years, correspond to larynges that are placed quite low in the neck.

The relationships observed in living mammals between the angulation of the skull base and the position of the larynx proved to be a most significant tool in the field of vocal tract reconstruction. Since we now knew that a consistent skull/larynx relationship exists in modern species, we could examine the skulls of fossil animals, particularly fossil human ancestors, and "reconstruct" the approximate level of the larynx and associated structures. If, for example, a skull was found to have a basicranium exhibiting little or no flexion, comparable to that of a living chimpanzee or monkey, we could reconstruct the position of its larynx high in the neck. Conversely, fossils exhibiting the marked flexion

These are reconstructions of an australopithecine drinking water from leaves. Because the high position of the larynx provided a direct airway from nose to lungs, liquids could flow around it en route to the esophagus. This allowed the early hominid to swallow and breathe simultaneously—as can the chimpanzee and human infant. This ability, while reducing the threat of choking, is lost by the adult human, who obtains instead the expanded pharynx that enables the production of fully articulate speech.

of modern adult humans could be reconstructed with a vocal tract like our own. Once the larynx is positioned in this manner, it is possible to infer the breathing, swallowing and vocalizing patterns of these fossil hominids (human ancestors).

The Evidence of Fossils

With this skull/larynx relationship in hand, those of us interested in vocal tract reconstruction had a reliable guide for gauging the position of the larynx. Through funding from the National Science Foundation, I have been able since then to examine the original fossil material housed in collections throughout Africa and Europe in order to evaluate their basicrania and, in turn, reconstruct their vocal tracts. This process is often more difficult than it sounds; fossil skulls dated at 2 to 3 million years before the present are seldom in the best of shape. Fortunately, however, a large enough sample of skulls with intact basicrania remains to give us a valuable look into the past.

The major thrust of our research in recent months has been to decipher the structure of the vocal tract of the earliest hominids, the austra-lopithecines (literally, southern ape-men). These hominids roamed the savannas of southern and eastern Africa about 4 to 1.5 million years before the present. We know from their post-cranial anatomy that they were erect bipeds whose brains were only slightly larger than those of modern apes. Our analysis of many of these australopithecines has revealed that their basicrania were essentially unflexed, much like those of chimpanzees. By the methods outlined above, we reconstructed these forms with a larynx positioned high in the neck, again in a configuration similar to that of a chimpanzee. In essence, we find that these early men probably had a vocal tract much like that of a living monkey or ape. In addition, they probably had the ability to swallow liquids and breathe simultaneously, much like any living non-human primate. These forms probably also had a very restricted vocal repertoire compared to that of modern man. The high position of the larynx in these forms would have made it impossible for them to produce some of the "universal" vowel sounds found in human speech patterns. These "first men" undoubtedly had

some sort of "language," probably slightly more advanced than the "languages" of the living apes, but they were not true speaking men, as we are today.

If the australopithecines had vocal tracts that were essentially ape-like, when did change begin to occur en route to the modern human condition? This is the question that our research is trying to answer at present. While we have not yet come to a definite conclusion, we have some preliminary data on the skulls of *Homo erectus*, creatures living some 1.5 million to 300,000 or 400,000 years ago who followed the australopithecines in evolutionary development. It is among specimens of this species that we find the first examples of basicranial flexion. This indicates to us that the larynx in *Homo erectus* may have begun to descend into the neck, increasing the area available to modify laryngeal sounds. While this crucial change thus seems to have begun more than a million years ago, it was probably not until the arrival of *Homo sapiens* about 300,000 years ago that a modern vocal tract appeared and man began to produce truly articulate speech.

Close Encounters

By Stephen Thayer

. . . .

IN MAY 1985, Brigitte Gerney was trapped beneath a 35-ton collapsed construction crane in New York City for six hours. Throughout her ordeal, she held the hand of rescue officer Paul Ragonese, who stayed by her side as heavy machinery moved the tons of twisted steel from her crushed legs. A stranger's touch gave her hope and the will to live.

Other means of communication can take place at a distance, but touch is the language of physical intimacy. And because it is, touch is the most powerful of all the communication channels—and the most carefully guarded and regulated.

From a mother's cradling embrace to a friend's comforting hug, or a lover's caress, touch has the special power to send messages of union and communion. Among strangers, that power is ordinarily held in check. Whether offering a handshake or a guiding arm, the toucher is careful to stay within the culture's narrowly prescribed limits lest the touch be misinterpreted. Touching between people with more personal relationships is also governed by silent cultural rules and restraints.

The rules of touch may be unspoken, but they're visible to anyone who takes the trouble to watch. Psychologist Richard Heslin at Purdue University, for instance, has proposed five categories of touch based on people's roles and relationships. Each category includes a special range of touches, best described by the quality of touch, the body areas touched and whether the touch is reciprocated.

FUNCTIONAL-PROFESSIONAL touches are performed while the toucher fulfills a special role, such as that of doctor, barber or tailor. For people in these occupations, touch must be devoid of personal messages.

SOCIAL-POLITE touches are formal, limited to greeting and separating and to expressing appreciation among business associates and among strangers and acquaintances. The typical handshake reflects cordiality more than intimacy.

FRIENDSHIP-WARMTH touches occur in the context of personal concern and caring, such as the relationships between extended-family members, friendly neighbors and close work mates. This category straddles the line between warmth and deep affection, a line where friendly touches move over into love touches.

LOVE-INTIMACY touches occur between close family members and friends in relationships where there is affection and caring.

SEXUAL-AROUSAL touches occur in erotic-sexual contexts.

These categories are not hard and fast, since in various cultures and subcultures the rules differ about who can touch whom, in what contexts and what forms the touch may take. In the Northern European "noncontact cultures," overall touch rates are usually quite low. People from these cultures can seem very cold, especially to people from "contact cultures" such as those in the Mediterranean area, where there are much higher rates of touching, even between strangers.

In the United States, a particularly low-touch culture, we rarely see people touch one another in public. Other than in sports and children's play, the most we see of it is when people hold hands in the street, fondle babies or say hello and goodbye. Even on television shows, with the odd exceptions of hitting and kissing, there is little touching.

The cultural differences in contact can be quite dramatic, as researcher Sidney Jourard found in the 1960s when he studied touch between pairs of people in coffee shops around the world. There was more touch in certain cities (180 times an hour between couples in San Juan, Puerto Rico, and 110 times an hour in Paris, France) than in others (2 times an hour between couples in Gainesville, Florida, and 0 times an hour in London, England).

Those cultural contact patterns are embedded early, through child-rearing practices. Psychologist Janice Gibson and her colleagues at the University of Pittsburgh took to the playgrounds and beaches of Greece, the Soviet Union and the United States and compared the frequency and nature of touch between caregivers and children 2 to 5 years old. When it came to retrieving or punishing the children, touching rates were similar in all three countries. But on touches for soothing, holding and play, American children had significantly less contact than those from the other cultures. (Is that why we need bumper stickers to remind us: "Have you hugged your child today?")

Generalizations about different national or ethnic groups can be tricky, however. For example, despite widespread beliefs that Latin Americans are highly contact-oriented, when researcher Robert Shuter at Marquette University compared public contact between couples in Costa Rica, Colombia and Panama, he found that the Costa Ricans both touched and held their partners noticeably more than the couples did in the other two countries.

Within most cultures the rules and meanings of touch are different for men and women, as one recent study in the United States illustrates. Imagine yourself in a hospital bed, about to have major surgery. The nurse comes in to tell you what your operation and after-care will be like. She touches you briefly twice, once on the hand for a few seconds after she introduces herself and again on the arm for a full minute during the instruction period. As she leaves she shakes your hand.

Does this kind of brief reassuring touch add anything to her talk? Does it have any kind of impact on your nervousness or how you respond to the operation? Your reaction is likely to depend upon your gender.

Psychologist Sheryle Whitcher, while working as a graduate student with psychologist Jeffrey Fisher of the University of Connecticut, arranged for a group of surgery patients to be touched in the way described above during their preoperative information session, while other patients got only the information. Women had strikingly positive reactions to being touched; it lowered their blood pressure and anxiety both before surgery and for more than an hour afterwards. But men found the experience upsetting; both their blood pressure and their anxiety rose and stayed elevated in response to being touched.

Why did touch produce such strikingly different responses? Part of the answer may lie in the fact that men in the United States often find it harder to acknowledge dependency and fear than women do; thus, for men, a well-intentioned touch may be a threatening reminder of their vulnerability.

These gender differences are fostered by early experiences, particularly in handling and caretaking. Differences in parents' use of touch with their infant children help to shape and model "male" and "female" touch patterns: Fathers use touch more for play, while mothers use it more for soothing and grooming. The children's gender also affects the kinds of touches they receive. In the United States, for example, girls receive more affectionate touches (kissing, cuddling, holding) than boys do.

By puberty, tactile experiences with parents and peers have already programmed differences in boys' and girls' touching behavior and their use of personal space (see "Body Mapping," this article). Some results of this training are evident when men and women greet people. In one study, psychologists Paul Greenbaum and Howard Rosenfeld of the University of Kansas watched how travelers at the Kansas City International Airport touched people who greeted them. Women greeted women and men more physically, with mutual lip kisses, embraces and more kinds of touch and holding for longer periods of time. In contrast, when men greeted men, most just shook hands and left it at that.

How do you feel about touching and being touched? Are you relaxed and comfortable, or does such contact make you feel awkward and tense? Your comfort with touch may be linked to your personality. Psychologist Knud Larsen and student Jeff LeRoux at Oregon State University looked at how people's personality traits are related to their attitudes toward touching between people of the same sex. The researchers measured touch attitudes through questions such as, "I enjoy persons of my sex who are comfortable with touching," "I sometimes enjoy hugging friends of the same sex" and "Physical expression of affection between persons of the same sex is healthy." Even though men were generally less comfortable about same-sex touching than women were, the more authoritarian and rigid people of both sexes were the least comfortable.

A related study by researchers John Deethardt and Debbie Hines at Texas Tech University in Lubbock, Texas, examined personality and attitudes toward being touched by opposite-sex friends and lovers and by same-sex friends. Touch attitudes were tapped with such questions as, "When I am with my girl/-boyfriend I really like to touch that person to show affection," "When I tell a same-sex intimate friend that I have just gotten a divorce, I want that person to touch me" and "I enjoy an opposite-sex acquaintance touching me when we greet each other." Regardless of gender, people who were comfortable with touching were also more talkative, cheerful, socially dominant and nonconforming; those discomforted by touch tended to be more emotionally unstable and socially withdrawn.

A recent survey of nearly 4,000 undergraduates by researchers Janis Andersen, Peter Andersen and Myron Lustig of San Diego State University revealed that, regardless of gender, people who were less comfortable about touching were also more apprehensive about communicating and had lower self-esteem. Several other studies have shown that people who are more comfortable with touch are less afraid and suspicious of other people's motives and intentions and have less anxiety and tension in their everyday lives. Not surprisingly, another study showed they are also likely to be more satisfied with their bodies and physical appearance.

These different personality factors play themselves out most revealingly in the intimacy of love relationships. Couples stay together and break apart for many reasons, including the way each partner expresses and reacts to affection and intimacy. For some, feelings and words are enough; for others, touch and physical intimacy are more critical.

In the film *Annie Hall*, Woody Allen and Diane Keaton are shown split-screen as each talks to an analyst about their sexual relationship. When the analyst asks how often they have sex, he answers, "Hardly ever, maybe three times a week," while she describes it as "constantly, three times a week."

How important is physical intimacy in close relationships? What role does touch play in marital satisfaction? Psychologists Betsy Tolstedt and Joseph Stokes of the University of Illinois at Chicago tried to find out by interviewing and observing couples. They used three measures of intimacy: emotional intimacy (feelings of closeness, support, tolerance); verbal intimacy (disclosure of emotions, feelings, opinions); and physical intimacy (satisfaction with "companionate" and sexual touch). The researchers also measured marital satisfaction and happiness, along with conflicts and actual separations and legal actions.

They found that each form of intimacy made its own contribution to marital satisfaction, but—perhaps surprisingly to some—physical intimacy mattered the least of the three. Conflict and divorce potential were most connected to dissatisfaction with emotional and verbal intimacy.

Touch intimacy may not usually have the power to make or break marriages, but it can sway strangers and even people close to you, often without their knowledge. The expressions "to put the touch on someone" and "that person is an easy touch" refer to the persuasive power of touch. Indeed, research shows that it is harder to say no to someone who makes a request when it is accompanied by a touch.

Politicians know this well. Ignoring security concerns, political candidates plunge into the crowd to kiss babies and "press the flesh." Even a quick handshake leaves a lasting impression—a personal touch—that can pay off later at election time.

A momentary and seemingly incidental touch can establish a positive, temporary bond between strangers, making them more helpful, compliant, generous and positive. In one experiment in a library, a slight hand brush in the course of returning library cards to patrons was enough to influence patrons' positive attitudes toward the library and its staff. In another study, conducted in restaurants, a fleeting touch paid off in hard cash. Waitresses who touched their customers on the hand or shoulder as they returned change received a larger percentage of the bill as their tip. Even though they risked crossing role boundaries by touching customers in such familiar ways, their ingratiating service demeanor offset any threat.

In certain situations, touch can be discomforting because it signals power. Psychologist Nancy Henley of the University of California, Los Angeles, after observing the touch behavior of people as they went about their daily lives, has suggested that higher-status individuals enjoy more touch liberties with their lower-status associates. To Henley, who has noted how touch signals one's place in the status-dominance hierarchy, there is even a sexist "politics of touch." She has found that women generally rank lower than men in the touch hierarchy, very much like the secretary-boss, student-teacher and worker-foreman relationships. In all of these, it is considered unseemly for lower-status individuals to put their hands on superiors. Rank does have its touching privileges.

The rules of the status hierarchy are so powerful that people can infer status differences from watching other people's touch behavior. In one experiment by psychologists Brenda Major and Richard Heslin of Purdue University, observers could see only the silhouettes of pairs of people facing each other, with one touching the other on the shoulder. They judged the toucher to be more assertive and of a higher status than the person touched. Had the touch been reciprocal, status differences would have disappeared.

Psychologist Alvin G. Goldstein and student Judy Jeffords at the University of Missouri have sharpened our understanding of touch and status through their field study of touch among legislators during a Missouri state legislative session. Observers positioned themselves in the gallery and systematically recorded who initiated touch during the many floor conversations. Based on a status formula that included committee leadership and membership, they discovered that among these male peers, the lower-status men were the ones most likely to initiate touch.

When roles are clearly different, so that one individual has control or power over the other, such as a boss and a secretary, then touch usually reflects major dominance or status differences in the relationship. But when roles are more diffuse and overlapping, so that people are almost equal in power—as the legislators were—then lower-status people may try to establish more intimate connections with their more powerful and higher-status colleagues by making physical contact with them.

Touching has a subtle and often ambivalent role in most settings. But there is one special circumstance in which touch is permitted and universally positive: In sports, teammates encourage, applaud and console each other generously through touch. In Western cultures, for men especially, hugs and slaps on the behind are permitted among athletes, even though they are very rarely seen between heterosexual men outside the sports arena. The intense enthusiasm legitimizes tactile expressions of emotion that would otherwise be seen as homosexually threatening.

Graduate student Charles Anderton and psychologist Robert Heckel of the University of South Carolina studied touch in the competitive context of all-male or all-female championship swim meets by recording each instance of touch after success and failure. Regardless of sex, winners were touched similarly, on average six times more than losers, with most of the touches to the hand and some to the back or shoulders; only a small percent were to the head or buttocks.

This swimming study only looked at touch between same-sex teammates, since swim meets have separate races for men and women. Would touch patterns be the same for mixed-gender teams, or would men and women be inhibited about initiating and receiving touches, as they are in settings outside of sports? Psychologists David Smith, Frank Willis and Joseph Gier at the University of Missouri studied touching behavior of men and women in bowling alleys in Kansas City, Missouri, during mixed-league competition. They found almost no differences between men and women in initiating or receiving touches.

Without the social vocabulary of touch, life would be cold, mechanical, distant, rational, verbal. We are created in the intimate union of two bodies and stay connected to the body of one until the cord is cut. Even after birth, we need touch for survival. Healthy human infants deprived of touch and handling for long periods develop a kind of infant depression that leads to withdrawal and apathy and, in extreme cases, wasting away to death.

As people develop, touch assumes symbolic meaning as the primary system for expressing and experiencing affection, inclusion and control. Deprived of those gestures and their meanings, the world might be more egalitarian, but it would also be far more frightening, hostile and chilly. And who would understand why a stranger's touch meant life to Brigitte Gerney?

5
Cultural Anthropology

Cultural anthropology has two main areas of study. One, termed *ethnography*, is the intensive study, description, and analysis of a specific group of people and their culture. The other, *ethnology*, is the systematic comparison of materials across cultural boundaries, with the aim of detecting and specifying accurate generalizations (formerly called laws) about human behavior and culture. The concept *culture* is central to both ethnography and ethnology.

What is *culture*? Surprisingly, although it is the central concept of anthropology, it is difficult to find exact agreement on the meaning of the term among anthropologists. Depending on their interests, scholars emphasize the symbolic nature of culture, its function as a mechanism of adaptation, the ways in which it structures our perception of the world, or the ways it patterns behavior. Nevertheless, it is possible to find agreement among anthropologists with regard to some basic aspects of culture:

1. Culture is central to human existence. The biological and cultural sides of humankind evolved together, constantly affecting each other's course. The concept *human being* and the concept *culture* are thus inseparable.

2. Culture is not inherited through the genes. Each person acquires his or her culture through interaction with other members of the group(s) into which she or he is born. In other words, culture is learned.

3. Not only is culture learned, but also everything that is learned is culture. All human knowledge, activities, beliefs, values, mores, schemes for organizing information about the world, languages, philosophical systems, technologies, art, and major behavioral patterns are learned and hence are aspects of culture.

4. Culture is a group phenomenon. The growing infant does not invent a culture for itself; it learns the culture of its society. Left all alone to its own devices, an infant *cannot* invent culture. Indeed, if a child is deprived of the opportunity to learn a language by the time it is five or six, it is probably unlikely ever to be able to learn one afterward.

5. Culture is patterned. All cultures of the world consist of many facets and elements. But these are not randomly thrown together like marbles in a bag or patches on a quilt. There are systematic relationships among the elements of a culture, and change in one area is likely to cause stress or change in other areas.

6. Culture is symbolic. This means that all cultural phenomena have meanings beyond their own existence. (A cat, in American culture, is not just an animal with the label *cat*. It "has nine lives," is "stealthy," and is "independent." A cat, then, as a part of our culture, represents a set of meanings; in other words, it is a symbol.) Culture, therefore, provides the backdrop of shared meanings against which all things are experienced.

As you can see, the subject of cultural anthropology is vast. It embodies the study of virtually every aspect of human behavior—from how you nourish yourself to how you feel about yourself and others, from your religion (or lack of one) to how you drive a car. For convenience, we have organized the articles in this part into seven topics, although we certainly have not come close to covering all areas of cultural anthropology. Nevertheless, we offer you interesting reading in some of the most important areas.

Fieldwork

....

For most anthropologists, fieldwork is one of the most significant experiences of their lives. Few anthropologists return home from the field unchanged, and for many, the personal changes are quite deep and enduring. In a distant place among strangers, the fieldworker is cut off from the people and patterns that gave his or her life meaning and in terms of which she or he built a sense of self. In a very real sense, the fieldworker becomes childlike: understanding little, incompetent to perform any locally valued tasks, utterly dependent on the good will of others for virtually everything. Like a child, the fieldworker starts to build a social identity; to a great measure, the success of the research will depend upon how well she or he succeeds in accomplishing this task. Not the least of fieldwork's challenges is to come to terms with the world view of the hosts and research subjects—which frequently is at significant variance with the fieldworker's own world view.

Napoleon A. Chagnon is very candid about the emotional stress he endured in the course of "Doing Fieldwork among the Yąnomamö." One can hardly imagine a society more different from our own. However, a word of caution is in order. Without giving away the whole story, we wish to indicate that one point made by Horace Miner's "Body Ritual among the Nacirema" is that the language used by the researcher in reporting on the behavior of his or her subjects can make them seem much more foreign than they really are.

"Shakespeare in the Bush," by Laura Bohannan, and "Eating Christmas in the Kalahari," by Richard B. Lee, both deal with the problem of cross-cultural (mis)understanding. It is inevitable that the fieldworker will misunderstand—and be misunderstood by—the people she or he is studying. Good researchers, however, use instances of misunderstanding as instruments of investigation into the divergent premises of the culture of their subjects, and their own culture as well. The result can be a much deeper understanding of both.

Doing Fieldwork Among the Yąnomamö

By Napoleon A. Chagnon

....

The Yąnomamö[1] Indians live in southern Venezuela and the adjacent portions of northern Brazil. Some 125 widely scattered villages have populations ranging from 40 to 250 inhabitants, with 75 to 80 people the most usual number. In total numbers their population probably approaches 10,000 people, but this is merely a guess. Many of the villages have not yet been contacted by outsiders, and nobody knows for sure exactly how many uncontacted villages there are, or how many people live in them. By comparison to African or Melanesian tribes, the Yąnomamö population is small. Still, they are one of the largest unacculturated tribes left in all of South America.

But they have a significance apart from tribal size and cultural purity: the Yąnomamö are still actively conducting warfare. It is in the nature of man to fight, according to one of the myths, because the blood of "Moon" spilled on this layer of the cosmos, causing men to become fierce. I describe the Yąnomamö as "the fierce people" because that is the most accurate single phrase that describes them. That is how they conceive them-

selves to be, and that is how they would like others to think of them.

I spent nineteen months with the Yąnomamö,[2] during which time I acquired some proficiency in their language and, up to a point, submerged myself in their culture and way of life. The thing that impressed me most was the importance of aggression in their culture. I had the opportunity to witness a good many incidents that expressed individual vindictiveness on the one hand and collective bellicosity on the other. These ranged in seriousness from the ordinary incidents of wife beating and chest pounding to dueling and organized raiding by parties that set out with the intention of ambushing and killing men from enemy villages (Fig. 1). One of the villages discussed in the chapters that follow was raided approximately twenty-five times while I conducted the fieldwork, six times by the group I lived among.

The fact that the Yąnomamö live in a state of chronic warfare is reflected in their mythology, values, settlement pattern, political behavior and marriage practices. Accordingly, I have organized this case study in such a way that students can appreciate the effects of warfare on Yąnomamö culture in general and on their social organization and politics in particular (Fig. 1).

I collected the data under somewhat trying circumstances, some of which I will describe in order to give the student a rough idea of what is generally meant when anthropologists speak of "culture shock" and "fieldwork." It should be borne in mind, however, that each field situation is in many respects unique, so that the problems I encountered do not necessarily exhaust the range of possible problems other anthropologists have confronted in other areas. There are a few problems, however, that seem to be nearly universal among anthropological fieldworkers, particularly those having to do with eating, bathing, sleeping, lack of privacy and loneliness, or discovering that primitive man is not always as noble as you originally thought.

1. The word Yąnomamö is nasalized through its entire length, indicated by the diacritical mark [ą]. When this mark appears on a word, the entire word is nasalized. The terminal vowel [-ö] represents a sound that does not occur in the English language. It corresponds to the phone [+] of linguistic orthography. In normal conversation, Yąnomamö is pronounced like "Yah-no-mama," except that it is nasalized. Finally, the words having the [-ä] vowel are pronounced at that vowel with the "uh" sound of "duck." Thus, the name Kąobawä would be pronounced "cow-ba-wuh," again nasalized.

2. I spent a total of twenty-three months in South America of which nineteen were spent among the Yąnomamö on three separate field trips. The first trip, November 1964 through February 1966, was to Venezuela. During this time I spent nineteen months in direct contact with the Yąnomamö, using my periodic trips back to Caracas to visit my family and to collate the genealogical data I had collected up to that point. On my second trip, January through March 1967, I spent two months among Brazilian Yąnomamö and one more month with Venezuelan Yąnomamö. Finally, I returned to Venezuela for three more months among the Yąnomamö, January through April 1968.

This is not to state that primitive man everywhere is unpleasant. By way of contrast, I have also done limited fieldwork among the Yąnomamö's northern neighbors, the Carib-speaking Makiritare Indians. This group was very pleasant and charming, all of them anxious to help me and honor bound to show any visitor the numerous courtesies of their system of etiquette. In short, they approached the image of primitive man that I had conjured up, and it was sheer pleasure to work with them. The recent work by Colin Turnbull (1966) brings out dramatically the contrast in personal characteristics of two African peoples he has studied.

Hence, what I say about some of my experiences is probably equally true of the experiences of many fieldworkers. I write about my own experiences because there is a conspicuous lack of fieldwork descriptions available to potential fieldworkers. I think I could have profited by reading about the private misfortunes of my own teachers; at least I might have been able to avoid some of the more stupid errors I made. In this regard there are a number of recent contributions by fieldworkers describing some of the discomforts and misfortunes they themselves sustained.[3] Students planning to conduct fieldwork are urged to consult them.

My first day in the field illustrated to me what my teachers meant when they spoke of "culture shock." I had traveled in a small, aluminum rowboat propelled by a large outboard motor for two and a half days. This took me from the Territorial capital, a small town on the Orinoco River, deep into Yąnomamö country. On the morning of the third day we reached a small mission settlement, the field "headquarters" of a group of Americans who were working in two Yąnomamö villages. The missionaries had come out of these villages to hold their annual conference on the progress of their mission work, and were conducting their meetings when I arrived. We picked up a passenger at the mission station, James P. Barker, the first non-Yąnomamö to make a sustained, permanent contact with the tribe (in 1950). He had just returned from a year's furlough in the United States, where I had earlier visited him before leaving for Venezuela. He agreed to accompany me to the village I had selected for my base of operations to introduce me to the Indians. This village was also his own home base, but he had not been there for over a year and did not plan to join me for another three months. Mr. Barker had been living with this particular group about five years.

3. Maybury-Lewis, 1967, "Introduction," and 1965b; Turnbull 1966; L.Bohannan, 1964. Perhaps the most intimate account of the tribulations of a fieldworker is found in the posthumous diary of Bronislaw Malinowski (1967). Since the diary was not written for publication, it contains many intimate, very personal details about the writer's anxieties and hardships.

We arrived at the village, Bisaasi-teri, about 2:00 P.M. and docked the boat along the muddy bank at the terminus of the path used by the Indians to fetch their drinking water. It was hot and muggy, and my clothing was soaked with perspiration. It clung uncomfortably to my body, as it did thereafter for the remainder of the work. The small, biting gnats were out in astronomical numbers, for it was the beginning of the dry season. My face and hands were swollen from the venom of their numerous stings. In just a few moments I was to meet my first Yąnomamö, my first primitive man. What would it be like? I had visions of entering the village and seeing 125 social facts running about calling each other kinship terms and sharing food, each waiting and anxious to have me collect his genealogy. I would wear them out in turn. Would they like me? This was important to me; I wanted them to be so fond of me that they would adopt me into their kinship system and way of life, because I had heard that successful anthropologists always get adopted by their people. I had learned during my seven years of anthropological training at the University of Michigan that kinship was equivalent to society in primitive tribes and that it was a moral way of life, "moral" being something "good" and "desirable." I was determined to work my way into their moral system of kinship and become a member of their society.

My heart began to pound as we approached the village and heard the buzz of activity within the circular compound. Mr. Barker commented that he was anxious to see if any changes had taken place while he was away and wondered how many of them had died during his absence. I felt into my back pocket to make sure that my notebook was still there and felt personally more secure when I touched it. Otherwise, I would not have known what to do with my hands.

The entrance to the village was covered over with brush and dry palm leaves. We pushed them aside to expose the low opening to the village. The excitement of meeting my first Indians was almost unbearable as I duck-waddled through the low passage into the village clearing.

I looked up and gasped when I saw a dozen burly, naked, filthy, hideous men staring at us down the shafts of their drawn arrows! Immense wads of green tobacco were stuck between their lower teeth and lips making them look even more hideous, and strands of dark-green slime dripped or hung from their noses. We arrived at the village while the men were blowing a hallucinogenic drug up their noses. One of the side effects of the drug is a runny nose. The mucus is always saturated with the green powder and the Indians usually let it run freely from their nostrils. My next discovery was that there were a dozen or so vicious, underfed dogs snapping at my legs, circling me as if I were going to be their next meal. I just stood there holding

Fig. 1. Members of allied villages engaged in a chest-pounding duel which followed a feast.

my notebook, helpless and pathetic. Then the stench of the decaying vegetation and filth struck me and I almost got sick. I was horrified. What sort of a welcome was this for the person who came here to live with you and learn your way of life, to become friends with you? They put their weapons down when they recognized Barker and returned to their chanting, keeping a nervous eye on the village entrances.

We had arrived just after a serious fight. Seven women had been abducted the day before by a neighboring group, and the local men and their guests had just that morning recovered five of them in a brutal club fight that nearly ended in a shooting war. The abductors, angry because they lost five of the seven captives, vowed to raid the Bisaasi-teri. When we arrived and entered the village unexpectedly, the Indians feared that we were the raiders. On several occasions during the next two hours the men in the village jumped to their feet, armed themselves, and waited nervously for the noise outside the village to be identified. My enthusiasm for collecting ethnographic curiosities diminished in proportion to the number of times such an alarm was raised. In fact, I was relieved when Mr. Barker suggested that we sleep across the river for the evening. It would be safer over there.

As we walked down the path to the boat, I pondered the wisdom of having decided to spend a year and a half with this tribe before I had even seen what they were like. I am not ashamed to admit, either, that had there been a diplomatic way out, I would have ended my fieldwork then and there. I did not look forward to the next day when I would be left alone with the Indians; I did not speak a word of their language, and they were decidedly different from what I had imagined them to be. The whole situation was depressing, and I wondered why I ever decided to switch from civil engineering to anthropology in the first place. I had not eaten all day, I was soaking wet from perspiration, the gnats were biting me, and I was covered with red pigment, the result of a dozen or so complete examinations I had been given by as many burly Indians. These examinations capped an otherwise grim day. The In-

Fig. 2. One way that warfare affects other aspects of Yǫnomamö social organization is in the great significance of intervillage alliances. Here members of an allied village dance excitedly in their hosts' village in anticipation of the feast and chest-pounding duel that will follow.

dians would blow their noses into their hands, flick as much of the mucus off that would separate in a snap of the wrist, wipe the residue into their hair, and then carefully examine my face, arms, legs, hair, and the contents of my pockets. I asked Mr. Barker how to say "Your hands are dirty"; my comments were met by the Indians in the following way: They would "clean" their hands by spitting a quantity of slimy tobacco juice into them, rub them together, and then proceed with the examination.

Mr. Barker and I crossed the river and slung our hammocks. When he pulled his hammock out of a rubber bag, a heavy, disagreeable odor of mildewed cotton came with it. "Even the missionaries are filthy," I thought to myself. Within two weeks, everything I owned smelled the same way, and I lived with that odor for the remainder of the fieldwork. My own habits of personal cleanliness reached such levels that I didn't

even mind being examined by the Indians, as I was not much cleaner than they were after I had adjusted to the circumstances.

So much for my discovery that primitive man is not the picture of nobility and sanitation I had conceived him to be. I soon discovered that it was an enormously time-consuming task to maintain my own body in the manner to which it had grown accustomed in the relatively antiseptic environment of the northern United States. Either I could be relatively well fed and relatively comfortable in a fresh change of clothes and do very little fieldwork, or, I could do considerably more fieldwork and be less well fed and less comfortable.

It is appalling how complicated it can be to make oatmeal in the jungle. First, I had to make two trips to the river to haul the water. Next, I had to prime my kerosene stove with alcohol and get it burning, a tricky procedure when you are trying to mix powdered milk and fill a coffee pot at the same time: the alcohol prime always burned out before I could turn the kerosene on, and I would have to start all over. Or, I would turn the kerosene on, hoping that the element was still hot enough to vaporize the fuel, and start a small fire in my palm-thatched hut as the liquid kerosene squirted all over the table and walls and ignited. It was safer to start over with the alcohol. Then I had to boil the oatmeal and pick the bugs out of it. All my supplies, of course, were carefully stored in Indian-proof, rat-proof, moisture-proof, and insect-proof containers, not one of which ever served its purpose adequately. Just taking things out of the multiplicity of containers and repacking them afterward was a minor project in itself. By the time I had hauled the water to cook with, unpacked my food, prepared the oatmeal, milk, and coffee, heated water for the dishes, washed and dried the dishes, repacked the food in the containers, stored the containers in locked trunks and cleaned up my mess, the ceremony of preparing breakfast had brought me almost up to lunch time!

Eating three meals a day was out of the question. I solved that problem by eating a single meal that could be prepared in a single container, or, at most, in two containers, washed my dishes only when there were no clean ones left, using cold river water, and wore each change of clothing at least a week to cut down on my laundry problem, a courageous undertaking in the tropics. I was also less concerned about sharing provisions with the rats, insects, Indians, and the elements, thereby eliminating the need for my complicated storage process. I was able to last most of the day on *café con leche,* heavily sugared espresso coffee diluted about five to one with hot milk. I would prepare this in the evening and store it in a thermos. Frequently, my single meal was no more complicated than a can of sardines and a package of crackers. But at least two or three times a week I would do something sophisticated, like make oatmeal or boil rice and add a can of tuna fish or tomato paste to it. I even saved time by devising a water system that obviated the trips to the river. I had a few sheets of zinc roofing brought in and made a rain-water trap; I caught the water on the zinc surface, funneled it into an emply gasoline drum, and then ran a plastic hose from the drum to my hut. When the drum was exhausted in the dry season, I hired the Indians to fill it with water from the river.

I ate much less when I traveled with the Indians to visit other villages. Most of the time my travel diet consisted of roasted or boiled green plantains that I obtained from the Indians, but I always carried a few cans of sardines with me in case I got lost or stayed away longer than I had planned. I found peanut butter and crackers a very nourishing food, and a simple one to prepare on trips. It was nutritious and portable, and

only one tool was required to prepare the meal, a hunting knife that could be cleaned by wiping the blade on a leaf. More importantly, it was one of the few foods the Indians would let me eat in relative peace. It looked too much like animal feces to them to excite their appetites.

I once referred to the peanut butter as the dung of cattle. They found this quite repugnant. They did not know what "cattle" were, but were generally aware that I ate several canned products of such an animal. I perpetrated this myth, if for no other reason than to have some peace of mind while I ate. Fieldworkers develop strange defense mechanisms, and this was one of my own forms of adaptation. On another occasion I was eating a can of frankfurters and growing very weary of the demands of one of my guests for a share in my meal. When he asked me what I was eating, I replied: "Beef." He then asked, "What part of the animal are you eating?" to which I replied, "Guess!" He stopped asking for a share.

Meals were a problem in another way. Food sharing is important to the Yąnomamö in the context of displaying friendship. "I am hungry," is almost a form of greeting with them. I could not possibly have brought enough food with me to feed the entire village, yet they seemed not to understand this. All they could see was that I did not share my food with them at each and every meal. Nor could I enter into their system of reciprocities with respect to food; every time one of them gave me something "freely," he would dog me for months to pay him back, not with food, but with steel tools. Thus, if I accepted a plantain from someone in a different village while I was on a visit, he would most likely visit me in the future and demand a machete as payment for the time that he "fed" me. I usually reacted to these kinds of demands by giving a banana, the customary reciprocity in their culture—food for food—but this would be a disappointment for the individual who had visions of that single plantain growing into a machete over time.

Despite the fact that most of them knew I would not share my food with them at their request, some of them always showed up at my hut during mealtime. I gradually became accustomed to this and learned to ignore their persistent demands while I ate. Some of them would get angry because I failed to give in, but most of them accepted it as just a peculiarity of the subhuman foreigner. When I did give in, my hut quickly filled with Indians, each demanding a sample of food that I had given one of them. If I did not give all a share, I was that much more despicable in their eyes.

A few of them went out of their way to make my meals unpleasant, to spite me for not sharing; for example, one man arrived and watched me eat a cracker with honey on it. He immediately recognized the honey, a particularly esteemed Yąnomamö food. He knew that I would not share my tiny bottle and that it would be futile to ask. Instead, he glared at me and queried icily, "Shaki!⁴ What kind of animal semen are you eating on that cracker?" His question had the desired effect, and my meal ended.

Finally, there was the problem of being lonely and separated from your own kind, especially your family. I tried to overcome this by seeking personal friendships among the Indians. This only complicated the matter because all my friends simply used my confidence to gain privileged access to my cache of steel tools and trade goods, and looted me. I would be bitterly disappointed that my "friend" thought no more of me than to finesse our relationship exclusively with the intention of getting at my locked up possessions, and my depression would hit new lows every time I discovered this. The loss of the possession bothered me much less than the shock that I was, as far as most of them were concerned, nothing more than a source of desirable items; no holds were barred in relieving me of these, since I was considered something subhuman, a non-Yąnomamö.

The thing that bothered me most was the incessant, passioned, and aggressive demands the Indians made. It would become so unbearable that I would have to lock myself in my mud hut every once in a while just to escape from it: Privacy is one of Western culture's greatest achievements. But I did not want privacy for its own sake; rather, I simply had to get away from the begging. Day and night for the entire time I lived with the Yąnomamö I was plagued by such demands as "Give me a knife, I am poor!"; "If you don't take me with you on your next trip to Widokaiya-teri I'll chop a hole in your canoe!"; "Don't point your camera at me or I'll hit you!"; "Share your food with me!"; "Take me across the river in your canoe and be quick about it!"; "Give me a cooking pot!"; "Loan me your flashlight so I can go hunting tonight!"; "Give me medicine . . . I itch all over!"; "Take us on a week-long hunting trip with your shotgun!"; and "Give me an axe or I'll break into your hut when you are away visiting and steal one!" And so I was bombarded by such demands day after day, months on end, until I could not bear to see an Indian.

It was not as difficult to become calloused to the incessant begging as it was to ignore the sense of urgency, the impassioned tone of voice, or the intimida-

4. "Shaki," or, rather, "Shakiwa," is the name they gave me because they could not pronounce "Chagnon." They like to name people for some distinctive feature when possible. *Shaki* is the name of a species of noisome bee; they accumulate in large numbers around ripening bananas and make pests of themselves by eating into the fruit, showering the people below with the debris. They probably adopted this name for me because I was also a nuisance, continuously prying into their business, taking pictures of them, and, in general, being where they did not want me.

tion and aggression with which the demands were made. It was likewise difficult to adjust to the fact that the Yąnomamö refused to accept "no" for an answer until or unless it seethed with passion and intimidation—which it did after six months. Giving in to a demand always established a new threshold; the next demand would be for a bigger item or favor, and the anger of the Indians even greater if the demand was not met. I soon learned that I had to become very much like the Yąnomamö to be able to get along with them on their terms: sly, aggressive, and intimidating.

Had I failed to adjust in this fashion I would have lost six months of supplies to them in a single day or would have spent most of my time ferrying them around in my canoe or hunting for them. As it was, I did spend a considerable amount of time doing these things and did succumb to their outrageous demands for axes and machetes, at least at first. More importantly, had I failed to demonstrate that I could not be pushed around beyond a certain point, I would have been the subject of far more ridicule, theft, and practical jokes than was the actual case. In short, I had to acquire a certain proficiency in their kind of interpersonal politics and to learn how to imply subtly that certain potentially undesirable consequences might follow if they did such and such to me. They do this to each other in order to establish precisely the point at which they cannot goad an individual any further without precipitating retaliation. As soon as I caught on to this and realized that much of their aggression was stimulated by their desire to discover my flash point, I got along much better with them and regained some lost ground. It was sort of like a political game that everyone played, but one in which each individual sooner or later had to display some sign that his bluffs and implied threats could be backed up. I suspect that the frequency of wife beating is a component of this syndrome, since men can display their ferocity and show others that they are capable of violence. Beating a wife with a club is considered to be an acceptable way of displaying ferocity and one that does not expose the male to much danger. The important thing is that the man has displayed his potential for violence and the implication is that other men better treat him with respect and caution.

After six months, the level of demand was tolerable in the village I used for my headquarters. The Indians and I adjusted to each other and knew what to expect with regard to demands on their part for goods, favors, and services. Had I confined my fieldwork to just that village alone, the field experience would have been far more enjoyable. But, as I was interested in the demographic pattern and social organization of a much larger area, I made regular trips to some dozen different villages in order to collect genealogies or to recheck those I already had. Hence, the intensity of begging and in-

Fig. 3. Kąobawä, the wise leader, listens to identify a strange noise in the jungle.

timidation was fairly constant for the duration of the fieldwork. I had to establish my position in some sort of pecking order of ferocity at each and every village.

For the most part, my own "fierceness" took the form of shouting back at the Yąnomamö as loudly and as passionately as they shouted at me, especially at first, when I did not know much of their language. As I became more proficient in their language and learned more about their political tactics, I became more sophisticated in the art of bluffing. For example, I paid one young man a machete to cut palm trees and make boards from the wood. I used these to fashion a platform in the bottom of my dugout canoe to keep my possessions dry when I traveled by river. That afternoon I was doing informant work in the village; the

long-awaited mission supply boat arrived, and most of the Indians ran out of the village to beg goods from the crew. I continued to work in the village for another hour or so and went down to the river to say "hello" to the men on the supply boat. I was angry when I discovered that the Indians had chopped up all my palm boards and used them to paddle their own canoes[5] across the river. I knew that if I overlooked this incident I would have invited them to take greater liberties with my goods in the future. I crossed the river, docked amidst their dugouts, and shouted for the Indians to come out and see me. A few of the culprits appeared, mischievous grins on their faces. I gave a spirited lecture about

5. The canoes were obtained from missionaries, who, in turn, got them from a different tribe.

Fig. 4. Koamashima, Kaobawä's youngest wife, playing with her son, who is holding a tree frog.

how hard I had worked to put those boards in my canoe, how I had paid a machete for the wood, and how angry I was that they destroyed my work in their haste to cross the river. I then pulled out my hunting knife and, while their grins disappeared, cut each of their canoes loose, set it into the current, and let them float away. I left without further ado and without looking back.

They managed to borrow another canoe and, after some effort, recovered their dugouts. The headman of the village later told me with an approving chuckle that I had done the correct thing. Everyone in the village, except, of course, the culprits, supported and defended my action. This raised my status.

Whenever I took such action and defended my

rights, I got along much better with the Yąnomamö. A good deal of their behavior toward me was directed with the forethought of establishing the point at which I would react defensively. Many of them later reminisced about the early days of my work when I was "timid" and a little afraid of them, and they could bully me into giving goods away.

Theft was the most persistent situation that required me to take some sort of defensive action. I simply could not keep everything I owned locked in trunks, and the Indians came into my hut and left at will. I developed a very effective means for recovering almost all the stolen items. I would simply ask a child who took the item and then take the person's hammock when he was not around, giving a spirited lecture to the others as I

Fig. 5. Rerebawä during an ebene *session sitting on the sidelines in an hallucinogenic stupor.*

marched away in a faked rage with the thief's hammock. Nobody ever attempted to stop me from doing this, and almost all of them told me that my technique for recovering my possessions was admirable. By nightfall the thief would either appear with the stolen object or send it along with someone else to make an exchange. The others would heckle him for getting caught and being forced to return the item.

With respect to collecting the data I sought, there was a very frustrating problem. Primitive social organization is kinship organization, and to understand the Yąnomamö way of life I had to collect extensive genealogies. I could not have deliberately picked a more difficult group to work with in this regard: They have very stringent name taboos. They attempt to name people in such a way that when the person dies and they can no longer use his name, the loss of the word in the language is not inconvenient. Hence, they name people for specific and minute parts of things, such as "toenail of some rodent," thereby being able to retain the words "toenail" and "(specific) rodent," but not being able to refer directly to the toenail of that rodent. The taboo is

maintained even for the living: One mark of prestige is the courtesy others show you by not using your name. The sanctions behind the taboo seem to be an unusual combination of fear and respect.

I tried to use kinship terms to collect genealogies at first, but the kinship terms were so ambiguous that I ultimately had to resort to names. They were quick to grasp that I was bound to learn everybody's name and reacted, without my knowing it, by inventing false names for everybody in the village. After having spent several months collecting names and learning them, this came as a disappointment to me: I could not cross-check the genealogies with other informants from distant villages.

They enjoyed watching me learn these names. I assumed, wrongly, that I would get the truth to each question and that I would get the best information by working in public. This set the stage for converting a serious project into a farce. Each informant tried to outdo his peers by inventing a name even more ridiculous than what I had been given earlier, or by asserting that the individual about whom I inquired was married to his mother or daughter, and the like. I would have the informant whisper the name of the individual in my ear, noting that he was the father of such and such a child. Everybody would then insist that I repeat the name aloud, roaring in hysterics as I clumsily pronounced the name. I assumed that the laughter was in response to the violation of the name taboo or to my pronunciation. This was a reasonable interpretation, since the individual whose name I said aloud invariably became angry. After I learned what some of the names meant, I began to understand what the laughter was all about. A few of the more colorful examples are: "hairy vagina," "long penis," "feces of the harpy eagle," and "dirty rectum." No wonder the victims were angry.

I was forced to do my genealogy work in private because of the horseplay and nonsense. Once I did so, my informants began to agree with each other and I managed to learn a few new names, real names. I could then test any new informant by collecting a genealogy from him that I knew to be accurate. I was able to weed out the more mischievous informants this way. Little by little I extended the genealogies and learned the real names. Still, I was unable to get the names of the dead and extend the genealogies back in time, and even my best informants continued to deceive me about their own close relatives. Most of them gave me the name of a living man as the father of some individual in order to avoid mentioning that the actual father was dead.

The quality of a genealogy depends in part on the number of generations it embraces, and the name taboo prevented me from getting any substantial information about deceased ancestors. Without this information, I could not detect marriage patterns through time. I had to rely on older informants for this information, but these were the most reluctant of all. As I became more proficient in the language and more skilled at detecting lies, my informants became better at lying. One of them in particular was so cunning and persuasive that I was shocked to discover that he had been inventing his information. He specialized in making a ceremony out of telling me false names. He would look around to make sure nobody was listening outside my hut, enjoin me to never mention the name again, act very nervous and spooky, and then grab me by the head to whisper the name very softly into my ear. I was always elated after an informant session with him, because I had several generations of dead ancestors for the living people. The others refused to give me this information. To show my gratitude, I paid him quadruple the rate I had given the others. When word got around that I had increased the pay, volunteers began pouring in to give me genealogies.

I discovered that the old man was lying quite by accident. A club fight broke out in the village one day, the result of a dispute over the possession of a woman. She had been promised to Rerebawä, a particularly agressive young man who had married into the village. Rerebawä had already been given her older sister and was enraged when the younger girl began having an affair with another man in the village, making no attempt to conceal it from him. He challenged the young man to a club fight, but was so abusive in his challenge that the opponent's father took offense and entered the village circle with his son, wielding a long club. Rerebawä swaggered out to the duel and hurled insults at both of them, trying to goad them into striking him on the head with their clubs. This would have given him the opportunity to strike them on the head. His opponents refused to hit him, and the fight ended. Rerebawä had won a moral victory because his opponents were afraid to hit him. Thereafter, he swaggered around and insulted the two men behind their backs. He was genuinely angry with them, to the point of calling the older man by the name of his dead father. I quickly seized on this as an opportunity to collect an accurate genealogy and pumped him about his adversary's ancestors. Rerebawä had been particularly nasty to me up to this point, but we became staunch allies: We were both outsiders in the local village. I then asked about other dead ancestors and got immediate replies. He was angry with the whole group and not afraid to tell me the names of the dead. When I compared his version of the genealogies to that of the old man, it was obvious that one of them was lying. I challenged his information, and he explained that everybody knew that the old man was deceiving me and bragging about it in the same village. The names the old man had given me were the dead ancestors of the members of a village so far away that he thought I would never have occasion to inquire about them. As it turned out, Rerebawä knew most of the people in that village and recognized the names.

I then went over the complete genealogical records with Rerebawä, genealogies I had presumed to be in final form. I had to revise them all because of the numerous lies and falsifications they contained. Thus, after five months of almost constant work on the genealogies of just one group, I had to begin almost from scratch!

Discouraging as it was to start over, it was still the first real turning point in my fieldwork. Thereafter, I began taking advantage of local arguments and animosities in selecting my informants, and used more extensively individuals who had married into the group. I began traveling to other villages to check the genealogies, picking villages that were on strained terms with the people about whom I wanted information. I would then return to my base camp and check with local informants the accuracy of the information. If the informants became angry when I mentioned the new names I acquired from the unfriendly group, I was almost certain that the information was accurate. For this kind of checking I had to use informants whose genealogies I knew rather well: they had to be distantly enough related to the dead person that they would not go into a rage when I mentioned the name, but not so remotely related that they would be uncertain of the accuracy of the information. Thus, I had to make a list of names I dared not use in the presence of each and every informant. Despite the precautions, I occasionally hit a name that put the informant into a rage, such as that of a dead brother or sister that other informants had not reported. This always terminated the day's work with that informant, for he would be too touchy to continue any further, and I would be reluctant to take a chance on accidentally discovering another dead kinsman so soon after the first.

These were always unpleasant experiences, and occasionally dangerous ones, depending on the temperament of the informant. On one occasion I was planning to visit a village that had been raided about a week earlier. A woman whose name I had on my list had been killed by the raiders. I planned to check each individual on the list one by one to estimate ages, and I wanted to remove her name so that I would not say it aloud in the village. I knew that I would be in considerable difficulty if I said this name aloud so soon after her death. I called on my original informant and asked him to tell me the name of the woman who had been killed. He refused, explaining that she was a close relative of his. I then asked him if he would become angry if I read off all the names on the list. This way he did not have to say her name and could merely nod when I mentioned the right one. He was a fairly good friend of mine, and I thought I could predict his reaction. He assured me that this would be a good way of doing it. We were alone in my hut so that nobody could overhear us. I read the names softly, continuing to the next when he gave a negative reply. When I finally spoke the name of the dead woman he flew out of his chair, raised his arm to strike me, and shouted: "You son-of-a-bitch! If you ever say that name again, I'll kill you!" He was shaking with rage, but left my hut quietly. I shudder to think what might have happened if I had said the name unknowingly in the woman's village. I had other, similar experiences in different villages, but luckily the dead person had been dead for some time and was not closely related to the individual into whose ear I whispered the name. I was merely cautioned to desist from saying any more names, lest I get people angry with me.

I had been working on the genealogies for nearly a year when another individual came to my aid. It was Kąobawä, the headman of Upper Bisaasi-teri, the group in which I spent most of my time. He visited me one day after the others had left the hut and volunteered to help me on the genealogies. He was poor, he explained, and needed a machete. He would work only on the condition that I did not ask him about his own parents and other very close kinsmen who were dead. He also added that he would not lie to me as the others had done in the past. This was perhaps the most important single event in my fieldwork, for out of this meeting evolved a very warm friendship and a very profitable informant-fieldworker relationship.

Kąobawä's familiarity with his group's history and his candidness were remarkable. His knowledge of details was almost encyclopedic. More than that, he was enthusiastic and encouraged me to learn details that I might otherwise have ignored. If there were things he did not know intimately, he would advise me to wait until he could check things out with someone in the village. This he would do clandestinely, giving me a report the next day. As I was constrained by my part of the bargain to avoid discussing his close dead kinsmen, I had to rely on Rerebawä for this information. I got Rerebawä's genealogy from Kąobawä.

Once again I went over the genealogies with Kąobawä to recheck them, a considerable task by this time: they included about two thousand names, representing several generations of individuals from four different villages. Rerebawä's information was very accurate, and Kąobawä's contribution enabled me to trace the genealogies further back in time. Thus, after nearly a year of constant work on genealogies, Yąnomamö demography and social organization began to fall into a pattern. Only then could I see how kin groups formed and exchanged women with each other over time, and only then did the fissioning of larger villages into smaller ones show a distinct pattern. At this point I was able to begin formulating more intelligent questions because there was now some sort of pattern to work with. Without the help of Rerebawä and Kąobawä I could not have made very much sense of the plethora of details I had collected from dozens of other informants.

I spent a good deal of time with these two men and their families and got to know them well. They frequently gave their information in a way which related themselves to the topic under discussion. We became very close friends. I will speak of them frequently in the following chapters, using them as "typical" Yąnomamö, if, indeed, one may speak of typical anything. I will briefly comment on what these men are like and their respective statuses in the village.

Kąobawä is about 40 years old (Fig. 3). I say "about" because the Yąnomamö numeration system has only three numbers: one, two, and more-than-two. He is the headman of Upper Bisaasi-teri. He has had five or six wives so far and temporary affairs with as many more women, one of which resulted in a child. At the present time he has just two wives, Bahimi and Koamashima. He has had a daughter and a son by Bahimi, his eldest and favorite wife. Koamashima, about 20 years old, recently had her first child, a boy (Fig. 4). Kąobawä may give Koamashima to his youngest brother. Even now the brother shares in her sexual services. Kaobawä recently gave his third wife to another of his brothers because she was beshi: "horny." In fact, this girl had been married to two other men, both of whom discarded her because of her infidelity. Kaobawä had one daughter by her; she is being raised by his brother.

Kaobawä's eldest wife, Bahimi, is about thirty-five years old. She is his first cross-cousin. Bahimi was pregnant when I began my fieldwork, but she killed the new baby, a boy, at birth, explaining tearfully that it would have competed with Ariwari, her nursing son, for milk. Rather than expose Ariwari to the dangers and uncertainty of an early weaning, she killed the new child instead. By Yanomamö standards, she and Kaobawä have a very tranquil household. He only beats her once in a while, and never very hard. She never has affairs with other men.

Kaobawä is quiet, intense, wise, and unobtrusive. He leads more by example than by threats and coercion. He can afford to be this way as he established his reputation for being fierce long ago, and other men respect him. He also has five mature brothers who support him, and he has given a number of his sisters to other men in the village, thereby putting them under some obligation to him. In short, his "natural" following (kinsmen) is large, and he does not have to constantly display his ferocity. People already respect him and take his suggestions seriously.

Rerebawä is much younger, only about twenty-two years old. (See Fig. 5.) He has just one wife by whom he has had three children. He is from Karohi-teri, one of the villages to which Kaobawä's is allied. Rerebawä left his village to seek a wife in Kaobawä's group because there were no eligible women there for him to marry.

Rerebawä is perhaps more typical than Kaobawä in the sense that he is concerned about his reputation for ferocity and goes out of his way to act tough. He is, however, much braver than the other men his age and backs up his threats with action. Moreover, he is concerned about politics and knows the details of intervillage relationships over a large area. In this respect he shows all the attributes of a headman, although he is still too young and has too many competent older brothers in his own village to expect to move easily into the position of leadership there.

He does not intend to stay in Kaobawä's group and has not made a garden. He feels that he has adequately discharged his obligations to his wife's parents by providing them with fresh game for three years. They should let him take the wife and return to his own village with her, but they refuse and try to entice him to remain permanently in Bisaasi-teri to provide them with game when they are old. They have even promised to give him their second daughter if he will stay permanently.

Although he has displayed his ferocity in many ways, one incident in particular shows what his character is like. Before he left his own village to seek a wife, he had an affair with the wife of an older brother. When he was discovered, his brother attacked him with a club. Rerebawä was infuriated so he grabbed an axe and drove his brother out of the village after soundly beating him with the flat of the blade. The brother was so afraid that he did not return to the village for several days. I recently visited his village with him. He made a point to introduce me to this brother. Rerebawä dragged him out of his hammock by the arm and told me, "This is the brother whose wife I had an affair with," a deadly insult. His brother did nothing and slunk back into his hammock, shamed, but relieved to have Rerebawä release the vise-grip on his arm.

Despite the fact that he admires Kaobawä, he has a low opinion of the others in Bisaasi-teri. He admitted confidentially that he thought Bisaasi-teri was an abominable group: "This is a terrible neighborhood! All the young men are lazy and cowards and everybody is committing incest! I'll be glad to get back home." He also admired Kaobawä's brother, the headman of Monou-teri. This man was killed by raiders while I was doing my fieldwork. Rerebawä was disgusted that the others did not chase the raiders when they discovered the shooting: "He was the only fierce one in the whole group; he was my close friend. The cowardly Monou-teri hid like women in the jungle and didn't even chase the raiders!"

Even though Rerebawä is fierce and capable of being quite nasty, he has a good side as well. He has a very biting sense of humor and can entertain the group for hours on end with jokes and witty comments. And he is one of few Yanomamö that I feel I can trust. When I returned to Bisaasi-teri after having been away for a year, Rerebawä was in his own village visiting his kinsmen. Word reached him that I had returned, and he immediately came to see me. He greeted me with an immense bear hug and exclaimed, "Shaki! Why did you stay away so long? Did you know that my will was so cold while you were gone that at times I could not eat for want of seeing you?" I had to admit that I missed him, too.

Of all the Yanomamö I know, he is the most genuine and the most devoted to his culture's ways and values. I admire him for that, although I can't say that I subscribe to or endorse these same values. By contrast, Kaobawä is older and wiser. He sees his own culture in a different light and criticizes aspects of it he does not like. While many of his peers accept some of the superstitions and explanatory myths as truth and as the way things ought to be, Kaobawä questions them and privately pokes fun at some of them. Probably, more of the Yanomamö are like Rerebawä, or at least try to be.

Shakespeare in the Bush

By Laura Bohannan

. . . .

Just before I left Oxford for the Tiv in West Africa, conversation turned to the season at Stratford. "You Americans," said a friend, "often have difficulty with Shakespeare. He was, after all, a very English poet, and one can easily misinterpret the universal by misunderstanding the particular."

I protested that human nature is pretty much the same the whole world over; at least the general plot and motivation of the greater tragedies would always be clear—everywhere—although some details of custom might have to be explained and difficulties of translation might produce other slight changes. To end an argument we could not conclude, my friend gave me a copy of *Hamlet* to study in the African bush: it would, he hoped, lift my mind above its primitive surroundings, and possibly I might, by prolonged meditation, achieve the grace of correct interpretation.

It was my second field trip to that African tribe, and I thought myself ready to live in one of its remote sections—an area difficult to cross even on foot. I eventually settled on the hillock of a very knowledgeable old man, the head of a homestead of some hundred and forty people, all of whom were either his close relatives or their wives and children. Like the other elders of the vicinity, the old man spent most of his time performing ceremonies seldom seen these days in the more accessible parts of the tribe. I was delighted. Soon there would be three months of enforced isolation and leisure, between the harvest that takes place just before the rising of the swamps and the clearing of new farms when the water goes down. Then, I thought, they would have even more time to perform ceremonies and explain them to me.

I was quite mistaken. Most of the ceremonies demanded the presence of elders from several homesteads. As the swamps rose, the old men found it too difficult to walk from one homestead to the next, and the ceremonies gradually ceased. As the swamps rose even higher, all activities but one came to an end. The women brewed beer from maize and millet. Men, women, and children sat on their hillocks and drank it.

People began to drink at dawn. By midmorning the whole homestead was singing, dancing, and drumming. When it rained, people had to sit inside their huts: there they drank and sang or they drank and told stories. In any case, by noon or before, I either had to join the party or retire to my own hut and my books. "One does not discuss serious matters when there is beer. Come, drink with us." Since I lacked their capacity for the thick native beer, I spent more and more time with *Hamlet*. Before the end of the second month, grace descended on me. I was quite sure that *Hamlet* had only one possible interpretation, and that one universally obvious.

Early every morning, in the hope of having some serious talk before the beer party, I used to call on the old man at his reception hut—a circle of posts supporting a thatched roof above a low mud wall to keep out wind and rain. One day I crawled through the low doorway and found most of the men of the homestead sitting huddled in their ragged cloths on stools, low plank beds, and reclining chairs, warming themselves against the chill of the rain around a smoky fire. In the center were three pots of beer. The party had started.

The old man greeted me cordially. "Sit down and drink." I accepted a large calabash full of beer, poured some into a small drinking gourd, and tossed it down. Then I poured some more into the same gourd for the man second in seniority to my host before I handed my calabash over to a young man for further distribution. Important people shouldn't ladle beer themselves.

"It is better like this," the old man said, looking at me approvingly and plucking at the thatch that had caught in my hair. "You should sit and drink with us more often. Your servants tell me that when you are not with us, you sit inside your hut looking at a paper."

The old man was acquainted with four kinds of "papers": tax receipts, bride price receipts, court fee receipts, and letters. The messenger who brought him letters from the chief used them mainly as a badge of office, for he always knew what was in them and told the old man. Personal letters for the few who had relatives in the government or mission stations were kept until someone went to a large market where there was a letter writer and reader. Since my arrival, letters were brought to me to be read. A few men also brought me bride price receipts, privately, with requests to change the figures to a higher sum. I found moral arguments were of no avail, since in-laws are fair game, and the technical hazards of forgery difficult to explain to an illiterate people. I did not wish them to think me silly enough to look at any such papers for days on end, and I hastily explained that my "paper" was one of the "things of long ago" of my country.

"Ah," said the old man. "Tell us."

I protested that I was not a storyteller. Storytelling is a skilled art among them; their standards are high, and the audiences critical—and vocal in their criticism. I protested in vain. This morning they wanted to hear a story while they drank. They threatened to tell me no more stories until I told them one of mine. Finally, the old man promised that no one would criticize my style "for we know you are struggling with our language." "But," put in one of the elders, "you must explain what we do not understand, as we do when we tell you our stories." Realizing that here was my chance to prove *Hamlet* universally intelligible, I agreed.

The old man handed me some more beer to help me on with my storytelling. Men filled their long wooden pipes and knocked coals from the fire to place in the pipe bowls; then, puffing contentedly, they sat back to listen. I began in the proper style, "Not yesterday, not yesterday, but long ago, a thing occurred. One night three men were keeping watch outside the homestead of the great chief, when suddenly they saw the former chief approach them."

"Why was he no longer their chief?"

"He was dead," I explained. "That is why they were troubled and afraid when they saw him."

"Impossible," began one of the elders, handing his pipe on to his neighbor, who interrupted, "Of course it wasn't the dead chief. It was an omen sent by a witch. Go on."

Slightly shaken, I continued. "One of these three was a man who knew things"—the closest translation for scholar, but unfortunately it also meant witch. The second elder looked triumphantly at the first. "So he spoke to the dead chief saying, 'Tell us what we must do so you may rest in your grave,' but the dead chief did not answer. He vanished, and they could see him no more. Then the man who knew things—his name was Horatio—said this event was the affair of the dead chief's son, Hamlet."

There was a general shaking of heads round the circle. "Had the dead chief no living brothers? Or was this son the chief?"

"No," I replied. "That is, he had one living brother who became the chief when the elder brother died."

The old men muttered: such omens were matters for chiefs and elders, not for youngsters; no good could come of going behind a chief's back; clearly Horatio was not a man who knew things.

"Yes, he was," I insisted, shooing a chicken away from my beer. "In our country the son is next to the father. The dead chief's younger brother had become the great chief. He had also married his elder brother's widow only about a month after the funeral."

"He did well," the old man beamed and announced to the others, "I told you that if we knew more about Europeans, we would find they really were very like us. In our country also," he added to me, "the younger brother marries the elder brother's widow and becomes the father of his children. Now, if your uncle, who married your widowed mother, is your father's full brother, then he will be a real father to you. Did Hamlet's father and uncle have one mother?"

His question barely penetrated my mind; I was too upset and thrown too far off balance by having one of the most important elements of *Hamlet* knocked straight out of the picture. Rather uncertainly I said that I thought they had the same mother, but I wasn't sure—the story didn't say. The old man told me severely that these genealogical details made all the difference and that when I got home I must ask the elders about it. He shouted out the door to one of his younger wives to bring his goatskin bag.

Determined to save what I could of the mother motif, I took a deep breath and began again. "The son Hamlet was very sad because his mother had married again so quickly. There was no need for her to do so, and it is our custom for a widow not to go to her next husband until she has mourned for two years."

"Two years is too long," objected the wife, who had appeared with the old man's battered goatskin bag. "Who will hoe your farms for you while you have no husband?"

"Hamlet," I retorted without thinking, "was old enough to hoe his mother's farms himself. There was no need for her to remarry." No one looked convinced. I gave up. "His mother and the great chief told Hamlet not to be sad, for the great chief himself would be a father to Hamlet. Furthermore, Hamlet would be the next chief: therefore he must stay to learn the things of a chief. Hamlet agreed to remain, and all the rest went off to drink beer."

While I paused, perplexed at how to render Hamlet's disgusted soliloquy to an audience convinced that Claudius and Gertrude had behaved in the best possible manner, one of the young men asked me who had married the other wives of the dead chief.

"He had no other wives," I told him.

"But a chief must have many wives! How else can he brew beer and prepare food for all his guests?"

I said firmly that in our country even chiefs had only one wife, that they had servants to do their work, and that they paid them from tax money.

It was better, they returned, for a chief to have many wives and sons who would help him hoe his farms and feed his people; then everyone loved the chief who gave much and took nothing—taxes were a bad thing.

I agreed with the last comment, but for the rest fell back on their favorite way of fobbing off my questions: "That is the way it is done, so that is how we do it."

I decided to skip the soliloquy. Even if Claudius was here thought quite right to marry his brother's widow, there remained the poison motif, and I knew they would disapprove of fratricide. More hopefully I resumed, "That night Hamlet kept watch with the three who had seen his dead father. The dead chief again appeared, and although the others were afraid, Hamlet followed his dead father off to one side. When they were alone, Hamlet's dead father spoke."

"Omens can't talk!" The old man was emphatic.

"Hamlet's dead father wasn't an omen. Seeing him might have been an omen, but he was not." My audience looked as confused as I sounded. "It *was* Hamlet's dead father. It was a thing we call a 'ghost.'" I had to use the English word, for unlike many of the neighboring tribes, these people didn't believe in the survival after death of any individuating part of the personality.

"What is a 'ghost'? An omen?"

"No, a 'ghost' is someone who is dead but who walks around and can talk, and people can hear him and see him but not touch him."

They objected. "One can touch zombis."

"No, no! It was not a dead body the witches had animated to sacrifice and eat. No one else made Hamlet's dead father walk. He did it himself."

"Dead men can't walk," protested my audience as one man.

I was quite willing to comprise. "A 'ghost' is the dead man's shadow."

But again they objected. "Dead men cast no shadows."

"They do in my country," I snapped.

The old man quelled the babble of disbelief that arose immediately and told me with that insincere, but courteous, agreement one extends to the fancies of the young, ignorant, and superstitious, "No doubt in your country the dead can also walk without being zombis." From the depths of his bag he produced a withered fragment of kola nut, bit off one end to show it wasn't poisoned, and handed me the rest as a peace offering.

"Anyhow," I resumed, "Hamlet's dead father said that his own brother, the one who became chief, had poisoned him. He wanted Hamlet to avenge him. Ham-let believed this in his heart, for he did not like his father's brother." I took another swallow of beer. "In the country of the great chief, living in the same homestead, for it was a very large one, was an important elder who was often with the chief to advise and to help him. His name was Polonius. Hamlet was courting his daughter, but her father and her brother . . . [I cast hastily about for some tribal analogy] warned her not to let Hamlet visit her when when was alone on her farm, for he would be a great chief and so could not marry her."

"Why not!" asked the wife, who had settled down on the edge of the old man's chair. He frowned at her for asking stupid questions and growled, "They lived in the same homestead."

"That was not the reason," I informed them. "Polonius was a stranger who lived in the homestead because he helped the chief, not because he was a relative."

"Then why couldn't Hamlet marry her!"

"He could have," I explained, "but Polonius didn't think he would. After all, Hamlet was a man of great importance who ought to marry a chief's daughter, for in his country a man could have only one wife. Polonius was afraid that if Hamlet made love to his daughter, then no one else would give a high price for her."

"That might be true" remarked one of the shrewder elders, "but a chief's son would give his mistress's father enough presents and patronage to more than make up the difference. Polonius sounds like a fool to me."

"Many people think he was," I agreed. "Meanwhile Polonius sent his son Laertes off to Paris to learn the things of that country, for it was the homestead of a very great chief indeed. Because he was afraid that Laertes might waste a lot of money on beer and women and gambling, or get into trouble by fighting, he sent one of his servants to Paris secretly, to spy out what Laertes was doing. One day Hamlet came upon Polonius's daughter Ophelia. He behaved so oddly he frightened her. "Indeed,"—I was fumbling for words to express the dubious quality of Hamlet's madness—"the chief and many others had also noticed that when Hamlet talked one could understand the words but not what they meant. Many people thought that he had become mad." My audience suddenly became much more attentive. "The great chief wanted to know what was wrong with Hamlet, so he sent for two of Hamlet's age mates [school friends would have taken long explanation] to talk to Hamlet and find out what troubled his heart. Hamlet, seeing that they had been bribed by the chief to betray him, told them nothing. Polonius, however, insisted that Hamlet was mad because he had been forbidden to see Ophelia, whom he loved."

"Why," inquired a bewildered voice, "should anyone bewitch Hamlet on that account?"

"Bewitch him?"

"Yes, only witchcraft can make anyone mad, unless of course, one sees the beings that lurk in the forest."

I stopped being a storyteller, took out my notebook and demanded to be told more about these two causes of madness. Even while they spoke and I jotted notes, I tried to calculate the effect of this new factor on the plot. Hamlet had not been exposed to the beings that lurk in the forest. Only his relatives in the male line could bewitch him. Barring relatives not mentioned by Shakespeare, it had to be Claudius who was attempting to harm him. And, of course, it was.

For the moment I staved off questions by saying that the great chief also refused to believe that Hamlet was mad for the love of Ophelia and nothing else. "He was sure that something much more important was troubling Hamlet's heart."

"Now Hamlet's age mates," I continued, "had brought with them a famous storyteller. Hamlet decided to have this man tell the chief and all his homestead a story about a man who had poisoned his brother because he desired his brother's wife and wished to be chief himself. Hamlet was sure the great chief could not hear the story without making a sign if he was indeed guilty, and then he would discover whether his dead father had told him the truth."

The old man interrupted, with deep cunning, "Why should a father lie to his son?" he asked.

I hedged: "Hamlet wasn't sure that it really was his dead father." It was impossible to say anything, in that language, about devil-inspired visions.

"You mean," he said, "it actually was an omen, and he knew witches sometimes send false ones. Hamlet was a fool not to go to one skilled in reading omens and divining the truth in the first place. A man-who-sees-the-truth could have told him how his father died, if he really had been poisoned, and if there was witchcraft in it; then Hamlet could have called the elders to settle the matter."

The shrewd elder ventured to disagree. "Because his father's brother was a great chief, one-who-sees-the-truth might therefore have been afraid to tell it. I think it was for that reason that a friend of Hamlet's father—a witch and an elder—sent an omen so his friend's son would know. Was the omen true?"

"Yes," I said, abandoning ghosts and the devil; a witch-sent omen it would have to be. "It was true, for when the storyteller was telling his tale before all the homestead, the great chief rose in fear. Afraid that Hamlet knew his secret he planned to have him killed."

The stage set of the next bit presented some difficulties of translation. I began cautiously. "The great chief told Hamlet's mother to find out from her son what he knew. But because a woman's children are always first in her heart, he had the important elder Polonius hide behind a cloth that hung against the wall of Hamlet's mother's sleeping hut. Hamlet started to scold his mother for what she had done."

There was a shocked murmur from everyone. A man should never scold his mother.

"She called out in fear, and Polonius moved behind the cloth. Shouting, 'A rat!' Hamlet took his machete and slashed through the cloth." I paused for dramatic effect. "He had killed Polonius!"

The old men looked at each other in supreme disgust. "That Polonius truly was a fool and a man who knew nothing! What child would not know enough to shout, 'It's me!'" With a pang, I remembered that these people are ardent hunters, always armed with bow, arrow, and machete; at the first rustle in the grass an arrow is aimed and ready, and the hunter shouts "Game!" If no human voice answers immediately, the arrow speeds on its way. Like a good hunter Hamlet had shouted, "A rat!"

I rushed in to save Polonius's reputation. "Polonius did speak. Hamlet heard him. But he thought it was the chief and wished to kill him to avenge his father. He had meant to kill him earlier that evening..." I broke down, unable to describe to these pagans, who had no belief in individual afterlife, the difference between dying at one's prayers and dying "unhousell'd, disappointed, unaneled."

This time I had shocked by audience seriously. "For a man to raise his hand against his father's brother and the one who has become his father—that is a terrible thing. The elders ought to let such a man be bewitched."

I nibbled at my kola nut in some perplexity, then pointed out that after all the man had killed Hamlet's father.

"No," pronounced the old man, speaking less to me than to the young men sitting behind the elders. "If your father's brother has killed your father, you must appeal to your father's age mates; *they* may avenge him. No man may use violence against his senior relatives." Another thought struck him. "But if his father's brother had indeed been wicked enough to bewitch Hamlet and make him mad that would be a good story indeed, for it would be his fault that Hamlet, being mad, no longer had any sense and thus was ready to kill his father's brother."

There was a murmur of applause. *Hamlet* was again a good story to them, but it no longer seemed quite the same story to me. As I thought over the coming complications of plot and motive, I lost courage and decided to skim over dangerous ground quickly.

"The great chief," I went on, "was not sorry that Hamlet had killed Polonius. It gave him a reason to send Hamlet away, with his two treacherous age mates, with letters to a chief of a far country, saying that Hamlet should be killed. But Hamlet changed the writing on their papers, so that the chief killed his age mates instead." I encountered a reproachful glare from one of the men whom I had told undetectable forgery was not merely immoral but beyond human skill. I looked the other way.

"Before Hamlet could return, Laertes came back for his father's funeral. The great chief told him Hamlet had killed Polonius. Laertes swore to kill Hamlet because of this, and because his sister Ophelia, hearing her father had been killed by the man she loved, went mad and drowned in the river."

"Have you already forgotten what we told you?" The old man was reproachful. "One cannot take vengeance on a madman; Hamlet killed Polonius in his madness. As for the girl, she not only went mad, she was drowned. Only witches can make people drown. Water itself can't hurt anything. It is merely something one drinks and bathes in."

I began to get cross. "If you don't like the story, I'll stop."

The old man made soothing noises and himself poured me some more beer. "You tell the story well, and we are listening. But is clear that the elders of your country have never told you what the story really means. No, don't interrupt! We believe you when you say your marriage customs are different, or your clothes and weapons. But people are the same everywhere; therefore, there are always witches and it is we, the elders, who know how witches work. We told you it was the great chief who wished to kill Hamlet, and now your own words have proved us right. Who were Ophelia's male relatives?"

"There were only her father and her brother." Hamlet was clearly out of my hands.

"There must have been many more; this also you must ask of your elders when you get back to your country. From what you tell us, since Polonius was dead, it must have been Laertes who killed Ophelia, although I do not see the reason for it."

We had emptied one pot of beer, and the old men argued the point with slightly tipsy interest. Finally one of them demanded of me, "What did the servant of Polonius say on his return?"

With difficulty I recollected Reynaldo and his mission. "I don't think he did return before Polonius was killed."

"Listen," said the elder, "and I will tell you how it was and how your story will go, then you may tell me if I am right. Polonius knew his son would get into trouble,

and so he did. He had many fines to pay for fighting, and debts from gambling. But he had only two ways of getting money quickly. One was to marry off his sister at once, but it is difficult to find a man who will marry a woman desired by the son of a chief. For if the chief's heir commits adultery with your wife, what do you do? Only a fool calls a case against a man who will someday be his judge. Therefore Laertes had to take the second way: he killed his sister by witchcraft, drowning her so he could secretly sell her body to the witches."

I raised an objection. "They found her body and buried it. Indeed Laertes jumped into the grave to see his sister once more—so, you see, the body was truly there. Hamlet, who had just come back, jumped in after him."

"What did I tell you?" The elder appealed to the others. "Laertes was up to no good with his sister's body. Hamlet prevented him, because the chief's heir, like a chief, does not wish any other man to grow rich and powerful. Laertes would be angry, because he would have killed his sister without benefit to himself. In our country he would try to kill Hamlet for that reason. Is this not what happened?"

"More or less," I admitted. "When the great chief found Hamlet was still alive, he encouraged Laertes to try to kill Hamlet and arranged a fight with machetes between them. In the fight both the young men were wounded to death. Hamlet's mother drank the poisoned beer that the chief meant for Hamlet in case he won the fight. When he saw his mother die of poison, Hamlet, dying, managed to kill his father's brother with his machete."

"You see, I was right!" exclaimed the elder.

"That was a very good story," added the old man, "and you told it with very few mistakes. There was just one more error, at the very end. The poison Hamlet's mother drank was obviously meant for the survivor of the fight, whichever it was. If Laertes had won, the great chief would have poisoned him, for no one would know that he arranged Hamlet's death. Then, too, he need not fear Laertes' witchcraft; it takes a strong heart to kill one's only sister by witchcraft.

"Sometime," concluded the old man, gathering his ragged toga about him, "you must tell us some more stories of your country. We, who are elders, will instruct you in their true meaning, so that when you return to your own land your elders will see that you have not been sitting in the bush, but among those who know things and who have taught you wisdom."

Eating Christmas in the Kalahari

By Richard Borshay Lee

The !Kung Bushmen's knowledge of Christmas is thirdhand. The London Missionary Society brought the holiday to the southern Tswana tribes in the early nineteenth century. Later, native catechists spread the idea far and wide among the Bantu-speaking pastoralists, even in the remotest corners of the Kalahari Desert. The Bushmen's idea of the Christmas story, stripped to its essentials, is "praise the birth of white man's god-chief"; what keeps their interest in the holiday high is the Tswana-Herero custom of slaughtering an ox for his Bushmen neighbors as an annual goodwill gesture. Since the 1930's, part of the Bushmen's annual round of activities has included a December congregation at the cattle posts for trading, marriage brokering, and several days of trance-dance feasting at which the local Tswana headman is host.

As a social anthropologist working with !Kung Bushmen, I found that the Christmas ox custom suited my purposes. I had come to the Kalahari to study the hunting and gathering subsistence economy of the !Kung, and to accomplish this it was essential not to provide them with food, share my own food, or interfere in any way with their food-gathering activities. While liberal handouts of tobacco and medical supplies were appreciated, they were scarcely adequate to erase the glaring disparity in wealth between the anthropologist, who maintained a two-month inventory of canned goods, and the Bushmen, who rarely had a day's supply of food on hand. My approach, while paying off in terms of data, left me open to frequent accusations of stinginess and hard-heartedness. By their lights, I was a miser.

The Christmas ox was to be my way of saying thank you for the co-operation of the past year; and since it was to be our last Christmas in the field, I determined to slaughter the largest, meatiest ox that money could buy, insuring that the feast and trance dance would be a success.

Through December I kept my eyes open at the wells as the cattle were brought down for watering. Several animals were offered, but none had quite the grossness that I had in mind. Then, ten days before the holiday, a Herero friend led an ox of astonishing size and mass up to our camp. It was solid black, stood five feet high at the shoulder, had a five-foot span of horns, and must have weighed 1,200 pounds on the hoof. Food consumption calculations are my specialty, and I quickly figured that bones and viscera aside, there was enough meat—at least four pounds—for every man, woman, and child of the 150 Bushmen in the vicinity of /ai/ai who were expected at the feast.

Having found the right animal at last, I paid the Herero £20 ($56) and asked him to keep the beast with his herd until Christmas day. The next morning word spread among the people that the big solid black one was the ox chosen by /ontah (my Bushman name; it means. roughly, "whitey") for the Christmas feast. That afternoon I received the first delegation. Ben!a, an outspoken sixty-year-old mother of five, came to the point slowly.

"Where were you planning to eat Christmas?"

"Right here at /ai/ai," I replied.

"Alone or with others?"

"I expect to invite all the people to eat Christmas with me."

"Eat what?"

"I have purchased Yehave's black ox, and I am going to slaughter and cook it."

"That's what we were told at the well but refused to believe it until we heard it from yourself."

"Well, it's the black one," I replied expansively, although wondering what she was driving at.

"Oh, no!" Ben!a groaned, turning to her group. "They were right." Turning back to me she asked, "Do you expect us to eat that bag of bones?"

"Bag of bones! It's the biggest ox at /ai/ai."

"Big, yes, but old. And thin.

EDITOR'S NOTE: *The !Kung and other Bushmen speak click languages. In the story, three different clicks are used:*

1. The dental click (/), as in /ai/ai, /ontah, and /gaugo. The click is sometimes written in English as tsk-tsk.

2. The alveopalatal click (!), as in Ben!a and !Kung.

3. The lateral click (//), as in //gom. Clicks function as consonants; a word may have more than one, as in /n!au.

Everybody knows there's no meat on that old ox. What did you expect us to eat off it, the horns?"

Everybody chuckled at Ben!a's one-liner as they walked away, but all I could manage was a weak grin.

That evening it was the turn of the young men. They came to sit at our evening fire. /gaugo, about my age, spoke to me man-to-man.

"/ontah, you have always been square with us," he lied. "What has happened to change your heart? That sack of guts and bones of Yehave's will hardly feed one camp, let alone all the Bushmen around /ai/ai." And he proceeded to enumerate the seven camps in the /ai/ai vicinity, family by family. "Perhaps you have forgotten that we are not few, but many. Or are you too blind to tell the difference between a proper cow and an old wreck? That ox is thin to the point of death."

"Look, you guys," I retorted, "that is a beautiful animal, and I'm sure you will eat it with pleasure at Christmas."

"Of course we will eat it; it's food. But it won't fill us up to the point where we will have enough strength to dance. We will eat and go home to bed with stomachs rumbling."

That night as we turned in, I asked my wife, Nancy: "What did you think of the black ox?"

"It looked enormous to me. Why?"

"Well, about eight different people have told me I got gypped; that the ox is nothing but bones."

"What's the angle?" Nancy asked. "Did they have a better one to sell?"

"No, they just said that it was going to be a grim Christmas because there won't be enough meat to go around. Maybe I'll get an independent judge to look at the beast in the morning."

Bright and early, Halingisi, a Tswana cattle owner, appeared at our camp. But before I could ask him to give me his opinion on Yehave's black ox, he gave me the eye signal that indicated a confidential chat. We left the camp and sat down.

"/ontah, I'm surprised at you;

you've lived here for three years and still haven't learned anything about cattle."

"But what else can a person do but choose the biggest, strongest animal one can find?" I retorted.

"Look, just because an animal is big doesn't mean that it has plenty of meat on it. The black one was a beauty when it was younger, but now it is thin to the point of death."

"Well I've already bought it. What can I do at this stage?"

"Bought it already? I thought you were just considering it. Well, you'll have to kill it and serve it, I suppose. But don't expect much of a dance to follow."

My spirits dropped rapidly. I could believe that Ben!a and /gaugo just might be putting me on about the black ox, but Halingisi seemed to be an impartial critic. I went around that day feeling as though I had bought a lemon of a used car.

In the afternoon it was Tomazo's turn. Tomazo is a fine hunter, a top trance performer (*see* "The Trance Cure of the !Kung Bushmen," NATURAL HISTORY, November, 1967), and one of my most reliable informants. He approached the subject of the Christmas cow as part of my continuing Bushmen education.

"My friend, the way it is with us Bushmen," he began, "is that we love meat. And even more than that, we love fat. When we hunt we always search for the fat ones, the ones dripping with layers of white fat: fat that turns into a clear, thick oil in the cooking pot, fat that slides down your gullet, fills your stomach and gives you a roaring diarrhea," he rhapsodized.

"So, feeling as we do," he continued, "it gives us pain to be served such a scrawny thing as Yehave's black ox. It is big, yes, and no doubt its giant bones are good for soup, but fat is what we really crave and so we will eat Christmas this year with a heavy heart."

The prospect of a gloomy Christmas now had me worried, so I asked Tomazo what I could do about it.

"Look for a fat one, a young one . . . smaller, but fat. Fat enough

to make us //*gom* ('evacuate the bowels'), then we will be happy."

My suspicions were aroused when Tomazo said that he happened to know of a young, fat, barren cow that the owner was willing to part with. Was Toma working on commission, I wondered? But I dispelled this unworthy thought when we approached the Herero owner of the cow in question and found that he had decided not to sell.

The scrawny wreck of a Christmas ox now became the talk of the /ai/ai water hole and was the first news told to the outlying groups as they began to come in from the bush for the feast. What finally convinced me that real trouble might be brewing was the visit from u!au, an old conservative with a reputation for fierceness. His nickname meant spear and referred to an incident thirty years ago in which he had speared a man to death. He had an intense manner; fixing me with his eyes, he said in clipped tones:

"I have only just heard about the black ox today, or else I would have come here earlier. /ontah, do you honestly think you can serve meat like that to people and avoid a fight?" He paused, letting the implications sink in. "I don't mean fight you, /ontah; you are a white man. I mean a fight between Bushmen. There are many fierce ones here, and with such a small quantity of meat to distribute, how can you give everybody a fair share? Someone is sure to accuse another of taking too much or hogging all the choice pieces. Then you will see what happens when some go hungry while others eat."

The possibility of at least a serious argument struck me as all too real. I had witnessed the tension that surrounds the distribution of meat from a kudu or gemsbok kill, and had documented many arguments that sprang up from a real or imagined slight in meat distribution. The owners of a kill may spend up to two hours arranging and rearranging the piles of meat under the gaze of a circle of recipients before handing them out. And I also knew that the

Christmas feast at /ai/ai would be bringing together groups that had feuded in the past.

Convinced now of the gravity of the situation, I went in earnest to search for a second cow; but all my inquiries failed to turn one up.

The Christmas feast was evidently going to be a disaster, and the incessant complaints about the meagerness of the ox had already taken the fun out of it for me. Moreover, I was getting bored with the wisecracks, and after losing my temper a few times, I resolved to serve the beast anyway. If the meat fell short, the hell with it. In the Bushmen idiom, I announced to all who would listen: "I am a poor man and blind. If I have chosen one that is too old and too thin, we will eat it anyway and see if there is enough meat there to quiet the rumbling of our stomachs."

On hearing this speech, Ben!a offered me a rare word of comfort. "It's thin," she said philosophically, "but the bones will make a good soup."

At dawn Christmas morning, instinct told me to turn over the butchering and cooking to a friend and take off with Nancy to spend Christmas alone in the bush. But curiosity kept me from retreating. I wanted to see what such a scrawny ox looked like on butchering, and if there *was* going to be a fight, I wanted to catch every word of it. Anthropologists are incurable that way.

The great beast was driven up to our dancing ground, and a shot in the forehead dropped it in its tracks. Then, freshly cut branches were heaped around the fallen carcass to receive the meat. Ten men volunteered to help with the cutting. I asked /gaugo to make the breast bone cut. This cut, which begins the butchering process for most large game, offers easy access for removal of the viscera. But it also allows the hunter to spot-check the amount of fat on the animal. A fat game animal carries a white layer up to an inch thick on the chest, while in a thin one, the knife will quickly cut to bone. All eyes fixed on his hand as /gaugo, dwarfed by the great car-

cass, knelt to the breast. The first cut opened a pool of solid white in the black skin. The second and third cut widened and deepened the creamy white. Still no bone. It was pure fat; it must have been two inches thick.

"Hey /gau," I burst out, "that ox is loaded with fat. What's this about the ox being too thin to bother eating? Are you out of your mind?"

"Fat?" /gau shot back, "You call that fat? This wreck is thin, sick, dead!" And he broke out laughing. So did everyone else. They rolled on the ground, paralyzed with laughter. Everybody laughed except me; I was thinking.

I ran back to the tent and burst in just as Nancy was getting up. "Hey, the black ox. It's fat as hell! They were kidding about it being too thin to eat. It was a joke or something. A put-on. Everyone is really delighted with it!"

"Some joke," my wife replied. "It was so funny that you were ready to pack up and leave /ai/ai."

If it had indeed been a joke, it had been an extraordinarily convincing one, and tinged, I thought, with more than a touch of malice as many jokes are. Nevertheless, that it was a joke lifted my spirits considerably, and I returned to the butchering site where the shape of the ox was rapidly disappearing under the axes and knives of the butchers. The atmosphere had become festive. Grinning broadly, their arms covered with blood well past the elbow, men packed chunks of meat into the big cast-iron cooking pots, fifty pounds to the load, and muttered and chuckled all the while about the thinness and worthlessness of the animal and /ontah's poor judgment.

We danced and ate that ox two days and two nights; we cooked and distributed fourteen potfuls of meat and no one went home hungry and no fights broke out.

But the "joke" stayed in my mind. I had a growing feeling that something important had happened in my relationship with the Bushmen and that the clue lay in the meaning of the joke. Several days later, when most of the people had dispersed back to the bush camps, I raised the

question with Hakekgose, a Tswana man who had grown up among the !Kung, married a !Kung girl, and who probably knew their culture better than any other non-Bushman.

"With us whites," I began, "Christmas is supposed to be the day of friendship and brotherly love. What I can't figure out is why the Bushmen went to such lengths to criticize and belittle the ox I had bought for the feast. The animal was perfectly good and their jokes and wisecracks practically ruined the holiday for me."

"So it really did bother you," said Hakekgose. "Well, that's the way they always talk. When I take my rifle and go hunting with them, if I miss, they laugh at me for the rest of the day. But even if I hit and bring one down, it's no better. To them, the kill is always too small or too old or too thin; and as we sit down on the kill site to cook and eat the liver, they keep grumbling, even with their mouths full of meat. They say things like, 'Oh this is awful! What a worthless animal! Whatever made me think that this Tswana rascal could hunt!'"

"Is this the way outsiders are treated?" I asked.

"No, it is their custom; they talk that way to each other too. Go and ask them."

/gaugo had been one of the most enthusiastic in making me feel bad about the merit of the Christmas ox. I sought him out first.

"Why did you tell me the black ox was worthless, when you could see that it was loaded with fat and meat?"

"It is our way," he said smiling. "We always like to fool people about that. Say there is a Bushman who has been hunting. He must not come home and announce like a braggard, 'I have killed a big one in the bush!' He must first sit down in silence until I or someone else comes up to his fire and asks, 'What did you see today?' He replies quietly, 'Ah, I'm no good for hunting. I saw nothing at all [pause] just a little tiny one.' Then I smile to myself," /gaugo continued, "because I know he has killed something big.

"In the morning we make up a party of four or five people to cut up and carry the meat back to the camp. When we arrive at the kill we examine it and cry out, 'You mean to say you have dragged us all the way out here in order to make us cart home your pile of bones? Oh, if I had known it was this thin I wouldn't have come.' Another one pipes up, 'People, to think I gave up a nice day in the shade for this. At home we may be hungry but at least we have nice cool water to drink.' If the horns are big, someone says, 'Did you think that somehow you were going to boil down the horns for soup?'

"To all this you must respond in kind. 'I agree,' you say, 'this one is not worth the effort; let's just cook the liver for strength and leave the rest for the hyenas. It is not too late to hunt today and even a duiker or a steenbok would be better than this mess.'

"Then you set to work nevertheless; butcher the animal, carry the meat back to the camp and everyone eats," /gaugo concluded.

Things were beginning to make sense. Next, I went to Tomazo. He corroborated /gaugo's story of the obligatory insults over a kill and added a few details of his own.

"But," I asked, "why insult a man after he has gone to all that trouble to track and kill an animal and when he is going to share the meat with you so that your children will have something to eat?"

"Arrogance," was his cryptic answer.

"Arrogance?"

"Yes, when a young man kills much meat he comes to think of himself as a chief or a big man, and he thinks of the rest of us as his servants or inferiors. We can't accept this. We refuse one who boasts, for someday his pride will make him kill somebody. So we always speak of his meat as worthless. This way we cool his heart and make him gentle."

"But why didn't you tell me this before?" I asked Tomazo with some heat.

"Because you never asked me," said Tomazo, echoing the refrain that has come to haunt every field ethnographer.

The pieces now fell into place. I had known for a long time that in situations of social conflict with Bushmen I held all the cards. I was the only source of tobacco in a thousand square miles, and I was not incapable of cutting an individual off for noncooperation. Though my boycott never lasted longer than a few days, it was an indication of my strength. People resented my presence at the water hole, yet simultaneously dreaded my leaving. In short I was a perfect target for the charge of arrogance and for the Bushmen tactic of enforcing humility.

I had been taught an object lesson by the Bushmen; it had come from an unexpected corner and had hurt me in a vulnerable area. For the big black ox was to be the one totally generous, unstinting act of my year at /ai/ai, and I was quite unprepared for the reaction I received.

As I read it, their message was this: There are no totally generous acts. All "acts" have an element of calculation. One black ox slaughtered at Christmas does not wipe out a year of careful manipulation of gifts given to serve your own ends. After all, to kill an animal and share the meat with people is really no more than Bushmen do for each other every day and with far less fanfare.

In the end, I had to admire how the Bushmen had played out the farce—collectively straight-faced to the end. Curiously, the episode reminded me of the *Good Soldier Schweik* and his marvelous encounters with authority. Like Schweik, the Bushmen had retained a thoroughgoing skepticism of good intentions. Was it this independence of spirit, I wondered, that had kept them culturally viable in the face of generations of contact with more powerful societies, both black and white? The thought that the Bushmen were alive and well in the Kalahari was strangely comforting. Perhaps, armed with that independence and with their superb knowledge of their environment, they might yet survive the future.

Body Ritual Among the Nacirema

By Horace Miner

....

The anthropologist has become so familiar with the diversity of ways in which different peoples behave in similar situations that he is not apt to be surprised by even the most exotic customs. In fact, if all of the logically possible combinations of behavior have not been found somewhere in the world, he is apt to suspect that they must be present in some yet undescribed tribe. This point has, in fact, been expressed with respect to clan organization by Murdock (1949:71). In this light, the magical beliefs and practices of the Nacirema present such unusual aspects that it seems desirable to describe them as an example of the extremes to which human behavior can go.

Professor Linton first brought the ritual of the Nacirema to the attention of anthropologists twenty years ago (1936:326), but the culture of this people is still very poorly understood. They are a North American group living in the territory between the Canadian Cree, the Yaqui and Tarahumare of Mexico, and the Carib and Arawak of the Antilles. Little is known of their origin, although tradition states that they came from the east. According to Nacirema mythology, their nation was originated by a culture hero, Notgnihsaw, who is otherwise known for two great feats of strength—the throwing of a piece of wampum across the river Pa-To-Mac and the chopping down of a cherry tree in which the Spirit of Truth resided.

Nacirema culture is characterized by a highly developed market economy which has evolved in a rich natural habitat. While much of the people's time is devoted to economic pursuits, a large part of the fruits of these labors and a considerable portion of the day are spent in ritual activity. The focus of this activity is the human body, the appearance and health of which loom as a dominant concern in the ethos of the people. While such a concern is certainly not unusual, its ceremonial aspects and associated philosophy are unique.

The fundamental belief underlying the whole system appears to be that the human body is ugly and that its natural tendency is to debility and disease. Incarcerated in such a body, man's only hope is to avert these characteristics through the use of the powerful influences of ritual and ceremony. Every household has one or more shrines devoted to this purpose. The more powerful individuals in the society have several shrines in their houses and, in fact, the opulence of a house is often referred to in terms of the number of such ritual centers it possesses. Most houses are of wattle and daub construction, but the shrine rooms of the more wealthy are walled with stone. Poorer families imitate the rich by applying pottery plaques to their shrine walls.

While each family has at least one such shrine, the rituals associated with it are not family ceremonies but are private and secret. The rites are normally only discussed with children, and then only during the period when they are being initiated into these mysteries. I was able, however, to establish sufficient rapport with the natives to examine these shrines and to have the rituals described to me.

The focal point of the shrine is a box or chest which is built into the wall. In this chest are kept the many charms and magical potions without which no native believes he could live. These preparations are secured from a variety of specialized practioners. The most powerful of these are the medicine men, whose assistance must be rewarded with substantial gifts. However, the medicine men do not provide the curative potions for their clients, but decide what the ingredients should be and then write them down in an ancient and secret language. This writing is understood only by the medicine men and by the herbalists who, for another gift, provide the required charm.

The charm is not disposed of after it has served its purpose, but is placed in the charm-box of the household shrine. As these magical materials are specific for certain ills, and the real or imagined maladies of the people are many, the charm-box is usually full to overflowing. The magical packets are so numerous that people forget what their purposes were and fear to use them again. While the natives are very vague on this

 Reproduced by permission of the American Anthropological Association from *American Anthropologist*, 58(3): 503–507, 1956.

point, we can only assume that the idea in retaining all the old magical materials is that their presence in the charm-box, before which the body rituals are conducted, will in some way protect the worshipper.

Beneath the charm-box is a small font. Each day every member of the family, in succession, enters the shrine room, bows his head before the charm-box, mingles different sorts of holy water in the font, and proceeds with a brief rite of ablution. The holy waters are secured from the Water Temple of the community, where the priests conduct elaborate ceremonies to make the liquid ritually pure.

In the hierarchy of magical practitioners, and below the medicine men in prestige, are specialists whose designation is best translated "holy-mouth-men." The Nacirema have an almost pathological horror of and fascination with the mouth, the condition of which is believed to have a supernatural influence on all social relationships. Were it not for the rituals of the mouth, they believe that their teeth would fall out, their gums bleed, their jaws shrink, their friends desert them, and their lovers reject them. They also believe that a strong relationship exists between oral and moral characteristics. For example, there is a ritual ablution of the mouth for children which is supposed to improve their moral fiber.

The daily body ritual performed by everyone includes a mouth-rite. Despite the fact that these people are so punctilious about care of the mouth, this rite involves a practice which strikes the uninitiated stranger as revolting. It was reported to me that the ritual consists of inserting a small bundle of hog hairs into the mouth, along with cer'ain magical powders, and then moving the bundle in a highly formalized series of gestures.

In addition to the private mouth-rite, the people seek out a holy-mouth-man once or twice a year. These practitioners have an impressive set of paraphernalia, consisting of a variety of augers, awls, probes, and prods. The use of these objects in the exorcism of the evils of the mouth involves almost unbelievable ritual torture of the client. The holy-mouth-man opens the client's mouth and, using the above mentioned tools, enlarges any holes which decay may have created in the teeth. Magical materials are put into these holes. If there are no naturally occurring holes in the teeth, large sections of one or more teeth are gouged out so that the supernatural substance can be applied. In the client's view, the purpose of these ministrations is to arrest decay and to draw friends. The extremely sacred and traditional character of the rite is evident in the fact that the natives return to the holy-mouth-men year after year, despite the fact that their teeth continue to decay.

It is to be hoped that, when a thorough study of the Nacirema is made, there will be careful inquiry into the personality structure of these people. One has but to watch the gleam in the eye of a holy-mouth-man, as he jabs an awl into an exposed nerve, to suspect that a certain amount of sadism is involved. It this can be established, a very interesting pattern emerges, for most of the population shows definite masochistic tendencies. It was to these that Professor Linton referred in discussing a distinctive part of the daily body ritual which is performed only by men. This part of the rite involves scraping and lacerating the surface of the face with a sharp instrument. Special women's rites are performed only four times during each lunar month, but what they lack in frequency is made up in barbarity. As part of this ceremony, women bake their heads in small ovens for about an hour. The theoretically interesting point is that what seems to be a preponderantly masochistic people have developed sadistic specialists.

The medicine men have an imposing temple, or *latipso*, in every community of any size. The more elaborate ceremonies required to treat very sick patients can only be performed at this temple. These ceremonies involve not only the thaumaturge but a permanent group of vestal maidens who move sedately about the temple chambers in distinctive costume and headdress.

The *latipso* ceremonies are so harsh that it is phenomenal that a fair proportion of the really sick natives who enter the temple ever recover. Small children whose indoctrination is still incomplete have been known to resist attempts to take them to the temple because "that is where you go to die." Despite this fact, sick adults are not only willing but eager to undergo the protracted ritual purification, if they can afford to do so. No matter how ill the supplicant or how grave the emergency, the guardians of many temples will not admit a client if he cannot give a rich gift to the custodian. Even after one has gained admission and survived the ceremonies, the guardians will not permit the neophyte to leave until he makes still another gift.

The supplicant entering the temple is first stripped of all his or her clothes. In every-day life the Nacirema avoids exposure of his body and its natural functions. Bathing and excretory acts are performed only in the secrecy of the household shrine, where they are ritualized as part of the body-rites. Psychological shock results from the fact that body secrecy is suddenly lost upon entry into the *latipso*. A man, whose own wife has never seen him in an excretory act, suddenly finds himself naked and assisted by a vestal maiden while he performs his natural functions into a sacred vessel. This sort of ceremonial treatment is necessitated by the fact that the excreta are used by a diviner to ascertain the course and nature of the client's sickness. Female clients, on the other hand, find their naked bodies are subjected to the scrutiny, manipulation and prodding of the medicine men.

Few supplicants in the temple are well enough to do anything but lie on their hard beds. The daily ceremonies, like the rites of the holy-mouth-men, involve discomfort and torture. With ritual precision, the vestals awaken their miserable charges each dawn and roll them about on their beds of pain while performing ablutions, in the formal movements of which the maidens are highly trained. At other times they insert magic wands in the supplicant's mouth or force him to eat substances which are supposed to be healing. From time to time the medicine men come to their clients and jab magically treated needles into their flesh. The fact that these temple ceremonies may not cure, and may even kill the neophyte, in no way decreases the people's faith in the medicine men.

There remains one other kind of practitioner, known as a "listener." This witch-doctor has the power to exorcise the devils that lodge in the heads of people who have been bewitched. The Nacirema believe that parents bewitch their own children. Mothers are particularly suspected of putting a curse on children while teaching them the secret body rituals. The countermagic of the witch-doctor is unusual in its lack of ritual. The patient simply tells the "listener" all his troubles and fears, beginning with the earliest difficulties he can remember. The memory displayed by the Nacirema in these exorcism sessions is truly remarkable. It is not uncommon for the patient to bemoan the rejection he felt upon being weaned as a babe, and a few individuals even see their troubles going back to the traumatic effects of their own birth.

In conclusion, mention must be made of certain practices which have their base in native esthetics but which depend upon the pervasive aversion to the natural body and its functions. There are ritual fasts to make fat people thin and ceremonial feasts to make thin people fat. Still other rites are used to make women's breasts larger if they are small, and smaller if they are large. General dissatisfaction with breast shape is symbolized in the fact that the ideal form is virtually outside the range of human variation. A few women afflicted with almost inhuman hypermammary development are so idolized that they make a handsome living by simply going from village to village and permitting the natives to stare at them for a fee.

Reference has already been made to the fact that excretory functions are ritualized, routinized, and relegated to secrecy. Natural reproductive functions are similarly distorted. Intercourse is taboo as a topic and scheduled as an act. Efforts are made to avoid pregnancy by the use of magical materials or by limiting intercourse to certain phases of the moon. Conception is actually very infrequent. When pregnant, women dress so as to hide their condition. Parturition takes place in secret, without friends or relatives to assist, and the majority of women do not nurse their infants.

Our review of the ritual life of the Nacirema has certainly shown them to be a magic-ridden people. It is hard to understand how they have managed to exist so long under the burdens which they have imposed upon themselves. But even such exotic customs as these take on real meaning when they are viewed with the insight provided by Malinowski when he wrote (1948:70):

> Looking from far and above, from our high places of safety in the developed civilization, it is easy to see all the crudity and irrelevance of magic. But without its power and guidance early man could not have mastered his practical difficulties as he has done, nor could man have advanced to the higher stages of civilization.

References

Linton, Ralph
    1936 The Study of Man. New York, D. Appleton-Century Co.
Malinowski, Bronislaw
    1948 Magic, Science, and Religion. Glencoe, The Free Press.
Murdock, George P.
    1949 Social Structure. New York, The Macmillan Co.

Kinship and Marriage

Each culture provides an accepted range of options for human activities. It thus sets limits on human behavior as well as creating its potential. Although the spectrum of accepted or normative behavior in human groups around the world is vast, there are certain patterns that reappear in virtually every culture. These are termed *cultural universals*.

The regulation of sexual behavior and mating is one such cultural universal. Sexual mores vary enormously from one culture to another, but all cultures apparently share one basic value—namely, that sexual intercourse between parents and their children is to be avoided. In addition, most cultures also prohibit sexual contact between brothers and sisters. The term for prohibited sex between relatives is *incest*, and because most cultures attach extremely strong feelings of revulsion to incest it is said to be *taboo*.

The universal presence of the incest taboo means that individuals must seek socially acceptable sexual partners and spouses outside their own families. All cultures provide definitions of the categories of persons who are eligible and ineligible to marry or have sex with one another. These definitions vary greatly across cultures. In our society, for instance, the incest taboo covers relatively few individuals—our own nuclear family, plus direct lineal relatives and their siblings. However, in societies organized primarily around kinship ties, the categories of sexually ineligible persons can be very large indeed, including almost all of an individual's relatives linked through either male (patrilineal) or female (matrilineal) kinship.

In the first article of Topic 9, "The Disappearance of the Incest Taboo," Yehudi Cohen follows the famous French anthropologist Claude Levi-Strauss in arguing that the incest taboo created the means for groups to form enduring relationships that promoted their survival through alliance building (by forcing what amounted to political marriages across group lines). Modern society has many other means of organizing enduring relationships among groups, hence the incest taboo may become obsolete if we look at the alliance-building function alone. However, we would add that this argument should not be taken to mean that incest is unproblematic in modern society. With sexual abuse in families apparently in the rise in our society, and with the abundance of clinical evidence of the enormous damage such abuse causes children, it may be more on the mark to say that with the disappearance of the socioeconomic and political bases of the incest taboo in modern society we can observe the uncovering of the profound psychological functions it serves.

In "Fission in an Amazonian Tribe," Napoleon A. Chagnon looks at the role played by kinship rules in regulating the size of preindustrial human groups. He also appreciates the role of kinship rules in cementing political alliances, and the pressure to increase group size in the presence of chronic warfare. This article reminds us how multidetermined all aspects of human behavior are—nothing is simple where humans are concerned, not even the choice of sexual and marriage partners.

Laurel Kendall's article "The Marriage of Yongsu's Mother" rounds out Topic 9. It could have fit equally well under the topic of fieldwork, but we put it here because it gives a graphic description of an arranged marriage that should put to rest once and for all the notion that research subjects' ways of doing things are somehow natural to them. Preindustrial or preliterate people are not simple, and at times what they have to do feels bad to them—even if it is culturally prescribed. In this they are not different from us. Indeed, suffering some degree of alienation, even within the realm of the culturally normal for one's group, may itself be a cultural universal.

The Disappearance of the Incest Taboo

By Yehudi Cohen

Several years ago a minor Swedish bureaucrat, apparently with nothing better to do, was leafing through birth and marriage records, matching people with their natural parents. To his amazement he found a full brother and sister who were married and had several children. The couple were arrested and brought to trial. It emerged that they had been brought up by separate sets of foster parents and never knew of each other's existence. By a coincidence reminiscent of a Greek tragedy, they met as adults, fell in love, and married, learning of their biological tie only after their arrest. The local court declared their marriage illegal and void.

The couple appealed the decision to Sweden's Supreme Court. After lengthy testimony on both sides of the issue, the court overturned the decision on the grounds that the pair had not been reared together. The marriage was declared legal and valid. In the wake of the decision, a committee appointed by Sweden's Minister of Justice to examine the question has proposed that criminal sanctions against incest be repealed. The committee's members were apparently swayed by Carl-Henry Alstrom, a professor of psychiatry. Alstrom argued that psychological deterrents to incest are stronger than legal prohibitions. The question will soon go to Sweden's Parliament, which seems prepared to follow the committee's recommendation.

Aside from illustrating the idea that the most momentous changes in human societies often occur as a result of unforeseen events, this landmark case raises questions that go far beyond Sweden's (or any other society's) borders. Some people may be tempted to dismiss the Swedish decision as an anomaly, as nothing more than a part of Sweden's unusual experiments in public welfare and sexual freedom.

But the probable Swedish decision to repeal criminal laws against incest cannot be regarded so lightly; this simple step reflects a trend in human society that has been developing for several thousand years. When we arrange human societies along a continuum from the least to the most complex, from those with the smallest number of interacting social groups to those with the highest number of groups, from those with the simplest technology to those with the most advanced technology, we observe that the incest taboo applies to fewer and fewer relatives beyond the immediate family.

Though there are exceptions, the widest extension of incest taboos beyond the nuclear family is found in the least complex societies. In a few societies, such as the Cheyenne of North America and the Kwoma of New Guinea, incest taboos extend to many remote relatives, including in-laws and the in-laws of in-laws. In modern industrial societies, incest taboos are usually confined to members of the immediate household. This contraction in the range of incest taboos is reaching the point at which they may disappear entirely.

The source of these changes in incest taboos lies in changing patterns of external trade. Trade is a society's jugular. Because every group lives in a milieu lacking some necessities that are available in other habitats, the flow of goods and resources is a society's lifeblood. But it is never sufficient merely to encourage people to form trade alliances with others in different areas. Incest taboos force people to marry outside their own group, to form alliances and to maintain trade networks. As other institutions— governments, business organizations—begin to organize trade, incest taboos become less necessary for assuring the flow of the society's lifeblood; they start to contract.

Other explanations of the incest taboo do not, under close examination, hold up. The most common assumption is that close inbreeding is biologically deleterious and will lead to the extinction of those who practice it. But there is strong evidence that inbreeding does not materially increase the rate of maladies such as albinism, total color blindness, or various forms of idiocy, which generally result when each parent carries the same recessive gene. In most cases these diseases result from chance combinations of recessive genes or from mutation.

According to Theodosius Dobzhansky, a geneticist, "The increase of the incidence of hereditary diseases in the

 From HUMAN NATURE, July 1978. Copyright © 1978 by Human Nature, Inc.

offspring of marriages between relatives (cousins, uncle and niece or aunt and nephew, second cousins, etc.) over that in marriages between persons not known to be related is slight—so slight that geneticists hesitate to declare such marriages disgenic." Inbreeding does carry a slight risk. The progeny of relatives include more stillbirths and infant and early childhood deaths than the progeny of unrelated people. But most of these deaths are due to environmental rather than genetic factors. Genetic disadvantages are not frequent enough to justify a prohibition. Moreover, it is difficult to justify the biological explanation for incest taboos when many societies prescribe marriage to one cousin and prohibit marriage to another. Among the Lesu of Melanesia a man must avoid sexual contact with his parallel cousins, his mother's sisters' daughters and his father's brothers' daughters, but is supposed to marry his cross cousins, his mother's brothers' daughters and his father's sisters' daughters. Even though both types of cousins have the same genetic relationship to the man, only one kind is included in the incest taboo. The taboo is apparently a cultural phenomenon based on the cultural classification of people and can not be explained biologically.

Genetic inbreeding may even have some advantages in terms of natural selection. Each time a person dies of a hereditary disadvantage, his detrimental genes are lost to the population. By such a process of genetic cleansing, inbreeding may lead to the elimination, or at least to reduced frequencies, of recessive genes. The infant mortality rate may increase slightly at first, but after the sheltered recessive genes are eliminated, the population may stabilize. Inbreeding may also increase the frequency of beneficial recessive genes, contributing to the population's genetic fitness. In the end, inbreeding seems to have only a slight effect on the offspring and a mixed effect, some good and some bad, on the gene pool itself. This mild consequence hardly justifies the universal taboo on incest.

Another explanation of the incest taboo is the theory of natural aversion, first propounded by Edward Westermarck in his 1891 book, *The History of Human Marriage*. According to Westermarck, children reared in the same household are naturally averse to having sexual relations with one another in adulthood. But this theory has major difficulties. First, it has a basic logical flaw: If there were a natural aversion to incest, the taboo would be unnecessary. As James Frazer pointed out in 1910, "It is not easy to see why any deep human instinct should need to be reinforced by law. There is no law commanding men to eat and drink or forbidding them to put their hands in the fire. . . . The law only forbids men to do what their instincts incline them to do; what nature itself prohibits and punishes, it would be superfluous for the law to prohibit and punish. . . . Instead of assuming,

Yehudi Cohen

therefore, from the legal prohibition of incest that there is a natural aversion to incest, we ought rather to assume that there is a natural instinct in favour of it."

Second, the facts play havoc with the notion of natural aversion. In many societies, such as the Arapesh of New Guinea studies by Margaret Mead, and the Eskimo, young children are betrothed and raised together, usually by the boy's parents, before the marriage is consummated. Arthur Wolf, an anthropologist who studied a village in northern Taiwan, describes just such a custom: "Dressed in the traditional red wedding costume, the bride enters her future husband's home as a child. She is seldom more than three years of age and often less than a year. . . . [The] last phase in the marriage process does not take place until she is old enough to fulfill the role of wife. In the meantime, she and her parents are affinally related to the groom's parents, but she is not in fact married to the groom."

One of the examples commonly drawn up to support Westermarck's theory of aversion is the Israeli *kibbutz*, where children who have been raised together tend to avoid marrying. But this avoidance has been greatly exaggerated. There is some tendency among those who have been brought up in the same age group in a communal "children's house" to avoid marrying one another, but this arises from two regulations that separate young adults from their *kibbutz* at about the age when they might marry. The first is a regulation of the Israel Defense Forces that no married woman may serve in the armed forces. Conscription for men and women is at 18, usually coinciding with their completion of secondary school, and military service is a deeply felt responsibility for most *kibbutz*-reared Israelis. Were women to marry prior to 18, they would be denied one of their principal goals. By the time they complete their military service, many choose urban spouses whom they have met in the army. Thus the probability of marrying a person one has grown up with is greatly reduced.

The second regulation that limits intermarriage on a *kibbutz* is a policy of the federations to which almost all *kibbutzim* belong. Each of the four major federations reserves the right to transfer any member to any other settlement, especially when a new one is being established. These "seeds," as the transferred members are called, are recruited individually from different settlements and most transfers are made during a soldier's third or fourth year of military service. When these soldiers leave the army to live on a *kibbutz*, they may be separated from those they were reared with. The frequency of marriage among people from working-class backgrounds who began and completed school together in an American city or town is probably higher than for an Israeli *kibbutz*; the proclivity among American college graduates to marry outside their neighborhoods or towns is no more an example of exogamy or incest avoidance than is the tendency in Israeli *kibbutzim* to marry out.

Just as marriage within a neighborhood is accepted in the United States, so is marriage within a *kibbutz* accepted in Israel. During research I conducted in Israel between 1967 and 1969, I attended the wedding of two people in a *kibbutz* who supposedly were covered by this taboo or rule of avoidance. As my tape recordings and photographs show, it would be difficult to imagine a more joyous occasion. When I questioned members of the *kibbutz* about this, they told me with condescending smiles that they had "heard of these things the professors say."

A third, "demographic," explanation of the incest taboo was originally set forth in 1950 by Wilson Wallis and elaborated in 1959 by Mariam Slater. According to this theory, mating within the household, especially between parents and children, was unlikely in early human societies because the life span in these early groups was so short that by the time offspring were old enough to mate, their parents would probably have died. Mating between siblings would also have been unlikely because of the average of eight years between children that resulted from breast-feeding and high rates of infant mortality. But even assuming this to have been true for the first human societies, there is nothing to prevent mating among the members of a nuclear family when the life span is lengthened.

A fourth theory that is widely subscribed to focuses on the length of the human child's parental dependency, which is the longest in the animal kingdom. Given the long period required for socializing children, there must be regulation of sexual activity so that children may learn

their proper roles. If the nuclear family's members are permitted to have unrestricted sexual access to one another, the members of the unit would be confused about their roles. Parental authority would be undermined, and it would be impossible to socialize children. This interpretation has much to recommend it as far as relationships between parents and children are concerned, but it does not help explain brother-sister incest taboos or the extension of incest taboos to include remote relatives.

The explanation closest to my interpretation of the changes in the taboo is the theory of alliance advocated by the French anthropologist Claude Levi-Strauss, which suggests that people are compelled to marry outside their groups in order to form unions with other groups and promote harmony among them. A key element in the theory is that men exchange their sisters and daughters in marriage with men of other groups. As originally propounded, the theory of alliance was based on the assumption that men stay put while the women change groups by marrying out, moved about by men like pieces on a chessboard. But there are many instances in which the women stay put while the men change groups by marrying out. In either case, the result is the same. Marriage forges alliances.

These alliances freed early human societies from exclusive reliance on their own limited materials and products. No society is self-sustaining or self-perpetuating; no culture is a world unto itself. Each society is compelled to trade with others and this was as true for tribal societies as it is for modern industrial nations. North America, for instance, was crisscrossed with elaborate trade networks before the Europeans arrived. Similar trade networks covered aboriginal New Guinea and Australia. In these trade networks, coastal or riverine groups gave shells and fish to hinterland people in exchange for cultivated foods, wood, and manufactured items.

American Indian standards of living were quite high before the Europeans destroyed the native trade networks, and the same seems to have been true in almost all other parts of the world. It will come as no surprise to economists that the material quality of people's lives improves to the extent that they engage in external trade.

But barter and exchange do not automatically take place when people meet. Exchange involves trust, and devices are needed to establish trust, to distinguish friend from foe, and to assure a smooth, predictable flow of trade goods. Marriage in the tribal world established permanent obligations and reciprocal rights and privileges among families living in different habitats.

For instance, when a young Cheyenne Indian man decided on a girl to marry, he told his family of his choice. If they agreed that his selection was good, they gathered a store of prized possessions—clothing, blankets, guns, bows and arrows—and carefully loaded them on a fine horse. A friend of the family, usually a respected old woman, led the horse to the tepee of the girl's elder brother. There the go-between spread the gifts for everyone to see while she pressed the suitor's case. The next step was for the girl's brother to assemble all his cousins for a conference to weigh the proposal. If they agreed to it, the cousins distributed the gifts among themselves, the brother taking the horse. Then the men returned to their tepees to find suitable gifts to give in return. Within a day or two, each returned with something roughly equal in value to what he had received. While this was happening, the bride was made beautiful. When all arrangements were completed, she mounted one horse while the return gifts were loaded on another. The old woman led both horses to the groom's camp. After the bride was received, her accompanying gifts were distributed among the groom's relatives in accordance with what each had given. The exchanges between the two families did not end with the marriage ceremony, however; they continued as a permanent part of the marriage ties. This continual exchange, which took place periodically, is why the young man's bridal choice was so important for his entire family.

Marriage was not the only integral part of external trade relationships. Another was ritualized friendship, "blood brotherhood," for example. Such bonds were generally established between members of different groups and were invariably trade partnerships. Significantly, these ritualized friendships often included taboos against marriage with the friend's sisters; sometimes the taboo applied to all their close relatives. This extension of a taboo provides an important key for understanding all incest taboos. Sexual prohibitions do not necessarily grow out of biological ties. Both marriage and ritualized friendships in primitive societies promote economic alliances and both are associated with incest taboos.

Incest taboos force people into alliances with others in as many groups as possible. They promote the greatest flow of manufactured goods and raw materials from the widest variety of groups and ecological niches and force people to spread their social nets. Looked at another way, incest taboos prevent localism and economic provincialism; they block social and economic inbreeding.

Incest taboos have their widest extensions outside the nuclear family in those societies in which technology is least well developed and in which people have to carry their own trade goods for barter or exchange with members of other groups. Often in these small societies, everyone in a community is sexually taboo to the rest of the group. When the technology surrounding trade improves and shipments of goods and materials can be concentrated (as when people learn to build and navigate ocean-going canoes or harness pack animals), fewer and fewer people have to be involved in trade. As this happens, incest taboos begin to contract, affecting fewer and fewer people outside the nuclear family.

This process has been going on for centuries. Today, in most industrial societies, the only incest taboos are those that pertain to members of the nuclear family. This contraction of the range of the taboo is inseparable from the fact that we no longer engage in personal alliances and trade agreements to get the food we eat, the clothes we wear, the tools and materials we use, the fuels on which we depend. Goods are brought to distribution points near our homes by a relatively tiny handful of truckers, shippers, merchants, entrepreneurs, and others. Most of us are only vaguely aware of the alliances, negotiations, and relationships that make this massive movement of goods possible. When we compare tribal and contemporary industrialized societies, the correspondence between the range of incest taboos and the material conditions of life cannot be dismissed as mere coincidence.

Industrialization does not operate alone in affecting the degree to which incest taboos extend beyond the nuclear family. In the history of societies, political institutions developed as technology advanced. Improvements in packaging and transportation have led not only to reductions in the number of people involved in external trade, but also to greater and greater concentrations of decision making in the hands of fewer and fewer people. Trade is no longer the responsibility of all members of a society, and the maintenance of relationships between societies has become the responsibility of a few people—a king and his bureaucracy, impersonal governmental agencies, national and multinational corporations.

To the extent that trade is conducted and negotiated by a handful of people, it becomes unnecessary to use incest taboos to force the majority of people into alliances with other groups. Treaties, political alliances, and negotiations by the managers of a few impersonal agencies have replaced marital and other personal alliances. The history of human societies suggests that incest taboos may have outlived their original purpose.

But incest taboos still serve other purposes. For social and emotional reasons rather than economic ones, people in modern industrial societies still need to prevent localism. Psychological well-being in a diversified society depends largely on the ability to tap different ideas, points of view, life styles, and social relationships. The jugulars that must now be kept open by the majority of people may no longer be for goods and resources, but for variety and stimulation. This need for variety is what, in part, seems to underlie the preference of Israelis to marry outside the communities in which they were born and brought up. The taboo against sex within the nuclear family leads young people to explore, to seek new experiences. In a survey of a thousand cases of incest, Christopher Bagley found that incestuous families are cut off from their society's social and cultural mainstream. Whether rural or urban, he writes, "the family seems to withdraw from the general community, and initiates its own 'deviant' norms of sexual behavior, which are contained within the family circle." "Such a family," he continues, "is an isolated cultural unit, relatively untouched by external social norms." This social and cultural inbreeding is the cause of the profound malaise represented by incest.

To illustrate the correspondence between incest and social isolation, let me describe an incestuous family reported by Peter Wilson, an anthropologist. Wilson sketched a sequence of events in which a South American family became almost totally isolated from the community in which it lived, and began to practice almost every variety of incest. The decline into incest began many years before Wilson appeared on the scene to do anthropological research, when the father of five daughters and four sons made the girls (who ranged in age from 18 to 33) sexually available to some sailors for a small sum of money. As a result, the entire household was ostracized by the rest of the village. "But most important," Wilson writes, "the Brown family was immediately cut off from sexual partners. No woman would have anything to do with a Brown man; no man would touch a Brown woman."

The Browns's isolation and incest continued for several years, until the women in the family rebelled—apparently because a new road connecting their hamlet to others provided the opportunity for social contact with people outside the hamlet. At the same time the Brown men began working in new light industry in the area and spending their money in local stores. The family slowly regained some social acceptance in Green Fields, the larger village to which their hamlet belonged. Little by little they were reintegrated into the hamlet and there seems to have been no recurrence of incest among them.

A second example is an upper-middle class, Jewish, urban American family that was described to me by a colleague. The Erva family (a pseudonym) consists of six people—the parents, two daughters aged 19 and 22, and two sons, aged 14 and 20. Mr. Erva is a computer analyst and his wife a dentist. Twenty-five years ago, the Ervas seemed relatively normal, but shortly after their first child was born, Mr. and Mrs. Erva took to wandering naked about their apartment, even when others were present. They also began dropping in on friends for as long as a week; their notion of reciprocity was to refuse to accept food, to eat very little of what was offered them, or to order one member of their family not to accept any food at all during a meal. Their rationale seemed to be that accepting food was receiving a favor, but occupying a bed was not. This pattern was accompanied by intense family bickering and inadvertent insults to their hosts. Not surprisingly, most of their friends wearied of their visits and the family was left almost friendless.

Reflecting Bagley's general description of incestuous families, the Ervas had withdrawn from the norms of the general community after the birth of their first child and had instituted their own "deviant" patterns of behavior. They thereby set the stage for incest.

Mr. Erva began to have intercourse with his daughters when they were 14 and 16 years old. Neither of them was self-conscious about the relationship and it was common for the father to take both girls into bed with him at the same time when they were visiting overnight. Mrs. Erva apparently did not have intercourse with her sons. The incest became a matter of gossip and added to the family's isolation.

The Erva family then moved to the Southwest to start over again. They built a home on a parcel of land that had no access to water. Claiming they could not afford a well of their own, the family began to use the bathrooms and washing facilities of their neighbors. In the end these neighbors, too, wanted nothing to do with them.

Mr. and Mrs. Erva eventually separated, he taking the daughters and she the sons. Later the younger daughter left her father to live alone, but the older daughter still shares a one bedroom apartment with her father.

Social isolation and incest appear to be related, and social maturity and a taboo on incest are also related. Within the modern nuclear family, social and emotional relationships are intense, and sexuality is the source of some of the strongest emotions in human life. When combined with the intensity of family life, sexually stimulated emotions can be overwhelming for children. Incest taboos are a way of limiting family relationships. They are assurances of a degree of emotional insularity, of detachment on which emotional maturity depends.

On balance, then, we can say that legal penalties for incest were first instituted because of the adverse economic effects of incestuous unions on society, but that today the negative consequences of incest affect only individuals. Some will say that criminal penalties should be retained if only to protect children. But legal restraints alone are unlikely to serve as deterrents. Father-daughter incest is regarded by many social workers, judges, and psychiatrists as a form of child abuse, but criminal penalties have not deterred other forms of child abuse. Moreover, incest between brothers and sisters cannot be considered child abuse. Some have even suggested that the concept of abuse may be inappropriate when applied to incest. "Many psychotherapists," claims psychologist James McCary in *Human Sexuality*, "believe that a child is less affected by actual incest than by seductive behavior on the part of a parent that never culminates in any manifest sexual activity."

Human history suggests that the incest taboo may indeed be obsolete. As in connection with changing attitudes toward homosexuality, it may be maintained that incestuous relations between consenting mature adults are their concern alone and no one else's. At the same time, however, children must be protected. But questions still remain about how they should be protected and until what age.

If a debate over the repeal of criminal laws against incest is to begin in earnest, as it surely will if the Swedish Parliament acts on the proposed reversal, one other important fact about the social history of sexual behavior must be remembered. Until about a century ago, many societies punished adultery and violations of celibacy with death. When it came time to repeal those laws, not a few people favored their retention on the grounds that extramarital sexual relationships would adversely affect the entire society. Someday people may regard incest in the same way they now regard adultery and violations of celibacy. Where the threat of punishment once seemed necessary, social and emotional dissuasion may now suffice.

For further information:

Bagley, Christopher. "Incest Behavior and Incest Taboos." *Social Problems*, Vol. 16, 1969, pp. 505-519.

Birdsell, J. B. *Human Evolution: An Introduction to the New Physical Anthropology.* Rand McNally, 1972.

Bischof, Norbert. "The Biological Foundations of the Incest Taboo." *Social Science Information*, Vol. 11, No. 6, 1972.

Fox, Robin. *Kinship and Marriage.* Penguin Books, 1968.

Slater, Mariam. "Ecological Factors in the Origin of Incest." *American Anthropologist*, Vol. 61, No. 6, 1959.

Wilson, Peter J. "Incest: A Case Study." *Social and Economic Studies*, Vol. 12, 1961, pp. 200-209.

Fission in an Amazonian Tribe

By Napoleon A. Chagnon

....

FOR MILLIONS OF YEARS our ancestors passed their lives in small groups that generally ranged in size from about a dozen individuals to no more than 200. The local, day-to-day groupings of the remaining primitive societies fall within that range, and studies of our own closest relatives in the animal world, the monkeys and apes, suggest that our primate ancestors also lived in social groups whose size stayed between what one anthropologist calls the "magic numbers," i.e. from 40 or 50 individuals to about 200. At this upper extreme, both the human and animal populations fission into two or more groups.

Anthropologists who concern themselves with tribal population size and distribution generally attempt to relate population to resource availability—water, game animals, cultivable land—and try to explain the population patterns in terms of these material needs. Thus, the focus has been on general ecological relationships between man and environment, between a region's "carrying capacity" and the actual numbers of exploiters. But why should there be ten communities of 100 people rather than one community of 1,000?

Most anthropologists would tend to assume, at least for egalitarian primitive societies, that it is ecologically more efficient for the population to subdivide into ten smaller groups than remain as a single, large nucleated group. Egalitarian societies, however, are organized along principles of kinship, marriage and descent from common ancestors. It is beginning to look as if there are intrinsic limits to the size which such groups can grow to when their organization consists of only those three principles.

Recent studies have shown the great significance that kinship recognition plays in non-human primate societies. Monkeys can recognize their relatives and, just like human beings, behave in very predictable, characteristic ways towards different categories of relative. Moreover, the organization of some of the well studied monkey societies is very much a matter of kinship ties; the fissioning of monkey troops, remarkably enough, shows very striking parallels to what happens in egalitarian societies that fission. One recent study in Japan revealed that a large troop of monkeys was organized into sixteen "matrilines," each consisting of an old female, her offspring and the offspring of her daughters. The troop was heavily provisioned and had no food limitation checking its growth. As the troop got larger, internal order began breaking down and the group fissioned into two new troops, the eight highest ranking matrilines forming one troop and the eight lowest ranking matrilines forming the other.

This is essentially the same pattern of fissioning I have found in 48 months spent in the egalitarian society of the Yąnomamö Indians of southern Venezuela and adjacent portions of Brazil. The area is vast and characterized by abundant resources, and the Yąnamamö population is growing and fissioning. The data considered here is mainly genealogical; some five generations deep, it encompasses approximately 3,500 individuals (about half of whom are dead) and approximately 1,600 marriages. Additionally, I have informants' accounts of population fissioning during the past 100 years, which led to the emergence of some dozen or so villages.

Nobody knows for certain how many Yąnomamö villages there are, or how many people comprise the total population. Large areas of the tribe have never been visited or studied, so we can only make a calculated estimate of the total population. During the course of our field research, my French colleague Jacques Lizot and I visited at least 100 villages and made detailed censuses on many of them. Putting our data together and estimating the sizes of the uncontacted groups, we come up with an estimate of about 15,000 Yąnomanö in total.

The Yąnomamö can be described as a "tribe" in the

following anthropological sense. Although they have no precise notion of their unity as a people, they can recognize another Yąnomamö by his or her language. Thus, the term tribe is more a linguistic notion than anything else: it does not imply any organization of a political kind that binds village to village.

The Yąnomamö language, incidentally, has not been demonstrably related to any other South American Indian language, attesting to the Yąnomamö's long separation and isolation from their neighbors. Like many primitive peoples, their word for human being is the word they use to describe themselves. Yąnomamö implies purity, if not superiority; all other people are "nabä" (foreigners, near human), potential enemies and somewhat degenerate forms of the "true" people.

The most significant social entity for the Yąnomamö is the village, a circular open structure with a cleared plaza at the center. Individual families live around the periphery of the village, under the common circular roof. There is no partitioning between households and almost everyone can hear and see almost everyone else in the village, so daily (and nightly) life is very public. Individuals know all the members of their village and are closely related to most of them. The villages range in size, as with the tribal world in general, from about 40 people to a maximum of about 250 people.

Village cohesion and social order derive mainly from the ties of kinship and the mutual obligations that stem from these ties. Daily life, economics, politics, religion and cooperation are embedded in and consequently affected by the ethical, moral and behavioral bonds inhering in kinship. There is no "economy" in a market sense: all exchanges are between kinsmen and "price" or "value" as we know it affect the transactions no more than they do within our own domestic households. Exchanges are first and foremost a component in transactions between kinsmen.

Nobody in such a community can escape the pervasive influence of the kinship system, not even the anthropologist. When I visit each village, I, too, must be incorporated into the system so that the individual residents know who I am and how to treat me. Since the headman, or leader, of the village usually has the largest number of kinsmen, I normally "relate" to him, usually by calling him "shoriwä," the Yąnomamö word that translates loosely into "brother-in-law" and "male cross-cousin."

This is a particularly affectionate relationship among the Yąnomamö. Thus, when I call the headman "shoriwä," it immediately establishes us as potential exchangers of women: I could marry the head-

man's sisters and he could marry mine. Furthermore, our children could marry each other, creating additional and important social bonds between us and our respective groups. As brothers-in-law we owe each other special services and must show generosity in our mutual dealings. If I have possessions the headman wants, I must give them to him—and vice-versa.

Being related to the headman of the village as brother-in-law also relates me to everyone else in the village; each person knows how he or she is related to the headman and it is a simple matter to do a little kinship arithmetic to figure out how one is related to the headman's brother-in-law. Thus, with the kin term "shoriwä" I become related to everyone in the village, and everyone knows how to behave with me. I become by extension the brother of the headman's wife, the mother's brother of his children, etc.

The villagers know that I am not really related to the headman, but the adoption of the kinship usage is the only basis for social interaction that exists. Within their own social system, villagers make very sharp and invidious distinctions. Some co-villagers are "better" than others and more trustworthy, and people in the next village over are always less trustworthy since they are less related. In this regard, the Yąnomamö operate in pretty much the same way we do when we deal with our own kin. We normally delight in a weekend visit from our parents or grandparents, but if a remote cousin and his family is passing through town and shows up for the weekend we are not likely to be so enthusiastic.

Each village may have several kinship groups of patrilineally related individuals; the oldest males in these groups will usually be politically prominent and represent the village in its dealings with other groups. The headman usually comes from the largest kinship group. It is as if a village were comprised of three or four large families—the Smiths, Joneses, Blacks and Greenes. The headman of the Smith family, "Smitty," has slightly more authority than the other heads of families.

Smitty and his family remain dependent on the others, however, especially for marriageable women; all the families are often bound together by several generations of reciprocal marriage exchanges. Smitty and his brothers (and their sons) might get wives from the Greenes and Blacks, for example, and give their sisters and daughters in return. The Yąnomamö marriage system contributes significantly to social solidarity by structuring first the kinds of kinship patterns that result from marriage and reproduction, and second the relative numbers of various types of genealogically specified marriages (such as the number of mother's brother's daughters' marriages vs. the number of father's sister's daughters').

The desire to obtain wives is very great among most of the men—the more wives the better. However, this is rather difficult. First, the Yąnomamö practice infanticide and kill more girls than boys. (When I point out that what they are doing will cause a shortage of marriageable females, they optimistically assert that with all those male babies they didn't kill, the village will become powerful and they can raid their neighbors for women!) Second, if some men are successful at acquiring many wives, then other men must go without wives. Although they may resign themselves to this fate, it becomes a serious problem in village life as the unmarried men persistently attempt to seduce the other men's wives. Most of the internal village squabbles begin with arguments and disputes over women.

A fission is usually the result of gradually accumulating strife and tension within the village: as the group gets larger and its composition becomes more complex, squabbles and fights grow in frequency. Finally, the village can no longer be held together by the ties of kinship, marriage obligations and the tenuous authority of the headman. Any fight or dispute might be the spark that touches off a division of the village.

The "Browns," for example, decide to move off, taking with them their children and their children's spouses (Joneses, Blacks and Greenes). The people who leave the group will be more closely related among themselves than they are to the ones who remain behind. The two new villages might remain on relatively peaceful terms with each other, but they could enter into hostilities as their populations grow and each is better able to fend for itself in war and politics. However, if the original group had a large number of enemies before it fissioned, members of both new groups know that it would be unwise to be too independent. Otherwise, their common enemies might attack each of the groups and destroy them. In such a situation the new groups might simply build two separate villages a few hundred feet apart, pursuing increasingly independent strategies as extra-village political pressures permit.

Over time, the two villages themselves would grow and fission, and the resulting new villages would disperse even further. In this fashion a whole area—a river drainage, for example—might come to have six or eight independent villages, all descended from the same original group. Each village would have people who are related, however remotely, to the members of other villages in the same river drainage.

One cannot live among the Yąnomamö for very long before realizing that if they had a choice in the matter, the villages would fission into even smaller entities—a few families—within which life would be very pleasant and happy. I have frequently heard the Yąnomamö comment, "We split up into two groups because we were many and therefore always fighting among ourselves." What keeps the village from fissioning into tiny units? It appears to be the subtle pressures of the warfare system.

As is the situation with internal village fights, wars between villages usually begin in a contest over the possession of some woman. In almost every case in which I attempted to get at the cause of a particular war, the Yąnomamö would look at me quizzically and hiss contemptuously: "Don't ask such stupid questions! Women! Women! Women! That's what started it! We fought over women!" The mortality rate in their wars, I might add, is staggering. In some areas as many as 30 per cent of the adult male deaths are attributable to warfare.

At the lower end of the village size scale—in the range of 40 to 60 people—warfare tactics and raiding strategies dictate that a village must contain approximately ten able-bodied men between the ages of 17 and 40. The age and sex distribution of the population require that a village must have about 40 members in order for there to be that many adult males capable of effective raiding. Therefore, a village rarely fissions until it reaches a size of about 80 inhabitants, i.e. until it reaches a size at which a fission will yield two viable villages of about 40 members.

Where warfare is particularly intense, a growing village of 80 to 100 people will probably not fission, since two smaller villages would be more vulnerable to raids than a single, larger village. Still, if a group of 150 is advantageous in the warfare system, why don't some villages grow even larger and have even more advantage? The answer to that question seems to be the limitations on organizational capacity imposed by kinship and marriage.

As most villages grow they make political alliances with other villages and exchange women with them. Young men from other villages may also move in, hoping to obtain wives. Their presence reduces the general amount of relatedness within the group. Over time, as the newcomers marry and reproduce, the composition of the village becomes more complex and the possibility for new alliance patterns increases: women can be given to create these alliances instead of to consolidate old ones. The more complex a village is, the greater the chance of sexual intrigues and, therefore, of arguments and disputes.

The conditions under which a new village is formed are crucial to its ability to grow larger. Suppose that a village is formed by twelve adults and their offspring—six men and six women who each have one spouse and several children. If the adults are not brothers and sisters, each man will be the "founder" of his own lineage; the village will have six small patrilineages at the outset, each attempting to get women from the other five. The amount and kinds of kinship and marriage interrelationships possible among their descendants will be relatively small.

Compare this to another situation in which two "families" of three brothers and three sisters each found a village. If the oldest brother of each family married all three sisters in the other family, we would have two large local descent groups whose members are very closely related to each other. Moreover, the grandchildren of the original founders would all be cousins (cross and parallel) to each other, and the cross-cousins could marry. Indeed it would be impossible to marry someone who is not a cross-cousin.

It is possible to measure the closeness of relationship between any pair of related individuals in a society by using genealogical data and a statistic known as the inbreeding coefficient. Technically the inbreeding coefficient specifies the probability that an individual will inherit, through both parents, a particular gene (allele) from some common ancestor. The statistic therefore makes it possible for anthropologists to discuss the terms "close kin" and "distant kin" objectively.

I have, with the aid of the computer, calculated these values among all 3,500 people in my sample and can characterize any village by an average amount of genealogical relationship obtaining between all possible pairs of individuals in the village. The data show that in very large villages, there is a correlation between village size and amount of relatedness in the population. The villages whose founders had a greater degree of relatedness tend to grow larger.

Since those villages that manage to grow particularly large have higher-than-usual frequencies of cross-cousin marriage, the amount of polygyny in the founding group seems to be significant in regard to village size. The effects of polygyny can be particularly dramatic in some of the Yąnomamö population blocs. In one bloc I studied, one founder had 45 children by eight wives. A number of his sons were also remarkably successful at acquiring spouses and, therefore, in producing large families: one of them had 33 children. Considering the population bloc as a whole (some six or seven villages), approximately 75 per cent of all the residents were descended from the one founder!

Given the explicitly stated desire of the Yąnomamö to live in smaller groups, it seems likely that military pressure is responsible for the fact that villages grow to 100 or 150 people, as it is for the minimum population size of 40. But whether villages grow to 200 or 250 depends on the nature of the marriage patterns and the amount of kinship relatedness that the group begins with and preserves as it grows. If there has been a modest amount of predatory or inter-group military pressure throughout the long history of human beings, then it would seem reasonable that there has been an advantage to maximizing group size. The data on the Yąnomamö suggests that there has likewise been a persistent tendency to arrange close marriages and to concentrate kinship relatedness as well. Thus, a significant amount of "inbreeding" may have been characteristic of the mating/marriage arrangement of *Homo sapiens* as a species.

The Marriage of Yongsu's Mother

By Laurel Kendall

The most nerve-wracking days come early in anthropological fieldwork. My assistant and I went from door to door in Enduring Pine Village, administering a routine questionnaire. How many people live in this house? What are their ages? We asked about childbirth, miscarriages, and abor-

Excerpted from *The Life and Hard Times of a Korean Shaman: Of Tales and the Telling of Tales*, by Laurel Kendall © 1988 University of Hawaii Press.

tions; about spirit possession, exorcisms, and divinations. We took great pains to explain the purpose of the survey, which was to compile background information on family life and women's experiences in this Korean community. But our carefully rehearsed and excessively polite introductions did not lull my own discomfort at intruding upon the lives of busy countrywomen. We were still seeking the least offensive way to ask our questions and struggling to make sense of the things that we were told.

In the lingering April dusk, we went to Yongsu's Mother's house because we needed a lift, and this would be an easy interview. I had already spent more than a month in the company of this *mansin*, or "shaman," observing her at divination sessions and rituals. She knew that my work included a barrage of questions, and I knew that she loved to talk. She fielded our queries with an air of amusement, prompting my giggling assistant to conduct the interview as if it were a parody.

"Do you practice birth control?"

"Am I a chicken? Can I lay eggs without a mate?"

The anthropologist and her assistant were an appreciative audience, a sympathetic audience, and the mansin would give us more than the routine answers our tedious questions solicited. She told us about the little sister who had contracted smallpox. To entertain and propitiate the smallpox spirit, the family held a *kut*, an elaborate ritual in which all of the family's gods and ancestors appear and speak in the person of the costumed, possessed shamans. The shamans jumped up and down on the porch with such enthusiasm that the floorboards caved in. When the smallpox spirit visits the house, nails should not be driven into wood. But her father ignored the prohibition and repaired the broken porch, and the sick child went blind. They searched for the nails, found one, pulled it out, washed it, and the little girl regained sight in one eye. Still, she remained sickly and soon died, cradled in her elder sister's arms.

Yongsu's Mother keeps the little girl's spirit with the gods and ancestors in her shrine. When she performs a kut to feast and entertain her own gods, she ties a child's brightly colored skirt and jacket to the belt of the costume

Reprinted from *The Life and Hard Times of a Korean Shaman: Of Tales and the Telling of Tales*, by Laurel Kendall, University of Hawaii Press, 1988, by permission of the publisher and the author. Photos: Courtesy of Homer Williams she wears to summon the Special Messenger, the smallpox spirit. Her dead sister comes to the kut in the god's entourage; I would meet her at a kut later that spring. Speaking through the lips of a possessed mansin, she would announce herself as a princess and claim that she had come to play.

From the loose threads of the survey questions, Yongsu's Mother began to spin bits of tales, constrained and abbreviated by the structure of our interview and the list of questions yet to be posed. When we asked about marriage, the dam burst and the words poured out, rising and falling until the tale was told:

It was market day, I can never forget it. We'd been boiling beans to make soy sauce. I was dressed up in a yellow jacket and a pink skirt, silky stuff, the best you could get back then. I had on my best Korean dress and fresh white stockings. I thought I'd go down and see what the Willow Market was like, and I was on my way out of the gate when a man and a woman arrived. The man asked me, "Is your elder sister home?" I just bawled back, "Sister, someone's here!" She came bustling out to greet them and took them straight to our mother's room. I told Mom I was going out, but she sent me to stoke the fire under the beans.

I kept tossing twigs into the flames while my sister, behind the paper door, kept saying, "Yes, yes, yes." I stuck my head in and asked, "What's going on?" She told me to get them some noodle soup from the Chinese restaurant. I asked, "What about me?" "You can do as you like." So I went and ordered their noodle soup, and when the restaurant boy delivered it, I set it on a tray with some kimchee and shouted in, "Here's the noodles!" My sister told me to come in and sit down. I just plopped the tray down and trudged back outside. I didn't think anything of it, didn't realize they'd come to look me over. I thought that they had come to see my sister and I'd just brought them some noodles for lunch. The man sat by the desk with a handkerchief on his lap and he looked very old. I remembered that afterward. I'd just walked in and out when I brought the noodles.

My sister called for me to take away the tray, so I went back in. That guy hadn't eaten more than three mouthfuls. I took his noodles out to the kitchen to save for later. When my mother came out, I asked her if I could go to the market. She said, "What's all this about going to the market? Where's the money?" I told her I had money, and she asked me where I'd kept it hidden. There wasn't anything to buy out in the country anyway. I just wanted to have a look around.

The man was ready to leave, and everyone stood around saying their goodbyes. I stayed in the kitchen, but as soon as the man left, the matchmaker came looking for me. She said she wanted to have a talk. I told her I was going to the market. She said, "You come right over here and tell me what you think of that guy."

"What do you mean?"

"He's looked you over and you please him. Just say the word and it's settled."

I was flabbergasted. "What nonsense is this? Who says I want to get married? Anyway, I wouldn't marry an old guy like that. Don't even say such things!"

The matchmaker went right back into my sister's room. I wasn't in the mood for the market anymore. I waited for the matchmaker to come out and she started in again, "Tell me what you thought of that guy, just say the word. He's all right, isn't he?"

I howled that I couldn't go through with it. I told them, "Do you think I can't find a husband anywhere? Do you think I have to settle for an old guy like that? I'm going back to Seoul."

Then my sister raised a fuss. "You're so stubborn. With your wretched horoscope, you should marry an older man, someone who's already been married once. I'm your sister. Do you think I'd arrange something that was bad for you?"

When she said that, I was so furious I couldn't hold it in, I ran to the chimney behind the house and sobbed. "She brought us down here because she was lonely. She's made us sell our house. Why is she doing this to me? When the right time comes, I'll gladly get married. Why do they have to marry me off to an old guy?" I raged and cried, and raged some more. . . .

We passed into the twelfth month, the empty time that we don't consider part of the old year. About five days before the wedding, the man gave my sister some money for my permanent and bride's makeup. I took the money and threw it on the ground. "What does this have to do with anything? Does he think I haven't gotten married because I can't afford to permanent my hair?" My sister tried to coax me, but this threw me into a deeper rage. "If I'm set against him, why are you all so anxious to throw me out like this? If our ages were similar it would be all right, but he's old. If you're so keen on this marriage, why not go and investigate him? Do you expect me to marry someone who lives so far away on just the strength of the matchmaker's words?"

"The matchmaker knows the whole story. How come you're so suspicious?"

After the wedding, I left Willow Market with him and cried all the way on the bus. My eyes were swollen. It must have been embarrassing for him.

We got to the Imjin River. That was as far as the bus would go. We needed passes to board the boat, but I said I didn't have one. We had a huge fight right there on the dock. Here I was, all done up in a Korean dress made of silk from Hong Kong, and the angrier I got, the more I wanted to throw myself into the river. By the time my husband had cleared things with the guards and dragged me away to the boat, my feet were frozen stiff. On the other side there was another checkpoint. The guard asked me, "Auntie, do you have a citizen's identification card?" This

time I just slipped out my Seoul registration card, showed it to the guard, and walked on through.

As we reached the far side of the river, someone rode up on a bicycle, parked it on the sand, and pulled in the boat. I thought it was just another passenger going to cross the river, but when I looked I saw that he resembled my husband. I'd heard that he had six brothers so I just assumed that this was one of them, but when I asked my husband, he denied it, said it was a distant relation. Even on the way to his home he lied to me.

We walked and walked. My feet swelled up like balloons. I wasn't used to walking. Finally, we came to the village. A girl emerged from one of the houses and threw out a basin of dishwater. She gave me the strangest look. In some odd way she seemed to resemble my husband. She was standing in front of a straw-roofed house, a tumbledown house. It was falling apart at the seams. I hoped

with all my might that we would not turn into that house. I followed behind my husband with my eyes cast down to the backs of his shoes. His feet turned into that very gateway. Could he just be stopping by? No such luck. As soon as we were inside the gate, I heard, "Daddy's home, Daddy's home!" Despair!

I stood there in the gateway, stunned. I heard them ask me, over and over again, to come in. There was a three-year-old boy, a little frog baby looking mischievous, and a nine-year-old daughter, the one who works in Seoul now. There was also a twenty-one-year-old daughter; I was barely five years older than her. I thought she was my husband's niece. I thought that she had just come over to help with the housework.

They kept asking me to come inside, so I went in and looked things over. It was laughable. The house was bare. The cupboard held one battered little dish for shrimp sauce. Oh, I was disappointed! I just stood there in the empty kitchen until my husband took me by the hand and led me to the inner room. It was a sorry show there too, only a wooden chest and some quilts piled up. I cursed my sister! Why did I deserve this? That bitch! I had told her to check everything before she married me off. I cried and cried. I couldn't stop. My husband said, "What's done is done. You won't get anywhere by crying about it." But I was fuming. If my sister had lived nearby, I'd have gone right over and grabbed her. I'd have dragged her there and said, "Feast your eyes on this!" But I didn't know the way back; I had never been in this village before.

The older girl brought in a tray of food. All of the relatives came over. The elder brothers' wives and the elder cousins' wives served the food—rice, toasted seaweed, and kimchee. Since it was the twelfth month, we ate winter kimchee. They kept asking me to eat and I kept saying that I didn't want any. They asked and I refused, again and again. That person, my husband, couldn't eat either. When the elder brother's wife came in and begged me to eat, I had a few mouthfuls just to make them happy.

Then I had to bow to them all. The room was full of people; they swarmed around like maggots. I had no idea who they were. There were relatives to the third degree and relatives to the fourth degree. I was dropping down to the floor and bobbing up all night. Finally, the third brother's wife said, "She's had a long journey. She must be tired. Those who haven't received her bows can come back tomorrow." My husband told them that my feet were swollen.

After everyone left, that man, my husband, went outside too. The brothers' wives were fixing a late-night snack. The girl came into the room to get something. She looked at my hand and said, "What a lovely hand!" She asked how old I was. My husband had told me to say that I was thirty-six but I told the truth, "I'm twenty-six."

The girl started. "Twenty-six?"

The elder brother's wife said, "Your skin is still soft like a baby's. With such a lovely face and hands, how can you do a countrywoman's work?" They said, "Your ages are too far apart." They chattered on about how young I was and how old he was while I just sat there. The girl came back into the room. I asked, "How old are you?"

She said, "One."

I said, "You mean twenty-one?"

She nodded.

The brother's wife explained, "My husband's brother is forty-one." Now it dawned on me that this girl was my husband's daughter. I thought, "It will be difficult enough to raise my own children, but how am I ever going to raise these?"

It was already one o'clock in the morning. They rolled out the quilts and told me to rest. My husband came in and sent them all home so I could sleep. He went out to see them off and came back. I couldn't even cry. I just sat there without a word. He came over and tried to take off my jacket. When he reached for the ribbon, I slapped his hand away. I said, "You should have told me the truth. You should have told me that you're forty-one years old and have a twenty-one-year-old daughter. After lying like this, how dare you put your hand to my body!"

Now he was angry. "Who told you that?" But then he said, "Don't worry about my daughter. I'll just marry her off. If I said I had so many daughters, they wouldn't have given you to me. I lied about that, but I really am thirty-seven."

I said, "All right, tomorrow we'll go to the district office and just see how you're registered. I've come all this way. If you turn out to be thirty-seven, I'll stay, but if that's not so, I'm leaving."

I didn't sleep. I held my ground all night. Whenever he reached out to touch me, I slapped his hand away. What could he do? He sat there smoking. He offered to help me take off my padded socks because my feet were sore. I said, "If my feet hurt, that's my business. You leave me alone."

In the morning, the older daughter fixed breakfast and the elder brother's wife came over to help. I stayed in the inner room. When the nine-year-old girl brought water for me to wash my face, she said, "How can this person be my mother?" My husband hit her. He scolded her in a loud voice that all the relatives could hear. It did not bode well for a daughter to be disrespectful to her new stepmother.

They brought in the breakfast tray and again I said that I wasn't going to eat. I hadn't eaten anything for so long that my eyes were turning back inside my head. My husband went out and spoke to his brother's wife. She came in and coaxed, "Since you're here, you might as well eat something. Here, let's eat together." I could have eaten everything on that tray, but I just had a couple of spoonfuls. When she took out the tray, I heard my husband ask how I was. I sat in the room all day without saying a word. He fretted and paced back and forth, back and forth. I can still

hear the sound of his feet. He was worried that I might run away.

Hours had passed as Yongsu's Mother narrated the tale of her wedding, a saga well polished by countless retellings for audiences of village women and clients. We were summoned to a late dinner while she hastened to cook up the evening rice for herself and Yongsu. We returned again in the evening and listened into the night. She told us how her elder stepdaughter ran away in rebellion and how, as a consequence, her husband began to drink himself to death in shame; how "that man" left her a widow when her own son, Yongsu, was barely a year old; and how she had been forced to survive on slim resources until, a few years later, the gods made her a shaman. Later, when we had translated all that we had heard and recorded, we knew that we were hooked, avid to hear more. Not only did Yongsu's Mother provide a rich ethnographic narrative, she was also a skilled storyteller, rendering her images with delicious turns of phrase. Her feet swelled up like balloons. She kept stoking the fire while her sister kept saying, "Yes, yes, yes." She modestly lowered her gaze to the backs of her husband's feet and saw them turn into the doorway of the hovel that would be her new home. She remembered details: the handkerchief on her future husband's lap, the pot of boiling beans, the half-eaten bowl of noodles, the basin of water in her stepdaughter's hands.

I toyed with the idea of recording a full biography, but was soon preoccupied by my research on shaman rituals. My assistant, who had relished the task of translating Yongsu's Mother's vivid language, left the field when she landed a promising job in Seoul. But Yongsu's Mother took the initiative, announcing that she would tell me the full story of her life. She had already mapped out the narrative: "The story of my childhood and of my father's taking a concubine, the story of my capture and escape during the war and my meeting with the Mountain God, the story of my lover and the birth of my daughter, the story of my marriage, and the story of my becoming a mansin." She told me that when I knew it all my tears would flow. The recurrent themes of her life had already been sounded in the initial interview: betrayal by kin, disappointment in human relationships, the bother and ingratitude of stepchildren, and the power of gods and ancestors to alter human destiny for good or ill.

I suspect that Yongsu's Mother often exaggerates, both to vindicate herself and also to heighten the drama of her performance. Hers is a melodramatic account, told among people who appreciate the purgative value of a good cry. This is not to say that she consciously deceives her audience, but rather that she plays her material for all it's worth. When she told us the story of her marriage, she re-created the innocent maiden of a fairy tale, oblivious to the machinations of a greedy sister who was sealing her fate behind closed doors. But how naïve could she have been? Not only was she twenty-six years old when she married the widower, she had already given birth to an illegitimate child. By the bitter standards of her own society, the bride was past marrying age and damaged goods besides. The scheming sister might rather have tried to make the best of her younger sibling's limited options. And although Yongsu's Mother protested every inch of the way to her husband's house, once there she recognized her lack of alternatives, cut her losses, made a life, and spun out her anger in a tale. Her art was to make old disappointment a good story.

I first heard Yongsu's Mother's account of her marriage in the spring of 1977. I returned in 1985 to tell her that I had finally translated the story of her life, to see if she was still willing to have me publish it, and to ask her help in completing the manuscript. I brought her a copy of my first book, inscribed "to my *mansin* honorable teacher," and heard her cap a discussion with "I've even come out in a book in America." But days passed before I could explain to Yongsu's Mother the real purpose of my visit. I wanted to be certain that she understood what I was about, and I wanted to discuss this project in privacy. This last condition was difficult to achieve in her sociable inner room, but one afternoon, when the last guest had departed and just before her son, Yongsu, returned home from another date, I brought out one of the old tapes and slipped it into my machine.

"You still have those old things?" I tell her about the translations and about the book I plan to publish. "But in America, what if Koreans read it? They'll think it's shameful." Her world has broadened. When I first knew her, America was on the other side of the earth, the home of the odd-complexioned soldiers who ran in formation on the road by her house, a land she had seen in movies. In 1985, America is where her brother and the kin of her neighbors live, a place where Koreans live. Appreciating her concern, I take a deep breath. I want to protect her and perhaps it is safest to abandon the project, but I also want her to know the worth of her storytelling.

"Americans won't find it shameful; they'll think it's inter-

esting, as interesting as a novel." "As interesting as a novel," she repeats the phrase to herself. "It has social and historical significance," I continue, using a Korean vocabulary that I read rather than speak, the words that do not ordinarily enter village conversation. "Of course, there are people who are incapable of understanding. I know this. I don't want any harm to come to you or Yongsu. As I have done in the past, I will try to keep your name a secret. In the book I've called you 'Yongsu's Mother.' When my friends from Seoul came here for the kut the other day, they kept asking, "Where's Yongsu's Mother?"" She laughs, and agrees to help me.

I was leaving again. About to depart for a kut with her closest friend and colleague, Songjuk Mansin, Yongsu's Mother presented me with some Korean accouterments for my American kitchen. She gave me a pair of covered rice bowls—a high *chubal*, such as men use, and a woman's short, broad *hap*—and a large rice pot, and then a smaller one, "so that your husband can cook rice when you are away." She saw the very un-Korean premise of my married life and was amused.

"What's her husband like?" Sonjuk Mansin asked Yongsu's Mother.

"Nice, steady-going," she said, and told a story from our visit in the summer of 1983. "It was the middle of the day, no one was around. I heard a faint splashing sound in the bath . . . I tiptoed in. . . . And there was the husband doing the laundry!" The prospect of my husband quietly doing laundry to surprise his absent wife was an image so droll as to provoke extended gales of laughter.

"And this," she said, returning to her bag of gifts and drawing out the gourd dipper that I had requested to replicate a birth charm for the American Museum, "this has historical significance. Why, people used to eat their rice out of these. We did that when we visited my grandfather in the country."

"Historical significance." She had taken my words because they intrigued and pleased her. She has observed my life and now tells stories about my household as I tell stories about her telling stories.

TOPIC *10*

Political and Economic Organization

All societies have means of molding their members' behavior to conform to group values (general orientations toward good and bad, right and wrong) and group norms (specific expectations of behavior depending on who the actor is and on the social context in which the behavior is taking place). Anthropologists call such means the mechanisms of social control, and they distinguish between internal means and external means.

Internal means of control rely on the individual's personal acceptance—through enculturation and socialization—of his or her culture's values and norms. In other words, the individual will feel uncomfortable when the moral order of the society is violated and therefore will be motivated not to transgress the society's moral code or expectations. External means of control are the responses of the society or its representatives to specific actions—either to reinforce (reward) such actions or to diminish the likelihood of their repetition. The former, reinforcing responses, are termed *positive sanctions*. The latter, punishments, are termed *negative sanctions*. Internalized values and norms, together with positive and negative sanctions, operate in all societies. However, there is enormous cross-cultural variation in the behaviors that are reinforced or punished and in the specific forms that the means of social control take.

In "Cannibalistic Revenge in Jalé Warfare," Klaus-Friedrich Koch examines intervillage feuding and its by-product—ritualistic cannibalism—as a means (among other things) to channel aggressive behavior into culturally acceptable patterns. Here, internalized means of social control seem quite prominent.

Despite accounts such as Koch's, however, it should be noted that not all anthropologists accept the idea that cannibalism exists or ever has existed in human societies. In his book, *The Man-Eating Myth* (1979), William Arens argues that good documentation of ritualistic or dietary cannibalism is nonexistent. Nearly all accounts ·of cannibalism, he writes, come down to one of three things: (1) accusations by other, usually neighboring, groups; (2) assertions that one's ancestors, but never oneself, were cannibals; or (3) fanciful travelers' tales. Other anthropologists, particularly those

who have conducted fieldwork in the Amazon and the South Pacific, disagree. They counter that cannibalism is both well-known and well-documented among the peoples they have studied.

Pat Shipman, a paleontologist at Johns Hopkins University, provides an early twentieth century example from the diaries of Richard Meinertzhagen, one of the last great explorer–soldiers of the British Empire. "An avid naturalist and hunter," she writes, "Meinertzhagen was an ideal witness. He took pains to learn the local languages, and was a meticulous observer." He encountered cannibalism during the struggle to "pacify" the Nandi, one of the most warlike peoples of western Kenya. In his diary for October 25, 1905, Meinertzhagen related the following story:

> I have a corporal in my company who is a Manyema, and this tribe practices cannibalism in so far as they eat their enemies, thereby gaining the enemy's strength. When this man returned from patrol yesterday he shouldered arms with his left hand level with his belt and to my amazement I saw five other black hands stuck in his belt. I asked him the reason and he said they were for his supper, explaining that fingers are the tenderest part of a man. I made him bury the hands and told him I would talk to him today. . . . This morning I had him up and told him he must not in the future mutilate his enemies. I then asked him about cannibalism; he tells me that fingers are the most succulent, adding: "But the best of all is the buttocks of a young girl."

Just as all societies have mechanisms of social control, so too do all societies have institutionalized production, distribution, and consumption of material goods and services. That is, they have an *economic system*. The form a society's economy takes will have a profound impact on many other social institutions. In "Subsistence Strategies and the Organization of Social Life," David E. K. Hunter reviews data from archaeology and ethnology to indicate ways in which

173

economics influence other aspects of social life. In doing so, he begins with an examination of the simplest hunting and food-gathering societies and ends with a sketch of modern industrial society. As you will see, one of the critical factors is not so much the specific subsistence strategy employed by a society, but whether or not the economy is organized around the production and distribution of surpluses.

The popular view of early human societies is that they were barely able to eke out a meager existence from a harsh and inhospitable environment. In "Murders in Eden," Marvin Harris argues that in fact, early hunting-and-gathering societies enjoyed an enviable standard of living and a great deal of leisure time—so long as they kept their population relatively stable, which they did through the practice of infanticide.

Allen Johnson, in his article "In Search of the Affluent Society," focuses on consumption rather than on production. He argues that the narrow view of economists is inadequate for assessing economic systems and that a critical variable is the quality of life an economic system permits its participants. In comparing an Amazonian society to French society, Johnson emphasizes a point made by Harris in the previous article: that the simple society provides its members with more time for visiting, play, conversation, and rest than does the complex society. And he shares with us some personal questions this raises for him.

Subsistence Strategies and the Organization of Social Life

By David E. K. Hunter

The sun beats down on the parched grasses, and its heat radiates from the rocky soil of the Kalahari Desert in southern Africa. Across the bleached landscape three men move slowly, in single file, keeping a line of thorny bushes between them and the herd of grazing giraffes. They have prayed and they have prepared their hunting arrows with poison freshly made from beetle paste. Now, with luck, one of them will wound a giraffe and they will follow it—for days, if necessary—until the poison works itself throughout the giant creature's bloodstream and slowly numbs and paralyzes it. Carefully avoiding its desperate last kicks, the men will use their clubs and spears to kill the animal. They will butcher it wherever it has fallen, cutting the meat into strips to dry in the sun. Then, finally, the men will return to their families camped in brush-and-hide windbreaks around a waterhole. The bones, the hide, and the meat will be passed from hand to hand, divided according to ancient customs, distributed along lines of family and kinship.

The people described here belong to the !Kung San (formerly known as the Bushmen); about 45,000 still live a semi-nomadic hunting and food-gathering existence in the Kalahari Desert. Their camps are small, numbering ten to thirty members, and they are communal and egalitarian. The sharing of food is fundamental to their way of life, and when, for whatever reasons, food sharing breaks down, the camp ceases to be a meaningful social unit: people pack their few belongings and move elsewhere, to camps of their relatives.

ECONOMY, SOCIETY, AND THE COMPARATIVE METHOD

In its most general sense, *economy* refers to the organized ways in which a society produces (or otherwise secures), distributes, and consumes its material goods (raw materials, products, and so on) and its services (that is, the patterns of behavior that supply individuals with their needs). Economic institutions are interlaced with the other social institutions of a society—indeed,

so much so, that separating them out for study is quite difficult. In order to do so here, and to indicate some of the ways in which economy and society are interwoven, this article focuses on strategies of subsistence and the ways in which such strategies affect and are affected by the organization of social groupings.

In order to keep this discussion reasonably brief and to the point, subsistence strategies will be considered under five main categories: hunting and food gathering, horticulture, pastoralism, agriculture, and industrialism. Inevitably, this classification has meant doing some violence to the actual facts—overlooking the ways in which the different strategies actually blend into or overlap with each other and stereotyping various social groups in terms of predominant features while downplaying (or even overlooking) other facets of their economic lives. This is the price one pays for using the comparative method; it is justified, however, if the main patterns it highlights nevertheless have something important to teach.

Anthropologists, in attempting to study and compare societies (both past and present) around the world, must take into account the tremendous impact of European imperialism and colonialism on the societies of Africa, Asia, and the Americas. Those societies that managed to survive into modern times often are distorted versions of their ancestral forms. Their populations were decimated by European diseases, their diversified subsistence systems were subordinated to the single cash-crop demands of European markets, their social life and political systems were torn apart by a tremendous increase in organized warfare (Sahlins 1972). However, while keeping these facts in mind, anthropologists have been able to note certain recurring patternings of social life that seem to be tightly tied to basic subsistence strategies.

Hunting and Food-Gathering Societies

The earliest human societies subsisted by foraging for vegetable foods and small game, fishing, collecting shellfish, and hunting larger animals. In modern times, the world's simplest and most marginal societies still subsist using these methods. They depend to a large degree on tools made of stone, wood, and bone.

Similarities among Hunting and Food-Gathering Societies. Although there are significant cultural differences among such groups, and in spite of the fact that they occupy environments varying from deserts to frozen wastelands, nevertheless there are certain recurring features of economic and social organizations that hunters and food-gatherers share—features that set them off from other kinds of societies. Contrary to both popular and scholarly preconceptions, hunting and food-gathering peoples do not work very hard. In fact, more time is spent socializing than in procuring food, which occupies perhaps some five hours per day (Sahlins 1972:1–39). Their communities are mobile and small. On the whole, social relationships among individuals tend to be quite egalitarian, at least in part because there is little private property. There is no social class differentiation, nor even institutionalized positions of prestige that are limited to favored subgroups.

In general, men are primarily responsible for hunting and for protecting the group. The women often hunt smaller game and forage for food (both animal and vegetable), typically providing some 60 to 70 percent of the total calories consumed by the group (Lee 1969). Women also take primary responsibility for raising the children. Marriage, in one or another form, in universally present, with monogamy the dominant form. Most social life is organized in terms of people's kinship relations. That is, the ways in which people are related to each other determines whether or not they may marry, what kinds of food or material goods they will exchange with each other, whether they observe the same taboos, and so on.

Differences among Hunting and Food-Gathering Societies. In spite of all these similarities, significant differences in societal organization do exist among contemporary hunting and food-gathering societies (Martin 1974). For one thing, political organization takes several forms, including male-centered kinship groups, female-centered kinship groups, and groups organized along kinship lines irrespective of gender. Those groups living in harsh climates and with a correspondingly low productivity are quite small, often numbering less than a few hundred individuals. But where nature is bountiful or affords special means of accumulating food surpluses (as on the Northwest Coast of North America, where annual salmon runs provided abundant food that could be stored for year-round consumption), hunting and food-gathering societies grew large, numbering into the thousands. Similarly, whereas most such groups are semi-nomadic because of their need to search for food, those who inhabit rich environments have developed sedentary village settlements. And with surplus food production and a sedentary life-style, social inequality is institutionalized among hunting and food-gathering groups just as it is in more technologically advanced societies (Martin and Voorhies 1975).

Horticultural Societies

Some 12,000 to 15,000 years ago, coinciding with the retreat of the last glaciers, a drying trend occurred in what previously had been rich, subtropical climates. The giant deserts of Africa, Asia, and the Middle East took shape. Even beyond their constantly expanding borders, new arid conditions made the age-old hunting and food-gathering way of life precarious. Some groups continued to eke out an existence using the old subsistence techniques. Others crowded together in the more abundant regions, harvesting wild grains until population pressures drove them out into less favorable environments. There they attempted to recreate the rich environments they had left. And in doing so, they created a whole new way of subsisting: the domestication of plants and animals (Flannery 1965, 1968). This process seems to have repeated itself at least three times in three different places: in the Far East in Thailand some 11,000 years ago; in the Middle East, about 10,000 years ago; and in Mesoamerica, some 6,000 to 9,000 years ago. From these three centers of origin, the domestication of plants and animals spread outward, until it became the most widespread means of subsistence and the economic base upon which all civilizations were built.

Recent research, reported in 1980 and 1981, indicates that people living in widely scattered areas of the world may well have domesticated some plant and animal species as early as 19,000 years ago. Wheat and barley, for example, apparently were being grown along the Nile fully 8,000 years before these grains were domesticated in Mesopotamia. And Charles Nelson, an anthropologist at the University of Massachusetts at Boston, reports evidence of early domestication of cattle in Kenya, southern Europe, and southwestern Egypt. But these societies did not develop civilizations on their own. Nelson theorizes that for civilization to arise, several elements must combine in a fertile environment. First, plants and animals must be domesticated, and the technology for harvesting and storing crops must be developed. Then, a society must come into contact with other societies, diversifying its domesticated plant and animal species and opening itself both to trade and to the new ideas that inevitably come with commerce. When this happens, food becomes more abundant and overpopulation ensues. The result, Nelson argues, is the birth of civilization. Apparently, though plants and animals were domesticated in many places, the *combination* of elements leading to the birth of civilization occurred in only three places: the Far East, the Middle East, and Mesoamerica.

You should not imagine that the domestication of plants and animals brought an easier work load or more leisure time to its inventors. Whereas hunting and food-foraging peoples work perhaps three to four days (averaging five hours per day) out of every week to secure their food, food *producers* (domesticators) must work every day—and long hours at that! Marvin Harris (1975:233–255), after comparing research on the energy spent and calories produced by five societies, concludes that the advantage of food production over hunting and food gathering lies in the ability of food producers to sustain settlements, rather than in any labor-saving improvements in productivity or in increased leisure time.

Horticulture is a technical term referring to the planting of gardens and fields using only human muscle power and the mechanical advantage of handheld tools (such as digging sticks and hoes), whereas *agriculture* refers to the use of an animal-drawn plow. There are two distinct approaches to horticulture: subsistence farming (producing only enough to feed the group) and surplus farming. The differences between the two are quite profound.

Subsistence Farming. Subsistence farmers live in environments that are unfavorable to cultivation. They are most often found in tropical or subtropical jungles where the forest constantly must be cleared away and always threatens to overgrow the fields. Every few years subsistence farmers must move their settlements when new fields have to be cleared. Their settlements are small, and competition among neighboring villages typically is high. In fact, ongoing feuding, raiding, and even prescheduled battles between the forces of nearby villages are not uncommon. Political organization rarely extends beyond the village, and usually it is based on positions that are inherited by males through the kinship system.

Where the environment is less difficult, competition and fighting among villages drop remarkably, and the political system frequently is organized around kinship-related women rather than men (Otterbein and Otterbein 1965). In this context, few differences in power and prestige exist between men and women. In fact, relationships between the sexes approach the egalitarian qualities generally found in hunting and food-gathering societies.

Although, in the richer environments, the production of surplus food is technologically possible, surplus production simply is not a culturally valued norm. Hence role specialization is relatively undeveloped—

not very much greater than among hunting and food-gathering groups. It seems, therefore, that with an abundant environment and little by way of tradable surpluses, social stratification and the institutionalization of prestige ranking are minimal.

Surplus Farming. Surplus farmers live in densely populated, permanent settlements. They have highly elaborated political institutions that tend to be male-dominated and structured by kinship relations. There is occupational specialization with the institutionalization of prestige differences, and social stratification is well established. Because the production of surpluses is a culturally valued norm, such societies often are expansionistic, with differentiated military force. Expansion means more land and more (captured) labor, which in turn allows the centralized accumulation of greater surpluses that can be used to pay for political support, specialized craftspeople, and conspicuous consumption.

As in hunting and food-gathering societies, women in horticultural societies perform most of the productive work associated with securing food. Although the men will do the heaviest work, such as clearing the fields, it is usually the women who prepare the fields, plant the crops, tend and harvest them, and share the food with their husbands and extended families (D'Andrade 1966, Murdock 1937).

Pastoralist Societies

Pastoralism is an approach to food production that relies on herding and animal husbandry to satisfy the bulk of a group's needs. Animal herds provide milk, dung (for fuel), skin, sheared fur, and even blood (which is drunk as a major source of protein in East Africa).

Pastoralist societies have flourished in many regions that are not suitable for plant domestication, such as semi-arid desert regions and the northern tundra plains of Europe and Asia. They are also found in less severe climates, including East African savannas and mountain grasslands. However, pastoralism almost never occurs in forest or jungle regions. It is an interesting fact, which scholars have not been able to explain, that no true pastoralist societies ever emerged in the Americas prior to the arrival of the Europeans.

Although many pastoralist groups rely partly on horticulture to subsist, most are nomads (or semi-nomads) who follow their herds in a never-ending quest for pasture lands and water. Hence, such societies typically consist of relatively small, mobile communities. When needed resources are predictable, pastoralist societies typically are composed of stable groups united under strong political figures. When resources are not predictable, they are quick to split apart and compete with each other. Hence, centralized political leadership does not appear (Salzman 1967). To the extent that political organization does exist, pastoralist societies generally are organized around male-centered kinship groups.

Pastoralism rests on three strategic resources: animal herds, pasture lands, and water. Animals usually are more or less equally available to all families in pastoralist groups. But access to the latter two resources often varies widely among families in such societies. Hence, although there are great differences of wealth in some pastoralist groups, rarely is there institutionalized stratification. When social classes and centralized political organization do develop, they appear to be responses to expansionist pressures from neighboring state-level societies.

When, through bonds of kinship, pastoralist societies have organized into those enormous sociopolitical entities called hordes, their extreme mobility, fierceness, and kinship-based fanatic loyalty have made them into extraordinary military powers. As such, nomadic pastoralists have influenced the course of civilization far more than their numbers alone would suggest. It was to keep out Central Asian hordes that the emperors of the Chou dynasty in China built the Great Wall in the third and fourth centuries B.C. And it was nomadic pastoralist armies who, in the fourth and fifth centuries A.D., drove the final nails into the coffin of the Roman Empire in the West. In fact, many of the states of ancient Asia, the Middle East, and Eastern Europe arose partly in protective response to pastoralist raids. But in fairness it must be said that pastoralists influenced civilizations not only through their destructiveness. In what is now Hungary, for example, the nomads themselves first established some of the oldest politically centralized societies in Europe (Cohen 1974).

Agricultural Societies

Agriculture, as we noted before, is plant cultivation that makes use of the plow. Agriculture is more efficient than horticulture. Plowing makes use of the far greater muscle power of draft animals, and it also turns the topsoil much deeper than does hoeing, allowing for better airing and fertilizing of the ground and thus improving the yield. Nevertheless, early agriculture probably did not yield much more than food gatherers in bountiful environments were able to harvest. However, by around 5500 B.C., farmers in the Middle East not only were using the plow, but *irrigation* as well. With irrigation, farming became capable of producing vast surpluses—enough to feed large numbers of people who did not produce food themselves.

Reliance on irrigated agriculture had several drastic and interrelated consequences for society. It pulled ever-growing populations together into those areas where irrigation could be practiced—into broad river valleys like those of the Nile in Egypt, the Tigris and Euphrates in the Middle East, the Huangho (Yellow River) in China, and the Danube and Rhine in Europe. This rapidly rising and geographically compressed population density gave rise to cities and to new social forms. For the first time, society was *not* organized principally in terms of kinship. Rather, occupational diversity and institutional specialization (including differentiated political, economic, and religious institutions) predominated.

Dependence on irrigation had additional, even more far-reaching, consequences. Irrigation projects are large and complicated. They consist of dams, canals and elaborate systems of ditches whose use must be carefully coordinated. The planning and building of such projects takes experts with the time and authority to direct the efforts of hundreds and even thousands of specialized laborers and farmers. This can be accomplished only by a society with centralized political organization. And it is clear that at least in the case of Chinese civilization, the organizational demands of irrigation farming led to the emergence of the centralized state (Wittfogel 1957).

Irrigated agriculture also made land that was suitable for farming into a scarce resource. Those who controlled access to arable land and its use soon were rich and powerful. They could command the payment of taxes and political support. By taxing the bulk of agricultural surpluses, political leaders could employ bureaucracies to implement their plans and armies to protect their privileges—both from external enemies and internal rebels. Thus social classes became entrenched, and the State evolved. Not surprisingly, the State is the most warlike of all sociopolitical forms (Otterbein 1970). For agricultural (and industrial) societies, conquest makes economic sense because it brings new farmlands and food producers under the State's control, increasing the surpluses at its disposal and thereby making possible ever more ambitious undertakings.

Industrial Society

The industrial revolution was a European and American phenomenon. Industrialism consists of the use of mechanical means (machines and chemical processes) for the production of goods. Contrary to its name the industrial "revolution" at first developed slowly. It had begun primarily in England early in the eighteenth century and gained momentum by the turn of the nineteenth century (Eli Whitney built a factory for the mass production of guns near New Haven, Connecticut in 1798). By the mid-1800s, it had swung into high gear with the invention of the steam locomotive and Henry Bessemer's development of large-scale production techniques at his steel works in England in 1858. It is called a "revolution" because of the enormous changes industrialism brought about in society.

Industrial society is characterized by more than just the use of mechanical means for production. It is an entirely new form of society that requires an immense, mobile, diversely specialized, highly skilled, and well-coordinated labor force. Among other things, this means that the labor force must be educated. Imagine the difficulties facing even the least skilled factory worker who cannot read. Hence an educational system open to all is a hallmark of industrial society—something that was not necessary in pre-industrial times. Industrialism also requires the creation of highly organized systems of exchange between the suppliers of raw materials and industrial manufacturers on the one hand, and between the manufacturers and consumers on the other.

Like agricultural societies, industrial societies inevitably are stratified. The nature of the stratification varies, depending on whether the society allows private ownership of capital (capitalism) or puts all capital in the hands of the State (socialism). However, all industrial societies may be said to have at least two social classes: (1) a large labor force that produces goods and services but has no say in what is done with them; and (2) a much smaller class that determines what shall be produced and how it shall be distributed.

Industrialism brought about a tremendous shift of populations. Over the past century and a half, vast numbers of rural peasants and farmers have migrated from the countryside to the cities, transforming themselves into what is called an urban proletariate. Kinship, which still played an important role in the organization of preindustrial agricultural society, now plays a much smaller role in patterning public affairs. (Some newly emergent industrial societies, such as those Arab states like Saudi Arabia that grew into existence from a nomadic pastoralist base, still are organized sociopolitically in terms of kinship relations.) Similarly, religious institutions, which in preindustrial society were very closely tied to political institutions, no longer dominate the scene—industrial society is highly secularized. (An exception to this generalization is the existence of so-called civil religions, such as Marxist-Leninism in socialist countries; another is the recent creation of a new Islamic state in Iran by followers of the Ayatollah Khomeini.) In general, the predominant form of social and political organization in industrial society is the bureaucracy—that least personal of all formal organizations, itself having been inspired by the model of the efficiently functioning machine the symbol of industrial production and of industrial society as a way of life.

SOCIETY AND ECONOMY

This article attempts to indicate some of the ways in which the economy and other social institutions are interwoven to make up the fabric of society. To accomplish this, it has focused on one aspect of economy—namely, the major strategies of subsistence that societies around the world employ. This is not meant to suggest that all social institutions are created only in response to—or caused by—subsistence strategies (or other aspects of the economy). That kind of a simplistic, one-way causal view, called economic determinism, enjoyed a vogue around the turn of this century before it was thoroughly refuted by careful research. Even those anthropologists who study cultural ecology—that is, the ways in which peoples' cultures adapt them to their environments—do not propose that environments or even subsistence strategies directly cause specific sociocultural forms to emerge. Rather, anthropologists recognize that human groups exist in dynamic relationships with the environment, that they both respond to and act upon the environment, and that the ways in which they interact with the environment have consequences for their social lives individually and as social groups.

Within this set of interdependent relationships, each society picks its way making use of culturally inherited patterns and also newly acquired, invented, or discovered techniques of production and distribution. Hence, in every generation, each society recreates and also modifies (to whatever degree) its design for living, its particular solutions to the problems of existence. Using the comparative method, anthropologists are able to point to some of the patterned commonalities and differences among societies. Here, I have highlighted these by organizing them in terms of the five major approaches to, or strategies for, subsistence.

References

Cohen, Yehudi A.
   1974 "Pastoralism," in Yehudi A. Cohen (ed.), *Man in Adaptation: The Cultural Present* (2nd ed.), Chicago: Aldine.
D'Andrade, Roy
   1966 "Sex differences and cultural institutions," in Eleanor Maccoby (ed.), *The Development of Sex Differences*, Stanford: Stanford University Press.
Flannery, Kent V.
   1965 "The ecology of early food production in Mesoamerica," *Science*, vol. 147:1247–1256.

1968 "Archaeological systems theory and early Mesopotamia," in Betty J. Meggars (ed.), *Anthropological Archaeology in the Americas*, Washington, D.C.: The Anthropological Society of Washington.

Harris, Marvin
1975 *Culture, People, Nature*, New York: Thomas Y. Crowell.

Martin, M. Kay, and Barbara Voorhies
1975 *The Female of the Species*, New York: Columbia University Press.

Murdock, George Peter
1937 "Comparative data on the division of labor by sex," *Social Forces*, vol. 16:551–553.

Otterbein, Keith
1970 *The Evolution of War*, New Haven, Conn.: Human Relations Area Files.

Otterbein, Keith, and Charlotte Swanson Otterbein
1965 "An eye for an eye, a tooth for a tooth: a cross-cultural study of feuding, "*American Anthropologist*, vol. 67:1470–1482.

Sahlins, Marshall
1972 *Stone Age Economics*, Chicago: Aldine

Salzman, Philip C.
1967 "Political organization among nomadic peoples," *Proceedings of the American Philosophical Society*, vol. 3:115–131.

Wittfogel, Karl
1957 *Oriental Despotism*, New Haven, Conn.: Yale University Press.

ARTICLE *31*

Cannibalistic Revenge in Jalé Warfare

By Klaus-Friedrich Koch

. . . .

In October, 1968, two white missionaries on a long trek between two stations were killed in a remote valley in the Snow Mountains of western New Guinea, and their bodies were eaten. A few days later, warriors armed with bows and arrows gave a hostile reception to a group of armed police flown to the site by helicopter. These people, described by the newspapers as "savages living in a stone-age culture," belong to a large population of Papuans among whom I lived for nearly two years, from 1964 to 1966.

People living to the west, in the high valley of the Balim River, call them "Jalé," and this is the name that I use for them. When I read of the killing of the missionaries I was reminded of how I had first heard that the people whom I had selected for ethnographic study had anthropophagic (man-eating) predilections. After arriving at Sentani airport on the north coast, I began negotiations for transport to a mission airstrip located in the Jalémó, the country of the Jalé. "I hope the Jalé will give us permission to land," one pilot said to me. "Just a few weeks ago the airstrip was blocked because the Jalé needed the ground for a dance and a cannibalistic feast to celebrate a military victory."

Our cultural heritage predisposes many people to view the eating of human meat with extreme horror. No wonder then that the literature on the subject is permeated with grossly erroneous and prejudicial ideas about the practice. Few anthropologists have been able to study cannibalism because missions and colonial governments have generally succeeded in eradicating a custom considered to epitomize, more than any other, the alleged mental primitiveness and diabolical inspirations of people with simple technologies. However, the Jalé, completely isolated from foreign influences until 1961, still practice cannibalism as an institutionalized form of revenge in warfare, which is itself an integral aspect of their life.

The Jalé live in compact villages along several valleys north and south of the Snow Mountains in east-central West New Guinea. Until the first missionaries entered the Jalémó in 1961, the Jalé were ignorant of the "outside" world. Five years later, when I left the area, many Jalé villages still had never been contacted, and culture change among the people living close to a mission station was largely limited to the acceptance of a few steel tools and to an influx of seashells imported by the foreigners.

Two weeks after I had set up camp in the village of Pasikni, a year-long truce with a neighboring village came to an end. Three days of fierce fighting ensued, during which the Pasikni warriors killed three enemies (among them a small boy), raided the defeated settlement, and drove its inhabitants into exile with friends and relatives in other villages of the region. At that time I understood little of the political realities of Jalé society, where neither formal government nor forensic institutions exist for the settlement of conflicts. Later, when I had learned their language, I began to comprehend the conditions that make military actions an inevitable consequence of the absence of an effective system of political control.

From an anthropological perspective any kind of war is generally a symptom of the absence, inadequacy, or breakdown of other procedures for resolving conflicts. This view is especially applicable to Jalé military operations, which aim neither at territorial gains and the conquest of resources nor at the suppression of one political or religious ideology and its forceful replacement by another. All armed conflicts in Jalémó occur as a result of bodily injury or killing suffered in retaliation for the infliction of a wrong. Violent redress may be exacted for adultery or theft or for a breach of obligation—usually a failure to make a compensatory payment of pigs.

Jalé warfare is structured by a complex network of kin relationships. The Jalé conceptually divide their society into two parts (moieties) whose members must marry someone from the opposite side. By a principle of patrilineal descent a person always belongs to the moiety of his father. Links between kin groups created by intervillage marriages—about half the wives in a village were born elsewhere—provide the structure of trade networks and alliance politics.

Most villages contain two or more residential compounds, or wards.

One hut among the group of dwellings forming a ward is considerably bigger than all the others. This is the men's house, a special domicile for men and for boys old enough to have been initiated. Women and uninitiated boys live in the smaller huts, each of which usually houses the family of one man. The residents of a men's house constitute a unified political and ritual community, and it is this community, not the village as a whole, that is the principal war-making unit.

As in all societies, there are some individuals who have more influence over the affairs of their fellows than most. In Jalémó a man gains a position of authority (which never extends much beyond the immediate kin group) through his acquisition of an esoteric knowledge of performing rituals and through the clever management of his livestock to the benefit of his relatives, for every important event demands the exchange of pigs—to solemnify or legitimate the creation of a new status or to settle a conflict. Most disputes are over women, pigs, or gardens, and any one of them may generate enough political enmity to cause a war in which many people may lose their lives and homes.

In every Jalé war one person on either side, called the "man-at-the-root-of-the-arrow," is held responsible for the outbreak of hostilities. These people are the parties to the original dispute, which ultimately escalates into armed combat. Being a man-at-the-root-of-the-arrow carries the liability of providing compensation for all injuries and deaths suffered by supporters on the battlefield as well as by all others—including women and children—victimized in clandestine revenge raids. This liability acts as a built-in force favoring an early end of hostilities.

On rare occasions blood revenge

Opposite page: By the time these young boys become warriors, they will be expert archers. Training begins early; boys who can hardly walk carry bows made by their fathers. Practice games perfect the proper stance.

has been prevented by delivery of wergild compensation, in the form of a pig to the kinsmen of a slain person. But only those people who, for one reason or another, cannot rally support for a revenge action and who shy away from solitary, surreptitious ambush attacks will accept such an offer if it is made at all. A negotiated peace settlement of this nature is most likely if the disputants are from the same village or if the whole settlement is at war with a common outside enemy.

When two villages are at war with each other, periods of daily combat are interrupted by short "cease-fires" during which the warriors attend to the more mundane task of garden work, but they are always prepared to counter a surprise attack launched by the enemy. After several weeks of discontinuous fighting, however, the threat of famine due to the prolonged neglect of proper cultivation induces the belligerents to maintain an informal and precarious truce. During this time small bands of kinsmen and members of the men's house of a victim whose death could not be avenged on the battlefield will venture clandestine expeditions into enemy territory, from which a successful raiding party may bring back

a pig as well. It is a revenge action of this kind that often precipitates a resumption of open warfare.

Fighting on the battlefield follows a pattern of haphazardly coordinated individual engagements, which rely on the tactic of "shoot-and-run." This technique requires a warrior to advance as far as the terrain affords him cover, discharge an arrow or two, and then run back to escape from the reach of enemy shots. When one side has been forced to retreat to its village, the fighting turns into sniping from behind huts and fences. Women and children always leave the village if an invasion is imminent and take refuge with friends and relatives in other villages. As a last resort the men retreat into the men's house, which a taboo protects from being burned. When a battle reaches this stage, the victorious warriors often plunder and burn family huts. Following a catastrophe of this extent the defeated side usually elects to abandon their village, and the warfare ceases, but the hostilities linger on until a formal peace ceremony reconciles the principal parties. Arranging the ceremony, which features the ritual slaughter and consumption of a pig, may take years of informal negotia-

Treacherous unbridged rivers are one of the obstacles the Jalé must surmount on revenge raids in distant valleys. Jalemo terrain is among the most rugged in New Guinea.

tions between people who have relatives on both sides. Afterward, dances in both villages and pig exchanges on a large scale consolidate the termination of the conflict.

"People whose face is known must not be eaten," say the Jalé. Consequently, cannibalism is normally not tolerated in wars between neighboring villages, and the few incidents that did occur during the lifetime of the oldest Pasikni men are remembered as acts of tragic perversion. In wars between villages separated by a major topographic boundary such as a mountain ridge, however, cannibalistic revenge is an integral part of the conflict.

While territorially confined hostilities usually end within a few years, interregional wars may last for more than a generation. During this long period revenge parties from either side venture sporadic expeditions into hostile areas, keenly avoiding any confrontation in battle and seeking instead to surprise lone hunters or small groups of women working in distant gardens. The geography of interregional wars favors long-lasting military alliances that have a stability quite unlike the temporary and shifting allegiances that personal kin connections and trading partner-ships create in local conflicts.

If an enemy is killed during a foray into hostile territory, the raiders will make every effort to bring the body home. If tactical exigencies demand that the revenge party retreat without the victim, an attempt is made to retrieve at least a limb. The avengers always present the body to an allied kin group that has lost a member in the war. In return they receive pigs and are feted at a victory dance, during which the victim's body is steam-cooked in an earth oven dug near the village. Before the butchering begins, the head is specially treated by ritual experts: eyelids and lips are clamped with the wing bones of a bat to prevent the victim's ghost from seeing through these apertures. Thus blinded, it will be unable to guide a revenge expedition against its enemies.

After the head has been severed, it is wrapped in leaves. To insure more revenge killings in the future, some men shoot reed arrows into the head while it is dragged on the ground by a piece of vine. Then the head is unwrapped and swung through the fire to burn off the hair. This is accompanied by loud incantations meant to lure the victim's kinsmen into sharing his fate.

Following this ritual overture the butchers use stone adzes and bamboo knives to cut the body apart. The fleshy portions are removed from the skull, and in an established order of step-by-step incisions, the limbs are separated from the trunk, which is split open to allow removal of the gastronomically highly prized entrails. Some small, choice cuts, especially rib sections, are roasted over the fire, but the bulk of the meat is cooked with a variety of leafy vegetables.

Before and during the operation, people who are preparing the oven, tending the fire, or just standing around appraise the victim. A healthy, muscular body is praised with ravenous exclamations, but a lesser grade body is also applauded.

When the meat is done, the pit is opened and the "owners of the body," as the Jalé call the recipients of a slain enemy, distribute much of the food among the attending relatives of the person whose death the killing has avenged. It is also distributed to the allied kin groups of a person maimed or killed in the war. Eligible people from other villages who could not participate in the celebrations are later sent pieces reserved for them. If mood so moves the Jalé, they may place some of the victim's bones in a tree near the cooking site to tell travelers of their brave deed.

In the course of the dancing and singing, a poetically gifted man may introduce a new song. If the lyrics appeal to others, it becomes a standard piece in the repertoire. The songs commemorate fortunate and tragic events from past wars, and a typical verse goes like this:

Ngingi, your mother
bakes only tiny potatoes for you.
Isel, your mother too
bakes only the ends of potatoes
for you.
We shall bake big potatoes for you
On the day of Kingkaen's return.

Several hundred loops of split liana vine are worn by Jalé men day and night. As an expression of masculinity, younger men wear more loops than their elders. Penis sheaths, cut from gourds, are tied around the body.

Three-day battle culminates in plunder of an enemy village and burning of selected huts, as victorious warriors watch from a nearby ridge. After such a drastic defeat, a village is usually abandoned and open hostilities cease.

Killed from ambush as he returned from
battle, the victim, below, is carried to his
funeral by members of his own village.
The body will be cremated.

Jalé warriors celebrate a battlefield triumph with a victory dance. Brilliant bird of paradise feathers punctuate the scene.

Ngingi and Isel are the names of two men from a hostile village, the home of a young woman named Kingkaen who was killed in an ambush attack in September, 1964. The lines make fun of the men who, because of Kingkaen's death, have to eat poor food prepared by the inept hands of senile women.

When the festival of revenge is over, the members of the men's house group of the owners of the body arrange for the ritual removal of the victim's ghost from their village. Rhythmically voicing efficacious formulas and whistling sounds, a ceremonial procession of men carries a special arrow into the forest, as far into enemy territory as is possible without risk. A small lump of pig's fat is affixed to the arrow by an expert in esoteric lore. (Pig's fat used for ritual purposes becomes a sacred substance that is applied in many different contexts.) The arrow is finally shot toward the enemy village. This, the Jalé believe, will make the ghost stay away from their own village, but as a further precaution they block the path with branches and plants over which spells are said.

Protective rites of this kind, and the vengeance ritual described above, are the only aspects of Jalé cannibalism that may be viewed as "religious." The actual consumption of human meat and organs does not constitute an act with intrinsic "supernatural" effects. Instead, as my Jalé friends repeatedly assured me, their reason for eating an enemy's body is that man tastes as good as pork, if not better. And they added that the bad enemies in the other valley had eaten some of their people.

These descriptions of Jalé rituals and beliefs do not sufficiently explain the practice of cannibalism. To do so would necessitate the compilation of all available information about this custom from every part of the world. On the basis of these data an extensive study would have to be made of the ecological and cultural variables found to be associated with institutionalized cannibalism. Perhaps it would then be possible to recognize specific ecological and sociological features that appear to be correlated with the consumption of human meat, but the task of interpreting the custom as a sociopsychological phenomenon would still remain.

It is obvious that the enigmatic nature of cannibalism has invited many writers to speculate about its origin and its biopsychic basis. Aristotle attributed anthropophagy among tribes around the Black Sea to their feral bestiality and morbid lust. In 1688 a treatise was published in Holland entitled *De natura et moribus anthropophagorum* ("On the Nature and Customs of Anthropophagi"), and some ethnographers writing in the nineteenth century still regarded the rejection of cannibalism as the "first step into civilization." Certainly, the consumption by man of a member of his own species is as much a problem for evolutionary bioanthropology as it is for ethnology and psychology. I have made an extensive survey of the various theories proposed by earnest scholars to elucidate the phenomenon, and I have found that, at best, a few hypotheses appear plausible for the interpretation of certain aspects of some cannibalistic practices.

In Jalémó the eating of a slain enemy, in addition to its dietary value, certainly indicates a symbolic expression of spite incorporated into an act of supreme vengeance. Violent retaliation, in turn, must be seen as a consequence of certain sociopsychological conditions that determine the degree of aggressive behavior expected and tolerated in their culture. Cross-cultural studies by anthropologists have supported theories that are applicable to Jalé society. An accepted model of personality development demonstrates that societies in which boys grow up in intimate association with their mothers, who dominate a household situation in which the boy's male elders, especially their fathers, do not take part, are characterized by a high level of physical violence. Sociological models developed from large-scale comparative research predict that in societies in which small kin groups operate as relatively independent political units, warfare within the society is a common means of resolving conflict.

Both models squarely apply to Jalé society. First, young boys, separated from the community of the men's house until their initiation, are socialized in a female environment. Second, the wards of a village are not integrated by a centralized system of headmanship, and no political cooperation exists between them until they are threatened by, or faced with, actual hostility from other villages. These are the critical variables that partially determine the bellicosity and violence I have observed.

No specific hypothesis can be given to explain the cannibalism that the Jalé incorporate in their vengeance. It is certain, however, that no understanding can be achieved by applying precepts of Western thought. In a missionary's travelogue published seventy years ago, the author, speaking of an African tribe, recounted:

Once, when told by a European that the practice of eating human flesh was a most degraded habit, the cannibal answered, "Why degraded? You people eat sheep and cows and fowls, which are all animals of a far lower order, and we eat man, who is great and above all; it is you who are degraded!"

Murders in Eden

By Marvin Harris

The accepted explanation for the transition from band life to farming villages used to go like this: Hunter-collectors had to spend all their time getting enough to eat. They could not produce a "surplus above subsistence," and so they lived on the edge of extinction in chronic sickness and hunger. Therefore, it was natural for them to want to settle down and live in permanent villages, but the idea of planting seeds never occurred to them. One day an unknown genius decided to drop some seeds in a hole, and soon planting was being done on a regular basis. People no longer had to move about constantly in search of game, and the new leisure gave them time to think. This led to further and more rapid advances in technology and thus more food—a "surplus above subsistence"—which eventually made it possible for some people to turn away from farming and become artisans, priests, and rulers.

The first flaw in this theory is the assumption that life was exceptionally difficult for our stone age ancestors. Archaeological evidence from the upper paleolithic period—about 30,000 B.C. to 10,000 B.C.—makes it perfectly clear that hunters who lived during those times enjoyed relatively high standards of comfort and security. They were no bumbling amateurs. They had achieved total control over the process of fracturing, chipping, and shaping crystalline rocks, which formed the basis of their technology, and they have aptly been called the "master stoneworkers of all times." Their remarkably thin, finely chipped "laurel leaf" knives, eleven inches long but only four-tenths of an inch thick, cannot be duplicated by modern industrial techniques. With delicate stone awls and incising tools called burins, they created intricately barbed bone and antler harpoon points, well-shaped antler throwing boards for spears, and fine bone needles presumably used to fashion animal-skin clothing. The items made of wood, fibers, and skins have perished, but these too must have been distinguished by high craftsmanship.

Contrary to popular ideas, "cave men" knew how to make artificial shelters, and their use of caves and rock overhangs depended on regional possibilities and seasonal needs. In southern Russia archaeologists have found traces of a hunter's animal-skin dwelling set in a shallow pit forty feet long and twelve feet wide. In Czechoslovakia winter dwellings with round floor plans twenty feet in diameter were already in use more than 20,000 years ago. With rich furs for rugs and beds, as well as plenty of dried animal dung or fat-laden bones for the hearth, such dwellings can provide a quality of shelter superior in many respects to contemporary inner-city apartments.

As for living on the edge of starvation, such a picture is hard to reconcile with the enormous quantities of animal bones accumulated at various paleolithic kill sites. Vast herds of mammoth, horses, deer, reindeer, and bison roamed across Europe and Asia. The bones of over a thousand mammoth, excavated from one site in Czechoslovakia, and the remains of 10,000 wild horses that were stampeded at various intervals over a high cliff near Solutré, France, testify to the ability of paleolithic peoples to exploit these herds systematically and efficiently. Moreover, the skeletal remains of the hunters themselves bear witness to the fact that they were unusually well-nourished.

The notion that paleolithic populations worked round the clock in order to feed themselves now also appears ludicrous. As collectors of food plants they were certainly no less effective than chimpanzees. Field studies have shown that in their natural habitat the great apes spend as much time grooming, playing, and napping as they do foraging and eating. And as hunters our upper paleolithic ancestors must have been at least as proficient as lions—animals which alternate bursts of intense activity with long periods of rest and relaxation. Studies of how present-day hunters and collectors allocate their time have shed more light on this issue. Richard Lee of the University of

Toronto kept a record of how much time the modern Bushman hunter-collectors spend in the quest for food. Despite their habitat—the edge of the Kalahari, a desert region whose lushness is hardly comparable to that of France during the upper paleolithic period—less than three hours per day per adult is all that is needed for the Bushmen to obtain a diet rich in proteins and other essential nutrients.

The Machiguenga, simple horticulturalists of the Peruvian Amazon studied by Allen and Orna Johnson, spend a little more than three hours per day per adult in food production and get less animal protein for this effort than do the Bushmen. In the rice-growing regions of eastern Java, modern peasants have been found to spend about forty-four hours per week in productive farm work—something no self-respecting Bushman would ever dream of doing—and Javanese peasants seldom eat animal proteins. American farmers, for whom fifty-and-sixty-hour work weeks are commonplace, eat well by Bushman standards but certainly cannot be said to have as much leisure.

I do not wish to minimize the difficulties inherent in comparisons of this sort. Obviously the work associated with a particular food-production system is not limited to time spent in obtaining the raw product. It also takes time to process the plants and animals into forms suitable for consumption, and it takes still more time to manufacture and maintain such instruments of production as spears, nets, digging sticks, baskets, and plows. According to the Johnsons' estimates, the Machiguenga devote about three additional hours per day to food preparation and the manufacture of essential items such as clothing, tools, and shelter. In his observations of the Bushmen, Lee found that in one day a woman could gather enough food to feed her family for three days and that she spent the rest of her time resting, entertaining visitors, doing embroidery, or visiting other camps. "For each day at home, kitchen routines, such as cooking, nut cracking, collecting firewood, and fetching water, occupy one to three hours of her time."

The evidence I have cited above leads to one conclusion: The development of farming resulted in an increased work load per capita. There is a good reason for this. Agriculture is a system of food production that can absorb much more labor per unit of land than can hunting and collecting. Hunter-collectors are essentially dependent on the natural rate of animal and plant reproduction; they can do very little to raise output per unit of land (although they can easily decrease it). With agriculture, on the other hand, people control the rate of plant reproduction. This means that production can be intensified without immediate adverse consequences, especially if techniques are available for combating soil exhaustion.

The key to how many hours people like the Bushmen put into hunting and collecting is the abundance and accessibility of the animal and plant resources available to them. As long as population density—and thus exploitation of these resources—is kept relatively low, hunter-collectors can enjoy both leisure and high-quality diets. Only if one assumes that people during the stone age were unwilling or unable to limit the density of their populations does the theory of our ancestors' lives as "short, nasty, and brutish" make sense. But that assumption is unwarranted. Hunter-collectors are strongly motivated to limit population, and they have effective means to do so.

Another weakness in the old theory of the transition from hunting and collecting to agriculture is the assumption that human beings naturally want to "settle down." This can scarcely be true given the tenacity with which people like the Bushmen, the aborigines of Australia, and the Eskimo have clung to their old "walk-about" way of life despite the concerted efforts of government and missionaries to persuade them to live in villages.

Each advantage of permanent village life has a corresponding disadvantage. Do people crave company? Yes, but they also get on each other's nerves. As Thomas Gregor has shown in a study of the Mehinacu Indians of Brazil, the search for personal privacy is a pervasive theme in the daily life of people who live in small villages. The Mehinacu apparently know too much about each other's business for their own good. They can tell from the print of a heel or a buttock where a couple stopped and had sexual relations off the path. Lost arrows give away the owner's prize fishing spot; an ax resting against a tree tells a story of interrupted work. No one leaves or enters the village without being noticed. One must whisper to secure privacy—with walls of thatch there are no closed doors. The village is filled with irritating gossip about men who are impotent or who ejaculate too quickly, and about women's behavior during coitus and the size, color and odor of their genitalia.

Is there physical security in numbers? Yes, but there is also security in mobility, in being able to get out of the way of aggressors. Is there an advantage in having a larger, cooperative labor pool? Yes, but larger concentrations of people lower the game supply and deplete natural resources.

As for the haphazard discovery of the planting process, hunter-collectors are not so dumb as this sequence in the old theory would suggest. The anatomical details in the paintings of animals found on the walls of caves in France and Spain bear witness to a people whose powers of observation were honed to great accuracy. And our admiration for their intellects has been forced to new heights by Alexander Marshak's discovery that the faint scratches on the surface of 20,000-year-old bone and antler artifacts were put there to keep track of the phases of the moon and other astronomical events. It is unreasonable to suppose that the people who made the great murals on the walls of Lascaux, and who were intelligent enough to make calendrical records, could have been ignorant of the biological significance of tubers and seeds.

Studies of hunter-collectors of the present and recent past reveal that the practice of agriculture is often forgone not for lack of knowledge but as a matter of convenience. Simply by gathering acorns, for example, the Indians of California probably obtained larger and more nutritious harvests than they could have derived from planting maize. And on the Northwest coast the great annual migrations of salmon and candlefish rendered agricultural work a relative waste of time. Hunter-collectors often display all the skills and techniques necessary for practicing agriculture minus the step of deliberate planting. The Shoshoni and Paiute of Nevada and California returned year after year to the same strands of wild grains and tubers, carefully refrained from stripping them bare, and sometimes even weeded and watered them. Many other hunter-collectors use fire to deliberately promote the growth of preferred species and to retard the growth of trees and weeds.

Finally, some of the most important archaeological discoveries of recent years indicate that in the Old World the earliest villages were built 1,000 to 2,000 years before the development of a farming economy, whereas in the New World plants were domesticated long before village life began. Since the early Americans had the idea for thousands of years before they made full use of it, the explanation for the shift away from hunting and collection must be sought outside their heads. I'll have more to say about these archaeological discoveries later on.

What I've shown so far is that as long as hunter-collectors kept their population low in relation to their prey, they could enjoy an enviable standard of living. But how did they keep their population down? This subject is rapidly emerging as the most important missing link in the attempt to understand the evolution of cultures.

Even in relatively favorable habitats, with abundant herd animals, stone age peoples probably never let their populations rise above one or two persons per square mile. Alfred Kroeber estimated that in the Canadian plains and prairies the bison-hunting Cree and Assiniboin, mounted on horses and equipped with rifles, kept their densities below two persons per square mile. Less favored groups of historic hunters in North America, such as the Labrador Naskapi and the Nunamuit Eskimo, who depended on caribou, maintained densities *below* .3 persons per square mile. In all of France during the late stone age there were probably no more than 20,000 and possibly as few as 1,600 human beings.

"Natural" means of controlling population growth cannot explain the discrepancy between these low densities and the potential fertility of the human female. Healthy populations interested in maximizing their rate of growth average eight pregnancies brought to term per woman. Childbearing rates can easily go higher. Among the Hutterites, a sect of thrifty farmers living in western Canada, the average is 10.7 births per woman. In order to maintain the estimated .001 percent annual rate of growth for the old stone age, each woman must have had on the average less than 2.1 children who survived to reproductive age. According to the conventional theory such a low rate of growth was achieved, despite high fertility, by disease. Yet the view that our stone age ancestors led disease-ridden lives is difficult to sustain.

No doubt there were diseases. But as a mortality factor they must have been considerably less significant during the stone age than they are today. The death of infants and adults from bacterial and viral infections—dysenteries, measels, tuberculosis, whooping cough, colds, scarlet fever—is strongly influenced by diet and general body vigor, so stone age hunter-collectors probably had high recovery rates from these infections. And most of the great lethal epidemic diseases—smallpox, typhoid fever, flu, bubonic plague, cholera—occur only among populations that have high densities. These are the diseases of state-level societies; they flourish amid poverty and crowded, unsanitary urban conditions. Even such scourges as malaria and yellow fever were probably less significant among the hunter-collectors of the old stone age. As hunters they would have preferred dry, open habitats to the wetlands where these diseases flourish. Malaria probably achieved its full impact only after agricultural clearings in humid forests had created better breeding conditions for mosquitoes.

What is actually known about the physical health of paleolithic populations? Skeletal remains provide important clues. Using such indices as average height and the number of teeth missing at time of death, J. Lawrence Angel has developed a profile of changing health standards during the last 30,000 years. Angel found that at the beginning of this period adult males averaged 177 centimeters (5' 11") and adult females about 165 centimeters (5' 6").

Twenty thousand years later the males grew no taller than the females formerly grew—165 centimeters—whereas the females averaged no more than 153 centimeters (5' 0"). Only in very recent times have populations once again attained statures characteristic of the old stone age peoples. American males, for example, averaged 175 centimeters (5' 9") in 1960. Tooth loss shows a similar trend. In 30,000 B.C. adults died with an average of 2.2 teeth missing; in 6500 B.C., with 3.5 missing; during Roman times, with 6.6 missing. Although genetic factors may also enter into these changes, stature and the condition of teeth and gums are known to be strongly influenced by protein intake, which in turn is predictive of general well-being. Angel concludes that there was "a real depression of health" following the "high point" of the upper paleolithic period.

Angel has also attempted to estimate the average age of death for the upper paleolithic, which he places at 28.7 years for females and 33.3 years for males. Since Angel's paleolithic sample consists of skeletons found all over Europe and Africa, his longevity estimates are not necessarily representative of any actual band of hunters. If the vital statistics of contemporary hunter-collector bands can be taken as representative of paleolithic bands, Angel's calculations err on the low side. Studies of 165 !Kung Bushman women by Nancy Howell show that life expectancy at birth is 32.5 years, which compares favorably with the figures for many modern developing nations in Africa and Asia. To put these data in proper perspective, according to the Metropolitan Life Insurance Company the life expectancy at birth for non-white males in the United States in 1900 was also 32.5 years. Thus, as paleodemographer Don Dumond has suggested, there are hints that "mortality was effectively no higher under conditions of hunting than under those of a more sedentary life, including agriculture." The increase in disease accompanying sedentary living "may mean that the mortality rates of hunters were more often significantly lower" than those of agricultural peoples.

Although a life span of 32.5 years may seem very short, the reproductive potential even of women who live only to Angel's 28.7 years of age is quite high. If a stone age woman had her first pregnancy when she was sixteen years old, and a live baby every two and a half years thereafter, she could easily have had over five live births by the time she was twenty-nine. This means that approximately three-fifths of stone age children could not have lived to reproductive age if the estimated rate of less than .001 percent population growth was to be maintained. Using these figures, anthropological demographer Ferki Hassan concludes that even if there was 50 percent infant mortality due to "natural" causes, another 23 to 35 percent of all potential offspring would have to be "removed" to achieve zero growth population.

If anything, these estimates appear to err in exaggerating the number of deaths from "natural" causes. Given the excellent state of health the people studied by Angel seemed to enjoy before they became skeletons, one suspects that many of the deceased died of "unnatural" causes.

Infanticide during the paleolithic period could very well have been as high as 50 percent—a figure that corresponds to estimates made by Joseph Birdsell of the University of California in Los Angeles on the basis of data collected among the aboriginal populations of Australia. And an important factor in the short life span of paleolithic women may very well have been the attempt to induce abortions in order to lengthen the interval between births.

Contemporary hunter-collectors in general lack effective chemical or mechanical means of preventing pregnancy—romantic folklore about herbal contraceptives notwithstanding. They do, however, possess a large repertory of chemical and mechanical means for inducing abortion. Numerous plant and animal poisons that cause generalized physical traumas or that act directly on the uterus are used throughout the world to end unwanted pregnancies. Many mechanical techniques for inducing abortion are also employed, such as tying tight bands around the stomach, vigorous massages, subjection to extremes of cold and heat, blows to the abdomen, and hopping up and down on a plank placed across a woman's belly "until blood spurts out of the vagina." Both the mechanical and chemical approaches effectively terminate pregnancies, but they are also likely to terminate the life of the pregnant woman. I suspect that only a group under severe economic and demographic stress would resort to abortion as its principal method of population regulation.

Hunter-collectors under stress are much more likely to turn to infanticide and geronticide (the killing of old people). Geronticide is effective only for short-run emergency reductions in group size. It cannot lower long-term trends of population growth. In the case of both geronticide and infanticide, outright conscious killing is probably the exception. Among the Eskimo, old people too weak to contribute to their own subsistence may "commit suicide" by remaining behind when the group moves, although children actively contribute to their parents' demise by accepting the cultural expectation that old people ought not to become a burden when food is scarce. In Australia, among the Murngin of Arnhem Land, old people are helped along toward their fate by being treated as if they were already dead when they become sick; the group begins to perform its last rites, and the old person responds by getting sicker. Infanticide runs a complex gamut from outright murder to mere neglect. Infants may be strangled, drowned, bashed against a rock, or exposed to the elements. More commonly, an infant is "killed" by neglect; the mother gives less care than is needed when it gets sick, nurses it less often, refrains from trying to find supplementary foods, or "accidentally" lets it fall from her arms. Hunter-collector women are strongly motivated to space out the age difference between their children since they must expend a considerable amount of effort merely lugging them about during the day. Richard Lee has calculated that over a four-year period of dependency a Bushman mother will carry her child a total of 4,900 miles on collecting expeditions and campsite moves. No Bushman woman wants to be burdened with two or three infants at a time as she travels that distance.

The best method of population control available to stone age hunter-collectors was to prolong the span of years during which a mother nursed her infant. Recent studies of menstrual cycles carried out by Rose Frisch and Janel McArthur have shed light on the physiological mechanism responsible for lowering the fertility of lactating women. After giving birth, a fertile woman will not resume ovulation until the percentage of her body weight that consists of fat has passed a critical threshold. This threshold (about 20-25 percent) represents the point at which a woman's body has stored enough reserve energy in the form of fat to accommodate the demands of a growing fetus. The average energy cost of a normal pregnancy is 27,000 calories—just about the amount of energy that must be stored before a woman can conceive. A nursing infant drains about 1,000 extra

calories from its mother per day, making it difficult for her to accumulate the necessary fatty reserve. As long as the infant is dependent on its mother's milk, there is little likelihood that ovulation will resume. Bushman mothers, by prolonging lactation, appear to be able to delay the possibility of pregnancy for more than four years. The same mechanism appears to be responsible for delaying menarche—the onset of menstruation. The higher the ratio of body fat to body weight, the earlier the age of menarche. In well-nourished modern populations menarche has been pushed forward to about twelve years of age, whereas in populations chronically on the edge of caloric deficits it may take eighteen or more years for a girl to build up the necessary fat reserves.

What I find so intriguing about this discovery is that it links low fertility with diets that are high in proteins and low in carbohydrates. On the one hand, if a woman is to nurse a child successfully for three or four years she must have a high protein intake to sustain her health, body vigor, and the flow of milk. On the other hand, if she consumes too many carbohydrates she will begin to put on weight, which will trigger the resumption of ovulation. A demographic study carried out by J. K. Van Ginneken indicates that nursing women in underdeveloped countries, where the diet consists mostly of starchy grains and root crops, cannot expect to extend the interval between births beyond eighteen months. Yet nursing Bushman women, whose diet is rich in animal and plant proteins and who lack starchy staples, as I have said, manage to keep from getting pregnant four or more years after each birth. This relationship suggests that during good times hunter-collectors could rely on prolonged lactation as their principal defense against overpopulation. Conversely, a decline in the quality of food supply would tend to bring about

an increase in population. This in turn would mean either that the rate of abortion and infanticide would have to be accelerated or that still more drastic cuts in the protein ration would be needed.

I am not suggesting that the entire defense against overpopulation among our stone age ancestors rested with the lactation method. Among the Bushmen of Botswana the present rate of population growth is .5 percent per annum. This amounts to a doubling every 139 years. Had this rate been sustained for only the last 10,000 years of the old stone age, by 10,000 B.C. the population of the earth would have reached 604,463,000,000,000,-000,000,000.

Suppose the fertile span were from sixteen years of age to forty-two. Without prolonged nursing, a woman might experience as many as twelve pregnancies. With the lactation method, the number of pregnancies comes down to six. Lowered rates of coitus in older women might further reduce the number to five. Spontaneous abortions and infant mortality caused by disease and accidents might bring the potential reproducers down to four— roughly two more than the number permissible under a system of zero population growth. The "extra" two births could then be controlled through some form of infanticide based on neglect. The optimal method would be to neglect only the girl babies, since the rate of growth in populations that do not practice monogamy is determined almost entirely by the number of females who reach reproductive age.

Our stone age ancestors were thus perfectly capable of maintaining a stationary population, but there was a cost associated with it—the waste of infant lives. This cost lurks in the background of prehistory as an ugly blight in what might otherwise be mistaken for a Garden of Eden.

In Search of the Affluent Society

By Allen Johnson

. . . .

One of the paradoxes of modern life is the persistence of suffering and deep dissatisfaction among people who enjoy an unparalleled abundance of material goods. The paradox is at least as old as our modern age. Ever since the benefits and costs of industrial technology became apparent, opinion has been divided over whether we are progressing or declining.

The debate grows particularly heated when we compare our civilization with the cultures of "primitive" or "simpler" peoples. At the optimistic extreme, we are seen as the beneficiaries of an upward development that has brought us from an era in which life was said to be "nasty, brutish, and short," into one of ease, affluence, and marvelous prospects for the future. At the other extreme, primitives are seen as enjoying idyllic lives of simplicity and serenity, from which we have descended dangerously through an excess of greed. The truth is a complex mix of these two positions, but it is striking how difficult it is to take a balanced view. We are attracted irresistibly to either the optimistic or the pessimistic position.

The issue is of more than academic interest. The modern world is trying to come to grips with the idea of "limits to growth" and the need to redistribute wealth. Pressures are mounting from the environment on which we depend and from the people with whom we share it. Scientists, planners, and policy makers are now talking about "alternative futures," trying to marshal limited resources for the greater good of humanity. In this context it is useful to know whether people living in much simpler economies than our own really do enjoy advantages we have lost.

In his book *The Affluent Society*, economist John Kenneth Galbraith accepts the optimistic view, with some reservations. According to him, the modern trend has been toward an increase in the efficiency of production; working time has decreased while the standard of living has risen through a growth in purchasing power. One of Galbraith's reservations is that he does not see this growth as an unmitigated good. He sees our emphasis on acquiring goods as left over from times when the experience of poverty was still real and thinks we are ready to acknowledge our wealth and reduce our rates of consumption. The trend over the last 100 years toward a shorter work week, he argues, demonstrates that we are relinquishing some of our purchasing power in exchange for greater leisure.

Galbraith's view that modern affluence both brings us greater leisure and fills our basic needs better than any previous economic system is widespread. Yet the first part of this view is almost certainly wrong, and the second is debatable. Anthropologist Marshall Sahlins has shown that hunting-and-gathering economies, such as those found among the Australian aborigines and the San of southern Africa, require little work (three to four hours per adult each day) to provide ample and varied diets. Although they lack our abundance of goods, material needs are satisfied in a leisurely way, and in their own view, people are quite well off.

Sahlins points out that there are two roads to affluence: our own, which is to produce more, and what he calls the Buddhist path, which is to be satisfied with less. Posing the problem of affluence in this way makes it clear that affluence depends not only on material wealth but also on subjective satisfaction. There is apparently plenty of room for choice in designing a life of affluence.

Recent studies of how people in different societies spend their time allow us to make a fairly objective comparison of primitive and modern societies. In one analysis, Alexander Szalai studied middle-class French couples residing in six cities in France—Arras, Besançon, Chalon-sur-Saône, Dunkerque, Épinal, and Metz. Orna Johnson and I, both of us anthropologists, collected similar data when we lived among the Machiguenga Indians of Peru for some 18 months, which were spread over one long and two shorter visits.

The Machiguenga live in extended family groups scattered throughout the Amazon rain forest. They spend approximately equal amounts of time growing food in gardens carved out of the surrounding forest and in hunting, fishing, and collecting wild foods. They are self-sufficient; almost everything they consume is produced by their own labors using materials that are found close at hand. Despite some similarities in how the French and the Machiguenga spend their time (for instance, in the way work is apportioned between the sexes), the differences between the societies are applicable to our purposes.

For reasons that will become clear, we divide ways of spending time into three categories: production time, consumption time, and free time. Production time refers to what we normally think of as work, in which goods and services are produced either for further production (capital goods) or for direct consumption (consumption goods). Consumption time refers to time spent using consumption goods. Eating, and what we think of as leisure time — watching television, visiting amusement parks, playing tennis — is spent this way. Free time is spent in neither production nor consumption; it includes sheer idleness, rest, sleep, and chatting.

Of course, these three categories of time are arbitrary. We could eliminate the difference between consumption time and free time, for example, by pointing out that the French consume beds and the Machiguenga consume mats during sleep. But we want to distinguish time spent at the movies or driving a car from time spent doing nothing — sitting idly by the door or casually visiting neighbors. This supports a main contention of our research: that little agreement now exists on exactly how to measure the differences between dissimilar societies.

For comparative purposes, we broke down our data into five categories of people, two for the Machiguenga and three for the French. For the relatively simple Machiguenga society, a division by gender was sufficient for studying patterns in time use. But for the more complex French society, a male-female breakdown was insufficient because such a division does not allow for working women. We divided the French data into three categories: men, working women, and housewives.

In production time French workers, both men and women, spend more time working outside the home than the Machiguenga do. French men work one and a half hours more per day away from home than do Machiguenga men;

employed French women work four hours more per day than do Machiguenga women. French housewives work less outside the home than Machiguenga women do, but they make up for this difference by exceeding their Machiguenga counterparts in work inside the home. French men spend more time working inside the home than do Machiguenga men. All told, French men spend more time engaged in production than do Machiguenga men, and French women (both working and housewives) spend more time in production activities than do Machiguenga women.

The French score equal to or higher than the Machiguenga on all measures of consumption. French men spend more

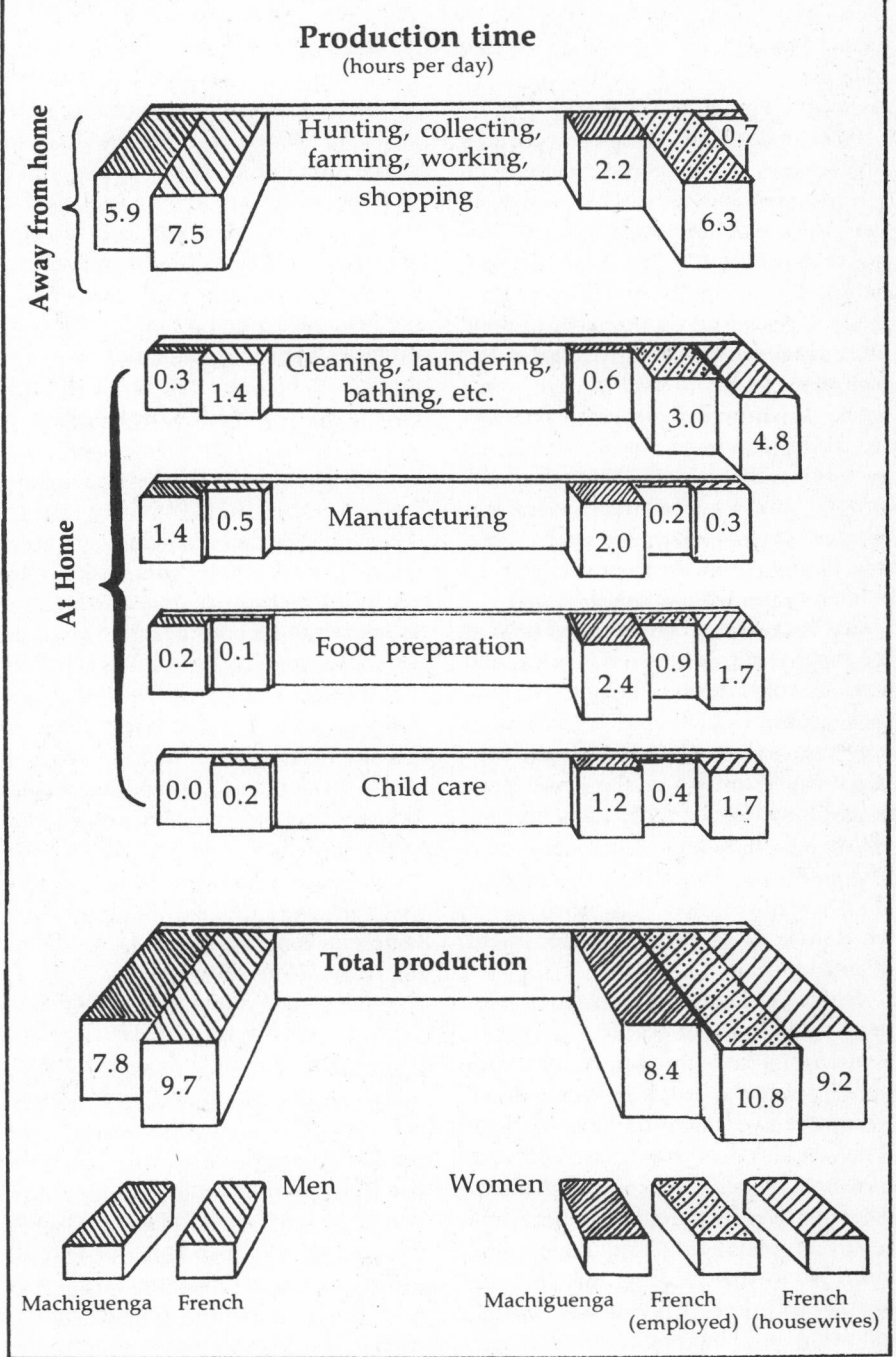

than three times as many hours in consumption as do Machiguenga men; French women consume goods at four or five times the rate of Machiguenga women, depending on whether they are employed or are housewives.

It is in the category of free time that the Machiguenga clearly surpass the French. Machiguenga men spend more than 14 hours per day engaged in free time, compared with nearly 10 hours for their French counterparts, and Machiguenga women have much more free time than French women do—whether or not the French women work.

The immediate question concerns differences in the overall pattern. It seems undeniable, as Sahlins has argued, that modern technological progress has not resulted in more free time for most people. The shrinking of the work week in the last century is probably nothing more than a short-term wrinkle in the historical trend toward longer work weeks. If our modern economy provides us with more goods, it is not simply because technical efficiency has increased. Indeed, the trend toward a shorter work week ended with World War II; since then, the length of the work week has remained about the same.

The increase of consumption time at the expense of free time is both a loss and a gain. Here we encounter a subtle, complex problem. Increased consumption may add excitement and pleasure to what would otherwise be considered boring time. On the other hand, this increase has the effect of crowding time with consumption activities so that people begin to feel that "time is short"—which may detract from the enjoyment of consumption.

Economist Staffan Burenstam Linder has looked at the effects of higher production and consumption of goods on our sense of time. To follow his argument we must move from the level of clock time to that of subjective time, as measured by our inner sense of the tempo of our lives. According to Linder, as a result of producing and consuming more, we are experiencing an increasing scarcity of time. This works in the following way. Increasing efficiency in production means that each individual

must produce more goods per hour; increased productivity means, though it is not often mentioned in this context, that to keep the system going we must consume more goods. Free time gets converted into consumption time because time spent neither producing nor consuming comes increasingly to be viewed as wasted. Linder's theory may account for the differences between the ways the Machiguenga and the French use their time.

The increase in the value of time (its increasing scarcity) is felt subjectively as an increase in tempo or pace. We are always in danger of being slow on the production line or late to work; and in our leisure we are always in danger of wasting time. I have been forcefully impressed with this aspect of time during several field visits to the Machiguenga. It happens each time I return to their communities that, after a period of two or three days, I sense a definite decrease in time pressure; this is a physiological as well as a psychological sensation.

This feeling of a leisurely pace of life reflects the fact that among the Machiguenga daily activities are never hurried or desperate. Each task is allotted its full measure of time, and free time is not felt to be boring or lost but is accepted as entirely natural. These feelings last throughout the field visit, but when I return home I am conscious of the pressure and sense of hurry building up to its former level. Something similar, though fleeting, happens on vacation trips—but here the pressure to consume, to see more sights while traveling, or to get one's money's worth in entertainment constantly asserts itself, and the tempo is usually kept up.

Linder sees a kind of evolutionary progression from "time surplus" societies through "time affluence" societies, ending with the "time famine" society of developed countries. The famine is expressed not only in a hectic pace, but also in a decline of activities in which goods are not consumed rapidly enough, such as spending time with the elderly and providing other social services. As Galbraith has pointed out, we neglect basic social needs because they are seen as economically unproductive.

Not only do we use our time for almost frantic consumption, but more of our time is also devoted to caring for the increasing number of goods we possess. The Machiguenga devote three to four times more of their production time at home to manufacturing (cloth and baskets, for example) than they do to maintenance activities, such as cleaning and doing the laundry; the French pattern is the reverse. This may help account for the failure of modern housewives to acquire more leisure time from their appliances, a situation that has prompted anthropologist Marvin Harris to refer to appliances as "labor-saving devices that don't save work."

On both objective and subjective grounds, then, it appears that economic growth has not given us more leisure time. If anything, the increasingly hectic pace of leisure activities detracts from our enjoyment of play, even when the increased stimulation they bring is taken into account. When we consider the abundance of goods, however, the situation is obviously different. The superiority of modern industrial technology in producing material goods is clear. The Machiguenga, and other people at a similar technological level, have no doubts on this score either. Despite their caution, which outsiders are apt to label "traditionalism," they really do undertake far-reaching changes in their ways of life in order to obtain even small quantities of industrial output.

One area in which the Machiguenga clearly need (and warmly welcome) Western goods is medicine. Despite hopeful speculations in popular writings that Amazon Indians have secret herbal remedies that are effective against infections, cancer, and other conditions, the curative powers of Machiguenga medicine are circumscribed. Antibiotics, even the lowly sulfa pill, are highly effective and much in demand for skin sores, eye infections, and other painful endemic health problems. Medicines to control such parasites as amoebae and intestinal worms bring immediate relief to a community, although people are eventually reinfected. In terms of human well-being, then, even the most romantic defender of the simple life must grant that modern medicines improve the lives of primitive people.

I am much less certain about what other Western goods to offer as evidence of the comparative lack of affluence among the Machiguenga. They have a great abundance of food, for example; they produce at least twice as many calories of food energy as they consume. (The excess production is not surplus so much as a security margin in case someone should fall ill or relatives unexpectedly come to stay for a time.) The Machiguenga diet is highly varied and at times very tasty. The people are attractive and healthy, with no apparent signs of malnutrition. Although they are somewhat underweight by modern standards, these standards may reflect average weights of modern populations that the Machiguenga would regard as overweight.

The highly productive food economy of the Machiguenga depends on metal tools obtained from Peruvian traders. Without an outside source of axes, the Machiguenga would have to give up their semisedentary existence and roam the forest as nomads. Should this happen, they could support fewer people in the same territory—but, if other hunter-collector groups can be used as evidence, nomadic life would result in even shorter workdays. Once again, in quantities of food as well as in quantities of time, the Machiguenga fit Sahlin's model of primitive affluence.

Our affluence exceeds Machiguenga affluence, but as in the case of time, there is the quality of life to take into account. My personal experiences in the field illustrate this aspect of the contrast. In preparing to leave for our first year-long visit to the Machiguenga, Orna and I decided to limit ourselves to the clothing and supplies that would fit into two trunks. This decision led to much agonizing over what to take and what to leave behind. Although we had both been in the field before, we had never gone anywhere quite so remote and we could not imagine how we would get along with so few goods.

The truth, however, was that we were absurdly oversupplied. As our field work progressed we used less and less of our store of goods. It even became a burden to us, since our possessions had to be dried in the sun periodically to prevent rot. As we grew close to the people we were living among, we began to be embarrassed by having so many things we did not really need.

Once, after a long rainy period, I laid my various footgear side by side in the sun to dry. There were a pair of hiking boots, a pair of canvas-topped jungle boots, and two pairs of sneakers. Some men came to visit and began inspecting the shoes, fingering the materials, commenting on the cleats, and trying them on for size. Then the discussion turned to how numerous my shoes were, and one man remarked that I had still another pair. There were protests of disbelief and I was asked if that was true. I said, "No, that's all I have." The man then said, "Wait," and went inside the house, returning with an "extra pair" of sneakers that I had left forgotten and unused in a corner of the room for months. This was not the only occasion on which I could not keep track of my possessions, a deficiency unknown to the Machiguenga.

My feelings about this incident were compounded when I discovered that, no matter which pair of shoes I wore, I could never keep up with these men, whose bare feet seemed magically to grip the slipperiest rocks or to find toe holds in the muddy trails. At about this time I was reading Alfred Russel Wallace's narrative of his years in the Amazon, in which he relates that his boots soon wore out and he spent his remaining time there barefoot—an achievement that continues to fill me with awe. My origi-

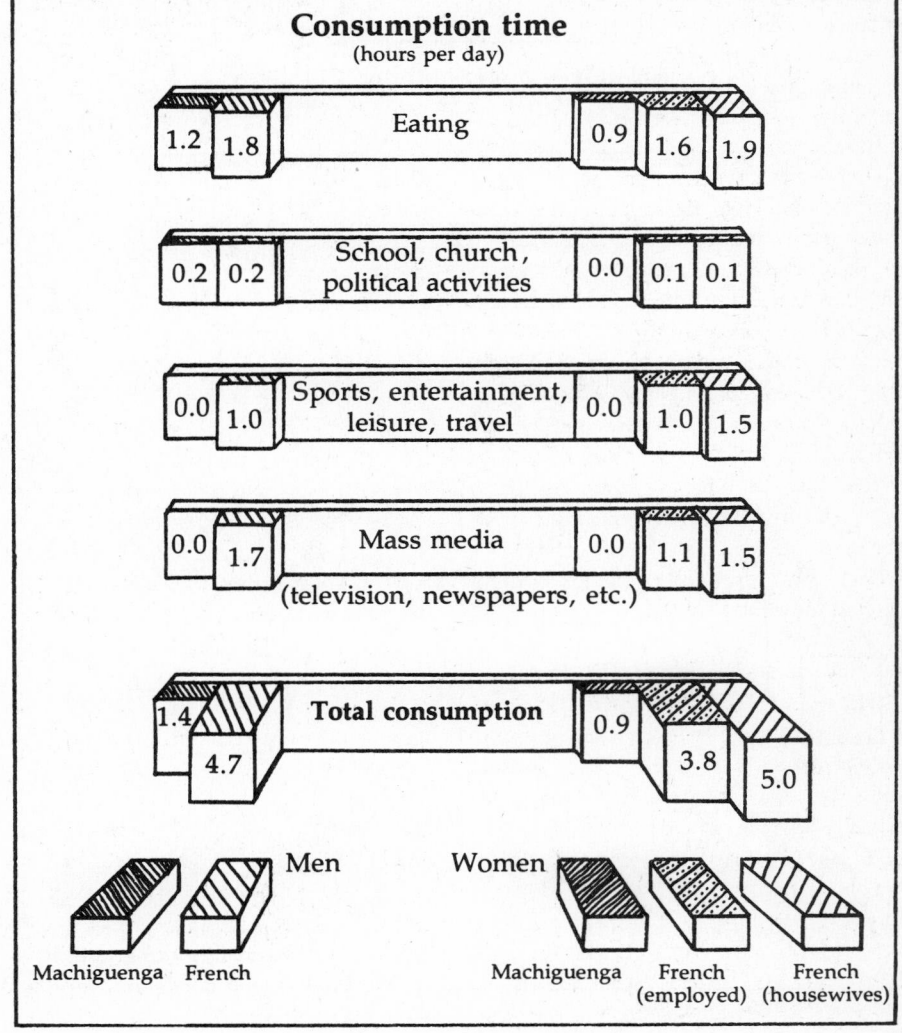

Consumption time
(hours per day)

	Men		Women		
	Machiguenga	French	Machiguenga	French (employed)	French (housewives)
Eating	1.2 / 1.8		0.9 / 1.6		1.9
School, church, political activities	0.2 / 0.2		0.0 / 0.1		0.1
Sports, entertainment, leisure, travel	0.0 / 1.0		0.0 / 1.0		1.5
Mass media (television, newspapers, etc.)	0.0 / 1.7		0.0 / 1.1		1.5
Total consumption	1.4 / 4.7		0.9 / 3.8		5.0

nal pride in being well' shod was diminished to something closely resembling embarrassment.

This experience brings up the question of whether goods are needed in themselves or because demand for them has been created by the producers. Galbraith stresses that we cannot simply assume that goods are produced to meet people's real needs. The billions of dollars spent each year on advertising indicate that not all consumer wants arise from basic needs of the individual, but that some are created in consumers by the producers themselves. This turns things around. Instead of arguing, as economists usually do, that our economic system serves us well, we are forced to consider that it may be we who serve the system by somehow agreeing to want the things it seems bent on producing, like dozens of kinds of shoes.

To most economists there is no justification for criticizing the purchasing habits of modern consumers. Purchases simply reflect personal preference, and it smacks of arrogance and authoritarianism to judge the individual decisions of free men and women. Economist Kenneth Boulding has referred sarcastically to such attempts as "theonomics." Economists assume that if there were more satisfying pathways of consumption, people would choose them. But the role of advertising in creating wants leaves open the question of the relationship between the consumption of goods and the fulfillment of needs.

When the task is to consume more, there are three ways of complying. One is to increase the amount of time spent consuming; this is one way the French differ from the Machiguenga. Another way is to increase the total number of goods we possess and to devote less time to each one individually. In a sense, this is what I was doing with the five pairs of shoes. The third way is to increase the elaborateness (and hence the cost of production) of the items we consume. The following instance, which took place at a Machiguenga beer feast, demonstrates that even those manufactured items we consider most practical are both elaborate and costly.

At Machiguenga beer feasts, which last for two or three days until the beer is gone, men often make recreational items like drums and toys. At one beer feast that had been going on for a day and a half, I watched a drum being made. The monkey-skin drumheads were being readied, and I noticed that the man next to me was about to make holes in the edge of the skin for the gut that would be used to tighten the drumhead. I had in my pocket an elaborate knife of fine steel, which had among its dozen separate functions (scissors, file, tweezers, etc.) a leather punch. By the time I had pulled the knife out and opened the punch, my neighbor had already made a

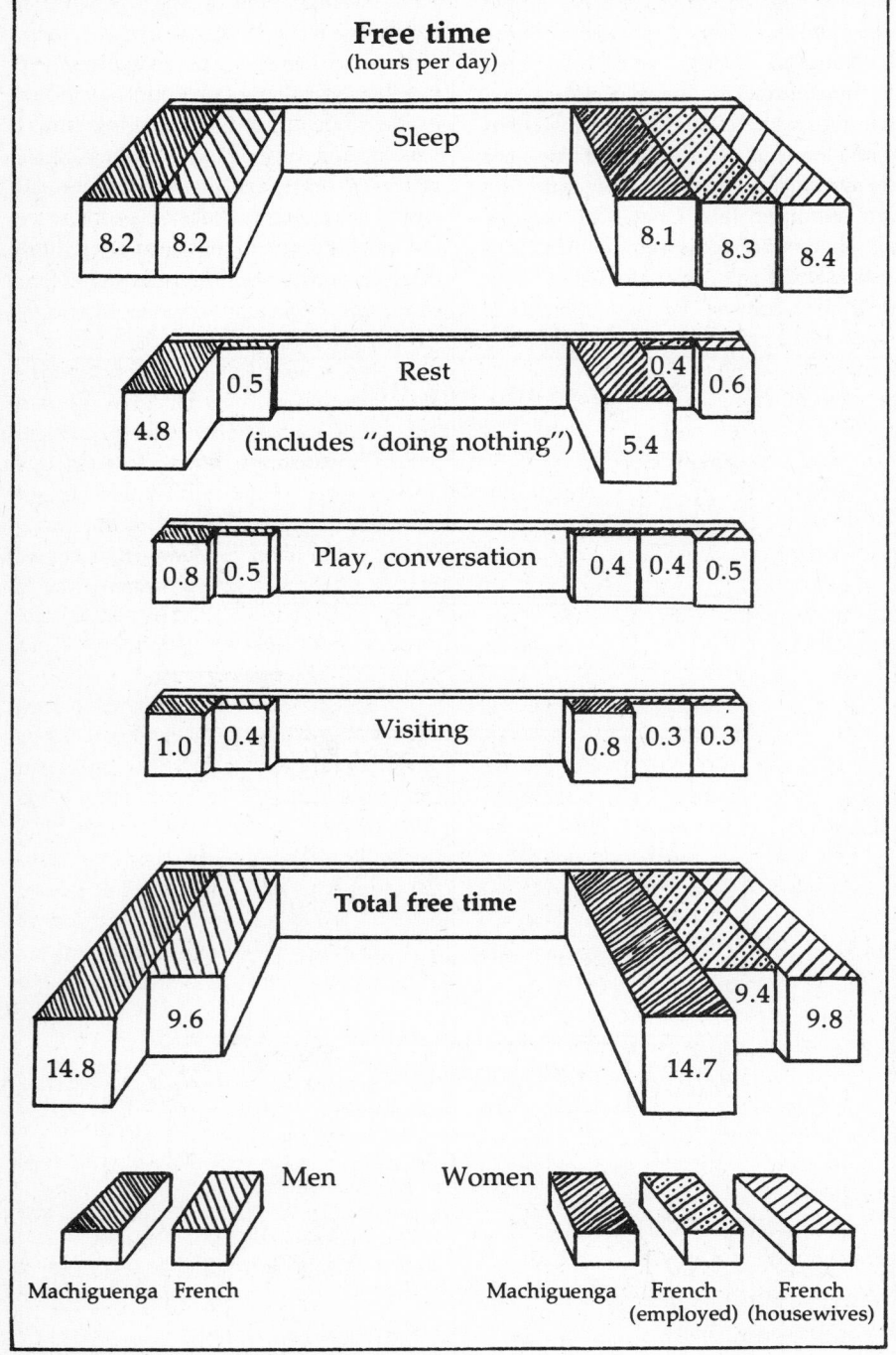

perfect hole with a scrap of broken kitchen knife he had kept close at hand.

Then he noticed my knife and wanted to see it. He noted its fine workmanship and passed it around to others, who tested its sharpness and opened all its parts, asking me to explain each one. They wanted to know how much it cost and how they could obtain one.

I interpret this experience in two ways. First, the knife was overelaborate. The Machiguenga met all their own needs for clothing, shelter, and containers with much simpler tools. Second, the elaborateness of the knife was itself an attraction, and its remarkable design and quality of materials could not help but draw the men's attention. They wanted the knife—not craving it, but willing to make serious efforts to get it or something similar if the opportunity arose. It is characteristic of a developed culture's contact with small, isolated societies that the developed culture is not met as a whole, but rather in highly selective ways that emphasize manufactured goods and the aura of the great, mysterious power that made them.

Our examples do not prove that the Machiguenga enjoy a higher quality of life than people who live in an industrial society, but they are not intended to. They do show that the quantitative abundance of consumption goods does not automatically guarantee an advantage to the consumer. And although our experiences among the Machiguenga make it easy to argue for the high quality of their lives—as reflected in their warm family ties, peaceable manners, good humor, intimacy with nature, and impressive integrity—it is also true that we would have regarded a permanent life there as a great personal sacrifice. Orna and I came home partly because it is home, where our lives have meaning, and partly because we did not want to go without some creature comforts that we, for better or worse, regard as highly desirable.

It seems likely, however, that an increasing supply of creature comforts and stimulation will bring us into a dangerous relationship with our environment. Such a confrontation might lead us to think about the costs involved in producing and consuming less. In traditional terms this is almost unthinkable, because the relative affluence of communities has been restricted to quantitative measures such as per capita income or gross national product, which can only increase (good), stay the same (bad), or decline (worse). But these numerical measures, which always discover the highest standard of living in the developed nations of the West, do not necessarily touch on all the factors that contribute to a good quality of life. The concept of quality of life suggests something more complex: a balancing-out of diverse satisfactions and dissatisfactions, not all of which are bought and sold in the marketplace.

Social scientists are trying to develop a broad range of indexes, such as those called "social indicators," that attempt to measure the quality of individual well-being. It has not been the theoreticians but the planners directly involved in applying economic thought to directed social changes, like urban renewal and rural development, who have insisted on such measures. Instead of relying on a single measure, like per capita income, they have added unemployment rates, housing, mental health, cultural and educational resources, air quality, government efficiency, and social participation. Communities, or nations, may rank low on one measure but high on another, and this makes comparisons both fairer and more realistic.

Even here problems remain. For one thing, the social indicators themselves sometimes sacrifice understanding of quality for measures of quantity. For example, the measure of "mental health" has been the suicide rate per 100,000 population—surely a restricted interpretation of the concept. Despite its obvious shortcomings, the measure has the advantage of specifying exactly what we mean by the term "mental health." In comparing communities or cultures we need standard measures, even though quality and quantity are ultimately incompatible.

When we discuss non-Western societies, the existing social indicators do not work very well. Unemployment, housing, and mental health all become hard to define. Economists, for example, often label free time in other cultures as "hidden unemployment"; by clever use of this negative term, they have transformed what might be a good thing into something that sounds definitely bad. In our case, Machiguenga housing, made of palm fronds, palm wood, and various tropical hardwoods, would never qualify as good housing in terms of a housing code, but it is cool, well ventilated, comfortable, and secure. Thus we are still far from developing criteria that allow us to compare the quality of life, or affluence, in diverse societies.

The economy of the United States is changing rapidly. Yet when we try to construct models of the alternative futures open to us, we falter because we lack the means to evaluate them. To turn this process over to the marketplace is not the same as turning it over to the "people" in some absolute democratic sense. People's behavior in the marketplace is strongly influenced, often by subterfuge, by producers who try to convince them that their interests coincide.

To accept the influence of the producers of goods without criticism, while labeling all other efforts to influence consumer patterns as "interference" or "theonomics," amounts to simple bias. Certainly a degree of open-mindedness about what a good quality of life is, and more efforts at learning about the quality of life in other communities, are invaluable as we chart our uncertain future.

For further information:

Andrews, Frank M. and Stephen B. Withey. *Social Indicators of Well-Being: Americans' Perception of Life Quality.* Plenum, 1976.

Galbraith, John Kenneth. *The Affluent Society.* Houghton Mifflin, 1958.

Linder, Staffan Burenstam. *The Harried Leisure Class.* Columbia University Press, 1970.

Sahlins, Marshall. *Stone Age Economics.* Aldine-Atherton, 1972.

Cultural Ecology

. . . .

Cultural ecology is the study of the ways in which patterns of culture serve to adapt human groups to the difficulties posed by their environment. This specialization grew out of a turn-of-the-century school of thought called *environmental determinism*—a misuse of evolutionary theory which argued that all facets of culture could be traced to the ways in which they helped adapt the group(s) in which they were found to the environment(s).

Modern cultural ecologists avoid such simplistic, A-leads-to-B kind of thinking—that is, a *deterministic* position—by acknowledging that there are many alternative patterns of thought and behavior that can adapt a group to a given environment. Therefore, when cultural ecologists explain a pattern of behavior in terms of its adaptive significance, they do not claim to be able to say why one particular pattern is adopted in preference to others. Instead, they merely contend that, given the facts of the environment, it is possible to make sense out of culturally normative patterns of behavior that at first glance seem to be curious or even foolish or destructive.

In the first article of Topic 11, Marvin Harris, perhaps the best known exponent of cultural ecology, seeks to explain the cultural ecology of "India's Sacred Cow"—that is, why in India starving people will refuse to eat beef. By the end of his argument you will find that *not* eating beef can, in the right context, result in having more food! Critics of cultural ecology say that this kind of analysis is reminiscent of the good Doctor Pangloss in Voltaire's *Candide*. Perhaps, but such research and analysis force us to rethink almost everything we think we know about why we do what we do.

John B. Calhoun's "Plight of the Ik and Kaiadilt Is Seen as a Chilling Possible End for Man" takes the horrifying testimony that came out of the research by Colin Turnbull among the Ik of Uganda and Geoffrey Bianchi among the Kaiadilt of Australia, and shows that the decay of virtually all sustaining aspects of a society is predictable in certain extreme contexts. Calhoun has investigated these contexts experimentally among populations of mice, and sees alarming parallels there to the fate of the two peoples discussed in his essay. One cannot read this article without becoming deeply concerned over the directions being taken by our own society.

India's Sacred Cow

By Marvin Harris

. . . .

News photographs that came out of India during the famine of the late 1960s showed starving people stretching out bony hands to beg for food while sacred cattle strolled behind them undisturbed. The Hindu, it seems, would rather starve to death than eat his cow or even deprive it of food. The cattle appear to browse unhindered through urban markets eating an orange here, a mango there, competing with people for meager supplies of food.

By Western standards, spiritual values seem more important to Indians than life itself. Specialists in food habits around the world like Fred Simoons at the University of California at Davis consider Hinduism an irrational ideology that compels people to overlook abundant, nutritious foods for scarcer, less healthful foods.

What seems to be an absurd devotion to the mother cow pervades Indian life. Indian wall calendars portray beautiful young women with bodies of fat white cows, often with milk jetting from their teats into sacred shrines.

Cow worship even carries over into politics. In 1966 a crowd of 120,000 people, led by holy men, demonstrated in front of the Indian House of Parliament in support of the All-Party Cow Protection Campaign Committee. In Nepal, the only contemporary Hindu kingdom, cow slaughter is severely punished. As one story goes, the car driven by an official of a United States agency struck and killed a cow. In order to avoid the international incident that would have occurred when the official was arrested for murder, the Nepalese magistrate concluded that the cow had committed suicide.

Many Indians agree with Western assessments of the Hindu reverence for their cattle, the zebu, or *Bos indicus*, a large-humped species prevalent in Asia and Africa. M. N. Srinivas, an Indian anthropologist states: "Orthodox Hindu opinion regards the killing of cattle with abhorrence, even though the refusal to kill the vast number of useless cattle which exists in India today is detrimental to the nation." Even the Indian Ministry of Information formerly maintained that "the large animal population is more a liability than an asset in view of our land resources." Accounts from many different sources point to the same conclusion: India, one of the world's great civilizations, is being strangled by its love for the cow.

The easy explanation for India's devotion to the cow, the one most Westerners and Indians would offer, is that cow worship is an integral part of Hinduism. Religion is somehow good for the soul, even if it sometimes fails the body. Religion orders the cosmos and explains our place in the universe. Religious beliefs, many would claim, have existed for thousands of years and have a life of their own. They are not understandable in scientific terms.

But all this ignores history. There is more to be said for cow worship than is immediately apparent. The earliest Vedas, the Hindu sacred texts from the Second Millennium B.C., do not prohibit the slaughter of cattle. Instead, they ordain it as a part of sacrificial rites. The early Hindus did not avoid the flesh of cows and bulls; they ate it at ceremonial feasts presided over by Brahman priests. Cow worship is a relatively recent development in India; it evolved as the Hindu religion developed and changed.

This evolution is recorded in royal edicts and religious texts written during the last 3,000 years of Indian history. The Vedas from the First Millennium B.C. contain contradictory passages, some referring to ritual slaughter and others to a strict taboo on beef consumption. A. N. Bose, in *Social and Rural Economy of Northern India, 600 B.C. — 200 A.D.*, concludes that many of the sacred-cow passages were incorporated into the texts by priests of a later period.

By 200 A.D. the status of Indian cattle had undergone a spiritual transformation. The Brahman priesthood exhorted the population to venerate the cow and forbade them to abuse it or to feed on it. Religious feasts involving the ritual slaughter and consumption of livestock were eliminated and meat eating was restricted to the nobility.

By 1000 A.D., all Hindus were forbidden to eat beef. Ahimsa, the Hindu belief in the unity of all life, was the spiritual justification for this restriction. But it is difficult to ascertain exactly when this change occurred. An important event that helped to shape the modern complex was the Islamic invasion, which took place in the Eighth Century A.D. Hindus may have found it politically expedient to set themselves off from the invaders, who were beefeaters, by emphasizing the need to prevent the slaughter of their sacred animals. Thereafter, the cow taboo assumed its modern form and began to function much as it does today.

The place of the cow in modern India is every place—on posters, in the movies, in brass figures, in stone and wood carvings, on the streets, in the fields. The cow is a symbol of health and abundance. It provides the milk that Indians consume in the form of yogurt and ghee (clarified butter), which contribute subtle flavors to much spicy Indian food.

This, perhaps, is the practical role of the cow, but cows provide less than half the milk produced in India. Most cows in India are not dairy breeds. In most regions, when an Indian farmer wants a steady, high-quality source of milk he usually invests in a female water buffalo. In India the water buffalo is the specialized dairy breed because its milk has a higher butterfat content than zebu milk. Although the farmer milks his zebu cows, the milk is merely a by-product.

More vital than zebu milk to South Asian farmers are zebu calves. Male calves are especially valued because from bulls come oxen, which are the mainstay of the Indian agricultural system.

Small, fast oxen drag wooden plows through late-spring fields when monsoons have dampened the dry, cracked earth. After harvest, the oxen break the grain from the stalk by stomping through mounds of cut wheat and rice. For rice cultivation in irrigated fields, the male water buffalo is preferred (it pulls better in deep mud), but for most other crops, including rainfall rice, wheat, sorghum, and millet, and for transporting goods and people to and from town, a team of oxen is preferred. The ox is the Indian peasant's tractor, thresher and family car combined; the cow is the factory that produces the ox.

If draft animals instead of cows are counted, India appears to have too few domesticated ruminants, not too many. Since each of the 70 million farms in India requires a draft team, it follows that Indian peasants should use 140 million animals in the fields. But there are only 83 million oxen and male water buffalo on the subcontinent, a shortage of 30 million draft teams.

In other regions of the world, joint ownership of draft animals might overcome a shortage, but Indian agriculture is closely tied to the monsoon rains of late spring and summer. Field preparation and planting must coincide with the rain, and a farmer must have his animals ready to plow when the weather is right. When the farmer without a draft team needs bullocks most, his neighbors are all using theirs. Any delay in turning the soil drastically lowers production.

Because of this dependence on draft animals, loss of the family oxen is devastating. If a beast dies, the farmer must borrow money to buy or rent an ox at interest rates so high that he ultimately loses his land. Every year foreclosures force thousands of poverty-stricken peasants to abandon the countryside for the overcrowded cities.

If a family is fortunate enough to own a fertile cow, it will be able to rear replacements for a lost team and thus survive until life returns to normal. If, as sometimes happens, famine leads a family to sell its cow and ox team, all ties to agriculture are cut. Even if the family survives, it has no way to farm the land, no oxen to work the land, and no cows to produce oxen.

The prohibition against eating meat applies to the flesh of cows, bulls, and oxen, but the cow is the most sacred because it can produce the other two. The peasant whose cow dies is not only crying over a spiritual loss but over the loss of his farm as well.

Religious laws that forbid the slaughter of cattle promote the recovery of the agricultural system from the dry Indian winter and from periods of drought. The monsoon, on which all agriculture depends, is erratic. Sometimes it arrives early, sometimes late, sometimes not at all. Drought has struck large portions of India time and again in this century, and Indian farmers and the zebus are accustomed to these natural disasters. Zebus can pass weeks on end with little or no food and water. Like camels, they store both in their humps and recuperate quickly with only a little nourishment.

During droughts the cows often stop lactating and become barren. In some cases the condition is permanent but often it is only temporary. If barren animals were summarily eliminated, as Western experts in animal husbandry have suggested, cows capable of recovery would be lost along with those entirely debilitated. By keeping alive the cows that can later produce oxen, religious laws against cow slaughter assure the recovery of the agricultural system from the greatest challenge it faces—the failure of the monsoon.

The local Indian governments aid the process of recovery by maintaining homes for barren cows. Farmers reclaim any animal that calves or begins to lactate. One police station in Madras collects strays and pastures them in a field adjacent to the station. After a small fine is paid, a cow is returned to its rightful owner when the owner thinks the cow shows signs of being able to reproduce.

During the hot, dry spring months most of India is like a desert. Indian farmers often complain they cannot feed their livestock during this period. They maintain the cattle by letting them scavenge on the sparse grass along the roads. In the cities cattle are encouraged to scavenge near food stalls to supplement their scant diet. These are the wandering cattle tourists report seeing throughout India.

Westerners expect shopkeepers to respond to these intrusions with the deference due a sacred animal; instead, their response is a string of curses and the crack of a long bamboo pole across the beast's back or a poke at its genitals. Mahatma Gandhi was well aware of the treatment sacred cows (and bulls and oxen) received in India. "How we bleed her to take the last drop of milk from her. How we starve her to emaciation, how we ill-treat the calves, how we deprive them of their portion of milk, how cruelly we treat the oxen, how we castrate them, how we beat them, how we overload them."

Oxen generally receive better treatment than cows. When food is in short supply, thrifty Indian peasants feed their working bullocks and ignore their cows, but rarely do they abandon the cows to die. When cows are sick, farmers worry over them as they would over members of the family and nurse them as if they were children. When the rains return and when the fields are harvested, the farmers again feed their cows regularly and reclaim their abandoned animals. The prohibition against beef consumption is a form of disaster insurance for all India.

Western agronomists and economists are quick to protest that all the functions of the zebu cattle can be improved with organized breeding programs, cultivated pastures, and silage. Because stronger oxen would pull the plow faster, they could work multiple plots of land, allowing farmers to share their animals. Fewer healthy, well-fed cows could provide Indians with more milk. But pastures and silage require arable land, land needed to produce wheat and rice.

A look at Western cattle farming makes plain the cost of adopting advanced technology in Indian agriculture. In a study of livestock production in the United States, David Pimentel of the College of Agriculture and Life Sciences at Cornell University found that 91 percent of the cereal, legume, and vegetable protein suitable for human consumption is consumed by livestock. Approximately three quarters of the arable land in the United States is devoted to growing food for livestock. In the production of meat and milk, American ranchers use enough fossil fuel to equal more than 82 million barrels of oil annually.

Indian cattle do not drain the system in the same way. In a 1971 study of livestock in West Bengal, Stewart Odend'hal of the University of Missouri found that Bengalese cattle ate only the inedible remains of subsistence crops—rice straw, rice hulls, the tops of sugar cane, and mustard-oil cake. Cattle graze in the fields after harvest and eat the remains of crops left on the ground; they forage for grass and weeds on the roadsides. The food for zebu cattle costs the human population virtually nothing. "Basically," Odend'hal says, "the cattle convert items of little direct human value into products of immediate utility."

In addition to plowing the fields and producing milk, the zebus produce dung, which fires the hearths and fertilizes the fields of India. Much of the estimated 800 million tons of manure produced annually is collected by the farmers' children as they follow the family cows and bullocks from place to place. And when the children see the droppings of another farmer's cattle along the road, they pick those up also. Odend'hal reports that the system operates with such high efficiency that the children of West Bengal recover nearly 100 percent of the dung produced by their livestock.

From 40 to 70 percent of all manure produced by Indian cattle is used as fuel for cooking; the rest is returned to the fields as fertilizer. Dried dung burns slowly, cleanly, and with low heat—characteristics that satisfy the household needs of Indian women. Staples like curry and rice can simmer for hours. While the meal slowly cooks over an unattended fire, the women of the household can do other chores. Cow chips, unlike firewood, do not scorch as they burn.

It is estimated that the dung used for cooking fuel provides the energy-equivalent of 43 million tons of coal. At current prices, it would cost India an extra 1.5 billion dollars in foreign exchange to replace the dung with coal. And if the 350 million tons of manure that are being used as fertilizer were replaced with commercial fertilizers, the expense would be even greater. Roger Revelle of the University of California at San Diego has calculated that 89 percent of the energy used in Indian agriculture (the equivalent of about 140 million tons of coal) is provided by local sources. Even if foreign loans were to provide the money, the capital outlay necessary to replace the Indian cow with tractors and fertilizers for the fields, coal for the fires, and transportation for the family would probably warp international financial institutions for years.

Instead of asking the Indians to learn from the American model of industrial agriculture, American farmers might learn energy conservation from the Indians. Every step in an energy cycle results in a loss of energy to the system. Like a pendulum that slows a bit with each swing, each transfer of energy from sun to plants, plants to animals, and animals to human beings involves energy losses. Some systems are more efficient than others; they provide a higher percentage of the energy inputs in a final, useful form. Seventeen percent of all energy zebus consume is returned in the form of milk, traction and dung. American cattle raised on Western range land return only 4 percent of the energy they consume.

But the American system is improving. Based on techniques pioneered by Indian scientists, at least one commercial firm in the United States is reported to be building plants that will turn manure from cattle feedlots into combustible gas. When organic matter is broken down by anaerobic bacteria, methane gas and carbon dioxide are produced. After the methane is cleansed of the carbon dioxide, it is available for the same purposes as natural gas—cooking, heating, electricity generation. The company constructing the biogasification plant plans to sell its product to a gas-supply company, to be piped through the existing distribution system. Schemes similar to this one could make cattle ranches almost independent of utility and gasoline companies, for methane can be used to run trucks, tractors, and cars as well as to supply heat and electricity. The relative energy self-sufficiency that the Indian peasant has achieved is a goal American farmers and industry are now striving for.

Studies like Odend'hal's understate

Cattle, like other living organisms, consume energy in one form and produce it in another. The diagrams below trace the consumption and production of energy by Indian and American cattle. The size of the colored arrows reflects the proportion of energy flow; the gray arrows indicate unmeasured quantities. Indian cattle transform 17 percent of

the efficiency of the Indian cow, because dead cows are used for purposes that Hindus prefer not to acknowledge. When a cow dies, an Untouchable, a member of one of the lowest ranking castes in India, is summoned to haul away the carcass. Higher castes consider

the body of the dead cow polluting; if they do handle it, they must go through a rite of purification.

Untouchables first skin the dead animal and either tan the skin themselves or sell it to a leather factory. In the privacy of their homes, contrary to the

teachings of Hinduism, untouchable castes cook the meat and eat it. Indians of all castes rarely acknowledge the existence of these practices to non-Hindus, but most are aware that beefeating takes place. The prohibition against beefeating restricts consumption by the higher castes and helps distribute animal pro-

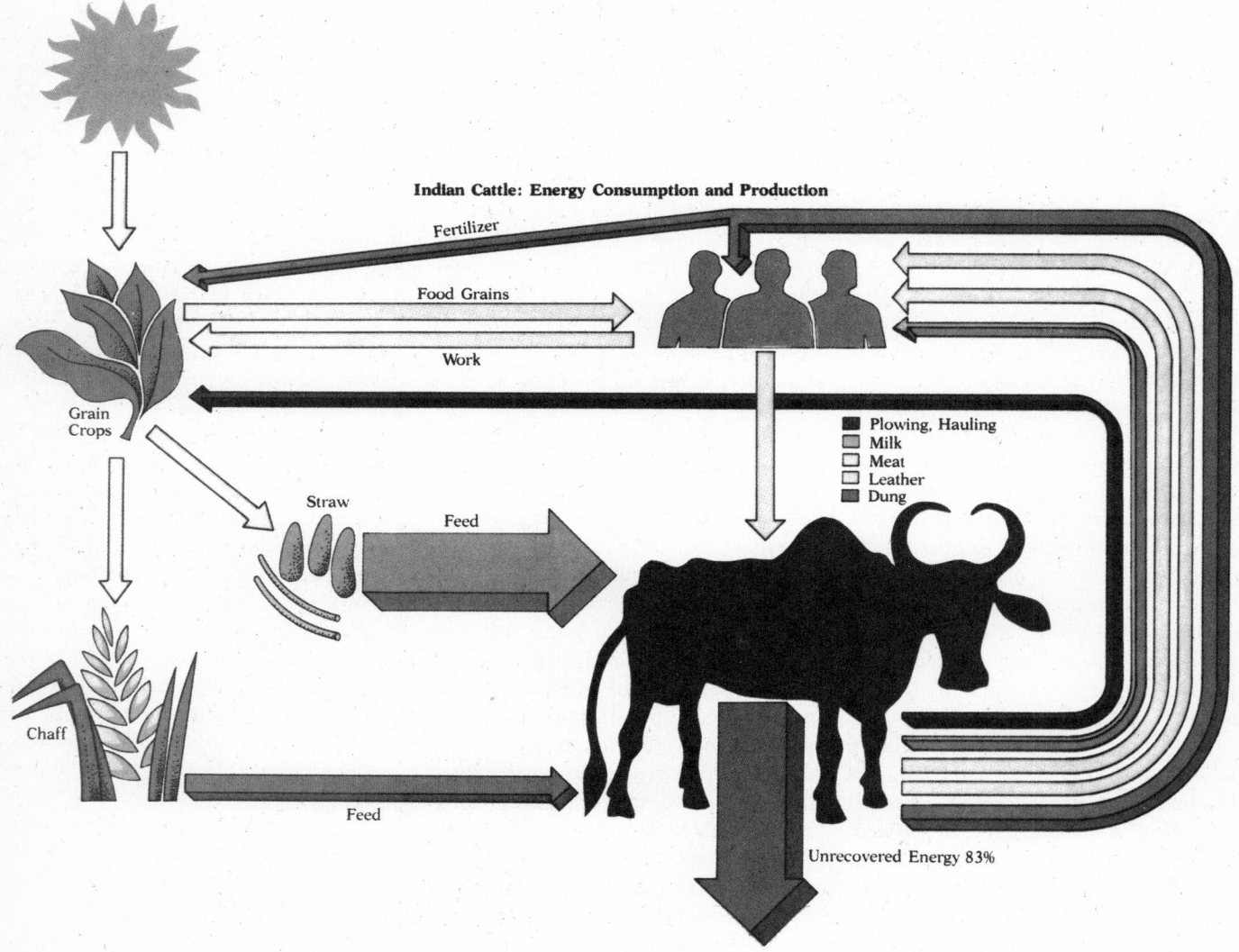

Indian Cattle: Energy Consumption and Production

Fertilizer

Food Grains

Work

Grain Crops

Straw

Feed

Plowing, Hauling
Milk
Meat
Leather
Dung

Chaff

Feed

Unrecovered Energy 83%

*the food they eat into useful goods.
American cattle transform only
4 percent of the energy used in their
production into useful forms. Indian
cattle eat agricultural waste products
unfit for human consumption. In
America, cattle eat grain that could
feed people, and beef and dairy
farming require fossil fuels that could
be put to more efficient use.*

tein to the poorest sectors of the population that otherwise would have no source of these vital nutrients.

Untouchables are not the only Indians who consume beef. Indian Muslims and Christians are under no restriction that forbids them beef, and its consumption is legal in many places. The Indian ban on cow slaughter is state, not national, law and not all states restrict it. In many cities, such as New Delhi, Calcutta, and Bombay, legal slaughterhouses sell beef to retail customers and to the restaurants that serve steak.

If the caloric value of beef and the energy costs involved in the manufacture of synthetic leather were included in the estimates of energy, the calculated efficiency of Indian livestock would rise considerably.

As well as the system works, experts often claim that its efficiency can be further improved. Alan

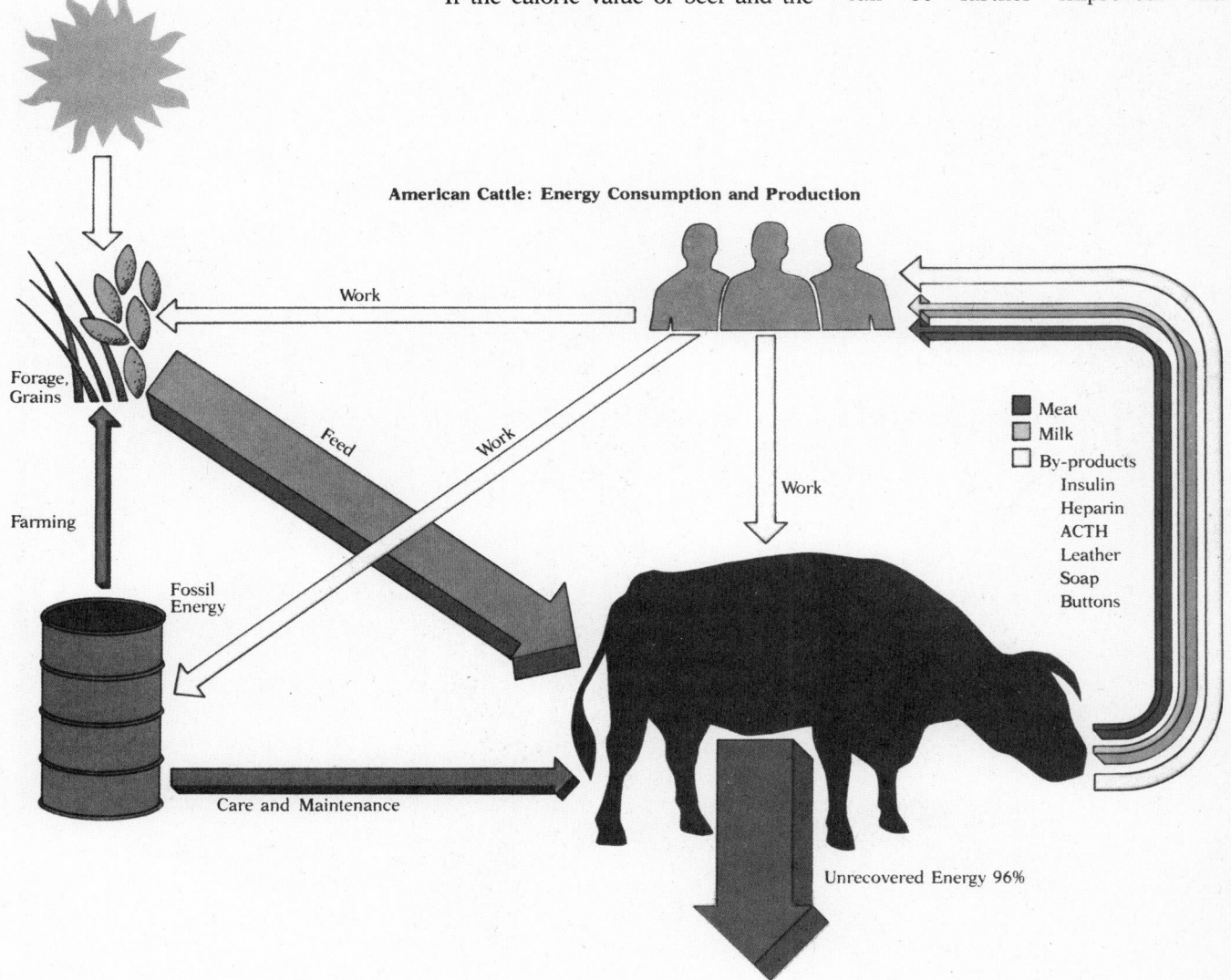

American Cattle: Energy Consumption and Production

Heston, an economist at the University of Pennsylvania, believes that Indians suffer from an overabundance of cows simply because they refuse to slaughter the excess cattle. India could produce at least the same number of oxen and the same quantities of milk and manure with 30 million fewer cows. Heston calculates that only 40 cows are necessary to maintain a population of 100 bulls and oxen. Since India averages 70 cows for every 100 bullocks, the difference, 30 million cows, is expendable.

What Heston fails to note is that sex ratios among cattle in different regions of India vary tremendously, indicating that adjustments in the cow population do take place. Along the Ganges River, one of the holiest shrines of Hinduism, the ratio drops to 47 cows for every 100 male animals. This ratio reflects the preference for dairy buffalo in the irrigated sectors of the Gangetic Plains. In nearby Pakistan, in contrast, where cow slaughter is permitted, the sex ratio is 60 cows to 100 oxen.

Since the sex ratios among cattle differ greatly from region to region and do not even approximate the balance that would be expected if no females were killed, we can assume that some culling of herds does take place; Indians do adjust their religious restrictions to accommodate ecological realities.

They cannot kill a cow but they can tether an old or unhealthy animal until it has starved to death. They cannot slaughter a calf but they can yoke it with a large wooden triangle so that when it nurses it irritates the mother's udder and gets kicked to death. They cannot ship their animals to the slaughterhouse but they can sell them to Muslims, closing their eyes to the fact that the Muslims will take the cattle to the slaughterhouse.

These violations of the prohibition against cattle slaughter strengthen the premise that cow worship is a vital part of Indian culture. The practice arose to prevent the population from consuming the animal on which Indian agriculture depends. During the First Millennium B.C., the Ganges Valley became one of the most densely populated regions of the world.

Where previously there had been only scattered villages, many towns and cities arose and peasants farmed every available acre of land. Kingsley Davis, a population expert at the University of California at Berkeley, estimates that by 300 B.C. between 50 million and 100 million people were living in India. The forested Ganges Valley became a windswept semidesert and signs of ecological collapse appeared; droughts and floods became commonplace, erosion took away the rich topsoil, farms shrank as population increased, and domesticated animals became harder and harder to maintain.

It is probable that the elimination of meat eating came about in a slow, practical manner. The farmers who decided not to eat their cows, who saved them for procreation to produce oxen, were the ones who survived the natural disasters. Those who ate beef lost the tools with which to farm. Over a period of centuries, more and more farmers probably avoided beef until an unwritten taboo came into existence.

Only later was the practice codified by the priesthood. While Indian peasants were probably aware of the role of cattle in their society, strong sanctions were necessary to protect zebus from a population faced with starvation. To remove temptation, the flesh of cattle became taboo and the cow became sacred.

The sacredness of the cow is not just an ignorant belief that stands in the way of progress. Like all concepts of the sacred and the profane, this one affects the physical world; it defines the relationships that are important for the maintenance of Indian society.

Indians have the sacred cow; we have the "sacred" car and the "sacred" dog. It would not occur to us to propose the elimination of automobiles and dogs from our society without carefully considering the consequences, and we should not propose the elimination of zebu cattle without first understanding their place in the social order of India.

Human society is neither random nor capricious. The regularities of thought and behavior called culture are the principal mechanisms by which we human beings adapt to the world around us. Practices and beliefs can be rational or irrational, but a society that fails to adapt to its environment is doomed to extinction. Only those societies that draw the necessities of life from their surroundings without destroying those surroundings, inherit the earth. The West has much to learn from the great antiquity of Indian civilization, and the sacred cow is an important part of that lesson.

For further information:

Gandhi, Mohandas K. *How to Serve the Cow:* Navajivan Publishing House, 1954.

Harris, Marvin. *Cows, Pigs, Wars and Witches: The Riddles of Culture.* Random House, 1974.

Heston, Alan, et al. "An Approach to the Sacred Cow of India." *Current Anthropology,* Vol. 12, 1971, pp. 191-209.

Odend'hal, Stewart. "Gross Energetic Efficiency of Indian Cattle in Their Environment." *Journal of Human Ecology,* Vol. 1, 1972, pp. 1-27.

Raj, K. N. "Investment in Livestock in Agrarian Economies: An Analysis of Some Issues Concerning 'Sacred Cows' and 'Surplus Cattle.'" *Indian Economic Review,* Vol. 4, 1969, pp. 1-33.

Plight of the Ik and Kaiadilt Is Seen as a Chilling Possible End for Man

By John B. Calhoun

....

The Mountain—how pervasive in the history of man. A still small voice on Horeb, mount of God, guided Elijah. There, earlier, Moses standing before God received the Word. And Zion: "I am the Lord your God dwelling in Zion, my holy mountain."

Then there was Atum, mountain, God and first man, one and all together. The mountain rose out of a primordial sea of nothingness—Nun. Atum, the spirit of life, existed within Nun. In creating himself, Atum became the evolving ancestor of the human race. So goes the Egyptian mythology of creation, in which the Judaic Adam has his roots.

And there is a last Atum, united in his youth with another mountain of God, Mt. Morungole in northeasternmost Uganda. His people are the Ik, pronounced eek. They are the subject of an important new book, *The Mountain People,* by Colin M. Turnbull (Simon and Schuster, $6.95). They still speak Middle-Kingdom Egyptian, a language thought to be dead. But perhaps their persistence is not so strange. Egyptian mythology held that the waters of the life-giving Nile had their origin in Nun. Could this Nun have been the much more extensive Lake Victoria of 40 to 50 millennia ago when, near its borders, man groped upward to cloak his biological self with culture?

Well might the Ik have preserved the essence of this ancient tradition that affirms human beginnings. Isolated as they have been in their jagged mountain fastness, near the upper tributaries of the White Nile, the Ik have been protected from cultural evolution.

What a Shangri-la, this land of the Ik. In its center, the Kidepo valley, 35 miles across, home of abundant game; to the south, mist-topped Mt. Morungole; to the west the Niangea range; to the north, bordering the Sudan, the Didinga range; to the east on the Kenya border, a sheer drop of 2,000 feet into the Turkanaland of cattle herdsmen. Through ages of dawning history few people must have been interested in encroaching on this rugged land. Until 1964 anthropologists knew little of the Ik's existence. Their very name, much less their language, remained a mystery until, quite by chance, anthropologist Colin M. Turnbull found himself among them. What an opportunity to study pristine man! Here one should encounter the basic qualities of humanity unmarred by war, technology, pollution, over-population.

Turnbull rested in his bright red Land Rover at an 8,000-foot-high pass. A bit beyond this only "navigable" pass into the Kidepo Valley, lay Pirre, a police outpost watching over a cluster of Ik villages. There to welcome him came Atum of the warm, open smile and gentle voice. Gray-haired at 40, appearing 65, he was the senior elder of the Ik, senior in authority if not quite so in age. Nattily attired in shorts and woolen sweater—in contrast to his mostly naked colleagues—Atum bounced forward with his ebony walking stick, greeted Turnbull in Swahili, and from that moment on took command as best he could of Turnbull's life. At Atum's village a plaintive woman's voice called out. Atum remarked that that was his wife—sick, too weak to work in the fields. Turnbull offered to bring her food and medicine. Atum suggested he handle Turnbull's gifts. As the weeks wore on Atum picked up the parcels that Turnbull was supplying for Atum's wife.

One day Atum's brother-in-law, Lomongin, laughingly asked Turnbull if he didn't know that Atum's wife had been dead for weeks. She had received no food or medicine. Atum had sold it. So she just died. All of this was revealed with no embarrassment. Atum joined the laughter over the joke played on Turnbull.

Another time Atum and Lojieri were guiding Turnbull over the mountains, and at one point induced him to push ahead through high grass until he broke through into a clearing. The clearing was a sheer 1,500-foot drop. The two Iks rolled on the ground, nearly bursting with laughter because Turnbull just managed to catch himself. What a lovable cherub this Atum! His laughter never ended.

New meaning of laughter

Laughter, hallmark of mankind, not shared with any other animal, not even primates, was an outstanding trait of the Ik. A whole village rushed to the edge of a low cliff and joined in communal laughter at blind old Lo'ono who lay thrashing on her back, near death after stumbling over. One evening Iks around a fire watched a child as it crawled toward the flames, then writhed back screaming after it grasped a gleaming coal. Laughter erupted. Quiet came to the child as its mother cuddled it in a kind of respect for the merriment it had caused. Then there was the laughter of innocent childhood as boys and girls gathered around a grandfather, too weak to walk, and drummed upon his head with sticks or pelted him with stones until he cried. There was the laughter that binds families together: Kimat, shrieking for joy as she dashed off with the mug of tea she had snatched from her dying brother Lomeja's hand an instant after Turnbull had given it to him as a last token of their friendship.

Laughter there had always been. A few old people remembered times, 25 to 30 years ago, when laughter mirrored love and joy and fullness of life, times when beliefs and rituals and traditions kept a bond with the "millions of years" ago when time began for the Ik. That was when their god, Didigwari, let the Ik down from heaven on a vine, one at a time. He gave them the digging stick with the instruction that they could not kill one another. He let down other people. To the Dodos and Turkana he gave cattle and spears to kill with. But the Ik remained true to their instruction and did not kill one another or neighboring tribesmen.

For them the bow, the net and the pitfall were for capturing game. For them the greatest sin was to overhunt. Mobility and cooperation ever were part of them. Often the netting of game required the collaboration of a whole band of 100 or more, some to hold the net and some to drive game into it. Between the big hunts, bands broke up into smaller groups to spread over their domain, then to gather again. The several bands would each settle for the best part of the year along the edge of the Kidepo Valley in the foothills of Mt. Morungole. There they were once again fully one with the mountain. "The Ik, without their mountains, would no longer be the Ik and similarly, they say, the mountains without the Ik would no longer be the same mountains, if indeed they continued to exist at all."

In this unity of people and place, rituals, traditions, beliefs and values molded and preserved a continuity of life. All rites of passage were marked by ceremony. Of these, the rituals surrounding death gave greatest meaning to life. Folded in a fetal position, the body was buried with favorite possessions, facing the rising sun to mark celestial rebirth. All accompanying rituals of fasting and feasting, of libations of beer sprinkled over the grave, of seeds of favorite foods planted on the grave to draw life from the dust of the dead, showed that death is merely another form of life, and reminded the living of the good things of life and of the good way to live. In so honoring the dead by creating goodness the Ik helped speed the soul, content, on its journey.

Such were the Ik until wildlife conservation intruded into their homeland. Uganda decided to make a national park out of the Kidepo Valley, the main hunting ground of the Ik. What then happened stands as an indictment of the myopia that science can generate. No one looked to the Ik to note that their hunter-gatherer way of life marked the epitome of conservation, that the continuance of their way of life would have added to the success of the park. Instead they were forbidden to hunt any longer in the Kidepo Valley. They were herded to the periphery of the park and encouraged to become farmers on dry mountain slopes so steep as to test the poise of a goat. As an example to the more remote villages, a number of villages were brought together in a tight little cluster below the southwest pass into the valley. Here the police post, which formed this settlement of Pirre, could watch over the Ik to see that they didn't revert to hunting.

These events contained two of the three strikes that knocked out the spirit of the Ik. *Strike No. 1:* The shift from a mobile hunter-gatherer way of life to a sedentary farming way of life made irrelevant the Ik's entire repertoire of beliefs, habits and traditions. Their guidelines for life were inappropriate to farming. They seemed to adapt, but at heart they remained hunters and gatherers. Their cultural templates fitted them for that one way of life.

Strike No. 2: They were suddenly crowded together at a density, intimacy and frequency of contact far greater than they had ever before been required to experience. Throughout their long past each band of 100 or so individuals only temporarily coalesced into a whole. The intervening breaking up into smaller groups permitted realignment of relationships that tempered conflicts from earlier associations. But at the resettlement, more than 450 individuals were forced to form a permanent cluster of villages within shouting distance of each other. Suppose the seven million or so inhabitants of Los Angeles County were forced to move and join the more than one million inhabitants of the more arid San Diego County. Then after they arrived all water, land and air communication to the rest of the world was cut off abruptly and completely. These eight million people would then have to seek survival completely on local resources without any communication with others. It would be a test of the ability of human beings to remain human.

Such a test is what Dr. Turnbull's book on the Mountain People is all about. The Ik failed to remain human. I have put mice to the same test and they failed to remain mice. Those of you who have been following SMITHSONIAN may recall from the April 1970 and the January 1971 issues something about the projected demise of a mouse population experiencing the same two strikes against it as did the Ik.

Fate of a mouse population

Last summer I spoke in London behind the lectern where Charles Darwin and Alfred Wallace had presented their papers on evolution—which during the next century caused a complete revision of our insight into what life is all about and what man is and may become. In summing up that session of 1858 the president remarked that nothing of importance had been presented before the Linnean Society at that year's meeting! I spoke behind this same lectern to a session of the Royal Society of Medicine during its symposium on "Man in His Place." At the end of my paper, "Death Squared: The Explosive Growth and Demise of a Mouse Population," the chairman admonished me to stick to my mice; the insights I had presented could have no implication for man. Wonderful if the chairman could be correct—but now I have read about the Mountain People, and I have a hollow feeling that perhaps we, too, are close to losing our "mountain."

Turnbull lived for 18 months as a member of the Ik tribe. His identity transfer became so strong that he acquired the Ik laughter. He laughed at seeing Atum suffer as they were completing an extremely arduous journey on foot back across the mountains and the Kidepo Valley from the Sudan. He felt pleasure at seeing Lokwam, local "Lord of the Flies," cry in agony from the beating given him by his two beautiful sisters.

Well, for five years I have identified with my mice, as they lived in their own "Kidepo Valley"—their contrived Utopia where resources are always abundant and all mortality factors except aging eliminated. I watched their population grow rapidly from the first few colonizers. I watched them fill their metal "universe" with organized social groups. I watched them bring up a host of young with loving maternal care and paternal territorial protection—all of these young well educated for mouse society. But then there were too many of these young mice, ready to become in-

Unwanted by Ik society, an old man, who remembered times of human caring, lies among the rocks of the mountain, quietly awaiting a lonely death.

volved in all that mice can become, with nowhere to go, no physical escape from their closed environment, no opportunity to gain a niche where they could play a meaningful role. They tried, but being younger and less experienced they were nearly always rejected.

Rejecting so many of these probing youngsters overtaxed the territorial males. So defense then fell to lactating females. They became aggressive. They turned against their own young and ejected them before normal weaning and before adequate social bonds between mother and young had developed. During this time of social tension, rate of growth of the population was only one third of that during the earlier, more favorable phase.

Strike No. 1 against these mice: They lost the opportunity to express the capacities developed by older mice born during the rapid population growth. After a while they became so rejected that they were treated as so many sticks and stones by their still relatively well-adjusted elders. These rejected mice withdrew, physically and psychologically, to live packed tightly together in large pools. Amongst themselves they became vicious, lashing out and biting each other now and then with hardly any provocation.

Strike No. 2 against the mice: They reached great numbers despite reduced conceptions and increased deaths of newborn young resulting from the dissolution of maternal care. Many had early been rejected by their mothers and knew little about social bonds.

Rains temporarily turned the Ik's mountain green just before Turnbull returned for a visit.

Often their later attempts at interaction were interrupted by some other mouse intervening unintentionally as it passed between two potential actors.

I came to call such mice the "Beautiful Ones." They never learned such effective social interactions as courtship, mating and aggressive defense of territory. Never copulating, never fighting, they were unstressed and essentially unaware of their associates. They spent their time grooming themselves, eating and sleeping, totally individualistic, totally isolated socially except for a peculiar acquired need for simple proximity to others. This produced what I have called the "behavioral sink," the continual accentuation of aggregations to the point that much available space was unused despite a population increase to nearly 15 times the optimum.

All true "mousity" was lost. Though physically they still appeared to be mice, they had no essential capacities for survival and continuation of mouse society.

Suddenly, population growth ceased. In what seemed an instant they passed over a threshold beyond which there was no likelihood of their ever recouping the capacity to become real mice again. No more young were born. From a peak population of 2,200 mice nearly three years ago, aging has gradually taken its toll until now there are only 46 sluggish near-cadavers comparable to people more than 100 years old.

It was just such a fading universe Colin Turnbull found in 1964. Just before he arrived, *Strike No. 3* had set in: starvation. Any such crisis could have added the coup de grace after the other two strikes. Normally the Ik could count on only making three crops every four years. At this time a two-year drought set in and destroyed almost all crops. Neighboring tribes survived with their cultures intact. Turkana herdsmen, facing starvation and death, kept their societies in contact with each other and continued to sing songs of praise to God for the goodness of life.

By the beginning of the long drought, "goodness" to the Ik simply meant to have food—to have food for one's self alone. Collaborative hunts were a thing of the past, long since stopped by the police and probably no longer possible as a social effort, anyway. Solitary hunting, now designated as poaching, became a necessity for sheer survival. But the solitary hunter took every precaution not to let others know of his success. He would gorge himself far off in the bush and bring the surplus back to sell to the police, who were not above profiting from this traffic. Withholding food from wife, children and aging parents became an accomplishment to brag and laugh about. It became a way of life, continuing after the government began providing famine relief. Those strong enough to go to the police station to get rations for themselves and their families would stop halfway home and gorge all the food, even though it caused them to vomit.

Village of mutual hatred

The village reflected this reversal of humanity. Instead of open courtyards around each group of huts within the large compound, there was a maze of walls and tunnels booby trapped with spears to ward off intrusion by neighbors.

In Atum's village a whole band of more than 100 individuals was crowded together in mutual hostility and aloneness. They would gather at their sitting place and sit for hours in a kind of suspended animation, not looking directly at each other, yet scanning slowly all others who might be engaged in some solitary task, watching for someone to make a mistake that would elicit the symbolic violence of laughter and derision. They resembled my pools of rejected withdrawn mice. Homemaking deteriorated, feces littered doorsteps and courtyard. Universal adultery and incest replaced the old taboo. The beaded virgins' aprons of eight-to-twelve-year-old girls became symbols that these were proficient whores accustomed to selling their wares to passing herdsmen.

One ray of humanity left in this cesspool was 12-year-old, retarded Adupa. Because she believed that food was for sharing and savoring, her playmates beat her. She still believed that parents were for loving and to be loved by. They cured her madness by locking her in her hut until she died and decayed.

The six other villages were smaller and their people could retain a few glimmers of the goodness and fullness of life. There was Kuaur, devoted to Turnbull, hiking four days to deliver mail, taunted for bringing food home to share with his wife and child. There was Losiké, the potter, regarded as a witch. She offered water to visitors and made pots for others. When the famine got so bad that there was no need for pots to cook in, her husband left her. She was no longer bringing in any income. And then there was old Nangoli, still capable of mourning when her husband died. She went with her family and village across Kidepo and into the Sudan where their village life turned for a while back to normality. But it was not normal enough to keep them. Back to Pirre, to death, they returned.

All goodness was gone from the Ik, leaving merely emptiness, valuelessness, nothingness, the chaos of Nun. They reentered the womb of beginning time from which there is no return. Urination beside the partial graves of the dead marked the death of God, the final fading of Mount Morungole.

My poor words give only a shadowy image of the cold coffin of Ik humanity that Turnbull describes. His two years with the Ik left him in a slough of despondency from which he only extricated himself with difficulty, never wanting to see them again. Time and distance brought him comfort. He did return for a brief visit some months later. Rain had come in abundance. Gardens had sprung up untended from hidden seeds in the earth. Each Ik gleaned only for his immediate needs. Granaries stood empty, not refilled for inevitable scarcities ahead. The future had ceased to exist. Individual and social decay continued on its downward spiral. Sadly Turnbull departed again from this land of lost hope and faith.

Last summer in London I knew nothing about the Ik when I was so publicly and thoroughly chastised for having the temerity to suspect that the behavioral and spiritual death my mice had exhibited might also befall man. But a psychiatrist in the audience arose in defense of my suspicion. Dr. Geoffrey N. Bianchi remarked that an isolated tribe of Australian Aborigines mirrored the changes and kinds of pathology I had seen among mice. I did not know that Dr. Bianchi was a member of the team that had studied these people, the Kaiadilt, and that a book about them was in preparation, Cruel, Poor and Brutal Nations by John Cawte (The University Press of Hawaii). In galley proof I have read about the Kaiadilt and find it so shattering to my faith in humanity that I now sometimes wish I had never heard of it. Yet there is some glimmer of hope that the Kaiadilt may recover—not what they were but possibly some new life.

A frail, tenacious people, the Kaiadilt never numbered more than 150 souls where they lived on Bentinck Island in the Gulf of Carpentaria. So isolated were they that not even their nearest Aboriginal neighbors, 20 miles away, had any knowledge of their existence until in this century; so isolated were the Kaiadilt from their nearest neighbors that they differ from them in such heredity markers as blood type and fingerprints. Not until the early years of this century did an occasional visitor from the Queensland Government even note their existence.

For all practical purposes the first real contact the Kaiadilt had with Western "culture" came in 1916 when a man by the name of McKenzie came to Bentinck with a group of male mainland Aborigines to try to establish a lime kiln. McKenzie's favorite sport was to ride about shooting Kaiadilt. His helpers' sport was to commandeer as many women as they could, and take them to their headquarters on a neighboring island. In 1948 a tidal wave poisoned most of the freshwater sources. Small groups of Kaiadilt were rounded up and transported to larger Mornington Island where they were placed under the supervision of a Presbyterian mission. They were crowded into a dense cluster settlement just as the Ik had been at Pirre.

Here they still existed when the psychiatric field team came into their midst 15 years later. They were much like the Ik: dissolution of family life, total valuelessness, apathy. I could find no mention of laughter, normal or pathological. Perhaps the Kaiadilt didn't laugh. They had essentially ceased the singing that had been so much a part of their traditional way.

The spiritual decay of the Kaiadilt was marked by withdrawal, depression, suicide and tendency to engage in such self-mutilation as ripping out one's testes or chopping off one's nose. In their passiveness some of the anxiety ridden children are accepting the new mold of life forced upon them by a benevolent culture they do not understand. Survival with a new mold totally obliterating all past seems their only hope.

So the lesson comes clear, and Colin Turnbull sums it up in the final paragraph of his book: "The Ik teach us that our much vaunted human values are not inherent in humanity at all, but are associated only with a particular form of survival called society, and that all, even society itself, are luxuries that can be dispensed with. That does not make them any the less wonderful or desirable, and if man has any greatness it is surely in his ability to maintain these values, clinging to them to an often very bitter end, even shortening an already pitifully short life rather than sacrifice his humanity. But that too involves choice, and the Ik teach us that man can lose the will to make it."

TOPIC *12*

Sex Roles

In the first part of this century, social events such as the Russian revolution and the rise of socialism, and academic schools of thought such as behaviorism in psychology underlined the view that human beings are extraordinarily malleable and that social, historical, and cultural factors are preeminent over biological causes in shaping human behavior. The noted anthropologist Franz Boas and his students led the intellectual movement that, among other things, attacked the viability of the concept of "race" and took an activist stance in combating racism.

In this context, the subject of differences between the human sexes became critical. One feature of the organization of social life that is present in all known societies is the cultural attribution of significance to differences between males and females. Notions of maleness and femaleness vary enormously across cultures, but the distinction between the sexes is made universally, and sex-role attributions and expectations are important organizers of social existence everywhere. Do innate biological differences between the sexes account for these distinctions?

In the early 1930s, Margaret Mead studied and lived with three societies in New Guinea. As she reported in her book *Sex and Temperament*, she found that in these societies the attribution of qualities of character to the two sexes differed remarkably—both among those societies and in contrast to ours. In her book, which quickly achieved notoriety, Mead argued for the point of view that human nature is "not rigid and unyielding" and that "cultural rhythms are stronger and more compelling than the physiological rhythms which they overlay and distort."

The public was more enthusiastic over *Sex and Temperament* than were anthropologists, who noted that her research was limited to a matter of months, that she relied on data provided by only one or two informants, that data and hypotheses were poorly separated, and that a subjective bias in the interpretation of the data was all too evident. Even Mead's husband, Reo Fortune, who had collaborated with her in this research, rejected her view that the Arapesh did not distinguish between male and female temperaments.

With the reemergence of feminism in America during the late 1960s and 1970s, *Sex and Temperament* was enshrined as a "classic," and its obvious shortcomings were overlooked because its contents could be used to validate feminist critiques of contemporary social life. Mead herself participated in the feminist movement, but at the same time she expressed unease about the overinterpretation of her New Guinea materials by the writers of feminist tracts.

In "Society and Sex Roles," Ernestine Friedl asks this question: Why do men have power over women in most societies? Her study of societies at differing levels of complexity shows a broad range of such dominance—from the extreme dominance of the Inuit (Eskimo) men to the relative social equality of the Hadza men and women of Tanzania. Friedl finds a positive correlation between the degree to which men control the production of food and the degree of sexual stratification of social life. She ends her article with some extrapolations to sex-role changes we might expect in modern industrial society.

In "Daughters of the Forest," Agnes Estioko-Griffin provides an example of a society in which men control neither the production of food nor the sexual stratification of social life. Among the Agta people of the Philippines, the women hunt large game animals and also have the primary responsibility for raising children.

Finally, in "Life Behind the Veil," Cherry and Charles Lindholm explore the secret world of Moslem women. Though it may appear to Westerners that Moslem women are the personifications of powerlessness, in fact, the Lindholms report, they are viewed in traditional Islamic society as powerful and dangerous beings.

Society and Sex Roles

By Ernestine Friedl

"Women must respond quickly to the demands of their husbands," says anthropologist Napoleon Chagnon describing the horticultural Yanomamo Indians of Venezuela. When a man returns from a hunting trip, "the woman, no matter what she is doing, hurries home and quietly but rapidly prepares a meal for her husband. Should the wife be slow in doing this, the husband is within his rights to beat her. Most reprimands . . . take the form of blows with the hand or with a piece of firewood. . . . Some of them chop their wives with the sharp edge of a machete or axe, or shoot them with a barbed arrow in some nonvital area, such as the buttocks or leg."

Among the Semai agriculturalists of central Malaya, when one person refuses the request of another, the offended party suffers *punan*, a mixture of emotional pain and frustration. "Enduring *punan* is commonest when a girl has refused the victim her sexual favors," reports Robert Dentan. "The jilted man's 'heart becomes sad.' He loses his energy and his appetite. Much of the time he sleeps, dreaming of his lost love. In this state he is in fact very likely to injure himself 'accidentally.'" The Semai are afraid of violence; a man would never strike a woman.

The social relationship between men and women has emerged as one of the principal disputes occupying the attention of scholars and the public in recent years. Although the discord is sharpest in the United States, the controversy has spread throughout the world. Numerous national and international conferences, including one in Mexico sponsored by the United Nations, have drawn together delegates from all walks of life to discuss such questions as the social and political rights of each sex, and even the basic nature of males and females.

Whatever their position, partisans often invoke examples from other cultures to support their ideas about the proper role of each sex. Because women are clearly subservient to men in many societies, like the Yanomamo, some experts conclude that the natural pattern is for men to dominate. But among the Semai no one has the right to command others, and in West Africa women are often chiefs. The place of women in these societies supports the argument of those who believe that sex roles are not fixed, that if there is a natural order, it allows for many different arrangements.

The argument will never be settled as long as the opposing sides toss examples from the world's cultures at each other like intellectual stones. But the effect of biological differences on male and female behavior can be clarified by looking at known examples of the earliest forms of human society and examining the relationship between technology, social organization, environment, and sex roles. The problem is to determine the conditions in which different degrees of male dominance are found, to try to discover the social and cultural arrangements that give rise to equality or inequality between the sexes, and to attempt to apply this knowledge to our understanding of the changes taking place in modern industrial society.

As Western history and the anthropological record have told us, equality between the sexes is rare; in most known societies females are subordinate. Male dominance is so widespread that it is virtually a human universal; societies in which women are consistently dominant do not exist and have never existed.

Evidence of a society in which women control all strategic resources like food and water, and in which women's activities are the most prestigious has never been found. The Iroquois of North America and the Lovedu of Africa came closest. Among the Iroquois, women raised food, controlled its distribution, and helped to choose male political leaders. Lovedu women ruled as queens, exchanged valuable cattle, led ceremonies, and controlled their own sex lives. But among both the Iroquois and the Lovedu, men owned the land and held other positions of power and prestige. Women were equal to men; they did not have ultimate authority over them. Neither culture was a true matriarchy.

Patriarchies are prevalent, and they appear to be strongest in societies in which men control significant goods that are exchanged with people outside the family. Regardless of who produces food, the person who gives it to others creates the obligations and alliances that are at the center of all political relations. The greater the male monopoly on the distribution of scarce items, the stronger their control of women seems to be. This is most obvious in relatively simple hunter-gatherer societies.

Hunter-gatherers, or foragers, subsist on wild plants, small land animals, and small river or sea creatures gathered by hand; large land animals and sea mammals hunted with spears, bows and arrows, and blow guns; and fish caught with hooks and nets. The 300,000 hunter-gatherers alive in the world today include the Eskimos, the Australian aborigines, and the Pygmies of Central Africa.

Foraging has endured for two million years and was replaced by farming and animal husbandry only 10,000 years ago; it covers more than 99 percent of human history. Our foraging ancestry is not far behind us and provides a clue to our understanding of the human condition.

Hunter-gatherers are people whose ways of life are technologically simple and socially and politically egalitarian. They live in small groups of 50 to 200 and have neither kings, nor priests, nor social classes. These conditions permit anthropologists to observe the essential bases for inequalities between the sexes without the distortions induced by the complexities of contemporary industrial society.

The source of male power among hunter-gatherers lies in their control of a scarce, hard to acquire, but necessary nutrient — animal protein. When men in a hunter-gatherer society return to camp with game, they divide the meat in some customary way. Among the !Kung San of Africa, certain parts of the animal are given to the owner of the arrow that killed the beast, to the first hunter to sight the game, to the one who threw the first spear, and to all men in the hunting party. After the meat has been divided, each hunter distributes his share to his blood relatives and his in-laws, who in turn share it with others. If an animal is large enough, every member of the band will receive some meat.

Vegetable foods, in contrast, are not distributed beyond the immediate household. Women give food to their children, to their husbands, to other members of the household, and rarely, to the occasional visitor. No one outside the family regularly eats any of the wild fruits and vegetables that are gathered by the women.

The meat distributed by the men is a public gift. Its source is widely known, and the donor expects a reciprocal gift when other men return from a successful hunt. He gains honor as a supplier of a scarce item and simultaneously obligates others to him.

These obligations constitute a form of power or control over others, both men and women. The opinions of hunters play an important part in decisions to move the village; good hunters attract the most desirable women; people in other groups join camps with good hunters; and hunters, because they already participate in an internal system of exchange, control exchange with other groups for flint, salt, and steel axes. The male monopoly on hunting unites men in a system of exchange and gives them power; gathering vegetable food does not give women equal power even among foragers who live in the tropics, where the food collected by women provides more than half the hunter-gatherer diet.

If dominance arises from a monopoly on big-game hunting, why has the male monopoly remained unchallenged? Some women are strong enough to participate in the hunt and their endurance is certainly equal to that of men. Dobe San women of the Kalahari Desert in Africa walk an average of 10 miles a day carrying from 15 to 33 pounds of food plus a baby.

Women do not hunt, I believe, because of four interrelated factors: variability in the supply of game; the different skills required for hunting and gathering; the incompatibility between carrying burdens and hunting; and the small size of seminomadic foraging populations.

Because the meat supply is unstable, foragers must make frequent expeditions to provide the band with gathered food. Environmental factors such as seasonal and annual variation in rainful often affect the size of the wildlife population. Hunters cannot always find game, and when they do encounter animals, they are not always successful in killing their prey. In northern latitudes, where meat is the primary food, periods of starvation are known in every generation. The irregularity of the game supply leads hunter-gatherers in areas where plant foods are available to depend on these predictable foods a good part of the time. Someone must gather the fruits, nuts, and roots and carry them back to camp to feed unsuccessful hunters, children, the elderly, and anyone who might not have gone foraging that day.

Foraging falls to the women because hunting and gathering cannot be combined on the same expedition. Although gatherers sometimes notice signs of game as they work, the skills required to track game are not the same as those required to find edible roots or plants. Hunters scan the horizon and the land for traces of large game; gatherers keep their eyes to the ground, studying the distribution of plants and the texture of the soil for hidden roots and animal holes. Even if a woman who was collecting plants came across the track of an antelope, she could not follow it; it is impossible to carry a load and hunt at the same time. Running with a heavy load is difficult, and should the animal be sighted, the hunter would be off balance and could neither shoot an arrow nor throw a spear accurately.

Pregnancy and child care would also present difficulties for a hunter. An unborn child affects a woman's body balance, as does a child in her arms, on her back, or slung at her side. Until they are two years old, many hunter-gatherer children are carried at all times, and until they are four, they are carried some of the time.

An observer might wonder why young women do not hunt until they become pregnant, or why mature women and men do not hunt and gather on alternate days, with some women staying in camp to act as wet nurses for the young. Apart from the effects hunting might have on a mother's milk production, there are two reasons. First, young girls begin to bear children as soon as they are physically mature and strong enough to hunt, and second, hunter-gatherer bands are so small that there are unlikely to be enough lactating women to serve as wet nurses. No hunter-gatherer group could afford to maintain a specialized female hunting force.

Because game is not always available, because hunting and gathering are specialized skills, because women carrying heavy loads cannot hunt, and because women in hunter-gatherer societies are usually either pregnant or caring for young children, for most of the last two million years of human history men have hunted and women have gathered.

If male dominance depends on controlling the supply of meat, then the degree of male dominance in a society should vary with the amount of meat available and the amount supplied by the men. Some regions, like the East African grasslands and the North American woodlands, abounded with species of large mammals; other zones, like tropical forests and semideserts, are thinly populated with prey. Many elements affect the supply of game, but theoretically, the less meat provided exclusively by the men, the more egalitarian the society.

All known hunter-gatherer societies fit into four basic types: those in which men and women work together in communal hunts and as teams gathering edible plants, as did the Washo Indians of North America; those in which men and women each collect their own plant foods although the men supply some meat to the group, as do the Hadza of Tanzania; those in which male hunters and female gatherers work apart but return to camp each evening to share their acquisitions, as do the Tiwi of North Australia; and those in which the men provide all the food by hunting large game, as do the Eskimo. In each case the extent of male dominance increases directly with the proportion of meat supplied by individual men and small hunting parties.

Among the most egalitarian of hunter-gatherer societies are the Washo Indians, who inhabited the valleys of the Sierra Nevada in what is now southern California and Nevada. In the spring they moved north to Lake Tahoe for the large fish runs of sucker and native trout. Everyone—men, women, and children—participated in the fishing. Women spent the summer gathering edible berries and seeds while the men continued to fish. In the fall some men hunted deer but the most important source of animal protein was the jack rabbit, which was captured in communal hunts. Men and women together drove the rabbits into nets tied end to end. To provide food for the winter, husbands and wives worked as teams in the late fall to collect pine nuts.

Since everyone participated in most food-gathering activities, there were no individual distributors of food and relatively little difference in male and female rights. Men and women were not segregated from each other in daily activities; both were free to take lovers after marriage; both had the right to separate whenever they chose; menstruating women were not isolated from the rest of the group; and one of the two major Washo rituals celebrated hunting while the other celebrated gathering. Men were accorded more prestige if they had killed a deer, and men directed decisions about the seasonal movement of the group. But if no male leader stepped forward, women were permitted to lead. The distinctive feature of groups such as the Washo is the relative equality of the sexes.

The sexes are also relatively equal among the Hadza of Tanzania but this near-equality arises because men and women tend to work alone to feed themselves. They exchange little food. The Hadza lead a leisurely life in the seemingly barren environment of the East African Rift Gorge that is, in fact, rich in edible berries, roots, and small game. As a result of this abundance, from the time they are 10 years old,

Hadza men and women gather much of their own food. Women take their young children with them into the bush, eating as they forage, and collect only enough food for a light family meal in the evening. The men eat berries and roots as they hunt for small game, and should they bring down a rabbit or a hyrax, they eat the meat on the spot. Meat is carried back to the camp and shared with the rest of the group only on those rare occasions when a poisoned arrow brings down a large animal—an impala, a zebra, an eland, or a giraffe.

Because Hadza men distribute little meat, their status is only slightly higher than that of the women. People flock to the camp of a good hunter and the camp might take on his name because of his popularity, but he is in no sense a leader of the group. A Hadza man and a woman have an equal right to divorce and each can repudiate a marriage simply by living apart for a few weeks. Couples tend to live in the same camp as the wife's mother but they sometimes make long visits to the camp of the husband's mother. Although a man may take more than one wife, most Hadza males cannot afford to indulge in this luxury. In order to maintain a marriage, a man must supply both his wife and his mother-in-law with some meat and trade goods, such as beads and cloth, and the Hadza economy gives few men the wealth to provide for more than one wife and mother-in-law. Washo equality is based on cooperation; Hadza equality is based on independence.

In contrast to both these groups, among the Tiwi of Melville and Bathurst Islands off the northern coast of Australia, male hunters dominate female gatherers. The Tiwi are representative of the most common form of foraging society, in which the men supply large quantities of meat, although less than half the food consumed by the group. Each morning Tiwi women, most with babies on their backs, scatter in different directions in search of vegetables, grubs, worms, and small game such as bandicoots, lizards, and opossums. To track the game, they use hunting dogs. On most days women return to camp with some meat and with baskets full of *korka*, the nut of a native palm, which is soaked and mashed to make a porridge-like dish. The Tiwi men do not hunt small game and do not hunt every day, but when they do they often return with kangaroo, large lizards, fish, and game birds.

The porridge is cooked separately by each household and rarely shared outside the family, but the meat is prepared by a volunteer cook, who can be male or female. After the cook takes one of the parts of the animal traditionally reserved for him or her, the animal's "boss," the one who caught it, distributes the rest to all near kin and then to all others residing with the band. Although the small game supplied by the women is distributed in the same way as the big game supplied by the men, Tiwi men are dominant because the game they kill provides most of the meat.

The power of Tiwi men is clearest in their betrothal practices. Among the Tiwi, a woman must always be married. To ensure this, female infants are betrothed at birth and widows are remarried at the gravesides of their late husbands. Men form alliances by exchanging daughters, sisters, and mothers in marriage and some collect as many as 25 wives. Tiwi men value the quantity and quality of the food many wives can collect and the many children they can produce.

The dominance of the men is offset somewhat by the influence of adult women in selecting their next husbands. Many women are active strategists in the political careers of their male relatives, but to the exasperation of some sons attempting to promote their own futures, widowed mothers sometimes insist on selecting their own partners. Women also influence the marriages of their daughters and granddaughters, especially when the selected husband dies before the bestowed child moves to his camp.

Among the Eskimo, representative of the rarest type of forager society, inequality between the sexes is matched by inequality in supplying the group with food. Inland Eskimo men hunt caribou throughout the year to provision the entire society, and maritime Eskimo men depend on whaling, fishing, and some hunting to feed their extended families. The women process the carcasses, cut and sew skins to make clothing, cook, and care for the young; but they collect no food of their own and depend on the men to supply all the raw materials for their work. Since men provide all the meat, they also control the trade in hides, whale oil, seal oil, and other items that move between the maritime and inland Eskimos.

Eskimo women are treated almost exclusively as objects to be used, abused, and traded by men. After puberty all Eskimo girls are fair game for any interested male. A man shows his intentions by grabbing the belt of a woman and if she protests, he cuts off her trousers and forces himself upon her. These encounters are considered unimportant by the rest of the group. Men offer their wives' sexual services to establish alliances with trading partners and members of hunting and whaling parties.

Despite the consistent pattern of some degree of male dominance among foragers, most of these societies are egalitarian compared with agricultural and industrial societies. No forager has any significant opportunity for political leadership. Foragers, as a rule, do not like to give or take orders, and assume leadership only with reluctance. Shamans (those who are thought to be possessed by spirits) may be either male or female. Public rituals conducted by women in order to celebrate the first menstruation of girls are common, and the symbolism in these rituals is similar to that in the ceremonies that follow a boy's first kill.

In any society, status goes to those who control the distribution of valued goods and services outside the family. Equality arises when both sexes work side by side in food production, as do the Washo, and the products are simply distributed among the workers. In such circumstances, no person or sex has greater access to valued items than do others. But when women make no contribution to the food supply, as in the case of the Eskimo, they are completely subordinate.

When we attempt to apply these generalizations to contemporary industrial society, we can predict that as long as women spend their discretionary income from jobs on domestic needs, they will gain little social recognition and power. To be an effective source of power, money must be exchanged in ways that require returns and create obligations. In other words, it must be invested.

Jobs that do not give women control over valued resources will do little to advance their general status. Only as managers, executives, and professionals are women in a position to trade goods and services, to do others favors, and therefore to obligate others to them. Only as controllers of valued resources can women achieve prestige, power, and equality.

Within the household, women who bring in income from jobs are able to function on a more nearly equal basis with their husbands. Women who contribute services to their husbands and children without pay, as do some middle-class Western housewives, are especially vulnerable to dominance. Like Eskimo women, as long as their services are limited to domestic distribution they have little power relative to their husbands and none with respect to the outside world.

As for the limits imposed on women by their procreative functions in hunter-gatherer societies, childbearing and child care are organized around work as much as work is organized around reproduction. Some foraging groups space their children three to four years apart and have an average of only four to six children, far fewer than many women in other cultures. Hunter-gatherers nurse their infants for extended periods, sometimes for as long as four years. This custom suppresses ovulation and limits the size of their families. Sometimes, although rarely, they practice infanticide. By limiting reproduction, a woman who is gathering food has only one child to carry.

Different societies can and do adjust the frequency of birth and the care of children to accommodate whatever productive activities women customarily engage in. In horticultural societies, where women work long hours in gardens that may be far from home, infants get food to supplement their mothers' milk, older children take care of younger children, and pregnancies are widely spaced. Throughout the world, if a society requires a woman's labor, it finds ways to care for her children.

In the United States, as in some other industrial societies, the accelerated entry of women with preschool children into the labor force has resulted in the development of a variety of child-care arrangements. Individual women have called on friends, relatives, and neighbors. Public and private child-care centers are growing. We should realize that the declining birth rate, the increasing acceptance of childless or single-child families, and a de-emphasis on motherhood are adaptations to a sexual division of labor reminiscent of the system of production found in hunter-gatherer societies.

In many countries where women no longer devote most of their productive years to childbearing, they are beginning to demand a change in the social relationship of the sexes. As women gain access to positions that control the exchange of resources, male dominance may become archaic, and industrial societies may one day become as egalitarian as the Washo.

For further information:

Friedl, Ernestine. *Women and Men: An Anthropologist's View.* Holt, Rinehart and Winston, 1975.

Martin, M. Kay, and Barbara Voorhies, eds. *Female of the Species.* Columbia University Press, 1977.

Murphy, Yolanda, and Robert Murphy. *Women of the Forest.* Columbia University Press, 1974.

Reiter, Rayna, ed. *Toward an Anthropology of Women.* Monthly Review Press, 1975.

Rosaldo, M. Z., and Louise Lamphere, eds. *Women, Culture, and Society.* Stanford University Press, 1974.

Schlegel, Alice, ed. *Sexual Stratification: A Cross-Cultural View.* Columbia University Press, 1977.

Strathern, Marilyn. *Women In Between: Female Roles in a Male World.* Academic Press, 1972.

Daughters of the Forest

By Agnes Estioko-Griffin

In the textbook-case foraging society, hunting is a man's job. Anthropologists argue that a sexual division of labor makes sense. Women seem less suited physically for such strenuous activity, and in any case, hunting entails many risks that might endanger their children. The woman's role is to bear and raise babies, dig roots, pick berries, and maybe catch the occasional rabbit. Discussing "The Evolution of Hunting," Sherwood L. Washburn and C.S. Lancaster wrote that "when males hunt and females gather, the results are shared and given to the young, and the habitual sharing between a male, a female, and their offspring becomes the basis for the human family" (in *Man the Hunter,* edited by Richard B. Lee and Irven DeVore).

Taytayan Taginod and other Agta women in the Philippines have not heard this anthropological wisdom and would laugh if they did. Taytayan, now a young grandmother, has long hunted wild "bearded pigs," deer, monkeys, and a variety of smaller forest animals and has spearfished in dangerous rivers.

The Agta live in the Sierra Madre, a heavily forested mountain range that parallels the rugged Pacific coast of northeastern Luzon. The Agta do exploit some ocean resources, but it is the humid rain forest and its streams and rivers that dominate their lives. Traditionally, the forest provided not only food but also bark for clothing, palm fronds and saplings for houses, leaves for bedding, and wood for tools. Today, the Agta obtain metal tools, manufactured cloth, cooking pots, tobacco, and rice in trade for forest products—meat and fish, rattan, orchids, and Manila copal, a tree resin.

Extended family groups—clusters of two or three brothers and sisters, the old folks, and the children—are the living and working units of Agta society. All men hunt, except those living where the encroachment of agricultural groups has decimated the forest and game. Where only Agta live, game is plentiful. Wild pig and deer are abundant, although they fluctuate in numbers through various cycles. Plant foods are less readily available. Wild roots are scattered, difficult to dig, and give low returns for the effort expended. Today, Agta dig wild roots only in times of real hardship or when they feel a desire for traditional foods. They grow upland (dry) rice, corn, cassava, and sweet potatoes, but the yield from these crops is low. Given this situation, the Agta say it makes sense for women to be hunters. Women vary in their patterns of living, but many hunt and nearly all join the men in driving game.

Agta women differ from men in hunting tactics. Men love to enter the forest alone, where they stalk with bow and arrow, wait in ambush for hours by fallen fruit, or spot game at night with flashlights tied to their heads. Women are team hunters. They work with other women or with their men. They almost always prefer to drive with dogs and favor killing with long knives instead of bows and arrows (arrows are apt to endanger the dogs). They are seldom the fanatics that men are, but for some women, love of the hunt dominates all their work.

Taytayan is one of the enthusiasts, as my husband, P. Bion Griffin, and I learned as anthropological guests of her family. Taytayan learned to hunt from her husband, Galpong, whose second wife she had become at age sixteen. Taytayan's older sister, Littawan, was Galpong's first wife. Littawan had been unable to conceive; rather than divorce her, Galpong had taken the younger sister as well. Taytayan soon loved hunting with Galpong or Littawan or both. By the time we became acquainted, all three were mature adults and very successful hunters. Taytayan hunts several times a week, choosing, as the more active women hunters often do, to carry the bow and arrow and to nurture a pack of hunting dogs.

I recall the time she ran a deer for two days, until its feet were raw and bloody and exhaustion had slowed it to the point it could be shot. She had given up the hunt the first day, but the next day, she took her dogs, found the deer, and chased it until it collapsed. Other times she and Littawan hunted, Taytayan leaping ahead to shoot and kill, then asking Littawan to carry the carcass home. The kill, she felt, was fun, but lugging a pig home was no joy at all.

Taytayan takes pleasure in the Agta pastime of telling the story of a hunt. The presence of a tape recorder spurs her and others on, and gives the anthropologists (who can seldom keep up during the actual chase) a better insight into the activity. While Taytayan readily tells the stories of both successful and unsuccessful hunts, the following excerpt reveals much of the character and action of a good hunt.

"Littawan and I took off and walked way upstream.... 'Say, here are some deer tracks,' I said. We went up the side of Tagemuyo Mountain. No tracks there. We walked up the stream bed and crossed. We saw more deer tracks. The dogs were all over the hillside. We kept on but saw nothing. We crossed the stream again and went farther upstream. Those deer were really hiding. 'Hala, ha, ha, ha,' a monkey cried. 'Huu, huu,' I called to the dogs. Upstream there were more tracks. We continued, and I said, 'There are too many tracks! Where are the dogs?' 'Aah,

Photographs by P. Bion Griffin

aah,' I called to the dogs. I grouped the dogs together where the tracks were clustered. The dogs wouldn't stay together, and one, Tighe, was off on his own.

" 'Listen! That's a pig!' I said; 'Quick, after it!' Littawan urged the dogs on by calling 'Arah, arah, arah, arah!' 'Hurry up to the next stream!' she yelled. I ran around a pile of fallen rocks and earth and into a swarm of bees. They started stinging me all over my body. My hands became swollen; I was so upset I almost threw away my bow. I ran through the bushes and saw the pig, a large boar. The dogs, Littawan, and I ran after it downstream. I nocked my arrow; Tighe really bit the pig, but it broke loose. I couldn't shoot for fear of hitting the dogs. I finally got an arrow into it but didn't kill it. I then stabbed it several times.

"Littawan arrived and tied the pig for carrying. 'Are we going to butcher it here or carry it home?' she asked. 'Let's butcher it over there,' I said, 'or we'll starve to death.' We roasted the liver and some sweet potatoes I was carrying, and then I said, 'Let's go downriver and spearfish.' On the way, we gathered grass for broom making to sell to the lowlanders. I spearfished but only got three fish.

"When we got home, I hollered, 'Bion, come and take our picture, as we are carrying meat.' I was carrying the grass and my bow and arrows over my shoulder. That would make a good picture."

While Taytayan learned to hunt after she married, most girls learn before they reach puberty. Later they develop into hunters or give it up, as it suits them. In our camp, which contained twenty-five people, girls of age ten and up accompanied fathers, mothers, aunts, and grandmothers on hunts. The girls carried knives or no weapons at all, but ran as game was taken, helped hold and control the dogs, and aided in butchering and carrying home the kills. They learned to recognize the signs of game animals, the fruit and leaves they eat, and how they behave under different conditions. Abey, Taytayan's elderly sister-in-law, recalls learning to hunt as a prepubescent girl:

"My mother and I left for the forest. We took the hunting dogs along. We walked upriver. 'The dogs are chasing a young wild pig!' called Mother. 'Hurry up before they chew it up.' 'I can't walk because of the thorns,' I answered. My mother got angry. 'I am going to leave you behind,' she threatened. I started to cry; I didn't want to be left in the forest. My

Just like boys, Agta girls also play with bow and arrows. This photo shows a father teaching his six-year-old daughter how to nock an arrow properly.

mother hit me on the head with a stick. She ran off through the undergrowth and I grudgingly followed.

"We reached the place where the dogs had cornered the wild pig. My mother stabbed it with a knife until it died. She also hit the dogs because they kept attempting to drag the pig away. Still angry at me, she told me to carry the pig on my back. I took it down to the river to soak. I wanted to head home since I was already hungry. My mother, however, called the dogs and we proceeded upriver.

"The dogs jumped a deer, chased it, and bit its legs. It got away and ran into the river. Mother ran to it, held one of its legs, and stabbed it. 'Oh!' she screamed, 'It will gore me!' 'Take it into the deeper water!' I called. She grabbed and held the deer's head. It finally collapsed. 'Drag it to where the pig is,' she said. She butchered the deer. I gathered firewood, built a fire, and burned the hair off the pig. After Mother finished the deer, she butchered the pig. I roasted the liver and we both ate.

"Mother sent me to cut vines for mak-

An Agta woman hunter returns from a hunting-fishing trip. She is carrying her bow and arrows, a pack of butchered wild pig, and a string of river fish. One of her hunting dogs follows behind.

ing a pack to carry the meat. She gave me three legs to carry and we proceeded downriver. My pack was so heavy I was really staggering."

Now a grandmother, Abey is again the weak one, as she hunts with her older daughter, Iring. On one trip, she and Iring killed a pig; Iring carried her one-year-old son on her back. We photographed the dead pig and recorded Iring's tale:

" 'Let's keep on walking, Mother,' I said. She answered, 'Wait there for me, because my thighs hurt from climbing up the mountainside.' I walked along with my baby on my back. I was annoyed at Talengteng [the baby] because he was noisy while I was running. We climbed up the steep trail, I on my hands and knees . . . .

"Mother asked, 'What is that howling?' 'Ho, ho, ho,' howled [the dog] Baklayan. I thought, this old woman has weak hearing. That's just a young pig, judging from the pitch of the howling. I had to go faster because my mother couldn't run fast enough. As soon as the old woman arrived, she clubbed the pig on the head, but it wouldn't die. She clubbed it again, but it

still would not die. I cut vines for tying the pig. She finished tying it, and I took the bow and arrows. The pig was still breathing hard tied to Mother's back. We walked and walked, rested, and chewed betel. While we descended the hill, Mother complained, 'That old dog is useless. It would have been better if I had reached the pig and stabbed it.' "

Just how effective are women hunters? My husband and I collected quantitative data and kept daily logs of activities. Of the 296 hunting trips we logged, men made 180, either singly or in groups that included no women. Another 61 trips were male–female team efforts. Trips involving only women numbered 55. Men, then, are more frequent hunters, but women also participate actively.

The greater frequency of hunting by men is reflected in the percentage of carcass weight they bring home. In our sample, men provided 43 percent of the animals by body weight. Hunting by women accounted for 22 percent, while mixed teams got 35 percent. These figures are

also the outcome of differences in hunting techniques.

Men use various tactics and often hunt alone. They lie in wait by fallen fruit to ambush the pigs and deer drawn to feed, or they stalk their prey under cover of jungle thickets. The average pig or deer killed by men using these tactics is larger than that brought down by women, although the better women hunters do kill large, adult game. The power of arrows shot from bows with sixty-pound pull also contributes to men's success in killing large animals. Women's bows seldom pull more than forty-five pounds. Of course, only the best hunters, male and female, regularly get the heaviest game.

While women's contribution by carcass weight is smaller, their hunting success rate is high. In the course of the 296 hunts we tabulated, 73 kills were made. The 180 "men only" trips brought in 31 kills, achieving a 17 percent rate of return. In comparison, women totaled 31 percent, and mixed teams of both men and women totaled 41 percent. These figures show that the use of teamwork and dogs yields the highest kill ratios.

Most of the trips by women involved dogs. Dog teams are expensive to maintain, perform poorly in rainy weather, and frequently die from game attacks, illness, or malnutrition. Well-trained, mature, healthy dogs, however, can be of critical importance to the hunt. Two different tactics may be used. In the first, hunters proceed into the forest and station themselves at ambush points where game is likely to pass. Then, one or more hunters with dogs enter the forest, hoping to surprise game and drive it to the ambushers. The second tactic is for a small team, say a husband and wife or two women, to travel with their dogs until an animal is located. Then, as Taytayan recounted, the chase is on, and the hunters expend huge amounts of energy covering rugged terrain. Very often the animal escapes, but good dogs help insure success.

Just as there is overlap, as well as a difference, in how men and women hunt in Agta society, so too the division of labor in other areas is a matter of emphasis. Everybody spearfishes, for example. Although women in foraging societies worldwide have usually been excluded from hunting, they have often been fishers in coastal and riverine environments.

Among the Agta, spearfishing is done under water, by swimmers wearing primitive goggles and using a large rubber band to propel a wire projectile. Some fishing is in deep, fast, cold rivers; some in slow and shallow streams. Children start learning to fish when little more than toddlers, eventually turning play into a skill. Boys and girls make forays to streams for safe, shallow-water fishing, their catches becoming picnic snacks. Teen-agers join adults in fishing the larger rivers where large fish abound. Women truly excel in this often daily activity. Nearly all females, from twelve years old to the very old, spearfish.

One of the most important of the Agta's food-getting pursuits, fishing may, in the dry season, provide nearly all their animal protein for days at a time. Even people who are not strong enough for the most rigorous fishing occasionally participate in the special fish drives. Women in advanced pregnancy, the elderly, and the lame may drag the rattan lines, tied with fronds, that span the river and chase fish to the swimmers.

Another large part of women's work among the Agta consists of gathering plant foods, shellfish, honey, and the multitude of items needed for medicines and camp maintenance. Even here, however, men are hardly excluded. Everybody collects honey, with women ably climbing the trees to cut down combs, except when young men can be talked into the task. (Women do not like to climb if they are wearing skirts; modest jogging shorts are the favored attire for work in the forest.) Frequently, all the adults and children in a camp take off for an outing along the beaches of rock and coral, where mollusks and crustaceans are to be had. Men limit their beach activities to spear and line fishing, however.

Women and children are the primary gatherers of wild roots and other plant foods. Men seldom join the women in digging up roots, whether cultivated or wild, and although they work at clearing and planting the family's small plot of dry rice, they are less likely to help harvest the crop. Whole families may work together in cutting the caryota palm tree, extracting the starch-laden pith, and packing the food home. More often, however, parties of women and girls do this arduous work, with lots of joking and horseplay throughout the long day.

As we examine all the work done by women, hunting and its supposed limitations on child rearing come into better perspective. Taytayan and her family exemplify efforts to harmonize food getting and general work with the bearing and raising of children.

Taytayan bore four children, two girls and two boys: only the two daughters survived. In this experience she was typical. We found that one-third to one-half of Agta children die before puberty. Tom Headland, a missionary-anthropologist working many miles to our south, found that about half the children die. In his area, the Agta have been more exposed to the destructive effects of newcomers—disease, alcohol, and depletion of game.

Children are a part of nearly all Agta activities. While older children may be left with baby sitters, nursing infants are carried on their mothers' backs not only on occasional hunting trips but also on forest excursions to secure building materials and food. This day in, day out exposure, which sometimes subjects them to wet and cold conditions, certainly contributes to the illnesses that kill many. Mothers shelter their children from bad weather whenever possible, however, and avoid hunting under such conditions. So although hunting is rigorous, it does not pose any special danger to infants.

Taytayan's two daughters are now rearing families. The elder has four surviving children, while the younger, married only in 1978, has two. Both women learned to hunt with their mother, but now hunt primarily with their husbands. They neglect bows and arrows, preferring to carry only knives. During pregnancy they hunted less, and not until the babies were about six months old did they begin to carry them on short hunts.

Taytayan continues to go after wild pigs, deer, and monkeys, while also tending her grandchildren, even adopting the eldest. Now her companions include nieces, nephews, and, of course, Littawan. Her daughters find her difficult to keep up with because of her vigor and enthusiasm. Taytayan once expressed her interest in rumored "fertility drugs" to me. I asked how in the world she would hunt if she had another baby. "No problem," she said, "Littawan can carry it while we hunt."

Mothers and females in general are most decidedly the major child tenders in Agta society. Mothers do the greatest share, followed by elder sisters and grandmothers. Fathers are fourth, but still spend a significant amount of time caring for their children. Young fathers of two or three children assist their wives in child care every day. These fathers often carry older children, aged about three to eight, on foraging trips outside of camp, tending the children while mothers spearfish or gather. My husband and I have often joined these family expeditions. One of my husband's favorite activities was to accompany a father or grandfather and children on some forest task; the anthropologist had no trouble keeping up with the smaller children!

We even know one little girl of about seven, an only child, who was taken by her devoted father on short hunts. Of course, she did not hunt, and she had to be carried for part of the trip. She did, however, begin to take in the whole world of hunting—the sights, sounds, feelings, and spirit of moving through the jungle in hopes of killing prey. As she grows older, she will learn that women and men are not identical in hunting or in any other aspect of their lives. A division of labor by sex does exist in Agta society. But it is flexible, subject to individual needs and preferences. Women adjust hunting and child rearing to each other and to their other subsistence efforts. If they choose, they too can "bring home the bacon."

Life Behind the Veil

By Cherry Lindholm and Charles Lindholm

....

The bazaar teems with activity. Pedestrians throng the narrow streets, wending past donkey carts, cyclists and overloaded vehicles. Vendors haggle in the dark doorways of their shops. Pitiful beggars shuffle among the crowds, while bearded religious mendicants wander about, their eyes fixed on a distant world.

Drifting among the mobs of men are, here and there, anonymous figures hidden beneath voluminous folds of material, who float along like ships in full sail, graceful, mysterious, faceless, instilling in the observer a sense both of awe and of curiosity. These are the Moslem women of the Middle East. Their dress is the customary *chador*, which they wear when obliged to leave the privacy of their homes. The *chador* is but one means by which women maintain their *purdah*, the institution of female seclusion, which requires that women should remain unseen by men who are not close relatives and strikes Westerners as so totally foreign and incomprehensible.

Sometimes the alien aspect is tempered with a touch of Western familiarity. A pair of plastic sunglasses may gleam from behind the lace that covers the eyes, or a platform shoe might peep forth from beneath the hem of the flowing *chador*. Nevertheless, the overall presence remains one of inscrutability and is perhaps the most striking image of Middle Eastern societies.

We spent nine months in one of the most strict of all the *purdah* societies, the Yusufzai Pakhtun of the Swat Valley in the North-West Frontier Province of Pakistan. ("Pakhtun" is the designation preferred by the tribesmen, who were generally called Pathans in the days of the British *raj*.)

We had come to the Swat Valley after a hair-raising ride on a rickety bus from Peshawar over the 10,280-foot Malakand Pass. Winston Churchill came this way as a young war correspondent attached to the Malakand Field Force in 1897. As we came into the valley, about half the size of Connecticut, we passed a sign that said WELCOME TO SWAT. We were fortunate to have entrée into the community through a Swati friend we had made eight years before. In Swat, women are secluded inside the domestic compound except for family rituals, such as marriage, circumcision and funerals, or visits to saints' tombs. A woman must always be in the protective company of other women and is never allowed out alone. It tells a great deal about the community that the word for husband in Pakhto, the language of the Pakhtun, is *khawund*, which also means God.

However, as everywhere, rules are sometimes broken or, more frequently, cleverly manipulated. Our Pakhtun host's stepmother, Bibi, an intelligent and forceful woman, was renowned for her tactics. Once, when all the females of the household had been forbidden to leave the compound to receive cholera inoculations at the temporary clinic next door, Bibi respectfully bowed her head and assured the men they could visit the mosque with easy minds. Once the men had gone, she promptly climbed the ladder to the flat roof and summoned the doctor to the door of her compound. One by one, the women extended their bare arms through the doorway and received their shots. Later, Bibi could honestly swear that no woman had set foot outside the compound walls.

Despite such circumventions, *purdah* is of paramount importance in Swat. As one Pakhtun proverb succinctly states: "The woman's place is in the home or the grave." Years ago in Swat, if a woman broke her *purdah*, her husband might kill her or cut off her nose as punishment and as a means of cleansing his honor. If a woman is caught alone with a unrelated man, it will always be assumed that the liaison is sexual, and public opinion will oblige her husband to shoot her, even if he does not desire her death; to go unavenged is to be known henceforth as *begherata*, or man without honor. As such, he would no longer have the right to call himself Pakhtun.

A shameless woman is a threat to the whole society. Our host remembered witnessing, 30 years ago when he was a child, the entire village stoning an adulteress. This punishment is prescribed by Islamic law, though the law requires there be four witnesses to the sexual act itself to establish guilt. Nowadays, punishments for wifely misdemeanors have become less harsh, though adulterous wives are still killed.

SEDUCTION

In the rural areas, poorer families generally cannot maintain *purdah* as rigorously as their wealthier neighbors, for often the wife must help her husband in the fields or become a servant. Nevertheless, she is required to keep her hair covered at all times and to interact with men to a minimum. Here again, the rules are sometimes flouted, and a poor woman might entice a man with her eyes or even, according to village men who claimed personal experiences, become more aggressive in her seductive attempts and actually seize a man in a deserted alleyway and lure him into her house. Often, the man is persuaded. Such a woman will accept money from her lover, who is usually a man from a wealthy family. Her husband is then a *begherata*, but some men acquiesce to the situation because of the money the wife is earning or because of fear of the wife's socially superior and more powerful lover. But most poor men,

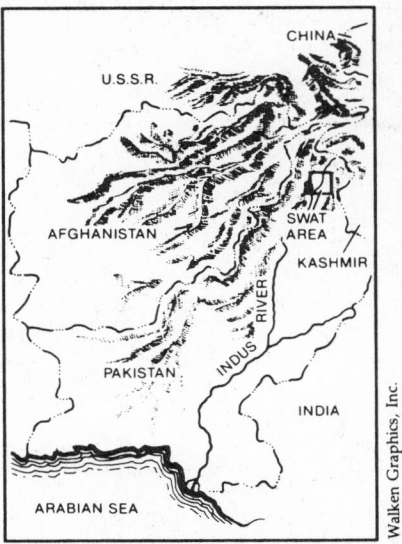

Swat is reached by a 10,280-foot deep pass in the mountains of the Hindu Kush.

and certainly all of the elite, keep their women under strict control.

In the Islamic Middle East, women are viewed as powerful and dangerous beings, highly sexual and lacking in personal discipline and discrimination. In Middle Eastern thought, sexual intercourse itself, though polluting, lacks the same negative connotations it has in the West. It has always been believed that women have sexual climaxes, and there is no notion of female frigidity. Male impotence, however, is well-documented, and some middle-aged and even young men admitted to us that they had lost their interest in women. Sometimes, though rarely, a young bridegroom will find himself incapable of consummating his marriage, either because he finds his bride unattractive or because he has been previously enchanted by a male lover and has become impotent in a heterosexual relationship. Homosexuality has never been seen as aberrant in the Middle East. As a famous Afghan saying humorously declares: "A woman is for bearing children, a boy is for pleasure, but ecstasy is a ripe watermelon!" However, with Western influence, homosexuality in the Middle East is now less overt. But even when it was common and open, the man was still expected to marry and produce children.

Men must marry, though women are regarded as a chaotic and anarchic force. They are believed to possess many times the sexual desire of men and constitute a potential threat to the family and the family's honor, which is based in large measure on the possession and control of women and their excessive and dangerous sexuality.

Among the Pakhtun of Swat, where the male-female relation is one of the most hostile in the Middle East, the man avoids showing affection to his wife, for fear she will become too self-confident and will begin to assert herself in ways that insult his position and honor. She may start by leaving the compound without his permission and, if unchecked, may end by bringing outside men into the house for sexual encounters, secure in the knowledge that her husband, weakened by his affection for her, will not take action. This course of events is considered inevitable by men and women alike and was illustrated by a few actual cases in the village where we lived.

Women are therefore much feared, despite the pronouncements of male supremacy. They must be controlled, in order to prevent their alarming basic natures from coming to the fore and causing dishonor to their own lineages. *Purdah* is generally described as a system that serves to protect the woman, but implicitly it protects the men and society in general from the potentially disruptive actions of the powerful female sex.

Changes are occurring, however, particularly in the modern urban centers. The educated urban woman often dispenses with the *chador,* replacing it with a simple length of veiling draped over the head or across the shoulders; she may even decide to adopt modest Western dress. The extent of this transformation will depend partly upon the attitude of the community in which she lives.

In the urban centers of the stricter *purdah* regions the public display of *purdah* is scrupulous, sometimes even more striking than that of the tribal village. Behind the scenes, though, the city-dwelling woman does have more freedom than she would have in the village. She will be able to visit not only relatives but friends without specific permission from her husband, who is out at work all day. She may, suitably veiled, go shopping in the bazaar, a chore her husband would have undertaken in the village. On the whole, the city woman will have a great deal more independence, and city men sometimes lament this weakening of traditional male domination.

The urbanized male may speak of the custom-bound tribesmen (such as the Swat Pakhtun, the Bedouin nomads of Saudi Arabia or the Qashqai herdsmen of Iran) as country bumpkins, yet he still considers their central values, their sense of personal pride, honor and autonomy, as cultural ideals and views the tribesmen, in a very real way, as exemplars of the proper mode of life. Elite families in the cities proudly emphasize their tribal heritage and sometimes send their sons to live for a year or so with distant tribal cousins, in order to expose them to the tribesman's integrity and moral code. The tribesman, on the other hand, views his urbanized relatives as weak and womanly, especially with reference to the slackening of *purdah* in the cities. Though the *purdah* female, both in the cities and in the tribal areas, rarely personifies the ideal virtues of silence, submission and obedience, the concept of *purdah* and male supremacy remains central to the male identity and to the ideology of the culture as a whole.

The dynamic beneath the notion of male supremacy, the institution of *purdah* and the ideology of women's sexual power becomes apparent when one takes an overall view of the social structure. The family in the Middle East, particularly in the tribal regions, is not an isolated element; kinship and marriage are the underlying principles that structure action and thought. Individuals interact not so much according to personal preference as according to kinship.

The Middle Eastern kinship system is known to anthropologists as a segmentary-lineage organization; the basic idea is that kinship is traced through one line only. In the Middle East, the system is patrilineal, which means that the male line is followed, and all the links through women are ignored. An individual can therefore trace his relationship to any other individual in the society and know the exact genealogical distance between them; i.e., the distance that must be traced to reach a common male ancestor. The system obliges men to defend their patrilineal relatives if they are attacked, but if there is no external force threatening the lineage, then men struggle against one another according to the principle of genealogical distance. This principle is nicely stated in a famous Middle Eastern proverb: "I against my brothers; my brothers and I against my cousins; my cousins, my brothers and I against the world." The cousins in question are of course patrilineal.

PROMISCUITY PHOBIA

Within this system, women appear to have no role, though they are the units of reproduction, the mothers of the sons who will carry on the patriline. Strange as it may seem, this is the core contradiction of the society: The "pure" patriline itself is actually descended from a woman. This helps explain the exaggerated fear of women's promiscuity and supposedly voracious sexuality. In order to protect the patriline, women must be isolated and guarded. Their sexuality, which threatens the integrity of the patriline, must be made the exclusive property of their husbands. Women, while being absolutely necessary for the perpetuation of the social order, are simultaneously the greatest threat to it.

The persistent denigration of women is explained by this core contradiction. Moslem society considers women naturally inferior in intelligence and ability—childlike, incapable of discernment, incompetent to testify in court, prey to whims and fancies. In tribal areas, women are prohibited from inheritance, despite a Koranic injunction, and in marriage they are purchased from their fathers like a commodity. Were women not feared, these denials of her personhood would be unnecessary.

Another unique element of Middle Eastern culture is the prevalence of marriage with the father's brother's daughter. In many areas, in fact, this marriage is so favored that a boy must give explicit permission to allow his patrilineal female cousin to marry elsewhere. This peculiar marriage form, which is found nowhere else in the world, also serves to negate the woman by merging her lineage with that of her husband, since both are members of the same patriline (indeed, are the offspring of brothers). No new blood enters, and the sanctity of the patriline is steadily maintained.

However, this ploy gives rise to other problems: Cousin marriage often divides the brothers rather than uniting them. Although the bride-price is usually reduced in such marriages, it is always demanded, thus turning the brothers into opponents in a business negotiation. Furthermore, giving a woman in Swat carries an implication of inferiority; historically, victors in war took women from the vanquished. Cousin marriage thus renders the brothers' equality questionable. Finally, the young couple's fights will further alienate the brothers, especially since such marriages are notoriously contentious. This is because patrilineal male cousins are rivals for the common grandfather's inheritance (in fact, the Swati term for father's brother's son is *tarbur*, which also means enemy), and a man who marries his patrilineal cousin is mar-

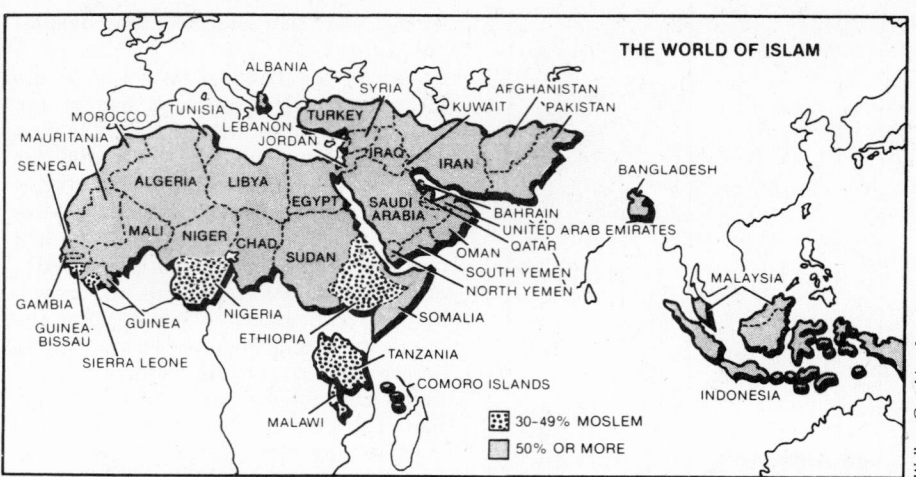

The world of Islam began when Mohammed preached in Saudi Arabia in the seventh century. It fanned out, carrying purdah with it, into Asia and into Africa south of the Sahara.

rying the sister of his lifelong opponent. Her loyalty is with her brother, and this is bound to cause frequent disputes.

Though the girl is treated like goods, she does not see herself as such. The fundamental premise of tribal life is the equality of the various landed families. There are very few hierarchies in these societies, and even the leaders are often no more than first among equals. Within this system, which has been described as a nearly perfect democracy, each *khan* (which means landowner and literally translates as king) family sees itself as superior to all others. The girls of the household feel the same pride in their lineage as their brothers and cannot help but regard their husbands' families through jaundiced eyes. The new bride is prepared to defend the honor of her family, even though they have partially repudiated her by negotiating the marriage. Her identity, like that of a man, rests on her lineage pride, which she will fight to uphold. The husband, meanwhile, is determined to demonstrate his domination and mastery, since control of women is the nexus of a man's sense of self-respect.

Hostility is thus built into marriage by the very structure of the society, which pits every lineage against every other in a never-ending contest to maintain an equilibrium of power within this markedly egalitarian culture. The hostility of the marriage bond is evident from its beginnings. The reluctant bride is torn from her cot in her family's house and ensconced on a palanquin that strongly resembles a bier. The war drums that announce the marriage procession indicate the nature of the tie, as does the stoning of the palanquin by the small boys of the

village as it is carried through the dusty streets. When the bride arrives at her new husband's house, his family triumphantly fires their rifles into the air. They have taken a woman! The young wife cowers in her veils as she is prodded and poked curiously by the females of the husband's house who try to persuade her to show her face. The groom himself is nowhere to be seen, having retreated to the men's house in shame. In three days, he will creep to her room and consummate the marriage. Taking the virginity of the bride is a highly charged symbolic act, and in some areas of the Middle East the display of the bloody nuptial sheet to the public is a vital part of the wedding rite. Breaking the hymen demonstrates the husband's possession of his wife's sexuality. She then becomes the most junior adult in the household, subordinate to everyone, but, most especially, under the heavy thumb of her mother-in-law.

The household the bride enters will be that of her husband's father, since the system, as well as being patrilineal, is also patrilocal. She will be surrounded by his relatives and will be alone with her husband only at night. During the day he will pay no attention to her, for it is considered shameful for a man to take note of his wife in front of others, particularly his father and mother. Within the compound walls, which shield the household from the rest of the world, she is at the mercy of her new family.

DOMESTIC BATTLES
Life within the compound is hardly peaceful. Wives squabble among themselves, and wives who have built a power base by having sons even quarrel with the

old matriarch, their mother-in law. This is usually a prelude to a couple moving out of the house into their own compound, and husbands always blame their wives for the breakup of the extended family, even though they, too, will be glad to become the masters of their own homes and households.

But the worst fights among women are the fights between women married to the same man. Islam permits polygamous marriage, and legally a man may have four wives. Not all men are financially able to take more than one wife, but most men dream of marrying again, despite the Swati proverb that says, "I may be a fool, but not so much of a fool as the man with two wives." Men who can afford it often do take a second wife. The reason is not sexual desire, for wives do not mind if their husbands have liaisons with prostitutes or promiscuous poor women. Rather, the second wife is brought in to humiliate an overly assertive first wife. Bringing in a second wife is a terrible insult; it is an expression of contempt for the first wife and her entire lineage. The insult is especially cutting in Swat, where divorce is prohibited (though it is permitted in the Koran) and where a disliked wife must either endure her lot or retreat to her family's house and a life of celibacy. Small wonder then that households with two wives are pits of intrigue, vituperation and magical incantation, as each wife seeks to expel the other. The Koran says a man should only practice polygamy if he is sure he can treat each wife equally; the only man we met who was able to approximate this ideal was a man who never went home. He spent his time in the men's house, talking with his cronies and having his meals sent to him.

The men's house is the best-built structure in any village, along with the mosque, which is also prohibited to women. It is a meeting place for the clan, the center for hospitality and refuge and the arena for political manipulation. This is where the visitor will be received, surrounded by men who gossip, doze or clean their rifles. Here, the guest might well imagine that women do not even exist. Only the tea and food that is sent over from the compound nearby tell him of the women working behind the walls.

Formerly, in Swat, most men slept in the men's house, visiting their wives secretly late at night and returning before daybreak. But now only a few elders and some ne'er-do-well youths live permanently in the elegant, aging buildings.

Sometimes, however, a man may be obliged to move to the men's house for a few days if his wife makes his home too uncomfortable, for women too have their own weapons in the household battles. Arguments may flare up over almost anything: the husband buying a rotten piece of meat or forgetting to bring home a length of material, the wife ruining some curd or gossiping too much with a neighbor. The wife may then angrily refuse to cook, obliging the husband to retreat to the men's house for food. The man's weapon in fights is violence, while the woman can withdraw domestic services at will.

In the early days of a marriage, when the bride is new to the household and surrounded by her husband's people, she may be fairly meek. But when her status has improved as a result of producing sons, she will become more aggressive. Her lacerating tongue is renowned, and she will also begin to fight back physically as well as verbally. Finally, her exasperated husband may silence her with a blow from a heavy stick he keeps for that purpose. No shame is attached to beating one's wife, and men laugh about beatings they have administered. The women themselves, though they decry their men's brutality, proudly display their scars and bruises, characterizing a neighbor who is relatively gentle to his wife as "a man with no penis."

The older a woman gets, the more powerful and fearless she becomes. She is aided by her sons who, though respecting their father, regard him as an obstacle to their gaining rights in land. The old man, who gains his stature from his landholding, is always reluctant to allot shares to his grown sons. Furthermore, the sons' ties of affection are much stronger with the mother. The elderly father, who is generally 10 or 15 years older than his wife, is thus surrounded by animosity in his own house. The situation of the earlier years has reversed itself, and the wife, who began alone and friendless, gains allies in her old age, while the husband becomes isolated. Ghani Khan, a modern Pakhtun writer, has described the situation well: "The Pakhtun thinks he is as good as anyone else and his father rolled into one and is fool enough to try this even with his wife. She pays for it in her youth, and he in his old age."

But many women do not live to see their triumph. In northern Swat, for every 100 women over the age of 60 there are 149 men, compared to the more equal

100 to 108 ratio below 60. The women are worn out by continual childbearing, breast-feeding and a lack of protein. Though fertile in places, the Swat valley is heavily overpopulated with an estimated one million people, and survival is always difficult. The diet consists chiefly of bread, rice, seasonal vegetables and some dairy products. Meat is a rarity and goes to the men and boys as a matter of course. They perpetuate the patrilineal clan and must survive, while women can always be replaced. The lives of men are hard, but the lives of women are harder, as witnessed by their early deaths.

In this environment, people must learn to be tough, just as they must learn to fit the structure of the patrilineal system. Child-rearing serves both functions.

The birth of a boy in Swat is greeted by rejoicing, while the birth of a girl is an occasion for gloom. But the first few years for both sexes are virtually identical. Like most Middle Easterners, the Swatis practice swaddling, binding the baby tightly so that it is immobilized. Ostensibly, this is to help the baby sleep and prevent it from blinding itself with its flailing hands, but anthropologists have hypothesized that swaddling actually serves to develop a certain character type: a type which can withstand great restraint but which also tends to uncontrolled bursts of temper. This hypothesis fits Swat, where privation and the exigencies of the social structure demand stoicism, but where violent temper is also useful. We often saw Swati children of all ages lose themselves in tantrums to coerce their parents, and such coercion was usually successful. Grown men and women as well are prone to fits of temper, and this dangerous aspect makes their enemies leery of pressing them too hard.

Both sexes are indoctrinated in the virtues of their family and its lineage. In marital fights this training is obvious, as both partners heatedly assert, "Your ancestor was nothing, and mine was great!" At a man's death his sister, not his wife, is his chief mourner. And if a woman is killed it is her brother, not her husband, who avenges her.

Child training in Swat produces strong characters. When they give affection, they give it wholeheartedly, and when they hate, they hate bitterly. The conditions under which they live are cruel and cramped, and they respond with cruelty and rigidity in order to survive. But at the same time, the people are able to bear their hard lives with pride and dignity.

Belief and Ritual

"As members of society, most of us see only what we expect to see, and what we expect to see is what we are conditioned to see when we have learned the definitions and classifications of our culture," anthropologist Victor Turner has observed. But the statement is incomplete; it omits any mention of *beliefs*—bodies of assumptions about the nature of things bolstered by selected facts—which are embedded in every culture and, along with the categories Turner mentions, powerfully organize our experiences of the world around us.

Belief systems deal with everything human beings can perceive and can imagine. Instrumental, or rational-technical, belief systems are concerned primarily with concrete phenomena and tasks. What kind of person makes a good spouse? Which stocks are likely to yield bushels of money to investors? What training methods and dietary regimens should Olympic swimmers undergo? Instrumental beliefs provide answers to these and countless other questions concerning day-to-day existence.

Other beliefs take us beyond daily concerns and address more profound issues, such as the purpose of human existence, the phenomenon of death, and the existence of entities that inherently cannot be verified by the human senses. Such transcendental beliefs always invoke the larger picture when they address concrete tasks or specific issues, as in the case of the Bolivian tin miners described by June Nash in "Devils, Witches, and Sudden Death." Without their instrumental and transcendental beliefs, these miners could hardly be expected to cope with the extreme stresses of their extraordinarily dangerous work.

Closer to home, Nathan L. Gerrard, in "The Serpent-Handling Religions of West Virginia," describes the beliefs of some fundamentalist Christian sects that have incorpo-rated deadly snakes into their religious services. The adherents of these sects see each recovery from snakebite as a miracle wrought by God, whereas each death is evidence of how dangerous and difficult it is to obey the Lord's commandments.

In "The Secrets of Haiti's Living Dead," Gino Del Guercio describes the fascinating world of voodoo. Legend has it that zombies are the living dead, raised from their graves by voodoo priests. When Harvard ethnobotanist Wade Davis went to Haiti in 1982, he definitely did not believe in zombies. He learned that voodoo is an integral aspect of a cohesive Haitian culture and social structure. What he discovered about zombies lies at the intersection of religious belief and modern science. Davis's book about his experiences, *The Serpent and the Rainbow*, was released as a motion picture in 1988.

Rituals are repeated and stereotyped activities, handed down from generation to generation, and they express certain transcendental and instrumental beliefs. Often, rituals mark important social transitions, such as birth, puberty, marriage, and death. In "Cargo Cults," Peter M. Worsley narrates the emergence of a complex of beliefs and rituals in the South Pacific as the indigenous cultures were subjected to severe stresses following contact with the industrial world. The cargo cults incorporated symbolic representations of industrial technology to bolster traditional belief systems, which were increasingly difficult to sustain in the context of invading armies during World War II—a paradox indeed. But rituals seem uniquely suited to the resolution, on an entirely different level, of those inevitable contradictions that people everywhere must cope with in their daily lives.

Cargo Cults

By Peter M. Worsley

Patrols of the Australian Government venturing into the "uncontrolled" central highlands of New Guinea in 1946 found the primitive people there swept up in a wave of religious excitement. Prophecy was being fulfilled: The arrival of the Whites was the sign that the end of the world was at hand. The natives proceeded to butcher all of their pigs—animals that were not only a principal source of subsistence but also symbols of social status and ritual preeminence in their culture. They killed these valued animals in expression of the belief that after three days of darkness "Great Pigs" would appear from the sky. Food, firewood and other necessities had to be stock-piled to see the people through to the arrival of the Great Pigs. Mock wireless antennae of bamboo and rope had been erected to receive in advance the news of the millennium. Many believed that with the great event they would exchange their black skins for white ones.

This bizarre episode is by no means the single event of its kind in the murky history of the collision of European civilization with the indigenous cultures of the southwest Pacific. For more than 100 years traders and missionaries have been reporting similar disturbances among the peoples of Melanesia, the group of Negro-inhabited islands (including New Guinea, Fiji, the Solomons and the New Hebrides) lying between Australia and the open Pacific Ocean. Though their technologies were based largely upon stone and wood, these peoples had highly developed cultures, as measured by the standards of maritime and agricultural ingenuity, the complexity of their varied social organizations and the elaboration of religious belief and ritual. They were nonetheless ill prepared for

the shock of the encounter with the Whites, a people so radically different from themselves and so infinitely more powerful. The sudden transition from the society of the ceremonial stone ax to the society of sailing ships and now of airplanes has not been easy to make.

After four centuries of Western expansion, the densely populated central highlands of New Guinea remain one of the few regions where the people still carry on their primitive existence in complete independence of the world outside. Yet as the agents of the Australian Government penetrate into ever more remote mountain valleys, they find these backwaters of antiquity already deeply disturbed by contact with the ideas and artifacts of European civilization. For "cargo"—Pidgin English for trade goods—has long flowed along the indigenous channels of communication from the seacoast into the wilderness. With it has traveled the frightening knowledge of the white man's magical power. No small element in the white man's magic is the hopeful message sent abroad by his missionaries: the news that a Messiah will come and that the present order of Creation will end.

The people of the central highlands of New Guinea are only the latest to be gripped in the recurrent religious frenzy of the "cargo cults." However variously embellished with details from native myth and Christian belief, these cults all advance the same central theme: the world is about to end in a terrible cataclysm. Thereafter God, the ancestors or some local culture hero will appear and inaugurate a blissful paradise on earth. Death, old age, illness and evil will be unknown. The riches of the white man will accrue to the Melanesians.

Although the news of such a movement in one area has doubtless often inspired similar movements in other areas, the evidence indicates that these cults have arisen independently in many places as parallel responses to the same enormous social stress and strain. Among the movements best known to students of Melanesia are the "Taro Cult" of New Guinea, the "Vailala Madness" of Papua, the "Naked Cult" of Espiritu Santo, the "John Frum Movement" of the New Hebrides and the "Tuka Cult" of the Fiji Islands.

At times the cults have been so well organized and fanatically persistent that they have brought the work of government to a standstill. The outbreaks have often taken the authorities completely by surprise and have confronted them with mass opposition of an alarming kind. In the 1930s, for example, villagers in the vicinity of Wewak, New Guinea, were stirred by a succession of "Black King" movements. The prophets announced that the Europeans would soon leave the island, abandoning their property to the natives, and urged their followers to cease paying taxes, since the government station was about to disappear into the sea in a great earthquake. To the tiny community of Whites in charge of the region, such talk was dangerous. The authorities jailed four of the prophets and exiled three others. In yet another movement, that sprang up in declared opposition to the local Christian mission, the cult leader took Satan as his god.

Troops on both sides in World War II found their arrival in Melanesia heralded as a sign of the Apocalypse. The G.I.'s who landed in the New Hebrides, moving up for the bloody fighting on Guadalcanal, found the natives furiously at work preparing airfields, roads and docks for the magic ships and planes that they believed were coming from "Rusefel" (Roosevelt), the friendly king of America.

The Japanese also encountered millenarian visionaries during their southward march to Guadalcanal. Indeed, one of the strangest minor military actions of World War II occurred in Dutch New Guinea, when Japanese forces had to be turned against the local Papuan inhabitants of the Geelvink Bay region. The Japanese had at first been received with great joy, not because their "Greater East Asia Co-Prosperity Sphere" propaganda had made any great impact upon the Papuans, but because the natives regarded them as harbingers of the new world that was dawning, the flight of the Dutch having already given the first sign. Mansren, creator of the islands and their peoples, would now return, bringing with him the ancestral dead. All this had been known, the cult leaders declared, to the crafty Dutch, who had torn out the first page of the Bible where these truths were inscribed. When Mansren returned, the existing world order would be entirely overturned. White men would turn black like Papuans, Papuans would become Whites; root crops would grow in trees, and coconuts and fruits would grow like tubers. Some of the islanders now began to draw together into large "towns"; others took Biblical names such as "Jericho" and "Galilee" for their villages. Soon they adopted military uniforms and began drilling. The Japanese, by now highly unpopular, tried to disarm and disperse the Papuans; resistance inevitably developed. The climax of this tragedy came when several canoe-loads of fanatics sailed out to attack Japanese warships, believing themselves to be invulnerable by virtue of the holy water with which they had sprinkled themselves. But the bullets of the Japanese did not turn to water, and the attackers were mowed down by machine-gun fire.

Behind this incident lay a long history. As long ago as 1857 missionaries in the Geelvink Bay region had made note of the story of Mansren. It is typical of many Melanesian myths that became confounded with Christian doctrine to form the ideological basis of the movements. The legend tells how long ago there lived an old man named Manamakeri ("he who itches"), whose body was covered with sores. Manamakeri was extremely fond of palm wine, and used to climb a huge tree every day to tap the liquid from the flowers. He soon found that someone was getting there before him and removing the liquid. Eventually he trapped the thief, who turned out to be none other than the Morning Star. In return for his freedom, the Star gave the old man a wand that would produce as much fish as he liked, a magic tree and a magic staff. If he drew in the sand and stamped his foot, the drawing would become real. Manamakeri, aged as he was, now magically impregnated a young maiden; the child of this union was a miracle-child who spoke as soon as he was born. But the maiden's parents were horrified, and banished her, the child and the old man. The trio sailed off in a canoe created by Mansren ("The Lord"), as the old man now became known. On this journey Mansren rejuvenated himself by stepping into a fire and flaking off his scaly skin, which changed into valuables. He then sailed around Geelvink Bay, creating islands where he stopped, and peopling them with the ancestors of the present-day Papuans.

The Mansren myth is plainly a creation myth full of symbolic ideas relating to fertility and rebirth. Comparative evidence—especially the shedding of his scaly skin—confirms the suspicion that the old man is, in fact, the Snake in another guise. Psychoanalytic writers argue that the snake occupies such a prominent part in mythology the world over because it stands for the penis, another fertility symbol. This may be so, but its symbolic significance is surely more complex than this. It is the "rebirth" of the hero, whether Mansren or the Snake, that exercises such universal fascination over men's minds.

The 19th-century missionaries thought that the Mansren story would make the introduction of Christianity easier, since the concept of "resurrection," not to mention that of the "virgin birth" and the "second coming," was already there. By 1867, however, the first cult organized around the Mansren legend was reported.

Though such myths were widespread in Melanesia, and may have sparked occasional movements even in the pre-White era, they took on a new significance in the late 19th century, once the European powers had finished parceling out the Melanesian region among themselves. In many coastal areas the long history of "blackbirding"—the seizure of islanders for work on the plantations of Australia and Fiji—had built up a reservoir of hostility to Europeans. In other areas, however, the arrival of the Whites was accepted, even welcomed, for it meant access to bully beef and cigarettes, shirts and paraffin lamps, whisky and bicycles. It also meant access to the knowledge behind these material goods, for the Europeans brought missions and schools as well as cargo.

Practically the only teaching the natives received about European life came from the missions, which emphasized the central significance of religion in European society. The Melanesians already believed that man's activities—whether gardening, sailing canoes or bearing children—needed magical assistance. Ritual without human effort was not enough. But neither was human effort on its own. This outlook was reinforced by mission teaching.

The initial enthusiasm for European rule, however, was speedily dispelled. The rapid growth of the plantation economy removed the bulk of the able-bodied men from the villages, leaving women, children and old men to carry on as best they could. The splendid vision of the equality of all Christians began to seem a pious deception in face of the realities of the color bar, the multiplicity of rival Christian missions and the open irreligion of many Whites.

For a long time the natives accepted the European mission as the means by which the "cargo" would eventually be made available to them. But they found that acceptance of Christianity did not bring the cargo any nearer. They grew disillusioned. The story now began to be put about that it was not the Whites who made the cargo, but the dead ancestors. To people completely ignorant of factory production, this made good sense. White men did not work; they merely wrote secret signs on scraps of paper, for which they were given shiploads of goods. On the other hand, the Melanesians labored week after week for pitiful wages. Plainly the goods must be made for Melanesians somewhere, perhaps in the Land of the Dead. The Whites, who possessed the secret of the cargo, were intercepting it and keeping it from the hands of the islanders, to whom it was really consigned. In the Madang district of New Guinea, after some 40 years' experience of the missions, the natives went in a body one day with a petition demanding

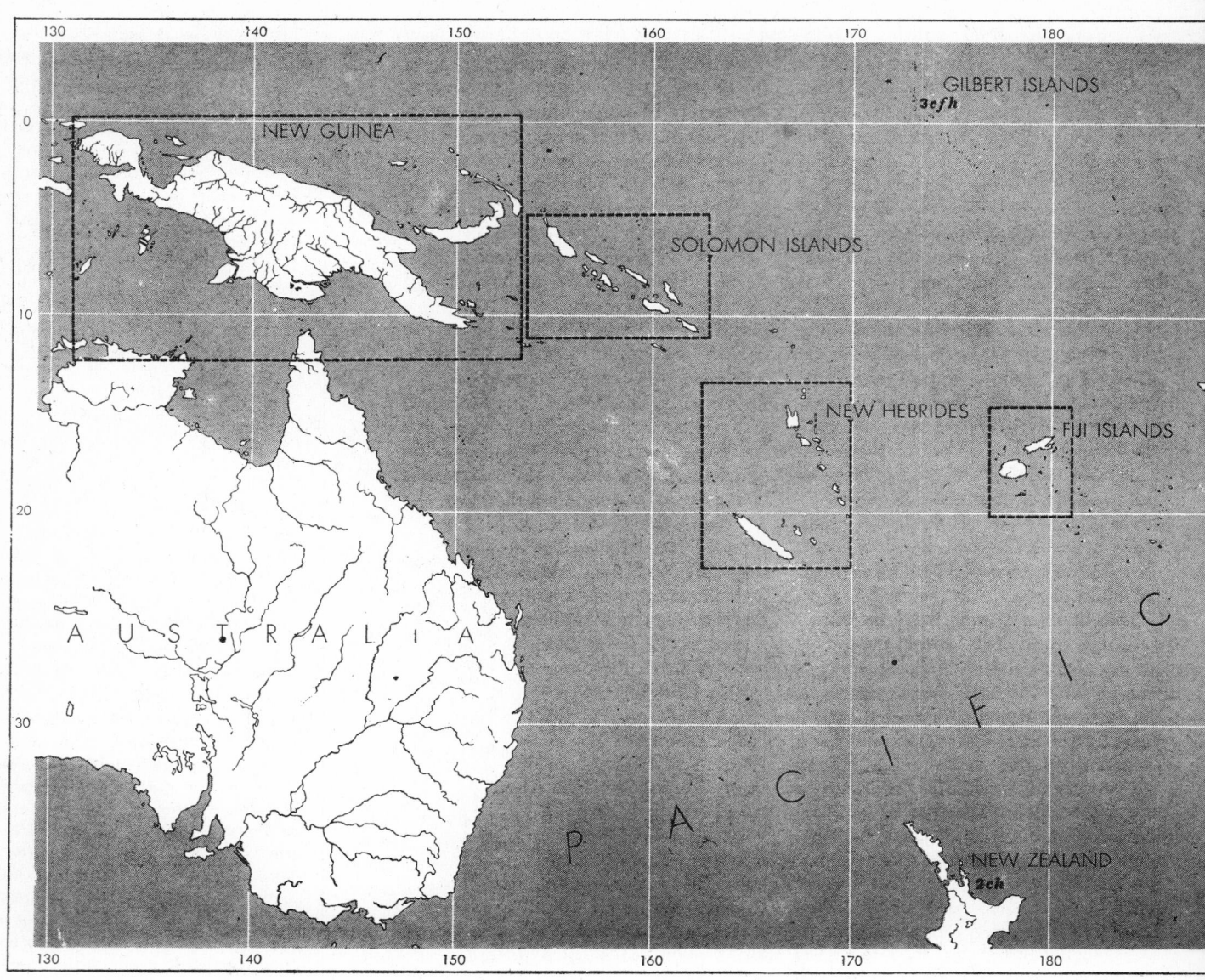

that the cargo secret should now be revealed to them, for they had been very patient.

So strong is this belief in the existence of a "secret" that the cargo cults generally contain some ritual in imitation of the mysterious European customs which are held to be the clue to the white man's extraordinary power over goods and men. The believers sit around tables with bottles of flowers in front of them, dressed in European clothes, waiting for the cargo ship or airplane to materialize; other cultists feature magic pieces of paper and cabalistic writing. Many of them deliberately turn their backs on the past by destroying secret ritual objects, or exposing them to the gaze of uninitiated youths and women, for whom formerly even a glimpse of the sacred objects would have meant the severest penalties, even death. The belief that they were the chosen people is further reinforced by their reading of the Bible, for the lives and customs of the people in the Old Testament resemble their own lives rather than those of the Europeans. In the New Testament they find the Apocalypse, with its prophecies of destruction and resurrection, particularly attractive.

Missions that stress the imminence of the Second Coming, like those of the Seventh Day Adventists, are often accused of stimulating millenarian cults among the islanders. In reality, however, the Melanesians themselves rework the doctrines the missionaries teach them, selecting from the Bible what they themselves find particularly congenial in it. Such movements have occurred in areas where missions of quite different types

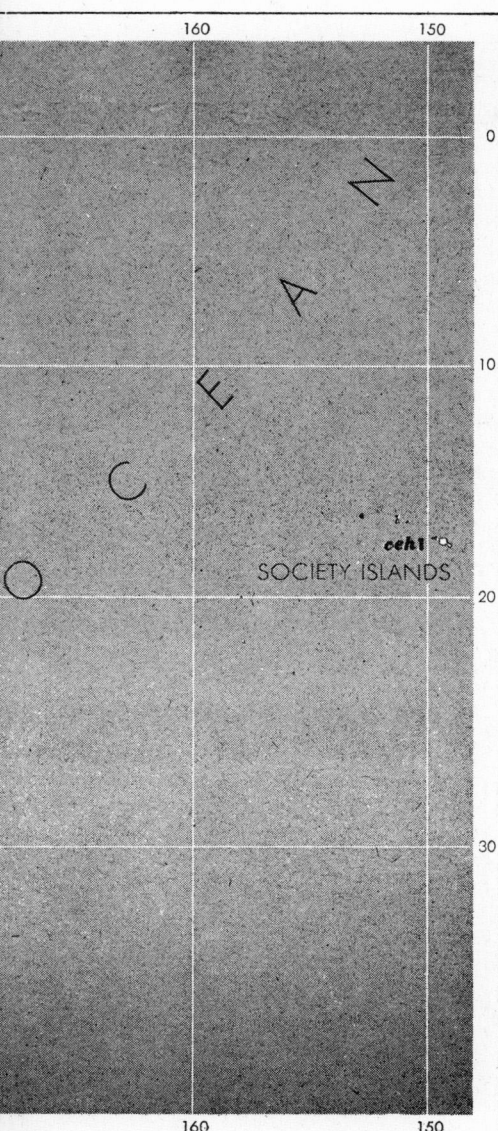

160   150

SOCIETY ISLANDS

SOUTH PACIFIC, scene of the religious disturbances known as cargo cults, is shown in this map. Most cargo cults have been in Melanesia, shown here as four regions enclosed in broken rectangles. Each of these regions is shown in a detailed map in the following pages. Also shown on this map are three outlying cargo cults, two of them Polynesian and the third Micronesian. Numbers on these maps indicate individual cults. Letters refer to typical features of cults (see number and letter keys accompanying each map).

1 MAMAIA MOVEMENT   TAHITI 1930-1944
2 HAU-HAU MOVEMENT   NEW ZEALAND
                                          1860-1871
3 ONOTOA TROUBLES GILBERT ISLANDS
                                          1932

a MYTH OF THE RETURN OF THE DEAD
b REVIVAL OR MODIFICATION OF
       PAGANISM
c INTRODUCTION OF CHRISTIAN
       ELEMENTS
d CARGO MYTH
e BELIEF THAT NEGROES WILL
       BECOME WHITE MEN AND
       VICE VERSA
f BELIEF IN A COMING MESSIAH
g ATTEMPTS TO RESTORE NATIVE
       POLITICAL AND ECONOMIC
       CONTROL
h THREATS AND VIOLENCE AGAINST
       WHITE MEN
i UNION OF TRADITIONALLY
       SEPARATE AND UNFRIENDLY
       GROUPS

ed overnight. Then came the Japanese, only to be ousted in turn largely by the previously unknown Americans. And among these Americans the Melanesians saw Negroes like themselves, living lives of luxury on equal terms with white G.I.'s. The sight of these Negroes seemed like a fulfillment of the old prophecies to many cargo cult leaders. Nor must we forget the sheer scale of this invasion. Around a million U. S. troops passed through the Admiralty Islands, completely swamping the inhabitants. It was a world of meaningless and chaotic changes, in which anything was possible. New ideas were imported and given local twists. Thus in the Loyalty Islands people expected the French Communist Party to bring the millennium. There is no real evidence, however, of any Communist influence in these movements, despite the rather hysterical belief among Solomon Island planters that the name of the local "Masinga Rule" movement was derived from the word "Marxian"! In reality the name comes from a Solomon Island tongue, and means "brotherhood."

Europeans who have witnessed outbreaks inspired by the cargo cults are usually at a loss to understand what they behold. The islanders throw away their money, break their most sacred taboos, abandon their gardens and destroy their precious livestock; they indulge in sexual license or, alternatively, rigidly separate men from women in huge communal establishments. Sometimes they spend days sitting gazing at the horizon for a glimpse of the long-awaited ship or airplane; sometimes they dance, pray and sing in mass congregations, becoming possessed and "speaking with tongues."

Observers have not hesitated to use such words as "madness," "mania," and "irrationality" to characterize the cults. But the cults reflect quite logical and rational attempts to make sense out of a social order that appears senseless and chaotic. Given the ignorance of the Melanesians about the wider European society, its economic organization and its highly developed technology, their reactions form a consistent and understandable pattern. They wrap up all their yearning and hope in an amalgam that combines the best counsel they can find in Christianity and their native belief. If the world is soon to end, gardening or fishing is unnecessary; everything will be provided. If the Melanesians are

have been dominant, from Roman Catholic to Seventh Day Adventist. The reasons for the emergence of these cults, of course, lie far deeper in the life-experience of the people.

The economy of most of the islands is very backward. Native agriculture produces little for the world market, and even the European plantations and mines export only a few primary products and raw materials: copra, rubber, gold. Melanesians are quite unable to understand why copra, for example,

fetches 30 pounds sterling per ton one month and but 5 pounds a few months later. With no notion of the workings of world-commodity markets, the natives see only the sudden closing of plantations, reduced wages and unemployment, and are inclined to attribute their insecurity to the whim or evil in the nature of individual planters.

Such shocks have not been confined to the economic order. Governments, too, have come and gone, especially during the two world wars: German, Dutch, British and French administrations melt-

NEW GUINEA has been a prolific breeder of cargo cults, resulting from the impact of Dutch, German, British and Japanese rule on its Stone Age cultures. At present the western portion is held by the Netherlands but claimed by Indonesia. The southeast (Papua) and northeast (U.N. Trust Territory of New Guinea) are governed by Australia.

a MYTH OF THE RETURN OF THE DEAD
b REVIVAL OR MODIFICATION OF
     PAGANISM
c INTRODUCTION OF CHRISTIAN
     ELEMENTS
d CARGO MYTH
e BELIEF THAT NEGROES WILL
     BECOME WHITE MEN AND
     VICE VERSA

f BELIEF IN A COMING MESSIAH
g ATTEMPTS TO RESTORE NATIVE
     POLITICAL AND ECONOMIC
     CONTROL
h THREATS AND VIOLENCE AGAINST
     WHITE MEN
i UNION OF TRADITIONALLY
     SEPARATE AND UNFRIENDLY
     GROUPS

 4 KORERI MOVEMENT   NUMFOR, DUTCH NEW GUINEA 1911
 5 KORERI MOVEMENT   BIAK, DUTCH NEW GUINEA 1939
 6 KORERI MOVEMENT   BIAK, DUTCH NEW GUINEA 1886
 7 KORERI MOVEMENT   BIAK, GEELVINK BAY, DUTCH NEW GUINEA   1942-1947
 8 SIMSON INCIDENT   HOLLANDIA, DUTCH NEW GUINEA 1940- ?
 9 PAMAI MOVEMENT   LAKE SENTANI, DUTCH NEW GUINEA 1928
10 NIMBORAN MOVEMENT   LAKE SENTANI, DUTCH NEW GUINEA 1945
11 NINIGO ISLANDS MOVEMENT   NINIGO ISLANDS, NEW GUINEA 1945- ?
12 BLACK KINGS MOVEMENT   AITAPE, WEWAK, NEW GUINEA 1930
13 GREAT PIGS   WEST-CENTRAL NEW GUINEA 1946
14 HINE MOVEMENT   WABAG, CENTRAL NEW GUINEA 1945
15 BLACK KINGS MOVEMENT   MOUNT HAGEN, NEW GUINEA 1940
16 NATIVE KING   KERAM RIVER, CENTRAL NEW GUINEA 1943-1945
17 GHOST WIND   KAINANTU, CENTRAL NEW GUINEA 1940-1947
18 TOMMY KABU COOPERATIVE MOVEMENT   PURARI DELTA, PAPUA   1945-1947
19 BATAWI INCIDENT   WESTERN PAPUA
20 GERMAN WISLIN   SAIBAI, TORRES STRAIT 1913-1915
21 VAILALA MADNESS   PAPUA 1919-1931
22 FILO INCIDENT   MEKEO, PAPUA 1940-1941
23 GOILALA AND GOGODARA CULT   PAPUA 1945
24 PIG KILLING   KAIRUKU, PAPUA 1937
25 THREE BLACK KINGS   WEWAK, NEW GUINEA 1948-1949
26 MAMBU MOVEMENT   MADANG, NEW GUINEA 1937-1940
27 TIFU INCIDENT   RAMU, MADANG, NEW GUINEA 1951
28 BLACK KING MOVEMENT   MADANG, NEW GUINEA 1935
29 KUKUAIK MOVEMENT   KARKAR ISLAND, NEW GUINEA 1940- ?
30 CARGO CULT   MADANG, NEW GUINEA 1940
31 CARGO CULT   MADANG, NEW GUINEA 1934
32 YALI INCIDENT   MADANG, NEW GUINEA 1945-1955
33 GARIA MOVEMENT   MADANG, NEW GUINEA 1940- ?
34 SECOND COMING OF CHRIST   RAI COAST, NEW GUINEA 1936
35 LETUB MOVEMENT   MADANG, NEW GUINEA 1939-1940
36 EEMASANG MOVEMENT   HUON PENINSULA, NEW GUINEA 1927- ?
37 COMING OF JESUS   EASTERN HIGHLANDS, CENTRAL NEW GUINEA   1943-1945
38 TIMO INCIDENT   HUON PENINSULA, NEW GUINEA 1922
39 THREE BLACK KINGS   FINSCHHAFEN, NEW GUINEA 1945- ?
40 LAZARUS MOVEMENT   HUON PENINSULA, NEW GUINEA 1933
41 SOSOM INCIDENT   MOUNT GOLDBERG, NEW GUINEA 1936
42 MOROBE MOVEMENT   MOROFE, NEW GUINEA 1933-1936
43 MARKHAM VALLEY MOVEMENT   MARKHAM VALLEY, NEW GUINEA   1932-1934
44 YERUMOT INCIDENT   TOEPFER RIVER, NEW GUINEA 1930- ?
45 SCHWAERMEREI   RAWLINSON RANGE, NEW GUINEA 1933
46 MARKHAM VALLEY MOVEMENT   MARKHAM VALLEY, NEW GUINEA   1932-1934
47 BAIGONA MOVEMENT   MASSIM, NEW GUINEA 1912-1919
48 TARO CULT   NORTHEAST NEW GUINEA 1914-1928
49 PIG KILLING   NORTH PAPUA 1930
50 PIG KILLING   NORTHEAST PAPUA 1930
51 ASSISI CULT   NORTHEAST PAPUA 1930-1944
52 MILNE BAY MOVEMENT   MASSIM, NEW GUINEA 1893- ?
53 PALIAU MOVEMENT   MANUS AND BALUAN, ADMIRALTY ISLANDS   1946-1954
54 THE NOISE   RAMBUDJON, ADMIRALTY ISLANDS 1946-1948 (?)
55 BATARI MOVEMENT   GALILO, NEW BRITAIN 1940-1946
56 BAINING TROUBLES   NEW BRITAIN 1955
57 BAINING MOVEMENT   NEW BRITAIN 1929-1930
58 KOKOPO MOVEMENT   NEW BRITAIN 1930 (?)
59 NAMATANAI MOVEMENT   NEW IRELAND 1939

to be part of a much wider order, the taboos that prescribe their social conduct must now be lifted or broken in a newly prescribed way.

Of course the cargo never comes. The cults nonetheless live on. If the millennium does not arrive on schedule, then perhaps there is some failure in the magic, some error in the ritual. New breakaway groups organize around "purer" faith and ritual. The cult rarely disappears, so long as the social situation which brings it into being persists.

At this point it should be observed that cults of this general kind are not peculiar to Melanesia. Men who feel

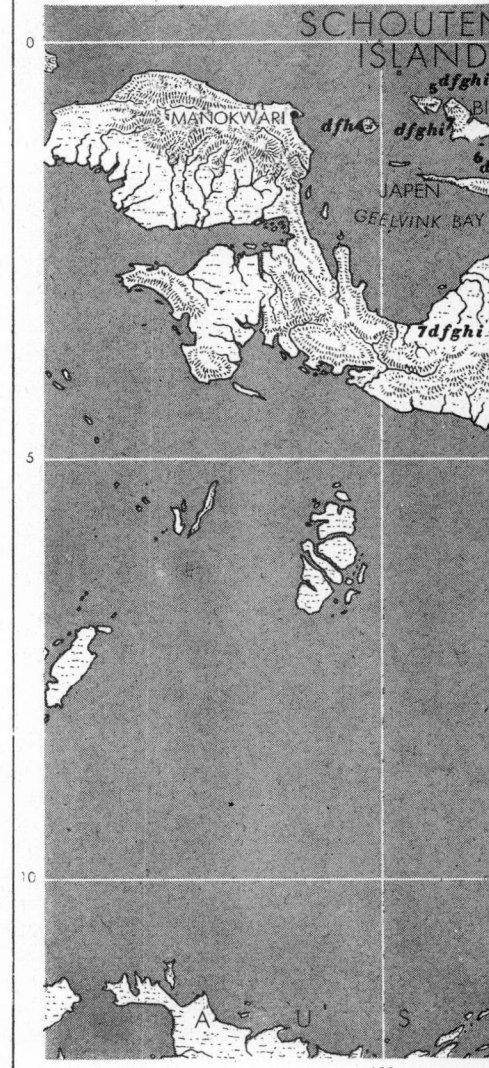

themselves oppressed and deceived have always been ready to pour their hopes and fears, their aspirations and frustrations, into dreams of a millennium to come or of a golden age to return. All parts of the world have had their counterparts of the cargo cults, from the American Indian ghost dance to the communist-millenarist "reign of the saints" in Münster during the Reformation, from medieval European apocalyptic cults to African "witch-finding" movements and Chinese Buddhist heresies. In some situations men have been content to wait and pray; in others they have sought to hasten the day by using their strong right arms to do the Lord's work. And always the cults serve to bring together scattered groups, notably the peasants and urban plebeians of agrarian societies and the peoples of "stateless" societies where the cult unites separate (and often hostile) villages, clans and tribes into a wider religio-political unity.

Once the people begin to develop secular political organizations, however, the sects tend to lose their importance as vehicles of protest. They begin to relegate the Second Coming to the distant future or to the next world. In Melanesia ordinary political bodies, trade unions and native councils are becoming the normal media through which the island-ers express their aspirations. In recent years continued economic prosperity and political stability have taken some of the edge off their despair. It now seems unlikely that any major movement along cargo-cult lines will recur in areas where the transition to secular politics has been made, even if the insecurity of prewar times returned. I would predict that the embryonic nationalism represented by cargo cults is likely in future to take forms familiar in the history of other countries that have moved from subsistence agriculture to participation in the world economy.

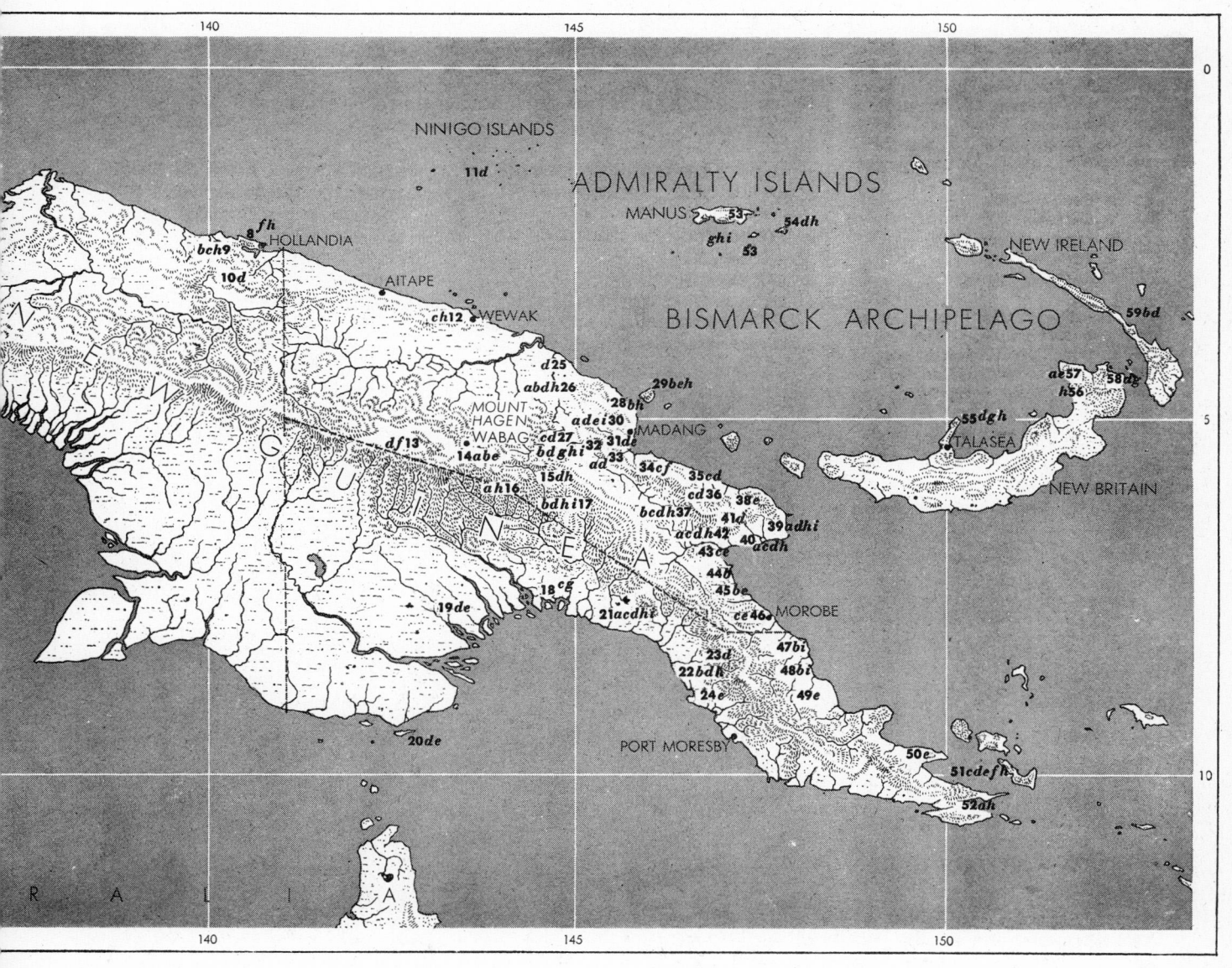

SOLOMON ISLANDS, *administered by Australia and Great Britain, are another center of cargo cults, some caused by the cataclysmic impact of World War II. The data contained in these maps and tables, prepared by the author and Jean Guiart of the Ecole des Hautes Etudes in Paris, are not a complete list of cargo cults. Many dates are only approximate.*

a MYTH OF THE RETURN OF THE DEAD
b REVIVAL OR MODIFICATION OF PAGANISM
c INTRODUCTION OF CHRISTIAN ELEMENTS
d CARGO MYTH
e BELIEF THAT NEGROES WILL BECOME WHITE MEN AND VICE VERSA
f BELIEF IN A COMING MESSIAH
g ATTEMPTS TO RESTORE NATIVE POLITICAL AND ECONOMIC CONTROL
h THREATS AND VIOLENCE AGAINST WHITE MEN
i UNION OF TRADITIONALLY SEPARATE AND UNFRIENDLY GROUPS

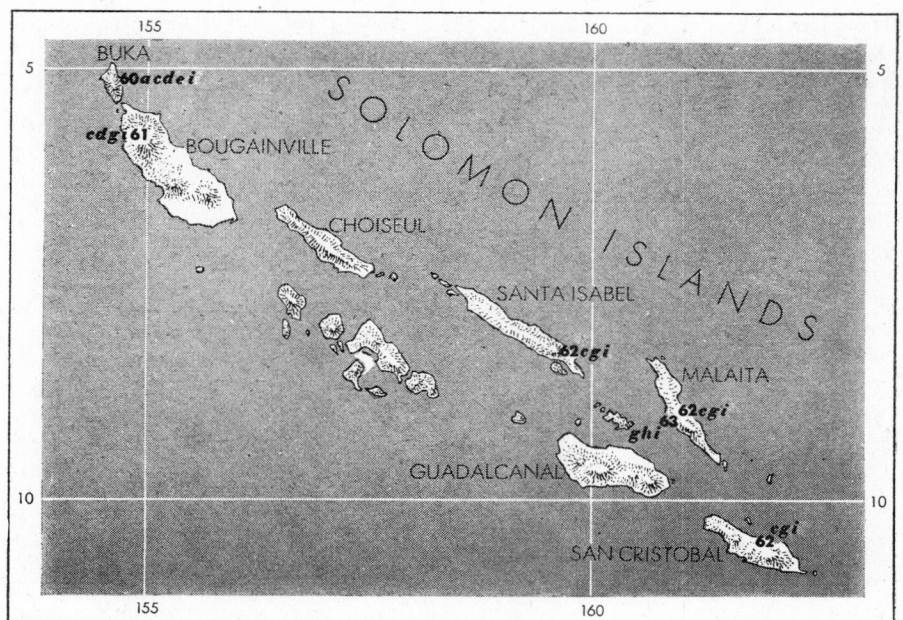

60 BUKA MOVEMENTS   NORTHERN SOLOMON ISLANDS   1913-1935
61 BOUGAINVILLE MOVEMENT   NORTHERN SOLOMON ISLANDS   1935-1939
62 MAASINA (MARCHING) RULE   MALAITA, SOLOMON ISLANDS   1945-1958
63 CHAIR AND RULE CULT   MALAITA, SOLOMON ISLANDS   1935

NEW HEBRIDES AND NEW CALEDONIA are, respectively, Anglo-French and French possessions. One New Caledonian cult placed Messianic hopes in the Communist Party.

FIJI ISLANDS are a British colony. Although generally Christianized, they have spawned several semi-Christian cargo cults.

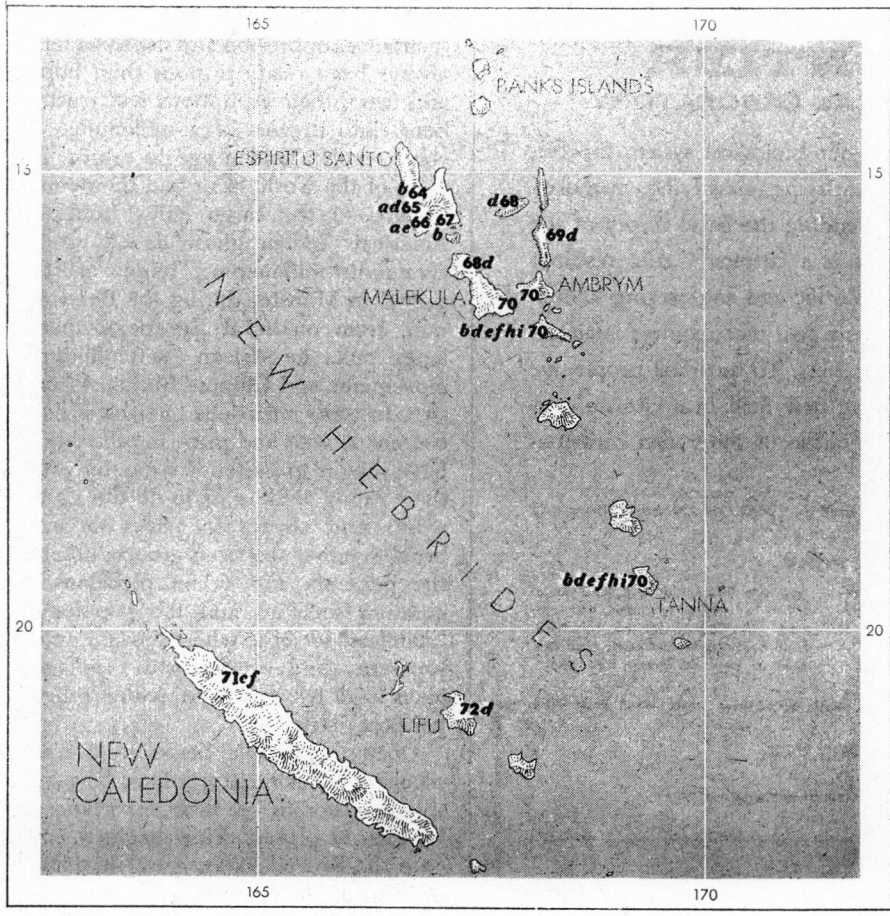

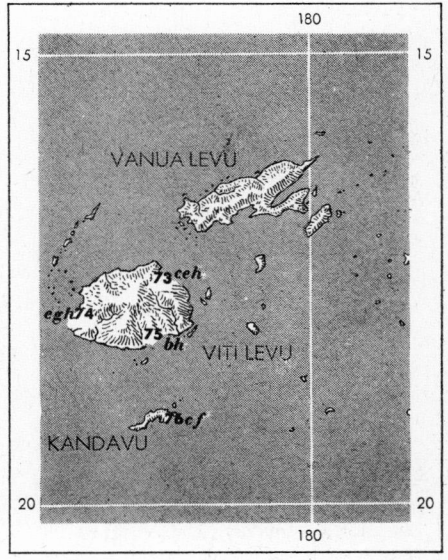

73 TUKA MOVEMENT CENTRAL VITI LEVU,
    FIJI 1873-1920
74 APOLOSI MOVEMENT WEST VITI LEVU,
    FIJI 1914-1940
75 LUVE-NI-WAI CENTRAL VITI LEVU,
    FIJI 1880- ?
76 KELEVI SECT KADAVU, FIJI 1945-1947

a MYTH OF THE RETURN OF THE DEAD
b REVIVAL OR MODIFICATION OF
    PAGANISM
c INTRODUCTION OF CHRISTIAN
    ELEMENTS
d CARGO MYTH
e BELIEF THAT NEGROES WILL
    BECOME WHITE MEN AND
    VICE VERSA
f BELIEF IN A COMING MESSIAH
g ATTEMPTS TO RESTORE NATIVE
    POLITICAL AND ECONOMIC
    CONTROL
h THREATS AND VIOLENCE AGAINST
    WHITE MEN
i UNION OF TRADITIONALLY
    SEPARATE AND UNFRIENDLY
    GROUPS

64 MAMARA MOVEMENT (NAKED CULT) WEST-CENTRAL ESPIRITU SANTO,
    NEW HEBRIDES 1945-1951
65 ATORI INCIDENT SOUTH ESPIRITU SANTO, NEW HEBRIDES 1945
66 RONGOFURO AFFAIR SOUTH ESPIRITU SANTO, NEW HEBRIDES 1914-1923
67 AVA-AVU INCIDENT SOUTH-CENTRAL ESPIRITU SANTO, NEW HEBRIDES 1937
68 MALEKULA NATIVE COMPANY CENTRAL NEW HEBRIDES 1950
69 BULE INCIDENT MELSISI, PENTECOST, NEW HEBRIDES 1947
70 JOHN FRUM MOVEMENT TANNA, NEW HEBRIDES 1938-1958
71 PWAGAC INCIDENT NORTHERN NEW CALEDONIA 1941
72 "COMMUNIST PARTY" LIFU, NEW CALEDONIA 1947

a MYTH OF THE RETURN OF THE DEAD
b REVIVAL OR MODIFICATION OF
    PAGANISM
c INTRODUCTION OF CHRISTIAN
    ELEMENTS
d CARGO MYTH
e BELIEF THAT NEGROES WILL
    BECOME WHITE MEN AND
    VICE VERSA

f BELIEF IN A COMING MESSIAH
g ATTEMPTS TO RESTORE NATIVE
    POLITICAL AND ECONOMIC
    CONTROL
h THREATS AND VIOLENCE AGAINST
    WHITE MEN
i UNION OF TRADITIONALLY
    SEPARATE AND UNFRIENDLY
    GROUPS

Devils, Witches, and Sudden Death

By June Nash

Tin miners in the high Andean plateau of Bolivia earn less than a dollar a day when, to use their phrase, they "bury themselves alive in the bowels of the earth." The mine shafts—as much as two miles long and half a mile deep—penetrate hills that have been exploited for more than 450 years. The miners descend to the work areas in open hauls; some stand on the roof and cling to the swaying cable as the winch lowers them deep into the mine.

Once they reach their working level, there is always the fear of rockslides as they drill the face of the mine, of landslides when they set off the dynamite, of gas when they enter unfrequented areas. And added to their fear of the accidents that have killed or maimed so many of their workmates is their economic insecurity. Like Wall Street brokers they watch international price quotations on tin, because a difference of a few cents can mean layoffs, loss of bonuses, a cut in contract prices—even a change of government.

Working in the narrow chimneys and corridors of the mine, breathing the dust- and silicate-filled air, their bodies numbed by the vibration of the drilling machines and the din of dynamite blasts, the tin miners have found an ally in the devil, or Tio (uncle), as he is affectionately known. Myths relate the devil to his pre-Christian counterpart Huari, the powerful ogre who owns the treasures of the hills. In Oruro, a 13,800-foot-high mining center in the western Andes of Bolivia, all the miners know the legend of Huari, who persuaded the simple farmers of the Uru Uru tribe to leave their work in the fields and enter the caves to find the riches he had in store. The farmers, supported by their ill-gained wealth from the mines, turned from a virtuous life of tilling the soil and praying to the sun god Inti to a life of drinking and midnight revels. The community would have died, the legend relates, if an Inca maiden, Nusta, had not descended from the sky and taught the people to live in harmony and industry.

Despite four centuries of proselyting, Catholic priests have failed to wipe out belief in the legend, but the principal characters have merged with Catholic deities. Nusta is identified with the Virgin of the Mineshaft, and is represented as the vision that appeared miraculously to an unemployed miner.

The miners believe that Huari lives on in the hills where the mines are located, and they venerate him in the form of the devil, or Tio. They believe he controls the rich veins of ore, revealing them only to those who give him offerings. If they offend the Tio or slight him by failing to give him offerings, he will withhold the rich veins or cause an accident.

Miners make images of the Tio and set them up in the main corridors of each mine level, in niches cut into the walls for the workers to rest. The image of the Tio varies in appearance according to the fancy of the miner who makes him, but his body is always shaped from ore. The hands, face, horns, and legs are sculptured with clay from the mine. Bright pieces of metal or burned-out bulbs from the miners' electric torches are stuck in the eye sockets. Teeth are made of glass or crystal sharpened "like nails," and the mouth is open, gluttonous and ready to receive offerings. Sometimes the plaster of Paris masks worn by the devil dancers at Carnival are used for the head. Some Tios wear embroidered vests, flamboyant capes, and miners' boots. The figure of a bull, which helps miners in contract with the devil by digging out the ore with its horns, occasionally accompanies the image, or there may be *chinas*, female temptresses who are the devil's consorts.

The Tio is a figure of power: he has what everyone wants, in excess. Coca remains lie in his greedy mouth. His hands are stretched out, grasping the bottles of alcohol he is offered. His nose is burned black by the cigarettes he smokes down to the nub. If a Tio is knocked out of his niche by an extra charge of dynamite and survives, the miners consider him to be more powerful than others.

Another spirit present in the mines but rarely represented in images is the Awiche, or old woman. Although some miners deny she is the Pachamama, the earth goddess worshiped by farmers, they relate to her in the same way. Many of the miners greet her when they enter the mine, saying, "Good-day, old woman. Don't let anything happen to me today!" They ask her to intercede with the Tio when they feel in danger; when they leave the mine safely, they thank her for their life.

Quite the opposite kind of feminine image, the Viuda, or widow, appears to miners who have been drinking *chicha*, a fermented corn liquor. Miners who have seen the Viuda describe her as a young and beautiful *chola*, or urbanized Indian, who makes men lose their minds—and sometimes their paychecks. She, too, is a consort of the devil and recruits men to make contracts with him, deluding them with promises of wealth.

When I started working in Oruro during the summer of 1969, the men told me about the *ch'alla*, a ceremonial offering of cigarettes, coca, and alcohol to the Tio. One man described it as follows:

"We make the *ch'alla* in the working areas within the mine. My partner and I do it together every Friday, but on the first Friday of the month we do it with the other workers on our level. We bring in banners, confetti, and paper streamers. First we put a cigarette in the mouth of the Tio and light it. After this we scatter alcohol on the ground for the Pachamama, then give some to the Tio. Next we take out our coca and begin to chew, and we also smoke. We serve liquor from the bottles each of us brings in. We light the Tio's cigarette, saying 'Tio, help us in our work. Don't let any accidents happen.' We do not kneel before him as we would before a saint, because that would be sacrilegious.

"Then everyone begins to get drunk. We begin to talk about our work, about the sacrifices that we make. When this is finished, we wind the streamers around the neck of the Tio. We prepare our *mesas* [tables of offerings that include sugar cakes, llama embryos, colored wool, rice, and candy balls].

"After some time we say, 'Let's go.' Some have to carry out those who are drunk. We go to where we change our clothes, and when we

come out we again make the offering of liquor, banners, and we wrap the streamers around each others' necks. From there on, each one does what he pleases."

I thought I would never be able to participate in a *ch'alla* because the mine managers told me the men didn't like to have women inside the mine, let alone join them in their most sacred rites. Finally a friend high in the governmental bureaucracy gave me permission to go into the mine. Once down on the lowest level of San José mine, 340 meters below the ground, I asked my guide if I could stay with one of the work crews rather than tour the galleries as most visitors did. He was relieved to leave me and get back to work. The men let me try their machines so that I could get a sense of what it was like to hold a 160-pound machine vibrating in a yard-wide tunnel, or to use a mechanical shovel in a gallery where the temperature was 100° F.

They told me of some of their frustrations—not getting enough air pumped in to make the machines work at more than 20 percent efficiency and constant breakdowns of machinery, which slowed them up on their contract.

At noon I refused the superintendent's invitation to eat lunch at level O. Each of the men gave me a bit of his soup or some "seconds," solid food consisting of noodles, potatoes, rice, and spicy meat, which their wives prepare and send down in the elevators.

At the end of the shift all the men in the work group gathered at the Tio's niche in the large corridor. It was the first Friday of the month and the gang leader, Lino Pino, pulled out a bottle of fruit juice and liquor, which his wife had prepared, and each of the men brought out his plastic bag with coca. Lino led the men in offering a cigarette to the Tio, lighting it, and then shaking the liquor on the ground and calling for life. "Hallalla! Hallalla!"

We sat on lumps of ore along the rail lines and Lino's helper served us, in order of seating, from a little

tin cup. I was not given any priority, nor was I forgotten in the rounds. One of the men gave me coca from his supply and I received it with two hands, as I had been taught in the rituals aboveground. I chewed enough to make my cheek feel numb, as though I had had an injection of novocaine for dental work. The men told me that coca was their gift from the Pachamama, who took pity on them in their work.

As Lino offered liquor to the Tio, he asked him to "produce" more mineral and make it "ripen," as though it were a crop. These rituals are a continuation of agricultural ceremonies still practiced by the farmers in the area. The miners themselves are the sons or grandsons of the landless farmers who were recruited when the gold and silver mines were reopened for tin production after the turn of the century.

A month after I visited level 340, three miners died in an explosion there when a charge of dynamite fell down a shoot to their work site and exploded. Two of the men died in the mine; the third died a few days later in the hospital. When the accident occurred, all the men rushed to the elevators to help or to stare in fascinated horror as the dead and injured were brought up to level O. They carried the bodies of their dead comrades to the social center where they washed the charred faces, trying to lessen the horror for the women who were coming. When the women came into the social center where the bodies were laid out, they screamed and stamped their feet, the horror of seeing their husbands or neighbors sweeping through their bodies.

The entire community came to sit in at the wake, eating and drinking in the feasting that took place before the coffins of their dead comrades. The meal seemed to confirm the need to go on living as well as the right to live.

Although the accident had not occurred in the same corridor I had been in, it was at the same level.

Shortly after that, when a student who worked with me requested permission to visit the mine, the manager told her that the men were hinting that the accident had happened because the gringa (any foreign-born, fair-haired person, in this case myself) had been inside. She was refused permission. I was disturbed by what might happen to my relations with the people of the community, but even more concerned that I had added to their sense of living in a hostile world where anything new was a threat.

The miners were in a state of uneasiness and tension the rest of that month, July. They said the Tio was "eating them" because he hadn't had an offering of food. The dead men were all young, and the Tio prefers the juicy flesh and blood of the young, not the tired blood of the sick older workers. He wanted a k'araku, a ceremonial banquet of sacrificed animals.

There had not been any scheduled k'arakus since the army put the mines under military control in 1965. During the first half of the century, when the "tin barons"—Patiño, Hochschild, and Arayamao—owned the mines, the administrators and even some of the owners, especially Patiño, who had risen from the ranks, would join with the men in sacrificing animals to the Tio and in the drinking and dancing that followed. After nationalization of the mines in 1952, the rituals continued. In fact, some of the miners complained that they were done in excess of the Tio's needs. One said that going into the mine after the revolution was like walking into a saloon.

Following military control, however, the miners had held the ritual only once in San José, after two men had died while working their shift. Now the Tio had again shown he was hungry by eating the three miners who had died in the accident. The miners were determined to offer him food in a k'araku.

At 10:30 P.M. on the eve of the devil's month, I went to the mine with Doris Widerkehr, a student, and Eduardo Ibañez, a Bolivian art-

ist. I was somewhat concerned about how we would be received after what the manager of the mine had said, but all the men seemed glad we had come. As we sat at the entry to the main shaft waiting for the yatiris, shamans who had been contracted for the ceremony, the miners offered us chicha and cocktails of fruit juice and alcohol.

When I asked one of the men why they had prepared the ritual and what it meant, his answer was:

"We are having the k'araku because a man can't die just like that. We invited the administrators, but none of them have come. This is because only the workers feel the death of their comrades.

"We invite the Pachamama, the Tio, and God to eat the llamas that we will sacrifice. With faith we give coca and alcohol to the Tio. We are more believers in God here than in Germany or the United States because there the workers have lost their soul. We do not have earthquakes because of our faith before God. We hold the crucifix to our breast. We have more confidence before God."

Most miners reject the claim that belief in the Tio is pagan sacrilege. They feel that no contradiction exists, since time and place for offerings to the devil are clearly defined and separated from Christian ritual.

At 11:00 P.M. two white llamas contributed by the administration were brought into level 0 in a company truck. The miners had already adorned the pair, a male and a female, with colored paper streamers and the bright wool earrings with which farmers decorate their flocks.

The four yatiris contracted for did not appear, but two others who happened to be staying at the house of a miner were brought in to perform the ceremony. As soon as they arrived, the miners took the llamas into the elevator. The male was on the right and the female to his left, "just the same as a marriage ceremony," one miner commented. Looking at the couple adorned with bright streamers and confetti, there was the feeling of a wedding.

Two men entered the elevator

with the llamas and eight more climbed on top to go down to level 340. They were commissioned to take charge of the ritual. All the workers of 340 entered to participate in the ceremony below and about 50 men gathered at level 0 to drink.

At level 340 the workers guided the yatiris to the spot where the accident had occurred. There they cast liquor from a bottle and called upon the Tio, the Awiche, and God to protect the men from further accidents—naming all the levels in the mine, the various work sites, the different veins of ore, the elevator shaft, and the winch, repeating each name three times and asking the Tio not to eat any more workers and to give them more veins to work. The miners removed their helmets during this ritual. It ended with the plea for life, "Hallalla, hallalla, hallalla." Two bottles of liquor were sprinkled on the face of the rock and in the various work places.

The yatiris then instructed the men to approach the llamas with their arms behind their backs so that the animals would not know who held the knife that would kill them. They were also told to beg pardon for the sacrifice and to kiss the llamas farewell. One miner, noting what appeared to be a tear falling from the female's eye, cried and tried to comfort her. As the men moved around the llamas in a circle, the yatiris called on the Malkus (eagle gods), the Awiche, the Pachamama, and finally the Tiyulas (Tios of the mines), asking for their care.

The female llama was the first to be sacrificed. She struggled and had to be held down by two men as they cut her jugular vein. When they disemboweled her, the men discovered that she was pregnant, to which they attributed the strength of her resistance. Her blood was caught in a white basin.

When the heart of the dying llama had pumped out its blood, the yatiri made an incision and removed it, using both his hands, a sign of respect when receiving an offering. He put the still palpitating heart in the basin with the blood and covered it with a white cloth on which the miners placed *k'oa*—an offering made up of herbs, coca, wool, and sweets—and small bottles of alcohol and wine.

The man in charge of the ceremony went with five aides to the site of the principal Tio in the main corridor. There they removed a piece of ore from the image's left side, creating a hole into which they put the heart, the blood, and the other offerings. They stood in a circle, their heads bent, and asked for safety and that there be no more accidents. In low voices, they prayed in Quechua.

When this commission returned, the *yatiris* proceeded to sacrifice the male llama. Again they asked the Tio for life and good ore in all the levels of the mine, and that there be no accidents. They took the heart, blood, *k'oa*, and bottles of alcohol and wine to another isolated gallery and buried it for the Tio in a place that would not be disturbed. There they prayed, "filled with faith," as one commented; then returned to the place of the sacrifice. The *yatiris* sprinkled the remaining blood on the veins of ore.

By their absorption and fervid murmuring of prayers, both young and old miners revealed the same faith and devotion. Many of them wept, thinking of the accident and their dead companions. During the ritual drinking was forbidden.

On the following day those men charged with responsibility for the ritual came to prepare the meat. They brought the two carcasses to the baker, who seasoned them and cooked them in large ovens. The men returned at about 1:15 P.M. to distribute the meat. With the meat, they served *chicha*. Some sprinkled *chicha* on the ground for the Pachamama, saying "Hallalla," before drinking.

The bones were burned to ashes, which were then offered to the Tio. The mine entrance was locked shut and left undisturbed for 24 hours. Some remarked that it should be closed for three days, but the company did not want to lose that much time.

During the *k'araku* the miners recognize the Tio as the true owner of the mine. "All the mineral that comes out from the interior of the mine is the 'crop' of the devil and whether one likes it or not, we have to invite the Tio to drink and eat so that the flow of metal will continue," said a young miner who studied evenings at the University of Oruro.

All the workers felt that the failure of the administrators to come to the *k'araku* indicated not only their lack of concern with the lives of the men but also their disregard of the need to raise productivity in the mine.

When the Tio appears uninvited, the miners fear that they have only a short time to live. Miners who have seen apparitions say the Tio looks like a gringo—tall, red-faced, with fair hair and beard, and wearing a cowboy hat. This description, hardly resembles the images sculptured by the miners, but it does fit the foreign technicians and administrators who administered the mines in the time of the tin barons. To the Indian workers, drawn from the highland and Cochabamba farming areas, the Tio is a strange and exotic figure, ruthless, gluttonous, powerful, and arbitrary in his use of that power, but nonetheless attractive, someone to get close to in order to share that power. I was beginning to wonder if the reason I was accepted with such good humor by the miners, despite their rule against women in the mines, was because they thought I shared some of these characteristics and was a match for the devil.

Sickness or death in the family can force a man in desperation to make a contract with the devil. If his companions become aware of it, the contract is destroyed and with it his life.

The miners feel that they need the protection of a group when they confront the Tio. In the *ch'alla* and the *k'araku* they convert the power of the Tio into socially useful production. In effect, the rituals are ways of getting the genie back into the bottle after he has done his miracles. Security of the group then depends upon respect toward the sacrificial offering, as shown by the following incident told me by the head of a work gang after the *k'araku*:

"I know of a man who had a vein of ore near where the bones of the sacrificial llama were buried. Without advising me, he made a hole with his drill and put the dynamite in. He knew very well that the bones were there. On the following day, it cost him his life. While he was drilling, a stone fell and cut his head off.

"We had to change the bones with a ceremony. We brought in a good shaman who charged us B$500 [about $40], we hired the best orchestra, and we sang and danced in the new location where we laid the bones. We did not work in that corridor for three days, and we spent all the time in the *ch'alla*."

Often the miners are frightened nearly to death in the mine. A rock falls on the spot they have just left, a man falls in a shaft and is saved by hitting soft clay at the bottom, a tunnel caves in the moment after a man leaves it—these are incidents in a day's work that I have heard men say can start a *haperk'a*, or fear, that can take their lives.

A shaman may have to be called in to bring back the spirit that the Tio has seized. In one curing, a frightened miner was told to wear the clothing he had on when the Tio seized his spirit and to enter and give a service to the Tio at the same spot where he was frightened. The shaman himself asked the Tio to cure his patient, flattering him, "Now you have shown your power, give back his spirit."

The fear may result in sexual impotency. At one of the mines, Siglo XX, when there is full production, a dynamite blast goes off every five minutes in a section called Block Haven. The air is filled with smoke and the miners describe it as an inferno. Working under such tension, a shattering blast may unnerve them. Some react with an erection, followed by sexual debilitation.

Mad with rage and fear, some miners have been known to seize a knife, the same knife they use to cut the dynamite leads, and castrate themselves. When I visited Block Haven, I noticed that the Tio on this level had a huge erection, about a foot long on a man-sized figure. The workers said that when they find themselves in a state of impotency they go to the Tio for help. By exemplifying what they want in the Tio, they seek to repair the psychic damage caused by fear.

After feasting on the meat of the llamas and listening to stories of the Tio, I left the mine. The men thanked me for coming. I could not express the gratitude I felt for restoring my confidence in continuing the study.

Shortly thereafter I met Lino Pino returning from a fiesta for a miraculous saint in a nearby village. He asked me if I would be *madrina* at his daughter's forthcoming confirmation, and when I agreed, his wife offered me a tin cup with the delicious cocktail she always prepares for her husband on the days of the *ch'alla*, and we all had a round of drinks.

Later, when I knelt at the altar rail with Lino and his daughter as we received the wafer and the wine, flesh and blood of another sacrifice victim, I sensed the unity in the miners' beliefs. The miraculous Virgin looked down on us from her marbelized, neon-lit niche, her jewelled finger held out in benediction. She was adequate for that scene, but in the mine they needed someone who could respond to their needs on the job.

In the rituals of the *ch'alla* and the *k'araku* the power of the Tio to destroy is transformed into the socially useful functions of increasing mineral yield and giving peace of mind to the workers. Confronted alone, the Tio, like Banquo's ghost, makes a man unable to produce or even to go on living. Properly controlled by the group, the Tio promises fertility, potency, and productivity to the miners. Robbed of this faith, they often lose the faith to continue drilling after repeated failure to find a vein, or to continue living when the rewards of work are so meager. Knowing that the devil is on your side makes it possible to continue working in the hell that is the mines.

ARTICLE *41*

The Serpent-Handling Religions of West Virginia

By Nathan L. Gerrard

. . . .

. . . And these signs shall follow them that believe; In my name shall they cast out devils; they shall speak with new tongues; They shall take up serpents; and if they drink any deadly thing, it shall not hurt them; they shall lay hands on the sick, and they shall recover.

Mark 16:17–18

In Southern Appalachia, two dozen or three dozen fundamentalist congregations take this passage literally and "take up serpents." They use copperheads, water moccasins, and rattlesnakes in their religious services.

The serpent-handling ritual was inaugurated between 1900 and 1910, probably by George Went Hensley. Hensley began evangelizing in rural Grasshopper Valley, Tenn., then traveled widely throughout the South, particularly in Kentucky, spreading his religion. He died in Florida at 70—of snakebite. To date, the press has reported about 20 such deaths among the serpent-handlers. One other death was recorded last year, in Kentucky.

For seven years, my wife and I have been studying a number of West Virginia serpent-handlers, primarily in order to discover what effect this unusual form of religious practice has on their lives. Although serpent-handling is outlawed by the state legislatures of Kentucky, Virginia, and Tennessee and by municipal ordinances in North Carolina, it is still legal in West Virginia. One center is the Scrabble Creek Church of All Nations in Fayette County, about 37 miles from Charleston. Another center is the Church of Jesus in Jolo, McDowell County, one of the most poverty-stricken areas of the state. Serpent-handling is also practiced sporadically elsewhere in West Virginia, where it is usually led by visitors from Scrabble Creek or Jolo.

The Jolo church attracts people from both Virginia and Kentucky, in addition to those from West Virginia.

Members of the Scrabble Creek church speak with awe of the Jolo services, where people pick up large handfuls of poisonous snakes, fling them to the ground, pick them up again, and thrust them under their shirts or blouses, dancing ecstatically. We attended one church service in Scrabble Creek where visitors from Jolo covered their heads with clusters of snakes and wore them as crowns.

Serpent-handling was introduced to Scrabble Creek in 1941 by a coal miner from Harlan, Ky. The practice really began to take hold in 1946, when the present leader of the Scrabble Creek church, then a member of the Church of God, first took up serpents. The four or five original serpent-handlers in Fayette County met at one another's homes until given the use of an abandoned one-room school house in Big Creek. In 1959, when their number had swelled several times over, they moved to a larger church in Scrabble Creek.

SNAKEBITES, SAINTS, AND SCOFFERS

During the course of our seven-year study, about a dozen members of the church received snakebites. (My wife and I were present on two of these occasions.) Although there were no deaths, each incident was widely and unfavorably publicized in the area. For their part, the serpent-handlers say the Lord causes a snake to strike in order to refute scoffers' claims that the snakes' fangs have been pulled. They see each recovery from snakebites as a miracle wrought by the Lord—and each death as a sign that the Lord "really had to show the scoffers how dangerous it is to obey His commandments." Since adherents believe that death brings one to the throne of God, some express an eagerness to die when He decides they are ready. Those who have been bitten and who have recovered seem to receive special deference from other members of the church.

The ritual of serpent-handling takes only 15 or 20 minutes in religious sessions that are seldom shorter than four hours. The rest of the service includes singing Christian hymns, ecstatic dancing, testifying, extemporaneous and impassioned sermons, faith-healing, "speaking in tongues," and foot-washing. These latter rituals are a part of the firmly-rooted Holiness movement, which encompasses thousands of churches in the Southern Appalachian region. The Holiness churches started in the 19th century as part of a perfectionist movement.

The social and psychological functions served by the Scrabble Creek church are probably very much the same as those served by the more conventional Holiness churches. Thus, the extreme danger of the Scrabble Creek rituals probably helps to validate the members' claims to holiness. After all, the claim that one is a living saint is pretentious even in a sacred society—and it is particularly difficult to maintain in a secular society. That the serpent-handler regularly risks his life for his religion is seen as evidence of his saintliness. As the serpent-handler stresses over and over, "I'm afraid of snakes like anybody else, but when God anoints me, I handle them with joy." The fact that he is usually not bitten, or if bitten usually recovers, is cited as further evidence of his claim to holiness.

After we had observed the Scrabble Creek serpent-handlers for some time, we decided to give them psychological tests. We enlisted the aid of Auke Tellegen, department of psychology, University of Minnesota, and three of his clinical associates: James Butcher, William Schofield, and Anne Wirt. They interpreted the Minnesota Multiphasic Personality Inventory that we administered to 50 serpent-handlers (46 were completed)—and also to 90 members of a conventional-denomination church 20 miles from Scrabble Creek. What we wanted to find out was how these two groups differed.

What we found were important personality differences not only between the serpent-handlers and the conventional church members, but also between the older and the younger generations within the conventional group. We believe that these differences are due, ultimately, to differences in social class: The serpent-handlers come from the nonmobile working class (average annual income: $3000), whereas members of the conventional church are upwardly mobile working-class people (average annual income: $5000) with their eyes on the future.

But first, let us consider the similarities between the two groups. Most of the people who live in the south central part of West Virginia, serpent-handlers or not, have similar backgrounds. The area is rural, nonfarm, with only about one-tenth of the population living in settlements of more than 2500. Until recently, the dominant industry was coal-mining, but in the last 15 years mining operations have been drastically curtailed. The result has been widespread unemployment. Scrabble Creek is in that part of Appalachia that has been officially declared a "depressed area"—which means that current unemployment rates there often equal those of the depression.

There are few foreign-born in this part of West Virginia. Most of the residents are of Scottish-Irish or Pennsylvania Dutch descent, and their ancestors came to the New World so long ago that there are no memories of an Old World past.

Generally, public schools in the area are below national standards. Few people over 50 have had more than six or seven years of elementary education.

Religion has always been important here. One or two generations ago, the immediate ancestors of both serpent-handlers and conventional-church members lived in the same mining communities and followed roughly the same religious practices. Today there is much "back-sliding," and the majority seldom attend church regularly. But there is still a great deal of talk about religion, and there are few professed atheists.

HYPOCHONDRIA AND THE HOLY SPIRIT

Though the people of both churches are native-born Protestants with fundamentalist religious beliefs, little education, and precarious employment, the two groups seem to handle their common problems in very different ways. One of the first differences we noticed was in the way the older members of both churches responded to illness and old age. Because the members of both churches had been impoverished and medically neglected during childhood and young adulthood, and because they had earned their livelihoods in hazardous and health-destroying ways, they were old before their time. They suffered from a wide variety of physical ailments. Yet while the older members of the conventional church seemed to dwell morbidly on their physical disabilities, the aged serpent-handlers seemed able to cheerfully ignore their ailments.

The serpent-handlers, in fact, went to the opposite extreme. Far from being pessimistic hypochondriacs like the conventional-church members, the serpent-handlers were so intent on placing their fate in God's benevolent hands that they usually failed to take even the normal precautions in caring for their health. Three old serpent-handlers we knew in Scrabble Creek were suffering from serious cardiac conditions. But when the Holy Spirit moved them, they danced ecstatically and violently. And they did this without any apparent harm.

No matter how ill the old serpent-handlers are, unless they are actually prostrate in their beds they manage to attend and enjoy church services lasting four to six hours, two or three times a week. Some have to travel long distances over the mountains to get to church. When the long sessions are over, they appear refreshed rather than weary.

One evening an elderly woman was carried into the serpent-handling church in a wheelchair. She had had a severe stroke and was almost completely paralyzed. Wheeled to the front of the church, she watched everything throughout the long services. During one particularly frenzied singing and dancing session, the fingers of her right hand tapped lightly against the arm of the chair. This was the only movement she was able to make, but obviously she was enjoying the service. When friends leaned over and offered to take her home, she made it clear she was not ready to go. She stayed until the end, and gave the impression of smiling when she was finally wheeled out. Others in the church apparently felt pleased rather than depressed by her presence.

Both old members of the conventional denomination and old serpent-handlers undoubtedly are frequently visited by the thought of death. Both rely on religion for solace, but the serpent-handlers evidently are more successful. The old serpent-handlers are not frightened by the prospect of death. This is true not only of those members who handle poisonous snakes in religious services, but also of the minority who do *not* handle serpents.

One 80-year-old member of the Scrabble Creek church—who did not handle serpents—testified in our presence: "I am not afraid to meet my Maker in Heaven. I am ready. If somebody was to wave a gun in my face, I would not turn away. I am in God's hands."

Another old church member, a serpent-handler, was dying from silicosis. When we visited him in the hospital he appeared serene, although he must have known that he would not live out the week.

The assertion of some modern theologians that whatever meaning and relevance God once may have had has been lost for modern man does not apply to the old serpent-handlers. To them, God is real. In fact, they often see Him during vivid hallucinations. He watches over the faithful. Misfortune and even death do not shake their faith, for misfortune is interpreted, in accordance with God's inscrutable will, as a hidden good.

Surprisingly, the contrast between the optimistic old serpent-handlers and the pessimistic elders of the conventional church all but disappeared when we shifted to the younger members of the two groups. Both groups of young people, on the psychological tests, came out as remarkably well adjusted. They showed none of the neurotic and depressive tendencies of the older conventional-church members. And this cheerful attitude prevailed despite the fact that many of them, at least among the young serpent-handlers, had much to be depressed about.

The young members of the conventional church are much better off, socially and economically, than the young serpent-handlers. The parents of the young conventional-church members can usually provide the luxuries that most young Americans regard as necessities. Many conventional-church youths are active in extracurricular activities in high school or are attending college. The young serpent-handlers, in contrast, are shunned and stigmatized as "snakes." Most young members of the conventional denomination who are in high school intend to go on to college, and they will undoubtedly attain a higher socioeconomic status than their parents have attained. But most of the young serpent-handlers are not attending school. Many are unemployed. None attend or plan to attend college, and they often appear quite depressed about their economic prospects.

The young serpent-handlers spend a great deal of time wandering aimlessly up and down the roads of the hollows, and undoubtedly are bored when not attending church. Their conversation is sometimes marked by humor, with undertones of cynicism and bitterness. We are convinced that what prevents many of them from becoming delinquent or demoralized is their wholehearted participation in religious practices that provide an acceptable outlet for their excess energy, and strengthen their self-esteem by giving them the opportunity to achieve "holiness."

Now, how does all this relate to the class differences between the serpent-handlers and the conventional-church group? The answer is that what allows the serpent-handlers to cope so well with their problems—what allows the older members to rise above the worries of illness and approaching death, and the younger members to remain relatively well-adjusted despite their grim economic prospects—is a certain approach to life that is typical of them as members of the stationary working class. The key to this approach is hedonism.

HOPELESSNESS AND HEDONISM

The psychological tests shows that the young serpent-handlers, like their elders, were more impulsive and spontaneous than the members of the conventional church. This may account for the strong appeal of the

Holiness churches to those members of the stationary working class who prefer religious hedonism to reckless hedonism, with its high incidence of drunkenness and illegitimacy. Religious hedonism is compatible with a puritan morality—and it compensates for its constraints.

The feeling that one cannot plan for the future, expressed in religious terms as "being in God's hands," fosters the widespread conviction among members of the stationary working class that opportunities for pleasure must be exploited immediately. After all, they may never occur again. This attitude is markedly different from that of the upwardly mobile working class, whose members are willing to postpone immediate pleasures for the sake of long-term goals.

Hedonism in the stationary working class is fostered in childhood by parental practices that, while demanding obedience in the home, permit the child license outside the home. Later, during adulthood, this orientation toward enjoying the present and ignoring the future is reinforced by irregular employment and the other insecurities of stationary working-class life. In terms of middle-class values, hedonism is self-defeating. But from a psychiatric point of view, for those who actually have little control of their position in the social and economic structure of modern society, it may very well aid acceptance of the situation. This is particularly true when it takes a religious form of expression. Certainly, hedonism and the associated trait of spontaneity seen in the old serpent-handlers form a very appropriate attitude toward life among old people who can no longer plan for the future.

In addition to being more hedonistic than members of the conventional church, the serpent-handlers are also more exhibitionistic. This exhibitionism and the related need for self-revelation are, of course, directly related to the religious practices of the serpent-handling church. But frankness, both about others and themselves, is typical of stationary working-class people in general. To a large extent, this explains the appeal of the Holiness churches. Ordinarily, their members have little to lose from frankness, since their status pretensions are less than those of the upwardly mobile working class, who are continually trying to present favorable images of themselves.

Because the young members of the conventional de-nomination are upwardly mobile, they tend to regard their elders as "old-fashioned," "stick-in-the-muds," and "ignorant." Naturally, this lack of respect from their children and grandchildren further depresses the sagging morale of the older conventional-church members. They respond resentfully to the tendency of the young "to think they know more than their elders." The result is a vicious circle of increasing alienation and depression among the older members of the conventional denomination.

RESPECT FOR AGE

There appears to be much less psychological incompatibility between the old and the young serpent-handlers. This is partly because the old serpent-handlers manage to retain a youthful spontaneity in their approach to life. Then too, the young serpent-handlers do not take a superior attitude toward their elders. They admire their elders for their greater knowledge of the Bible, which both old and young accept as literally true. And they also admire their elders for their handling of serpents. The younger church members, who handle snakes much less often than the older members do, are much more likely to confess an ordinary, everyday fear of snakes—a fear that persists until overcome by strong religious emotion.

Furthermore, the young serpent-handlers do not expect to achieve higher socioeconomic status than their elders. In fact, several young men said they would be satisfied if they could accomplish as much. From the point of view of the stationary working class, many of the older serpent-handlers are quite well-off. They sometimes draw two pensions, one from Social Security and one from the United Mine Workers.

Religious serpent-handling, then—and all the other emotionalism of the Holiness churches that goes with it—serves a definite function in the lives of its adherents. It is a safety valve for many of the frustrations of life in present-day Appalachia. For the old, the serpent-handling religion helps soften the inevitability of poor health, illness, and death. For the young, with their poor educations and poor hopes of finding sound jobs, its promise of holiness is one of the few meaningful goals in a future dominated by the apparent inevitability of lifelong poverty and idleness.

The Secrets of Haiti's Living Dead

By Gino Del Guercio

Five years ago, a man walked into l'Estère, a village in central Haiti, approached a peasant woman named Angelina Narcisse, and identified himself as her brother Clairvius. If he had not introduced himself using a boyhood nickname and mentioned facts only intimate family members knew, she would not have believed him. Because, eighteen years earlier, Angelina had stood in a small cemetery north of her village and watched as her brother Clairvius was buried.

The man told Angelina he remembered that night well. He knew when he was lowered into his grave, because he was fully conscious, although he could not speak or move. As the earth was thrown over his coffin, he felt as if he were floating over the grave. The scar on his right cheek, he said, was caused by a nail driven through his casket.

The night he was buried, he told Angelina, a voodoo priest raised him from the grave. He was beaten with a sisal whip and carried off to a sugar plantation in northern Haiti where, with other zombies, he was forced to work as a slave. Only with the death of the zombie master were they able to escape, and Narcisse eventually returned home.

Legend has it that zombies are the living dead, raised from their graves and animated by malevolent voodoo sorcerers, usually for some evil purpose. Most Haitians believe in zombies, and Narcisse's claim is not unique. At about the time he reappeared, in 1980, two women turned up in other villages saying they were zombies. In the same year, in northern Haiti, the local peasants claimed to have found a group of zombies wandering aimlessly in the fields.

But Narcisse's case was different in one crucial respect; it was documented. His death had been recorded by doctors at the American-directed Schweitzer Hospital in Deschapelles. On April 30, 1962, hospital records show, Narcisse walked into the hospital's emergency room spitting up blood. He was feverish and full of aches. His doctors could not diagnose his illness, and his symptoms grew steadily worse. Three days after he entered the hospital, according to the records, he died. The attending physicians, an American among them, signed his death certificate. His body was placed in cold storage for twenty hours, and then he was buried. He said he remembered hearing his doctors pronounce him dead while his sister wept at his bedside.

At the Centre de Psychiatrie et Neurologie in Port-au-Prince, Dr. Lamarque Douyon, a Haitian-born, Canadian-trained psychiatrist, has been systematically investigating all reports of zombies since 1961. Though convinced zombies were real, he had been unable to find a scientific explanation for the phenomenon. He did not believe zombies were people raised from the dead, but that did not make them any less interesting. He speculated that victims were only made to *look* dead, probably by means of a drug that dramatically slowed metabolism. The victim was buried, dug up within a few hours, and somehow reawakened.

The Narcisse case provided Douyon with evidence strong enough to warrant a request for assistance from colleagues in New York. Douyon wanted to find an ethnobotanist, a traditional-medicines expert, who could track down the zombie potion he was sure existed. Aware of the medical potential of a drug that could dramatically lower metabolism, a group organized by the late Dr. Nathan Kline—a New York psychiatrist and pioneer in the field of psychopharmacology—raised the funds necessary to send someone to investigate.

The search for that someone led to the Harvard Botanical Museum, one of the world's foremost institutes of ethnobiology. Its director, Richard Evans Schultes, Jeffrey professor of biology, had spent thirteen years in the tropics studying native medicines. Some of his best-known work is the investigation of curare, the substance used by the nomadic people of the Amazon to poison their darts. Refined into a powerful muscle relaxant called D-tubocurarine, it is now an essential component of the anesthesia used during almost all surgery.

Schultes would have been a natural for the Haitian investigation, but he was too busy. He recommended another Harvard ethnobotanist for the assignment, Wade Davis, a 28-year-old Canadian pursuing a doctorate in biology.

Davis grew up in the tall pine forests of British Columbia and entered Harvard in 1971, influenced by a Life magazine story on the student strike of 1969. Before Harvard, the only Americans he had known were draft dodgers, who seemed very exotic. "I used to fight forest fires with them," Davis says. "Like everybody else, I thought America was where it was at. And I wanted to go to Harvard because of that Life article.

When I got there, I realized it wasn't quite what I had in mind."

Davis took a course from Schultes, and when he decided to go to South America to study plants, he approached his professor for guidance. "He was an extraordinary figure," Davis remembers. "He was a man who had done it all. He had lived alone for years in the Amazon." Schultes sent Davis to the rain forest with two letters of introduction and two pieces of advice: wear a pith helmet and try ayahuasca, a powerful hallucinogenic vine. During that expedition and others, Davis proved himself an "outstanding field man," says his mentor. Now, in early 1982, Schultes called him into his office and asked if he had plans for spring break.

"I always took to Schultes's assignments like a plant takes to water," says Davis, tall and blond, with inquisitive blue eyes. "Whatever Schultes told me to do, I did. His letters of introduction opened up a whole world." This time the world was Haiti.

Davis knew nothing about the Caribbean island—and nothing about African traditions, which serve as Haiti's cultural basis. He certainly did not believe in zombies. "I thought it was a lark," he says now.

Davis landed in Haiti a week after his conversation with Schultes, armed with a hypothesis about how the zombie drug—if it existed—might be made. Setting out to explore, he discovered a country materially impoverished, but rich in culture and mystery. He was impressed by the cohesion of Haitian society; he found none of the crime, social disorder, and rampant drug and alcohol abuse so common in many of the other Caribbean islands. The cultural wealth and cohesion, he believes, spring from the country's turbulent history.

During the French occupation of the late eighteenth century, 370,000 African-born slaves were imported to Haiti between 1780 and 1790. In 1791, the black population launched one of the few successful slave revolts in history, forming secret societies and overcoming first the French plantation owners and then a detachment of troops from Napoleon's army, sent to quell the revolt. For the next hundred years Haiti was the only independent black republic in the Caribbean, populated by people who did not forget their African heritage. "You can almost argue that Haiti is more African than Africa," Davis says. "When the west coast of Africa was being disrupted by colonialism and the slave trade, Haiti was essentially left alone. The amalgam of beliefs in Haiti is unique, but it's very, very African."

Davis discovered that the vast majority of Haitian peasants practice voodoo, a sophisticated religion with African roots. Says Davis, "It was immediately obvious that the stereotypes of voodoo weren't true. Going around the countryside, I found clues to a whole complex social world." Vodounists believe they communicate directly with, indeed are often possessed by, the many spirits who populate the everyday world. Vodoun society is a system of education, law, and medicine; it embodies a code of ethics that regulates social behavior. In rural areas, secret vodoun societies, much like those found on the west coast of Africa, are as much or more in control of everyday life as the Haitian government.

Although most outsiders dismissed the zombie phenomenon as folklore, some early investigators, convinced of its reality, tried to find a scientific explanation. The few who sought a zombie drug failed. Nathan Kline, who helped finance Davis's expedition, had searched unsuccessfully, as had Lamarque Douyon, the Haitian psychiatrist. Zora Neale Hurston, an American black woman, may have come closest. An anthropological pioneer, she went to Haiti in the Thirties, studied vodoun society, and wrote a book on the subject, *Tell My Horse*, first published in 1938. She knew about the secret societies and was convinced zombies were real, but if a powder existed, she too failed to obtain it.

Davis obtained a sample in a few weeks.

He arrived in Haiti with the names of several contacts. A BBC reporter familiar with the Narcisse case had suggested he talk with Marcel Pierre. Pierre owned the Eagle Bar, a bordello in the city of Saint Marc. He was also a voodoo sorcerer and had supplied the BBC with a physiologically active powder of unknown ingredients. Davis found him willing to negotiate. He told Pierre he was a representative of "powerful but anonymous interests in New York," willing to pay generously for the priest's services, provided no questions were asked. Pierre agreed to be helpful for what Davis will only say was a "sizable sum." Davis spent a day watching Pierre gather the ingredients—including human bones—and grind them together with mortar and pestle. However, from his knowledge of poison, Davis knew immediately that nothing in the formula could produce the powerful effects of zombification.

Three weeks later, Davis went back to the Eagle Bar, where he found Pierre sitting with three associates. Davis challenged him. He called him a charlatan. Enraged, the priest gave him a second vial, claiming that this was the real poison. Davis pretended to pour the powder into his palm and rub it into his skin. "You're a dead man," Pierre told him, and he might have been, because this powder proved to be genuine. But, as the substance had not actually touched him, Davis was able to maintain his bravado, and Pierre was impressed. He agreed to make the poison and show Davis how it was done.

The powder, which Davis keeps in a small vial, looks like dry black dirt. It contains parts of toads, sea worms, lizards, tarantulas, and human bones. (To obtain the last ingredient, he and Pierre unearthed a child's grave on a nocturnal trip to the cemetery.) The poison is rubbed into the victim's skin. Within hours he begins to feel nauseated and has difficulty breathing. A pins-and-needles sensation afflicts his arms and legs, then progresses to the whole body. The subject becomes paralyzed; his lips turn blue for lack of oxygen. Quickly—sometimes within six hours—his metabolism is lowered to a level almost indistinguishable from death.

As Davis discovered, making the poison is an inexact science. Ingredients varied in the five samples he eventually acquired, although the active agents were always the same. And the poison came with no guarantee. Davis speculates that sometimes instead of merely paralyzing the victim, the compound kills him. Sometimes the victim suffocates in the coffin before he can be resurrected. But clearly the potion works well enough often enough to make zombies more than a figment of Haitian imagination.

Analysis of the powder produced another surprise. "When I went down to Haiti originally," says Davis, "my hypothesis was that the formula would contain *concombre zombi*, the 'zombie's cucumber,' which is a *Datura* plant. I thought somehow *Datura* was used in putting people down." *Datura* is a powerful psychoactive plant, found in West Africa as well as other tropical areas and used there in ritual as well as criminal activities. Davis had found *Datura* growing in Haiti. Its popular name suggested the plant was used in creating zombies.

But, says Davis, "there were a lot of problems with the *Datura* hypothesis. Partly it was a question of how the drug was administered. *Datura* could create a stupor in huge doses, but it just wouldn't produce the kind of immobility that was key. These people had to appear dead, and there aren't many drugs that will do that."

One of the ingredients Pierre included in the second formula was a dried fish, a species of puffer or blowfish, common to most parts of the world. It gets its name from its ability to fill itself with water and swell to several times its normal size when threatened by predators. Many of these fish contain a powerful poison known as tetrodotoxin. One of the most powerful nonprotein poisons known to man, tetrodotoxin turned up in every sample of zombie powder that Davis acquired.

Numerous well-documented accounts of puffer fish poisoning exist, but the most famous accounts come from the Orient, where *fugu* fish, a species of puffer, is considered a delicacy. In Japan, special chefs are licensed to prepare *fugu*. The chef removes enough poison to make the fish nonlethal, yet enough remains to create exhilarating physiological effects—tingles up and down the spine, mild prickling of the tongue and lips, euphoria. Several dozen Japanese die each year, having bitten off more than they should have.

"When I got hold of the formula and saw it was the *fugu* fish, that suddenly threw open the whole Japanese literature," says Davis. Case histories of *fugu* poisoning read like accounts of zombification. Victims remain conscious but unable to speak or move. A man who had "died" after eating *fugu* recovered seven days later in the morgue. Several summers ago, another Japanese poisoned by *fugu* revived after he was nailed into his coffin. "Almost all of Narcisse's symptoms correlated. Even strange things such as the fact that he said he was conscious and could hear himself pronounced dead. Stuff that I thought had to be magic, that seemed crazy. But,

in fact, that is what people who get *fugu*-fish poisoning experience."

Davis was certain he had solved the mystery. But far from being the end of his investigation, identifying the poison was, in fact, its starting point. "The drug alone didn't make zombies," he explains. "Japanese victims of puffer-fish poisoning don't become zombies, they become poison victims. All the drug could do was set someone up for a whole series of psychological pressures that would be rooted in the culture. I wanted to know why zombification was going on," he says.

He sought a cultural answer, an explanation rooted in the structure and beliefs of Haitian society. Was zombification simply a random criminal activity? He thought not. He had discovered that Clairvius Narcisse and "Ti Femme," a second victim he interviewed, were village pariahs. Ti Femme was regarded as a thief. Narcisse had abandoned his children and deprived his brother of land that was rightfully his. Equally suggestive, Narcisse claimed that his aggrieved brother had sold him to a *bokor*, a voodoo priest who dealt in black magic; he made cryptic reference to having been tried and found guilty by the "masters of the land."

Gathering poisons from various parts of the country, Davis had come into direct contact with the vodoun secret societies. Returning to the anthropological literature on Haiti and pursuing his contacts with informants, Davis came to understand the social matrix within which zombies were created.

Davis's investigations uncovered the importance of the secret societies. These groups trace their origins to the bands of escaped slaves that organized the revolt against the French in the late eighteenth century. Open to both men and women, the societies control specific territories of the country. Their meetings take place at night, and in many rural parts of Haiti the drums and wild celebrations that characterize the gatherings can be heard for miles.

Davis believes the secret societies are responsible for policing their communities, and the threat of zombification is one way they maintain order. Says Davis, "Zombification has a material basis, but it also has a societal logic." To the uninitiated, the practice may appear a random criminal activity, but in rural vodoun society, it is exactly the opposite—a sanction imposed by recognized authorities, a form of capital punishment. For rural Haitians, zombification is an even more severe punishment than death, because it deprives the subject of his most valued possessions: his free will and independence.

The vodounists believe that when a person dies, his spirit splits into several different parts. If a priest is powerful enough, the spiritual aspect that controls a person's character and individuality, known as *ti bon ange*, the "good little angel," can be captured and the corporeal aspect, deprived of its will, held as a slave.

From studying the medical literature on tetrodotoxin poisoning, Davis discovered that if a victim survives the first few hours of the poisoning, he is likely to recover fully from the ordeal. The subject simply revives spontaneously. But zombies remain without will, in a trance-like state, a condition vodounists attribute to the power of the priest. Davis thinks it possible that the psychological trauma of zombification may be augmented by *Datura* or some other drug; he thinks zombies may be fed a *Datura* paste that accentuates their disorientation. Still, he puts the material basis of zombification in perspective: "Tetrodotoxin and *Datura* are only templates on which cultural forces and beliefs may be amplified a thousand times."

Davis has not been able to discover how prevalent zombification is in Haiti. "How many zombies there are is not the question," he says. He compares it to capital punishment in the United States: "It doesn't really matter how many people are electrocuted, as long as it's a possibility." As a sanction in Haiti, the fear is not of zombies, it's of becoming one.

Davis attributes his success in solving the zombie mystery to his approach. He went to Haiti with an open mind and immersed himself in the culture. "My intuition unhindered by biases served me well," he says. "I didn't make any judgments." He combined this attitude with what he had learned earlier from his experiences in the Amazon. "Schultes's lesson is to go and live with the Indians as an Indian." Davis was able to participate in the vodoun society to a surprising degree, eventually even penetrating one of the Bizango societies and dancing in their nocturnal rituals. His appreciation of Haitian culture is apparent. "Everybody asks me how did a white person get this information? To ask the question means you don't understand Haitians— they don't judge you by the color of your skin."

As a result of the exotic nature of his discoveries, Davis has gained a certain notoriety. He plans to complete his dissertation soon, but he has already finished writing a popular account of his adventures. To be published in January by Simon and Schuster, it is called *The Serpent and the Rainbow*, after the serpent that vodounists believe created the earth and the rainbow spirit it married. Film rights have already been optioned; in October Davis went back to Haiti with a screenwriter. But Davis takes the notoriety in stride. "All this attention is funny," he says. "For years, not just me, but all Schultes's students have had extraordinary adventures in the line of work. The adventure is not the end point, it's just along the way of getting the data. At the Botanical Museum, Schultes created a world unto itself. We didn't think we were doing anything above the ordinary. I still don't think we do. And you know," he adds, "the Haiti episode does not begin to compare to what others have accomplished—particularly Schultes himself."

TOPIC *14*

The Social Costs of Modernization

Modernization refers to the global transformation of society, a transformation that has its roots in the emergence of the industrial revolution. Although its particular manifestations vary widely due to local social, historical, cultural, political, and economic conditions (and also environmental riches and limitations), students of modernization have noted that certain elements characterize this phenomenon everywhere. As summarized by anthropologist Helen Henderson, these include the following:

1. Subsistence farming gives way to cultivation of agricultural products for the market, and new jobs are created in trade, manufacturing, and administration.

2. New sources of energy are exploited, and individual wage earners operate machines within the industrial system.

3. Specialized educational institutions are created to bring literacy to the masses and impart new skills and knowledge.

4. Urban areas develop rapidly as rural immigrants flow into cities in search of economic opportunities. Urbanites cut their ties with their extended kin, are freed from many traditional restraints, and step into new social roles.

5. The functions of the family change (and the form may as well). The family is no longer a unit of production but instead specializes in the socialization of offspring and the organization of consumption.

6. Some scholars would add that modernization also introduces new forms of alienation into the lives of industrial workers, who lose control over the product of their labor and whose work tends to be repetitive and dull.

Modernization, therefore, means far more than a series of adjustments in indigenous economic systems. Rather, it refers to qualitative changes in the organization of society, in culture, and even in individual personalities.

Modernization is a European invention. It was exported from Europe (and America, its descendant) to the so-called Third World through the politics of colonialism and the sociopolitical economy of imperialism. Although its benefits to indigenous societies have been tabulated in terms of increased life spans, better health conditions, rising literacy, and broadened opportunities, the social costs of modernization have been high.

Imperialist nations systematically destroyed indigenous societies' subsistence economies, converting them to specialized cash-crop (rubber, tobacco) or mineral (metal ores, diamonds) economies. Whereas before modernization the native populations could easily provide for their own subsistence needs, they were suddenly forced to participate in an economic system that was controlled from afar, that kept down the prices of what they had to offer, that made them dependent on high-priced imported goods, and that kept their wages low. Thus, modernization created poverty in many areas of the world where, before, the concept simply had no meaning.

In "Requiem for a Lost People," William W. Howells documents the horrifying story of the complete annihilation of the aboriginal population of Tasmania (an island south of Australia) by land-hungry European settlers in the nineteenth century. In "Societies on the Brink," David Maybury-Lewis lays out current rationales for the continuing destruction of small, semi-isolated societies and also presents anthropologically based arguments against this ongoing trend. He advocates social pluralism and suggests that the alternatives are grim.

Lauriston Sharp's classic article, "Steel Axes For Stone-Age Australians," illustrates Maybury-Lewis's point. She recounts how the introduction by missionaries of one small item of Western technology—the steel axe—totally disrupted and destabilized the culture of an aboriginal people, the Yir Yoront.

Although it appears inevitable that small-scale societies will be transformed and absorbed as they come into contact with modern civilization, the final article strikes a somewhat hopeful, as well as pragmatic, note. Earlier in this book (Article 23), Napoleon A. Chagnon described some of his fieldwork experiences among the Yąnomamö of Venezuela. Since the 1960s, he has returned several times to live among the Yąnomamö and to observe the changes that increasing contact with modern industrial society has wrought among "his" people. In "The Beginning of Western Acculturation," Chagnon argues that anthropologists have a special responsibility to see to it that the transformation and absorption of tribal societies occur in humane and enlightened ways. And he describes some of the measures he has taken to ease the Yąnomamö into the twentieth century.

Requiem for a Lost People

By William W. Howells

No segment of humankind can have been rushed into oblivion as speedily as the aboriginals of Tasmania. Dark-skinned and woolly-haired, superficially they looked like Africans, though this is only skin-deep. Anthropologists regret their rapid passing; there is a great deal they would have liked to ask the Tasmanians, but in the early nineteenth century anthropology was a science unborn. There are other things to regret.

Tasmania is the shield-shaped island lying south of Australia's southeast corner. Its towns today give off a staid provincial air, and its countryside is rich in apples and flowers, but a hundred and fifty years ago the keynotes were kangaroos and violence. The island is a little like New England—north for south of course, since it lies in the other hemisphere. Its northern coast, nearest Australia, has the same latitude in the south as has New York in the north, and its southern end, with the city of Hobart, has about the latitude of Portland, Maine. But Tasmania lacks New England's antic weather. Deep snow may fall in the high interior, which is colder than the coast, and there are glaciers in the mountains. Still, while there was some risk from exposure if they were separated from companions and fire, the native Tasmanians essentially wore no clothes. On the shore, winters are mild and summers are cool. Over the year, the average temperature for the day changes only about eighteen degrees, from 46° to 64° Fahrenheit, compared with a swing of well over forty degrees in coastal New England. In fact, the thermometer may go up and down more during a single Tasmanian day than does the day's average during the whole year. Tell that in Boston.

During the late ice age it was colder, with larger glaciers in the center. Almost 25,000 years ago, while it was still a peninsula of Australia, aboriginal hunters are known to have entered Tasmania, to be marooned about twelve thousand years later, when the world's major ice sheets melted and the seas rose.

They were a culturally simple people, like their surviving cousins in Australia, and as time went on they became simpler still, their recent equipment being the most modest on record. When seen by Europeans, they lacked boomerangs, dogs, and hafted stone tools, all of which were invented or acquired in Australia after the original Tasmanians had left. And for some mysterious reason they gave up the catching of fish, although they continued to appreciate shellfish. Evidently the land was good to them, with kangaroos and other marsupials to hunt, and the climate temperate enough so that an occasional cape of animal skin was all they ever wore. Two centuries ago about four thousand natives lived all over the island, except in the rugged mountains. Then, in thirty years, settlers from Australia and England wiped them out.

In the last crisis two men tried to stave off the extermination but only facilitated it, each in his own way. They were Governor George Arthur, with his printed proclamations and "picture boards," and G. A. Robinson, who went out to talk to the natives directly, in their own language. The Tasmanians themselves were neither ferocious nor hostile at first, as much testimony made clear too late. They were dangerous enough when provoked, and they fought to a limited extent among themselves over such things as trespass on hunting grounds or abduction of women, two offenses that the whites at once carried to intolerable excess. As for the "settlers," there could hardly have been a better team to carry out the annihilation. They were convicts, mostly hard cases from Australia. The first lot was accompanied by a handful of freemen given very small land grants to work with convict labor. Since a person might in those days be transported for what now pass as minor crimes (like stealing cars in Massachusetts?), some convicts were fairly decent men, but many, along with the soldiers sent to guard them, were capable of vicious brutality and in fact took pleasure in it. For a hundred years now, the fate of the Tasmanians has been a source of shame and lamentation, in today's high-minded Hobart as in the world at large. But in that time and place, it seems clear now, no other outcome was likely, as the repellent tragedy ran its course.

It started early, with the Risdon Massacre. The first arrivals from Sydney set up camp in 1803 along the mouth of the Derwent River in the vicinity of Hobart, founded a little later. They had already been officially enjoined to treat the natives with kindness, and threatened with punishment for violence to them. But there seems to have been little contact with Tasmanians as the first small farms were set up. Then, on a day in May 1804, about three hundred aboriginals—men, women, and children—appeared out of the woods forming a half-circle to surround kangaroos driven ahead of them. They had no spears, only clubs, and the fact that women and children joined in shows that they were not a war party. But a farmer a short distance away appears to have been frightened, and the semicircle seemed to be surrounding the camp. The officer in command of the soldiers (drunk, by accounts) was persuaded by the camp surgeon to fire on them with cannon loaded with grapeshot, killing a number. How many was not known, since the natives carried off some badly wounded members. The surgeon entertained the chaplain with a dissection of one corpse, and sent some pickled bones to Australia. Children were captured as well.

A few days later, the aboriginals retaliated with an attack on sailors gathering oysters, though no one was killed. In the next couple of years inexpert farming (the settlers were largely townspeople originally) and inept government supply led to a serious food shortage in the colony, which the governor met by setting a good price on kangaroo meat and encouraging hunting. Off into the bush went all who could be given a gun—not homesteaders, but their convict bond servants. Many of these saw at once how much better a free bush life was than harsh treatment and forced labor in the colony. Bushrangers increased in number as time went on, becoming dangerous men skilled in bushcraft, desperadoes of the worst sort who preyed on and murdered settlers, costing successive governors much effort in capturing and hanging them.

They also figured prominently in the long erosion of the native Tasmanians. But hostilities grew up gradually, and developed into the Black War only twenty years later. In spite of the Risdon Massacre, the local natives seemed not to be vindictive, only careful, and of course for some years aboriginals elsewhere in the large island knew little about the whites. Witnesses say they were friendly and helpful at the very start. Later, even when most settlers considered the Tasmanians enemies, other settlers could wander safely in the bush, and their young people joined aboriginal groups in hunting.

Nevertheless, new colonists were pressing up the whole fertile eastern side of the island, and from about 1818 people with more money and importance were taking out large grants of land. Beyond them roamed the bushrangers, capturing native women and often killing off a husband in the process—Tasmanian

men were very jealous of their wives. Wifeless settlers often did the same; Robinson, for example, was told of cases in which "stockkeepers had chained the females to their huts with bullock chains for the purpose of fornication." Partners in all this were seal hunters along the north coast, who had established themselves even before the colony in the south, and who remained effectively out of its control. They were American, British, New Zealander, or Polynesian, and as free of restraint or scruple as the bushrangers. Such a man usually supplied himself with two to five aboriginal women for sex and slavery, to help in sealing, hunting kangaroos, and skinning birds, and to be shot out of hand if they failed to get the work done or tried to escape. This glib description covers many specific accounts of atrocities, which we will do without. The point is that, whether or not a Tasmanian husband was actually dispatched for every woman taken, the women were removed as aboriginal mothers, with devastating effects on the next generation. When they gave birth to half-caste children, the women regarded them as despicable and usually killed them.

Bear in mind that the testimony, nauseating as it is, comes from our side, the European. If all the things Tasmanians saw and suffered could be known, the effect would be even more appalling. Settlers were outraged at

The Conciliation, *oil painting by Benjamin Duterrau, 1840. George Augustus Robinson, protector of aboriginals, is shown with native Tasmanians on Bruny Island. The woman beside him is thought to be Truganini. Reproduced courtesy of the Tasmanian Museum and Art Gallery.*

interference with their land-clearing, and the occasional spearing of cattle by natives; it did not occur to them that Tasmanians, not using the land for farming, might likewise have a sense of outrage—apart from their feelings at being shot up by any white man who took it into his mind. Of course, the Tasmanians were not passive, although reprisal on their part was long in becoming common. Their weapons were simple: carefully chosen stones, and long wooden javelins with fire-hardened points, both thrown with extraordinary marksmanship even at a distance. In later years they used ruses to draw a farmer away from his house, spearing the family in his absence. They were always skilled stalkers and ambushers. They developed the trick of walking while dragging a javelin, between the big toe and the next, through the grass where it could not be seen. Stark naked, such a man seemed to be unarmed—certainly with nothing up his sleeve—until he could approach a settler within easy spearing distance. (Tit for tat, one farmer taught himself to do the same thing with a shotgun.) Some such

Truganini, the last full-blooded Tasmanian aboriginal to live in Tasmania, died May 8, 1876, and was buried near Hobart. She reportedly had feared a fate similar to the last aboriginal male, William Lanne, who had died seven years before. On the eve of his funeral, a surgeon acting for a scientific society allegedly removed Lanne's skull and substituted another, and competitors made off with his hands and feet. The night after the burial, what remained of the corpse was removed from the grave and was never recovered.

Two years after Truganini's burial, she was exhumed and her skeleton put on display in the Tasmanian Museum and Art Gallery. There it remained for nearly a hundred years. Last April, in response to pressure from people of Tasmanian-aboriginal descent, Truganini's skeleton was cremated and the ashes scattered in Tasmania's D'Entrecasteaux Channel.

This photograph of Truganini was taken in 1866 by Charles A. Wooley and is reproduced courtesy of the Tasmanian Museum and Art Gallery.

things they invented on their own, and others they picked up from white bush-rangers. They even made up bush-ranging groups themselves in a few instances. An Australian aboriginal convict named Mosquito was sent to Hobart to be a police scout. Bored, he ended by forming a gang of shantytown Tasmanians and taking to the bush, where he enjoyed a long outburst of crime before he was apprehended and suspended.

Back at the center, officialdom tried to control things, with ever smaller success, until at last its hand was forced against the natives willy-nilly, as a result of the cumulative acts of its own unruly subjects. Governor after governor tried in good conscience to carry out the early admonition not to harm the aboriginals, at least as far as words would serve. David Collins in 1810 ordered that violence against the natives be dealt with in the same manner as violence against a "civilized person." Thomas Davey in 1814 proclaimed that recent hostility of the natives was traceable to ill-treatment, especially the kidnapping of children. William Sorrell in 1817-1819 said the same, at great length, sternly forbidding such abductions. Governor Arthur arrived in 1824 and promptly issued a proclamation that he would punish ill-treatment of natives. And he did so, handing out 25 lashes to some colonists who had brutalized native women. (Such brutalities, which usually escaped punishment, were chaining a woman to a log, burning another with firebrands, and making another wear the head of her fresh-killed husband around her neck, and do not include outright murders by shooting, pushing onto a fire, and so on.)

In 1828, Arthur posted another proclamation, again admitting the depredations of the whites, but now trying to calm things by ordering the Tasmanians to stay out of the settled areas unless they procured official passports to gather shellfish on the coast. Of course the natives could not read this document even if they should see it; and the governor had no hot line to the interior—in fact one problem all along was that chiefs who one would expect could be negotiated with did not exist. So in early 1830, Arthur made one more try at proclaiming even-handed treatment for the natives, in a way they might grasp, with his famous picture boards.

They were the 1830 equivalent of propaganda leaflets dropped behind enemy lines. The message is clear enough, to us; its intentional simplicity read something like this: "Natives and whites can mingle in amity; natives should come meet Governor (recognize him by cocked hat); black spear white, black hang; white shoot black, white hang." Citizens who saw them thought them hilarious. But the idea was ingenious, and at least better than printed officialese in its promise of getting

across. (It seems to have been suggested by a colonist who had seen a charcoal drawing on a tree done by aboriginals, which showed a settler cart train they had been watching from hiding.) The boards were hung in trees where it was thought aboriginals would see them.

The picture boards had no effect. And the message was false, as earlier proclamations had been. Blacks had indeed been hanged in plenty, some for killing settlers and some who were falsely accused of murders committed by whites. But in the whole story no white was ever hanged for killing a black, in spite of cases of solid testimony to the killing. And little other punishment was handed out for all the murders, kidnappings, maimings, and other crimes against the blacks. This was not, however, squeamishness about using the gallows; on one occasion a single sitting of judges sentenced 37 whites to hang for offenses against whites.

The picture boards were a watershed—the last attempt at asserting native rights to justice. Actually, the wind had been blowing the other way ever more strongly, and the end came rather quickly. Although the governors wanted to protect the Tasmanians, or said they did, nobody else cared; and anyhow, a governor's constituency was the colonists, not the Tasmanians. Nor was a sense of moral responsibility the same as moral conviction. The government, whether local or back home in Britain, was nonplussed by the seemingly homeless, wandering naked savages, and compassion for these uncivilized folk did not extend to letting them interfere with the civilized spreading of farms and towns in a supposedly new and open land. As to spreading the gospel, for once the clergy sat on its hands and did nothing worth mentioning in behalf of the aboriginals. And the ordinary colonist's sense of humanity is epitomized by one of them. This jolly specimen amused a perfectly friendly black by holding an empty pistol to his own head and clicking the trigger. Then he suggested it was the native's turn at the same silly game, handed him a loaded pistol, and watched with satisfaction as the poor man blew his own brains out.

In any case, there was no road back. From about 1825 the Black War was on in earnest. After a generation of their special education by the whites, the

Tasmanians were waging total war, with their own cruelties and killings of personally innocent (not always, of course) settlers and their families. The Tasmanians were so successful, in spite of their primitive weapons and their dwindling numbers, that they were actually driving homesteaders back into the towns. The settlers demanded protection, and the government decided that the only solution to the aboriginal problem was extermination (certainly the settlers' choice) or holing them up somewhere out of the way. Governor Arthur's attempt to apply the second expedient was his most bizarre scheme of all, the Black Line.

This came in 1830, just after the picture boards, which were a last despairing cry and far too late. The Line was supposed to operate like a vast kangaroo surround, as used by the natives, starting at the perimeter of the whole settled southeastern third of the island and driving the Tasmanians before it into a cul-de-sac in the Tasman Peninsula at the island's corner. Such a drive had actually been used on the Australian mainland, with a degree of success. But the plains of Victoria were not the rugged and forested terrain of Tasmania. And the Black Line was not black, or thin red, but white, being composed partly of soldiers and partly of convicts but mostly of civilians, taking leave from whatever they were doing in farm or town to become instant woodsmen. It was a major effort for the still modest colony, although it was like executing the Schlieffen Plan with something over three thousand men having little or no training. The government doubtless had no idea how far aboriginal numbers had already ebbed, but there were still significant tribes in the area.

Governor Arthur organized the whole thing on paper in detail. D-day was October 7 and the Line, 120 miles long, started off with a man supposedly at every sixty yards. The story of the operation is a novel in itself. It would be superhuman, in that country, to maintain such a line in order. There were a few actual encounters with natives, and a few fancied ones. Some of these "Down Under Deerslayers" were wounded by their own comrades. One Tasmanian man was caught, as well as a boy about fifteen. Two more were shot dead. After seven weeks, the Line arrived at the neck of the Tasman Peninsula in great excitement and anticipation of the bag of aboriginals hemmed in there by the human net. The peninsula was scoured; it was empty. Newspapers poured scorn on the campaign for having spent £30,000 of His Majesty's money to catch one black man. But the £30,000 had, after all, gone into colonial pockets, and the participants agreed they had had a very good time.

The operation was perhaps the least harmful thing that was ever visited on the Tasmanians, who must have been amazed as they slipped through the Line or watched it pass them by. More effective measures against them were already afoot. One was "roving parties."

With the Black War heating up and with settlers and natives shooting on sight, Governor Arthur in 1826 had proclaimed the need to capture certain natives who had become adept in directing attacks (by learning from the whites), and the next year he divided the country into military districts and then proclaimed martial law—all this, remember, before the picture boards and the Black Line. In 1829 Arthur authorized six parties, staffed by convicts but headed by relatively responsible men, to hunt for natives, and in 1830—but still before the ambitious Line—he offered rewards of £5 a head (£2 for a child) for natives taken alive. This is just the system that has brought the orang-utan to the verge of extinction because, as a newspaper predicted correctly at the time, several would be killed for one captured. The methods of such parties, official or informal, varied from attempts to capture with limited loss of life to outright search-and-destroy missions. In 1827 an informal posse to avenge the death of a settler reported killing or wounding about sixty Tasmanians; and in another case, a party of police that had come under a stone-throwing attack caught the attackers in a defile and killed seventy of them, dashing the brains of the children. The formal roving parties had by the end of 1832 captured 236 aboriginals, obviously at great cost to tribal life.

The other arm of the pincers was George Augustus Robinson, who earned the title of Conciliator. He was raised in the building trades in London, had come to Tasmania to improve himself, and would retire at last to England, living in affluence and mingling with the gentry in Bath, where he died. He was goodhearted though jealous of his prerogatives. He was a devout Wesleyan; he missionized and preached to the Tasmanians as opportunity afforded, but did not let it interfere with his main object of communication. He had great fortitude, self-possession, and persistence. He became convinced by everything he heard, and by his own contacts, that the aboriginals were essentially mild and inoffensive, that their rights had been trampled on, and that they could be conciliated by decent treatment, if it were honest and official. His method was to go out among them everywhere; he had a few helpers, black and white, all unarmed, but he put himself at the head of his party and usually kept the other whites out of sight.

He had arrived in Tasmania in 1824, the same year as Governor Arthur. He soon formed his opinions but had no way of acting on them. Then in March 1829, the governor, in one of his deeds of good intention, published an advertisement in The Hobart Town Gazette seeking a man of good character who would try to effect friendly connections with the Tasmanians by taking charge of those on Bruny Island, across the bay from Hobart. The island was already partly settled by whites of the bad sort, and the surviving blacks needed protection and provisions, having little of either.

Robinson at once applied for and got the job, insisting on the salary being raised from £50 to £100 a year. He started his work in a week and carried it on for some months, but it does not seem to have been much of a success in helping the natives, who were a little too close to white civilization. However, it was an experience for Robinson. He observed a surprising mortality rate among the natives, from afflictions of unclear nature. In less than two months he had accumulated a vocabulary of 115 words of the local language and was also preaching in it to the aboriginals. With little formal education and no training he went on recording names and some words on his travels, noting where the languages were different; in spite of his crude renderings this has been an important source of information on these lost tongues. Finally, on Bruny he had met Truganini, an extraordinary girl of sixteen or seventeen, small of build, obviously intelligent, lively, resourceful, brave, and attractive. During his stay she was married (rather against her will) to Wooraddy, who had been mooning after her as the story opened. These two, and a few more Tasmanians from Bruny Island and elsewhere, were to accompany Robinson in all his travels, with Truganini as a constant source of intelligence he could not otherwise get, even when she did not know the language of an area.

At the beginning of 1830, Robinson started on his mission to conciliate outlying natives, a mission that would last some five years. He set out from Hobart westward along the coast, with his aboriginals and a few whites, including convicts. He was supported by a whaleboat and a schooner, but he himself went on foot—a trek sometimes extremely arduous—all around the shore, with inland excursions, until he reached Launceston in the northeast, just as the Black Line was kicking off to the south. He spent the next twelve months ranging through the northern interior and visiting the sealers, actually getting many of them to part with their Tasmanian women by threatening government action. The governor was impressed with the apparent success of Robinson in conciliating and bringing in natives, and promised him full support, giving him as his next objective the rounding up of the feared Big River tribe. On the last day of 1831, Robinson made friendly contact with two "sanguinary tribes," the Big River and Oyster Bay, and found that they came to a total of 26 persons: sixteen men, nine women, and one child, who put themselves under his protection. These figures alone reveal a people without a future.

Robinson made three more expeditions between 1832 and 1834, to remnant peoples in the still-wild west. In September 1832, a group of blacks he met in the northwest decided to spear him and his own natives, and he barely escaped by crossing a river on pieces of floating wood—he could not swim—pushed by Truganini. This was his closest call, as recorded in his long, immensely detailed journal. It is full of action, showing that his mission was no triumphal parade, but a long tussle of making contact in unmapped places through unknown languages, persuading aboriginals of his good intentions, and seeing many of those he persuaded change their minds and run off again. It contains his enumeration and naming of natives as he tried to learn facts; and it is larded with stories, some quite fresh, of horrors perpetrated by blacks and whites—though mostly by the latter and sometimes more sickening than any already mentioned. All this time he was bringing in parties of submitted aboriginals. The presumed last lot of Tasmanians was found at the

Tasmanian aboriginals at Oyster Cove. Taken in 1858 by Francis Russell (Bishop) Nixon, the photograph shows nearly all of the members of the race then living.

end of 1834 (by Robinson's sons after he had gone back to Hobart in August): it was made up of four women, one man, and three boys, who had wanted to turn themselves in but had been shot at by every white who saw them. One family or small group, however, is known to have remained at large until 1842.

The Conciliator had succeeded: he had rounded up Tasmania's aboriginals in a way everyone—official, humanitarian, or extirpationist—could approve. He was given public praise and reward, though he felt it was not prompt enough nor in a measure he was entitled to (he was recompensed for his captures at a kind of wholesale rate, less than the £5 a head previously offered). At his request he was made commandant of the new aboriginal settlement on Flinders Island, off the northeast corner of Tasmania, where all the natives were placed, after some smaller and less hospitable islands had been tried out.

In this windy place, now wearing clothing, which was probably often damp, the captives declined rapidly. There were not many, anyhow. Robinson's listing of natives he met is less than 300, showing how the population beyond the settlement zone had already shrunk, and he brought in less than 200—the roving parties rather more. Many Tasmanians never reached the settlement: of the tribe that had tried to kill him in September 1832, he and his people obtained the submission of eleven in July 1833; nine of these died inside three

weeks. When he took up residence on Flinders in 1835, there were only 106 on the island, not counting some he brought with him. Tuberculosis, influenza, and pneumonia continued the execution: in 1837 alone there were 29 deaths. There were a few births, but all infants died in a matter of weeks. Robinson left Tasmania in 1839, to become Protector of the Aborigines in Victoria, Australia. It is possible he took a few Tasmanians with him.

So aboriginal life was extinguished in Tasmania thirty years after the Risdon Massacre. Aboriginal bodies, it is true, went on breathing a while longer, like the mythical dead snake wriggling until sundown. Forty-four survivors (including some half-castes) were taken off Flinders in 1847 and brought down to Oyster Cove near Hobart. By 1854 sixteen were left. By 1870 there was one: hardy little Truganini herself.

She died in 1876, and so they ended. Actually, Robinson had been forced, some time earlier, to return a dozen or so aboriginal women to their sealer consorts on Cape Barren Island, and for all we know one or more of these may have outlived her. At any rate, from such unions there has grown up a present-day population of perhaps two thousand part-aboriginals. But with Truganini's death there went out the last known spark of native speech and ideas and memories. After twenty thousand years.

Societies on the Brink

By David Maybury-Lewis

....

Small societies around the world are currently threatened with extinction. The threat, either implicit or explicit, that they must die so that we may live is something we normally conceal from ourselves under comfortable phrases like "the social costs of development," or "the price of progress." The assumptions behind this sort of thinking need to be examined.

We need first to try to develop some perspective on a problem that is often debated with considerable passion. If we consider the whole span of human history, then it is clear that the majority of the peoples of the world lived until quite recent times in relatively small and relatively isolated societies. The emergence of powerful tribes, nations, or empires threatened the physical existence and certainly the cultural continuity of smaller, weaker peoples. This is a process that is as old as humankind itself. What has rendered it more dramatic in recent centuries is the development of what we are pleased to call "Western technology." This placed the nations of Western Europe and, later, North America at an enormous advantage and hastened the process of physical and cultural extinction of weaker peoples. Even China, an ancient and powerful civilization which hardly qualifies as a small-scale society, was shaken to its very foundations by the impact of the West. It was able to recover because of its vast reserves, demographic and otherwise. Small societies cannot recover. Instead, they face destruction, either by physical extinction or by absorption into the larger ones that press in on them.

The process has long been recognized; scholars have tried to grapple with its implications since the earliest days of the European expansion. For a while it was a matter for serious debate whether humanoid creatures encountered in other lands were really humans at all. The people in the other lands were equally puzzled. A British party was at first kept in cages by the Singhalese, who tried to determine whether or not they were actually human. We have similar reports from other parts of the world. In fact, even when the conventional attributes of humanity were granted to alien peoples, debate still raged as to whether they were fully human and therefore entitled to fully human treatment (whatever that might be by the standards of the time and place). Thus it became a matter of grave consequence whether they were or were not considered to be endowed with souls. Similarly, arguments raged as to whether peoples who apparently possessed the basic physical and mental equipment of human beings could nevertheless put themselves beyond the pale by practicing "inhuman" customs.

Cannibalism was usually regarded as one such practice. One can imagine with what *frisson* the Europeans of the sixteenth century read Hans Staden's *True History and Description of the Land of the Savage, Naked and Ugly Maneating Peoples of the New World of America* (1557). The Tupinamba Indians, who once held Staden captive, regularly and ritually killed and ate their prisoners. It was considered a heroic death. A captive warrior, who in some cases might have been living with his captors for years and might even have raised a family there, was led out and clubbed to death in a ceremonial duel, after which the entire community ate him to partake of his heroic essence. Staden also pointed out that the same Tupinamba were horrified by the cruelty of the Europeans with whom they came in contact. They considered the Europeans to be in some sense beyond the pale because of their inhuman customs, such as the routine use of torture in trials and punishments, and the practice of slavery.

The relativistic implications of the Tupinamba view were not, unfortunately, taken seriously by European scholars. The debates concerning the essential humanity of alien peoples and the rights to which they were entitled were conducted in strictly European terms. Even when the arguments were genuine—as in the case of the famous series of debates before the Spanish crown between Las Casas and Sepúlveda—the results were self-serving. When the debate went against the Indians, the local authorities considered that they had learned opinion on their side. When it came out favorably to the Indians, the local authorities refused to abide by its outcome. In the last analysis, the principal argument was power. The stronger tended to find justifications for using the weaker, or at the very least for making the weaker over in the image of the conqueror.

I have referred to these centuries-old arguments because modern versions of them still persist in our own thinking, both in our conventional wisdom and in the assumptions made by our theorists. On the one hand we have what may be called the liberal, neo-Darwinian view that small, weak societies are fated for extinction and that there is not much that can be done about it. Perhaps indeed, according to this view, there is not much that should be done about it, for why expend energy and resources in trying to interfere with irreversible processes that are part of the order of things? On the other hand, there is an orthodox Marxist position that holds that such societies are backward and out of step historically. They must therefore be assisted in getting in phase with history as rapidly as possible or they will be crushed by the relentless and irreversible force of historical process. But the results in practical terms of these two views are monotonously similar. Small societies are extinguished, culturally, or physically, or both.

These arguments are unsatisfactory. There is no natural or historical law that militates against small societies. There are only political choices. In fact the rhetoric of both the United States and the Soviet Union, to take the two strongest powers in the world today, stresses cultural pluralism as a goal for their own

In the northern Kalahari of Botswana, a San boy squeezes water from a grass sponge into his sister's mouth. The scene reflects the traditional San hunting-and-gathering way of life; the water comes from a depression in the trunk of a monongo tree, whose protein-rich nuts are a vital food source. In the years since this picture was taken, however, cultural change among the San has increased dramatically as a neighboring cattle-keeping people, the Herero, have encroached on their territories.

societies and indeed for the world at large. The fact that this rhetoric is not often put into practice is not a matter of natural or historical necessity but of political convenience.

A small society is of course a relative concept. Many nations are small compared with the superpowers but overwhelmingly large compared with some peoples in remote jungle regions who have just come into contact with the outside world. It is the societies at the lower end of this continuum with which I am primarily concerned, although the fact that it is a continuum and that the problem transcends the fate of isolated, tribal populations has certain implications, which I shall also discuss.

Anthropologists have often come to the defense of these tiny, tribal peoples. When they do, these anthropologists are

normally attacked with a battery of arguments that need to be explicitly stated and examined.

First it is contended that anthropologists want tribal peoples left alone simply to preserve a traditional way of life. They therefore want to halt the push to explore and exploit the resources of the earth. They are sentimentalists who stand up for the right of a few to live their own lives in backwardness and ignorance as against the right of the many to use the resources available. Anthropologists are therefore the enemies of development.

This is a serious misrepresentation, which makes the defenders of the rights of small-scale societies seem like the nineteenth-century Luddites, who went around smashing machines in a futile effort to halt the Industrial Revolution. Whether isolated, tribal societies would be better off if the world left them alone is an academic matter. They are not going to be permitted to live in isolation. The people who speak up for them do not argue that they should be left alone or that all exploration and development should be halted. On the contrary, we assume that isolated societies will not be left alone and are therefore concerned with how to soften the impact of inevitable contact so that it will not destroy them in the name of progress. To return to the Luddite analogy for a moment, we do not try to stem the Industrial Revolution by breaking the machines. We accept its inevitability but question the necessity of chaining children to the machines (as was done in nineteenth-century England) as a means of capital formation.

A second argument is a malicious variation on the first one. According to that, it is claimed that anthropologists would like to keep tribal peoples isolated in what amount to human zoos for their own research purposes.

Again this is a misrepresentation. Anthropologists and others who take an interest in such small societies argue that these peoples' contacts with the outside world should be regulated if they are not to prove destructive. A small society must therefore have a guaranteed territory that it can call its own. This should not be a reservation in the sense that its inhabitants are confined to and imprisoned on it, but rather a home base, which the members of the society can use as a springboard in their efforts to come to terms with the outside world.

Another variation on these arguments stresses the immorality of preventing "backward" peoples from enjoying the benefits of civilization. Who, it is asked, has the right to insist that a relatively isolated society be left alone, to manage without modern medicine and modern consumer goods? Some ardent proponents of this theme wax so eloquent that they make the anxious anthropologist seem like a puritan who is determined to deny color TV to the natives. But the argument, once again, is a distortion of a position that gets little hearing.

Those people who are concerned about the effects of contact are merely urging caution, based on an understanding of the possible harmful effects of such contact. One would have thought that the grim historical record of death, disease, and despair that also accompany the arrival of civilization in remote areas would be sufficient grounds for advocating a cautious approach. We now know a good deal about the diseases that are introduced and we know too that they tend to be unremitting, while the provision of modern medicine is often fitful or inadequate. At a later stage in the process, we know too that the introduction of new industries in remote and not-so-remote areas can lead to cultural breakdown and personal despair within the local population *as well as* providing jobs, increasing income, and so on. This is a familiar dilemma even in advanced societies, which is why people are so anxious to have a say in what happens to their own communities. There is an uneasy suspicion that the arrival of, say, an oil refinery may on balance produce costs for the people of the community where it is located and benefits for people elsewhere. We understand this element of trade-off keenly enough in advanced societies and yet we often seek to impose oil refineries or their equivalents on societies much less able to cope with them. When the results are not cottages and TV sets but disruption and even death, we tend to shrug our shoulders and reassure ourselves that such costs are unavoidable. I am arguing here that this is not so, and that such costs can be minimized even if not avoided altogether.

But the most insidious argument used against those who speak up for small societies is insidious precisely because it seems so reasonable. Why, it is asked, should such societies be protected anyway? What are the advantages of protecting their way of life? There are in fact many that have been claimed. We can learn from their life styles, since we are clearly so desperately unhappy with our own. We can learn from their views of the world, particularly as concerns the general interrelatedness of things on earth. Many Americans are, for example, discovering a harmony in American Indian views of the world which they find conducive not only to inner peace but also to a more effective use of the environment. There are other arguments that are frequently advanced as reasons for protecting the life style of small societies in different parts of the world. We need to do so in order to further our understanding of human cultural variation. We know too little about how societies work and about how they can be made to work *for* people rather than against them. Besides, it is claimed, the members of the small society will be more useful citizens in the larger one if they come into it with something of their own heritage intact. Then again, there may be genetic advantages in seeing that such groups are not physically extinguished, and so on.

But these are the wrong questions. Supposing we decided that we had nothing more to learn from small societies; that there was no particular genetic advantage in seeing them survive physically and no particular social or philosophical advantage in seeing them survive culturally. Would that then give us the right to eliminate these cultures? Would we be willing to apply a similar reasoning to the sick, the weak, or the aged in our own culture? The question, put that way, is horrifying, which is precisely why I called the original question insidious. If we accept it as a legitimate question, then we find ourselves debating the question of whether it is *useful* to permit another culture to survive. But useful to whom? Presumably the usefulness of their physical and social existence is not in doubt for the members of that culture. What we are in fact debating is whether their existence is useful to *us*. Such thinking can lead to the gas chambers and has done so in our own time. That is why the original question is the wrong one. The fundamental reason why we must help other cultures to survive is because in all conscience we have no alternative. It is a moral imperative of the sort that insists that the strong ought not to trample on the rights of the weak.

Some writers have referred to the process by which a powerful society extinguishes a weaker culture as *ethnocide*, and have argued that this is (and should be recognized as) a crime analogous to genocide. I understand and sympathize with the passion that informs this view, but I find the formulation of it unhelpful. Homicide is hard enough to define and the arguments concerning the circumstances under which it may or may not be justified are complex. Genocide is even more difficult and its use as a term of opprobrium all too often depends on the point of view of the user. I find the concept of ethnocide more difficult still, and much too vague to be helpful. The moment of a culture's death, even more so than that of a person, is difficult to perceive. The manner of its passing, save in the most obvious cases, is hard to evaluate.

Take some hypothetical cases. A society may occupy the territory of another so that the members of the latter are deprived of their livelihood. Or it may send missionaries into a territory, who then seek to undermine the culture they find. Alternatively, a timber company may move into an area and pay the local people for cutting down the forests off which they have traditionally lived. Again, a new industry may move into an area and effect profound changes in its way of life. Now, all of these changes have some disruptive effect on the local culture. At the same time all of them, save presumably the first instance, bring some benefits. How is one to decide on the precise ratio of costs to benefits that constitutes ethnocide? Indeed, how does one deal with the paradox of a society that may collaborate in its own ethnocide, permitting its culture to be extinguished in exchange for the benefits obtained from another society? In my view, the concept of *ethnocide* is too much of an either/or, life-or-death concept, and does little to help us understand situations where often it is not clear how to knock the gun out of the murderer's hand, or even who the murderer is or which is the gun.

I would insist instead that we are dealing with processes of contact and rapidly induced change that have in the past been known to have serious and even fatal consequences. The problem then is how to soften the contact and how to regulate the change so that its consequences for the small societies are minimally harmful. We are seeking to minimize the costs and to maximize the benefits for the people contacted.

This is not easy to do, however, since the benefits usually accrue to the wider society while the costs are borne largely by the contacted culture. We are thus dealing with a problem as old as humankind itself, namely that of protecting the weak against the strong. It is a problem that is unlikely to disappear and for which there are no easy solutions. Yet there are some things that can be done.

In the first place it is important to insist, as I have done here, on the right of other societies to their own ways of life. Such an insistence is not banal. This right is neither generally accepted nor generally understood. That is why it must be established that small-scale societies are not condemned to disappear by the workings of some abstract historical process. On the contrary, small societies may be shattered and their members annihilated, but this happens as a result of political choices made by the societies that impinge upon them, and for which the powerful must take responsibility. It is not, in any case, inevitable. The smaller societies can be assisted to deal with the impact of the outside world at comparatively little cost to those who bear down upon them. We have now come to recognize the principle that it is reasonable to set aside some part of the profits from the extraction of resources from the earth to be used to offset the ecological damage that may have been done in the process of extracting them. A similar understanding of the human costs of development and a willingness to deal with them is all that is necessary.

Such understanding and willingness cannot be taken for granted. It has to be cultivated and the attempt to cultivate it will not always be successful. It is unlikely, for example, that anybody, however eloquent or theoretically brilliant, could have convinced Hitler of the right of German Jews to their own cultural integrity. In such cases there may be no redress other than warfare or revolution. In many instances, however, the ways of persuasion have hardly been tried, and it is largely out of ignorance that planners make decisions that have such fatal costs for the small societies caught up in their plans. It is therefore vital that anthropologists and others concerned about the problem make people aware of its dimensions and point out that the cost of assisting small societies to become successful ethnic minorities is a comparatively small one, which may well be offset in the long run by the benefits the wider society will reap as a result.

Of course, attempts to protect threatened small-scale societies will not always be successful. The politics of some situations indicate that the minorities are doomed, if not physically, then at least as distinct cultures or subcultures. Yet this is no reason to abandon the effort in despair, any more than we abandon the efforts to avoid war or to construct just societies because these efforts are so often frustrated. I consider the effort to protect the cultural integrity of small-scale societies an issue of equal importance. We are talking not merely about the fate of tiny enclaves of people, buried in the last jungle refuges of this earth. What we are really talking about is the ability of human beings to discover ways to live together in plural societies. It seems to me that this is the critical issue of our times. Our success or failure in this endeavor may well decide whether people anywhere will be able to live in societies based on a minimum of mutual tolerance and respect. The alternatives are unpleasant to contemplate.

Steel Axes for Stone-Age Australians

By Lauriston Sharp

I.

Like other Australian aboriginals, the Yir Yoront group which lives at the mouth of the Coleman River on the west coast of Cape York Peninsula originally had no knowledge of metals. Technologically their culture was of the old stone age or paleolithic type. They supported themselves by hunting and fishing, and obtained vegetables and other materials from the bush by simple gathering techniques. Their only domesticated animal was the dog; they had no cultivated plants of any kind. Unlike some other aboriginal groups, however, the Yir Yoront did have polished stone axes hafted in short handles which were most important in their economy.

Towards the end of the 19th century metal tools and other European artifacts began to filter into the Yir Yoront territory. The flow increased with the gradual expansion of the white frontier outward from southern and eastern Queensland. Of all the items of western technology thus made available, the hatchet, or short handled steel axe, was the most acceptable to and the most highly valued by all aboriginals.

In the mid 1930's an American anthropoligist lived alone in the bush among the Yir Yoront for 13 months without seeing another white man. The Yir Yoront were thus still relatively isolated and continued to live an essentially inde-

pendent economic existence, supporting themselves entirely by means of their old stone age techniques. Yet their polished stone axes were disappearing fast and being replaced by steel axes which came to them in considerable numbers, directly or indirectly, from various European sources to the south.

What changes in the life of the Yir Yoront still living under aboriginal conditions in the Australian bush could be expected as a result of their increasing possession and use of the steel axe?

II. THE COURSE OF EVENTS

Events leading up to the introduction of the steel axe among the Yir Yoront begin with the advent of the second known group of Europeans to reach the shores of the Australian continent. In 1623 a Dutch expedition landed on the coast where the Yir Yoront now live.[1] In 1935 the Yir Yoront were still using the few cultural items recorded in the Dutch log for the aboriginals they encountered. To this cultural inventory the Dutch added beads and pieces of iron which they offered in an effort to attract the frightened "Indians." Among these natives metal and beads have disappeared, together with any memory of this first encounter with whites.

The next recorded contact in this area was in 1864. Here there is more positive assurance that the natives

concerned were the immediate ancestors of the Yir Yoront community. These aboriginals had the temerity to attack a party of cattle men who were driving a small herd from southern Queensland through the length of the then unknown Cape York Peninsula to a newly established government station at the northern tip.[2] Known as the "Battle of the Mitchell River," this was one of the rare instances in which Australian aboriginals stood up to European gunfire for any length of time. A diary kept by the cattle men records that: " . . . 10 carbines poured volley after volley into them from all directions, killing and wounding with every shot with very little return, nearly all their spears having already been expended. . . . About 30 being killed, the leader thought it prudent to hold his hand, and let the rest escape. Many more must have been wounded and probably drowned, for 59 rounds were counted as discharged." The European party was in the Yir Yoront area for three days; they then disappeared over the horizon to the north and never returned. In the almost three-year long anthropological investigation conducted some 70 years later—in all the material of hundreds of free association interviews, in texts of hundreds of dreams and myths, in genealogies, and eventually in hundreds of answers to direct and indirect questioning on just this particular matter—there was nothing that could be interpreted as a reference to this shocking contact with Europeans.

The aboriginal accounts of their first remembered contact with whites begin in about 1900 with references to persons known to have had sporadic but lethal encounters with them. From that time on whites continued to remain on the southern periphery of Yir Yoront territory. With the establishment of cattle stations (ranches) to the south, cattle men made occasional excursions among the "wild back-fellows" in order to inspect the country and abduct natives to be trained as cattle boys and "house girls." At least one such expedition reached the Coleman River where a number of Yir Yoront men and women were shot for no apparent reason.

About this time the government was persuaded to sponsor the establishment of three mission stations along the 700-mile western coast of the Peninsula in an attempt to help regulate the treatment of natives. To further this purpose a strip of coastal territory was set aside as an aboriginal reserve and closed to further white settlement.

In 1915, an Anglican mission station was established near the mouth of the Mitchell River, about a three-day march from the heart of the Yir Yoront country. Some Yir Yoront refused to have anything to do with the mission, others visited it occasionally, while only a few eventually settled more or less permanently in one of the three "villages" established at the mission.

Thus the majority of the Yir Yoront continued to live their old self-supporting life in the bush, protected until 1942 by the government reserve and the intervening mission from the cruder realities of the encroaching new order from the south. To the east was poor, uninhabited country. To the north were other bush tribes extending on along the coast to the distant Archer River Presbyterian mission with which the Yir Yoront had no contact. Westward was the shallow Gulf of Carpentaria on which the natives saw only a mission lugger making its infrequent dry season trips to the Mitchell River. In this protected environment for over a generation the Yir Yoront were able to recuperate from shocks received at the hands of civilized society. During the 1930's their raiding and fighting, their trading and stealing of women, their evisceration and two- or three-year care of their dead, and their totemic ceremonies continued, apparently uninhibited by western influence. In 1931 they killed a European who wandered into their territory from the east, but the investigating police never approached the group whose members were responsible for the act.

As a direct result of the work of the Mitchell River mission, all Yir Yoront received a great many more western artifacts of all kinds than ever before. As part of their plan for raising native living standards, the missionaries made it possible for aboriginals living at the mission to earn some western goods, many of which were then given or traded to natives still living under bush conditions; they also handed out certain useful articles gratis to both mission and bush aboriginals. They prevented guns, liquor, and damaging narcotics, as well as decimating diseases, from reaching the tribes of this area, while encouraging the introduction of goods they considered "improving." As has been noted, no item of western technology available, with the possible exception of trade tobacco, was in greater demand among all groups of aboriginals than the short handled steel axe. The mission always kept a good supply of these axes in stock; at Christmas parties or other mission festivals they were given away to mission or visiting aboriginals in-discriminately and in considerable numbers. In addition, some steel axes as well as other European goods were still traded in to the Yir Yoront by natives in contact with cattle stations in the south. Indeed, steel axes had probably come to the Yir Yoront through established lines of aboriginal trade long before any regular contact with whites had occurred.

III. RELEVANT FACTORS

If we concentrate our attention on Yir Yoront behavior centering about the original stone axe (rather than on the axe—the object—itself) as a cultural trait or item of cultural equipment, we should get some conception of the role this implement played in aboriginal culture. This, in turn, should enable us to foresee with considerable accuracy some of the results stemming from the displacement of the stone axe by the steel axe.

The production of a stone axe required a number of simple technological skills. With the various details of the axe well in mind, adult men could set about producing it (a task not considered appropriate for women or children). First of all a man had to know the location and properties of several natural resources found in his immediate environment: pliable wood for a handle, which could be doubled or bent over the axe head and bound tightly; bark, which could be rolled into cord for the binding; and gum, to fix the stone head in the haft. These materials had to be correctly gathered, stored, prepared, cut to size and applied or manipulated. They were in plentiful supply, and could be taken from anyone's property without special permission. Postponing consideration of stone head, the axe could be made by any normal man who had a simple knowledge of nature and of the technological skills involved, together with fire (for heating the gum), and a few simple cutting tools—perhaps the sharp shells of plentiful bivalves.

The use of the stone axe as a piece of capital equipment used in producing other goods indicates its very great importance to the subsistence economy of the aboriginal. Anyone—man, woman, or child—could use the axe; indeed, it was used primarily by women, for their's was the task of obtaining sufficient wood to keep the family campfire burning all day, for cooking or other purposes, and all night against mosquitoes and cold (for in July, winter temperature might drop below 40 degrees). In a normal lifetime a woman would use the axe to cut or knock down literally tons of firewood. The axe was also used to make other tools or weapons, and a variety of material equipment required by the aboriginal in his daily life. The stone axe was essential in the construction of the wet season domed huts which keep out some rain and some insects; of platforms which provide dry storage; of shelters which give shade in the dry summer when days are bright and hot. In hunting and fishing and in gathering vegetable or animal food the axe was also a necessary tool, and in this tropical culture, where preservatives or other means of storage are lacking, the natives spend more time obtaining food than in any other occupation—except sleeping. In only two instances was the use of the stone axe strictly limited to adult men: for gathering wild honey, the most prized food known to the Yir Yoront; and for making the secret paraphernalia for ceremonies. From this brief listing of some of the activities involving the use of the axe, it is easy to understand why there was at least one stone axe in every camp, in every hunting or fighting party, and in every group out on a "walkabout" in the bush.

The stone axe was also promi-

nent in interpersonal relations. Yir Yoront men were dependent upon interpersonal relations for their stone axe heads, since the flat, geologically-recent alluvial country over which they range provides no suitable stone for this purpose. The stone they used came from quarries 400 miles to the south, reaching the Yir Yoront through long lines of male trading partners. Some of these chains terminated with the Yir Yoront men, others extended on farther north to other groups, using Yir Yoront men as links. Almost every older adult man had one or more regular trading partners, some to the north and some to the south. He provided his partner or partners in the south with surplus spears, particularly fighting spears tipped with the barbed spines of sting ray which snap into vicious fragments when they penetrate human flesh. For a dozen such spears, some of which he may have obtained from a partner to the north, he would receive one stone axe head. Studies have shown that the sting ray barb spears increased in value as they move south and farther from the sea. One hundred and fifty miles south of Yir Yoront one such spear may be exchanged for one stone axe head. Although actual investigations could not be made, it was presumed that farther south, nearer the quarries, one sting ray barb spear would bring several stone axe heads. Apparently people who acted as links in the middle of the chain and who made neither spears nor axe heads would receive a certain number of each as a middleman's profit.

Thus trading relations, which may extend the individual's personal relationships beyond that of his own group, were associated with spears and axes, two of the most important items in a man's equipment. Finally most of the exchanges took place during the dry season, at the time of the great aboriginal celebrations centering

about initiation rites or other totemic ceremonials which attracted hundreds and were the occasion for much exciting activity in addition to trading.

Returning to the Yir Yoront, we find that adult men kept their axes in camp with their other equipment, or carried them when travelling. Thus a woman or child who wanted to use an axe—as might frequently happen during the day—had to get one from a man, use it promptly, and return it in good condition. While a man might speak of "my axe," a woman or child could not.

This necessary and constant borrowing of axes from older men by women and children was in accordance with regular patterns of kinship behavior. A woman would expect to use her husband's axe unless he himself was using it; if unmarried, or if her husband was absent, a woman would go first to her older brother or to her father. Only in extraordinary circumstances would she seek a stone axe from other male kin. A girl, a boy, or a young man would look to a father or an older brother to provide an axe for their use. Older men, too, would follow similar rules if they had to borrow an axe.

It will be noted that all of these social relationships in which the stone axe had a place are pair relationships and that the use of the axe helped to define and maintain their character and the roles of the two individual participants. Every active relationship among the Yir Yoront involved a definite and accepted status of superordination or subordination. A person could have no dealings with another on exactly equal terms. The nearest approach to equality was between brothers, although the older was always superordinate to the younger. Since the exchange of goods in a trading relationship involved a mutual reciprocity, trading partners usually stood in a brotherly type of relationship, although one was always classified as older than the other and would have some advantage in case of dispute. It can be seen that repeated and widespread conduct centering around the use of the axe helped to generalize and standardize these sex, age, and kinship roles both in their normal benevolent and exceptional malevolent aspects.

The status of any individual Yir Yoront was determined not only by sex, age, and extended kin relationships, but also by membership in one of two dozen patrilineal totemic clans into which the entire community was divided.[3] Each clan had literally hundreds of totems, from one or two of which the clan derived its name, and the clan members their personal names. These totems included natural species or phenomena such as the sun, stars, and daybreak, as well as cultural "species": imagined ghosts, rainbow serpents, heroic ancestors; such external cultural verities as fires, spears, huts; and such human activities, conditions, or attributes as eating, vomiting, swimming, fighting, babies and corpses, milk and blood, lips and loins. While individual members of such totemic classes or species might disappear or be destroyed, the class itself was obviously ever-present and indestructable. The totems, therefore, lent a permanence and stability to the clans, to the groupings of human individuals who generation after generation were each associated with a set of totems which distinguished one clan from another.

The stone axe was one of the most important of the many totems of the Sunlit Cloud Iguana clan. The names of many members of this clan referred to the axe itself, to activities in which the axe played a vital part, or to the clan's mythical ancestors with whom the axe was prominently associated. When it was necessary to represent the stone axe in totemic ceremonies,

only men of this clan exhibited it or pantomimed its use. In secular life, the axe could be made by any man and used by all; but in the sacred realm of the totems it belonged exclusively to the Sunlit Cloud Iguana people.

Supporting those aspects of cultural behavior which we have called technology and conduct, is a third area of culture which includes ideas, sentiments, and values. These are most difficult to deal with, for they are latent and covert, and even unconscious, and must be deduced from overt actions and language or other communicating behavior. In this aspect of the culture lies the significance of the stone axe to the Yir Yoront and to their cultural way of life.

The stone axe was an important symbol of masculinity among the Yir Yoront (just as pants or pipes are to us). By a complicated set of ideas the axe was defined as "belonging" to males, and everyone in the society (except untrained infants) accepted these ideas. Similarly spears, spear throwers, and fire-making sticks were owned only by men and were also symbols of masculinity. But the masculine values represented by the stone axe were constantly being impressed on all members of society by the fact that females borrowed axes but not other masculine artifacts. Thus the axe stood for an important theme of Yir Yoront culture: the superiority and rightful dominance of the male, and the greater value of his concerns and of all things associated with him. As the axe also had to be borrowed by the younger people it represented the prestige of age, another important theme running through Yir Yoront behavior.

To understand the Yir Yoront culture it is necessary to be aware of a system of ideas which may be called their totemic ideology. A fundamental belief of the aboriginal divided time into two great epochs: (1) a distant and sacred period at the

beginning of the world when the earth was peopled by mildly marvelous ancestral beings or culture heroes who are in a special sense the forebears of the clans; and (2) a period when the old was succeded by a new order which includes the present. Originally there was no anticipation of another era supplanting the present. The future would simply be an eternal continuation and reproduction of the present which itself had remained unchanged since the epochal revolution of ancestral times.

The important thing to note is that the aboriginal believed that the present world, as a natural and cultural environment, was and should be simply a detailed reproduction of the world of the ancestors. He believed that the entire universe "is now as it was in the beginning" when it was established and left by the ancestors. The ordinary cultural life of the ancestors became the daily life of the Yir Yoront camps, and the extraordinary life of the ancestors remained extant in the recurring symbolic pantomimes and paraphernalia found only in the most sacred atmosphere of the totemic rites.

Such beliefs, accordingly, opened the way for ideas of what *should* be (because it supposedly *was*) to influence or help determine what actually is. A man called Dog-chases-iguana-up-a-tree-and-barks-at-him-all-night had that and other names because he believed his ancestral alter ego had also had them; he was a member of the Sunlit Cloud Iguana clan because his ancestor was; he was associated with particular countries and totems of this same ancestor; during an initiation he played the role of a dog and symbolically attacked and killed certain members of other clans because his ancestor (conveniently either anthropomorphic or kynomorphic) really did the same to the ancestral alter egos of these men; and he would avoid his mother-in-law, joke with a mother's distant brother, and make spears in a certain way because his and other people's ancestors did these things. His behavior in these specific ways was outlined, and to that extent determined for him, by a set of ideas concerning the past and the relation of the present to the past.

But when we are informed that Dog-chases-etc. had two wives from the Spear Black Duck clan and one from the Native Companion clan, one of them being blind, that he had four children with such and such names, that he had a broken wrist and was left handed, all because his ancestor had exactly these same attributes, then we know (though he apparently didn't) that the present has influenced the past, that the mythical world has been somewhat adjusted to meet the exigencies and accidents of the inescapably real present.

There was thus in Yir Yoront ideology a nice balance in which the mythical was adjusted in part to the real world, the real world in part to the ideal pre-existing mythical world, the adjustments occurring to maintain a fundamental tenet of native faith that the present must be a mirror of the past. Thus the stone axe in all its aspects, uses, and associations was integrated into the context of Yir Yoront technology and conduct because a myth, a set of ideas, had put it there.

IV. THE OUTCOME

The introduction of the steel axe indiscriminately and in large numbers into the Yir Yoront technology occurred simultaneously with many other changes. It is therefore impossible to separate all the results of this single innovation. Nevertheless, a number of specific effects of the change from stone to steel axes may be noted, and the steel axe may be used as an epitome of the increasing quantity of European goods and implements received by the aboriginals and of their general influence on the native culture. The use of the steel axe to illustrate such influences would seem to be justified. It was one of the first European artifacts to be adopted for regular use by the Yir Yoront, and whether made of stone or steel, the axe was clearly one of the most important items of cultural equipment they possessed.

The shift from stone to steel axes provided no major technological difficulties. While the aboriginals themselves could not manufacture steel axe heads, a steady supply from outside continued; broken wooden handles could easily be replaced from bush timbers with aboriginal tools. Among the Yir Yoront the new axe was never used to the extent it was on mission or cattle stations (for carpentry work, pounding tent pegs, as a hammer, and so on); indeed, it had so few more uses than the stone axe that its practical effect on the native standard of living was negligible. It did some jobs better, and could be used longer without breakage. These factors were sufficient to make it of value to the native. The white man believed that a shift from steel to stone axe on his part would be a definite regression. He was convinced that his axe was much more efficient, that its use would save time, and that it therefore represented technical "progress" towards goals which he had set up for the native. But this assumption was hardly born out in aboriginal practice. Any leisure time the Yir Yoront might gain by using the steel axes or other western tools was not invested in "improving the conditions of life," nor, certainly, in developing aesthetic activities, but in sleep—an art they had mastered thoroughly.

Previously, a man in need of an axe would acquire a stone axe head through regular trading partners from whom he knew what to expect, and was then dependent solely upon a known and adequate natural environment, and his own skills or easily acquired techniques. A man wanting a steel axe, however, was in no such self-reliant position. If he attended a mission festival when steel axes were handed out as gifts, he might receive one either by chance or by happening to impress upon the mission staff that he was one of the "better" bush aboriginals (the missionaries definition of "better" being quite different from that of his bush fellows). Or, again almost by pure chance, he might get some brief job in connection with the mission which would enable him to earn a steel axe. In either case, for older men a preference for the steel axe helped change the situation from one of self-reliance to one of dependence, and a shift in behavior from well-structured or defined situations in technology or conduct to ill-defined situations in conduct alone. Among the men, the older ones whose earlier experience or knowledge of the white man's harshness made them suspicious were particularly careful to avoid having relations with the mission, and thus excluded themselves from acquiring steel axes from that source.

In other aspects of conduct or social relations, the steel axe was even more significantly at the root of psychological stress among the Yir Yoront. This was the result of new factors which the missionary considered beneficial: the simple numerical increase in axes per capita as a result of mission distribution, and distribution directly to younger men, women, and even children. By winning the favor of the mission staff, a woman might be given a steel axe which was clearly intended to be hers, thus creating a situation quite different from the previous custom which necessitated her borrowing an axe from a male relative. As a result a woman would refer to the axe as "mine," a possessive form she was never able to use for the stone axe. In the same fashion, young men or even boys also obtained steel axes directly from the mission, with the result that older men no longer had a complete monopoly of all the axes in the bush community. All this led to a revolutionary confusion of sex, age, and kinship roles, with a major gain in independence and loss of subordination on the part of those who now owned steel axes when they had previously been unable to possess stone axes.

The trading partner relationship was also affected by the new situation. A Yir Yoront might have a trading partner in a tribe to the south whom he defined as a younger brother and over whom he would therefore have some authority. But if the partner were in contact with the mission or had other access to steel axes, his subordination obviously decreased. Among other things, this took some of the excitement away from the dry season fiesta-like tribal gatherings centering around initiations. These had traditionally been the climactic annual occasions for exchanges between trading partners, when a man might seek to acquire a whole year's supply of stone axe heads. Now he might find himself prostituting his wife to almost total strangers in return for steel axes or other white man's goods. With trading partnerships weakened, there was less reason to attend the ceremonies, and less fun for those who did.

Not only did an increase in steel axes and their distribution to women change the character of the relations between individuals (the paired relationships that have been noted), but a previously rare type of relationship was created in the Yir Yoront's conduct towards whites. In the aboriginal society there were few occasions outside of the immediate family when an individual would initiate action to several other people at once. In any average group, in accordance with the kin-

ship system, while a person might be superordinate to several people to whom he could suggest or command action, he was also subordinate to several others with whom such behavior would be tabu. There was thus no overall chieftanship or authoritarian leadership of any kind. Such complicated operations as grass-burning animal drives or totemic ceremonies could be carried out smoothly because each person was aware of his role.

On both mission and cattle stations, however, the whites imposed their conception of leadership roles upon the aboriginals, consisting of one person in a controlling relationship with a subordinate group. Aboriginals called together to receive gifts, including axes, at a mission Christmas party found themselves facing one or two whites who sought to control their behavior for the occasion who disregarded the age, sex, and kinship variables of which the aboriginals were so conscious, and who considered them all at one subordinate level. The white also sought to impose similar patterns on work parties. (However, if he placed an aboriginal in charge of a mixed group of post-hole diggers, for example, half of the group, those subordinate to the "boss," would work while the other half, who were superordinate to him, would sleep.) For the aboriginal, the steel axe and other European goods came to symbolize this new and uncomfortable form of social organization, the leader-group relationship.

The most disturbing effects of the steel axe, operating in conjunction with other elements also being introduced from the white man's several sub-cultures, developed in the realm of traditional ideas, sentiments, and values. These were undermined at a rapidly mounting rate, with no new conceptions being defined to replace them. The result was the erection of a mental and moral void which foreshad-

owed the collapse and destruction of all Yir Yoront culture, if not, indeed, the extinction of the biological group itself.

From what has been said it should be clear how changes in overt behavior, in technology and conduct, weakened the values inherent in a reliance on nature, in the prestige of masculinity and of age, and in the various kinship relations. A scene was set in which a wife, or a young son whose initiation may not yet have been completed, need no longer defer to the husband or father who, in turn, became confused and insecure as he was forced to borrow a steel axe from them. For the woman and boy the steel axe helped establish a new degree of freedom which they accepted readily as an escape from the unconscious stress of the old patterns—but they, too, were left confused and insecure. Ownership became less well defined with the result that stealing and trespassing were introduced into technology and conduct. Some of the excitement surrounding the great ceremonies evaporated and they lost their previous gaiety and interest. Indeed, life itself became less interesting, although this did not lead the Yir Yoront to discover suicide, a concept foreign to them.

The whole process may be most specifically illustrated in terms of totemic system, which also illustrates the significant role played by a system of ideas, in this case a totemic ideology, in the breakdown of a culture.

In the first place, under pre-European aboriginal conditions where the native culture has become adjusted to a relatively stable environment, few, if any, unheard of or catastrophic crises can occur. It is clear, therefore, that the totemic system serves very effectively in inhibiting radical cultural changes. The closed system of totemic ideas, explaining and categorizing a well-known universe as it was fixed at the beginning of time, presents a considerable obstacle to the adoption of new or the dropping of old culture traits. The obstacle is not insurmountable and the system allows for the minor variations which occur in the norms of daily life. But the inception of major changes cannot easily take place.

Among the bush Yir Yoront the only means of water transport is a light wood log to which they cling in their constant swimming of rivers, salt creeks, and tidal inlets. These natives know that tribes 45 miles further north have a bark canoe. They know these northern tribes can thus fish from midstream or out at sea, instead of clinging to the river banks and beaches, that they can cross coastal waters infested with crocodiles, sharks, sting rays, and Portuguese men-of-war without danger. They know the materials of which the canoe is made exist in their own environment. But they also know, as they say, that they do not have canoes because their own mythical ancestors did not have them. They assume that the canoe was part of the ancestral universe of the northern tribes. For them, then, the adoption of the canoe would not be simply a matter of learning a number of new behavioral skills for its manufacture and use. The adoption would require a much more difficult procedure; the acceptance by the entire society of a myth, either locally developed or borrowed, to explain the presence of the canoe, to associate it with some one or more of the several hundred mythical ancestors (and how to decide which?), and thus establish it as an accepted totem of one of the clans ready to be used by the whole community. The Yir Yoront have not made this adjustment, and in this case we can only say that for the time being at least, ideas have won out over very real pressures for technological change. In the elaborateness and explicitness of the totemic ideolo-

gies we seem to have one explanation for the notorious stability of Australian cultures under aboriginal conditions, an explanation which gives due weight to the importance of ideas in determining human behavior.

At a later stage of the contact situation, as has been indicated, phenomena unaccounted for by the totemic ideological system begin to appear with regularity and frequency and remain within the range of native experience. Accordingly, they cannot be ignored (as the "Battle of the Mitchell" was apparently ignored), and there is an attempt to assimilate them and account for them along the lines of principles inherent in the ideology. The bush Yir Yoront of the mid-thirties represent this stage of the acculturation process. Still trying to maintain their aboriginal definition of the situation, they accept European artifacts and behavior patterns, but fit them into their totemic system, assigning them to various clans on a par with original totems. There is an attempt to have the myth-making process keep up with these cultural changes so that the idea system can continue to support the rest of the culture. But analysis of overt behavior, of dreams, and of some of the new myths indicates that this arrangement is not entirely satisfactory, that the native clings to his totemic system with intellectual loyalty (lacking any substitute ideology), but that associated sentiments and values are weakened. His attitudes towards his own and towards European culture are found to be highly ambivalent.

All ghosts are totems of the Head-to-the-East Corpse clan, are thought of as white, and are of course closely associated with death. The white man, too, is closely associated with death, and he and all things pertaining to him are naturally assigned to the Corpse clan as totems. The steel axe, as a totem, was thus associated with the

Corpse clan. But as an "axe," clearly linked with the stone axe, it is a totem of the Sunlit Cloud Iguana clan. Moreover, the steel axe, like most European goods, has no distinctive origin myth, nor are mythical ancestors associated with it. Can anyone, sitting in the shade of a *ti* tree one afternoon, create a myth to resolve this confusion? No one has, and the horrid suspicion arises as to the authenticity of the origin myths, which failed to take into account this vast new universe of the white man. The steel axe, shifting hopelessly between one clan and the other, is not only replacing the stone axe physically, but is hacking at the supports of the entire cultural system.

The aboriginals to the south of the Yir Yoront have clearly passed beyond this stage. They are engulfed by European culture, either by the mission or cattle station subcultures or, for some natives, by a baffling, paradoxical combination of both incongruent varieties. The totemic ideology can no longer support the inrushing mass of foreign culture traits, and the myth-making process in its native form breaks down completely. Both intellectually and emotionally, a saturation point is reached so that the myriad new traits which can neither be ignored nor any longer assimilated simply force the aboriginal to abandon his totemic system. With the collapse of this system of ideas, which is so closely related to so many other aspects of the native culture, there follows an appallingly sudden and complete cultural disintegration, and a demoralization of the individual such as has seldom been recorded elsewhere. Without the support of a system of ideas well devised to provide cultural stablity in a stable environment, but admittedly too rigid for the new realities pressing in from outside, native sentiments and values are simply dead. Apathy reigns. The aboriginal has passed beyond the realm of any outsider who might wish to do him well or ill.

Returning from the broken natives huddled on cattle stations or on the fringes of frontier towns to the ambivalent but still lively aboriginals settled on the Mitchell River mission, we note one further devious result of the introduction of European artifacts. During a wet season stay at the mission, the anthropologist discovered that his supply of toothpaste was being depleted at an alarming rate. Investigation showed that it was being taken by old men for use in a new toothpaste cult. Old materials of magic having failed, new materials were being tried out in a malevolent magic directed towards the mission staff and some of the younger aboriginal men. Old males, largely ignored by the missionaries, were seeking to regain some of their lost power and prestige. This mild aggression proved hardly effective, but perhaps only because confidence in any kind of magic on the mission was by this time at a low ebb.

For the Yir Yoront still in the bush, a time could be predicted when personal deprivation and frustration in a confused culture would produce an overload of anxiety. The mythical past of the totemic ancestors would disappear as a guarantee of a present of which the future was supposed to be a stable continuation. Without the past, the present could be meaningless and the future unstructured and uncertain. Insecurities would be inevitable. Reaction to this stress might be some form of symbolic aggression, or withdrawal and apathy, or some more realistic approach. In such a situation the missionary with understanding of the processes going on about him would find his opportunity to introduce his forms of religion and to help create a new cultural universe.

Notes

[1] An account of this expedition from Amboina is given in R. Logan Jack, *Northmost Australia* (2 vols.), London, 1921, Vol. 1, pp. 18–57.

[2] Ibid, pp. 298–335.

[3] The best, although highly concentrated, summaries of totemism among the Yir Yoront and the other tribes of North Queensland will be found in R. Lauriston Sharp, "Tribes and Totemism in Northeast Australia," *Oceania*, Vol. 8, 1939, pp. 254–275 and 439–461 (especially pp. 268–275); also "Notes on Northeast Australian Totemism," in *Papers of the Peabody Museum of American Archaeology and Ethnology*, Vol. 20, *Studies in the Anthropology of Oceania and Asia*, Cambridge, 1943, pp. 66–71.

The Beginning of Western Acculturation

By Napoleon A. Chagnon

Those of us who live in industrialized societies look on change and progress as being "good" and "desirable." Our entire system of values and goals is constituted in such a way that we strive to make changes, improve and tinker with rules and technology, and reward those who are skillful at it. "Progress" for its own sake is beneficial by definition. The Yąnomamö are now entering a new and potentially hazardous time in their history, for our kind of culture is confronting them and urging, in the name of "progress," that they give up their way of life and adopt some rural form of ours. The agents of progress among the Yąnomamö are mostly missionaries—Salesian Catholics and several independent groups of Protestant Evangelists—whose presence among the Yąnomamö is permitted by Venezuelan and Brazilian law. Incorporation of the Yąnomamö into the national culture has been left almost entirely in the hands of the missionaries, who have been and continue to remain free to use whatever means or techniques they have to accomplish this objective. While the explicit goal of all the missionaries is the conversion of the Yąnomamö to Christianity and the salvation of their souls, a few far-sighted individuals in both groups have independently realized that they likewise have an obligation to prepare the Yąnomamö in other ways for their inevitable absorption into Western culture—teaching them to speak the Spanish or Portuguese language, reading, writing and counting, introducing domesticated animals that can later serve as predictable sources of protein, market principles, the use of money, scales of economic values, and so on. Other missionaries are more narrowly dedicated to saving souls at any cost, and are insensitive to the point of being inhumane in the techniques they use to bring salvation to the Yąnomamö.

It is inevitable that the Yąnomamö, and all tribal peoples, will be absorbed by the national cultures in whose territories they coincidentally reside. The process of acculturation is nearly as old as culture itself: all dominant cultures impinge on and transform their less-dominant neighbors. There are, however, enlightened and humane ways of accomplishing this . . . and there are insensitive and inhumane ways. Knowing that acculturation is inevitable, I must conclude that it is essential that a rational and sympathetic policy of acculturation be developed for the Yąnomamö, for the process of change has already begun at a number of mission villages, and it is off to a poor start. Such a policy will require the cooperation of missionaries, government officials, and field-experienced, informed anthropologists. It is yet to be developed.

This raises a dilemma for me. Anthropologists who have worked in "traditional" or "tribal" cultures are often frustrated and saddened by the vectors of change that transform the peoples they have grown to admire during their studies, especially when the changes diminish the freedom and dignity of those peoples. Many anthropologists are, in fact, alarmed by any change and would prefer to see native cultures persist indefinitely while the rest of the maddening world mires itself deeper and deeper into the technological, ecological, and political morass that is one certain artifact of cultural evolution and "progress." It is an open question whether particular anthropologists are attracted to primitive cultures because such cultures seemingly represent a more rational, more comprehensible means for coping with the external world . . . that is to say, a more human way. It is jokingly said that psychiatrists become what they are to better understand their own personal problems, and I suspect that some anthropologists, by analogy, are attracted to their craft for equally personal reasons. A few of my colleagues have even good-naturedly suggested to me that my own intensive involvement with the Yąnomamö is not without reason, for they suspect that I might fit as well in Yąnomamö culture as I do in my own!

But any similarity between an anthropologist and the people with whom he or she has spent a significant portion of his or her life is probably due more to association and learning than to initial equivalencies of personality. Anthropology as a science differs radically from, let us say, chemistry or genetics. Our subject matter is made essentially of the same kind of stuff as the observer—the "subject matter" itself has hopes, fears, desires, and emotions. It is easy to identify with people and become intimate with them; a chemist or geneticist cannot have much empathy for carbon or the genes that determine eye color.

My long association with the Yąnomamö, my intimate friendships among them, and my awareness of the values in their culture account for my sense of frustration and alarm when I reflect on the changes that are taking place in the mission posts and the means by which some of the changes have been effected. Some of them are wrong, in my estimation, perhaps even cruel. Others are ineffective and harmless. Still others are amusing and downright funny.

Acculturation is a subject that has all but become a major subdiscipline within anthropology. Perhaps the most appropriate way to end this case study would be to cast the process into academic terms and adopt a strictly formal, pedagogical stance as I discuss what is now happening to the Yąnomamö. I should like, however, to communicate something about the human dimension of the process, to relate a few incidents and anecdotes that reveal more than a neutral description can expose. What the Yąnomamö must now endure has happened to countless other tribesmen. Perhaps if more citizens of the twentieth century and industrialized culture knew, from the tribesman's point of view, what acculturation means, we might have more compassion and sympathy for the traumas they must endure as they are required to make, usually unwillingly, their transformation. Hopefully such knowledge will be used to a good end, and rational policies of directed change will be forged.

In addition, by looking at the means and methods of the changes that are being made in Yąnomamöland through their eyes we can gain insights into the nature of our own culture. Very often the things that we ourselves take to be normal, progressive, and desirable look very different when viewed through a tribal lens. Sometimes they appear to be merely humorous. At other times they appear to be hideous.

YĄNOMAMÖ GLIMPSES OF US

Rerebawä looked frail and dwarfed in my trousers and shirt as we sat in the blistering sun on the savannah of Esmeralda waiting for the Venezuelan Air Force cargo plane to appear out of the cloudy north. The *piums*—tiny, biting black gnats—were out in astronomical numbers; their annoying bites left miniscule blood clots, that itched for a day and then turned black. The *piums* liked the larger rivers and savanna areas, and I speculated about the distribution of the Yąnomamö villages—inland, on tiny streams, away from this an-

noying *plaga*. I pitied those groups that had started moving out to the Orinoco River to make contact with foreigners—to obtain the highly desirable steel tools that they brought with them. Life without clothing for them was unbearable in the dry season, and they would come to the mission stations to work for days at hard labor to earn a tattered garment that some charity had sent into the missions gratis. The Yąnomamö always looked so pathetic in European hand-me-downs, especially after wearing them for several months and not washing them. They would be crusted with filth and rancid, and their skins would begin to have boils and sores all over them.

I was in a gloomy mood, reflecting on the changes that I noticed were taking place among the Yąnomamö. Each year I returned to them there were more missionaries, new mission posts, and now alarming numbers of tourists were beginning to arrive. I did not like what I was seeing and it was no longer possible to ignore the problems that acculturation would bring the Yąnomamö. My personal relationships with the Yąnomamö had deepened and grown more intimate every year. As I observed what some mission activities and the tourists were doing to the Yąnomamö, my attitude hardened.

Rerebawä had indicated to me several times in the past few years that he would like to see Caracas and how the Caraca-teri lived, especially the Caracateri-yoma: "Perhaps I could abduct a few when nobody is looking and drag them back to Bisaasi-teri in the plane!" he would tease mischievously. "But they eat only cows and bread and sugar and would run away from you if you brought them only monkeys and *yei* fruits!" I teased back. "You have warts on your forehead!" he insulted me good-naturedly, and jabbed me in the ribs to make me laugh, for he knew I was ticklish. "You'd better be careful in Caraca-teri," I warned, "almost all the men run around with large guns like shotguns and they will ask you for your 'decorated leaves' they call 'papers' and if you don't have any, they will take you away . . . and me with you!" He puffed his chest out and said: "Huh! I'll just grab a large club and insult them and then we'll see who takes who away!" He adjusted the wad of chewing tobacco he always carried in his lip. "Will we bump into the upper layer when we fly to Caraca-teri?" he asked anxiously. I chuckled to myself. Rerebawä had spent many months with me during my annual returns to his people and he was quite cosmopolitan by Yąnomamö standards, but nevertheless a firm believer in the Yąnomamö notion of the cosmos—a series of rigid bowl-like layers, one over the other, separated by only a few hundred feet or yards. "No, the *Hedu kä misi* layer is too high for the plane to reach," I responded, choosing to confirm his beliefs about the cosmic layers rather than rouse his anxiety further by denying their existence. This would be his first plane ride and his first glimpse of the civilization that lay beyond Yąnomamöland, and I wanted him to enjoy his experience.

It was always difficult for me to impress the Yąnomamö with the size of the world beyond their villages and tropical forest, including Rerebawä. I recall being teased by my companions on one of my inland trips as we sat around the campfire before retiring to our hammocks for the evening. They were bantering me about how numerous the Yąnamamö were and how few foreigners there were by comparison. Rerebawä was among them, and just as vociferous. I stood up to underscore my argument, pointing dramatically to the north, northeast, east, reciting names of cities as they came indiscrimately to my mind: "Over there lie the New York-teri, the Boston-teri, the Washington-teri, the Miami-teri; and over there the London-teri, the Paris-teri, and Madrid-teri, and Berlin-teri . . ." and on, around the globe. They chuckled confidently, and one of them rose. "Over there lie the Shibariwä-teri, the Yabroba-teri, the Wabutawä-teri, the Yeisi-teri, the Auwei-teri and over there the Niyaiyoba-teri, the Maiyo-teri, the Boreta-teri, the Ihirubö-teri . . ." and on around the cardinal points of the compass. I protested, arguing that ". . . Caraca-teri is huge! There are many people there and you are just a few by comparison!" Their response would be, inevitably, "But have you seen the new Patanowä-teri *shabono* or Mishimishimaböwe-teri *shabono*? They stretch in a great arc, like this . . ." and an arm would slowly describe the vast arc while the others listened intently, clicking their tongues to exaggerate the size. Caracas, to them, was just another large *shabono*, with a large, thatched roof, and I knew that the only way to convince them otherwise was to bring one of them there to see it with his own eyes.

Perhaps if Rerebawä saw the scope and magnitude of the culture that was moving inexorably to assimilate his own he would be more prepared to understand and deal with it when it eventually came. Would the same thing happen to Yąnomamö culture that happened to so many North American Indian societies? Would the Yąnomamö be reduced biologically and culturally to a mere shadow of the proud and free people I had grown to know and admire during 12 years of research among them? My personal dilemma was that I hoped that the Yąnomamö would be permitted to remain sovereign and unchanged, but my sense of history and understanding of culture contact told me that change was inevitable.

Storm clouds were piling up over Duida, the massive, abrupt cliff that rose 10,000 feet up from the small savanna at Esmeralda, and I hoped the plane would arrive soon, for in an hour the clouds would obscure the landing strip and it might be weeks or months before another flight would be scheduled to Esmeralda. A free lift out to Caracas with Rerebawä today would be very convenient, for I could spend five days with him working in comfort on myth translations and return with my bush-pilot, who was coming in with my medical colleagues. There would be space for us in the plane.

"Avion! Avion!" shouted the Makiritare Indians who idly waited for the plane to arrive, for it always brought cargo for them. Rerebawä was on his feet in an instant, his hand over his brow, peering intently into the cloud-blackened northern sky. *"Kihamö kä a! A ösöwa he barohowä!"* he jabbered excitedly, and I agreed that indeed it was visible and very high. He raced over to his possessions, a small cluster of tightly bound cloth bags made from the remains of a shirt I had given him last year. "Hold on! It will not get here for a while yet. It has to circle the landing area and chase the Makiritare cows off the savanna." He sat down, clutching his bags and grinning. I hadn't noticed his bags until now, and asked him what he had in them. "Just some 'things,' " he responded nonchalantly. "What kind of 'things'?" I asked suspiciously. He untied the knot and opened the larger bag: it was full of grey wood ashes, about a quart of them. Before I could ask him why in the world he was bringing ashes to Caracas, he had opened the other bag: it was full of tightly bound cured tobacco leaves. I clicked my tongue approvingly and he wrapped them back up. The ashes were to mix with the chewing tobacco, and I recall that he had asked me earlier if the Caraca-teri made fires on the floor on their houses to cook by. He was way ahead of me.

The gigantic transport plane—a C-123 designed for paratroop drops and hauling heavy cargo—lumbered to a dusty stop and the Makiritare descended on it to unload the cargo. The crew was in a hurry, for they had caught the edge of the storm and wanted to be airborne as soon as possible. They were reluctant to fly over Amazonas, a vast jungle with no radio communications or emergency landing strips, in a tropical storm.

Within an hour the plane was unloaded and the crew motioning for any passengers who wanted a lift to get aboard. We stepped into the giant, empty belly of the plane and I strapped Rerebawä into his safety harness. He had grown very quiet and was now obviously worried . . . if we weren't going to crash into the upper layer, why is it necessary to tie ourselves into the seats? The plane lumbered to the end of the savanna, turned, and screeched to a halt. The pilot tested the motors, and the roar was deafening: Rerebawä's knuckles were white as he clutched the edge of his seat. The plane lurched forward and gathered speed, bouncing unpredictably over the irregularities of the unimproved dirt landing stirp. Then the nose tipped upward sharply and we were airborne.

It was one of the worst flights I ever had, for we hit the storm soon after we gained cruising altitude. The plane jerked and twisted violently, dipping first one wing and then, suddenly, the other. Gusts of wind bounced us around, and jarring losses of altitude would leave us breathless, pinning us against our safety harnesses and then, as the frail plane fought back upwards, forcing us into our canvas seats. We could hear the ominous beating of rain on the fuselage above the roar of the motors. In an hour we were over the llanos and the flight had become more calm, but the noise was still deafening as the two motors labored incessantly. I unsnapped my harness and walked around the plane, but I was unsuccessful in persuading Rerebawä to untie himself or look out one of the fogged-up portholes. He just sat there, staring blankly at the opposite side of the plane, his tobacco buried deeply between his lower lip and teeth, clutching his seat. He relaxed a bit when I told him that we were approaching our landing strip at Maracay, and whispered cautiously that he was very cold. I assured him that I, too, was cold but that it would be warm when we landed. He rolled his eyes back and nodded his understanding.

The tires squealed and gave off a puff of blue smoke as we touched the concrete runway, taxied in, and coasted to a stop in front of the gigantic hanger that Rerebawä immediately recognized as the "den" of the creature in which we were riding. The crew opened the tiny side doors of the plane, and a blast of hot, dry air burst in. Our ears continued to ring, even though the deafening engines had stopped. We climbed out and stood on the concrete pad that stretched as far as our eyes could see, disappearing in the shimmering heatwaves near the horizon. Rerebawä touched it carefully and asked me how we found so much flat stone to make such a huge trail. Before I could answer that question, a dozen more, equally startling, came from his dry lips. One of the crew asked me if I wanted a lift up to the headquarters, from which we could call a taxi to take us to Caracas, some 35 miles away. I accepted, and told Rerebawä that we were going to have a ride in a "car." "What is a 'car'?" he asked suspiciously, remembering his airplane trip. I pointed to the white Ford parked a short way off. "Why don't you get into it and wait for me there while I unload our things?" I suggested. He headed slowly for the car and I gathered our things from the plane. When I stepped out of the plane, he was standing by the car, examining it carefully, glancing periodically at me, then at the car. "Get into it!" I shouted, "I'll be right there!" I watched

him walk slowly around the car, scratch his head, and look up at me with a puzzled expression. "Don't be afraid!" I shouted as I walked toward him. "Get in it!" He adjusted the tobacco in his mouth, took a half-step toward the car, and dived through the open window on the passenger's side, his feet and legs hanging curiously out the gaping hole in the side! I had forgotten to tell him about doors, and realized how much I had taken things for granted, and how incredibly bizarre much of our culture would be to the Yąnomamö.

The next week proved to be both sobering and outrageously funny at times as Rerebawä discovered what Caraca-teri and its customs and ways were like, and how much he would have to report to his co-villagers. The staggering size of the buildings reaching to the sky, built of stone laid upon stone, elevators, people staying up all night, the bright lights of the automobiles coming at an incredible speed at you during night travel, looking like the piercing eyes of the *bore* spirits, the ridiculous shoes that women wore with high heels and how they would cause you to trip if you tried to walk through the jungle in them, and the marvels of flush toilets and running water. He was astounded at how clean the floors were in the houses, was afraid to climb suspended stairs for fear they would collapse and could not drink enough orange soda pop, or get over the fact that a machine would dispense it when you put a coin in and pushed a button. "How could you invite these things to a feast?" he queried. "They certainly are generous and give their 'goods' away, but they expect to be reciprocated on the spot!"

He enjoyed himself in Caracas but was happy to return to his village, and spoke grandiloquently to his peers about the size of Caraca-teri. "Is it bigger than Patanowä-teri's *shabono*?" they asked him skeptically, and he looked at me, somewhat embarrassed, and knew that he could not explain it to them. We both knew that they would not be able to conceive of what Rerebawä had seen. His arm stretched out and he described a large arc, slowly, saying with the greatest of exaggeration his language permitted: "it stretches from here to . . . way over . . . there!" And they clicked their tongues, for it was bigger than they imagined.

In a few days Rerebawä had ceased discussing Caracas and his exciting trip there. He was busily and happily going about his normal Yąnomamö activities as if nothing extraordinary had happened. I marvelled at his resiliency and was relieved that the experience in Caracas had not diminished his enthusiastic view of his own culture as being inherently superior to and dominant over the ways of the *nabä*—the rest of the world that fell short of full humanness, the Non-Yąnomamö.

6
Anthropology in the Modern World

Contemporary Applications

In 1928 the "father" of American anthropology, Franz Boas, wrote a classic text, *Anthropology and Modern Life*. In it he argued that anthropology should not be mistaken for what it sometimes appears to be—the collection of curiosities, of tales and artifacts that merely entertain. Rather, if anthropology is to be a viable scholarly discipline, it should shed light on our own society and, if we are willing to learn its lessons, teach us as a society what to do and what to avoid.

In compiling the articles for this reader we have often felt like collectors—searching and sifting the literature, hoping to find those gems of anthropological scholarship that would stimulate and entertain you while teaching you useful things. In doing so we have never lost our view that in almost every anthropological undertaking, no matter how remote its concerns seem from modern living, there is a message for the contemporary world.

For this reason we debated the question of whether it made any sense to include this final topic. After all, virtually all of anthropology has its contemporary implications, if not direct applications. Would not adding a topic on contemporary applications undermine that message?

We finally decided to add this topic, but to do it in a way that underlines our view of the vitality and relevance of anthropology to contemporary life. Thus, we confine ourselves to two issues: birth and death, our coming and going both as individuals and as a species.

To open Topic 15 we have chosen an original article by Robbie Elizabeth Davis-Floyd, "Ritual in the Hospital: Giving Birth the American Way." Like other articles in this reader, this one can be read on several levels. On the surface, it is a bleak description of the dehumanizing processes that women are subjected to when giving birth in hospitals; by extension, it is about the dehumanizing of all of us in many of the public institutions of our society (schools, the legal system, and so on). It is also a brilliant analysis of the components of ritual and the reasons rituals actually work to transform the sense of self and meaning in their participants. At times the author may seem to overstate her case; and at

times she may seem to generalize too easily from individual to collective experience, but these can be useful techniques—as when, for instance, the irregular tracings on a crumbling stone pillar leap sharply into focus when a bright light is shone across the surface. We expect that you will be disturbed by this article, and that it will change forever your perception of medical technology. It was such an experience that Clyde Kluckhohn, a great American anthropologist, had in mind when he called our discipline a "mirror for man."

In "The Stone-Age Diet: Cuisine Sauvage," Melvin Konner talks about our birth as a species—specifically, what our evolving ancestors ate. He argues that we may be doing ourselves in by shifting our diet away from that of hunter-gatherers, and he provides anthropological evidence to support health educators who advocate a return to a simpler, high-fiber, low-fat diet.

Finally, we end our reader with Barry Bogin's thoughts about "The Extinction of *Homo sapiens*." By looking at both the biological and cultural processes that underlay the evolution of our species, Bogin extrapolates from current social, economic, and cultural trends in order to forecast our extinction. By depleting our environment by diminishing the range of resources we are willing to depend on; by savagely extinguishing hundreds, and soon thousands, of other animal species and thereby creating environmental instability through the elimination of diversity; and by homogenizing world culture, thereby reducing the availability of alternative visions and options, we are rapidly making ourselves into an overspecialized species with reduced adaptive flexibility in a context of rapid environmental changes—a surefire recipe for creating for ourselves an evolutionary dead-end.

Only an educated world population becoming aware of this hazard will be able to pressure those in power to alter the course of history. And certainly it is a noble goal of anthropology to contribute to the fund of knowledge that could help in this most essential process.

Ritual in the Hospital:
Giving Birth the American Way

By Robbie Elizabeth Davis-Floyd

Why is childbirth, which should be such a unique and individual experience for the woman, treated in such a highly standardized way in the United States? To find out, over the past seven years I interviewed over eighty-five mothers, as well as many of the obstetricians, nurses, childbirth educators, and midwives who attended them during pregnancy and birth. What I discovered was that childbirth in the United States is transformed into a cultural rite of passage designed to initiate the birthing woman into the core value and belief system of American society. The rituals to accomplish such initiation take the form of a set of standardized obstetrical procedures performed upon birthing women, regardless of the nature of their individual labors and desires.

Almost every woman in my study, no matter how long or short, how easy or hard her labor, had been hooked up to an electronic fetal monitor and an IV (intravenously administered fluids and/or medication), had been encouraged to use some form of pain-relieving drug, had an episiotomy (a surgical incision in her vagina to widen the birth outlet in order to prevent tearing) at the moment of birth, and was separated from her baby shortly after birth. Most of them had also received doses of the synthetic hormone pitocin to speed their labors, and had given birth flat on their backs; one-quarter of them, as of all American women today, gave birth by Cesarean section.

I knew from my study of anthropology that there were many other ways to give birth, and I wondered how such standardization of treatment was possible and what it meant. I was told by the obstetricians I interviewed that these procedures were medically and scientifically necessary, but the cross-cultural evidence I had did not confirm that they were. For example, the Mayan Indians of Highland Chiapas hold onto a rope while squatting for birth, a position which is far more physiologically efficacious than the flat-on-your-back-with-your-feet-in-stirrups (lithotomy) position required of most American women. Mothers in many low-technology cultures give birth sitting, squatting, or on their hands and knees, and are nurtured through the pain of labor by experienced midwives and supportive female relatives. Yet we

seemed to believe that the hospital management of birth represented its *de-ritualization*—the freeing of physiology from primitive custom and taboo.

Was this perception correct? Anthropologists have never found a society that does not ritualize important life transitions like birth, puberty, and death. Most societies, in fact, turn such events into cultural rites of passage, which serve to make it appear that society itself effects the biological transformation of the individual. Our culture is not so different from others as we sometimes assume, so I began to look beneath the veneer of "medical necessity" covering obstetrical procedures for the rituals that were, in some form or other, likely to be there.

It is hard to see the cognitive filter one is looking through! While poring over the transcriptions of my interviews, I began to understand that the forces shaping American hospital birth are invisible to us because they stem from the conceptual foundations of our society. I realized that American society's deepest values and beliefs center around science, technology, and the institutions which control and disseminate them, and that there could be no better transmitter of these core values and beliefs than the very obstetrical procedures whose *raison d'être* I had been questioning.

A *ritual* is a patterned, repetitive, and symbolic enactment of a cultural belief or value; its primary purpose is alignment of the belief system of the individual with that of society. A *rite of passage* may be simply defined as a series of rituals through which individuals are conveyed from one social status to another (for example, from boyhood to manhood, girlhood to womanhood, or from the womb to the world of culture), thereby transforming both society's perception of the individual and the individual's perceptions of herself or himself. Rites of passage generally consist of three stages, as outlined by van Gennep (1966): (1) *separation* of the individuals from their preceding social state; (2) a period of *transition* in which they are neither one thing nor the other; and (3) an *integration* phrase, in which through various rites of incorporation they are absorbed into their new social state. In the year-long pregnancy/childbirth rite of passage in American society, the separation phase begins with the woman's first awareness of pregnancy; the transitional stage lasts until several days after the birth; and the integration phase ends gradually in the newborn's first few months of life, when the new mother begins to feel that, as one woman put it, she is "mainstreaming it again."

The most important feature of all rites of passage is that they place their participants in a transitional realm which has few of the attributes of the past or coming state (Turner 1979). Existing in such a non-ordinary realm facilitates the gradual psychological opening of the initiates to profound interior change. In many initiation rites involving major transitions into new social roles (such as military basic training), this openness is achieved through a ritualized combination of physical and mental hardships that serve to break down the initiates' *belief systems*—the internal mental structure of concepts and categories through which the initiates perceive and interpret the world and their relationship to it. The breakdown of their belief systems leaves the initiates profoundly open to new learning and to the construction of new categories. The rite of passage then restructures the initiates' category systems in accordance with the dominant belief and value system of the society or group into which they are being initiated.

By making the naturally transformative process of birth into a cultural rite of passage, a society can ensure that its basic values will be transmitted to the three new members born out of the birth process: the new baby, the woman reborn into the new social role of mother, and the man reborn as father. Society must make especially certain that the new mother is very clear about these values and the belief system which underlies them, as she is generally the one primarily responsible for instilling this belief system in the minds of her children—society's new members and the guarantors of its future. This goal is accomplished through ritualizing the birth process.

CHARACTERISTICS OF RITUAL

Some primary characteristics of ritual are particularly relevant to understanding how this process of cognitive restructuring is accomplished in hospital birth. We will examine each of these characteristics in order to understand (1) how ritual works and (2) how the natural process of childbirth is transformed in the United States into a cultural rite of passage.

Symbolism

Ritual works by sending messages in the form of symbols to those who perform and those who receive or observe it. A *symbol*, most simply, is an object, idea, or action that is loaded with cultural meaning. The left hemisphere of the human brain decodes and analyzes straightforward verbal messages, enabling the recipient to either accept or reject

their content. Symbols, on the other hand, are received by the right hemisphere of the brain, where they are interpreted holistically. Instead of being analyzed intellectually, a symbol's message will be *felt* in its totality through the body and the emotions. Thus, even though the recipient may be unaware of her incorporation of the symbol's message, its ultimate effect may be extremely powerful.

Routine obstetrical procedures are highly symbolic. For example, to be seated in a wheelchair upon entering the hospital, as many laboring women are, is to receive through their bodies the symbolic message that they are disabled; to then be put to bed is to receive the symbolic message that they are sick. Although no one pronounces, "You are disabled, you are sick," such graphic demonstrations of disability and illness can be far more powerful than words. One woman told me:

> I can remember just almost being in tears by the way they would wheel you in. I would come into the hospital on top of this, breathing, you know, all in control. And they slap you in a wheelchair! It made me suddenly feel like maybe I wasn't in control any more.

Another elaborated:

> It's funny—it seems so normal to lie down in labor—just to be in the hospital seems to mean "to lie down." But as soon as I did, I felt that I had lost something. I felt defeated. And it seems to me now that my lying down tacitly permitted the Demerol, or maybe entailed it. And the Demerol entailed the pitocin, and the pitocin entailed the Cesarean. It was as if, in laying down my body as I was told to, I also laid down my autonomy and my right to self-direction.

The intravenous drips commonly attached to the hands or arms of birthing women make a very powerful symbolic statement: they are umbilical cords to the hospital. The long cord connecting her body to the fluid-filled bottle places the woman in the same relation to the hospital as the baby in her womb is to her. By making her dependent on the institution for her life, the IV conveys to her one of the most profound messages of her initiation experience: in American society, we are all dependent on institutions for our lives. This message is even more compelling in her case, for *she* is the real giver of life. Society and its institutions cannot exist unless women give birth, yet the birthing woman in the hospital is shown, not that *she* gives life, but rather that the *institution* does.

A Cognitive Matrix

A *matrix* (from the Latin *mater* = mother), like a womb, is something from within which something else comes. Rituals are not arbitrary; they come from within the belief system of a group. Their primary purpose is to enact and, thereby, to transmit that belief system into the emotions, minds, and bodies of their participants. Thus, analysis of a culture's rituals can lead to a profound understanding of its belief system. Analysis of the rituals of hospital birth reveals their cognitive matrix to be the technological model of reality which forms the philosophical basis of both Western biomedicine and American society.

This model was originally developed in the 1600s by Descartes, Bacon, and Hobbes, among others. It assumes that the universe is mechanistic, following predictable laws which those enlightened enough to free themselves from the limitations of medieval superstition could discover through science and manipulate through technology, in order to decrease their dependence on nature (Merchant 1983). This model views the human body as a machine that can be taken apart and put back together to ensure proper functioning. In the 17th century, the practical utility of this metaphor of the body-as-machine lay in its separation of body, mind, and soul. The soul could be left to religion, the mind to the philosophers, while the body could be opened up to scientific investigation.

The dominant religious belief system of Western Europe at that time held that women were inferior to men—closer to nature and feebler both in body and intellect. Consequently, the men who developed the idea of the body-as-machine also firmly established the male body as the prototype of this machine. Insofar as it deviated from the male standard, the female body was regarded as abnormal, inherently defective, and dangerously under the influence of nature. The metaphor of the body-as-machine and the related image of the female body as a defective machine eventually formed the philosophical foundations of modern obstetrics (Rothman 1982). Wide cultural acceptance of these metaphors accompanied the demise of the midwife and the rise of the male-attended, mechanically manipulated birth. Obstetrics was thus enjoined by its own conceptual origins to develop tools and technologies for the manipulation and improvement of the inherently defective, and therefore anomalous and dangerous, process of birth.

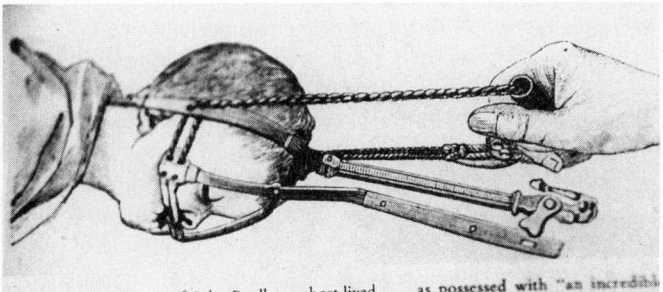

Fig. 9-33. The *sericeps* of Jules Poullet, a short-lived fetal extractor of the mid nineteenth century. Witkowski described the obstetricians of this period as possessed with "an incredibl[e] instruments, sometimes danger[ous], always ingenious."

The rising science of obstetrics ultimately accomplished this goal by adopting the model of the assembly-line production of goods as its template for hospital birth. Accordingly, a woman's reproductive tract is treated like a birthing machine by skilled technicians working under semiflexible timetables to meet production and quality-control demands. As one fourth-year resident observed,

We shave 'em, we prep 'em, we hook 'em up to the IV and administer sedation. We deliver the baby, it goes to the nursery and the mother goes to her room. There's no room for niceties around here. We just move 'em right on through. It's hard not to see it like an assembly line.

The hospital itself is a highly sophisticated technological factory; the more technology the hospital has to offer, the better it is considered to be. As an institution, the hospital constitutes a more significant social unit than an individual or a family, so it can require that the birth process conform more to institutional than personal needs. As one resident explained, "There is a set, established routine for doing things, usually for the convenience of the doctors and nurses, and the laboring woman is someone you work around, rather than with."

The most desirable end-product of the birth process is the new social member, the baby; the new mother is a secondary by-product. One obstetrician commented, "It was what we were all trained to always go after—the perfect baby. That's what we were trained to produce. The quality of the mother's experience—we rarely thought about that."

Repetition and Redundancy

For maximum effectiveness, a ritual concentrates on sending one basic set of messages which it will repeat over and over again in different forms. Hospital birth takes place in a series of ritual procedures, many of which convey the same basic messages in different forms. The open and exposing hospital gown, the ID bracelet, the intravenous fluid, the bed in which she is placed—all these convey to the laboring woman that she is dependent on the institution.

She is also reminded in myriad ways of the potential defectiveness of her birthing machine. These include periodic and sometimes continuous electronic monitoring of that machine, frequent manual examinations of her cervix to make sure it is dilating on schedule, and, if it is not, administration of the synthetic hormone pitocin to speed up her labor. All three of these procedures convey the same messages over and over: time is important, you must produce on time, and you cannot do that without technological assistance because your machine is defective.

In the hospital, production timetables indicate that delivery must take place within 26 hours lest the product have defects. (Home birthers often have much longer labors than hospital birthers, as they generally respect the mother's internal rhythms, and allow the labor to set its own pace.)

When a woman's labor fails to conform to the timetable, the administration of pitocin through the "umbilical" IV graphically conveys to the woman the message that her machine is defective. The additional and powerful message of this technological ritual is that the institution's schedule is much more important than her body's internal rhythms and her personal experience of labor. Cultural metaphors must be consistent. Since hospital birth is the process that reproduces society, it is only fitting that these messages should be repeatedly conveyed during the birth of a new social member. Hospital birth reflects and reproduces this culture's standard for handling time.

Cognitive Simplification

In any culture, the intellectual abilities of ritual participants are likely to differ, often markedly. It is not practical for society to design different rituals for persons of different levels of intellectual ability, so ritual utilizes specific techniques such as rhythmic repetition to attempt to reduce all participants to the same simpler level of cognitive functioning. This low level of cognitive operation involves thinking in either/or patterns of little cognitive complexity that do not allow for consideration of options or alternative views (McManus 1979a). Such cognitive simplification must precede the conceptual reorganization accompanying true psychological transformation.

Three other techniques are often employed by ritual to accomplish this end. One of these is the *hazing* familiar to undergraduates in fraternity initiation rites. Another is *strange-making*—making the commonplace appear strange by juxtaposing it with the unfamiliar (Abrahams 1972). A third is *symbolic inversion*—metaphorically turning things upside down and inside-out in order to generate "the power attendant upon confusion" (Abrahams 1973; Babcock 1978).

For example, in the rite of passage of military basic training, the initiate's normal patterns of action and thought are turned topsy-turvy. He is made strange to himself: his head is shaved, so that he does not even recognize himself in the mirror. He must give up his clothes, those expressions of individual identity and personality, to put on a uniform identical to that of the other initiates. Constant and apparently meaningless hazing (e.g., orders to dig six ditches and then fill them up) breaks down his cognitive structure. Then through repetitive and highly symbolic rituals (such as sleeping with his rifle), the basic values, beliefs, and practices of the Marines are literally incorporated into his body and his mind.

The transformative nature of ritual is a key to understanding the thorough internalization of the technological model by the medical students, residents, and physicians who are society's representatives-in-charge of the rite of passage of birth in American society. These medicine men must go through an extraordinarily intensive eight-year long rite of passage (four years of medical school and four years of residency), because, in any society, those responsible for the welfare of the human body (whether physician, shaman, priest—or all of these) are also responsible for conducting many of the rituals that will properly enculturate that body and the social member it carries.

In medical school and again in residency, the same ritual techniques which transform a youth into a Marine are employed to transform college graduates into physicians. Reduced from the high status of graduate to the lowly status of first-year medical student, initiates are subjected to hazing techniques of rote memorization of endless facts and formulas, absurdly long hours of work, and intellectual and sensory overload. As one physician explained:

> *Medical school is not difficult in terms of what you have to learn—there's just so much of it. You go through, in a six-week course, a thousand-page book. The sheer bulk of information is phenomenal. You have pop quizzes in two or three courses every day the first year. We'd get up around six, attend classes till five, go home and eat, then head back to school and be in anatomy lab working with a cadaver, or something, until 1 or 2 in the morning, and then go home and get a couple of hours sleep and then go out again. And you did that virtually day in and day out for four years, except for vacations.*

Subjected to such a process, medical students often gradually lose any idealistic goals of "helping humanity" they had upon entering medical school. A successful rite of passage produces new professional values structured in accordance with the technological and scientific values of the dominant medical system. The emotional impact of this cognitive narrowing is aptly summarized by a former resident:

> *Most of us went into medical school with pretty humanitarian ideals. I know I did. But the whole process of medical education makes you inhuman. . . . I've seen people devastated when they didn't know an answer. . . . The whole thing can get you pretty warped. I think that's where the feelings begin that somebody owes you something, 'cause you really, you know, you've blocked out a good part of your life. People lost boyfriends and girlfirends, fiancées and marriages. There were a couple of attempted suicides. . . . So you forget about the rest of life, and so by the time you get to residency, you end up not caring about anything beyond the latest techniques you can master and how sophisticated the tests are that you can perform.*

Likewise, the birthing woman is socialized by ritual techniques. She is made strange to herself by being dressed in a hospital gown, tagged with an ID bracelet, and by the shaving of her pubic hair, which symbolically de-sexualizes the lower portion of her body, returning it to a conceptual state of childishness. (Official hospital rationale for this procedure holds that shaving reduces the danger of infection, since hair cannot be sterilized. But shaving in fact *increases* the risk of infection in the open abrasions often left by the razor.) The physiological process of labor itself is painful, and is often rendered more so by the hazing techniques of frequent and very painful insertion of someone's fingers into her vagina to see how far her cervix has dilated. This technique also functions as a strange-making device. Since almost any nurse or resident in need of practice may check her cervix, the birthing woman's most private and intimate parts are symbolically inverted into institutional property. One respondent's obstetrician said to her, "It's a wonder you didn't get an infection, with so many people sticking their hands inside of you."

Cognitive Stabilization

When humans are subjected to extremes of stress and pain, they are likely, at least temporarily, to retrogress cognitively past the level of simplicity into a dysfunctional condition in which the individual becomes unreasonable and out of touch with reality. Whenever the danger of such retrogression is present, ritual plays a critical role, since it stabilizes individuals under stress by giving them a conceptual handle-hold to keep from "falling apart" or "losing it." When the airplane starts to falter, even passengers who don't go to church are likely to pray! Ritual mediates between cognition and chaos by making reality appear to conform to accepted cognitive categories. To perform a ritual in the face of chaos is to restore order to the world. Ritual has high evolutionary value, for it must have been one of the adaptive techniques our hominoid ancestors utilized to help them continue to function at a survival level whenever they faced conditions of extreme environmental stress (McManus 1979).

The labor process itself subjects most women to extremes of pain, which are often intensified by the hospital environment. Women who choose to birth at home generally expe-

rience more support from and control over their environments. These factors better enable the home birth mother to cope with the pain of labor without cognitively retrogressing to dysfunctional behavior. Most hospital birthers, on the other hand, no matter how supportive their husbands, must constantly cope with an unsupportive and alien environment over which they have no control. They look to obstetrical rituals to relieve the cognitive distress resulting from their pain and fear. Thus they utilize techniques to prevent cognitive retrogression through breathing rituals taught in hospital-sponsored childbirth classes. If these prove insufficient, they turn to drugs for pain relief, and to the reassuring presence of medical technology for relief from fear. One woman expressed it this way:

> *I was terrified when my daughter was born. I just knew I was going to split open and bleed to death right there on the table, but she was coming so fast they didn't have time to do anything to me. . . . I like Cesarean sections, because you don't have to be afraid.*

When you come from within a belief system, its rituals will comfort and calm you. Accordingly, those women in my study who espoused the technological model of birth to some degree before going into the hospital (54%) expressed general satisfaction with their hospital births, even if they were distressed with some of the specific procedures used. Nine percent of the women interviewed entered the hospital determined to give birth without technological intervention, yet ended up with highly technological births. These women, by contrast, experienced extreme cognitive dissonance between their previously held self-images and those internalized in the hospital. Most of them suffered severe emotional wounding and short-term post-partum depression as a result.

Order, Formality, and a Sense of Inevitability

Its exaggerated and precise order and formality set ritual apart from other modes of social interaction, enabling ritual to establish an atmosphere that feels both inevitable and inviolate. In hospital birth, this sense of inevitability is created by the order and formality of obstetrical procedures such as electronic monitoring of fetal heart tones, the administration of pitocin, and the ever-present possibility of the performance of a Cesarean section. These procedures, while often bothersome and painful, work to give the laboring woman a sense that society is using the best it has to offer—the full force of its technology—to inevitably ensure that she will have a safe birth. When women who have placed their faith in the technological model are denied its rituals, they often react with fear and a feeling of being neglected:

My husband and I got to the hospital, and we thought they would take care of everything. I kept sending my husband out to ask them to give me something for the pain, to check me—anything—but they were short-staffed and they just ignored me until the shift changed in the morning.

To perform a series of rituals is to feel oneself locking onto a set of "cosmic gears" which will safely crank the individual right on through the danger to safety on the other side. The Trobriand sea fisherman who performs an elaborate series of rituals in precise order believes that, if he does his part with precision, so must the gods of the sea do their part to bring him safely home. Likewise, the obstetrician feels that if he performs all the procedures correctly, they should result in a healthy baby. Without their rituals, neither obstetrician nor fisherman would have the courage daily to face the challenge and caprice of nature.

Once these gears have been set in motion, however, there is often no stopping them. Childbirth activists have noted that the very inevitability of hospital procedures makes them almost antithetical to the possibility of normal, natural birth. Such activists observe that a "cascade of interventions" occurs when one obstetrical procedure alters the natural birthing process, causing complications, and so inexorably "necessitates" the next procedure, and the next. Many of the women in my study experienced such a "cascade" when they received some form of pain relief, such as an epidural, which resulted in slowing their labor. Then pitocin was administered through the IV in order to speed up the labor, but pitocin very suddenly induced longer and stronger contractions. Unprepared for the additional pain, the woman asked for more pain relief, which ultimately necessitated more pitocin. Pitocin-induced contractions, together with the fact that the mother must lie flat on her back because of the electronic monitor strapped around her waist, can cause the supply of blood and oxygen to the fetus to drop, affecting the fetal heart rate. In response to the "distress" registered on the fetal monitor, an emergency Cesarean is performed.

Acting, Stylization, and Staging

Ritual's set-apartness is enhanced by the fact that it is usually highly stylized and self-consciously acted, like a part in a play. Those who perform the rituals of hospital birth are often aware of their dramatic elements. The physician becomes the protagonist in the play. The woman's body is the stage upon which he performs, often for an appreciative audience of medical students, residents, and nurses. Here is how one obstetrician played to his audience of students observing the delivery he was performing:

"In honest-to-God natural conditions babies were sometimes born without tearing the perineum and without an episiotomy, but without artificial things

like anesthesia and episiotomy, the muscle is torn apart, and if it is not cut, it is usually not repaired. Even today, if there is no episiotomy and repair, those women quite often develop a retoceole and a relaxed vaginal floor. This is what I call the saggy, baggy bottom." Laughter by the students. *A student nurse asks if exercise doesn't help strengthen the perineum. . . . "No, exercises may be for the birds, but they're not for bottoms. When the woman is bearing down, the leveator muscles of the perineum contract too. This means the baby is caught between the diaphragm and the perineum. Consequently, anesthesia and episiotomy will reduce the pressure on the head and, hopefully, produce more Republicans."* More laughter from the students. [Shaw 1974:90]

Cognitive Transformation

The goal of most initiatory rites of passage is cognitive transformation. It occurs in ritual when "symbol and object seem to fuse and are experienced as a perfectly undifferentiated whole, and insight, belief and emotion are called into play, altering our conceptions. . . . at a stroke" (Moore and Myerhoff 1977:13). This transformation, or conceptual reorganization, must usually be preceded by the cognitive simplification described above.

The following quote from a practicing obstetrician presents the outcome for him of such transformative learning:

I think my training was valuable. The people who trained us, and their philosophy, were unbeatable. Dr. Pritchard—he's the top man in obstetrics today in this country. And his philosophy was one of teaching one way to do it, and that was his way. And it was basically the right way. . . . I like the set hard way. I like the riverbanks that confine you in a direction. Later on, you can incorporate a little bit of this or that as things change, but you learn one thing real well, and that's the way.

For both nascent physicians and nascent mothers, cognitive transformation of the initiate occurs when reality as presented by the technological model, and reality as the initiate perceives it, become one and the same. This process is gradual. Routine obstetrical procedures cumulatively map the technological model of birth onto the birthing woman's perceptions of her labor experience, thereby aligning her belief system with that of society. One woman described her experience of this process:

As soon as I got hooked up to the monitor, all everyone did was stare at it. The nurses didn't even look at me anymore when they came into the room—they went straight to the monitor. I got the weirdest feeling that it was having the baby, not me.

The electronic fetal monitor—a machine which utilizes ultrasound to measure the rate of the baby's heartbeat through electrodes belted onto the mother's abdomen—has itself become *the* symbol of high technology hospital birth. Observers and participants alike report that the monitor, once attached, becomes the focal point of the labor, as nurses, physicians, husbands, and even the mother herself become visually and conceptually glued to the machine, which then shapes their perceptions and interpretations of the birth process. The above statement illustrates the successful progression of conceptual fusion between the woman's perceptions of her birth experience and the technological model. So thoroughly was this model mapped onto her experience that she began to *feel* that the machine itself was having the baby, and that she was a mere onlooker. Soon after the monitor was in place, she requested a Cesarean section, stating that there was "no more point in trying."

Consider the visual and kinesthetic images that the laboring woman experiences—herself in bed, in a hospital gown, staring up at an IV pole, bag, and cord on one side and a big whirring machine on the other side, and down at a steel bed and a huge belt encircling her waist. Her entire sensory field conveys one overwhelming message about our culture's deepest values and beliefs: technology is supreme, and the individual is utterly dependent upon it.

Internalizing the technological model, women come to accept the notion that the female body is inherently defective. This notion then shapes their perceptions of the labor experience, as exemplified by one woman's story:

> It seemed as though my uterus had suddenly tired! When the nurses in attendance noted a contraction building on the recorder, they instructed me to begin pushing, not waiting for the urge to push, so that by the time the urge pervaded, I invariably had no strength remaining, but was left gasping, dizzy, and diaphoretic. The vertigo so alarmed me that I became reluctant to push firmly for any length of time, for fear that I would pass out. I felt suddenly depressed by the fact that labor, which had progressed so uneventfully up to this point, had now become unproductive.

Note that she does not say, "The nurses had me pushing too soon," but "my uterus had tired," and labor had "become unproductive." These responses reflect another basic tenet of the technological model of birth: when something goes wrong, it is the woman's fault. One critic, a female physician, commented:

> Yesterday on rounds I saw a baby with a cut on its face, and the mother said, "My uterus was so thinned that when they cut into it for the section, the baby's face got cut." The patient is always blamed in medicine. The doctors don't make mistakes. "Your uterus is too thin," not "We cut too deeply." "We had to take the baby," (meaning forceps or Cesarean) instead of "The medicine we gave you interfered with your ability to give birth." [Harrison 1982:174]

Affectivity and Intensification

The repetitious bombardment of the woman with symbolic messages will often, in ritual, intensify toward a climax, heightening the emotional affect of the event. Behavioral psychologists have long understood that people are far more likely to remember, and to absorb lessons from, those events that carry an emotional charge. The order and stylization of ritual, combined with its rhythmic repetitiveness and the intensification of its messages, methodically create just the sort of highly charged emotional atmosphere which works to ensure long-term learning.

As the moment of physical transformation approaches, the number of ritual procedures performed upon the woman will intensify toward the climax of birth. For example, once the woman's cervix reaches full dilation (10 cm), the nursing staff immediately begins to exhort the woman to push with each contraction, whether or not she actually feels the urge to push. When delivery is imminent, the woman must be transported, often with a great deal of drama and haste, down the hall to the delivery room. Lest the baby be born *en route*, the laboring woman is then exhorted, with equal vigor, *not* to push. Such commands constitute a complete denial of the natural rhythmic imperatives of the woman's body. They intensify the messages of the mechanicity of her labor and her subordination to the institution's expectations and schedule, as well as the atmosphere of drama which will pervade the rest of her birthing experience.

Preservation of the Status Quo

Through explicit enactment of a culture's belief system, ritual works both to preserve and to transmit that belief system, and so becomes an important force in the preservation of the status quo in any society. Wherever this stabilizing characteristic of ritual is paramount, one usually will find that those in positions of power have unique control over its performance. They utilize the effectiveness of ritual to reinforce both their own importance and the importance of the belief and value system which legitimates their positions. It is no cultural accident that over 95% of American women give birth in hospitals, where only physicians have final authority over the performance of the rituals through which births are culturally conducted.

In spite of tremendous advances in equality for women, the United States is still a patriarchy. Nowhere is this reality more visible than in the lithotomy position. Despite years of effort on the part of childbirth activists, including many obstetricians, the majority of American women still give birth lying flat on their backs. This position is physiologically dysfunctional. One of its many disadvantages is that it quite literally makes the baby, who follows the curve of the birth canal, be born heading upward, against gravity, thus making birth more difficult and increasing the need for a forceps delivery. We gain a clue to the peculiar tenacity of this position from an obstetrical text:

> *The lithotomy position is the best. Here the patient lies with her legs in stirrups and her buttocks close to the lower edge of the table. The patient is in the ideal position for the attendant to deal with any complications which may arise. [Oxorn and Foote 1975:110]*

Of course, this position itself *creates* many complications: besides often necessitating the use of forceps, it narrows the pelvic outlet, making birth longer and more difficult; it compresses major blood vessels, lowering the mother's circulation and thus the baby's oxygen supply; and it increases the likelihood of tearing and the need for episiotomy because of disproportionate stretching of the perineum.

This lithotomy position completes the process of symbolic inversion that has been in motion since the woman was put into that "upside-down" hospital gown. The woman's normal bodily patterns are turned, quite literally, upside down—her legs are in the air, her buttocks at the table's edge, her vagina totally exposed. As the ultimate symbolic inversion, it is ritually appropriate that this position be reserved for the peak cognitive *and* physiological transformational moments of the initiation experience—the birth itself. The official representative of society and its core values of science, technology, patriarchy, and institutions stands, in control, not at the mother's head nor at her side, but at her bottom, where the baby's head is beginning to emerge.

Structurally speaking, this puts the woman's vagina where her head should be. Such total inversion is perfectly appropriate from a social perspective, as the technological model promises us that we can have babies with our cultural heads instead of our natural bottoms. The cultural value here is clearly on the *baby*. In our culture, "up" is good and "down" is bad, so the babes born of science and technology must be born "up" toward the positively valued cultural world of men, in *opposition* to the natural force of gravity, instead of "down" toward the negatively valued natural world of women.

The overthrow of the initiate's category system is now complete: this position marks and reinforces her now-total openness to the new messages she is about to receive. The inversion itself constitutes one of those messages, because it speaks so eloquently to her of her powerlessness and of the power of society at the supreme moment of her own individual transformation.

The episiotomy performed by the obstetrician just before birth also plays a valuable role in preserving the status quo in American society. This procedure, which is used on over 90% of all first-time mothers giving birth in the United States (Inch 1984:126), conveys to the birthing woman the value and importance of one of the most fundamental markers of our separation from nature—the straight line.

The vagina constitutes the cross-cultural symbol *par excellence* of the natural, powerfully sexual, creative and male-threatening aspects of women. This symbol has long been honored in myth as the *vagina dentata*, the vagina with teeth which threatens to consume or castrate the impotent male. Through episiotomies, physicians (society's representatives) can deconstruct the vagina (and by extension, its representations), then reconstruct it in accord with our cultural belief and value system. Doctors perform episiotomies partly because they are taught (incorrectly) that straight cuts heal faster than jagged tears—a teaching which mirrors our Western belief in the superiority of culture over nature. The episiotomy reflects and reinforces the straight line as one of our most basic cultural categories. Because it virtually does not exist in nature, the line is most useful in aiding us in our constant conceptual efforts to separate ourselves from nature.

The episiotomy is also conceptually useful to obstetrics. From its inception, the obstetrical profession was constrained to justify itself as having value equal to other branches of medicine in which the inherent pathology of the disease was perhaps clearer than is the inherent "pathology" of natural birth (Wertz and Wertz 1977). Since surgery constitutes the ultimate form of manipulation of the human body-machine in Western medicine, the legitimation of obstetrics necessitated the transformation of childbirth into a surgical procedure. By routinizing the episiotomy, and, increasingly, the Cesarean section, obstetrics has moved childbirth into the *sanctum sanctorum* of modern medicine, the operating room.

Effecting Social Change

Paradoxically, ritual, with all of its insistence on continuity and order, can be an important factor not only in individual transformation but also in social change (Turner 1974). New belief and value systems are most effectively spread through new rituals designed to enact and transmit them; entrenched belief and value systems are most effectively altered through alterations in the rituals which enact them.

In the cultural arena of birth, some of our society's most visible battles over cultural values are being waged. Medical personnel, pressured by the threat of malpractice suits, work to develop increasing control over the birth process, and place ever-greater reliance on technology, while growing numbers of women demand more options in birth and seek greater autonomy and self-responsibility.

Twelve percent of the women in my study (and 2–3% in

the wider society) chose not to participate in the technological socialization of women and gave birth at home. These women adopted an alternative paradigm which is based on systems theory, and offers a holistic, integrated approach to childbirth as well as to daily life. This approach stresses the inherent trustworthiness of the female body, communication and oneness between mother and child, the integrity and self-sufficiency of the family, and self-responsibility. Home birth mothers enact this paradigm and send its messages to themselves through creative rituals such as chanting, Blessing Way ceremonies, and the preparation of special foods.

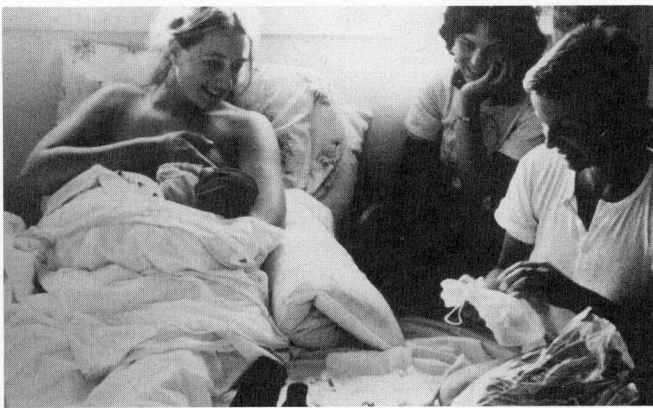

Another 25% of the women in my study gave birth in the hospital but were able to avoid conceptual fusion with the technological model by adhering to and achieving their goals of "natural childbirth," or by choosing and controlling the technological procedures administered. These women were personally empowered by their birth experiences. They tended to view technology as a resource that they could choose to utilize or ignore, and often consciously subverted their socialization processes by replacing technological symbols with self-empowering alternatives. For example, they wore their own clothes and ate their own food, rejecting the hospital gown and the IV. They walked the halls instead of going to bed. They chose perineal massage instead of episiotomy, and gave birth, like "primitives," sitting up, squatting, or on their hands and knees. One woman, confronted with the wheelchair, said "I don't need this," and used it as a luggage cart.

These respondents have many counterparts in the wider society. The technological model is under attack in the birthplace: feminists, natural childbirth activists, childbirth educators, humanistic obstetricians and nurses, midwives, and consumers are joining forces to subvert the core value system underlying this model, seeking to place science, technology, and institutions at the service of birthing women and their families, instead of the other way around. The alternative paradigms that these groups espouse, and the changes in birth that they have effected, increasingly threaten the conceptual hegemony of our technological model of reality.

A common cultural response to this type of threat is to step up the performance of the rituals designed to preserve and transmit the reality model under attack. Malpractice suits against physicians have risen dramatically in recent years. Physicians know that the risk of losing a lawsuit is lower if they cleave to the strict interpretation of the technological model. As one of them explained:

> *Certainly I've changed the way I practice since malpractice became an issue. I do more C-sections, that's the major thing. And more and more tests to cover myself. We don't do risky things that women ask for— we're very conservative in our approach to everything. In 1970 before all this came up, my C-section rate was around 4%. It has gradually climbed every year since then. In 1985 it was 16%, and now it's 23%.*

From this perspective, the increase in malpractice suits emerges as society's effort to make sure that its representatives, the obstetricians, perpetuate our technological core value system by continuing to socialize birthing women into that system. Its perpetuation seems imperative, for in our technology we see the promise of our eventual transcendance of our bodily and earthly limitations—already we grow babies in test tubes, replace some body parts with computerized devices, and build space stations.

The outcome of this core value struggle over birth is of critical importance for the future directions our society will take. Changes in the values transmitted through birth could profoundly alter those directions. Students of American society need to be aware of the implications of this struggle for the kind of culture that future generations of our society will acquire through the ritualization of birth.

SUMMARY: BIRTH RITUALS AND SOCIETY

Obstetrical procedures can be understood as ritual. They are patterned and repetitive; they are profoundly symbolic, communicating messages concerning our culture's deepest beliefs about the necessity for cultural control of natural processes. These procedures provide an ordered structure to the chaotic flow of the natural birth process. In so doing, they both enhance the natural affectivity of that process and create a sense of inevitability about their performance. Obstetrical interventions are also transformative in intent. They attempt to contain and control the inherently transformative process of birth, and to transform the birthing woman into a mother in the full social sense of the word—that is, into a woman who has internalized the core values of American society: one who believes in science, relies on technology, and recognizes her inferiority (either consciously or unconsciously) and so at some level accepts the principles of patriarchy. Such a woman will conform to society's dictates and meet the demands of its institutions.

Because the technological model of birth encapsulates the core values of the wider culture, it offers the American woman the opportunity to participate *in* that culture. The technological model itself replaces an earlier paradigm of birth—that of motherhood as the defining feature of woman. This paradigm still retains a certain symbolic force, and modern women still have many reasons for wishing to escape it. That hospital birth is a socialization process is neither inherently negative nor inherently positive; every society in the world has felt the need to thoroughly socialize its citizens into conformity with its norms, and the citizens derive many benefits from such socialization. If a culture had to rely on policemen to make sure that everyone would obey its laws, it would disintegrate into chaos, as there would not be enough policemen to go around. It is much more practical for cultures to find ways to socialize their members from the *inside*, by making them *want* to conform to society's needs. Yet human beings are not automatons, and the extent to which this type of socialization succeeds depends to a great extent on the individual involved. One woman succinctly sums up:

> *It's almost like programming you. You get to the hospital. They put you in this wheelchair. They whisk you off from your husband. And I mean just start in on you. Then they put you in another wheelchair, and send you home. And then they say, well, we need to give her something for the depression. [Laughs] Get away from me! That will help my depression!*

Through hospital ritual procedures, obstetrics deconstructs birth, then reverses, inverts, and reconstructs it as a technological process. But unlike most transformations effected by ritual, birth does *not* depend upon the performance of ritual to make it happen. The physiological process of labor itself transports the birthing woman into a naturally transitional situation that carries its own affectivity. Hospital procedures take advantage of that affectivity to transmit the core values of American society to birthing women. From society's perspective, the birth process will not be successful unless the woman and child are properly socialized during the experience, transformed as much by the rituals as by the physiology of birth.

REFERENCES

Abrahams, Roger D. 1973. Ritual for Fun and Profit (or The Ends and Outs of Celebration). Paper delivered at the Burg Wartenstein Symposium No. 59, on "Ritual: Reconciliation in Change," Wenner-Gren Foundation for Anthropological Research, New York, NY.

Babcock, Barbara, ed. 1978. *The Reversible World: Symbolic Inversion in Art and Society*. Ithaca and London: Cornell University Press.

Harrison, Michelle, M.D. 1982. *A Woman in Residence*. New York: Random House.

Inch, Sally. 1984. *Birth-Rights: What Every Parent Should Know about Childbirth in Hospitals*. New York: Pantheon Books.

McManus, John. 1979a. Ritual and Ontogenetic Development. In *The Spectrum of Ritual: A Bio-Genetic Analysis*, edited by Eugene G. d'Aquili, Charles D. Laughlin, and John McManus. New York: Columbia University Press. pp. 183–215.

McManus, John. 1979b. Ritual and Human Social Cognition. In *The Spectrum of Ritual*, edited by Eugene G. d'Aquili, Charles D. Laughlin, and John McManus. New York: Columbia University Press. pp. 216–248.

Merchant, Carolyn. 1983. *The Death of Nature: Women, Ecology, and the Scientific Revolution*. San Francisco: Harper & Row.

Moore, Sally Falk and Myerhoff, Barbara, eds. 1977. *Secular Ritual*. Assen and Amsterdam: Van Gorcum and Co.

Oxorn, Harry and Foote, William R. 1975. *Human Labor and Birth*, 3rd. ed. New York: Appleton Century Crofts.

Rothman, Barbara K. 1982. *In Labor: Women and Power in the Birthplace*. New York: W.W. Norton and Co. (Reprinted in paperback under the title *Giving Birth: Alternatives in Childbirth*. New York: Penguin Books, 1985.)

Shaw, Nancy Stoller. 1974. *Forced Labor: Maternity Care in the United States*. New York: Pergamon Press.

Turner, Victor. 1979. Betwixt and Between: The Liminal Period in *Rites de Passage*. In *Reader in Comparative Religion*, 4th ed. edited by Lessa and Vogt. New York: Harper & Row. pp. 234–243.

Turner, Victor. 1974. *Dramas, Fields and Metaphors: Symbolic Action in Human Society*. Ithaca: Cornell University Press.

Van Gennep, Arnold. 1966. *The Rites of Passage*. Chicago: University of Chicago Press.

Wertz, Richard W. and Wertz, Dorothy C. 1977. *Lying-In: A History of Childbirth in America*. New York: The Free Press.

RECOMMENDED READING

Following are a number of primary sources for some of the scientific and medical data demonstrating the dangers of hospital procedures and the safety of planned, midwife-attended home births over hospital births.

Burnett, C., Jones, J., Rooks, J., Tyler, C., and Miller, A. 1980. Home Delivery and Neonatal Mortality in North Carolina. *Journal of the American Medical Association* **244** (No. 24). An excellent study showing safety of planned, attended home births with direct-entry midwives or family physicians. Authors include medical doctors, government statisticians, a nurse-midwife, and a past-president of the American Public Health Association (Arden Miller, M.D.)

Hinds, M., Bergeisen, G., and Allen, D. 1985. Neonatal Outcome in Planned vs. Unplanned Out-of-Hospital

Births in Kentucky. *Journal of the American Medical Association* **253** (No. 11):1578–1582. Gives data showing safety of home birth attended by direct-entry midwives. Corroborates data for North Carolina study cited above.

Mehl, L., Peterson, G., Whitt, M., et al. 1977. Outcomes of Elective Home Births: A Series of 1146 Cases. *Journal of Reproductive Medicine* **19**:281–290. Gives data showing safety of home births attended by direct-entry midwives.

Tew, Marjorie. 1985. The Place of Birth and Perinatal Mortality. *Journal Royal College General Practitioners* **35**:390–394. Marjorie Tew holds position of research statistician in Nottingham Medical School, Nottingham, England. Analysis of statistical data for Britain shows that even when all appropriate statistical allowances are made, mortality rates in hospitals with board-certified obstetricians are much higher than for general practitioners or for home births, and that it is questionable to what extent even high-risk mothers benefit from hospitalization.

Tew, Marjorie. 1985. The Practices of Birth Attendants and the Safety of Birth. *Journal of Midwifery* (November issue). An excellent statistical study showing that beyond a certain point, increased hospitalization makes birth less safe and that the natural approach of midwifery results in better outcomes for most women and babies than sophisticated obstetrics.

The following books contain succinct and easily accessible summations of the scientific and medical evidence which demonstrates that most obstetrical procedures cause more physiological harm than good to most mothers and babies:

Brackbill, Yvonne., Rice, J., and Young, Diony. 1984. *Birth Trap: The Legal Low-Down on High-Tech Obstetrics*. St. Louis: C.V. Mosby Co.

Inch, Sally. 1984. *Birth-Rights: What Every Parent Should Know About Childbirth in Hospitals*. New York: Pantheon Books.

Parfitt, Rebecca. 1977. *The Birth Primer: A Source Book of Traditional and Alternative Methods in Labor and Delivery*. Philadelphia: Running Press.

Stewart, David and Stewart, Lee, eds. 1976. *Safe Alternatives in Childbirth*. Marble Hill, MO: NAPSAC (National Association of Parents and Professionals for Safe Alternatives in Childbirth).

Stewart, David and Stewart, Lee, eds. 1977. *21st Century Obstetrics Now!*. Vols 1,2. Marble Hill, MO: NAPSAC.

Stewart, David and Stewart, Lee, eds. 1979. *Compulsory Hospitalization or Freedom of Choice in Childbirth?*. Vols. 1,2,3. Marble Hill, MO: NAPSAC.

Stewart, David and Stewart, Lee, eds. 1981. *The Five Standards for Safe Childbearing*. Marble Hill, MO: NAPSAC.

The Stone-Age Diet: Cuisine Sauvage

By Melvin Konner

T. L. Solien, Victim of Doubt, *1983*

In 1972, when I left the Kalahari Desert, and the !Kung San bands that reside there, I had a vastly enriched comprehension of hunter-gatherer cultures, enough data for a doctoral dissertation, and a very enlightening sense of embarrassment. I had gone to Africa to pursue not only specific scientific goals but also some personal philosophic ones, among them the confirmation of a naïve, almost Rousseauian vision of a rather noble savage. On the plains of Botswana, I expected to find the beauty of the human spirit in "pure" form, unadulterated by the corrupting influences of civilization. The not-so-noble savages I in fact encoun-

tered—and came to know so well and, in some instances, to love—proved capable of selfishness, greed, jealousy, envy, adultery, wife abuse, and frequent conflict ranging from petty squabbles to homicidal violence. Not that they were any worse than we are; they just weren't evidently better. Thus I learned a lesson that sooner or later impresses itself on almost every anthropologist: it is a risky business, at best, to project human ideals onto our evolutionary past. The noble savage does not exist—and never did.

It was with a sense of irony, then, that I read an editorial in *The New York Times* this past June suggesting that a paper I had

recently written with a colleague perpetuated "the myth of the Noble Savage." Perhaps my surprise was unjustified; by then I should have been inured to odd and unflattering characterizations of the paper. The preceding months had seen a flurry of publicity about it. It had been billed in the popular press as espousing a "caveman diet," and *The Washington Post* had ventured the tongue-in-cheek prediction that my co-author and I would soon publish a best-selling book with such a title. Meanwhile, *The New England Journal of Medicine,* which published the paper, had received letters of more serious intent, questioning on scientific

Reprinted from *The Sciences,* September/October 1985, by permission of the author grounds the merit of our argument.

The episode had begun innocently enough. During the summer of 1983, I got a call from S. Boyd Eaton, an Atlanta radiologist and advocate of preventive medicine who wanted to collaborate on a study of hunter-gatherer societies. Eaton, I soon discovered, believed that in the study of such societies were to be found critical insights into the human condition as well as, perhaps, the key to a comprehensive theory of human biology and behavior. That is not to say that he believed the myth of the noble savage. Rather, he simply subscribed to what anthropologists call the hunter-gatherer party line: regardless of whether ancient hunter-gatherer societies were in any sense noble, their genetic endowment was very similar to ours. This belief rests on the considerable body of evidence suggesting that 95 or 98 or 99 percent of human evolution—depending on what you want to call human—took place in societies sustained by hunting and gathering. Inasmuch as genetic change in the mere ten thousand years since the advent of agriculture has probably been trivial, the argument goes, we are in essence hunter-gatherers transplanted out of skins and huts into three-piece suits and high-rise condominiums.

My once faithful adherence to that party line had been shaken in an oblique way by my experience in Africa. The trip to the Kalahari, after all, had been motivated by both my belief in the existence of the noble savage and my commitment to the hunter-gatherer hypothesis; the ensuing disillusionment had somewhat indiscriminately diluted both. But as I talked with Eaton, I regained some respect for the party line—enough, certainly, to proceed with our collaboration.

We set out to study the diet of ancient hunter-gatherer societies against the backdrop of recent research on nutrition. Using anthropological data on the few extant groups (including the !Kung San) as well as paleontological and archaeological findings about various hunter-gatherer societies that flourished between two million and ten thousand years ago, we proposed a model of what human beings ate during the better part of their evolution. Broadly similar studies had been conducted before, but we enjoyed the benefit of quite good numbers—credible data amassed over decades of modern research. Moreover, we added what proved to be a provocative comparison between our hypothesized paleolithic diet

and two other diets: that of the average American today, on the one hand, and that recommended by physicians and scientists, on the other.

The results were mostly predictable but no less impressive for it. The paleolithic diet consistently met or exceeded the standards being proposed for shifting the American diet toward a more healthful pattern. For example, the ratio of polyunsaturated to saturated fat consumed by the typical American is 0.44. It is now recommended that this ratio be moved closer to 1.00 to protect against atherosclerosis—the epidemic illness underlying most heart disease and strokes. In the paleolithic age, we estimated, this ratio was even higher—around 1.41. Sodium, a suspected cause of high blood pressure, is consumed by the average American at the rate of 2,300 to 6,900 milligrams per day, despite recommendations that the rate be cut to between 1,100 and 3,300. Our hunter-gatherer ancestors, it appears, consumed only about 690 milligrams of sodium per day. For fiber, which may protect against several diseases of the bowel, including cancer, the figures were 19.7 grams per day for Americans, 30 to 60 grams recommended, and 45.7 grams estimated for paleolithic man. The high level of fiber intake among hunter-gatherers also implies a low intake of sugars and other simple carbohydrates widely considered too common in the American diet. Once complex carbohydrates, such as those found in fruits and vegetables, are added, the percentage of daily calories derived from carbohydrates in the late Paleolithic period amounts to about the same as it does today. But the percentage of protein was much higher and the percentage of fat markedly lower. (Large quantities of fat are thought to contribute to cancer of the colon, breast, uterus, and prostate.)

The paleolithic estimate corresponds to the typical American diet rather than to the nutritional ideal in one respect: cholesterol intake. Like the high paleolithic protein level, this is due to heavy reliance on meat; cholesterol, being the major constituent of animal cell membranes, is abundant even in lean meats. Nonetheless, contemporary hunter-gatherers have extremely low levels of serum cholesterol, which reinforces the recent finding that the major dietary determinant of serum cholesterol is not, paradoxically, cholesterol, but saturated fat.

Our paper concluded that there was an impressive convergence between the paleolithic diet—the diet that evolution designed us to eat—and the generally

healthful diet prescribed by modern nutritional science. "The diet of our remote ancestors," we wrote, "may be a reference standard for modern human nutrition and a model for defense against certain 'diseases of civilization.' "

In a burst of optimism, we sent the paper to *The New England Journal of Medicine*, arguably the most prestigious medical periodical in the world. To our pleasant surprise, the journal accepted the paper and published it on January 31 of this year, under the title "Paleolithic Nutrition: A Consideration of Its Nature and Current Implications." I knew that the health and medicine sections of many newspapers regularly report the journal's more arresting findings. Still, I was not prepared for the reaction that our rather offbeat paper (offbeat, at least, by the journal's standards) generated.

Days before we even saw the published paper, Eaton and I began to receive telephone calls from an array of newspaper and broadcast journalists ranging from science reporters to food editors. Several reporters adopted the phrase "caveman diet" and went on to use it despite our insistence that it was not only misleading but it was also insulting to contemporary hunting-and-gathering peoples. A few representative headlines: "Cavemen Cooked Up a Healthy Diet" *(USA Today);* "Cave Man Takes a Healthy Bite Out of Today's 'Civilized' Diet" *(The Atlanta Journal);* "Check Ads for Specials on Saber-toothed Tigers *(The Atlanta Constitution).* There were many amusing cartoons and drawings, but the graphics award surely must go to *The Fort Lauderdale News/Sun-Sentinel,* which ran a series of "paleolithic" recipes accompanied by a color photograph of an actor grotesquely made up as a caveman—skins, club, tooth necklace, and all. Even distinguished journalistic institutions were not above this sort of humor. *The Washington Post,* after predicting the appearance of our book-to-be on the best-sellers' list, added, "Some day in the near future you'll look out at daybreak and see people all up and down your street come loping out of their homes wearing designer skins and wielding L.L. Bean stoneaxes while every dog, cat and squirrel in the neighborhood runs for cover."

Ellen Goodman, the much loved syndicated columnist based at *The Boston Globe,* ridiculed us in an uncharacteristically harsh tone. Her piece was accompanied by an etching of savages dancing, captioned "Make mine mastodon." The column seemed marred by resentment—the resentment of a noncompliant patient sermonized yet again by high-minded, pesky physicians. "But I am convinced," she concluded, "that the average Paleolithic person was the very role model of good health when he died at the ripe old age of 32."

By and large, though, I got a good laugh out of the copy. I am enough of a writer to realize what a superb target our article made. Most of the jokes and cartoons were presented side by side with fairly serious summaries of the paper, and the pieces generally got the message across—and to a much larger audience than we could have reached without such help. (Fellow physicians and scientists had sent us scores of letters, the majority of them positive.) As Eaton pointed out after we had stopped laughing and finished licking our wounds, the attention to our ideas was what counted, and we had now become one more small force for preventive medicine in a sea of cultural forces aligned against it.

Needless to say, the critiques that appeared in the journal itself were more serious in intent than was the popular commentary. One reader pointed out that paleolithic hunter-gatherers would likely have eaten a lot of honey—a challenge to our contention that their consumption of simple carbohydrates was meager. (In fact, the Pygmies of Zaire have recently been found to gorge themselves on caches of honey.) But we countered that there was no way our ancient ancestors could have consumed anywhere near the 108 pounds of sugar a year now eaten by the average American child, and that the archaeological record shows a massive increase in tooth decay accompanying the rising consumption of refined carbohydrates. Another critic questioned one of our basic premises—that there has been little genetic change since the hunting-gathering era. This is an important issue and it calls for further research; but all studies of modern hunter-gatherers suggest an overwhelming genetic continuity between them and us.

For the present, then, our model of paleolithic nutrition seems to have some claim on the truth. Still, the criticisms published by the journal were serious enough to lend weight to the barb thrown by *The New York Times*: "Did people of the early Stone Age eat more healthily than their urban successors? The issue is being vigorously chewed in the New England Journal of Medicine, and it tastes like the myth of the Noble Savage."

Had we indeed projected today's medical ideals onto our evolutionary past? I won't speak for Eaton, but I know myself well enough to concede that possibility; I don't purport to be conscious of all my motivations, and it may well be that I was inspired to accept Eaton's invitation to collaborate by the same naïveté that drew me to the Kalahari as a graduate student. But whatever the inspiration for our study, we took pains to conduct it by the rules. We spent months examining and re-examining our premises and our data, and we were very hard on any interpretation that even hinted at romanticism. But a solid core of good data survived our harshest scrutiny, and the burden of proof now rests with those who doubt that the diet of hunter-gatherers, whether recent or ancient, was qualitatively better than the average American's.

A scientific hypothesis, after all, should be evaluated not on the basis of its authors' motives but on the basis of its merits. It does not find its way into a respectable journal because it was nobly conceived or because it is guaranteed to be right, but because it is sufficiently interesting and sufficiently supported by facts to warrant admission, at least temporarily, into the stream of scientific discourse. Scientists' motivations must come from somewhere, and the realities of research are such that the pure pursuit of truth is often asked to coexist with a certain amount of advocacy. The best we can hope is that the resulting discourse resembles the contending thoughts in a single, rather superior mind—contradiction progressing toward synthesis.

The Extinction of *Homo sapiens*

By Barry Bogin

Population explosions, mass starvation, social revolution, and nuclear winter are just a few of the prophesied fates awaiting our species. Any one, or combination, of these catastrophes could lead to our annihilation from the face of the earth. As if these were not enough, showers of asteroids and comets may periodically bombard the earth causing the catastrophic extinction of many life forms. Fortunately, the periods between showers are long (by human standards), lasting about 30 million years. The next one is predicted to occur 15 million years from now.

For some reason we usually think of our eventual demise as a species in terms of catastrophes. Perhaps the Old Testament accounts of mass destruction provide a cultural rationale for this ethnocentric preoccupation. The Bible claims a unique privilege for people: last to be created with dominion over all living things. We think of ourselves as so special a species that nothing short of nuclear holocaust, or its equivalent, could do us in. After all, we have eliminated most of the childhood diseases that were threats to our health, we can transplant major body organs, and we think of population growth and increasing longevity as problems rather than benefits of our technology. The fact is, however, that we are just one of more than two million animal species presently living on this planet. Many more millions of species once existed and are now extinct. Many, if not most, of these species became extinct in noncatastrophic ways that occurred gradually over the vast course of geologic time. Extinction of this gradual type is such a common occurrence that the biologist George Gaylord Simpson observed, "In the grand pattern of evolution nothing is more dramatic than the prevalence of extinction."[1]

The evolutionary history of non-human life needs few spectacular catastrophes to explain the extinction of species. Most biologists view extinction as the result of a mismatch between a species' repertoire of adaptive characteristics and changes in the environment. Extinction is natural. "[E]xtinction is part and parcel of the process of evolution; it is not 'failure.'"[2]

Paleontologist Leigh Van Valen and geneticist Richard C. Lewontin theorize that the environment is constantly changing with respect to any species. Temperature, humidity, food resources, etc. are always one step removed from a species' ability to adapt perfectly to them. Thus, like the Red Queen in *Alice in Wonderland*, who had to run as fast as she could just to stay in the same place, a species must constantly change just to maintain its imperfectly adapted state.[3] Through the process of evolution by mutation and natural selection, species are constantly "tracking" the pace of environmental change. These changes are essentially random, or at least unpredictable, from the point of view of the species. In terms of evolutionary time, tomorrow's environment will not be the same as today's. Thus, it is highly unlikely that an organism could ever "improve," in the sense of becoming perfectly adapted, to a given environment. Another problem is that species have genetic limits to the extent of their adaptability, but the environment has an almost unlimited capacity for change. This results in the inevitable extinction of most species, and their replacement by new forms of life more closely adapted to the prevailing environment.

The Red Queen hypothesis of adaptation predicts the high levels of extinction we observe in the fossil record. These include the thousands of extinctions of individual species and the spectacular mass extinctions of hundreds of species, such as the "Great Dying" of the dinosaurs that occurred about 65 million years ago. High extinction rates over the long run of geologic time are statistically constant for several classes of animals for which we have suitable fossil records (e.g. echinoderms, pelecypods, gastropods). No species has a "lock" on adaptation. Whether long-lived or short-lived, all eventually become extinct.

The question is, at this point, are humans subject to this same possibility? Can *Homo sapiens* become extinct due to a lack of adaptability to environmental change? To answer this question I shall discuss the evidence for the extinction of one of our early relatives, a member of the genus *Australopithecus*, and also discuss the possibility of extinction for the species *Homo neandertalensis*, the Neandertals of Ice Age Europe. Lastly, I will consider the case for the ecologically caused extinction of our own species.

Reprinted from the *Michigan Quarterly Review*, Spring 1985, by permission of the author

THE EARLIEST HOMINIDS

The oldest fossil organisms that are considered to be hominids (living humans or our direct ancestors) are members of the genus *Australopithecus*. This is a group of creatures that lived between 4 million and 1 million years ago. The first fossil of this type was discovered in South Africa in 1924. Since then hundreds of additional australopithecine skeletal parts, stone tools, and archaeological sites have been found in South and East Africa.

The australopithecines were bipedal walkers, with arms and hands free for carrying objects and making and using tools. Their cranial capacity was small by our standards, about 450cc versus a 1400cc average for living humans (750cc equals a fifth of whisky). However, the small body size of the australopithecines, about 65 pounds, gives them a favorable brain size to body size ratio. They had about 7cc of cranial space for every pound of body. The gorilla averages 500cc of cranial capacity and weighs about 400 pounds. This gives a ratio of only 1.25cc of cranial space per pound. Clearly, *Australopithecus* was "brainier" than the ape.

Somewhat like apes, australopithecines have proportionally longer arms and finger bones that curve more than modern humans. Actually the arm length and finger curvature are in between that seen in humans and chimpanzees. Australopithecines did not use arms or hands for terrestrial locomotion. On the ground they were bipedal. But they may have used their forelimbs for tree climbing, in search of food and for protection from predators. Their hands were well suited for making and using a variety of tools. Though tools of bone and wood were probably used, only the stone tools survive.

For reasons of brain size and anatomy the australopithecines are placed in a unique genus. But due to their bipedalism, tool use, and brain to body size they are similar enough to humans to be called hominids.

Australopithecus fossils have these traits in common. But all australopithecine individuals are not alike. There are differences in overall size, the size and shape of teeth and jaws, and in specific brain size to body size proportions. These differences may be grouped into two basic types of fossils: gracile and robust. The robust variety has a huge face, with large jaws filled with enormous premolar and molar teeth. The robust type molar tooth has about three times the surface area of a modern human molar. The jaws are large and thick boned to hold these teeth. The flaring cheek bones and crest of bone along the midline of the top of the skull are places for the attachment of the massive chewing muscles needed to close the lower jaw. This robust type was obviously capable of generating powerful chewing forces. The robust fossils are formally designated as two distinct species. They are called either *Australopithecus robustus*, a form found mainly in southern Africa, or *A. boisei*, a hyper-robust form found only in eastern Africa.

The gracile variety is less massive in face, jaws and teeth. There are no crests of bone on the top of the skull nor are there flaring cheek bones. The cheek teeth are smaller than in the robust species, though still larger than those found in modern humans. The graciles were less dependent on powerful chewing than the robust types. The gracile species, *A. afarensis*, is found in East Africa. Its descendent species, *A. africanus*, is found in southern and eastern Africa.

Anthropologists and paleontologists accept that two, three, or more species of early hominids co-existed in Africa. They also accept the fact that all but one of these species became extinct, since today there is only one species of living hominid. However, to my knowledge no one has offered an hypothesis explaining how any of these relatively large-brained, tool-using hominids could become extinct.

The regulation of species evolution patterns, including extinction, is now recognized as a normal ecological process. One part of ecology is concerned with the distribution of trophic (food) resources in the environment. Paleontologists also are concerned with trophic ecology in the study of human evolution. For instance, since 1954 a "dietary hypothesis" explaining the differences in skull, tooth and jaw size between the gracile and robust australopithecines has been proposed by John Robinson. A co-discoverer of many of the South African *Australopithecus* fossils, Robinson believes that the huge masticatory apparatus of the robust type is adapted for chewing and grinding tough vegetable foods, especially seeds. The gracile dentition, according to Robinson, is better suited for softer foods, including greater quantities of meat. Robinson does not argue that the two types consumed totally different diets. Rather, the proportion of tough versus softer foods differed between gracile and robust species. Other researchers present models of hominid evolution that relate dental, cranio-facial, and postural changes in the early hominids with the evolution of new trophic niches. No single model is completely reconcilable with all the fossil evidence, but this line of research does indicate that the trophic approach to hominid evolution can be fruitful (no pun intended).

Most of these models are basically special cases of G. G. Simpson's general model for evolution. Since Simpson's model explains the basic process of speciation and extinction it is worthwhile to state its basic tenets. There are four evolutionary stages in this model. The first stage is the evolution of new environments. This can occur due to climate change, geologic activity, or even to the evolution of previously existing ecosystems. These changes in the physical environment often lead to geographic or ecological isolation of populations of organisms that previously coexisted in a single locale. The new environments and the isolation of populations challenge the adaptive abilities of existing species. Some will meet the challenges and survive, others will not and die. There is also the possibility of more drastic changes in some species leading to diversification and the evolution of one or more new species from some ancestral group. The evolution of Darwin's finches in the Galapagos Islands is a classic example of evolutionary diversification in a new environment. Though in this case the finches migrated to the Galapagos, similar kinds of evolutionary change may occur when the environment alters and species, *in situ*, respond. In stage two, competition occurs between old and new species vying for similar resources. The competition drives some of the contestants to extinction. The survivors usually specialize further, which increases the ecological isolation between species and reduces competition. Such specialization exaggerates the physical differences between species that relate to their specific adaptations. As far as trophic adaptations are concerned, the specializations would relate to the ways a species acquires or processes its food. Darwin's finches, for example, differ mostly in beak size and shape in relation to the foods each beak type can process. By stage three this process of specialization results in only one species per niche. The fourth stage is one of new environmental change. Old niches close and new ones open, returning us to stage one again.

For hominid evolution, stage one begins with climate change in Africa and Asia during the late Miocene and early Pliocene (6–4 million years ago). During this time tropical forests begin to shrink in size as rainfall becomes more seasonal and possibly less abundant as well. As a consequence, the woodland-savanna areas expand in size. Hominids were one of the new mammalian species to evolve and adapt to these woodland-savanna environments. Several hominid species may have evolved and quickly become extinct as they competed for new woodland-savanna niches (stage two). By stage three, two or more hominid species appear to have successfully established themselves. These species are the robust and gracile australopithecines. Continued climate change during the Pliocene and early Pleistocene (4–2 million years ago) may have resulted in the closing of some of the hominid niches, with the extinction of the associated species. To substantiate this, we must determine the kind of niche to which each species was adapted.

There is general agreement that the early hominids were basically adapted to the woodland-savanna habitat. The evolution of bipedal locomotion, hairlessness, copious sweating, and other aspects of hominid anatomy and physiology could probably only have occurred in a relatively open environment.[4]

But, the tropical woodland-savanna habitat is ecologically diverse. It ranges from the periphery of the tropical rainforest and the gallery forests along rivers and streams, to the scrub-forests and woodlands, to the open grassy savannas. Humidity decreases from the first to the last of these. With the decrease in humidity come changes in vegetation type and trophic resources. Early hominids could have lived in any one of these habitats. But to effectively exploit these environments the different species of australopithecines may have specialized in one habitat more than the others. Trophic specialization within different habitats would have de-

creased competition and allowed for an increase in each species' population size. Following this evolutionary pattern, the australopithecines would be like Darwin's finches adapting to the different habitats of the Galapagos Islands. As with the finches, we should expect each hominid species to show specializations characteristic of its niche adaptations.

Robinson argues persuasively that the differences in dental and skeletal anatomy between the gracile and robust australopithecines relate to feeding adaptations. The gracile species was a savanna and scrub forest form. The robust species was adapted to the woodland and forest periphery habitats. E. L. DuBrul agrees with Robinson that the *Australopithecus* fossils represent two species adapted for different kinds of feeding behavior. DuBrul believes that the gracile form was omnivorous, eating a wide variety of foods, including some meat. The robust form ". . . exhibits all the features of extreme herbivory."[5] These conclusions are based on an analysis of australopithecine cranio-facial biomechanics and tooth morphology. This analysis reveals many parallels in dental structure and function between the australopithecines and two species of the Ursidae, the bear family. Gracile australopithecines are dentally similar to the grizzly bear, an omnivore. Robust australopithecines are similar in tooth and jaw structure to the giant panda, a highly specialized, forest-living herbivore. Of course, hominids and bears also show a great many differences in craniofacial structure. But the point is that the diversity of species in the bear family and the hominid family both can be related to dietary specializations.

Diversity tells only half of the early hominid story. That is, about 1.5 million years ago *Homo erectus* appears, and for about 1 million years it is the only species of hominid alive on earth. Thus, the other half of the early hominid story relates to the extinction of the australopithecine species, and the evolution of *H. erectus*.

The same general factors that resulted in the evolution and diversification of early hominid species probably resulted in their extinction as well. The climate change leading to the expansion of savanna and woodland habitats and the shrinking of forest habitats continued all during the late Pliocene and early Pleistocene. Species adapted to the forests were under constant pressure to compete for an ever dwindling supply of resources. Robust austrolopithecines were only one of these forest species. Hundreds of others were under similar pressure. The value of originally adapting to the forest may therefore have been self-limiting for many of these species. As paleontologist N. D. Jago observes:

> *When the process of speciation . . . is viewed against the geological time scale, one is led irresistibly to the conclusion that the tropical forest is not a great generator of new species. Admittedly it induces oddity and specialization, but in the long term such species are (if we can judge by the experience of recent cli-*

matic fluctuations) doomed to quicker extinction than their more adaptable brethren in the more continuous savanna and savanna-woodland zones.[6]

Jago finds that in tropical environments, the savanna and woodland zones are "species dynamos," generating a greater variety of new species.

Gracile australopithecines, *Homo erectus* and other latter hominids were all savanna-living species. In contrast, trophic and anatomical evidence places the robust australopithecines in the forest. With their flaring cheekbones, huge jaws, and enormous molars they adapted to eating vast quantities of forest vegetation. The robust australopithecines are also different from other hominids in that they show no increase in cranial capacity during their evolutionary history. From about 3.0 to 1.5 million years ago the robust brain size hovers around 500cc. This contrasts with the gracile species in which cranial capacity increases from 400cc at 3.0 million years to 750cc by the time *Homo erectus* appears. While robust australopithecine brains do not enlarge, their cheek teeth and jaws markedly increase in size with time. It seems that as the forest habitat shrank, robust australopithecines just kept making greater investments in forest adaptations. Bigger jaws and teeth may have temporarily allowed them to successfully compete for increasingly scarce forest resources. As food became tougher to find, they ate tougher food. But as they adaptively tracked the environmental change, they were sealing their own doom. The rate of forest shrinkage outpaced their adaptive capabilities and they became extinct.

Out on the savannas a different evolutionary sequence occurred. The gracile australopithecines never achieved the anatomical specializations of their robust brethren. Rather, the graciles excelled in trophic generalization (e.g. their omnivorous diet) and neural specialization (e.g. brains). Modern humans are also dietary generalists and neural specialists. One way of arranging the available fossil evidence has the gracile australopithecines evolving into the genus *Homo*. Even if the graciles are not our direct ancestors, any other arrangement of the fossil evidence supports the view that for human evolution the savanna was a species dynamo. Essentially modern post-cranial anatomy appears by 1.5 million years ago (*H. erectus*). Cranial capacity reaches 750cc by that time and then almost doubles in size again by 100,000 years ago (early *H. sapiens*). Teeth and jaws decrease in size while tool technology, social structure, and ritual behavior increase in sophistication. By 35,000 years ago fully modern humans, in all our social and cultural splendor, appear.

NEANDERTAL EXTINCTION

The evolutionary history of our species from *H. erectus* to *H. sapiens* seems to be fairly straightforward. But there is at least one problem, the "Neandertal problem." Neandertals were not the stoop-shouldered, bent-kneed cavemen of cartoons. They were fully erect, large-brained hominids, with a highly developed stone tool technology. They buried their dead and practiced various kinds of ritual behavior (e.g. cave bear cults). However, their anatomy, their tools, and their rituals were different from those of other contemporary hominid populations. They lived isolated from those other populations for about 65,000 years, and then "disappeared" in less than 5,000 years. The problem is, where did the Neandertals come from and where did they go?

Neandertals lived in western Europe during the last major glacial period. This lasted from about 100,000 to 35,000 years ago. Glaciers moving southward from Scandinavia and down the slopes of the Alps isolated western Europe from the rest of the world. Hominids, various forms of early *H. sapiens*, lived all over the Old World. The European glaciers prevented contact, and interbreeding, between the Neandertals and their peers living elsewhere. Recall that geographic and reproductive isolation are part of the first stage in the process of biological speciation. The isolated population of organisms, in this case hominids, can no longer exchange genes or culture with other members of the species. The isolated group may begin to adapt to its local environment and specialize in anatomy and behavior. Eventually this specialization may lead to the inability or undesirability of matings between the isolated population and the ancestral population. At this point the isolate has speciated.

It is uncertain if the Neandertals were isolated long enough to have truly speciated from other hominids. But they did evolve a variety of unusual anatomical and behavioral specializations. These include very robust, thick-boned skeletons with evidence for large and powerful muscles attached to these skeletons. Male, female, and child skeletons show this robusticity, indicating that it was a genetically-controlled population characteristic rather than the result of individual muscular development. Skulls are also thick-boned with powerful jaws and deeply-rooted molar teeth. Arm and leg bones are curved, probably to provide greater muscular power. Fossils from other parts of the world showing evidence for heavy muscularity do not show limb curvature. This may be another genetic adaptation particular to the Neandertals. Their skulls are larger in overall size and in cranial capacity (about 1600cc) than modern humans. Judging from the size of their nasal apertures and the remaining nasal bones, Neandertals must have had truly enormous noses. Large nose size may have been an adaptation designed to warm glacial air upon inspiration, since cold air can cause damage to sinus and lung tissue. In sum, arranging each of these Neandertal features into one living creature, we would find that to us, and possibly to their contemporaries in other parts of the world, the Neandertals "looked different."

The physical features of the Neandertals were adaptations

to the arctic-like conditions of western Europe during the height of the glaciations. Neandertal adaptations, in fact, seem to be highly exaggerated versions of some of the living Eskimo adaptations. Neandertals did not have the advantage of the cultural and technological innovations of the modern Eskimo, so they invested more heavily in their biological adaptations. Fossil evidence shows that it took about 50,000 years for the Neandertal physical adaptations to fully develop. They "tracked" their environment very closely for at least 2,500 generations. In so doing they may have successfully adapted to the glacial environment; indeed, they may have overspecialized.

The Neandertal physical and cultural type persists for more than 65,000 years, but is replaced by more modern humans (physically and culturally) in less than 5,000 years (between 40,000 and 35,000 years ago). It is possible that as the glaciers retreated, the Neandertals rapidly evolved, *in situ*, into modern humans. Several American paleontologists and the majority of European workers doubt this possibility.[7] They argue that the appearance of modern humans predates the disappearance of the Neandertals. Essentially modern-looking fossils are known from Africa and the Near East from the time period 65,000 to 45,000 years ago. This means that if the Neandertals survived, they either evolved into modern humans at a later date, 35,000 years ago, or they were assimilated by modern human populations. Such assimilation could result from large scale interbreeding between Neandertals and moderns as the glacial ice retreated and populations mixed.

The first possibility, of independent evolution, is unlikely due to the short time involved, less than 5,000 years, and the low probability that two independent lines of evolution could lead to the same species. The second possibility, interbreeding, may have occurred if the physical and cultural differences between Neandertals and moderns were not barriers to sexual desirability. However, imagining that this happened at the level required for racial assimilation amounts to what Steven Stanley calls a paleontological "sexual fantasy."

European paleontologists argue that the Neandertals were "replaced." This is the euphemistic term employed in place of extinction. The evidence for extinction is the rapid disappearance of Neandertal physical and cultural life. In less than 5,000 years, an eye blink of geological time, modern humans appear in western Europe. They bring with them their less robust and straight-limbed skeletons, and more sophisticated tools and sociocultural systems. The technology and culture of the modern humans was far different from anything that the Neandertals had ever devised (e.g. art work and calendar systems). The Neandertals had adapted to the world of glaciers and cold, to collecting and eating sub-arctic vegetation, and to the hunting of large Pleistocene mammals (woolly rhinoceros and mammoth). When that world ceased to exist, the plants and animals adapted to it disappeared as well. As the climate, plant life, and game animals changed, the Neandertals may have just continued trying to follow their old way of life, the way that had been safe for them for more than fifty millennia. In so doing, the Neandertals may have followed their environment and their way of life into oblivion.

THE EXTINCTION OF *HOMO SAPIENS*

Extinction, more than a diamond, is forever. Robust australopithecines and Neandertals are gone now and will never return. Their adaptive abilities were outpaced by environmental change. These hominids were, possibly, the most intelligent and adaptable creatures of their times. Modern humans are a highly flexible and adaptable species due to our complex nervous systems, sophisticated technology, and cultural behavior. With our "brain power" we can modify and adapt our technology and culture much faster than biological evolution can change physical characteristics. We have been able to keep pace with most kinds of environmental change since the end of the last Ice Age. However, we now have the ability to induce environmental change to take place at a faster rate than ever before. Carbon dioxide build-up in the atmosphere and acid rain are just two examples of our ability to drastically alter the ecological balance. The consequences of our technological and cultural activity have been documented by many ecologists. The most far-reaching consequence of our activity is that we can, and have, become a major force of extinction for other plants and animals.

David Day, in *The Doomsday Book of Animals*, states that before the expansion of Western culture and technology, the extinction of animal species was a rare occurrence when measured against a human lifetime. Though extinction is a common event in the geological record, even during the "Great Dying" of the dinosaurs the rate of extinction was no more than one species per thousand years. Extinctions during the last 300 years have occurred at a far greater rate. Since the last dodo died in 1680, at least 150 vertebrate animal species have vanished. Only rough estimates of plant extinctions are available, but at least several thousand such extinctions occurred in the same period. In the Hawaiian Islands alone, 300 plant species have become extinct since European contact.

Humans are part of the web of life. We are connected to the organisms we destroy in many complex and important ways. From animals and plants we derive our food, medicine, energy, and many raw materials for industry. The organisms we directly exploit are dependent on other species for their food, energy, protection against disease, etc. The interconnections of life's web continue to levels of living things most humans have never seen or heard about. As we convert more land and water for the needs of our species we take these resources from other species. Mostly through habitat alteration (cutting forests, damming rivers, draining marshes) we accelerate the pace of environmental change beyond the adaptive capabilities of other species. Each time a species fails to keep pace with environmental change it becomes extinct. Each extinction breaks one strand in the web of life. In itself, a single extinction generally has few consequences, just as breaking one strand of a spider's web leaves the rest of the web largely unaffected. But the accumulation of many broken strands destroys the spider's home. Similarly, the accumulation of many extinctions weakens the web of life beyond its ability to support itself.

G. E. Hutchinson observes that the web of interconnections between organisms makes the biological world more complex, but also more stable.[8] The tremendous diversity of life forms (2 million species of animals alone) helps insure that each species will have multiple connections of support for critical resources. Thus, even if one species should die, the multitude of species will survive. Connected in this way, whole ecological systems, like individual species, evolve and adapt to meet the challenge of an ever-changing world.

It has taken 3,500 million years of biological evolution to reach the present ecological conditions of our planet. Human activity is changing these conditions by decreasing the diversity of life on a time scale measured in decades. Compounding this problem is the fact that our species is concentrating its efforts on the exploitation of only a few species of plants and animals for food and raw materials. Our species eats more wheat, rice, potatoes and corn than the total for the next 26 most often consumed plants combined (when did you last eat a turnip?). Survey your supermarket for the variety of animal protein sources and you will find a similar lack of culinary diversity (when did you last eat squirrel or rabbit?). I think that the limited variety of foods available in fast food restaurants depicts our current diet quite well. We worry so much about the health consequences of our diet that we pay millions of dollars annually for nutritional supplements and "health foods."

Taking vitamin pills to compensate for a narrow diet was not the trophic pattern followed by our ancestors. From the time of *Australopithecus* until about 10,000 years ago (a time period that covers 99% of our evolutionary history) hominids lived by gathering and hunting wild foods. Studies of the few remaining cultures of gathering and hunting peoples demonstrate that the diversity of food resources utilized is very high compared to agricultural-based cultures. For instance, the !Kung San people of southern Africa eat about 100 species of plants and 144 species of animals. The Australian North Queensland Aborigines exploit 240 species of plants and 120 species of animals. Both groups include insects, reptiles, birds, and mammals in their animal diet. Archaeological evidence indicates that our ancestors consumed a similarly diverse diet. With such a great variety of foods these people had and have no problem satisfying their need for vitamins, minerals, and other essential nutrients.

Though there are attempts today to promote more eclectic diets and alternative food resources, none has proved so far to be popular and, therefore, commercially successful. For the time being, most of us will continue to depend on a dangerously small variety of foods for subsistence. Some human groups have already followed this path to cultural extinction. The Caribou Eskimo became totally dependent on migrating herds of caribou for food, clothing, housing, and tools. In the 1950s the caribou changed migration routes and bypassed the Eskimo. The people would have starved to death had not the Canadian government moved them to coastal areas to live with groups of maritime Eskimo. The people barely survived, but the Caribou Eskimo culture is extinct. Just as robust australopithecines and Neandertals overspecialized and are now known only from fossil remains, modern humans, as cultural isolates, can also become extinct.

On a global basis, we are following the example of the robust australopithecines, Neandertals, and the Caribou Eskimo. We are growing more dependent on fewer resources. We are narrowing our ecological niche and, perhaps, overspecializing. At the same time our environmental shenanigans are decreasing the diversity of life, and our biological web of support, at an ever accelerated rate. As we narrow our food base we will become susceptible to ecological instability. Recall the social and political unrest caused by the Irish potato blight of the last century, the United States "dust bowl" of the 1930s, and the African droughts of the last two decades. Each of these events was partially caused by human overspecialization in one or a few crops or misuse of available resources. These were only local ecological disturbances. A major world change in climate or the appearance of a new plant disease could lead to widespread crop failure and the starvation death of millions. The social unrest created by this ecological catastrophe could bring death to tens of millions more.

If our pattern of ecological specialization and environmental degradation continues, we will determine the conditions of our own extinction. Paul and Anne Ehrlich write in their book *Extinction*:

> As nature is progressively impoverished, its ability to provide a moderate climate, cleanse air and water, recycle wastes, protect crops from pests, replenish soils, and so on, will be increasingly degraded. The human population will be growing as the capacity of Earth to support people is shrinking. Rising death rates and a falling quality of life will lead to a crumbling of post-industrial civilization. The end may come so gradually that the hour of its arrival may not be recognizable, but the familiar world of today will disappear within the life span of many people now alive.

Caring about the fate of other species is one way in which we can care about ourselves. This means that we must leave enough space, both geographic and ecological, for other species to survive. Ironically, the more species we exploit for food and raw materials the more we will come to appreciate and sustain ecological diversity. Another way we may be able to forestall the crumbling of civilization is by retaining our own species' biological and cultural variability. Human bio-cultural diversity provides for genetic, technological, social, and ideological alternatives that may be used to solve small problems and avoid the large problems that threaten the life of our species. Our bio-cultural variability has sustained us so far in our evolution. However, as the world "modernizes" and "Westernizes," cultural diversity is reduced. This is as much a danger to our species as is the extinction of non-human life.

As was argued earlier, modern humans adapt to environmental change via cultural modifications of behavior rather than biological change. However, our Western cultural penchant for technological domination of the environment is leading us to the brink of ecological disaster. Coupled with the increased rate of cultural homogenization, our path toward environmental deterioration may be unstoppable. If Western culture becomes the only culture we will have no choices for change and adaptation. As the Ehrlichs predict we will go merrily on our way toward oblivion without realizing that our end is in sight. Our ethnocentric belief in the "rightness" of our culture will fail us, and Western culture will crumble and die. Since we are *the* cultural animal—that is, culture is our ecological niche—our culture's death will surely be the cause of our biological death.

The next hominid extinction will differ in one major way from all previous hominid extinctions. There is only one hominid species alive today. If we become extinct there will be no more chances. Given our apparent contempt for the consequences of our activity on the environment and the fate of other cultures of our species, *Homo sapiens* will be-

come extinct. Not with the bang of nuclear or cosmic catastrophe, but with the whimper of ecological deterioration.[9]

Notes

[1]G. G. Simpson, *The Major Features of Evolution* (New York: Columbia University Press, 1953), p. 281.

[2]F. J. Ayala and J. W. Valentine, *Evolving: The Theory and Process of Organic Evolution* (Menlo Park: Benjamin/Cummings, 1979), p. 323.

[3]R. C. Lewontin, "Adaptation," *Scientific American*, September, 1978.

[4]See C. O. Lovejoy, "The evolution of Man," *Science*, 211, 1981, pp. 341–350, for a discussion of this topic.

[5]E. L. DuBrul, "Early hominid feeding mechanisms," *American Journal of Physical Anthropology*, 47, 1977, pp. 305–320.

[6]N. D. Jago, "The genesis and nature of tropical forest and savanna grasshopper faunas, with special reference to Africa." In B. J. Meggers, E. S. Ayensu and W. D. Duckworth (eds.), *Tropical Forest Ecosystems in Africa and South America: A Comparative Review* (Washington, D.C.: Smithsonian Institution Press, 1971), pp. 187–196.

[7]M. H. Wolpoff, *Paleoanthropology* (New York: Knopf, 1980); S. Stanley, *The New Evolutionary Timetable* (New York: Basic Books, 1981); G. E. Kennedy, "The emergence of *Homo sapiens*: the post-cranial evidence," *Man*, 19, 1984, pp. 94–110.

[8]G. E. Hutchinson, "Homage to Santa Rosalia, or why are there so many kinds of animals?" *American Naturalist*, 93, 1959, pp. 145–159.

[9]With apologies to T. S. Eliot and thanks to Alan Mann, whose ideas on early hominid evolution stimulated many of the ideas expressed in this paper. Jack Schuster and Daniel Moerman provided criticisms of this essay that helped to improve its presentation.

Glossary

Abbevillean (or Chellean) culture The earlier of two stages in the hand ax (bifacial core tool) tradition, lasting approximately 1,000,000 to 400,000 B.P.; found across southerly and medium latitudes of the Old World, radiating out from Africa to southwest Europe and as far east as India; associated with *Homo erectus.*

absolute dating Physical-chemical dating methods that tie archaeologically retrieved artifacts into clearly specified time ranges calculated in terms of an abstract standard, such as the calendar.

acclimatization The process by which an organism's sweat glands, metabolism, and associated mechanisms adjust to a new and different climate.

acculturation Those adaptive cultural changes that come about in a minority culture when its adherents come under the influence of a more dominant society and take up many of the dominant culture's traits.

Acheulian culture The second stage of the hand ax bifacial core tool tradition; associated primarily with *Homo erectus;* found in southern and middle latitudes all across the Old World from India to Africa and West Europe; lasting in toto from about 400,000 to 60,000 B.P.

adaptation The processes by which groups become fitted, physically and culturally, to particular environments over several generations. This comes about through natural selection on the biological level and the modification and selective passing on of cultural traits and practices on the cultural level.

adaptational approach A theoretical approach to cultural change with the underlying assumption that, in order to survive, human beings must organize themselves into social, economic, and political groups that somehow fit in with the resources and challenges of a particular environment.

adultery Sexual intercourse by a married person with a person other than the legal spouse.

Aegyptopithecus An especially important Oligocene ape form, dated to 28 million years ago, and found in the Fayum area of Egypt. It represents a probable evolutionary link between the prosimian primates of the Paleocene and Eocene, and the apes of the Miocene and Pliocene. *Aegyptopithecus* probably was ancestral to *Dryopithecus,* and thus possibly to modern apes and humans.

affinal kin A kin relationship involving one marriage link (for example, a husband is related by affinity to his wife and her consanguineals).

age grades Specialized hierarchical associations based on age that cut across entire societies.

agnatic kin Kin related to one through males.

agonistic interactions A term used mostly to refer to animal behavior that is aggressive or unfriendly, including the behavior of both the initiator and the recipient of aggression.

agriculture Domesticated food production involving minimally the cultivation of plants but usually also the raising of domesticated animals; more narrowly, plant domestication making use of the plow (versus horticulture).

alleles Alternative forms of a single gene.

alliance theory A theoretical approach to the study of descent that emphasizes reciprocal exchanges among descent groups as the basic mechanism of social integration.

allomorph In language, one of the different-sounding versions of the same morpheme (unit of meaning).

allophone In language, one of the different sounds (phones) that represent a single phoneme.

alveolar ridge Thickened portions of the upper and lower interior jaws in which the teeth are set.

ambilineal descent The reckoning of descent group membership by an individual through either the mother's or the father's line—at the individual's option. See also *cognatic descent.*

androgens The hormones, present in relatively large quantities in the testes, that are responsible for the development of the male secondary sex characteristics.

angular gyrus An area of the brain crucial to human linguistic ability that serves as a link between the parts of the brain that receive stimuli from the sense organs of sight, hearing, and touch.

animatism The attribution of life to inanimate objects.

animism The belief that objects (including people) in the concretely perceivable world have a nonconcrete, spiritual element. For human beings, this element is the soul.

anomie The state of normlessness, usually found in societies undergoing crises, that renders social control over individual behavior ineffective.

Anthropoidea Suborder of the order of Primates that includes monkeys, apes, and humans.

anthropology The systematic study of the nature of human beings and their works, past and present.

anthropometry A subdivision of physical anthropology concerned with measuring and statistically analyzing the dimensions of the human body.

anthropomorphism The ascription of human characteristics to objects not human—often deities or animals.

antigens Proteins with specific molecular properties located on the surface of red blood cells.

ape A large, tailless, semi-erect primate of the family *Pongidae*. Living species include the orangutan, gorilla, chimpanzee, gibbon, and siamang.

applied anthropology The use of anthropological concepts, methods, theories, and findings to achieve a desired social goal.

archaeological site See *site*.

archaeology The systematic retrieval, identification, and study of the physical and cultural remains that human beings and their ancestors have left behind them deposited in the earth.

aristocracy The privileged, usually land-owning, class of a society (for example, the ruling nobility of prerevolutionary France).

articulatory features Speech events described in terms of the speech organs employed in their utterance rather than from the nature of the sounds themselves.

artifact Any object manufactured, modified, or used by human beings to achieve a culturally defined goal.

ascribed status The social position a person comes to occupy on the basis of such uncontrollable characteristics as sex, age, or circumstances of birth.

assemblage The artifacts of one component of a site.

assimilation The disappearance of a minority group through the loss of particular identifying physical or sociocultural characteristics.

associated regions Broad regions surrounding the three geographical centers where agriculture was invented. Here different plants and animals were domesticated, and then spread individually throughout the whole area.

Aurignacian culture Upper Paleolithic culture that some scholars claim may represent a separate Middle Eastern migration into Europe; flourished in western Europe from 33,000 to 25,000 B.P. The Aurignacians began the European tradition of bone carving. The skeletal remains associated with this culture are the famous Cro-Magnon fossils.

australopithecine An extinct grade in hominid evolution found principally in early to mid-Pleistocene in eastern and southern Africa, usually accorded subfamily status (*Australopithecinae*, within *Hominidae*).

Australopithecus afarensis Early australopithecine form, dating to about 5.5 million years ago, found in the Afar region of Ethiopia and other parts of East Africa. Current debate centers on whether or not this form was directly ancestral to human beings.

Australopithecus africanus The original type specimen of australopithecines discovered in 1924 at Taung, South Africa, and dating from approximately 3.5 million years ago to approximately 1.6 million years ago. Belongs to the gracile line of the australopithecines.

Australopithecus boisei One of two species of robust australopithecines, appearing approximately 1.6 million years ago in sub-Saharan Africa.

Australopithecus habilis See *Homo habilis*.

Australopithecus robustus One of two species of robust australopithecines, found in both eastern and southern Africa, and dating from about 3.5 million years ago to about 1 million years ago.

avunculocal residence The practice by which a newlywed couple establishes residence with, or in the locale of, the groom's maternal uncle. A feature of some matrilineal societies that facilitates the men's maintaining their political power.

Aztec civilization Final Postclassic Mesoamerican civilization, dated from about A.D. 1300 to 1521, when Cortes conquered and destroyed the empire. The Aztec capital at Tenochtitlán (now Mexico City) housed some 300,000 people. Aztec society was highly stratified, dominated by a military elite.

balanced reciprocity The straightforward exchange of goods or services that both parties regard as equivalent at the time of the exchange.

baboon Large, terrestrial Old World monkey. Baboons have long, doglike muzzles, short tails, and are highly organized into troops.

band The simplest level of social organization; marked by very little political organization and consisting of small groups (50 to 300 persons) of families.

bartering The exchange of goods whose equivalent value is established by negotiation, usually in a market setting.

bifaces Stone artifacts that have been flaked on two opposite sides, most typically the hand axes produced by *Homo erectus*.

bifurcation Contrast among kin types based on the distinction between the mother's and father's kinfolk.

bilateral descent The reckoning of descent through both male and female lines. Typically found in Europe, the United States, and Southeast Asia.

bilateral kin A kin relationship in which an individual is linked equally to relatives of both sexes on both sides of the family.

bilocal residence The practice by which a newlywed couple has a choice of residence, but must establish residence with, or in the locale of, one or the other set of parents.

bipedalism The predominant use of the hind (two) legs for locomotion.

blade tool A long and narrow flake tool that has been knocked off a specially prepared core.

bound morpheme In language, a unit of meaning (represented by a sound sequence) that can only occur when linked to another morpheme (for example, suffixes and prefixes).

B.P. An abbreviation used in archaeology, meaning before the present.

brachiation A method of locomotion, characteristic of the pongids, in which the animal swings hand over hand through the trees, while its body is suspended by the arms.

breeding population In population genetics, all individuals in a given population who potentially, or actually, mate with one another.

brideprice A gift from the groom and his family to the bride and her family prior to their marriage. The custom legitimizes children born to the wife as members of her husband's descent group.

Broca's area An area of the brain located toward the front of the dominant side of the brain that activates, among other things, the muscles of the lips, jaw, tongue, and larynx. A crucial biological substratum of speech.

brow ridge A continuous ridge of bone in the skull, curving over the eyes and connected across the bridge of the nose.

burins Chisel-like Upper Paleolithic stone tools produced by knocking small chips off the end(s) of a blade, and used for carving wood, bone, and antlers to fashion spear and harpoon points. Unlike end scrapers, burins were used for fine engraving and delicate carving.

call systems Systems of communication of nonhuman primates, consisting of a limited number of specific sounds (calls) conveying specific meanings to members of the group, largely restricted to emotional or motivational states.

capitalism Economic system featuring private ownership of the means of production and distribution.

cargo cults Revitalization movements (also designated as revivalist, nativistic, or millenarian) that received their name from movements in Melanesia early in the twentieth century. Characterized by the belief that the millenium will be ushered in by the arrival of great ships or planes loaded with European trade goods (cargo).

carotene A yellowish pigment in the skin.

caste A hereditary, endogamous group of people bearing a common name and often having the same traditional occupation.

caste system A stratification system within which the social strata are hereditary and endogamous. The entire system is sanctioned by the mores, laws, and usually the religion of the society in question.

Catarrhini Old World anthropoids; one of two infraorders of the suborder of *Anthropoidea*, order of Primates. Includes Old World monkeys, apes, and humans.

catastrophism A school of thought, popular in the late eighteenth and early nineteenth centuries, proposing that old life forms became extinct through natural catastrophes, of which Noah's flood was the latest.

cephalic index A formula for computing long-headedness and narrow-headedness:

$$\frac{\text{head breadth}}{\text{head length}} \times 100$$

A low cephalic index indicates a narrow head.

Cercopithecoidea One of two superfamilies of the infraorder *Catarrhini*, consisting of the Old World monkeys.

cerebral cortex The "grey matter" of the brain, associated primarily with thinking and language use. The expansion of the cortex is the most recent evolutionary development of the brain.

ceremonial center Large permanent site that reveals no evidence of occupation on a day-to-day basis. Ceremonial centers are composed almost exclusively of structures used for religious purposes.

Chavin culture Highland Peruvian culture dating from about 1000 to 200 B.C. It was the dominant culture in the central Andes for some 700 years.

Chellean handax A bifacial core tool from which much (but not all) of the surface has been chipped away, characteristic of the Abbevillean (or Chellean) culture. Produced by *Homo erectus*.

chiefdom Estate, place, or dominion of a chief. Currently the term is used also to refer to a society at a level of social integration a stage above that of tribal society, characterized by a redistributive economy and centralized political authority.

chimpanzee (*Pan troglodytes*) Along with the gorilla and the orangutan, one of the great apes; found exclusively in Africa; one of *Homo sapiens'* closest relatives.

choppers Unifacial core tools, sometimes called pebble tools, found associated with *Homo habilis* in Olduvai sequence, and also with *Homo erectus* in East Asia.

chromosomal sex The sex identity of a person determined by the coded message in the sex chromosome contributed by each parent.

chromosome Helical strands of complex protein molecules found in the nuclei of all animal cells, along which the genes are located. Normal human somatic cells have forty-six chromosomes.

circumcision The removal of the foreskin of a male or the clitoral sheath of a female.

circumscription theory Theory of the origins of the state advanced by Robert Carneiro and others that emphasizes natural and social barriers to population expansion as major factors in producing the state.

civilization Consists of all those life-styles incorporating at least four of the following five elements: (1) agriculture; (2) urban living; (3) a high degree of occupational specialization and differentiation; (4) social stratification; and (5) literacy.

clan An exogamous unilineal kin group consisting of two or more lineages tracing descent from an unknown, perhaps legendary, founder.

class A stratum in a hierarchically organized social system; unlike a caste, endogamy is not a requirement (though it is often favored), and individuals do have the possibility (though not the probability) of moving to a neighboring stratum.

class consciousness An awareness by members of a social stratum of their common interests.

Classical archaeology A field within archaeology that concerns itself with the reconstruction of the classical civilizations, such as Greece, Rome, and Egypt.

Classic period Spectacular and sophisticated Mesoamerican cultural period dated from A.D. 300 to 900; marked by the rise of great civilizations and the building of huge religious complexes and cities. By A.D. 500, the Classical city of Teotihuacán housed some 120,000 people.

class system A stratification system in which the individual's position is usually determined by the economic status of the family head, but the individual may potentially rise or fall from one class to another through his or her own efforts or failings.

cognatic descent A form of descent by which the individual may choose to affiliate with either the mother's or father's kinship group. See also *ambilineal descent*.

cognatic kin Those relatives of all generations on both sides of the family, out to some culturally defined limit.

collateral kin Those nonlineal relatives in one's own generation on both sides of the family, out to some culturally defined limit.

colonialism The process by which a foreign power holds

political, economic, and social control over another people and establishes outposts of its own citizens among that people.

comparative linguistics (historical linguistics) A field of linguistics that attempts to describe formally the basic elements of languages and the rules by which they are ordered into intelligible speech.

communication The exchange of information between two or more organisms.

communist society A society marked by public or state ownership of the means of production and distribution.

composite family The situation in which multiple marriages are practiced or in which the residence rule requires a couple to reside with parents. See also *extended family; polygamy.*

consanguineal kin A kin relationship based on biological connections only.

continental drift Hypothesis introduced by Alfred Wegener, in the early twentieth century, of the breakup of a supercontinent, Pangaea, beginning around 225 million years ago and resulting in the present positions of the continents.

core tool A rough, unfinished stone tool shaped by knocking off flakes, used to crush the heads of small game, to skin them, and to dissect the carcasses.

couvade The custom, in many societies, for fathers to participate in the period of recuperation, after their wives give birth, by remaining inactive for a long period of time—often much longer than the women.

cranial index Anatomical measure computed on skeletal material, otherwise similar to the cephalic index.

cranium The skull, excluding the jaw.

creation myth A religiously validated tale, unique to each culture, in which ancestors become separated from the rest of the animal kingdom, accounting for the society's biological and social development.

Cro-Magnon A term broadly referring to the first modern humans, from 40,000 to 10,000 B.P. Specifically refers to humans living in southwestern France during the same period.

cross-cousins Cousins related through ascending generation linking kin (often parental siblings) of the opposite sex (for example, mother's brother's children or father's sister's children).

cultural anthropology The study of the cultural diversity of contemporary societies. It can be divided into two aspects: ethnography and ethnology.

cultural area A part of the world in which the inhabitants share many of the elements of culture, such as related languages, similar economic systems, social systems, and ideological systems; an outmoded concept that is seldom used.

cultural assemblage See *assemblage.*

cultural components (of a site) All the different divisions that can be found in a site.

cultural ecology (of a group) The ways in which a group copes with and exploits the potentials of its environment.

cultural evolution The process of invention, diffusion, and elaboration of the behavior that is learned and taught in groups and is transmitted from generation to generation; often used to refer to the development of social complexity.

cultural relativism A methodological orientation in an-thropology, the basis of which is the idea that every culture is unique and therefore each cultural item must be understood in its own terms.

culture The patterned behavior and mental constructs that individuals learn, are taught, and share within the context of the groups to which they belong.

cuneiform Wedged-shaped writing developed by the Sumerian civilization.

cytoplasm The living matter in a cell, except the nucleus.

Darwinism The theoretical approach to biological evolution first presented by Charles Darwin and Alfred Russel Wallace in 1858. The central concept of the theory is natural selection, referring to the greater probability of survival and reproduction of those individuals of a species having adaptive characteristics for a given environment.

demographic study Population study, primarily concerned with such aspects of population as analyses of fertility, mortality, and migration.

dental formula The number of incisors, canines, premolars, and molars found in one upper and one lower quandrant of a jaw. The human formula, which we share with the apes and Old World monkeys, is shown below:

I	C	P	M
2	1	2	3
2	1	2	3

deoxyribonucleic acid (DNA) The hereditary material of the cell, capable of self-replication and of coding the production of proteins carrying on metabolic functions.

descent The practice of bestowing a specific social identity on a person as a consequence of his or her being born to a specific mother and/or father.

descent group A corporate entity whose membership is acquired automatically as a consequence of the genealogical connections between members and their offspring.

descent rule The principle used to trace lineal kin links from generation to generation. A child is filiated to both of its parents, but the descent rule stresses one parent's line and sex as links with others, over the other parent's line and sex.

descriptive kinship terminology The classification of kinspeople in ego's (the individual's) own generation, with a separate kin term for each kin type.

descriptive linguistics The careful recording, description of, and structural analysis of existing languages.

diachronics The comparative study of culture and society as they change through time in a specified geographical area.

differential fertility A major emphasis in the modern (or synthetic) theory of evolution, which stresses the importance of an organism actually reproducing and transmitting its genes to the next generation.

diffusion The spread of cultural traits from one people to another.

diffusionism The belief held by some European cultural anthropologists of the nineteenth and early twentieth century that all culture began in one or a few areas of the world and then spread outward.

diluvialism A school of thought, popular in the late eighteenth and early nineteenth centuries, claiming that Noah's flood accounted for the existence of extinct fossil forms.

diploid number The number of chromosomes normally found in the nucleus of somatic cells. In humans, the number is forty-six.

displacement The process by which sexual, aggressive, or other energies are diverted into other outlets. When these outlets are socially approved, the process is called sublimation.

divination The use of magic to predict the behavior of another person or persons, or even the course of natural events.

division of labor The universally practiced allotment of different work tasks to subgroupings of a society. Even the least complex societies allot different tasks to the two sexes and also distinguish different age groups for work purposes.

DNA See *deoxyribonucleic acid.*

domesticants Domesticated plants and/or animals.

dominance hierarchy The social ranking order supposed to be present in most or all primate species.

dominant allele The version of a gene that masks out other versions' ability to affect the phenotype of an organism when both alleles co-occur heterozygotically.

double descent A form of descent by which an individual belongs both to a patriline and a separate matriline, but usually exercises the rights of membership in each group separately and situationally.

dowry The wealth bestowed on a bride or a new couple by her parents.

Dryopithecus The most common Miocene ape genus, known from Africa, Europe, and Asia, and dated from 20 to 10 million years ago. A forest-dwelling ape with about six or seven species, *Dryopithecus* was most probably ancestral to modern apes and may have been ancestral to humans.

duality of patterning A feature of human language, it consists of sequences of sounds that are themselves meaningless (phonemes) and also of units of meaning (morphemes).

ecological niche Features of the environment(s) that an organism inhabits, that pose problems and create opportunities for the organism's survival.

ecology The science of the interrelationships between living organisms and their natural environments.

ecosystem A system containing both the physical environment and the organisms that inhabit it.

egalitarian society A society that makes all achieved statuses equally accessible to all its adult members.

emics The culturally organized cognitive constructs of a people being investigated (the "folk perspective"). See *etics.*

enculturation The lifelong process of learning one's culture and its values and learning how to act within the acceptable limits of behavior in culturally defined contexts.

endogamy The custom by which members of a group marry exclusively within the group.

environment All aspects of the surroundings in which an individual or group finds itself, from the geology, topography, and climate of the area to its vegetational cover and insect, bird, and animal life.

estrogens The hormones, produced in relatively large quantities by the ovaries, that are responsible for the development of female secondary sex characteristics.

estrous cycle The approximately four-week reproductive cycle of female mammals.

estrus The phase of the approximately four-week cycle in female mammals during which the female is receptive to males and encourages copulation.

ethnic group A group of people within a larger social and cultural unit who identify themselves as a culturally and historically distinct entity, separate from the rest of that society.

ethnicity The characteristic cultural, linguistic, and religious traditions that a given group of people use to establish their distinct social identity—usually within a larger social unit.

ethnocentrism The tendency of all human groups to consider their own way of life superior to all others and to judge the life-styles of other groups (usually negatively) in terms of their own value system.

enthnographic analogy A method of archaeological interpretation in which the behavior of the ancient inhabitants of an archaeological site is inferred from the similarity of their artifacts to those used by living peoples.

ethnography The intensive description of individual societies, usually small, isolated, and relatively homogeneous.

ethnology The systematic comparison and analysis of ethnographic materials, usually with the specification of evolutionary stages of development of legal, political, economic, technological, kinship, religious, and other systems.

etics The perspective of Western social science in general and anthropology in particular, as applied to the study of different cultures. See *emics.*

evolution The progress of life forms and social forms from the simple to the complex. In Herbert Spencer's terms, evolution is "change from an indefinite, incoherent homogeneity to a definite, coherent heterogeneity; through continuous differentiations and integrations." In narrow biological terms, evolution is the change in gene and allele frequencies within a breeding population over generations.

evolutionary progress The process by which a social or biological form can respond to the demands of the environment by becoming more adaptable and flexible. In order to achieve this, the form must develop to a new stage of organization that makes it more versatile in coping with problems of survival posed by the environment.

excessive fertility The notion that organisms tend to reproduce more offspring than actually survive; one of the principal points in Darwin's theory of organic evolution.

exchange marriage Usually describes the situation in which two men marry each other's sister. The term is sometimes used for more complicated patterns in which groups exchange women to provide wives for the men.

exogamy The custom by which members of a group regularly marry outside the group.

extended family A linking together of two or more nuclear families: horizontally, through a sibling link; or vertically, through the parent-child link.

family A married couple or other group of adult kinsfolk and their immature offspring, all or most of whom share a common dwelling and who cooperate economically.

family of orientation (family of origin) Nuclear or elementary family (consisting of husband, wife, and offspring) into which an individual is born and is reared and in which he or she is considered a child in relation to the parents.

family of procreation Nuclear or elementary family (consisting of husband, wife, and offspring) formed by the marriage of an individual, in which he or she is a parent.

feudalism The sociopolitical system characterizing medieval Europe, in which all land was owned by a ruling aristocracy that extracted money, goods, and labor (often forced) from the peasant class in return for letting the peasants till the soil.

fictive kin Extensions of the affect and social behavior usually shown toward genealogically related kin to particular persons with whom one has special relationships— godparents, blood brothers, and so on.

field study The principal methods by which anthropologists gather information, using either the participant-observation technique to investigate social behavior, excavation techniques to retrieve archaeological data, or recording techniques to study languages.

flake tool A tool made by preparing a flint core, then striking it to knock off a flake, which then can be worked further to produce the particular tool needed.

folklore Refers to a series of genres or types of culturally standardized stories transmitted from person to person (usually orally or by example).

folk taxonomy The cognitive categories and their hierarchical relations characteristic of a particular culture by which a specific group classifies all the objects of the universe it recognizes.

foraging society A society with an economy based solely on the collection of wild plant foods, the hunting of animals, and/or fishing.

Foramen magnum The "large opening" in the cranium of vertebrates through which the spinal cord passes.

formal negative sanction Deliberately organized, social response to individuals' behavior that usually takes the form of legal punishment.

formal positive sanction Deliberately organized, social response to individuals' behavior that takes the form of a ceremony sponsored by a central authority conveying social approval.

formal sanction Socially organized (positive or negative) response to individuals' behavior that is applied in a very visible, patterned manner under the direct or indirect leadership of authority figures.

fossils Remains of plant and animal forms that lived in the past and that have been preserved through a process by which they either leave impressions in stone or become stonelike themselves.

free morpheme In language, a unit of meaning (represented by a sound sequence) that can stand alone.

functionalism A mode of analysis, used particularly in the social sciences, that attempts to explain social and cultural phenomena in terms of the contributions they make to the maintenance of sociocultural systems.

functionalist anthropology A perspective of anthropology associated with Bronislaw Malinowski and A. R. Radcliffe-Brown. The former emphasized the meeting of biological and psychological "needs," the latter social "needs."

gametes The sex cells that, as sperm in males and eggs in females, combine to form a new human being as a fetus in a mother's womb.

gender identity The attachment of significance to a self-identification as a member of a sexually defined group and the adopting of behavior culturally appropriate to that group.

gender roles Socially learned behaviors that are typically manifested by persons of one sex and rarely by persons of the opposite sex in a particular culture.

gene The unit of biological heredity; a segment of DNA that codes for the synthesis of a single protein.

gene flow (admixture) The movement of genes from one population into another as a result of interbreeding in cases where previous intergroup contact had been impossible or avoided because of geographical, social, cultural, or political barriers.

gene frequency The relative presence of one allele in relation to another in a population's gene pool.

gene pool The sum total of all individuals' genotypes included within a given breeding population.

generalized exchange (reciprocity) The giving of gifts without expecting a direct return but in expectation of an "evening out" of gifts in the long run.

generative grammar (transformational grammar) A theory about a specific language that accounts in a formal manner for all the possible (permitted) strings of elements of that language and also for the structural relationships among the elements constituting such strings.

genetic drift The shift of gene frequencies as a consequence of genetic sampling errors that come from the migration of small subpopulations away from the parent group, or natural disasters that wipe out a large part of a population.

genetic load The number of deleterious or maladaptive genes that exist in the gene pool of a population or entire species.

genetic plasticity A characteristic of the human species that allows humans to develop a variety of limited physiological and anatomical responses or adjustments to a given environment.

genotype The genetic component that each individual inherits from his or her parents.

geographic center One of three regions in the world—the Middle East, East Asia, and the Americas—in which agriculture probably was invented independently.

gift exchange The giving of a gift from one group or individual to another with the expectation that the gift will be returned in similar form and quantity at the time or at a later date.

glottochronology A mathematical technique for dating language change.

gonadal sex Refers to the form, structure, and position of the hormone-producing gonads (ovaries, located within the pelvic cavity in females, and testes, located in the scrotum in males).

gorilla (*Gorilla gorilla*) The largest of the anthropoid (Great) apes and of the living primates; found exclusively in Africa.

government The administrative apparatus of the political organization in a society.

gracile australopithecines One of the two lines of australopithecine development, first appearing about 5.5 million years ago; usually refers to the fossil forms *Australopithecus africanus* and *Australopithecus afarensis*.

grammar According to Leonard Bloomfield, "the meaningful arrangements of forms in a language."

grid system A method of retrieving and recording the positions of remains from an archaeological dig.

Habilis. See *Homo habilis*.

habitation site A place where whole groups of people spent some time engaged in the generalized activities of day-to-day living.

hand ax An unspecialized flint bifacial core tool, primarily characteristic of the Lower and Middle Paleolithic, made by chipping flakes off a flint nodule and using the remaining core as the tool; produced by *Homo erectus*, later by *Homo sapiens neanderthalensis*.

hand ax tradition A technological tradition developed out of the pebble tool tradition, occuring from about 600,000 to about 60,000 years ago during the Lower and Middle Paleolithic; primarily associated with *Homo erectus*.

haploid number The number of chromosomes normally occurring in the nucleus of a gamete (sex cell). For humans, the number is twenty-three (one-half the diploid number).

Harappan civilization Civilization in the northwest corner of the Indian subcontinent (roughly, in present-day Pakistan), which reached its peak about 2000 B.C. Its major cities were Mohenjo-Daro and Harappa.

Hardy-Weinberg law The principle that in large breeding populations, under conditions of random mating and where natural selection is not operating, the frequencies of genes or alleles will remain constant from one generation to the next.

hemoglobin Complex protein molecule that carries oxygen through the bloodstream, giving blood its red color.

heredity (genetics) The innate capacity of an individual to develop characteristics possessed by its parents and other lineal ancestors.

heritability The proportion of the measurable variation in a given trait in a specified population estimated to result from hereditary rather than environmental factors.

heterozygote The new cell formed when the sperm and egg contain different alleles of the same gene.

heterozygous A condition in which two different alleles occur at a given locus (place) on a pair of homologous (matched pair of) chromosomes.

historical archaeology The investigation of all literate societies through archaeological means.

historical linguistics The study of the evolutionary tree of language. Historical linguistics reconstructs extinct "proto" forms by systematically comparing surviving language branches.

holism The viewing of the whole context of human behavior—a fundamental theme of anthropology.

Holocene The most recent geologic epoch; it began about 10,000 years ago.

homeostasis The process by which a system maintains its equilibrium using feedback mechanisms to accommodate inputs from its environment.

home range (of a primate group) An area through which a primate group habitually moves in the course of its daily activities.

hominid The common name for those primates referred to in the taxonomic family *Hominidae* (modern humans and their nearest evolutionary predecessors).

Hominidae Human beings, one of *Hominoidea*. See also *hominid*.

Hominoidea One of two superfamilies of *Catarrhini*, consisting of apes and human beings.

Homo erectus Middle Pleistocene hominid form that is the direct ancestor of *Homo sapiens*. It appeared about 1.9 million years ago, flourished until about 200,000 to 250,000 years ago. *H. erectus* was at least five feet tall, with a body and limbs that were within the range of variation of modern humans, and had a cranial capacity ranging from 900 to 1200 cubic centimeters.

Homo habilis ("handy man") A fossil form, dating from more than 2 million years ago, whose evolutionary status is disputed. Some physical anthropologists regard it as early *Homo*—the first members of our own genus. Others regard it as an advanced form of gracile australopithecine. This is the earliest hominid with which stone tools have been found in unambiguous relationship.

Homo sapiens neanderthalensis The first subspecies of *Homo sapiens*, appearing some 300,000 years ago and becoming extinct about 35,000 B.P. Commonly known as Neanderthal man.

Homo sapiens sapiens The second subspecies of *Homo sapiens*, including all contemporary humans, appearing about 60,000 years ago. The first human subspecies was the now extinct *Homo sapiens neanderthalensis*.

homologous A matched pair; usually refers to chromosomes, one from each parent, having the same genes in the same order.

homozygote The new cell formed when the sperm and egg contain the same allele of a particular gene.

homozygous A condition in which identical genes occur at a certain locus on homologous (matched pair) chromosomes.

horizontal extended family A household and cooperating unit of two siblings and their respective spouses and children.

hormonal sex The type of hormone mix (estrogens or androgens) produced by the gonads.

horticulture The preparation of land for planting and the tending of crops using only the hoe or digging stick; characterized especially by the absence of use of the plow.

hunting and gathering society A society that subsists on the collection of plants and animals existing in the natural environment. See *foraging society*.

hybrid vigor The phenomenon that occurs when a new generation, whose parent groups were from previously separated breeding populations, is generally healthier and larger than either of the parent populations.

hydraulic theory A theory of the origins of the state advanced by Karl Wittfogel that traces the rise of the state to the organization, construction, and maintenance of vast dam and irrigation projects.

hypothesis A tentative assumption, which must be tested, about the relationship(s) between specific events or phenomena.

ideology A belief system linked to and legitimating the political and economic interests of the group that subscribes to it.

imperialism The expansionist policy of nation-states by

which one state assumes political and economic control over another.

Inca Empire Empire of the Late Horizon period of Peruvian prehistory, dated about A.D. 1438 to 1540. The ninth and tenth Incas (kings) seized control of a 3,000-mile-long empire stretching from Quito to central Chile. The Incas had a highly sophisticated political organization.

incest Usually refers to sexual relations between father and daughter, mother and son, or brother and sister. In some societies the definition is extended to include larger numbers of consanguineal relatives, especially if the society is organized along the principle of lineages and clans.

incest taboo The nearly universal prohibition against sexual intercourse between family members, with the limits of incest varying from culture to culture on the basis of the society's kinship system and forms of social organization.

independent invention The process whereby two or more cultures develop similar elements without the benefit of cultural exchange or even contact.

independent assortment See *Law of Independent Assortment*.

Indus Valley civilization See *Harappan civilization*.

industrialism The form of production characterizing post-agricultural societies, in which goods are produced by mechanical means using machines and labor organized into narrowly defined task groups that engage in repetitive, physically simplified, and highly segmented work.

industrialization The process involving the growth of manufacturing industries in hitherto predominantly agrarian, pastoral, or foraging societies.

industrial society A society with a high degree of economic development that largely utilizes mechanization and highly segmented labor specialization for the production of its goods and services.

infanticide The killing of a baby soon after birth.

informal sanction A social response to an individual's behavior that is enacted individually by group members, with minimal organization by social authority.

informant A member of a society who establishes a working relationship with a fieldworker, providing him or her with information regarding that society.

instrumental belief system An organized set of ideas about phenomena necessary for survival and for performing day-to-day (functional) tasks.

integration, cultural The condition of harmonious pattern maintenance potentially characterizing cultural systems.

interglacial Refers to periods during which glaciers retreat and a general warming trend occurs in the climate.

internalized controls An individual's beliefs and values that mirror the beliefs and values of the group culture and that induce the individual to behave in ways appropriate to that culture.

invention The development of new ideas, techniques, resources, aptitudes, or applications that are adopted by a society and become part of its cultural repertoire.

involution Evolution through which a biological or social form adapts to its environment by becoming more and more specialized and efficient in exploiting the resources of that environment. Sometimes called specific evolution.

irrigation The artificial use of water for agriculture by means of human technology when naturally available water (rainfall or seasonal flooding) is insufficient or potentially too destructive to sustain desired crop production.

ischial callosities Bare, calloused areas of skin on the hindquarters, frequently found in terrestrial or semiterrestrial Old World monkeys.

kill site A place where prehistoric people killed and butchered animals.

kibbutz A collective settlement in Israel with strong emphasis on communal life and values; one of the forms of cooperative agricultural villages in Israel that is collective (to a greater or less degree) in the organization of work, ownership of all resources, child rearing, and living arrangements.

kin category A terminologically distinguished aggregate of persons with whom one might or might not have frequent interaction, but who are conceived to stand in a clearly understood genealogical relationship to the user of the term.

kindred The network of relatives linked genealogically to a person in a culturally specified manner. Each such network is different for each person, with the exception of siblings.

kinesics The study of body movement as a mode of communication.

kin group A terminologically distinguished aggregate of persons with whom one stands in specified genealogical relationships and with whom one interacts frequently in terms of these relationships.

kinship The social phenomenon whereby people establish connections with each other on the basis of genealogical linkages in culturally specified ways.

kinship terminology The set of contrasting terms that designate the culturally significant genealogical linkages between people and the social networks these perceived relationships generate.

knuckle walking The characteristic mode of terrestrial locomotion of orangutans, chimpanzees, and gorillas. These apes walk with a partially erect body posture, with the forward weight of the body supported by the arms and the hands touching the ground, fingers curled into the palm so that the back of the fingers bear the weight.

language The characteristic mode of communication practiced by all human beings, consisting of sounds (phonemes) that are strung together into a virtually limitless number of meaningful sequences.

Law of Independent Assortment Gregor Mendel's second principle. It refers to the fact that the particular assortment of alleles found in a given gamete is independently determined.

Law of Segregation Gregor Mendel's first principle. It states that, in reproduction, a set of paired alleles separate (segregate) in a process called meiosis into different sex cells (gametes); thus, either allele can be passed on to offspring.

legal sanction A formal, socially enacted negative response to an individual's or group's noncompliance with the law, or a legal decision meant to compel that compliance.

lemur A diurnal, semiterrestrial prosimian having stereoscopic vision. Lemurs are found only on the island of Madagascar.

levirate The practice by which a man is expected to marry the wife or wives of a deceased brother.

lineage A unilineal, consanguineal kin group tracing descent from a known ancestor and found in two forms: patrilineage, in which the relationship is traced through males; and matrilineage, in which the relationship is traced through females.

linguistic anthropology A subfield of anthropology entailing the study of language forms across space and time and their relation to culture and social behavior.

linguistics The study of language, consisting of two large subcategories: (1) historical linguistics, which is concerned with the evolution of languages and language groups through time, and with reconstructing extinct proto-languages from which historically known languages differentiate; and (2) descriptive linguistics, which focuses on recording, transcribing, and analyzing the structures of languages distributed across the world today.

little tradition The localized cultures of rural villagers living in the broader cultural and social contexts of mass industrial society, with its "great tradition." Currently the term is rarely used because it is very ethnocentric.

locus The position of a gene on a chromosome.

"Lucy" See *Australopithecus afarensis*.

Magdalenian culture The most advanced of the Upper Paleolithic cultures, dating from 17,000 to 10,000 B.P. Confined to France and northern Spain, the Magdalenian culture marks the climax of the Upper Paleolithic in Europe. The Magdalenians produced a highly diversified tool kit but are most famous for their spectacular cave art.

magic The usually ritualized behavior that is intended to control, or at least to influence significantly, the basic processes of the universe without recourse to perceptibly instrumental acts.

mana A diffuse force or energy-like entity that suffuses through various objects, places, and even people; recognized in various parts of the world but especially well known in Polynesia and Melanesia.

market economy A system in which goods and services are exchanged, and their relative values established, in marketplaces, generally via the use of money as a standard of value.

market exchange The process of distributing goods and services and establishing their relative value (frequently in terms of money) at centers of trade known as markets.

marriage A difficult term to define, given enormous cross-cultural variety. However, all societies recognize (publicly) connections between two or more persons that confer social legitimacy to their children—which is the basic minimum of marriage.

matriarchy A form of family organization characterized by the domination of domestic life or society as a whole by women.

matricentric family A family that is headed by a woman, often serially married to a number of men.

matrifocal family A family form in which the mother, sometimes assisted by other women of the household, is the most influential socializing agent and is central in terms of cultural values, family finances, patterns of decision-making, and affective ties.

matrilateral prescriptive cross-cousin marriage The rule by which a man must choose his spouse from among his mother's brother's daughters or their social equivalents.

matrilineage A kinship group made up of people all of whom trace relationships to one another through female links and are descended from a known female ancestor.

matrilineal descent The principle by which lineal kin links are traced exclusively through females—that is, a child is descended from his or her mother, mother's mother, and so on.

matrilocal residence The practice by which a newlywed couple moves into residence with, or in the locale of, the bride's mother's kin group.

Maya civilization The best-known Classic Mesoamerican civilization, located on the Yucatan peninsula and dated from before A.D. 300 to 900. Less intensely urban than Teotihuacán, it is marked by the building of huge ceremonial centers, such as Tikal in Guatemala.

melanin The brown, granular sustance found in the skin, hair, and some internal organs that gives a brownish tint or color to the areas in which it is found.

Mesolithic (Middle Stone Age) A term of convenience used by archaeologists to designate immediately preagricultural societies in the Old World, 13,000 to 6,000 B.C. A frequently used diagnostic characteristic is the presence of microliths, small blades often set into bone or wood handles to make sickles for the harvesting of wild grains. In Europe, this period also featured the invention of the bow and arrow as a response to the emergence of forests with the shift from Pleistocene to Holocene climate.

messianic movement A revitalization movement based on the belief that a person or god will arrive to cure the evils of the world.

metallurgy The techniques of separating metals from their ores and working them into finished products.

microlith A small stone tool made from bladettes, or fragments of blades, associated with the Mesolithic period, approximately 13,000 to 6,000 B.C.

migration A permanent or semipermanent change of residence by a group, usually involving movement over large distances.

millenarianism A revivalistic movement reacting to the perceived disparity between ideal and real social conditions, with the belief that this gap is about to close, usually with disastrous consequences for nonbelievers.

minority A group that is distinguished from the larger society of which it is a part by particular traits, such as language, national origin, religion, values, or customs. The term may also be used to refer to groups that, though a plurality in numbers, are nevertheless discriminated against socially, politically, and/or economically by the society's dominant patterns (for example, women in the United States).

modernization The process whereby traditional social units (such as tribes or villages) are integrated into larger, over-arching units (such as nation-states), while at the same time being split into units of production (such as factories) and consumption (such as nuclear families) that are characteristic of industrial societies.

moiety The name used to refer to a group that is one of two units of a larger group (for example, each clan of a society composed of two clans is a moiety). Both groups are usually, but not always, based on unilineal descent and are exogamous.

money A medium of exchange characteristic of market economies that is easily replaceable and/or exchangeable for another of like kind, portable, divisible into combinable units, and accepted by all participants in the market system in which it is used.

monkey A small or medium-sized quadrupedal primate. There are two groups of monkeys: Old World and New World. Only New World monkeys have prehensile tails. Most monkeys are arboreal, have long tails, and are vegetarians.

monogamy The marriage rule that permits both the man and the woman only one spouse at a time.

monogenesis The theory that the human species had only one origin.

mores The important norms of a society. They have compelling social and emotional commitment and are rationalized by the society's belief system.

morpheme The smallest unit of meaning in a language.

morphological sex The physical appearance of a person's genitals and secondary sex characteristics.

multilinear evolution The study of cultural evolution recognizing regional variation and divergent evolutionary sequences.

mutation A rapid and permanent change in genetic material.

myths Sacred tales or narratives that usually deal with the issue of origins (of nature, society, humans) and/or transformations.

nasal index The ratio calculated from the width and height measurements of the nose; it was used by early physical anthropoligists to classify human "races."

national character Personality characteristics shared by the inhabitants of a nation—no longer a scientifically valued concept.

nativism A revitalization movement initiated by members of a society to eliminate foreign persons, customs, and objects in order to improve their own way of life.

natural selection The process through which certain environmentally adaptive biological features are perpetuated at the expense of less adaptive features.

Neanderthal man (*Homo sapiens neanderthalensis*) A subspecies of *Homo sapiens* living from approximately 300,000 years ago to about 35,000 years ago and thought to have been descended from *Homo erectus*. See also *Homo sapiens neanderthalensis*.

negative reciprocity A form of gift exchange in which the giver attempts to get the better of the exchange.

negative sanction A punitive social response to an individual's behavior that does not meet with group approval.

neoclassicism A new school of geneticists who propose that most of the molecular variations in natural populations are selectively neutral.

Neolithic (New Stone Age) A stage in cultural evolution marked by the appearance of ground stone tools and frequently by the domestication of plants and animals, starting some 10,000 years ago.

neolocal residence The practice by which a newlywed couple is expected to establish its own independent residence, living with neither the husband's nor the wife's parents or relatives.

neontology A division of physical anthropology that deals with the comparative study of living primates, with special emphasis on the biological features of human beings.

network study An analysis of interpersonal relations, usually focused on a particular individual (ego), that examines the character of interactions between ego and other individuals.

New Archaeology Primarily an American development, the New Archaeology attempts to develop archaeological theory by using rigorous, statistical analysis of archaeological data within a deductive, logical framework.

nomadism A characteristic trait associated with a number of ecologically adaptive systems, in which continuing residential mobility is necessary for the subsistence of the group, with a resulting lack of permanent abode.

nonverbal communication The transmission of communication between organisms without the use of speech. Modes of communication include gesturing (with voice and body) and manipulating space between the communicating organisms.

norm A standard shared by members of a social group to which members are expected to conform.

nuclear family A small social unit consisting of a husband and wife and their children, typical of a monogamous marriage with neolocal residence; also forms a functioning subunit of extended and otherwise composite families.

oasis hypothesis A theory of plant and animal domestication advanced by V. Gordon Childe, in which he suggests that in the arid Pleistocene environment, humans and animals congregated around water resources, where they developed patterns of mutual dependence.

Oldowan culture The oldest recognized Lower Paleolithic assemblage, whose type site is Olduvai Gorge (Tanzania), dating from about 2.2 to 1 million years ago and comprising unifacial core (pebble) tools and crude flakes

Olmec culture The first civilization in Mesoamerica and the base from which all subsequent Mesoamerican civilizations evolved. Located in the Yucatan peninsula, it is dated from 1500 to 400 B.C., Olmec art first appeared in 1250 B.C., and the civilization flourished at its height from 1150 to 900 B.C.

order A taxonomic rank. *Homo sapiens* belongs to the order of Primates.

orangutan (*Pongo pygmaeus*) A tree-dwelling great ape found only in Borneo and Sumatra. It has four prehensile limbs capable of seizing and grasping, and very long arms. The orangutan is almost completely arboreal.

ovaries The female gonads, located within the pelvic cavity.

Paleolithic (Old Stone Age) A stage in cultural evolution, dated from about 2.5 million to 10,000 years ago, during which chipped stone tools, but not ground stone tools, were made.

paleontology, human A subdivision of physical anthropology that deals with the study of human and hominid fossil remains.

paradigm, scientific A concept introduced by Thomas Kuhn (1962): the orthodox doctrine of a science, its training exercises, and a set of beliefs with which new scientists are enculturated.

paralinguistics The study of the nonphonemic phonetic overlays onto the phonological system used to convey special (connotative) meanings.

parallel cousins Cousins linked by ascending generation relatives (often parental siblings) of the same generation and sex (for example, mother's sister's or father's brother's children).

participant observation A major anthropological field research method formally conceptualized by Bronislaw Malinowski, in which the ethnographer is immersed in the day-to-day activities of the community being studied.

pastoralism A type of ecological adaptation found in geographically marginal areas of Europe, Asia, and Africa where natural resources cannot support agriculture, and hence the people are partially or entirely devoted to the care and herding of animals.

patriarchy A form of family organization in which power and authority are vested in the males and in which descent is usually in the male line, with the children being members of the father's lineage, clan, or tribe.

patrilateral parallel cousin marriage A marriage between brothers' children.

patrilineage An exogamous descent group based on genealogical links between males that are traceable back to a known male ancestor.

patrilineal descent The principle by which lineal kin links are traced through males (that is, a child is descended from his or her father, father's father, and so forth).

patrilocal residence A postmarital residence rule by which a newlywed couple takes up permanent residence with or near the groom's father's extended kin group.

peasants Rural, agricultural members of civilizations who maintain a very traditional life-style (often rejecting urban values) while tied into the wider economic system of the whole society through markets, where they sell their produce and purchase goods.

pebble tool The first manufactured stone tools consisting of somewhat larger than fist-sized pieces of flint that have had some six or seven flakes knocked off them; unifacial core tools; associated with *Homo habilis* in Africa and also *Homo erectus* in East Asia.

persistence hunting A unique hunting ability of humans in which prey is hunted over vast distances, often for days at a time.

pharynx The throat above the larynx.

phenotype The visible expression of a gene or pair of genes.

phoneme In language, the basic unit of recognized but meaningless sound.

phylogeny The tracing of the history of the evolutionary development of a life form.

phonetic laws Patterns of change in the sounds used by languages as they evolved, expressed as rules or principles of change.

phonological system The articulatory phonetics and the phonemic system of a language.

phonology The combined study of phonetics and phonemics.

phratry A unilineal descent group composed of at least two clans claiming to be related by kinship. When there are only two such clans, each is called a moiety.

physical anthropology The study of human beings as biological organisms across space and time. Physical anthropology is divided into two areas: (1) paleontology, which is the study of the fossil evidence of primate evolution, and (2) neontology, which is the comparative biology of living primates.

pigmentation Skin color.

Piltdown man A human skull and ape jaw "discovered" in England in 1911 and thought by some to be a "missing link" in human evolution. It was exposed as a fraud in 1953.

Pithecanthropus erectus See *Homo erectus*.

plate tectonics The branch of geology that studies the movement of the continental plates over time; popularly known as "continental drift."

Platyrrhini One of two infraorders of the primate suborder *Anthropoidea*, consisting of all the New World monkeys; characterized by vertical nostrils and, often, prehensile tails.

plow An agricultural tool generally requiring animal power, used to loosen, aerate, and invert the soil so as to cover weeds, expose a large area of soil to weathering, and prepare a seed bed. Its presence differentiates agriculture from horticulture (limited to the use of digging sticks and hoes).

pluralism A characteristic of many complex societies, marked by the presence of several or numerous subgroups that coexist within a common political and economic system.

political anthropology The field of cultural anthropology that deals with that aspect of social behavior known as political organization and that concerns itself specifically with the organization and management of the public affairs of a society, especially pertaining to the sources and uses of power.

political economy The interpretation of the economy and the system of power and authority in a society, most frequently studied from a conflict theory perspective.

political organization That subsystem of social organization that specifically relates to the individuals or groups who are responsible for managing affairs of public policy or who control the appointment or action of those individuals or groups.

polyandrous family A family in which a woman has more than one husband at the same time.

polyandry A relatively rare form of multiple marriage in which a woman has more than one husband at the same time.

polygamy Any form of marriage in which more than two persons are married to one another.

polygenesis The theory that the human species had more than one origin.

polygynous family A family in which a man has more than one wife at the same time.

polygyny The most common form of multiple marriage, allowing a man to have more than one wife at the same time.

pongid A common term for the members of the *Pongidae* family, including the five modern apes: the orangutan, gorilla, chimpanzee, gibbon, and siamang.

positive sanctions A social response to an individual's behavior that takes the form of a reward.

positivism An approach to knowledge embodying empiricism and the scientific method, with its built-in tests for truth.

possession A trance state based on the culturally supported belief that curative or malevolent spirits may displace people's personalities and use their bodies as vehicles for temporary residence.

potassium-argon (KAr) dating An absolute dating technique that uses the rate of decay of radioactive potassium (K^{40}) into argon (Ar^{40}) as its basis. The half-life of K^{40} is 1.3 billion ± 40 million years.

potlatch Ceremonial feasting accompanied by the giving of gifts to guests according to rank; practiced by the Indians of the Northwest Coast of the United States and Canada; a form of economic redistribution.

power, political The ability of leaders to compel compliance with their orders.

prehistoric archaeology The use of archaeology to reconstruct prehistoric times.

Primates The order of mammals that includes humans, the apes, Old and New World monkeys, and prosimians.

primatologist One who studies primates.

profane All that which is ordinary, or not sacred.

prosimii (prosimian) The most primitive suborder of Primates, including lemurs, lorises, tarsiers, and similar creatures.

Protestant ethic A set of values, originally associated with the rise and spread of Protestantism in Europe, that celebrates the virtues of self-discipline, hard work, initiative, acquisitiveness, and thrift.

proxemics The study of the manipulation and meaning of space.

psychological sex The self-image that a person holds about his or her own sexual identity.

quadrupedalism Locomotion by the use of four feet.

quarry site In archaeology, a place where prehistoric people dug for flint, tin, copper, and other materials.

race A folk category of the English language that refers to discrete groups of human beings who are uniformly separated from one another on the basis of arbitrarily selected phenotypic traits.

racial minorities Groups that are categorically separated from the majority members of the larger society on the basis of arbitrarily selected phenotypic traits.

radiocarbon (C^{14}) dating An absolute physical-chemical dating technique that uses the rate of decay of radioactive carbon (C^{14}) which is present in all plants, to stable carbon (C^{12}) as its basis. The half-life of C^{14} is 5568 ± 30 years. The technique is useful for dating remains from 5000 to 50,000 years old, although a new technique may extend its range to about 100,000 years while reducing the margin of error.

Ramapithecus A late Miocene hominoid, found in India, Kenya, and Europe, who lived from 14 to 9 million years ago. Until recently, *Ramapithecus* was accepted by some scholars as the first true hominid, though recent discoveries have placed this form in the evolutionary lineage of the orang-utan.

random (genetic) drift A shift in gene and allele frequencies in a population due to sampling "error." When a small breeding population splits off from a larger one, its collection of genes may not adequately represent the allele frequencies of the larger population. These differences compound over succeeding generations, until the two populations are quite distinct. Along with mutation, gene flow, and natural selection, random drift is one of the mechanisms of organic evolution.

range (of a primate) See *home range*.

rank society A society in which there is equal access to land and other economic resources but unequal access to positions of prestige.

recessive allele A version of a gene that is not able to influence an organism's phenotype when it is homologous with another version of the gene. See also *dominant allele*.

reciprocity The giving and receiving of gifts, usually consisting of material items, favors, or specific forms of labor.

redistribution The enforced giving of surplus goods to a centralized authority, who then distributes them back to members of the society according to social conventions and his own predilections.

reference group The aggregate of people that an individual uses for comparison when assessing or evaluating his or her own and others' behavior.

reformulation The modification of a new cultural trait, or cluster of traits, by a group to fit its own traditions and circumstances; part of the process of culture trait diffusion.

relative dating In archaeology, the determination of the sequence of events; a relative date specifies that one thing is older or younger than another.

religious beliefs The sets of convictions held by members of a society with regard to the supernatural, transcendental, and fundamental issues, such as life's meaning.

revitalization movements Religious movements of a reformative nature that arise among exploited or disorganized groups (often after socioeconomic or political traumas) and that attempt to reinject culturally salient meaning into people's lives—often through a radical assault on existing conditions and/or institutions.

revivalistic movement A revitalization movement espousing the reintroduction of previous religious (or political) forms.

ribonucleic acid (RNA) Any of the nucleic acids containing ribose. One type—messenger RNA—carries the information encoded in the DNA to the site of protein synthesis located outside the nucleus.

rifting The sliding of the continental masses against one another's edges.

rites of passage Rituals marking changes in status or social position undergone as a person passes through the culturally recognized life phases of his or her society.

rites of solidarity Various rituals, usually but not necessarily religious, which in addition to their intended purposes also develop and maintain feelings of group cohesiveness among participants.

rituals Culturally prescribed, consistently repeated, patterned sequences of (group) behavior.

RNA See *Ribonucleic acid*.

robust australopithecines One of two lines of australopithecines, appearing some 3.5 million years ago and surviving until approximately 1 million years ago or even later; thought to have embodied two successive species, *Australopithecus robustus* and *Australopithecus boisei*.

role conflict The emotional stress experienced by a person whose socially expected behaviors are irreconcilable. This happens when a person occupies diverse social positions (statuses) yet in a given situation must act in terms of two or more of them (for instance, a U.S. senator who is also a stockholder asked to vote on legislation that would affect the corporation in which he or she owns shares).

roles The expected (normative) behaviors that every society associates with each of its statuses.

Rosetta stone A tablet containing three parallel texts written in Egyptian hieroglyphics, demotic script, and Greek. In 1822, Jean François Champollion used the stone to decode the hieroglyphics.

sacred A category of things, actions, and so on set apart as holy and entitled to reverence.

salvage archaeology The attempt to preserve archaeological remains from destruction by large-scale projects of industrial society (such as a dam or highway construction).

sanctions, social The responses a social group makes as a consequence of an individual's behavior.

savanna Tropical or subtropical grasslands.

scapulimancy The use of charred cracks in the burned scapula (shoulder bone) of an animal to divine the future.

scientific racism Research strategies based on the assumption that groups' biological features underlie significant social and cultural differences. Not surprisingly, this kind of research always manages to find "significant" differences between "races."

scraper An Upper Paleolithic stone tool made from blades with a retouched end; used for carving wood, bone, and antlers to make spear points.

secondary sex characteristics Physiological changes developing at and after puberty, such as body hair, breasts, and voice changes.

Segregation, Law of See *Law of Segregation*.

self-concept A person's perceptions and evaluative feelings about his or her continuity, boundaries, and qualities.

semantics The relationship between signs and what they represent; the study of semantics is essentially the study of meaning.

semiotic The study of signs and sign-using behavior in general.

serial marriage The process by which a man or woman marries and divorces a series of partners in succession.

seriation A technique of relative dating in which the relative dates of artifacts may be reconstructed by arranging them so that variations in form or style can be inferred to represent a developmental sequence and, hence, chronological order.

sexual dimorphism A difference between the males and females of a species that is not related directly to reproductive functions.

sexual identity The expectations about male and female behavior that affect the individual's learning ability, choice of work, and feelings about herself or himself.

shamanism The process by which certain gifted persons establish (usually with the aid of a trance or an ecstatic state of excitement) direct communication with the supernatural for the benefit of their social group.

sickle cell A red blood cell that has lost its normal circular shape and has collapsed into a half-moon shape.

sickle-cell anemia An often fatal disease caused by a chemical mutation that changes one of the amino acids in normal hemoglobin. The mutant sickle-cell gene occurs in unusually high frequency in parts of Africa and the Arabian peninsula. Individuals heterozygotic for the sickle-cell gene have a special resistance to malaria; homozygots suffer the severe anemia.

sign An object, gesture, or sound that represents something else.

silent trade A form of exchange with no face-to-face interaction between the parties involved, often practiced where potential for conflict between groups exists. Traded items are simply left at agreed-upon places by both parties.

site A concentration of the remains of (human) activities, or artifacts.

Sivapithecus A late Miocene hominoid found in India and Kenya, closely related to *Ramapithecus,* and thought by some scholars to be the first true hominid.

slash-and-burn agriculture A shifting form of cultivation with recurrent, alternate clearing and burning of vegetation and planting in the burnt fields; also called swidden (or shifting) cultivation.

slavery An extreme form of coerced work organization wherein the rights to people and their labor are owned by others, and in which both subordinate and superordinate positions are inherited.

social class A stratum in a social hierarchy based on differential group access to means of production and control over distribution; usually but not necessarily endogamous, with little—but some—openness.

social control Practices that induce members of a society to conform to the expected behavior patterns of their culture; also, mechanisms through which a society's rulers ensure the masses' conformity with the rules of the social order.

Social Darwinism The doctrine that makes use, or misuse, of Charles Darwin's biological evolutionary principles to explain or justify existing forms of social organization. The theory was actually formulated by Herbert Spencer.

social identity The socially recognized characteristics of a person that indicate his or her social position(s).

socialism A socioeconomic form characterized by public ownership of all strategic resources and major distribution mechanisms. It features centralized economic and social planning, and it is conceived by some Marxists to be a transitional stage to communism, in which centralized bureaucracies will "wither away."

social mobility The upward or downward movement of individuals or groups of individuals in a society consisting of social hierarchies and unequal distribution of such social resources as occupations, education, power, and wealth.

social organization The ordering of social relations within social groups whereby individuals' choices and decisions are visibly patterned.

social stratification An arrangement of statuses or groups within a society into a pattern of socially superior and inferior ranks (or groups) that are open to a greater or lesser degree.

social structure The total pattern of eco-centered relationships (such as kinship systems and friendship networks) that occur within a society.

societal structure The total aggregate of discrete, bounded subgroups that compose a society.

society A socially bounded, spacially contiguous aggregation of people who participate in a number of overarching institutions and share to some degree an identifiable culture, and that contains within its boundaries some means of production and units of consumption—with relative stability across generations.

sociobiology The systematic study of the biological basis of social behavior.

sociogram The full description, in the form of a catalog, of all the social behaviors of a species.

sociolinguistics The study of the societal correlates to variations in the patterning of linguistic behavior.

somatic cells The cells that make up all the bodily parts and that are constantly dying and being replaced; does not include central nervous system cells or sex cells.

sorcery A negatively connotative term to refer to magic—the use of supernatural agencies—to further the practitioner's goals.

sororal polygyny A marriage involving two or more sisters as wives of the same man at one time.

sororate The practice by which women are expected to marry the husband of a deceased sister.

spacing mechanisms The behaviors between neighboring groups of animals that help to maintain them at some distance from each other.

speciation The process of gradual separation of one interbreeding population into two or more separate, noninterbreeding populations.

species The largest naturally occurring population that interbreeds (or is capable of interbreeding) and produces fully fertile offspring.

speech community An aggregate of persons who share a set of conventions about how verbal communication is to take place.

state A set of institutions in a stratified society that operates to maintain the status quo by: (1) organizing the provision of needed services; (2) planning the production and use of needed resources; (3) quelling internal discontent by buying off or subduing rebellious minorities or subordinate classes; and (4) organizing, administering, and financing the protection of the society against hostile external forces.

statuses The interrelated positions in a society, with each position carrying certain expectations of behavior (roles) with respect to those persons occupying the same and/or interrelated positions.

stereoscopic vision Overlapping fields of vision resulting when the eyes are located toward the front of the skull, improving depth perception.

stereotype The attribution of certain presumed, invariable personality or behavioral characteristics to all members of a particular group, most notably those groups defined by religion, sex, nationality, or ethnicity.

stimulus diffusion The transfer of a basic idea from one culture to another, in which the idea is reinterpreted and modified to the extent that it becomes unique to the receiving group.

strategic resources The category of resources vital to a group's survival.

stratified society A society in which there is a structured inequality of access among groups not only to power and prestige, but also to the strategic resources that sustain life.

stratigraphy The arrangement of archaeological deposits in superimposed layers, or strata.

structural-functionalism An anthropological school of thought emphasizing the mutual interdependence of all parts and subgroups of a society, interpreting relationships between such groupings as contributing to the ongoing pattern maintenance of the society.

structuralism An analytical approach based on the assumption that observed phenomena are specific instances of the underlying, generalized principles of relationship or structure.

structural linguistics The study of the internal structures of the world's languages.

subculture The culture of a subgroup of a society that shares its fundamental values, but that also has its own distinctive folkways, mores, values, and world view.

subsistence strategies Technological skills, tools, and behaviors that a society uses to meet its subsistence needs.

substantivists A group of economic anthroplogists who deny that economic models derived from developed market economies can be applied universally to all economic systems.

supernatural Refers to all things that are believed to exist but are beyond verifiability through the human senses.

supernatural beliefs Organized systems of thoughts, ideas, and concerns regarding entities whose existence is not verifiable through the human senses.

superposition In archaeology, the perception that, under normal circumstances, a stratum found lying under another stratum is relatively older than the stratum under which it is lying.

supraorbital ridge The torus, or bony bar, surmounting orbital (eyeball) cavities; it is large and continuous in apes and quite small and divided in *Homo sapiens*.

swidden farming Shifting cultivation, with recurrent, alternate clearing and burning of vegetation and planting in the burnt fields. Fallow periods for each plot last many times longer than the periods of cultivation. See also *slash-and-burn agriculture*.

symbol A sign that represents some other (complex) thing with which it has no intrinsic connection.

synchronics The comparison of biological, linguistic, archaeological, and ethnographic data across a wide geographical area at one arbitrarily selected point in time.

syntax The relationships between signs. The study of syntax is the study of the rules of sequence and combination of signs.

synthetic theory (of evolution) A modern theory of evolution based on the Darwinian theory but emphasizing differential fertility (as opposed to differential mortality).

systematics The study of the kinds and diversity of objects and of the types of relationships existing among them.

taboo (tabu) The belief in negative supernatural consequences that attach to the performance of certain acts or the violation of certain objects or places.

tabula rasa The concept proposed by John Locke (1690) that people are born with blank minds and that they learn everything they come to know through their life experiences, socialization, and enculturation into groups.

taxonomy The science of constructing classifications of ganisms.

technology A society's use of knowledge, skills, implemer and sources of power in order (1) to exploit and partia control the natural environment and (2) to engage in p duction and reproduction of its goods and services.

tell A stratified mound created entirely through long peric of successive occupation by a series of groups.

tenancy A form of forced agricultural labor under which f mers plant their crops in the land owner's fields but o the land owner a certain proportion of the crops they h vest.

territoriality Defense by an animal of a geographically de- limited area.

testes The male gonads, suspended outside the body cavity in the scrotum.

test pit In archaeology, a pit that is dug at carefully selected positions in a site to reveal information about buried ar- tifacts and stratigraphy.

thalassemia Like sickle-cell anemia, a blood anemia carried by populations that are or have been in malaria-infested areas of the world—especially around the Mediterranean, Asia Minor, and southern Asia. Like sickle-cell anemia, it also represents an example of balanced polymorphism.

Third World Originally referred to non-Western peoples of the colonized societies of Asia, Africa, and Latin America. More recently, the term has also been associated with na- tional minorities within the United States and Canada, such as Chicanos, blacks, Native Americans, Puerto Ri- cans, and Asian-Americans.

Three-Age System The concept delineated by Christian Thomsen (1836) in which he identified three successive stages in cultural evolution: the Stone Age, the Bronze Age, and the Iron Age.

Toltec civilization Postclassic Mesoamerican civilization, dated from A.D. 900 to about 1300. The Toltecs perpetuated many of the themes of Classic culture. Their capital of Tula was sacked around 1160, and they were eventually re- placed by the Aztecs.

totemism The symbolic association of plants, animals, and objects with groups of people, especially the association of exogamous clans with animal species as their emblems and/or mythological ancestors.

trade The exchange of goods between people.

traditionalizm The organizing of behavior in terms of stan- dards derived from the past.

tradition (archaeological) The similarity in cultural elements and forms over a considerable span of time at a given site or group of sites in a geographically delimited area.

transcendental belief system A belief system providing people with organized ideas regarding states of existence inherently beyond the capacities of their senses to register and about things that are impossible for them to learn from their personal experience.

transhumance The seasonal migration of domesticated live- stock and their herders for the purpose of grazing different pastures at different times of the year; usually rotation between highlands and lowlands.

tribalism The orientation toward tribal membership—rather than toward citizenship in nation-states—as the criterion

of political allegiance and behavior.

tribe A relatively small group of people (small society) who share a culture, speak a common language or dialect, and share a perception of their common history and unique- ness. Often refers to unstratified social groups with a minimum of (or no) centralized political authority at all, organized around kinship lines.

type site In archaeology, a site used to represent the charac- teristic features of a culture.

typology A method of classifying objects according to hierar- chically arranged sets of diagnostic criteris.

underdevelopment The condition of state-level societies that have been exploited by the industrialization of the Euro- pean, American, and Japanese nations and that have themselves failed to benefit from industrialization.

underwater archaeology The retrieval and study of ships, dwellings, and other human remains that have been cov- ered over by waters in the course of time.

undifferentiated (social) system A social system in which the ascriptive qualities of sex, age, or kinship determine social relations in most domains of society.

Uniformitarianism The theory, developed by Charles Lyell, that the geological processes shaping the earth are uniform and continuous in character.

unilineal descent The reckoning of kinship connections through either exclusively female (matrilineal descent) or male (patrilineal descent) links.

unilineal evolution The theory that all human societies evolve through specific stages that are usually defined in terms of the occurrence of increasingly complex social and cultural elements.

unit of deposition All the contents of each stratum in an archaeological site that are conceived to have been depo- sited at the same point in time (as measured by ar- chaeologists).

unit of excavation Subdivision of an archaeological site made by an archaeologist to record the context in which each remain is found.

Upper Paleolithic culture The culture produced by modern *Homo sapiens sapiens*, beginning about 35,000 years ago. It is characterized by pervasive blade tool production, an "ex- plosion" of artistic endeavors (cave painting), highly or- ganized large-game hunting, and the efficient exploitation of previously uninhabited ecological niches—including the population of the New World, perhaps beginning as early as 40,000 years ago.

urban anthropology The application of anthropological re- search techniques and methods of analysis to the study of people living in cities.

urbanism An ill-defined term designating those qualities of life that presumably characterize all city life-styles.

urbanization The worldwide process of the growth of cities at the expense of rural populations.

uterine kin Kin related to one through female links.

uxorilocal residence The practice by which a newlywed couple takes up residence near the bride's mother's family but does not become a subordinate group contained within a larger extended family.

Valdivian culture A coastal Ecuadorian culture, dated from 3200 B.C., in which the earliest pottery found in the

Americas has been unearthed. Some archaeologists believe the pottery was introduced to the New World by Japanese visitors from the Jomon culture—a view hotly disputed by others.

values The ideals of a culture that are concerned with appropriate goals and behavior.

verbal communication The uniquely human use of language to communicate.

vertical extended family A family in which parents, their married children, and their grandchildren share a residence and constitute a functioning social unit.

virilocal residence The practice by which a newlywed couple moves near the residence of the groom's father but does not become a subordinate group contained within a larger extended family.

voluntary association A group of persons who join together for a common objective or on the basis of a mutual interest.

Wernicke's area The brain site where verbal comprehension takes place, located in the temporal lobe of the dominant hemisphere.

Westernization The transplanting of industrial European-American institutions to developing countries.

witchcraft The use of magic to control the behavior of another person or persons.

world view *(Weltanschauïng)* The corpus of beliefs about the world shared by members of a society, and represented in their myths, lore, ceremonies, social conduct, general values, and so on.

yeomanry In feudal societies, those who were granted special privileges in land and produce in exchange for military service in the militia of the lord.

Zinjanthropus A 1.75-million-year-old australopithecine fossil found in Kenya by Mary Leakey and thought to be a form of *Australopithecus robustus.*